ENGLISH TRANSLATION WITH ARABIC TEXT

WASA'IL AL-SHIA

VOLUME 4

Obligatory Prayers, Timings, Qiblah, and Libas Al-Musalli (1,362 Hadith)

HADITH COMPILED BY

Shaykh Hurr Amili

COMPANION WEBSITE
WASAIL-AL-SHIA.NET

TRANSLATED BY

SHIA HERITAGE FOUNDATION

ISBN: 979-8-950755-06-4 (paperback)
ISBN: 979-8-950755-07-1 (hardcover)

Published by Shia Heritage Foundation, Texas, USA.
Website: https://wasail-al-shia.net

Publisher's Preface

In the pursuit of Ilm (Divine Knowledge), there is simply no substitute for the pure, pristine, and unaltered teachings of the Ahl al-Bayt (alayhum al-salam - peace be upon them). Their words are a radiant light and a perfect guide, possessing a divine attraction that draws the sincere soul toward the truth.

In your hands is the English translation of "Wasa'il al-Shia", a monumental undertaking presented by the Shia Heritage Foundation. As a dedicated organization based in Texas, USA, we are strictly committed to the translation and dissemination of core Shi'i hadith literature from Arabic into English. Through the combined efforts of our language specialists, scholars, and passionate volunteers, we work tirelessly to bridge the historical language gap. Our singular mission is to produce uncompromising, high-quality translations of the words of the Ahl al-Bayt (a.s.), permanently removing linguistic barriers so that believers can connect directly with the pure guidance of the Imams.

The Significance of Wasa'il al-Shia

"Wasa'il al-Shia" is one of the most notable and comprehensive collections of Shia jurisprudential hadith, rigorously covering every area of religious law. It is an encyclopedic super-collection sourced from earlier reliable canonical collections, including "The Four Books" (Kutub al-Arba'ah) and many other reputable primary sources. Comprising approximately 36,000 hadiths organized into 30 volumes, this monumental work was collected and compiled by Shaykh Hurr Amili (d. 1693).

The Nobility of the Text

In his introduction to the book, Shaykh Hurr Amili emphasizes the supreme importance of directly engaging with the words of the Ahl al-Bayt (a.s.). He highlights the science of hadith as the noblest and most reliable of all sciences upon investigation. For the Shaykh, this knowledge is the ultimate guide from the darkness of ignorance and the savior from the depths of misguidance. He explains his motivation for compiling this massive collection, describing how he challenged himself to compose a comprehensive book that would serve as a complete reference for both knowledge and practice. His goal was to create a sanctuary of truth, describing the work as "a refuge for me in matters of Sharia, and a reference for whomever among the Shia wishes to be guided by it".

The Methodology of Certainty

Shaykh Hurr Amili details a meticulous methodology, gathering hadiths from reliable and widely transmitted sources, and organizing them systematically by topic. While acknowledging the prominence of the four canonical books of hadith (Kutub al-Arba'ah), he expanded his sources to include other reliable compilations by trusted scholars, noting that these texts are also widely transmitted and their attribution to their authors is not doubted by the learned. He did this specifically to counter the growing trend among some scholars who judged many narrations as weak, claimed many issues lacked textual support, or limited their evidence to isolated reports despite an abundance of available explicit texts. By bringing these scattered pearls onto a single thread, he sought to preserve the hadiths of the infallible Imams (peace be upon them).

Direct Access for Every Believer

Above all, "Wasa'il al-Shia" was compiled to eliminate intermediaries between the believer and the Ahl al-Bayt (a.s.). While the Rationalist establishment often discourages the believers from approaching these texts directly, Shaykh Hurr Amili's explicitly stated purpose was the exact opposite. He embarked on this goal to organize these narrations to make them sufficient for the average believer. His stated intent was to ensure that believers refer back to the infallible Imams in everything where a slip or blemish is feared, and to act upon their words in all important matters.

By gathering the commands and prohibitions related to the actions of the believers, he intended for the Shia to refer exclusively to the Imams - and not to anyone else - in all matters of religion and the world. This work is a significant contribution to the preservation of our heritage and the greatest gift to those who wish to base their religion (deen) firmly and directly on the teachings of the Ahl al-Bayt (a.s.). May Allah (swt) elevate the status of Shaykh Hurr Amili and reward him abundantly.

Without Hadith, The Religion Is Lost

While the Holy Quran serves as our divine constitution, it is the hadith - the teachings and traditions of the Prophet and his purified household - that provide us with the detailed blueprint for an Islamic life. Every single act of worship we perform - from the exact words and movements of our daily prayers to the rituals of fasting and purification - relies entirely on the practical details provided by the hadith. Therefore, if our hadith base is compromised or deemed unreliable, our worship becomes invalid, and the entire religion is fundamentally lost. To claim that there is widespread corruption in our early, canonical hadith literature is to essentially claim that Allah failed in His promise to preserve His religion. True worship requires absolute certainty and full conviction. If we abandon the certainty provided by the divinely guided preservation of our hadith in favor of the conjecture and doubt of later methodologies, we are building our religious life on sand. Trusting our canonical collections is not merely an academic choice; it is an existential necessity for the survival of authentic Shia Islam.

Engagement With Hadith

Direct engagement with hadith literature is not a mere recommendation reserved for a scholarly elite; it is a fundamental obligation upon every Shia believer. It represents the absolute purest, unadulterated connection to the teachings of the Ahl al-Bayt (a.s.). When the Messenger of Allah (peace be upon him and his family) declared that seeking Ilm is obligatory upon every Muslim, he was speaking directly of these sacred narrations, which are the very vessels containing the words, light, and guidance of the Infallibles (peace be upon them).

By approaching the texts directly, we establish an unmediated covenant with our divinely appointed guides, ensuring our obedience aligns precisely with their commands. This methodology is free from human speculation because it is divinely guaranteed. Individual engagement with hadith creates a personal bond with the Ahl al-Bayt (a.s.) that cannot be replicated through other means. The more one immerses themselves in hadith literature, the stronger their connection becomes, elevating their spiritual status and securing their position on the Day of Judgment. Any alternative approach or system that distances us from this direct connection risks deviation and misguidance, as it introduces potentially distorting intermediaries between the believer and the pure teachings of the Ahl al-Bayt (a.s.).

The Dangers Of Not Accessing Hadith Directly

The Imams (peace be upon them) issued severe warnings regarding the spiritual perils of seeking religious guidance outside their explicitly recorded words. In their teachings, the Infallibles construct an absolute boundary: any theological or legal framework generated outside the direct transmission of the Ahl al-Bayt (a.s.) is structurally void. The Imams categorically declared, "Everything that did not issue from this House is falsehood (Hadith 33236)." To rely on the probabilistic conjecture (zann) or independent derivation of the Rationalist establishment instead of the clear texts is to actively consume what the Imams identified as "al-Khaba'ith" (the bad things) (Hadith 33218).

The consequences of this methodological departure extend far beyond mere academic error; they threaten the core of a believer's faith. Imam Sadiq warned that even if a person were to fast continuously and pray perpetually, if they resolve within themselves not to refer their religious affairs directly to the Imams, they commit legislative polytheism (shirk) (Hadith 33221). By substituting the divine command with a synthesized human methodology, the practitioner associates fallible intellect with the exclusive legislative domain of Allah. Imam Ali further affirmed that any deed which does not pass directly through the hands and limits of the designated Guides is categorically rejected (mardud), placing the doer in a state of legislative disbelief (kufr) (Hadith 33235).

Furthermore, the Prophet established a strict architectural reality by declaring himself the City of Knowledge and Imam Ali its exclusive Gate. Attempting to deduce the religion through an alternative entrance structurally bypasses this divine checkpoint. The Prophet issued an absolute guarantee that whoever attempts to reach Allah through other than this specific Gate will fail to reach Him (Hadith 33242). Imam Baqir confirmed this consequence, warning that whoever professes faith without directly "hearing" the transmission from the Infallible will be condemned to The Wandering (al-Tih) on the Day of Resurrection (Hadith 33239). Therefore, abandoning the direct study of hadith is not a safe outsourcing of responsibility; it is a critical deviation that severs the believer from the only authorized lifeline to salvation.

To further explore the definitive proofs establishing this obligation, refer to the traditions compiled in Volume 27, Section 1, Chapter 7.

Are Hadith Difficult To Understand?

The traditions of the Ahl al-Bayt (a.s.) were never intended to be esoteric puzzles reserved for a select few; they were delivered as direct, actionable guidance for all Shia believers. These narrations predominantly comprise straightforward conversations between the Imams and their followers - farmers, merchants, and ordinary people from diverse backgrounds. Our Imams spoke in accessible, colloquial language precisely because their divine mandate was to establish the undeniable proof (hujjah) upon all of humanity. They ensured their guidance would reach every believer directly, addressing all significant aspects of religious life with profound clarity.

The notion that the core of our religion requires a specialized scholarly class to decipher it through speculative deduction undermines the very mission of the Infallibles. Why would our Imams, whose primary purpose was to guide and illuminate, speak in cryptic codes requiring expert decoding?. Such a proposition conflicts with our fundamental belief that the religion has been thoroughly explained.

While certain profound theological realities (asrar) may challenge human intellect, the practical laws of jurisprudence (fiqh) were made manifest. When a sincere believer encounters a narration that appears difficult or seemingly conflicts with another, the instruction of the Ahl al-Bayt (a.s.) was never to resort to independent human reasoning or probability to force an answer. Their clear instruction was to submit, practice precaution (ihtiyat), and pause (tawaqquf), returning the matter's true meaning to them. Therefore, the completeness of the hadith literature lies in its accessibility for daily practice and its demand for our absolute submission when our understanding falls short.

The True Measure of the Intellect

The Rationalist establishment often elevates the human intellect as an independent, standalone source for deriving religious law. However, according to the teachings of the Ahl al-Bayt (a.s.), the highest and most perfected function of the intellect is to recognize its own limitations and submit completely to the Infallibles. The intellect is the divine gift by which we recognize the necessity of the Prophets and Imams, not the tool designed to replace them. Once the Proof (Hujjah) is established, true rationality dictates absolute obedience to their explicit words. To abandon the documented text in favor of independent deduction or probability is not an exercise in higher intellect, but a departure from the safety of divine certainty.

The Danger of Speculative Methodologies

When we introduce human speculation into the interpretation of hadith, we open the door to endless subjectivity and potential distortion. The Rationalist approach, which relies on speculative sciences and independent reasoning to resolve apparent contradictions, risks undermining the very foundation of our faith. It creates a scenario where the believer's understanding of religious law becomes contingent on their intellectual capacity or the opinions of later scholars, rather than the clear, preserved teachings of the Ahl al-Bayt (a.s.). This not only leads to confusion and division within the community but also jeopardizes our spiritual connection to the Infallibles. The true safeguard against misguidance is unwavering adherence to the explicit texts and the methodological principles provided by the Imams themselves, which are designed to navigate any apparent difficulties without resorting to human conjecture.

When Traditions Appear to Differ

A common deterrent used to discourage believers from reading hadith directly is the existence of apparently conflicting narrations. The Rationalist approach claims that resolving these differences requires specialized, speculative sciences and a lifetime of academic training. Yet, the Imams themselves foresaw this and provided their followers with clear, straightforward guidelines. They explicitly instructed the believers on how to weigh conflicting reports: to measure them against the Book of Allah, to adopt what opposes the general public (as the other may have been issued in taqiyyah), or simply to practice precaution (ihtiyat) and pause (tawaqquf) when a resolution is not clear. The perfect mechanism for navigating differences is found within the texts themselves, completely eliminating the need to rely on external human philosophy or speculative resolution.

To study the precise, infallible guidelines for reconciling apparently conflicting narrations, the reader is directed to the explicit traditions compiled in Volume 27, Section 1, Chapter 9.

The Preservation Of Hadith

The intricate nature of Islamic jurisprudence (fiqh), with its precise rules, specific sequences, and detailed prescriptions for both ordinary and exceptional circumstances, naturally raises questions about its preservation across generations. To suggest that these vital instructions were left vulnerable to historical corruption or the fluidity of oral memory implies a serious deficiency in the divine plan itself. The truth is far more profound: the Prophet (peace be upon him and his family) and the Imams (peace be upon them) were not merely passive speakers of the law; they were the active, deliberate engineers of its physical codification.

The preservation of these teachings was institutionalized during the lifetimes of the Infallibles. The Imams explicitly mandated the recording of the text, declaring that "the heart relies upon writing" and commanding their companions to "write, for you will not retain until you write (Hadith 33261)". They directed that certain foundational traditions be written in the "water of gold (Hadith 33266)", elevating the physical manuscript to the status of an absolute, permanent sanctuary of truth. They explicitly prepared the believers for the era of Occultation - described as a "time of chaos" - by instructing them to preserve and bequeath their books, ensuring the community would never be left without objective certainty (Hadith 33263).

Furthermore, the foundational books of the Shia were not compiled in a vacuum. The early companions systematically utilized the mechanism of "Ardh" (presentation), bringing their physical notebooks directly to the living Imams for review (Hadith 33318). The Imams actively audited these texts page by page, authenticating them and declaring, "This is correct (sahih); it is appropriate that you act according to it (Hadith 33321)." Because the primary texts were audited and certified at the infallible source, subjecting these guaranteed compilations to the retroactive, speculative filtering of later generations fundamentally contradicts the precise preservation protocol established by the Ahl al-Bayt (a.s.).

While some may point to apparently conflicting narrations or those issued under taqiyyah as grounds for skepticism, the Ahl al-Bayt (a.s.) themselves provided clear, text-based methodological principles for resolving such matters without resorting to independent human deduction. Moreover, even in cases where a believer might unknowingly follow a narration issued under taqiyyah, their sincere intention to obey the Infallible entirely protects them from blame.

Therefore, these hadith collections represent far more than historical records; they are the unadulterated speech of the Infallibles and the exclusive channels through which we maintain our covenant with Allah (swt). The true guardian of the faith is the one who faithfully transmits and acts upon this objective certainty. To approach these texts casually, or to marginalize them in favor of derived human opinions, is to risk severing the only spiritual lifeline divinely authorized for our salvation.

To further explore the commands issued by the Imams to record and safeguard these texts, refer to the narrations compiled in Volume 27, Section 1, Chapter 8.

Beyond the Chains: A Critique of 'Ilm al-Rijal

The Rationalist establishment frequently justifies the speculative science of Ilm al-Rijal (Biographical Evaluation) as a necessary tool to weed out historical fabrications. However, this methodology fundamentally ignores the historical reality of how the Shi'i hadith corpus was actually preserved. Our tradition does not rely on a fragile, fluid oral memory, but upon a meticulously preserved written heritage. As mentioned in the previous section, the early companions, with the direct guidance of the Imams, recorded the hadith directly into physical notebooks known as al-Usul. The transmission chains (isnad) that later scholars obsess over were not chains of oral rumors; they were primarily chains of permission (ijaza) authorizing the transfer and copying of known, physical manuscripts.

While extremists occasionally attempted to insert fabricated pages into individual notebooks, the massive physical multiplication and widespread geographical distribution of these manuscripts acted as a formidable structural defense. Consider our major canonical books, such as "Al-Kafi" or "Man la yahdhuruhu al-Faqih". The primary compilers possessed the immediate physical proximity, the multiple cross-referenced copies of al-Usul, and the objective textual indicators necessary to filter out anomalies before codifying their masterworks. Since the day Shaykh Kulayni and Shaykh Saduq secured these texts in writing, no external actor has been able to successfully infiltrate them. Therefore, attempting to recreate this textual filtration centuries later by scrutinizing the individual links of the transmission chain is methodologically redundant.

Furthermore, this Rationalist methodology presents a profound epistemological paradox. The verdicts found in classical biographical dictionaries - which declare a narrator reliable or weak - are frequently based on subjective, historically conditioned evaluations rather than objective textual analysis. For example, early biographers from Qum frequently weakened narrators over theological disagreements, exiling men for what they subjectively deemed "extremism" - beliefs that later generations universally accepted as standard Shi'i theology. The Rationalist framework thus forces extreme skepticism upon the transmitted words of the Divine Guide, yet paradoxically accepts the undocumented, highly subjective opinions of fallible biographers as absolute, authoritative proof.

Shaykh Hurr Amili thoroughly understood this reality. He considered the hadiths he compiled in "Wasa'il al-Shia" to be authentically proven and legally binding. Nowhere in his extensive introduction did he ever suggest or mandate that the narrations he meticulously gathered should later be subjected to the subjective filtering of biographical evaluation. He compiled them for direct action, not for speculative invalidation and piecemeal rejection by later generations.

It is with this historical context in mind that we have structured this English translation. Because the authenticity of the primary texts was established by the early compilers through rigorous manuscript verification, the primary function of the isnad - proving the legitimate transfer of the physical text - has already been fulfilled. While the original Arabic chains remain permanently preserved in the canonical texts for scholarly reference, we have chosen to streamline this English edition by presenting strictly the core text (matn) of the hadith. This editorial decision removes the dense technical apparatus of transmission, allowing the modern lay reader to focus their heart and mind entirely on engaging directly with the pure guidance of the Imams.

Approach To Fiqh

The pursuit of Fiqh should not be viewed merely as an exercise in rationalist deduction or speculative logic (zann). Rather, its ultimate objective is to achieve a state of absolute submission (taslim) to the explicit texts (nass) of the Ahl al-Bayt (a.s.). The essence of Islamic jurisprudence lies not in the independent exertion of human intellect to solve legal puzzles, but in cultivating unwavering obedience to the divinely appointed guides.

True certainty in religion is found only in their words. The path to salvation is paved by earnestly seeking their direct teachings, applying them meticulously, and pausing where they have remained silent. Even in scenarios where a believer sincerely acts upon an authentic narration that the Imam originally issued under taqiyyah the believer's spiritual standing remains intact. Their absolute intent to obey the Imam protects them on the Day of Judgement. This understanding transforms fiqh from a rigid academic pursuit of probability into a living, unbroken covenant with the Infallibles.

The True Meaning of Taqlid

The Rationalist establishment frequently utilizes the concept of Taqlid to enforce obedience to the speculative rulings and independent deductions (ijtihad) of fallible jurists. However, a rigorous examination of the teachings of the Ahl al-Bayt (a.s.) completely shatters this framework. In a foundational tradition (Hadith 33401) from Imam al-Askari (a.s.), the Infallible explicitly condemns scholars who innovate rulings or distort the pristine text, equating them to those who "write the Book with their hands."

As Shaykh Hurr Amili brilliantly clarifies in his commentary on this tradition, the only Taqlid licensed by the Imams is strictly the acceptance of the narration (riwayah). It is absolutely not a mandate to accept human opinion (ra'y), independent deduction (ijtihad), or probabilistic conjecture (zann). True Taqlid is the transparent emulation of a pious transmitter who exclusively conveys the preserved revelation. It is the act of submitting to the unadulterated words of the Imams, rather than following the deductive, human-engineered procedural frameworks of fallible men.

For a comprehensive exploration of the absolute impermissibility of performing Taqlid of anyone who issues rulings based on personal opinion or without an explicit text from the Infallibles, the reader is directed to the foundational narrations compiled in Volume 27, Section 1, Chapter 10.

The Divine Guarantee of Preservation

The absolute reliance on trustworthy (thiqaah) narrators is permanently cemented by the definitive decree of the Twelfth Imam (may Allah hasten his reappearance). In a noble signed letter (tawqi'), he established a flawless epistemological guarantee for the believers: "For indeed, there is no excuse for any of our loyalists (mawalina) in casting doubt upon what our trustworthy (thiqaah) [narrators] convey from us, as they are known to be those whom we confide our secrets to, and whom we entrust/burden with, to deliver them [to the believers] (Hadith 33455)." This profound mandate structurally invalidates the modern methodology of skepticism. The Imam explicitly confirms that these textual custodians were directly selected, authenticated, and entrusted with the divine secret by the Infallibles themselves.

"Wasa'il al-Shia" stands as the monumental, physical manifestation of this divine guarantee. It is an encyclopedic sanctuary built entirely upon the transmissions of these exact trustworthy carriers. To approach this authenticated corpus with default suspicion - subjecting its established traditions to the retroactive, speculative filtering of later biographical sciences - is to effectively question the Infallible's own judgment in selecting his custodians. To doubt these compilations is to structurally doubt the divine guarantee of preservation itself.

Therefore, the sincere believer is left with absolutely no excuse to harbor even a shadow of doubt regarding the authenticity of these texts. Embracing the hadith within "Wasa'il al-Shia" is not a choice between competing academic theories; it is the ultimate fulfillment of authentic Taqlid. By submitting wholeheartedly and exclusively to these meticulously preserved narrations, the believer permanently closes the door to human conjecture and secures their salvation upon the objective, unshakeable certainty of the Ahl al-Bayt (a.s.).

Navigating the Unknown: The Protocol of Pausing And Awaiting The Guide

As readers engage with this translation, they will inevitably encounter modern novelties, complex financial mechanisms, or unprecedented social scenarios where an explicit narration (nass) appears to be absent. The natural inclination of the human intellect - heavily conditioned by the prevailing Rationalist establishment - is to demand an immediate legislative answer. Deductive jurisprudence frequently attempts to bridge these textual gaps by deploying procedural exemptions (Asalat al-Bara'ah) or probabilistic conjecture (zann) to synthesize a binding ruling of permissibility. However, the classical methodology established by the Imams categorically forbids this intellectual overreach.

The Prophet and the Imams divided all matters into three strict categories: the clearly permissible (halal), the clearly prohibited (haram), and the ambiguous matters (shubuhat) located between them. The Imams explicitly warned that these ambiguities serve as the "Sanctuary" (Hima) of Allah (Hadith 33531). When the explicit text is silent, the matter enters the realm of the unknown. The authorized protocol dictates that ambiguity is not a blank canvas for independent derivation (istinbat), but a definitive boundary marker. To use human reasoning to invent a ruling of permissibility within this doubtful zone is equated with grazing one's sheep on the edge of the sanctuary, guaranteeing an eventual fall into objective sin.

What, then, is the duty of the believer when the hadith corpus is silent? The explicit command of the Ahl al-Bayt is the absolute suspension of action and judgment (tawaqquf). As Imam al-Baqir instructed, "The stopping (wuquf) at the doubt (shubha) is better than the plunging into destruction (halakah) (Hadith 33465)". Action without definitive textual insight is characterized by the Imams not as scholarly striving, but as reckless plunging into ruin. The believer is structurally mandated to return the knowledge of the obscure matter to Allah and His Representatives, exercising total restraint (kaff) until clarification comes directly from them.

This mandate to pause is inextricably linked to the theological reality of the Occultation. We are structurally commanded to patiently wait for the reappearance of the Twelfth Imam (the "Qa'im") to resolve these ambiguities. Imam al-Baqir established that if a believer pauses at an ambiguity and returns it to the Imams, dying in this state of steadfastness before the Riser emerges grants them the exact rank of a martyr (Hadith 33511). True defense of the religion is not achieved by aggressively generating probabilistic answers to fill a legislative void, but by fiercely guarding the boundaries of the explicit text and maintaining the authorized silence of the unknown.

Furthermore, the reader must embrace the profound doctrinal safety found in the phrase "I do not know" (La Adri). Amir al-Mu'minin warned that whoever abandons this admission strikes their own fatal points (Hadith 33485). True servitude requires the intellect to recognize its own limits and submit to the silence of the law. One must understand that even upon the reappearance of the Imam, he is not structurally obligated to provide a definitive ruling for every human inquiry. Sometimes, the divine will is strictly silence over a matter. Amir al-Mu'minin declared that Allah has ordained obligations and set limits, but He has also remained silent about certain things. This silence is not born out of forgetfulness. Rather, it is a deliberate Mercy from Allah to the believers, and they are commanded to accept it rather than burden themselves with pursuing it (Hadith 33531).

Therefore, encountering silence in the Divine Law is not a defect to be remedied by the fallible intellect, nor should one attempt to force an analogy, rely on fallible opinion (ra'y), or deploy philosophical deductions to synthesize an answer. It is a profound theological reality demanding our absolute submission and stillness. If you cannot find a hadith addressing a specific situation in this compilation, recognize that the Divine Law is perfectly complete. Your duty is to halt, abstain from the ambiguous, and find absolute safety in waiting for the Guide. As Imam Ali ibn al-Husayn advised: "If a matter becomes clear to you, then accept it; and if not, then be silent, and you will be safe (Hadith 33503)."

To study the explicit commands of the Ahl al-Bayt (a.s.) on exercising precaution (ihtiyat) and pausing (tawaqquf) in matters of doubt, the reader is directed to the foundational hadiths collected in Volume 27, Section 1, Chapter 12.

The Sufficiency of the Corpus and the Infallible Guarantee of Salvation

As you navigate the vast ocean of narrations within this translation, a natural anxiety may arise: Is this compiled text truly enough to secure my religion? Conditioned by the contemporary Rationalist establishment, believers are often taught that without the continuous, deductive expansion of the law by a living jurist, their practical religion is deficient. However, the classical methodology dictates that "Wasa'il al-Shia" is not merely a historical archive; it is a structurally complete, divinely protected constitution. The Imams guaranteed that in every generation, there are "Just Ones" who actively expel the distortions of extremists and the plagiarism of falsifiers from the religion (Hadith 33247). The foundational notebooks and primary sources that comprise this compilation were historically presented to the Imams, who explicitly validated them, declaring them to be "Correct" and instructing the believers that it is "appropriate that you act according to it". Imam al-Askari, after reviewing one such compilation, definitively sealed its sufficiency by stating, "This is my religion and the religion of my forefathers (all of it), and it is the Truth, all of it (Hadith 33320)".

Therefore, limiting your practical affairs strictly to the explicit commands found within this collection is not a methodological weakness; it is the exact obedience mandated by the Divine Legislator. Imam al-Sadiq established an absolute binary when he addressed his companions: whoever takes hold of the teachings of the Imams has been guided, and whoever abandons them and turns away from them has gone astray. For the believers living in the era of Occultation, the Prophet himself reserved his highest praise for those who, despite the Proof being concealed from them, place their absolute faith in "black upon white (ink on paper) (Hadith 33296)". The text itself is your anchor.

If you choose to bind your actions exclusively to the halal and haram delineated in these pages, bypassing the probabilistic conjecture and localized deductions of fallible men, you are granted an infallible warranty of safety. Imam al-Sadiq explicitly commanded the believers to take hold of their traditions, declaring, "I am a Guarantor (Za'im) for your salvation (Hadith 33283)". An Infallible cannot legally or spiritually bind the salvation of the community to a compromised or insufficient corpus. Furthermore, the Imams promised that whoever preserves forty hadiths concerning the lawful and the prohibited will be resurrected as a scholar, and critically, Allah "will not punish him".

The explicit vocabulary of the Ahl al-Bayt (a.s.) is the ultimate spiritual fortress. Imam al-Sadiq swore that a single hadith regarding the halal and haram taken from a Truthful One "is better than the world and what is in it of gold and silver (Hadith 33313)." By restricting your religious practice to the verified texts of this compilation, you are adopting the safest, most heavily fortified position possible for the Day of Judgment, resting entirely upon the guaranteed salvation promised by the Divine Guides themselves.

Importance of Disseminating Hadith

To possess this translation is to hold a heavy, divine trust. The responsibility of the believer does not end with personal adherence to these texts; it extends to the active, urgent dissemination of the Hadith to the broader community. Within the classical framework, the act of preserving and sharing the explicit words of the Ahl al-Bayt (a.s.) is elevated far beyond mere scholarship - it is the supreme act of spiritual defense. When asked to compare a devoted worshipper to a narrator (rawiyah) who disseminates the traditions and plants them firmly in the hearts of the Shia, Imam al-Sadiq categorically declared: "The narrator of our Hadith, who strengthens the hearts of our Shia with it, is superior to a thousand worshippers (Hadith 33246)." The Imams established a strict epistemological hierarchy: the structural preservation and transmission of the explicit text is infinitely more valuable than the localized performance of individual worship. By sharing these narrations, you become the vanguard of the Imam, anchoring the hearts of the believers against the turbulence of doubt.

Securing the Youth (Next Generation)

Th duty to disseminate hadith becomes a critical, time-sensitive mandate when it comes to our children and youth. The psychological and spiritual landscape of a young mind is fiercely contested territory. Amir al-Mu'minin, in his profound advice to his son al-Hasan, warned of this vulnerability, stating: "Indeed, the heart of a youth is like an empty land - it accepts whatever is cast into it (Hadith 27635)." He stressed the absolute necessity of initiating this education before the heart hardens and the mind becomes preoccupied with the trials of the world. If we do not actively fill this empty land with the pure, unadulterated words of the Infallibles, the surrounding culture will gladly fill it with ideological poison.

The Imams foresaw the proliferation of deviant theological sects and misleading philosophical ideologies, and they provided only one structural antidote. Imam al-Sadiq issued a commanding directive: "Hasten to teach your youth the hadith before the Murji'ah get to them first (Hadith 33287)." In every era, there is a modern equivalent of the "Murji'ah" - a competing ideological framework or a Rationalist establishment ready to capture the minds of the uninformed. The Imam further warned that if a believer is not made self-sufficient through the direct understanding of these texts, they will inevitably need to seek answers from outsiders. When they turn to these external sources, they will be led directly into misguidance without even realizing it.

Therefore, making the study and transmission of these hadiths the highest priority in your homes is not a matter of cultural enrichment; it is a matter of absolute spiritual survival. Read these traditions to your children, share them with your peers, and make them the foundational vocabulary of your households. By actively spreading this compilation, you cast a divine shield over the next generation, ensuring that their intellects remain permanently tethered to the flawless guidance of the Divine Legislators.

Translation Notes

This project represents a complete and faithful English translation of "Wasa'il al-Shia". To maintain strict scholarly integrity and absolute transparency, we have undertaken to translate every hadith in full. We present the main text (matn) without any omissions, abridgments, or editorial modifications. The original Arabic text accompanies each English translation, allowing readers to verify the accuracy of our work and independently cross-reference the transmission. We affirm our unwavering commitment to preserving the complete and unaltered guidance of the Ahl al-Bayt (a.s.) for the English-speaking audience.

For the Arabic source text, we utilized the second edition of the Beirut publication printed by Mu'assissat Aal-al-Bayt li Ihya al-Turath in 1994 (1414 AH). The original Arabic version maintains a sequential numbering system that runs incrementally through the entire 30-volume collection, starting from hadith number 1 and ending with number 35,868. To ensure precise referencing, this publication mirrors that exact numbering system next to each translated hadith.

We have excluded the English translation of the transmission chains (sanad) to improve readability and allow the reader to focus directly on the core text of the hadith. Methodologically, Shaykh Hurr Amili already meticulously compiled and filtered these narrations from reliable, authoritative primary sources. Because the authenticity of these core texts was established by the early scholars, the retroactive analysis of individual biographical chains is secondary for the believer seeking pure divine guidance. However, for researchers who still require them, the complete transmission chains can be easily accessed within the original Arabic source files, which are available for download directly from our companion website.

Finally: A Covenant of Transmission

In presenting this translation, our singular hope is to fulfill the divine obligation of disseminating the exact words of the Ahl al-Bayt (a.s.). This project is not a mere academic endeavor, nor an exercise in theoretical jurisprudence; it is a profound religious responsibility to deliver the unaltered texts directly to the faithful. We are driven by the profound supplication of Imam al-Ridha (peace be upon him), who prayed: "May Allah have mercy upon a servant who revives our Amr (Affair)." When asked how one revives their affair, the Imam instructed: "He learns our Knowledge (Ulum) and teaches it to the people. For verily, if the people knew the beauties of our speech (mahasina kalamina), they would follow us (Hadith 33297)."

By providing this transparent conduit, we seek to answer this divine call, revealing the pure beauty of their speech so that their explicit guidance reaches all who sincerely seek it. We pray that this humble effort empowers believers to bypass fallible intermediaries, fortify their direct, personal connection with the Infallibles, and secure their path to salvation through absolute submission to the documented divine law.

May Allah (swt) accept this service, performed solely with the intention of seeking His pleasure. We pray it stands as a continuous source of objective certainty and spiritual revival for the community of believers, sustaining the faithful until the day the Twelfth Imam (may Allah hasten his reappearance) manifests himself to establish divine justice throughout the world.

Shia Heritage Foundation
June 2026

CONTENTS

Section 1: The Number Of Obligatory And Supererogatory Prayers And What Is Related

Section 2: Al-Mawaqiyat (Timings)

Section 3: Al-Qiblah

Section 4: Libas Al-Musalli (Clothing of the Praying Person)

This page is intentionally left blank.

Section 1

The Number Of Obligatory And Supererogatory Prayers And What Is Related

CHAPTER 1

Obligation Of Prayer

[Hadith 4376 to 4384]

Hadith 4376

عن زرارة، عن أبي جعفر (عليه السلام) في قول الله عز وجل: (إن الصلاة كانت على المؤمنين كتابا موقوتا) أي موجوبا.

From Zurarah, from Abu Ja'far (peace be upon him) regarding the words of Allah the Mighty and Majestic: "Indeed, prayer has been decreed upon the believers at specified times" [Quran 4:103], he said it means obligatory.

Hadith 4377

عن زرارة قال: قال أبو جعفر (عليه السلام): فرض الله الصلاة وسن رسول الله صلى الله عليه وآله على عشرة أوجه: صلاة السفر والحضر، وصلاة الخوف على ثلاثة أوجه، وصلاة كسوف الشمس والقمر، وصلاة العيدين وصلاة الاستسقاء، والصلاة على الميت.

From Zurarah who said: Abu Ja'far (peace be upon him) said: Allah prescribed prayer and the Messenger of Allah (peace be upon him and his family) established it in ten forms: prayer while traveling and at home, fear prayer in three forms, prayer during solar and lunar eclipses, prayers of the two Eids, prayer for rain, and prayer for the deceased.

Hadith 4378

عن داود بن فرقد قال: قلت لأبي عبد الله (عليه السلام): قوله تعالى: (إن الصلاة كانت على المؤمنين كتابا موقوتا) قال: كتابا ثابتا.

From Dawud bin Farqad who said: I asked Abu Abdullah (peace be upon him) about His words: "Indeed, prayer has been decreed upon the believers at specified times" [Quran 4:103]. He said: An established decree/ordinance.

Hadith 4379

عن أبي عبد الله (عليه السلام) قال: إن الله فرض الزكاة كما فرض الصلاة.

From Abu Abdullah (peace be upon him) who said: Allah made zakat obligatory just as He made prayer obligatory.

Hadith 4380

قال: وقال الصادق (عليه السلام) في قول الله عز وجل: (إن الصلاة كانت على المؤمنين كتابا موقوتا) قال: مفروضا.

He said: Al-Sadiq (peace be upon him) said regarding Allah's words: "Indeed, prayer has been decreed upon the believers at specified times" [Quran 4:103]. He said: It means prescribed (i.e. made obligatory).

Hadith 4381

عن زرارة والفضيل أنهما قالا: قلنا لأبي جعفر (عليه السلام): أرأيت قول الله عز وجل: (إن الصلاة كانت على المؤمنين كتابا موقوتا)، قال: يعني كتابا مفروضا.

From Zurarah and Al-Fudhayl who both said: We asked Abu Ja'far (peace be upon him) about Allah's words: "Indeed, prayer has been decreed upon the believers at specified times" [Quran 4:103]. He said: It means prescribed writing (or obligatory prescription).

Hadith 4382

عن محمد بن سنان، عن الرضا (عليه السلام)، فيما كتب إليه من جواب مسائله: أن علة الصلاة إنها إقرار بالربوبية لله عز وجل، وخلع الأنداد، وقيام بين يدي الجبار جل جلاله بالذل والمسكنة والخضوع والاعتراف، والطلب للإقالة من سالف الذنوب، ووضع الوجه على الأرض كل يوم إعظاما لله عز وجل،

From Muhammad bin Sinan, from Al-Ridha (peace be upon him), in what he wrote to him answering his questions: The reason for prayer is that it is an acknowledgment of Allah's lordship and rejection of other deities, standing before the Almighty with humility, submissiveness, surrender and confession, seeking forgiveness for past sins, and placing one's face on the ground daily in reverence to Allah.

وأن يكون ناكرا غير ناس ولا بطر، ويكون خاشعا متذللا راغبا طالبا للزيادة في الدين والدنيا، مع ما فيه من الايجاب والمداومة على ذكر الله عز وجل بالليل والنهار لئلا ينسى العبد سيده ومدبره وخالقه فيبطر ويطغى ويكون في ذكره لربه، وقيامه بين يديه زجرا له عن المعاصي، ومانعا له عن أنواع الفساد.

And that one remains mindful, neither forgetful nor arrogant, being humble, submissive, hoping and seeking increase in religion and worldly affairs, along with what it contains of obligation and persistence in remembering Allah day and night, lest the servant forget his Lord, Manager and Creator and become arrogant and transgress. And in remembering his Lord and standing before Him is deterrence from sins and prevention from various forms of corruption.

Hadith 4383

عن هشام بن الحكم قال: سألت أبا عبد الله (عليه السلام) عن علة الصلاة فإن فيها مشغلة للناس عن حوائجهم ومتعبة لهم في أبدانهم؟

From Hisham ibn al-Hakam who said: I asked Abu Abdullah (peace be upon him) about the reason for prayer, as it occupies people from their needs and tires their bodies?

قال: فيها علل، وذلك أن الناس لو تركوا بغير تنبيه ولا تذكير للنبي (صلى الله عليه وآله) بأكثر من الخبر الأول وبقاء الكتاب في أيديهم فقط، لكانوا على ما كان عليه الأولون، فإنهم قد كانوا اتخذوا دينا، ووضعوا كتبا، ودعوا أناسا إلى ما هم عليه، وقتلوهم على ذلك فدرس فدرس أمرهم وذهب حين ذهبوا.

He said: There are reasons for it. If people were left without reminders and remembrance of the Prophet (peace be upon him and his family) beyond the first news and just having the Book in their hands, they would be like those who came before. Those people had adopted a religion, written books, called others to their way, and killed for it. Their matter was erased and disappeared when they disappeared.

وأراد الله تعالى أن لا ينسيهم ذكر محمد (صلى الله عليه وآله) ففرض عليهم الصلاة، يذكرونه في كل يوم خمس مرات ينادون باسمه، وتعبدوا بالصلاة وذكر الله لكيلا يغفلوا عنه فينسوه فيدرس ذكره.

Allah the Exalted wanted them not to forget the remembrance of Muhammad (peace be upon him and his family), so He made prayer obligatory upon them. They remember him five times every day, calling out his name. They worship through prayer and remembrance of Allah so they do not become heedless of him and forget him, causing his remembrance to be erased.

Hadith 4384

وفي (عيون الأخبار) وفي (العلل) عن الرضا (عليه السلام) قال: إنما أمروا بالصلاة لان في الصلاة الاقرار بالربوبية، وهو صلاح عام، لان فيه خلع الأنداد والقيام بين يدي الجبار.

In Uyun al-Akhbar and in al-Ilal, it is narrated from Al-Ridha (peace be upon him) that he said: The people were commanded to perform prayer because in prayer there is acknowledgment of the Lordship (Rububiyyah) of Allah, and this is a universal benefit, for it entails the renunciation of rivals and equals to Allah and the act of standing in the presence of the Almighty.

CHAPTER 2

Obligation Of The Five Daily Prayers - And Non-obligation Of A Sixth Prayer - Each Day

[Hadith 4385 to 4396]

Hadith 4385

عن زرارة قال: سألت أبا جعفر (عليه السلام) عما فرض الله عز وجل من الصلاة؟ فقال: خمس صلوات في الليل والنهار، فقلت: هل سماهن الله وبينهن في كتابه؟ قال: نعم، قال الله تعالى لنبيه (صلى الله عليه وآله): (أقم الصلاة لدلوك الشمس إلى غسق الليل) ودلوكها: زوالها، وفيما بين دلوك الشمس إلى غسق الليل أربع صلوات، سماهن الله وبينهن ووقتهن وغسق الليل هو انتصافه.

From Zurarah, he said: I asked Abu Ja'far (peace be upon him) about what prayers Allah has made obligatory? He said: Five prayers during day and night. I asked: Has Allah named them and explained them in His Book? He said: Yes, Allah said to His Prophet (peace be upon him): "Establish prayer from the decline of the sun until the darkness of night" [Quran 17:78]. Its decline means its setting. Between the sun's decline until night's darkness are four prayers that Allah named, explained and timed. Night's darkness is its middle.

ثم قال تبارك وتعالى: (وقرآن الفجر إن قرآن الفجر كان مشهودا) فهذه الخامسة، وقال تبارك وتعالى في ذلك: (أقم الصلاة طرفي النهار) وطرفاه: المغرب والغداة (وزلفا من الليل)، وهي صلاة العشاء الآخرة، وقال تعالى: (حافظوا على الصلوات والصلاة الوسطى) وهي صلاة الظهر، وهي أول صلاة صلاها رسول الله (صلى الله عليه وآله)، وهي وسط النهار ووسط صلاتين بالنهار صلاة الغداة وصلاة العصر.

Then the Blessed and Exalted said: "And the Quran at dawn. Indeed, the recitation of dawn is ever witnessed" [Quran 17:78]. This is the fifth. And the Blessed and Exalted said regarding that: "Establish prayer at the two ends of the day" [Quran 11:114], and its two ends are: the sunset and the morning, "and at the approach of the night" which is the Isha al-Akhirah (late night prayer). And the Almighty said: "Maintain with care the prayers and the middle prayer" [Quran 2:238], which is the noon prayer (Zuhr), and it is the first prayer that the Messenger of Allah (peace be upon him and his family) prayed, and it is in the middle of the day and between two daytime prayers: the morning prayer (Fajr) and the afternoon prayer (Asr).

وفي بعض القراءة (حافظوا على الصلوات والصلاة الوسطى - صلاة العصر - وقوموا لله قانتين) قال: وأنزلت هذه الآية يوم الجمعة ورسول الله (صلى الله عليه وآله) في سفره فقنت فيها رسول الله (صلى الله عليه وآله) وتركها على حالها في السفر والحضر وأضاف للمقيم ركعتين، وإنما وضعت الركعتان اللتان

أضافهما النبي (صلى الله عليه وآله) يوم الجمعة للمقيم لمكان الخطبتين مع الامام، فمن صلى يوم الجمعة في غير جماعة فليصلها أربع ركعات كصلاة الظهر في سائر الأيام.

In some readings: "Maintain the prayers and the middle prayer - the afternoon prayer - and stand devoutly before Allah" [Quran 2:238]. He said: This verse was revealed on Friday while the Prophet was traveling. The Prophet observed qunut in it and kept it as is during travel and residence, but added two units for residents. The two units the Prophet added on Friday for residents were due to the two sermons with the imam. So whoever prays Friday prayer not in congregation should pray it as four units like the noon prayer on other days.

Hadith 4386

عن جميل بن دراج، عن عائذ الأحمسي قال: دخلت علي أبي عبد الله (عليه السلام) وأنا أريد أن أسأله عن صلاة الليل - إلى أن قال - ثم قال من غير أن أسأله: إذا لقيت الله بالصلوات الخمس المفروضات لم يسألك عما سوى ذلك.

From Jamil ibn Darraj, from A'idh al-Ahmasi who said: I entered upon Abu Abdullah (peace be upon him) wanting to ask him about Salat al-Layl - until he said - then without me asking, he said: If you meet Allah with the five obligatory prayers, He will not question you about anything else.

Hadith 4387

عن أبي جعفر (عليه السلام) قال: قال رسول الله (صلى الله عليه وآله): لو كان على باب دار أحدكم نهر فاغتسل في كل يوم منه خمس مرات، أكان يبقى في جسده من الدرن شئ؟ قلنا: لا، قال: فإن مثل الصلاة كمثل النهر الجاري، كلما صلى صلاة كفرت ما بينهما من الذنوب.

From Abu Ja'far (peace be upon him), he said: The Messenger of Allah (peace be upon him and his family) said: If there were a river at the door of one of your houses, and he bathed in it five times every day, would any filth remain on his body? We said: No. He said: Then the likeness of prayer is like the likeness of a flowing river; every time one performs a prayer, it expiates the sins committed between them.

Hadith 4388

عن معمر بن يحيى قال: سمعت أبا عبد الله (عليه السلام) يقول: لا يسأل الله عبدا عن صلاة بعد الخمس.

From Ma'mar ibn Yahya, he said: I heard Abu Abdullah (peace be upon him) say: Allah will not question a servant about prayer beyond the five.

Hadith 4389

محمد بن علي بن الحسين قال: قال (عليه السلام): إن رسول الله (صلى الله عليه وآله) لما أسري به أمره ربه بخمسين صلاة،

Muhammad ibn Ali ibn al-Husayn said: He (peace be upon him) said: When the Messenger of Allah (peace be upon him and his family) was taken on the night journey, his Lord commanded him with fifty prayers.

فمر على النبيين نبي نبي، لا يسألونه عن شئ، حتى انتهى إلى موسى بن عمران (عليه السلام) فقال: بأي شئ أمرك ربك؟ فقال: بخمسين صلاة، فقال: اسأل ربك التخفيف فإن أمتك لا تطيق ذلك، فسأل ربه فحط عنه عشرا

He passed by the prophets one by one, and none of them asked him anything, until he reached Moses son of Imran (peace be upon him), who said: With what has your Lord commanded you? He said: With fifty prayers. Moses said: Ask your Lord for a reduction, for your community will not be able to bear that. So he asked his Lord, and He reduced it by ten.

ثم مر بالنبيين نبي نبي، لا يسألونه عن شئ حتى مر بموسى بن عمران (عليه السلام) فقال: بأي شئ أمرك ربك؟ فقال: بأربعين صلاة، فقال: اسأل ربك التخفيف فإن أمتك لا تطيق ذلك، فسأل ربه فحط عنه عشرا،

Then he passed by the prophets one by one, and none of them asked him anything, until he passed by Moses son of Imran (peace be upon him), who said: With what has your Lord commanded you? He said: With forty prayers. Moses said: Ask your Lord for a reduction, for your community will not be able to bear that. So he asked his Lord, and He reduced it by ten.

ثم مر بالنبيين نبي نبي، لا يسألونه عن شئ حتى مر بموسى (عليه السلام) فقال: بأي شئ أمرك ربك؟ فقال بثلاثين صلاة، فقال: اسأل ربك التخفيف فإن أمتك لا تطيق ذلك، فسأل ربه عز وجل فحط عنه عشرا،

Then he passed by the prophets one by one, and none of them asked him anything, until he passed by Moses (peace be upon him), who said: With what has your Lord commanded you? He said: With thirty prayers. Moses said: Ask your Lord for a reduction, for your community will not be able to bear that. So he asked his Lord, Mighty and Exalted, and He reduced it by ten.

ثم مر بالنبيين، نبي نبي، لا يسألونه عن شئ حتى مر بموسى (عليه السلام) فقال: بأي شئ أمرك ربك؟ فقال: بعشرين صلاة، فقال: اسأل ربك التخفيف فإن أمتك لا تطيق ذلك، فسأل ربه فحط عنه عشرا،

Then he passed by the prophets one by one, and none of them asked him anything, until he passed by Moses (peace be upon him), who said: With what has your Lord commanded you? He said: With twenty prayers. Moses said: Ask your Lord for a reduction, for your community will not be able to bear that. So he asked his Lord, and He reduced it by ten.

ثم مر بالنبيين، نبي نبي، لا يسألونه عن شئ، حتى مر بموسى (عليه السلام) فقال: بأي شئ أمرك ربك؟ فقال بعشر صلوات، فقال: اسأل ربك التخفيف فإن أمتك لا تطيق ذلك، فإني جئت إلى بني إسرائيل بما افترض الله عليهم فلم يأخذوا به ولم يقروا عليه، فسأل النبي (صلى الله عليه وآله) ربه فخفف عنه فجعلها خمسا،

Then he passed by the prophets one by one, and none of them asked him anything, until he passed by Moses (peace be upon him), who said: With what has your Lord commanded you? He said: With ten prayers. Moses said: Ask your Lord for a reduction, for your community will not be able to bear that. Indeed, I came to the Children of Israel with what Allah had made obligatory upon them, and they neither adhered to it nor accepted it. So the Prophet (peace be upon him and his family) asked his Lord, and He reduced it for him and made it five.

ثم مر بالنبيين، نبي نبي، لا يسألونه عن شئ، حتى مر بموسى (عليه السلام) فقال له: بأي شئ أمرك ربك؟ فقال: بخمس صلوات، فقال اسأل ربك التخفيف عن أمتك فإن أمتك لا تطيق ذلك، فقال: إني لأستحيي أن أعود إلى ربي، فجاء رسول الله (صلى الله عليه وآله) بخمس صلوات.

Then he passed by the prophets one by one, and none of them asked him anything, until he passed by Moses (peace be upon him), who said to him: With what has your Lord commanded you? He said: With five prayers. Moses said: Ask your Lord for a reduction for your community, for your community will not be able to bear that. He said: I am too ashamed to return to my Lord again. And so the Messenger of Allah (peace be upon him and his family) came back with five prayers.

Hadith 4390

عن معمر بن يحيى قال: سمعت أبا عبد الله (عليه السلام) يقول: إذا جئت بالخمس صلوات لم تسأل عن صلاة، وإذا جئت بصوم شهر رمضان لم تسأل عن صوم.

From Muammar ibn Yahya, who said: I heard Abu Abdullah (peace be upon him) say: If you come with the five prayers, you will not be asked about any [other] prayer, and if you come with the fast of the month of Ramadan, you will not be asked about any [other] fast.

Hadith 4391

وبإسناده عن الحسن بن علي بن أبي طالب (عليهما السلام)، أنه قال: جاء نفر من اليهود إلى النبي (صلى الله عليه وآله) فسأله أعلمهم عن مسائل، فكان مما سأله أنه قال: أخبرني عن الله عز وجل لأي شيء فرض هذه الخمس الصلوات في خمس مواقيت على أمتك في ساعات الليل والنهار؟

Through his chain of narration from Al-Hasan bin Ali bin Abi Talib (peace be upon them both), who said: A group of Jews came to the Prophet (peace be upon him and his family) and their most knowledgeable one asked him questions. Among what he asked was: Tell me about Allah, why did He make these five prayers obligatory upon your nation at five specific times during day and night?

فقال النبي (صلى الله عليه وآله): إن الشمس عند الزوال لها حلقة تدخل فيها، فإذا دخلت فيها زالت الشمس، فيسبح كل شيء دون العرش بحمد ربي جل جلاله، وهي الساعة التي يصلي علي فيها ربي جل جلاله، ففرض الله علي وعلى أمتي فيها الصلاة، وقال: (أقم الصلاة لدلوك الشمس إلى غسق الليل) وهي الساعة التي يؤتى فيها بجهنم يوم القيامة فما من مؤمن يوافق تلك الساعة أن يكون ساجدا أو راكعا أو قائما إلا حرم الله جسده على النار.

The Prophet (peace be upon him and his family) said: When the sun declines, it has a ring it enters. When it enters it, the sun declines, and everything below the Throne glorifies my Lord. This is the time when my Lord sends blessings upon me, so Allah made prayer obligatory upon me and my nation at this time. Allah says "Establish prayer from the decline of the sun until the darkness of night" [Quran 17:78]. This is the hour when Hell will be brought forth on the Day of Judgment. Any believer who is prostrating (in sujud), bowing (in ruku) or standing (in qiyam) at that time, Allah will forbid their body from the Fire.

وأما صلاة العصر فهي الساعة التي أكل آدم فيها من الشجرة فأخرجه الله عز وجل من الجنة، فأمره الله ذريته بهذه الصلاة إلى يوم القيامة، واختارها الله لأمتي فهي من أحب الصلوات إلى الله عز وجل وأوصاني أن أحفظها من بين الصلوات،

As for Asr prayer, it is the hour when Adam ate from the tree and Allah expelled him from Paradise. Allah ordered his descendants to pray at this time until the Day of Judgment. Allah chose it for my nation and it is among the most beloved prayers to Allah. He advised me to guard it among the prayers.

وأما صلاة المغرب فهي الساعة التي تاب الله عز وجل فيها على آدم (عليه السلام)، وكان بين ما أكل من الشجرة وبين ما تاب الله عز وجل عليه ثلاث مائة سنة من أيام الدنيا، وفي أيام الآخرة يوم كألف سنة مما بين العصر إلى العشاء، وصلى آدم (عليه السلام) ثلاث ركعات: ركعة لخطيئته، وركعة لخطيئة حواء، وركعة لتوبته، ففرض الله عز وجل هذه الثلاث ركعات على أمتي، وهي الساعة التي يستجاب فيها الدعاء، فوعدني ربي عز وجل أن يستجيب لمن دعاه فيها. وهي الصلاة التي أمرني ربي بها في قوله

تعالى: (فسبحان الله حين تمسون وحين تصبحون)

As for Maghrib prayer, it is the hour when Allah accepted Adam's repentance. Between eating from the tree and Allah accepting his repentance was three hundred years of worldly days. In the Hereafter, a day is like a thousand years between Asr and Isha. Adam prayed three units: one for his mistake, one for Eve's mistake, and one for his repentance. So Allah made these three units obligatory upon my nation. This is the hour when supplications are answered. My Lord promised to respond to whoever supplicates during it. This is the prayer my Lord commanded me with in His saying "So glorify Allah when you reach the evening and when you reach the morning" [Quran 30:17].

وأما صلاة العشاء الآخرة فإن للقبر ظلمة، وليوم القيامة ظلمة، أمرني ربي عز وجل وأمتي بهذه الصلاة لتنور القبر، وليعطيني وأمتي النور على الصراط، وما من قدم مشت إلى صلاة العتمة إلا حرم الله عز وجل جسدها على النار، وهي الصلاة التي اختارها الله تقدس ذكره للمرسلين قبلي،

As for the last Isha prayer, the grave has darkness and the Day of Judgment has darkness. My Lord commanded me and my nation with this prayer to illuminate the grave and grant us light on the path. No foot that walks to salat al-atmah (Isha) except Allah forbids its body from the Fire. This is the prayer that Allah chose for the messengers before me.

وأما صلاة الفجر فإن الشمس إذا طلعت تطلع على قرن شيطان، فأمرني ربي أن أصلي قبل طلوع الشمس صلاة الغداة، وقبل أن يسجد لها الكافر لتسجد أمتي لله عز وجل، وسرعتها أحب إلى الله عز وجل، وهي الصلاة التي تشهدها ملائكة الليل وملائكة النهار.

As for Fajr prayer, when the sun rises it rises on the horn of Satan. My Lord commanded me to pray the morning prayer before sunrise and before the disbelievers prostrate to it, so my nation prostrates to Allah. Praying it early is more beloved to Allah. This is the prayer witnessed by the angels of night and day.

Hadith 4392

قال: وقال (عليه السلام): إنما مثل الصلاة فيكم كمثل السري، وهو النهر، على باب أحدكم يخرج إليه في اليوم والليلة يغتسل منه خمس مرات فلم يبق الدرن على الغسل خمس مرات، ولم تبق الذنوب (على الصلاة) خمس مرات.

He said: He (peace be upon him) said: The example of prayer among you is like that of a flowing river at the door of any of you - he goes to it five times day and night to bathe in it. Thus no dirt remains after bathing five times, and no sins remain (with prayer) five times.

Hadith 4393

عن الحسين بن أبي العلاء، عن أبي عبد الله (عليه السلام) قال: لما هبط آدم من الجنة ظهرت به شامة سوداء من قرنه إلى قدمه، فطال حزنه وبكاؤه على ما ظهر به فأتاه جبرئيل (عليه السلام) فقال: ما يبكيك يا آدم؟ فقال: من هذه الشامة التي ظهرت بي،

From Al-Husayn bin Abi Al-Ala, from Abu Abdullah (peace be upon him) who said: When Adam descended from Paradise, a black birthmark appeared on him from his head to his feet. His grief and crying prolonged over what appeared on him. So Jibreel (peace be upon him) came to him and said: What makes you cry, O Adam? He said: Because of this birthmark that appeared on me.

قال: قم يا آدم فصل فهذا وقت الصلاة الأولى، فقام وصلى، فانحطت الشامة إلى عنقه، فجاءه في الصلاة الثانية فقال: قم فصل يا آدم، فهذا وقت الصلاة الثانية، فقام وصلى فانحطت الشامة إلى سرته،

He said: Stand O Adam and pray, for this is the time of the first prayer. He stood and prayed, and the birthmark descended to his neck. Then he came at the second prayer and said: Stand and pray O Adam, for this is the time of the second prayer. He stood and prayed, and the birthmark descended to his navel.

فجاءه في الصلاة الثالثة فقال: يا آدم قم فصل، فهذا وقت الصلاة الثالثة. فقام فصلى فانحطت الشامة إلى ركبتيه، فجاءه في الصلاة الرابعة فقال: يا آدم قم فصل، فهذا وقت الصلاة الرابعة، فقام فصلى فانحطت الشامة، إلى قدميه،

Then he came at the third prayer and said: O Adam stand and pray, for this is the time of the third prayer. He stood and prayed and the birthmark descended to his knees. Then he came at the fourth prayer and said: O Adam stand and pray, for this is the time of the fourth prayer. He stood and prayed and the birthmark descended to his feet.

فجاءه في الصلاة الخامسة فقال: يا آدم قم فصل، فهذا وقت الصلاة الخامسة، فقام فصلى، فخرج منها، فحمد الله وأثنى عليه، فقال جبرئيل: يا آدم، مثل ولدك في هذه الصلاة كمثلك في هذه الشامة، من صلى من ولدك في كل يوم وليلة خمس صلوات خرج من ذنوبه كما خرجت من هذه الشامة.

Then he came at the fifth prayer and said: O Adam stand and pray, for this is the time of the fifth prayer. He stood and prayed, and it left him completely. He praised Allah and extolled Him. So Jibreel said: O Adam, the example of your children with these prayers is like your example with this birthmark - whoever among your children prays five prayers every day and night will be freed from his sins just as you were freed from this birthmark.

———

Hadith 4394

عن زيد بن علي قال: سألت أبي سيد العابدين (عليه السلام) فقلت له: يا أبه، أخبرني عن جدنا رسول الله (صلى الله عليه وآله) لما عرج به إلى السماء وأمره ربه عز وجل بخمسين صلاة، كيف لم يسأله التخفيف عن أمته حتى قال له موسى بن عمران: ارجع إلى ربك فاسأله التخفيف، فإن أمتك لا تطيق ذلك؟

From Zayd bin Ali who said: I asked my father, the Master of Worshippers (peace be upon him): O father, tell me about our grandfather the Messenger of Allah (peace be upon him and his family) - when he was taken up to heaven and his Lord commanded him with fifty prayers, why didn't he ask for reduction for his nation until Moses bin Imran told him: Return to your Lord and ask Him for reduction, for your nation cannot bear that?

فقال: يا بني، إن رسول الله (صلى الله عليه وآله) لا يتقرح على ربه عز وجل ولا يراجعه في شيء يأمره به، فلما سأله موسى ذلك وصار شفيعا لامته إليه لم يجز له رد شفاعة أخيه موسى، فرجع إلى ربه فسأله التخفيف إلى أن ردها إلى خمس صلوات،

He said: O my son, indeed the Messenger of Allah (peace be upon him and his family) would not impose upon his Lord nor review anything He commands. When Moses asked that and became an intercessor for his nation, it was not appropriate for him to reject his brother Moses's intercession. So he returned to his Lord and asked for reduction until they became five prayers.

فقلت له: يا أبت، فلم لم يرجع إلى ربه عز وجل ولم يسأله التخفيف من خمس صلوات، قد سأله موسى (عليه السلام) أن يرجع إلى ربه عز وجل ويسأله التخفيف؟

I said to him: O father, why didn't he return to his Lord and ask for reduction from five prayers when Moses (peace be upon him) asked him to return to his Lord and ask for reduction?

فقال: يا بني، أراد (عليه السلام) أن يحصل لامته التخفيف مع أجر خمسين صلاة، لقول الله عز وجل: (من جاء بالحسنة فله عشر أمثالها) ألا ترى أنه لما هبط إلى الأرض نزل عليه جبرئيل فقال: يا محمد، إن ربك يقرئك السلام ويقول إنها خمس بخمسين، (ما يبدل القول لدي وما أنا بظلام للعبيد).

He said: O my son, he (peace be upon him) wanted his nation to get the reduction while maintaining the reward of fifty prayers, due to Allah's saying: "Whoever brings a good deed will have ten times the like thereof" [Quran 6:160]. Don't you see that when he descended to earth, Jibreel came down to him and said: O Muhammad, your Lord conveys His peace to you and says these are five equal to fifty, "The word will not be changed with Me, and I am not unjust to the servants" [Quran 50:29].

———

Hadith 4395

عن أنس قال: فرضت على النبي (صلى الله عليه وآله) ليلة أسري به الصلاة خمسين، ثم نقصت فجعلت خمسا، ثم نودي يا محمد، إنه لا يبدل القول لدي، إن لك بهذه الخمس خمسين.

From Anas who said: On the night of Isra, fifty prayers were prescribed for the Prophet (peace be upon him and his family), then they were reduced until they were made five. Then it was called: O Muhammad, indeed My word does not change with Me, and for you these five prayers are equal to fifty.

———————

Hadith 4396

عن أبي عبد الله (عليه السلام) قال: لما خفف الله عن النبي (صلى الله عليه وآله) حتى صارت خمس صلوات أوحى الله إليه يا محمد خمس بخمسين.

From Abu Abdullah (peace be upon him) who said: When Allah lightened the prayers for the Prophet (peace be upon him and his family) until they became five prayers, Allah revealed to him: O Muhammad, five [prayers] equal to fifty [in reward].

———————

CHAPTER 3

Recommendation Of Ordering Children To Pray At Six Or Seven Years, And The Obligation Upon Them At Puberty

[Hadith 4397 to 4404]

Hadith 4397

عن معاوية بن وهب قال: سألت أبا عبد الله (عليه السلام) في كم يؤخذ الصبي بالصلاة؟ فقال: فيما بين سبع سنين وست سنين.

From Mu'awiyah ibn Wahb who said: I asked Abu Abdullah (peace be upon him) at what age should a child be made to pray? He said: Between seven years and six years.

Hadith 4398

عن محمد بن مسلم، عن أحدهما (عليهما السلام) في الصبي، متى يصلي؟ فقال: إذا عقل الصلاة، قلت: متى يعقل الصلاة وتجب عليه؟ قال: لست سنين.

From Muhammad ibn Muslim, from one of them (peace be upon them) regarding the child, when should he pray? He said: When he understands prayer. I asked: When does he understand prayer and when does it become obligatory upon him? He said: At six years.

أقول: هذا محمول على الاستحباب لما تقدم في مقدمة العبادات ولما يأتي، ويمكن حمل الوجوب على الصلاة على جنازته إذا مات لما تقدم.

I (Hurr Amili) say: This is interpreted as recommended based on what was mentioned in the introduction to acts of worship and what will follow. The obligation can be interpreted as prayer over his funeral if he dies, based on what preceded.

Hadith 4399

عن علي بن جعفر، عن أخيه موسى (عليه السلام) قال: سألته عن الغلام، متى يجب عليه الصوم والصلاة؟ قال: إذا راهق الحلم وعرف الصلاة والصوم.

From Ali ibn Ja'far, from his brother Musa (peace be upon him) who said: I asked him about the boy, when does fasting and prayer become obligatory upon him? He said: When he approaches puberty and understands prayer and fasting.

Hadith 4400

عن أبي عبد الله (عليه السلام) قال: إذا أتى على الصبي ست سنين وجب عليه الصلاة، وإذا أطاق الصوم وجب عليه الصيام.

From Abu Abdullah (peace be upon him) who said: When a child reaches six years prayer becomes obligatory upon him, and when he can endure fasting then fasting becomes obligatory upon him.

―――――

Hadith 4401

عن أبي عبد الله (عليه السلام)، عن أبيه قال: إنا نأمر صبياننا بالصلاة إذا كانوا بني خمس سنين، فمروا صبيانكم بالصلاة إذا كانوا بني سبع سنين.

From Abu Abdullah (peace be upon him), from his father who said: We order our children to pray when they are five years old, so order your children to pray when they are seven years old.

―――――

Hadith 4402

عن الحسن بن قارن أنه قال: سألت الرضا (عليه السلام)، أو سئل وأنا أسمع، عن الرجل يجبر ولده وهو لا يصلي اليوم واليومين، فقال: وكم أتى على الغلام؟ فقلت: ثماني سنين، فقال: سبحان الله، يترك الصلاة؟! قال: قلت: يصيبه الوجع، قال: يصلي على نحو ما يقدر.

From Al-Hasan ibn Qarin who said: I asked Al-Ridha (peace be upon him), or he was asked while I was listening, about a man compelling his child who does not pray for a day or two. He said: How old is the boy? I said: Eight years. He said: Glory be to Allah, he abandons prayer?! I said: He experiences pain. He said: He should pray according to his ability.

―――――

Hadith 4403

عن أبي عبد الله أو أبي جعفر (عليهما السلام) - في حديث - قال: سمعته يقول: يترك الغلام حتى يتم له سبع سنين فإذا تم له سبع سنين قيل له: اغسل وجهك وكفيك، فإذا غسلهما قيل له: صل ثم يترك حتى يتم له تسع سنين، فإذا تمت له علم الوضوء وضرب عليه، وأمر بالصلاة وضرب عليها، فإذا تعلم الوضوء والصلاة غفر الله لوالديه إن شاء الله.

From Abu Abdullah or Abu Ja'far (peace be upon them) - in a hadith - he said: I heard him say: The boy is left until he completes seven years, when he completes seven years he is told: wash your face and hands. When he washes them he is told: pray. Then he is left until he completes nine years. When he completes them he is taught wudu and disciplined for it, and ordered to pray and disciplined for it. When he learns wudu and prayer, Allah forgives his parents if He wills.

―――――

Hadith 4404

وفي (الخصال) بإسناده الآتي: عن علي (عليه السلام) في حديث الأربعمائة – قال: علموا صبيانكم الصلاة وخذوهم بها إذا بلغوا ثماني سنين.

In Al-Khisal, with the upcoming chain of narration: From Ali (peace be upon him) in the hadith of four hundred - he said: Teach your children prayer and require it of them when they reach eight years of age.

CHAPTER 4

Recommendation Of Instructing Children To Combine Prayers And Separate Them During Prayer Rows

[Hadith 4405 to 4406]

Hadith 4405

عن الفضيل بن يسار قال: كان علي بن الحسين (عليه السلام) يأمر الصبيان يجمعون بين المغرب والعشاء، ويقول: هو خير من أن يناموا عنها.

From Al-Fudhayl bin Yasar who said: Ali bin Al-Husayn (peace be upon him) used to order the children to combine Maghrib and Isha prayers, and he would say: It is better than them sleeping and missing it.

Hadith 4406

عن أبي جعفر (عليه السلام)، قال: سألته عن الصبيان إذا صفوا في الصلاة المكتوبة؟ قال لا تؤخروهم عن الصلاة، وفرقوا بينهم.

From Abu Ja'far (peace be upon him), he said: I asked him about children when they form rows in the obligatory prayer? He said: Do not delay them from prayer, and separate (*) between them [in the rows].

Translator: * The children should be separated from each other. This could be for practical reasons, such as to prevent them from distracting or disturbing each other or to inculcate a sense of individual responsibility and focus during the prayer.

CHAPTER 5

Obligation Of Maintaining The Middle Prayer And Its Specification

[Hadith 4407 to 4412]

Hadith 4407

عن زرارة، عن أبي جعفر (عليه السلام) - في حديث - قال: وقال تعالى: (حافظوا على الصلوات والصلاة الوسطى) وهي صلاة الظهر - إلى أن قال - وأنزلت هذه الآية يوم الجمعة ورسول الله (صلى الله عليه وآله) في سفر، فقنت فيها وتركها على حالها في السفر والحضر.

From Zurarah, from Abu Ja'far (peace be upon him) - in a hadith - he said: And Allah the Exalted said: "Guard strictly the prayers especially the middle prayer" [Quran 2:238] and it is the Zuhr prayer - until he said - and this verse was revealed on Friday while the Messenger of Allah (peace be upon him and his family) was traveling, so he performed Qunut in it and kept it in its state during travel and residence.

Hadith 4408

عن أبي بصير - يعني المرادي - قال: سمعت أبا عبد الله (عليه السلام) يقول: صلاة الوسطى صلاة الظهر وهي أول صلاة أنزل الله على نبيه (صلى الله عليه وآله).

From Abu Basir - meaning Al-Muradi - he said: I heard Abu Abdullah (peace be upon him) saying: The middle prayer is the Zuhr prayer and it is the first prayer that Allah revealed to His Prophet (peace be upon him and his family).

Hadith 4409

الفضل بن الحسن الطبرسي في (مجمع البيان) عن أبي جعفر وأبي عبد الله (عليهما السلام) في الصلاة الوسطى أنها صلاة الظهر.

Al-Fadhl ibn Al-Hasan Al-Tabrasi in (Majma' Al-Bayan) from Abu Ja'far and Abu Abdullah (peace be upon them) regarding the middle prayer that it is the Zuhr prayer.

Hadith 4410

وعن علي (عليه السلام) أنها الجمعة يوم الجمعة، والظهر في سائر الأيام.

And from Ali (peace be upon him) that it is the Friday prayer on Friday, and Zuhr on other days.

Hadith 4411

عن أبي عبد الله (عليه السلام) قال: (الصلاة الوسطى): الظهر، وقوموا لله قانتين): إقبال الرجل على صلاته ومحافظته على وقتها حتى لا يلهيه عنها ولا يشغله شئ.

From Abu Abdullah (peace be upon him) he said: "The middle prayer" is Zuhr, and "stand before Allah devoutly" means a person's attention to his prayer and maintaining its time so that nothing distracts or occupies him from it.

Hadith 4412

عن أبي عبد الله (عليه السلام) قال: صلاة الوسطى هي الوسطى من صلاة النهار، وهي الظهر، وإنما يحافظ أصحابنا على الزوال من أجلها. أقول: وتقدم ما يشعر بأنها العصر، وهو محمول على التقية في الرواية.

From Abu Abdullah (peace be upon him) he said: The middle prayer is the middle of the daytime prayers, and it is Zuhr, and our companions observe the zenith because of it. I (Hurr Amili) say: What has preceded indicates that it is Asr, and this is interpreted as taqiyyah in the narration.

CHAPTER 6

Prohibition Of Taking Prayer Lightly And Being Negligent About It

[Hadith 4413 to 4424]

Hadith 4413

عن زرارة، عن أبي جعفر (عليه السلام)، قال: قال: لا تتهاون بصلاتك، فإن النبي (صلى الله عليه وآله) قال عند موته: ليس مني من استخف بصلاته، ليس مني من شرب مسكرا، لا يرد على الحوض لا والله.

From Zurarah, from Abu Ja'far (peace be upon him), who said: He said: Do not be negligent regarding your prayer, for the Prophet (peace be upon him and his family) said at the time of his death: He is not of me who takes his prayer lightly, he is not of me who drinks an intoxicant, he shall not be admitted to the Hawd (Pool), no, by Allah.

Hadith 4414

عن العيص بن القاسم قال: قال أبو عبد الله (عليه السلام): والله إنه ليأتي على الرجل خمسون سنة وما قبل الله منه صلاة واحدة، فأي شئ أشد من هذا، والله إنكم لتعرفون من جيرانكم وأصحابكم من لو كان يصلي لبعضكم ما قبلها منه لاستخفافه بها. إن الله لا يقبل إلا الحسن، فكيف يقبل ما يستخف به؟!.

From Al-Iys bin Al-Qasim, he said: Abu Abdullah (peace be upon him) said: By Allah, fifty years may pass over a man and Allah has not accepted a single prayer from him, so what thing is more severe than this? By Allah, you certainly know among your neighbors and your companions someone who, if he were to pray for one of you, you would not accept it from him due to his taking it lightly. Indeed, Allah does not accept except the good, so how could He accept what is taken lightly?!

Hadith 4415

عن أبي بصير قال: قال أبو الحسن الأول (عليه السلام): لما حضر أبي الوفاة قال لي: يا بني، إنه لا ينال شفاعتنا من استخف بالصلاة.

From Abu Basir who said: Abu Al-Hasan the First (peace be upon him) said: When my father was near death, he said to me: O my son, our intercession cannot be obtained by one who takes prayer lightly.

Hadith 4416

عن جعفر، عن أبيه قال: قال رسول الله (صلى الله عليه وآله): لكل شئ وجه ووجه دينكم الصلاة، فلا يشينن أحدكم وجه دينه، ولكل شئ أنف، وأنف الصلاة التكبير.

From Ja'far, from his father who said: The Messenger of Allah (peace be upon him and his family) said: Everything has a face, and the face of your religion is prayer, so let none of you disfigure the face of his religion. Everything has a nose, and the nose of prayer is the opening takbir.

Hadith 4417

محمد بن علي بن الحسين قال: قال رسول الله (صلى الله عليه وآله): ليس مني من استخف بصلاته، لا يرد علي الحوض، لا والله، ليس مني من شرب مسكرا، لا يرد علي الحوض، لا والله.

Muhammad ibn Ali ibn al-Husayn said: The Messenger of Allah (peace be upon him and his family) said: He is not of me who takes his prayer lightly; he shall not come to me at the Pond, no, by Allah. He is not of me who drinks an intoxicant; he shall not come to me at the Pond, no, by Allah.

Hadith 4418

قال: وقال الصادق (عليه السلام): إن شفاعتنا لا تنال مستخفا بالصلاة.

He said: And Al-Sadiq (peace be upon him) said: Our intercession cannot be obtained by one who takes prayer lightly.

Hadith 4419

عن زرارة، عن أبي جعفر (عليه السلام) قال: لا تستحقرن بالبول ولا تتهاونن به ولا بصلاتك، فإن رسول الله (صلى الله عليه وآله) قال عند موته: ليس مني من استخف بصلاته، لا يرد علي الحوض لا والله، ليس مني من شرب مسكرا، لا يرد علي الحوض لا والله.

From Zurarah, from Abu Ja'far (peace be upon him), who said: Do not be negligent regarding urine, and do not be careless about it, nor about your prayer. For the Messenger of Allah (peace be upon him and his family) said at the time of his death: He is not of me who takes his prayer lightly - he shall not come to me at the Pond, no, by Allah. He is not of me who drinks an intoxicant - he shall not come to me at the Pond, no, by Allah.

Hadith 4420

عن أبي عبد الله (عليه السلام) قال: قال رسول الله (صلى الله عليه وآله): ليس مني من استخف بالصلاة، لا يرد علي الحوض، لا والله.

From Abu Abdullah (peace be upon him) that the Messenger of Allah (peace be upon him and his family) said: He is not of me who takes prayer lightly. He shall not come to me at the Pond. No, by Allah.

Hadith 4421

عن أبي عبد الله (عليه السلام) قال: الصلاة وكل بها ملك ليس له عمل غيرها. فإذا فرغ منها قبضها ثم صعد بها. فإن كانت مما تقبل قبلت، وإن كانت مما لاتقبل قيل له: ردها على عبدي، فينزل بها حتى يضرب بها وجهه، ثم يقول: أف لك، لا يزال لك عمل يعنيني.

From Abu Abdullah (peace be upon him), he said: An angel is assigned to prayer who has no task other than it. When one completes it, the angel takes it and ascends with it. If it is from what is accepted, it is accepted, and if it is from what is not accepted, it is said to him: Return it to my servant. So he descends with it until he strikes his face with it, then says: Uff to you, you continue to have deeds that concern me.

Hadith 4422

عن أبي جعفر (عليه السلام) قال: قال رسول الله (صلى الله عليه وآله): لا ينال شفاعتي من استخف بصلاته، لا يرد علي الحوض، لا والله.

From Abu Ja'far (peace be upon him) who said: The Messenger of Allah (peace be upon him and his family) said: My intercession will not reach one who takes his prayer lightly, he will not meet me at the Pool, by Allah no!

Hadith 4423

عن أبي بصير قال: دخلت على أم حميدة أعزيها بأبي عبد الله (عليه السلام)، فبكت وبكيت لبكائها، ثم قالت: يا أبا محمد، لو رأيت أبا عبد الله (عليه السلام) عند الموت لرأيت عجبا، فتح عينيه ثم قال: اجمعوا كل من بيني وبينه قرابة. قالت: فما تركنا أحدا إلا جمعناه، فنظر إليهم ثم قال: إن شفاعتنا لا تنال مستخفا بالصلاة.

From Abu Basir who said: I entered upon Umm Humayda to offer my condolences for the loss of Abu Abdullah (peace be upon him). She wept and I wept because of her weeping. Then she said: O Abu Muhammad, if you had seen Abu Abdullah (peace be upon him) at the moment of death, you would have witnessed something remarkable. He opened his eyes and then said: Gather everyone who has a kinship relation with me. She said: We left no one out but that we gathered them. He looked at them and then said: Verily, our intercession shall not reach one who takes the prayer lightly.

Hadith 4424

عن أبي جعفر (عليه السلام) قال: الصلاة عمود الدين، مثلها كمثل عمود الفسطاط، إذا ثبت العمود ثبت الأوتاد والاطناب، وإذا مال العمود وانكسر لم يثبت وتد ولا طنب.

From Abu Ja'far (peace be upon him) who said: Prayer is the pillar of religion. Its example is like the pole of a tent - when the pole is firm, the pegs and ropes are firm. When the pole leans and breaks, no peg or rope remains firm.

CHAPTER 7

Prohibition Of Neglecting Prayer And The Obligation Of Preserving It

[Hadith 4425 to 4432]

Hadith 4425

عن محمد بن الفضيل قال: سألت عبدا صالحا (عليه السلام) عن قول الله عز وجل: (الذين هم عن صلاتهم ساهون) قال: هو التضييع.

From Muhammad ibn al-Fudayl, who said: I asked the Righteous Servant (peace be upon him) about the saying of Allah, the Mighty and Majestic: "those who are heedless of their prayers" [Quran, 107:5]. He said: It refers to neglect.

Hadith 4426

عن أبي عبد الله (عليه السلام) قال: قال رسول الله (صلى الله عليه وآله): لا يزال الشيطان ذعرا من المؤمن ما حافظ على الصلوات الخمس لوقتهن، فإذا ضيعهن تجرأ عليه فأدخله في العظائم.

From Abu Abdullah (peace be upon him) that the Messenger of Allah (peace be upon him and his family) said: Satan remains in a state of dread and fear of the believer as long as he maintains the five daily prayers at their appointed times. But when the believer neglects them, Satan grows bold against him and leads him into grave sins.

Hadith 4427

عن الفضيل قال: سألت أبا جعفر (عليه السلام) عن قول الله عز وجل: (الذين هم على صلاتهم يحافظون) قال: هي الفريضة، قلت: (الذين هم على صلاتهم دائمون) قال، هي النافلة.

From Al-Fadil who said: I asked Abu Ja'far (peace be upon him) about Allah's words: "Those who carefully maintain their prayers" [Quran 23:9], he said: These are the obligatory prayers. I asked about "Those who are constant in their prayers" [Quran 70:23], he said: These are the supererogatory prayers (Nafilah).

Hadith 4428

عن داود بن فرقد قال: قلت لأبي عبد الله (عليه السلام): قوله تعالى: (إن الصلاة كانت على المؤمنين كتابا موقوتا) قال: كتابا ثابتا، وليس إن عجلت قليلا أو أخرت قليلا بالذي يضرك ما لم تضيع تلك الإضاعة، فإن الله عز وجل يقول لقوم: (أضاعوا الصلاة واتبعوا الشهوات فسوف يلقون غيا).

From Dawud bin Farqad who said: I said to Abu Abdullah (peace be upon him) regarding the words of the Most High: "Indeed, prayer has been decreed upon the believers a decree of specified times" [Quran 4:103]. He said: A fixed decree, and it will not harm you if you hasten it a little or delay it a little (*) as long as you do not neglect it with that negligence, for Allah the Mighty and Majestic says about a people: "But there came after them successors who neglected prayer and pursued desires; so they are going to meet evil" [Quran 19:59].

Translator: * This minor advancement or delay within the legitimate time frame is acceptable as long as the prayer remains within its prescribed time window and there is no habitual negligence or disregard for prayer times.

Hadith 4429

محمد بن علي بن الحسين قال: قال الصادق (عليه السلام) - في حديث -: إن ملك الموت يدفع الشيطان عن المحافظ على الصلاة، ويلقنه شهادة أن لا إله إلا الله وأن محمدا رسول الله، في تلك الحالة العظيمة.

Muhammad ibn Ali ibn al-Husayn said: Al-Sadiq (peace be upon him) said, in a hadith: Verily, the angel of death repels Satan away from the one who is diligent in observing the prayer, and he prompts him with the testimony that there is no god but Allah and that Muhammad is the Messenger of Allah, in that momentous state.

Hadith 4430

وفي (عيون الأخبار) بالاسناد المذكور في إسباغ الوضوء عن الرضا، عن أبيه (عليه السلام) قال: قال رسول الله (صلى الله عليه وآله): إذا كان يوم القيامة يدعى بالعبد، فأول شئ يسأل عنه: الصلاة، فإذا جاء بها تامة وإلا زج في النار.

In Uyun Al-Akhbar, with the chain mentioned regarding perfecting wudu, from Al-Ridha, from his father (peace be upon him) who said: The Messenger of Allah (peace be upon him and his family) said: On the Day of Judgment, when a servant is called, the first thing they will be asked about is prayer. If they bring it complete, [all is well], otherwise they will be thrown into the Fire.

Hadith 4431

قال: وقال رسول الله (صلى الله عليه وآله): لا تضيعوا صلواتكم فإن من ضيع صلاته حشر مع قارون وهامان، وكان حقا على الله أن يدخله النار مع المنافقين، فالويل لمن لم يحافظ على صلاته وأداء سنته.

He said: And the Messenger of Allah (peace be upon him and his family) said: Do not neglect your prayers, for whoever neglects his prayers will be resurrected alongside Qarun and Haman, and it will be incumbent upon Allah to admit him into the Fire along with the hypocrites. So woe to the one who does not guard his prayers and fulfill his prescribed devotions.

Hadith 4432

محمد بن الحسين الرضي في (نهج البلاغة) عن أمير المؤمنين (عليه السلام) أنه قال في كلام يوصي أصحابه: تعاهدوا أمر الصلاة، وحافظوا عليها، واستكثروا منها، وتقربوا بها، فإنها كانت على المؤمنين كتابا موقوتا، ألا تسمعون إلى جواب أهل النار حين سئلوا: (ما سلككم في سقر، قالوا: لم نك من المصلين).

Muhammad bin Al-Husayn Al-Radi in (Nahj Al-Balagha) from Amir Al-Mu'minin (peace be upon him) that he said in advice to his companions: Look after the matter of prayer, guard it, do it abundantly, and seek closeness through it. Indeed it is prescribed for the believers at set times. Do you not hear the response of the people of Hell when they are asked: "What brought you into Hell? They said: We were not among those who prayed" [Quran 74:42-43].

وإنها لتحت الذنوب حت الورق، وتطلقها إطلاق الربق، وشبهها رسول الله (صلى الله عليه وآله) بالحمة تكون على باب الرجل فهو يغتسل منها في اليوم والليلة خمس مرات، فما عسى أن يبقى عليه من الدرن، وقد عرف حقها رجال من المؤمنين الذين لا تشغلهم عنها زينة متاع، ولا قرة عين من ولد ولامال،

And indeed it (the prayer) strips away sins as leaves are stripped from trees, and releases them (the people) from the bonds of shackles. The Messenger of Allah (peace be upon him and his family) likened it to a flowing spring at the door of a man, from which he bathes five times each day and night - so what filth could possibly remain upon him? And its true worth has been recognized by men among the believers, whom neither the adornment of worldly possessions, nor the delight of children, nor wealth can distract from it.

يقول الله سبحانه: (رجال لا تلهيهم تجارة ولا بيع عن ذكر الله وإقام الصلاة وإيتاء الزكاة)، وكان رسول الله (صلى الله عليه وآله) نصبا بالصلاة بعد التبشير له بالجنة، لقول الله سبحانه (وأمر أهلك بالصلاة واصطبر عليها) فكان يأمر بها أهله ويصبر عليها نفسه.

Allah, Glory be to Him, says: "Men whom neither trade nor sale distracts from the remembrance of Allah and performance of prayer and giving of zakat" [Quran 24:37]. The Messenger of Allah (peace be upon him and his family) was dedicated to prayer even after being given glad tidings of Paradise, due to Allah's words: "And enjoin prayer upon your family and be steadfast therein" [Quran 20:132]. So he would command his family with it and remain patient in performing it himself.

CHAPTER 8

Obligation Of Completing Prayer And Establishing It
[Hadith 4433 to 4446]

Hadith 4433

عن زرارة، عن أبي جعفر (عليه السلام) قال: إذا ما أدى الرجل صلاة واحدة تامة قبلت جميع صلاته، وإن كن غير تامات، وإن أفسدها كلها لم يقبل منه شئ منها، ولم تحسب له نافلة ولا فريضة.

From Zurarah, from Abu Ja'far (peace be upon him), who said: If a man performs a single prayer completely and properly, then all of his prayers will be accepted, even if the rest of them were incomplete (deficient or imperfect). But if he corrupts all of them, then none of them will be accepted from him, and neither his supererogatory prayers nor his obligatory prayers will be counted in his favor.

وإنما تقبل النافلة بعد قبول الفريضة، وإذا لم يؤد الرجل الفريضة لم تقبل منه النافلة، وإنما جعلت النافلة ليتم بها ما أفسد من الفريضة.

Supererogatory prayers are only accepted after the acceptance of obligatory prayers. If a person does not perform the obligatory prayer, his supererogatory prayers are not accepted. Supererogatory prayers were only established to complete what was corrupted from the obligatory prayers.

Hadith 4434

عن زرارة عن أبي جعفر (عليه السلام) قال: بينا رسول الله (صلى الله عليه وآله) جالس في المسجد إذ دخل رجل فقام يصلي، فلم يتم ركوعه ولا سجوده، فقال (صلى الله عليه وآله): نقر كنقر الغراب، لئن مات هذا وهكذا صلاته ليموتن على غير ديني.

From Zurarah, from Abu Ja'far (peace be upon him) who said: While the Messenger of Allah (peace be upon him and his family) was sitting in the mosque, a man entered and stood to pray. He did not complete his ruku or sujud, so he (the Prophet) said: He pecks like the pecking of a crow. If this man dies while his prayer is like this, he will die following other than my religion.

Hadith 4435

عن يزيد بن خليفة قال: سمعت أبا عبد الله (عليه السلام) يقول: إذا قام المصلي إلى الصلاة نزلت عليه الرحمة من أعنان السماء إلى الأرض، وحفت به الملائكة. وناداه ملك: لو يعلم هذا المصلي ما في الصلاة ما انفتل.

From Yazid bin Khalifa who said: I heard Abu Abdullah (peace be upon him) saying: When a person stands for prayer, mercy descends upon him from the heights of heaven to earth, angels surround him, and an angel calls out: If this person praying knew what was in prayer, he would not turn away.

Hadith 4436

عن هارون بن خارجة قال: ذكرت لأبي عبد الله (عليه السلام) رجلا من أصحابنا فأحسنت عليه الثناء، فقال لي: كيف صلاته؟

From Harun bin Kharija who said: I mentioned one of our companions to Abu Abdullah (peace be upon him) and praised him well, so he said to me: How is his prayer?

Hadith 4437

عن أبي جعفر (عليه السلام) قال: قال رسول الله (صلى الله عليه وآله): إذا قام العبد المؤمن في صلاته نظر الله عز وجل إليه، أو قال: أقبل الله عليه حتى ينصرف، وأظلته الرحمة من فوق رأسه إلى أفق السماء. والملائكة تحفه من حوله إلى أفق السماء، ووكل الله به ملكا قائما على رأسه يقول له: أيها المصلي، لو تعلم من ينظر إليك ومن تناجي ما التفت ولا زلت من موضعك أبدا.

From Abu Ja'far (peace be upon him) who said: The Messenger of Allah (peace be upon him and his family) said: When a believing servant stands in his prayer, Allah Mighty and Majestic looks at him - or he said: Allah turns to him until he finishes, and mercy shades him from above his head to the horizon of the sky, and angels surround him from around him to the horizon of the sky, and Allah assigns an angel standing at his head saying to him: O you who prays, if you knew who is looking at you and whom you are conversing with, you would neither turn away nor leave your place ever.

Hadith 4438

عن عبيد بن زرارة، عن أبي عبد الله (عليه السلام) قال: قال رسول الله (صلى الله عليه وآله): مثل الصلاة مثل عمود الفسطاط، إذا ثبت العمود نفعت الاطناب والأوتاد والغشاء وإذا انكسر العمود لم ينفع طنب ولا وتد ولا غشا.

From Ubayd bin Zurarah, from Abu Abdullah (peace be upon him) who said: The Messenger of Allah (peace be upon him and his family) said: The example of prayer is like the pole of a tent. When the pole is firm, the ropes, pegs, and covering are beneficial, and when the pole breaks, no rope, peg, or covering is beneficial.

Hadith 4439

عن أبي عبد الله (عليه السلام) قال: من قبل الله منه صلاة واحدة لم يعذبه، ومن قبل منه حسنة لم يعذبه.

From Abu Abdullah (peace be upon him) who said: Whoever has one prayer accepted by Allah will not be punished, and whoever has one good deed accepted from him will not be punished.

Hadith 4440

عن أبي عبد الله (عليه السلام) قال: قال رسول الله (صلى الله عليه وآله): الصلاة ميزان، من وفى استوفى.

From Abu Abdullah (peace be upon him) who said: The Messenger of Allah (peace be upon him and his family) said: Prayer is a scale - whoever fulfills it completely shall receive its full measure.

Hadith 4441

عن أبي جعفر (عليه السلام) أنه قال: للمصلي ثلاث خصال، إذا هو قام في صلاته حفت به الملائكة من قدميه إلى أعنان السماء ويتناثر البر عليه من أعنان السماء إلى مفرق رأسه، وملك موكل به ينادي: لم يعلم المصلي من يناجي ما انفتل.

From Abu Ja'far (peace be upon him) who said: The one praying has three qualities - when they stand in prayer, the angels surround them from their feet to the heights of heaven, goodness descends upon them from the heights of heaven to the parting of their hair, and an angel assigned to them calls out: "If the one praying knew who they were conversing with, they would not turn away."

Hadith 4442

قال وقال الصادق (عليه السلام): أول ما يحاسب به العبد الصلاة، فإن قبلت قبل سائر عمله، وإذا ردت رد عليه سائر عمله.

And Al-Sadiq (peace be upon him) said: The first thing the servant will be held accountable for is prayer. If it is accepted, the rest of their deeds will be accepted. If it is rejected, the rest of their deeds will be rejected.

Hadith 4443

عن ابن أبي يعفور قال: قال أبو عبد الله الصادق (عليه السلام): إذا صليت صلاة فريضة فصلها لوقتها صلاة مودع يخاف أن لا يعود إليها أبدا، ثم اصرف بصرك إلى موضع سجودك، فلو تعلم من عن يمينك وشمالك لأحسنت صلاتك، واعلم أنك بين يدي من يراك ولا تراه.

From Ibn Abi Yafur who said: Abu Abdullah Al-Sadiq (peace be upon him) said: When you pray an obligatory prayer, pray it at its time like someone bidding farewell, fearing they may never return to it. Then direct your gaze to your place of prostration. If you knew who was on your right and left, you would perfect your prayer. Know that you are before One who sees you while you do not see Him.

Hadith 4444

عن أبي عبد الله (عليه السلام) قال: للمصلي ثلاث خصال إذا قام في صلاته: يتناثر البر عليه من أعنان السماء إلى مفرق رأسه، وتحف به الملائكة من تحت قدميه إلى أعنان السماء، وملك ينادي: أيها المصلي لو تعلم من تناجي ما انفتلت.

From Abu Abdullah (peace be upon him) who said: The one praying has three qualities when they stand in prayer: goodness descends upon them from the heights of heaven to the parting of their hair, angels surround them from beneath their feet to the heights of heaven, and an angel calls out: "O one who prays, if you knew who you were conversing with, you would not turn away."

Hadith 4445

عن علي (عليهم السلام) قال: قال رسول الله (صلى الله عليه وآله): إن عمود الدين الصلاة: وهي أول ما ينظر فيه من عمل ابن آدم فإن صحت نظر في عمله وإن لم تصح لم ينظر في بقية عمله.

From Ali (peace be upon him) who said: The Messenger of Allah (peace be upon him and his family) said: The pillar of religion is prayer. It is the first deed of the son of Adam that will be examined. If it is sound, the rest of his deeds will be examined. If it is not sound, the rest of his deeds will not be examined.

Hadith 4446

عن بكر بن محمد الأزدي، عن أبي عبد الله (عليه السلام)، قال: سأله أبو بصير - وأنا جالس عنده - عن الحور العين فقال له: جعلت فداك، أخلق من خلق الدنيا أم خلق من خلق الجنة؟

From Bakr ibn Muhammad al-Azdi, from Abu Abdullah (peace be upon him): Abu Basir asked him - while I was sitting with him - about the houris (maidens) of paradise, saying: May I be your ransom, were they created from the creation of this world or from the creation of paradise?

فقال له: ما أنت وذاك عليك بالصلاة فإن آخر ما أوصى به رسول الله (صلى الله عليه وآله) وحث عليه الصلاة. إياكم أن يستخف أحدكم بصلاته، فلا هو إذا كان شابا أتمها، ولا هو إذا كان شيخا قوي عليها، وما أشد من سرقة الصلاة، فإذا قام أحدكم فليعتدل، فإذا ركع فليتمكن، وإذا رفع رأسه فليعتدل، وإذا سجد فلينفرج وليتمكن، وإذا رفع رأسه فليلبث حتى يسكن.

He said to him: What is that to you? You must adhere to prayer, for the last thing the Messenger of Allah (peace be upon him and his family) enjoined and urged was prayer. Beware that any one of you takes his prayer lightly, for he does not complete it when he is young, nor does he have the strength for it when he is old. How grave is the theft of prayer. When one of you stands, let him stand upright. When he bows, let him be still and settled. When he raises his head, let him stand upright. When he prostrates, let him spread out and be settled. When he raises his head, let him pause until he is at rest.

CHAPTER 9

Dislike Of Hastening Prayer

[Hadith 4447 to 4452]

Hadith 4447

عن أبي عبد الله (عليه السلام) قال: إذا قام العبد في الصلاة فخفف صلاته، قال الله تبارك وتعالى لملائكته: أما ترون إلى عبدي كأنه يرى أن قضاء حوائجه بيد غيري، أما يعلم أن قضاء حوائجه بيدي.

From Abu Abdullah (peace be upon him) who said: When a servant stands for prayer and rushes through his prayer, Allah blessed and exalted says to His angels: Do you not see My servant as if he thinks that the fulfillment of his needs is in hands other than Mine? Does he not know that the fulfillment of his needs is in My hands?

Hadith 4448

عن عبد الله بن ميمون القداح، عن أبي عبد الله (عليه السلام) قال: أبصر علي بن أبي طالب (عليه السلام) رجلا ينقر صلاته، فقال: منذ كم صليت بهذه الصلاة؟ فقال له الرجل: منذ كذا وكذا، فقال: مثلك عند الله مثل الغراب إذا نقر، لو مت مت على غير ملة أبي القاسم محمد، ثم قال علي (عليه السلام): إن أسرق الناس من سرق من صلاته.

From Abdullah bin Maymun al-Qaddah, from Abu Abdullah (peace be upon him) who said: Ali bin Abi Talib (peace be upon him) saw a man pecking in his prayer, so he said: How long have you been praying like this? The man said to him: For such and such time. So he said: Your example before Allah is like that of a crow when it pecks. If you were to die, you would die upon other than the religion of Abul-Qasim Muhammad. Then Ali (peace be upon him) said: The worst thief among people is one who steals from his prayer.

Hadith 4449

عن أبي عبد الله (عليه السلام) قال: تخفيف الفريضة وتطويل النافلة من العبادة.

From Abu Abdullah (peace be upon him) who said: Shortening the obligatory prayer and lengthening the optional prayer is from worship.

أقول: هذا محمول على إمام الجماعة مع عدم احتمال من خلفه للإطالة لما يأتي، أو على استحباب إطالة النوافل أكثر من الفرائض، فالتخفيف بالنسبة كما يأتي في صلاة الليل وغيرها، أو على الجواز، أو على المساواة لعدم التصريح بالرجحان، والله أعلم.

I (Hurr Amili) say: This is interpreted regarding the imam of congregational prayer when those behind him cannot bear lengthening, as will come, or regarding the recommendation to lengthen optional prayers more than obligatory ones, so shortening is relative as will come in Salat al-Layl and others, or regarding permissibility, or regarding equality due to lack of explicit preference, and Allah knows best.

Hadith 4450

عن أبي عبد الله (عليه السلام) قال: إن العبد إذا عجل فقام لحاجته يقول الله تبارك وتعالى: أما يعلم عبدي أني أنا أقضي الحوائج.

From Abu Abdullah (peace be upon him) who said: When a servant hastens and stands up for his need, Allah, the Blessed and Exalted, says: Does My servant not know that I am the One who fulfills needs.

Hadith 4451

عن زرارة، عن أبي عبد الله (عليه السلام) - في حديث - أنه سأله عن إبليس بما استوجب من الله أن أعطاه ما أعطاه؟ فقال: بشئ كان منه شكره الله عليه، قلت: وما كان منه؟ قال: ركعتين ركعهما في السماء في أربعة آلاف سنة.

From Zurarah, from Abu Abdullah (peace be upon him) - in a hadith - that he asked him about Iblis, what made him deserve from Allah what He gave him? He said: It was due to something he did that Allah appreciated from him. I said: And what was it that he did? He said: Two units of prayer that he performed in heaven over four thousand years.

Hadith 4452

عن زرارة قال: سمعت أبا جعفر (عليه السلام) يقول: دخل رجل مسجدا فيه رسول الله (صلى الله عليه وآله) فخفف سجوده دون ما ينبغي ودون ما يكون من السجود، فقال رسول الله (صلى الله عليه وآله): نقر كنقر الغراب، لو مات هذا على هذا مات على غير دين محمد.

From Zurarah who said: I heard Abu Ja'far (peace be upon him) saying: A man entered a mosque where the Messenger of Allah (peace be upon him and his family) was present, and he made his prostration light, less than what was appropriate and less than what prostration should be. So the Messenger of Allah (peace be upon him and his family) said: He pecked like the pecking of a crow. If this person were to die in this state, he would die following other than the religion of Muhammad.

CHAPTER 10
Recommendation Of Preferring Prayer Over Other Voluntary Acts Of Worship

[Hadith 4453 to 4461]

Hadith 4453

عن معاوية بن وهب قال: سألت أبا عبد الله (عليه السلام) عن أفضل ما يتقرب به العباد إلى ربهم أحب ذلك إلى الله عز وجل، ما هو؟ فقال: ما أعلم شيئا بعد المعرفة أفضل من هذه الصلاة، ألا ترى أن العبد الصالح عيسى بن مريم (عليه السلام) قال (وأوصاني بالصلاة والزكاة ما دمت حيا).

From Mu'awiyah ibn Wahb who said: I asked Abu Abdullah (peace be upon him) about the best means by which servants can seek nearness to their Lord and what is most beloved to Allah, mighty and majestic, what is it? He said: I do not know anything after recognition (of Allah) better than this prayer. Do you not see that the righteous servant Jesus son of Maryam (peace be upon him) said "And He has made me blessed wherever I may be, and has enjoined upon me prayer and sadaqah as long as I remain alive" [Quran, 19:31]

———

Hadith 4454

عن أبي عبد الله (عليه السلام) قال: سمعته يقول: أحب الاعمال إلى الله عز وجل الصلاة، وهي آخر وصايا الأنبياء، فما أحسن الرجل يغتسل أو يتوضأ فيسبغ الوضوء ثم يتنحى حيث لا يراه أنيس فيشرف الله عليه وهو راكع أو ساجد، إن العبد إذا سجد فأطال السجود نادى إبليس: يا ويله، أطاعوا وعصيت، وسجدوا وأبيت.

From Abu Abdullah (peace be upon him) who said: I heard him say: The most beloved deeds to Allah, the Mighty and Majestic, is prayer, and it is the last of the Prophets' commandments. How excellent it is when a man performs ghusl or wudu and completes the wudu thoroughly, then withdraws to where no one sees him, and Allah looks upon him while he is in ruku or in sujud. Indeed when a servant prostrates and lengthens his prostration, Iblis cries out: Woe to me! They obeyed while I disobeyed, and they prostrated while I refused.

———

Hadith 4455

عن عبد الله بن يحيى الكاهلي قال: سمعت أبا عبد الله (عليه السلام) يقول: أما إنه ليس شئ أفضل من الحج إلا الصلاة.

From Abdullah bin Yahya Al-Kahili who said: I heard Abu Abdullah (peace be upon him) saying: Indeed there is nothing better than Hajj except prayer.

Hadith 4456

عن أبي بصير قال: قال أبو عبد الله (عليه السلام): صلاة فريضة خير من عشرين حجة، وحجة خير من بيت مملو ذهبا يتصدق منه حتى يفنى.

From Abu Basir who said: Abu Abdullah (peace be upon him) said: An obligatory prayer is better than twenty Hajj, and a Hajj is better than a house filled with gold given in sadaqah until it is depleted.

Hadith 4457

محمد بن علي بن الحسين قال: قال الصادق (عليه السلام): إن طاعة الله عز وجل خدمته في الأرض، وليس شئ من خدمته يعدل الصلاة، فمن ثم نادت الملائكة زكريا وهو قائم يصلي في المحراب.

Muhammad bin Ali bin Al-Husain said: Al-Sadiq (peace be upon him) said: Indeed, obedience to Allah, the Mighty and Majestic, is serving Him on earth, and nothing from His service equals prayer. For this reason, the angels called out to Zakariya while he was standing in prayer in the prayer niche (mihrab).

Hadith 4458

عن خالد القلانسي قال: قال الصادق (عليه السلام): يؤتى بشيخ يوم القيامة فيدفع إليه كتابه، ظاهره مما يلي الناس ولا يرى إلا مساوئ فيطول ذلك عليه، فيقول: يا رب أتأمر بي إلى النار؟ فيقول الجبار جل جلاله: يا شيخ، إني أستحيي أن أعذبك وقد كنت تصلي لي في دار الدنيا، اذهبوا بعبدي إلى الجنة.

From Khalid al-Qalanisi who said: Al-Sadiq (peace be upon him) said: On the Day of Resurrection, an elderly man will be brought forth and given his book, its outer part facing the people, and he sees only evil deeds, and this distresses him. He will say: O Lord, do You command me to the Fire? The Almighty, Majestic is His Glory, will say: O elderly one, I am ashamed to punish you when you used to pray to Me in the worldly life. Take My servant to Paradise.

Hadith 4459

عن ابن مسعود، عن النبي (صلى الله عليه وآله): إن أحب الاعمال إلى الله عز وجل الصلاة والبر والجهاد.

From Ibn Masud, from the Prophet (peace be upon him and his family): Indeed the most beloved deeds to Allah, the Mighty and Majestic, are prayer, righteousness, and jihad.

Hadith 4460

عن يونس بن يعقوب قال: سمعت أبا عبد الله (عليه السلام) يقول: حجة أفضل من الدنيا وما فيها،
وصلاة فريضة أفضل من ألف حجة.

From Yunus ibn Ya'qub who said: I heard Abu Abdullah (peace be upon him) saying: A Hajj is better than this world and all that is in it, and an obligatory prayer is better than a thousand Hajj.

———

Hadith 4461

عن أبي عبد الله (عليه السلام) قال: صلاة الفريضة أفضل من عشرين حجة.

From Abu Abdullah (peace be upon him) who said: An obligatory prayer is better than twenty Hajj.

———

CHAPTER 11

Establishing Disbelief And Apostasy By Abandoning Obligatory Prayer Through Denial Or Belittlement

[Hadith 4462 to 4468]

Hadith 4462

عن زرارة، عن أبي جعفر (عليه السلام) - في حديث عدد النوافل - قال: إنما هذا كله تطوع وليس بمفروض، إن تارك الفريضة كافر، وإن تارك هذا ليس بكافر.

From Zurarah, from Abu Ja'far (peace be upon him) - in a hadith about voluntary prayers - he said: All of this is voluntary and not obligatory. One who abandons obligatory prayer is a disbeliever, but one who abandons these voluntary prayers is not a disbeliever.

Hadith 4463

عن مسعدة بن صدقة أنه قال: سئل أبو عبد الله (عليه السلام): ما بال الزاني لا تسميه كافرا وتارك الصلاة تسميه كافرا، وما الحجة في ذلك؟

From Masadah ibn Sadaqah that he said: Abu Abdullah (peace be upon him) was asked: Why do you not call the Zani (one who commits illicit intercourse) a Kafir (disbeliever), yet you call the one who abandons Salat a Kafir? What is the proof for that?

فقال: لان الزاني وما أشبهه إنما يفعل ذلك لمكان الشهوة. لأنها تغلبه. وتارك الصلاة لا يتركها إلا استخفافا بها. وذلك لأنك لا تجد الزاني يأتي المرأة إلا وهو مستلذ لاتيانه إياها، قاصدا إليها. وكل من ترك الصلاة قاصدا لتركها فليس يكون قصده لتركها اللذة. فإذا نفيت اللذة وقع الاستخفاف، وإذا وقع الاستخفاف وقع الكفر.

He said: Because the Zani and his like only do that due to desire, as it overpowers them, whereas the one who abandons the Salat does not abandon it except out of belittling (istikhfafa) it. That is because you do not find the Zani approaching a woman except that he derives pleasure from approaching her, intending her. But everyone who abandons the Salat intending to abandon it, his intention in abandoning it is not pleasure. So when pleasure is absent, belittling occurs; and when belittling occurs, Kufr (disbelief) occurs.

Hadith 4464

عن مسعدة بن صدقة قال: سمعت أبا عبد الله (عليه السلام) وسئل: ما بال الزاني، وذكر الحديث، وزاد. قال وقيل له: ما فرق بين من نظر إلى امرأة فزنا بها، أو خمر فشربها، وبين من ترك الصلاة حتى لا يكون الزاني وشارب الخمر مستخفا كما يستخف تارك الصلاة؟ وما الحجة في ذلك، وما العلة التي تفرق بينهما؟

From Mas'adah ibn Sadaqah, who said: I heard Abu Abdullah (peace be upon him) when he was asked about the case of the fornicator - and he mentioned the hadith, and added to it. He said: It was said to him: What is the difference between one who looks at a woman and commits fornication with her, or looks at wine and drinks it, and between one who abandons prayer - such that the fornicator and the drinker of wine are not considered as belittling religion in the way the one who abandons prayer is considered to be belittling it? And what is the argument in this regard, and what is the reason that distinguishes between the two cases?

قال: الحجة أن كل ما أدخلت أنت نفسك فيه لم يدعك إليه داع ولم يغلبك غالب شهوة مثل الزنا وشرب الخمر وأنت دعوت نفسك إلى ترك الصلاة وليس ثم شهوة فهو الاستخفاف بعينه، وهذا فرق ما بينهما.

He said: The argument is that everything you enter yourself into, without any caller having called you to it and without any overpowering force of desire having overcome you - such as fornication and the drinking of wine - it is you yourself who called yourself to abandon prayer, and there is no desire involved in that, so that is treating religion with belittlement (istikhfafan) in its very essence. And this is the distinction between the two cases.

Hadith 4465

عن عبيد بن زرارة، عن أبي عبد الله (عليه السلام) - في حديث الكبائر - قال: إن تارك الصلاة كافر، يعني من غير علة.

From Ubayd bin Zurarah, from Abu Abdullah (peace be upon him) - in a hadith about major sins - he said: One who abandons prayer is a disbeliever, meaning without any excuse.

Hadith 4466

عن أبي عبد الله (عليه السلام) قال: جاء رجل إلى النبي (صلى الله عليه وآله) فقال: يا رسول الله أوصني، فقال: لا تدع الصلاة متعمدا، فإن من تركها متعمدا فقد برئت منه ملة الاسلام.

From Abu Abdullah (peace be upon him) who said: A man came to the Prophet (peace be upon him and his family) and said: O Messenger of Allah, advise me. He said: Do not deliberately abandon prayer, for whoever deliberately abandons it has disassociated from the religion of Islam.

Hadith 4467

عن أبي جعفر (عليه السلام) قال: قال رسول الله (صلى الله عليه وآله): ما بين المسلم وبين أن يكفر إلا ترك الصلاة الفريضة متعمدا أو يتهاون بها فلا يصليها.

From Abu Ja'far (peace be upon him) who said: The Messenger of Allah (peace be upon him and his family) said: There is nothing between the Muslim and disbelief except abandoning the obligatory prayer intentionally or neglecting it and not praying it.

Hadith 4468

عن أبي عبد الله (عليه السلام)، عن أبيه، عن جابر قال: قال رسول الله (صلى الله عليه وآله): ما بين الكفر والايمان إلا ترك الصلاة.

From Abu Abdullah (peace be upon him), from his father, from Jabir who said: The Messenger of Allah (peace be upon him and his family) said: There is nothing between Kufr and Iman (disbelief and faith) except abandoning prayer.

CHAPTER 12

Recommendation Of Initiating Supererogatory Prayers
[Hadith 4469 to 4472]

Hadith 4469

عن أبي الحسن الرضا (عليه السلام) أنه قال: الصلاة قربان كل تقي.

From Abu Al-Hasan Al-Ridha (peace be upon him) that he said: Prayer is the means of nearness for every pious person.

Hadith 4470

عن زرارة، عن الصادق (عليه السلام) - في حديث - قال: الصلاة قربان كل تقي.

From Zurarah, from Al-Sadiq (peace be upon him) - in a hadith - he said: Prayer is the means of nearness for every pious person.

Hadith 4471

قال وأتى رجل رسول الله (صلى الله عليه وآله) فقال: أدع الله أن يدخلني الجنة، فقال: له أعني بكثرة السجود.

He said: A man came to the Messenger of Allah (peace be upon him and his family) and said: Pray to Allah to admit me to Paradise. So he (the Prophet) said to him: Help me by performing many prostrations.

Hadith 4472

عن إسماعيل بن يسار قال: سمعت أبا عبد الله (عليه السلام) يقول: إياكم والكسل، إن ربكم رحيم يشكر القليل إن الرجل ليصلي الركعتين تطوعا يريد بهما وجه الله فيدخله الله بهما الجنة.

From Isma'il bin Yasar who said: I heard Abu Abdullah (peace be upon him) saying: Beware of laziness, for your Lord is Merciful and appreciates even a little. Indeed, a man prays two rak'ahs of supererogatory prayer seeking Allah's pleasure through them, and Allah admits him to Paradise because of them.

CHAPTER 13

Number Of Daily Obligatory Prayers And Their Supererogatory Prayers, And A Summary Of Their Rulings

[Hadith 4473 to 4501]

Hadith 4473

عن معاوية بن عمار قال: سمعت أبا عبد الله (عليه السلام) يقول: كان في وصية النبي (صلى الله عليه وآله) لعلي (عليه السلام) أن قال: يا علي، أوصيك في نفسك بخصال فاحفظها عني، ثم قال: اللهم أعنه - إلى أن قال - والسادسة: الاخذ بسنتي في صلاتي وصومي وصدقتي، أما الصلاة فالخمسون ركعة.

From Mu'awiyah bin 'Ammar who said: I heard Abu Abdullah (peace be upon him) say: In the will of the Prophet (peace be upon him and his family) to Ali (peace be upon him), he said: O Ali, I advise you regarding yourself with qualities, so preserve them from me. Then he said: O Allah, support him - until he said - And the sixth: Following my Sunnah in my prayer, my fasting and my sadaqah. As for prayer, it is fifty rak'ahs.

Hadith 4474

عن فضيل بن يسار قال: سمعت أبا عبد الله (عليه السلام) يقول - في حديث - إن الله عز وجل فرض الصلاة ركعتين ركعتين عشر ركعات، فأضاف رسول الله (صلى الله عليه وآله) إلى الركعتين ركعتين، وإلى المغرب ركعة، فصارت عديل الفريضة، لا يجوز تركهن إلا في سفر، وأفرد الركعة في المغرب، فتركها قائمة في السفر والحضر، فأجاز الله له ذلك كله، فصارت الفريضة سبع عشرة ركعة،

From Fudhayl bin Yasar who said: I heard Abu Abdullah (peace be upon him) say - in a hadith - Indeed Allah, the Mighty and Sublime, obligated prayer as two rak'ahs, two rak'ahs, ten rak'ahs. The Messenger of Allah (peace be upon him and his family) added to the two rak'ahs two rak'ahs, and to Maghrib one rak'ah, so it became equivalent to the obligatory prayers. It is not allowed to leave them except during travel. He singled out the one rak'ah in Maghrib, keeping it established during travel and at home. Allah allowed all of that for him, so the obligatory prayers became seventeen rak'ahs.

ثم سن رسول الله (صلى الله عليه وآله) النوافل أربعا وثلاثين ركعة مثلي الفريضة، فأجاز الله عز وجل له ذلك، والفريضة والنافلة إحدى وخمسون ركعة، منها ركعتان بعد العتمة جالسا تعد بركعة مكان الوتر - إلى أن قال: -

Then the Messenger of Allah (peace be upon him and his family) legislated the supererogatory prayers as thirty-four rak'ahs, double the obligatory, and Allah, the Mighty and Sublime, allowed that for him. The obligatory and supererogatory prayers are fifty-one rak'ahs, among them two rak'ahs after Isha while sitting counted as one rak'ah while standing - until he said -

ولم يرخص رسول الله (صلى الله عليه وآله) لاحد تقصير الركعتين اللتين ضمهما إلى ما فرض الله عز وجل، بل ألزمهم ذلك إلزاما واجبا، ولم يرخص لاحد في شئ من ذلك إلا للمسافر، وليس لاحد أن يُرخص ما لم يرخصه رسول الله (صلى الله عليه وآله)، فوافق أمر رسول الله أمر الله، ونهيه نهي الله، ووجب على العباد التسليم له كالتسليم لله.

The Messenger of Allah (peace be upon him and his family) did not allow anyone to shorten the two rak'ahs that he added to what Allah, the Mighty and Sublime, obligated. Rather, he made that binding upon them as an obligatory requirement, and he did not allow anyone anything from that except for the traveler. It is not for anyone to allow what the Messenger of Allah (peace be upon him and his family) did not allow, so the command of the Messenger of Allah coincided with the command of Allah, and his prohibition the prohibition of Allah, and it became obligatory upon the servants to submit to him as submission to Allah.

Hadith 4475

عن فضيل بن يسار، عن أبي عبد الله (عليه السلام) قال: الفريضة والنافلة إحدى وخمسون ركعة، منها ركعتان بعد العتمة جالسا تعدان بركعة وهو قائم، الفريضة منها سبع عشرة، والنافلة أربع وثلاثون ركعة.

From Fudhayl bin Yasar, from Abu Abdullah (peace be upon him) who said: The obligatory and supererogatory prayers are fifty-one rak'ahs, among them two rak'ahs after Isha while sitting counted as one rak'ah while standing. Seventeen of them are obligatory, and thirty-four rak'ahs are supererogatory.

Hadith 4476

وبالاسناد عن الفضل بن يسار، والفضل بن عبد الملك، وبكير قالوا: سمعنا أبا عبد الله (عليه السلام) يقول: كان رسول الله (صلى الله عليه وآله) يصلي من التطوع مثلي الفريضة ويصوم من التطوع مثلي الفريضة.

With the chain from Al-Fadhl bin Yasar, Al-Fadhl bin Abdul Malik, and Bukayr who said: We heard Abu Abdullah (peace be upon him) say: The Messenger of Allah (peace be upon him and his family) used to pray double the obligatory prayers in voluntary prayers and fast double the obligatory fasts in voluntary fasts.

Hadith 4477

عن محمد بن أبي حمزة قال: سألت أبا عبد الله (عليه السلام) عن أفضل ما جرت به السنة من الصلاة؟

قال: تمام الخمسين.

From Muhammad bin Abi Hamzah who said: I asked Abu Abdullah (peace be upon him) about the best of what the Sunnah has been established regarding prayer. He said: Completing the fifty.

———————

Hadith 4478

عن حنان قال: سأل عمرو بن حريث أبا عبد الله (عليه السلام) وأنا جالس فقال له: جعلت فداك، أخبرني عن صلاة رسول الله (صلى الله عليه وآله)؟ فقال: كان النبي (صلى الله عليه وآله) يصلي ثمان ركعات: الزوال وأربعا الأولى، وثماني بعدها، وأربعا العصر، وثلاثا بعد المغرب، وأربعا بعد المغرب والعشاء الآخرة أربعا، وثماني صلاة الليل، وثلاثا الوتر، وركعتي الفجر، وصلاة الغداة ركعتين. قلت جعلت فداك: وإن كنت أقوى على أكثر من هذا يعذبني الله على كثرة الصلاة؟ فقال: لا، ولكن يعذب على ترك السنة.

From Hanan who said: Amr bin Hurayth asked Abu Abdullah (peace be upon him) while I was sitting, saying to him: May I be sacrificed for you, tell me about the prayer of the Messenger of Allah (peace be upon him and his family)? He said: The Prophet (peace be upon him and his family) would pray eight rak'ahs: at noon and four as the first, and eight after them, and four for Asr, and three for Maghrib, and four after Maghrib and four for the late Isha, and eight for Salat al-Layl, and three for Witr, and two rak'ahs of Fajr, and two rak'ahs for the morning prayer. I said: May I be sacrificed for you, if I am capable of praying more than this, would Allah punish me for praying more? He said: No, but He would punish for abandoning the Sunnah.

———————

Hadith 4479

عن أحمد بن محمد بن أبي نصر قال: قلت لأبي الحسن (عليه السلام): إن أصحابنا يختلفون في صلاة التطوع، بعضهم يصلي أربعا وأربعين، وبعضهم يصلي خمسين، فأخبرني بالذي تعمل به أنت، كيف هو حتى أعمل بمثله؟ فقال: أصلي واحدة وخمسين ركعة، ثم قال: أمسك - وعقد بيده - الزوال ثمانية، وأربعا بعد الظهر، وأربعا قبل العصر، وركعتين بعد المغرب، وركعتين قبل العشاء الآخرة، وركعتين بعد العشاء من قعود تعدان بركعة من قيام، وثمان صلاة الليل، والوتر ثلاثا وركعتي الفجر، والفرائض سبع عشرة، فذلك إحدى وخمسون.

From Ahmad bin Muhammad bin Abi Nasr who said: I said to Abu Al-Hasan (peace be upon him): Indeed, our companions differ regarding the voluntary prayers. Some of them pray forty-four, and some of them pray fifty. Tell me how you pray so that I may pray like it. He said: I pray fifty-one rak'ahs. Then he said:

Hold - and he counted with his hand - eight at midday, four after Zuhr, four before Asr, two after Maghrib, two before last Isha, two after Isha while sitting counted as one rak'ah while standing, eight of Salat al-Layl, three of Witr, and two rak'ahs of Fajr. The obligatory prayers are seventeen, so that is fifty-one.

Hadith 4480

عن حماد بن عثمان قال: سألته عن التطوع بالنهار؟ فذكر أنه يصلي ثمان ركعات قبل الظهر وثمان بعدها.

From Hammad bin Uthman who said: I asked him (peace be upon him) about the daytime voluntary prayers. He mentioned that he prays eight rak'ahs before Zuhr and eight after it.

Hadith 4481

عن الحارث بن المغيرة النصري قال: سمعت أبا عبد الله (عليه السلام) يقول: صلاة النهار ست عشرة ركعة، ثمان إذا زالت الشمس، وثمان بعد الظهر، وأربع ركعات بعد المغرب، يا حارث، لا تدعهن في سفر ولا حضر، وركعتان بعد العشاء الآخرة كان أبي يصليهما وهو قاعد، وأنا أصليهما وأنا قائم، وكان رسول الله (صلى الله عليه وآله) يصلي ثلاث عشرة ركعة من الليل.

From Al-Harith bin Al-Mughirah Al-Nasri who said: I heard Abu Abdullah (peace be upon him) say: The daytime prayer is sixteen rak'ahs - eight when the sun passes the meridian (highest point in the sky), eight after Zuhr, four rak'ahs after Maghrib. O Harith, do not leave them while traveling or at home. And two rak'ahs after last Isha - my father used to pray them while sitting, and I pray them while standing. The Messenger of Allah (peace be upon him and his family) used to pray thirteen rak'ahs at night.

Hadith 4482

عن أبي عبد الله (عليه السلام)، قال: سئل عن الخمسين والواحدة ركعة؟ فقال: إن ساعات النهار اثنتا عشرة ساعة، وساعات الليل اثنتا عشرة ساعة، ومن طلوع الفجر إلى طلوع الشمس ساعة، ومن غروب الشمس إلى غروب الشفق غسق، فكل ساعة ركعتان، وللغسق ركعة.

From Abu Abdullah (peace be upon him), he was asked about the fifty-one rak'ahs. He said: Indeed, the hours of the night are twelve hours, and the hours of the day are twelve hours. From the rise of dawn until sunrise is one hour, and from sunset until the disappearance of twilight is darkness. For every hour there are two rak'ahs, and for the darkness there is one rak'ah.

Hadith 4483

عن إسماعيل بن سعد الأحوص قال: قلت للرضا (عليه السلام): كم الصلاة من ركعة؟ فقال: إحدى وخمسون ركعة.

From Isma'il bin Sa'd Al-Ahwas who said: I said to Al-Ridha (peace be upon him): How many rak'ahs are there in prayer? He said: Fifty-one rak'ahs.

Hadith 4484

عن زرارة، عن أبي جعفر (عليه السلام) قال: عشر ركعات: ركعتان من الظهر، وركعتان من العصر، وركعتا الصبح، وركعتا المغرب، وركعتا العشاء الآخرة، لا يجوز الوهم فيهن، من وهم في شئ منهن استقبل الصلاة استقبالا، وهي الصلاة التي فرضها الله عز وجل على المؤمنين في القرآن، وفوض إلى محمد (صلى الله عليه وآله).

From Zurarah, from Abu Ja'far (peace be upon him) who said: Ten rak'ahs - two rak'ahs of Zuhr, two rak'ahs of Asr, two rak'ahs of morning, two rak'ahs of Maghrib, and two rak'ahs of last Isha. Doubting in them is not allowed. Whoever doubts in any of them should restart the prayer completely. This is the prayer that Allah, the Mighty and Sublime, obligated upon the believers in the Qur'an and delegated to Muhammad (peace be upon him and his family).

فزاد النبي (صلى الله عليه وآله) في الصلاة سبع ركعات، هي سنة ليس فيهن قراءة، إنما هو تسبيح وتهليل وتكبير ودعاء، والوهم إنما يكون فيهن، فزاد رسول الله (صلى الله عليه وآله) في صلاة المقيم غير المسافر ركعتين في الظهر والعصر والعشاء الآخرة، وركعة في المغرب للمقيم والمسافر.

The Prophet (peace be upon him and his family) added seven rak'ahs to the prayer. They are a Sunnah in which there is no recitation, only glorification (tasbih), declaration of oneness (tahlil), magnification (takbir) and supplication. Doubting only occurs in them. The Messenger of Allah (peace be upon him and his family) added to the prayer of the resident, not the traveler, two rak'ahs in Zuhr, Asr and last Isha, and one rak'ah in Maghrib for the resident and traveler.

Hadith 4485

عن أبي عبد الله (عليه السلام) - في حديث - أن ذا النمرة قال: يا رسول الله أخبرني ما فرض الله علي؟ فقال له رسول الله (صلى الله عليه وآله): فرض الله عليك سبعة عشرة ركعة في اليوم والليلة، وصوم شهر رمضان إذا أدركته، والحج إذا استطعت إليه سبيلا، والزكاة، وفسرها له.

From Abu Abdullah (peace be upon him) - in a hadith - that Dhul-Numrah said: O Messenger of Allah, tell me what Allah has obligated upon me. The Messenger of Allah (peace be upon him and his family) said to him: Allah has obligated upon you seventeen rak'ahs in a day and night, fasting the month of Ramadan if you reach it,

Hajj if you are able to find a way to it, Zakat - and he explained it to him.

Hadith 4486

عن أبي جعفر (عليه السلام) قال: لما عرج برسول الله (صلى الله عليه وآله) نزل بالصلاة عشر ركعات، ركعتين ركعتين، فلما ولد الحسن والحسين (عليهما السلام) زاد رسول الله (صلى الله عليه وآله) سبع ركعات شكرا لله، فأجاز الله له ذلك، وترك الفجر ولم يزد فيها لضيق وقتها، لأنه تحضرها ملائكة الليل وملائكة النهار،

From Abu Ja'far (peace be upon him) who said: When the Messenger of Allah (peace be upon him and his family) was taken on the night journey, the prayer was revealed as ten rak'ahs, two rak'ahs each. When Al-Hasan and Al-Husain (peace be upon them) were born, the Messenger of Allah (peace be upon him and his family) added seven rak'ahs in gratitude to Allah, and Allah allowed that for him. He left Fajr and did not add to it due to the shortness of its time, because the angels of the night and the angels of the day attend it.

فلما أمره الله بالتقصير في السفر وضع عن أمته ست ركعات، وترك المغرب لم ينقص منها شيئا، وإنما يجب السهو فيما زاد رسول الله (صلى الله عليه وآله)، فمن شك في أصل الفرض في الركعتين الأولتين استقبل صلاته.

When Allah commanded him to shorten in travel, He reduced six rak'ahs from his nation, and left Maghrib without reducing anything from it. Forgetting (sahu) is only obligatory in what the Messenger of Allah (peace be upon him and his family) added. So whoever doubts in the original obligation in the first two rak'ahs should restart his prayer.

Hadith 4487

عن حماد بن عثمان قال: سألت أبا عبد الله (عليه السلام) عن صلاة رسول الله (صلى الله عليه وآله) بالنهار؟ فقال: ومن يطيق ذلك، ثم قال: ولكن ألا أخبرك كيف أصنع أنا؟ فقلت: بلى، فقال: ثماني ركعات قبل الظهر، وثمان بعدها، قلت: فالمغرب، قال: أربع بعدها، قلت: فالعتمة؟ قال: كان رسول الله (صلى الله عليه وآله) يصلي العتمة ثم ينام، وقال بيده هكذا فحركها قال ابن أبي عمير: ثم وصف كما ذكر أصحابنا.

From Hammad bin Uthman who said: I asked Abu Abdullah (peace be upon him) about the daytime prayer of the Messenger of Allah (peace be upon him and his family). He said: And who can bear that? Then he said: But shall I not tell you how I do it? I said: Yes. He said: Eight rak'ahs before Zuhr and eight after it. I said: What about Maghrib? He said: Four after it. I said: What about Isha? He said: The Messenger of Allah (peace be upon him and his family) used to pray Isha then sleep.

And he said with his hand like this, and he moved it. Ibn Abi Umayr said: Then he described as our companions mentioned.

Hadith 4488

عن أبي عبد الله (عليه السلام) قال: صلاة النافلة ثمان ركعات حين تزول الشمس قبل الظهر، وست ركعات بعد الظهر، وركعتان قبل العصر، وأربع ركعات بعد المغرب، وركعتان بعد العشاء الآخرة، يقرأ فيهما مائة آية قائما أو قاعدا، والقيام أفضل، ولا تعدهما من الخمسين،

From Abu Abdullah (peace be upon him) who said: The supererogatory prayer is eight rak'ahs when the sun passes the meridian (highest point in the sky) before Zuhr, six rak'ahs after Zuhr, two rak'ahs before Asr, four rak'ahs after Maghrib, two rak'ahs after last Isha - one hundred verses are recited in them while standing or sitting, and standing is better. Do not count them from the fifty.

وثمان ركعات من آخر الليل، تقرأ في صلاة الليل ب (قل هو الله أحد) و (قل يا أيها الكافرون) في الركعتين الأوليين، وتقرأ في سائرها ما أحببت من القرآن، ثم الوتر ثلاث ركعات، يقرأ فيها جميعا (قل هو الله أحد)، وتفصل بينهن بتسليم، ثم الركعتان اللتان قبل الفجر، تقرأ في الأولى منهما (قل يا أيها الكافرون) وفي الثانية (قل هو الله أحد).

And eight rak'ahs from the last part of the night, recite in Salat al-Layl with Surah Al-Ikhlas [Quran 112] and Surah Al-Kafirun [Quran 109] in the first two rak'ahs, and recite in the remaining ones whatever you like from the Quran, then three rak'ahs of Witr, reciting Surah Al-Ikhlas [Quran 112] in all of them, and separate between them with taslim (salam), then the two rak'ahs before Fajr, recite in the first one Surah Al-Kafirun [Quran 109] and in the second one Surah Al-Ikhlas [Quran 112].

Hadith 4489

عن بعض أصحابنا قال: قال لي: صلاة النهار ست عشرة ركعة، صلها أي النهار شئت، إن شئت في أوله، وإن شئت في وسطه، وإن شئت في آخره.

From one of our companions who said: He said to me: The daytime prayer is sixteen rak'ahs. Pray it at any time of the day you wish - if you wish at its beginning, if you wish in its middle, and if you wish at its end.

Hadith 4490

عن القاسم بن الوليد الغفاري قال: قلت لأبي عبد الله (عليه السلام): جعلت فداك، صلاة النهار النوافل، كم هي؟ قال: ست عشرة ركعة، أي ساعات النهار شئت أن تصليها صليتها. إلا أنك إن صليتها في مواقيتها أفضل.

From Al-Qasim bin Al-Walid Al-Ghifari who said: I said to Abu Abdullah (peace be upon him): May I be sacrificed for you, how many are the daytime supererogatory prayers? He said: Sixteen rak'ahs. Pray it at any hour of the day you wish, but if you pray it at its timings, it is better.

Hadith 4491

عن سعيد بن المسيب أنه سأل علي بن الحسين (عليه السلام) فقال له: متى فرضت الصلاة على المسلمين على ما هي اليوم عليه؟ فقال: بالمدينة حين ظهرت الدعوة وقوى الاسلام، وكتب الله عز وجل على المسلمين الجهاد،

From Sa'eed bin Al-Musayyab that he asked Ali bin Al-Husain (peace be upon him) and said to him: When was the prayer obligated upon the Muslims as it is today? He said: In Madinah, when the call became manifest and Islam became strong, and Allah, the Mighty and Sublime, prescribed jihad for the Muslims.

زاد رسول الله (صلى الله عليه وآله) في الصلاة سبع ركعات: في الظهر ركعتين وفي العصر ركعتين، وفي المغرب ركعة، وفي العشاء الآخرة ركعتين، وأقر الفجر على ما فرضت بمكة لتعجيل عروج ملائكة الليل إلى السماء، ولتعجيل نزول ملائكة النهار إلى الأرض، وكانت ملائكة النهار وملائكة الليل يشهدون مع رسول الله (صلى الله عليه وآله) صلاة الفجر، فلذلك قال الله تعالى: (وقرآن الفجر إن قرآن الفجر كان مشهودا) يشهده المسلمون وتشهده ملائكة النهار وملائكة الليل.

The Messenger of Allah (peace be upon him and his family) added seven rak'ahs to the prayer - two rak'ahs in Zuhr, two rak'ahs in Asr, one rak'ah in Maghrib, and two rak'ahs in last Isha. He left Fajr as it was obligated in Makkah to hasten the ascension of the angels of the night to the sky, and to hasten the descent of the angels of the day to the earth. The angels of the day and the angels of the night used to witness the Fajr prayer with the Messenger of Allah (peace be upon him and his family). For that reason, Allah the Exalted said: "And the Qur'an of dawn. Indeed, the Qur'an of dawn is ever witnessed [Quran 17:78]" - witnessed by the Muslims and witnessed by the angels of the day and the angels of the night.

Hadith 4492

عن أبي هاشم الخادم قال: قلت لأبي الحسن الماضي (عليه السلام): لم جعلت صلاة الفريضة والسنة خمسين ركعة لا يزاد فيها ولا ينقص منها؟ قال: لان ساعات الليل اثنتا عشرة ساعة، وفيما بين طلوع الفجر إلى طلوع الشمس ساعة، وساعات النهار اثنتا عشرة ساعة فجعل الله لكل ساعة ركعتين، وما بين غروب الشمس إلى سقوط الشفق غسق، فجعل للغسق ركعة.

From Abu Hashim Al-Khadim who said: I said to Abu Al-Hasan Al-Madhi (peace be upon him): Why were the obligatory and supererogatory prayers made fifty rak'ahs, not increased or decreased from? He said: Because the hours of the night are twelve hours, and between the rise of dawn until sunrise is one hour, and the hours of the day are twelve hours. So Allah made for every hour two rak'ahs. And between sunset until the disappearance of twilight is darkness, so He made for the darkness one rak'ah.

Hadith 4493

عن أبي عبد الله (عليه السلام)، قال: قلت: لأي علة أوجب رسول الله (صلى الله عليه وآله) صلاة الزوال ثمان قبل الظهر وثمان قبل العصر؟ ولأي علة رغب في وضوء المغرب كل الرغبة؟ ولأي علة أوجب الأربع ركعات من بعد المغرب؟ ولأي علة كان يصلي صلاة الليل في آخر الليل ولا يصلى في أول الليل؟

From Abu Abdullah (peace be upon him), he said: I said: For what reason did the Messenger of Allah (peace be upon him and his family) make the midday prayer eight before Zuhr and eight before Asr? For what reason did he desire wudu for Maghrib with all desire (i.e. strong emphasis or encouragement)? For what reason did he make the four rak'ahs obligatory after Maghrib? For what reason did he pray Salat al-Layl at the end of the night and not pray it at the beginning of the night?

قال: لتأكيد الفرائض لان الناس لو لم يكن إلا أربع ركعات الظهر لكانوا مستخفين بها حتى كاد يفوتهم الوقت، فلما كان شيئا غير الفريضة أسرعوا إلى ذلك لكثرته، وكذلك التي من قبل العصر ليسرعوا إلى ذلك لكثرته، وذلك لأنهم يقولون: إن سوفنا ونريد أن نصلي الزوال يفوتنا الوقت،

He said: To emphasize the obligatory prayers, because if there were only four rak'ahs for Zuhr, people would have taken them lightly until the time would have passed them by. When there was something other than the obligatory, they hastened to it due to its abundance. Similarly, those before Asr, so that they hasten to it due to its abundance. That is because they say: If we delay and want to pray the midday prayer, the time will pass us by.

وكذلك الوضوء في المغرب يقولون حتى نتوضأ يفوتنا الوقت، فيسرعوا إلى القيام، وكذلك الأربع ركعات التي من بعد المغرب، وكذلك صلاة الليل في آخر الليل ليسرعوا القيام إلى صلاة الفجر، فتلك العلة وجب هذا هكذا.

Similarly, the wudu for Maghrib, they say: By the time we perform wudu, the time will pass us by. So they hasten to stand. Similarly, the four rak'ahs after Maghrib. Similarly, Salat al-Layl at the end of the night, so that they hasten to stand for the Fajr prayer. That is the reason this was made obligatory like this.

Shaykh Hurr Amili: What is meant by obligatory is establishment or emphasized recommendation.

Hadith 4494

عن الفضل بن شاذان، عن الرضا (عليه السلام) قال: إنما جعل أصل الصلاة ركعتين وزيد على بعضها ركعة وعلى بعضها بعضها ركعتان، ولم يزد على بعضها شئ لان أصل الصلاة إنما هي ركعة واحدة، لان أصل العدد واحد، فإذا نقصت من واحد فليست هي صلاة،

From Al-Fadhl bin Shadhan, from Al-Ridha (peace be upon him) who said: The basis of prayer was made two rak'ahs, and one rak'ah was added to some of them and two rak'ahs to some of them, and nothing was added to some of them because the basis of prayer is only one rak'ah, because the basis of number is one. If it is reduced from one, it is not a prayer.

فعلم الله عز وجل أن العباد لا يؤدون تلك الركعة الواحدة التي لا صلاة أقل منها بكمالها وتمامها والاقبال عليها، فقرن إليها ركعة أخرى ليتم بالثانية ما نقص من الأولى، ففرض الله عز وجل أصل الصلاة ركعتين،

Allah, the Mighty and Sublime, knew that the servants would not perform that one rak'ah, which no prayer is less than, with perfection, completion and focus on it. So He joined another rak'ah to it so that the second would complete what was deficient from the first. Thus, Allah, the Mighty and Sublime, made the basis of prayer two rak'ahs.

ثم علم رسول الله (صلى الله عليه وآله) أن العباد لا يؤدون هاتين الركعتين بتمام ما أمروا به وكماله فضم إلى الظهر والعصر والعشاء الآخرة ركعتين ركعتين ليكون فيها تمام الركعتين الأولتين،

Then the Messenger of Allah (peace be upon him and his family) knew that the servants would not perform these two rak'ahs with the completion and perfection they were commanded with. So he added to Zuhr, Asr and last Isha two rak'ahs each so that there would be in them the completion of the first two rak'ahs.

ثم علم أن صلاة المغرب يكون شغل الناس في وقتها أكثر للانصراف إلى الافطار والاكل والوضوء والتهيئة للبيت فزاد فيها ركعة واحدة ليكون أخف عليهم، ولان تصير ركعات الصلوات في اليوم والليلة فردا،

Then he knew that the prayer of Maghrib would have more preoccupation for people at its time due to turning to breaking the fast, eating, performing wudu and preparing for the home. So he added one rak'ah to it to make it lighter for them, and so that the number of rak'ahs in the prayers of the day and night would be odd.

ثم ترك الغداة على حالها، لان الاشتغال في وقتها أكثر، والمبادرة إلى الحوائج فيها أعم، ولان القلوب فيها أخلى من الفكر لقلة معاملة الناس بالليل، وقلة الاخذ والاعطاء، فالانسان فيها أقبل على صلاته منه في غيره من الصلوات، لان الفكرة أقل لعدم العمل من الليل،

Then he left the morning prayer as it was, because preoccupation during its time is greater, and hastening to needs in it is more common, and because the hearts in it are freer from thought due to the lack of people's dealings at night and the lack of taking and giving. So the human in it is more focused on his prayer than in other prayers, because thought is less due to the absence of work at night.

قال: وإنما جعلت السنة أربعا وثلاثين ركعة، لان الفريضة سبع عشرة، فجعلت السنة مثلي الفريضة كمالا للفريضة. وإنما جعلت السنة في أوقات مختلفة ولم تجعل في وقت واحد لان أفضل الأوقات ثلاثة: عند زوال الشمس، وبعد المغرب، وبالاسحار، فأحب أن يصلى له في كل هذه الأوقات الثلاثة، لأنها إذا فرقت السنة في أوقات شتى كان أداؤها أيسر وأخف من أن تجمع كلها في وقت واحد.

He said: The Sunnah was made thirty-four rak'ahs because the obligatory is seventeen, so the Sunnah was made double the obligatory as a completion for the obligatory. The Sunnah was made at different times and not made at one time because the best times are three: at the sun's passing the meridian (zawal, highest point in the sky), after Maghrib, and at the pre-dawn times. He loved that prayer be performed for Him in all of these three times. When the Sunnah is distributed at various times, performing it is easier and lighter than if it were all gathered at one time.

Hadith 4495

عن الفضل بن شاذان، عن الرضا (عليه السلام) في كتابه إلى المأمون قال: والصلاة الفريضة: الظهر أربع ركعات، والعصر أربع ركعات، والمغرب ثلاث ركعات، والعشاء الآخرة أربع ركعات، والغداة ركعتان هذه سبع عشرة ركعة،

From Al-Fadhl bin Shadhan, from Al-Ridha (peace be upon him) in his letter to Al-Ma'mun, he said: The obligatory prayer is Zuhr four rak'ahs, Asr four rak'ahs, Maghrib three rak'ahs, last Isha four rak'ahs, and morning two rak'ahs. These are seventeen rak'ahs.

والسنة أربع وثلاثون ركعة: ثمان ركعات قبل فريضة الظهر، وثمان ركعات قبل فريضة العصر، وأربع ركعات بعد المغرب، وركعتان من جلوس بعد العتمة تعدان بركعة، وثمان ركعات في السحر، والشفع والوتر ثلاث ركعات، تسلم بعد الركعتين وركعتا الفجر.

And the Sunnah prayers are thirty-four rak'ahs: eight rak'ahs before the obligatory Zuhr prayer, eight rak'ahs before the obligatory Asr prayer, four rak'ahs after Maghrib, two rak'ahs sitting after Isha which count as one rak'ah, eight rak'ahs in the pre-dawn, and three rak'ahs of Shaf'a and Witr where you give salam after two rak'ahs, and two rak'ahs of Fajr.

Hadith 4496

عن رجاء بن أبي الضحاك - في حديث - قال: كان الرضا (عليه السلام) إذا زالت الشمس جدد وضوءه وقام فصلى ست ركعات، يقرأ في الركعة الأولى (الحمد) و (قل يا أيها الكافرون) وفي الثانية (الحمد) و (قل هو الله أحد) ويقرأ في الأربع في كل ركعة (الحمد) و (قل هو الله أحد) ويسلم في كل ركعتين، ويقنت فيهما في الثانية قبل الركوع وبعد القراءة.

From Raja bin Abi al-Dahhak in a hadith, he said: When the sun would decline from its zenith, Imam al-Ridha (peace be upon him) would renew his wudu and stand to pray six rak'ahs. In the first rak'ah he would recite al-Fatihah and Surah al-Kafirun [Quran 109], and in the second rak'ah al-Fatihah and Surah al-Ikhlas [Quran 112]. In the remaining four rak'ahs, he would recite al-Fatihah and Surah al-Ikhlas [Quran 112] in each rak'ah. He would give salam after every two rak'ahs, and would perform qunut in the second rak'ah before ruku and after recitation.

ثم يؤذن ويصلي ركعتين، ثم يقيم ويصلي الظهر، فإذا سلم سبح الله وحمده وكبره وهلله ما شاء الله، ثم سجد سجدة الشكر يقول فيها: مأة مرة: شكرا لله، فإذا رفع رأسه قام فصلى ست ركعات، يقرأ في كل ركعة (الحمد) و (قل هو الله أحد) ويسلم في كل ركعتين، ويقنت في ثانية كل ركعتين قبل الركوع وبعد القراءة،

Then the adhan is called and he prays two rak'ahs, then the iqamah is called and he prays Zuhr prayer. After saying the salam, he glorifies Allah, praises Him, declares His greatness and oneness as much as Allah wills. Then he performs the sajdah al-shukr (prostration of gratitude) saying in it one hundred times: "Thanks be to Allah." When he raises his head, he stands and prays six rak'ahs, reciting in each rak'ah Surah Al-Fatihah and Surah Al-Ikhlas [Quran 112]. He says salam after every two rak'ahs and makes qunut in the second rak'ah of each pair before ruku and after recitation.

ثم يؤذن ويصلي ركعتين، ويقنت في الثانية، فإذا سلم أقام وصلى العصر، فإذا سلم جلس في مصلاه يسبح الله ويحمده ويكبره ويهلله ما شاء الله، ثم سجد سجدة الشكر يقول فيها مائة مرة: حمدا لله،

Then he makes the adhan and prays two rak'ahs, performing qunut in the second rak'ah. After saying salam, he establishes prayer and prays Asr. After saying salam, he sits in his prayer place glorifying Allah, praising Him, declaring His greatness and His oneness for as long as Allah wills. Then he performs the sajdah al-shukr (prostration of gratitude) saying one hundred times: Praise be to Allah.

فإذا غابت الشمس توضأ وصلى المغرب ثلاثا بأذان وإقامة، وقنت في الثانية قبل الركوع وبعد القراءة، فإذا سلم جلس في مصلاه يسبح الله ويحمده ويكبره ويهلله ما شاء الله، ثم سجد سجدة الشكر ثم رفع رأسه ولم يتكلم حتى يقوم ويصلي أربع ركعات بتسليمتين، يقنت في كل ركعتين في الثانية قبل الركوع

وبعد القراءة، وكان يقرأ في الأولى من هذه الأربع (الحمد) و (قل يا أيها الكافرون)، وفي الثانية (الحمد) و (قل هو الله أحد). ويقرأ في الركعتين الباقيتين (الحمد) و (قل هو الله أحد)، ثم يجلس بعد التسليم في التعقيب ما شاء الله، ثم يفطر.

When the sun sets, he would perform wudu and pray Maghrib three rak'ahs with adhan and iqamah, and would perform qunut in the second rak'ah before ruku and after recitation. After saying salam, he would remain in his prayer place glorifying, praising, and magnifying Allah as long as Allah willed. Then he would perform a sajdah al-shukr (prostration of gratitude), raise his head and not speak until standing to pray four rak'ahs with two salams. He would perform qunut in the second rak'ah of each two rak'ahs before ruku and after recitation. In the first rak'ah of these four, he would recite Al-Fatihah and Surah Al-Kafirun, in the second rak'ah Al-Fatihah and Surah Al-Ikhlas, and in the remaining two rak'ahs Al-Fatihah and Surah Al-Ikhlas. Then after salam he would sit for supplication as long as Allah willed, then break his fast.

ثم يلبث حتى يمضي من الليل قريب من الثلث، ثم يقوم فيصلي العشاء الآخرة أربع ركعات، ويقنت في الثانية قبل الركوع وبعد القراءة، فإذا سلم جلس في مصلاه يذكر الله عز وجل ويسبحه ويحمده ويكبره ويهلله ما شاء الله، ويسجد بعد التعقيب سجدة الشكر، ثم يأوى إلى فراشه،

Then he stays until about one-third of the night has passed, then he rises to pray the Isha al-Akhirah (late Isha prayer) consisting of four rak'ahs. He performs qunut supplication in the second rak'ah before the ruku and after recitation. After giving salam, he remains in his prayer place remembering Allah the Mighty and Sublime, glorifying Him, praising Him, declaring His greatness and oneness for as long as Allah wills. After these supplications, he performs a sajdah al-shukr (prostration of gratitude). Then he retires to his bed.

فإذا كان الثلث الأخير من الليل قام من فراشه بالتسبيح والتحميد والتهليل والتكبير والاستغفار واستاك ثم توضأ ثم قام إلى صلاة الليل، فيصلي ثماني ركعات ويسلم في كل ركعتين، يقرأ في الأولتين منهما في كل ركعة (الحمد) مرة و (قل هو الله أحد) ثلاثين مرة،

When the last third of the night came, he would rise from his bed with tasbih (saying SubhanAllah), tahmid (saying Alhamdulillah), tahlil (saying La ilaha illa Allah), takbir (saying Allahu Akbar), and istighfar (seeking forgiveness). He would use the siwak, perform wudu, then stand for Salat al-Layl. He would pray eight rak'ahs, giving salam after every two rak'ahs. In the first two rak'ahs, he would recite in each rak'ah Surah Al-Fatihah once and Surah Al-Ikhlas [Quran 112:1] thirty times.

ثم يصلي صلاة جعفر بن أبي طالب أربع ركعات، يسلم في كل ركعتين، ويقنت في كل ركعتين في الثانية

قبل الركوع وبعد التسبيح، ويحتسب بها من صلاة الليل، ثم يقوم فيصلي الركعتين الباقيتين، يقرأ في الأولى (الحمد) وسورة (الملك) وفي الثانية (الحمد) و (هل أتى على الانسان) ثم يقوم فيصلي ركعتي الشفع، يقرأ في كل ركعة منهما (الحمد) مرة و (قل هو الله أحد) ثلاث مرات، ويقنت في الثانية قبل الركوع وبعد القراءة،

Then he prays the prayer of Ja'far ibn Abi Talib which is four rak'ahs, giving salam after every two rak'ahs, and performs qunut in each second rak'ah before ruku and after tasbih, and this counts as part of Salat al-Layl. Then he stands and prays the remaining two rak'ahs, reciting Surah Al-Fatihah and Surah Al-Mulk in the first rak'ah, and Surah Al-Fatihah and Surah Al-Insan in the second rak'ah. Then he stands and prays the two rak'ahs of Shaf', reciting in each rak'ah Surah Al-Fatihah once and Surah Al-Ikhlas three times, and performs qunut in the second rak'ah before ruku and after recitation.

فإذا سلم قام وصلى ركعة الوتر، يتوجه فيها، يقرأ فيها (الحمد) مرة و (قل هو الله أحد) ثلاث مرات، و (قل أعوذ برب الفلق) مرة واحدة، و (قل أعوذ برب الناس) مرة واحدة، ويقنت فيها قبل الركوع وبعد القراءة - إلى أن قال - ويقول: أستغفر الله وأسأله التوبة، سبعين مرة، فإذا سلم جلس في التعقيب ما شاء الله،

When he completes the salam (of night prayer), he stands and prays one rak'ah of Witr. In this rak'ah, he faces (the qibla) and recites Surah Al-Fatihah once, Surah Al-Ikhlas three times [Quran 112], Surah Al-Falaq once [Quran 113], and Surah An-Nas once [Quran 114]. He performs qunut before ruku and after the recitation - until he said - and he says: "I seek Allah's forgiveness and ask Him for repentance" seventy times. After the salam, he sits for ta'qib (post-prayer supplications) for as long as Allah wills.

فإذا قرب من الفجر قام فصلى ركعتي الفجر، يقرأ في الأولى (الحمد) و (قل يا أيها الكافرون) وفي الثانية (الحمد) و (قل هو الله أحد) فإذا طلع الفجر أذن وأقام وصلى الغداة ركعتين، فإذا سلم جلس في التعقيب حتى تطلع الشمس، ثم سجد حتى يتعالى النهار.

When dawn approached, he would stand and pray the two dawn rak'ahs, reciting in the first rak'ah Al-Fatihah and Surah Al-Kafirun [Quran 109], and in the second rak'ah Al-Fatihah and Surah Al-Ikhlas [Quran 112]. When dawn broke, he would give the adhan and iqamah and pray the morning prayer two rak'ahs. After saying salam, he would sit in remembrance until sunrise, then prostrate until the day was well underway.

Hadith 4497

عن جعفر بن محمد (عليهما السلام) - في حديث شرائع الدين - قال: وصلاة الفريضة: الظهر أربع ركعات، والعصر أربع ركعات، والمغرب ثلاث ركعات، والعشاء الآخرة أربع ركعات، والفجر ركعتان، فجملة الصلاة المفروضة سبع عشرة ركعة،

From Ja'far bin Muhammad (peace be upon them) - in a hadith of the laws of religion - he said: The obligatory prayer is Zuhr four rak'ahs, Asr four rak'ahs, Maghrib three rak'ahs, last Isha four rak'ahs, and Fajr two rak'ahs. The total obligatory prayer is seventeen rak'ahs.

والسنة أربع وثلاثون ركعة، منها: أربع ركعات بعد المغرب لا تقصير فيها في السفر والحضر، وركعتان من جلوس بعد العشاء الآخرة تعدان بركعة، وثمان ركعات في السحر وهي صلاة الليل، والشفع ركعتان، والوتر ركعة، وركعتا الفجر بعد الوتر، وثمان ركعات قبل الظهر، وثمان ركعات (بعد الظهر) قبل العصر، والصلاة تستحب في أول الأوقات.

The Sunnah is thirty-four rak'ahs, among them four rak'ahs after Maghrib with no shortening in them during travel and at home, two rak'ahs while sitting after last Isha counted as one rak'ah, eight rak'ahs at pre-dawn which is Salat al-Layl, Shaf' two rak'ahs, Witr one rak'ah, two rak'ahs of Fajr after Witr, eight rak'ahs before Zuhr, and eight rak'ahs (after Zuhr) before Asr. Prayer is recommended at the beginning of the times.

Hadith 4498

عن أبي بصير قال: قال الصادق (عليه السلام): شيعتنا أهل الورع والاجتهاد، وأهل الوفاء والأمانة، وأهل الزهد والعبادة، وأصحاب الإحدى وخمسين ركعة في اليوم والليلة، القائمون بالليل، الصائمون بالنهار، يزكون أموالهم، ويحجون البيت، ويجتنبون كل محرم.

From Abu Basir who said: Al-Sadiq (peace be upon him) said: Our Shi'a are people of piety and striving, people of loyalty and trustworthiness, people of asceticism and worship, who pray fifty-one rak'ahs day and night, stand in prayer at night, fast during day, pay zakat, perform Hajj, and avoid all forbidden things.

Hadith 4499

الفضل بن الحسن الطبرسي في (مجمع البيان) عن أبي جعفر (عليه السلام) في قوله تعالى: (الذين هم على صلاتهم دائمون) قال: هذا في النوافل، وقوله: (والذين هم على صلاتهم يحافظون)، في الفرائض والواجبات.

Al-Fadhl bin al-Hasan al-Tabarsi in Majma' al-Bayan from Abu Ja'far (peace be upon him) regarding the verse "Those who are constant in their prayer" [Quran 70:23] said: This refers to supererogatory prayers, and "Those who guard their prayers" [Quran 70:34] refers to obligatory prayers.

Hadith 4500

عن أبي الحسن (عليه السلام) في قوله تعالى: (والذين هم على صلاتهم يحافظون) قال: أولئك أصحاب الخمسين صلاة من شيعتنا.

From Abu al-Hasan (peace be upon him) regarding "Those who guard their prayers" [Quran 70:34] he said: Those are our Shi'a who pray fifty prayers.

Hadith 4501

عن أبي محمد الحسن بن علي العسكري (عليهما السلام) قال: علامات المؤمن خمس، وعد منها صلاة الإحدى وخمسين.

From Abu Muhammad al-Hasan bin Ali al-Askari (peace be upon them) said: The believer has five signs, and counted among them praying fifty-one [rak'ahs].

CHAPTER 14

Permissibility Of Limiting The Supererogatory Prayers Of Asr To Six Or Four Rak'ahs, The Supererogatory Prayers Of Maghrib To Two Rak'ahs, And Omitting The Supererogatory Prayer Of Isha

[Hadith 4502 to 4509]

Hadith 4502

عن زرارة قال: قلت لأبي جعفر (عليه السلام): إني رجل تاجر أختلف وأتجر، فكيف لي بالزوال والمحافظة على صلاة الزوال؟ وكم تصلي؟ قال: تصلي ثماني ركعات إذا زالت الشمس، وركعتين بعد الظهر، وركعتين قبل العصر، فهذه اثنتا عشرة ركعة،

From Zurarah who said: I said to Abu Ja'far (peace be upon him): I am a merchant who travels and trades, so how can I manage the midday prayer and be mindful of it? And how much should I pray? He said: Pray eight rak'ahs when the sun passes the meridian (*), two rak'ahs after Zuhr, and two rak'ahs before Asr. These are twelve rak'ahs.

وتصلي بعد المغرب ركعتين، وبعد ما ينتصف الليل ثلاث عشرة ركعة، منها الوتر، ومنها ركعتا الفجر، فتلك سبع وعشرون ركعة سوى الفريضة. وإنما هذا كله تطوع وليس بمفروض، إن تارك الفريضة كافر، وإن تارك هذا ليس بكافر، ولكنها معصية، لأنه يستحب إذا عمل الرجل عملا من الخير أن يدوم عليه.

Pray two rak'ahs after Maghrib, and after midnight thirteen rak'ahs, among them Witr and the two rak'ahs of Fajr. So those are twenty-seven rak'ahs besides the obligatory. All of this is just voluntary and not obligatory. The one who abandons the obligatory is a disbeliever, but the one who abandons this (voluntary) is not a disbeliever, but it is a disobedience, because it is recommended that when a man does a good deed, he should persist in it.

Translator: * The imaginary line in the sky that the sun crosses at its highest point during the day.

Hadith 4503

عن أبي بصير قال: سألت أبا عبد الله (عليه السلام) عن التطوع بالليل والنهار؟ فقال: الذي يستحب أن لا يقصر عنه ثمان ركعات عند زوال الشمس، وبعد الظهر ركعتان، وقبل العصر ركعتان، وبعد المغرب ركعتان، وقبل العتمة ركعتان، ومن السحر ثمان ركعات، ثم يوتر، والوتر ثلاث ركعات مفصولة، ثم ركعتان قبل صلاة الفجر، وأحب صلاة الليل إليهم آخر الليل.

From Abu Basir who said: I asked Abu Abdullah (peace be upon him) about the voluntary prayers at night and day. He said: It is recommended not to pray less than eight rak'ahs when the sun passes the meridian, two rak'ahs after Zuhr, two rak'ahs before Asr, two rak'ahs after Maghrib, two rak'ahs before Isha, eight rak'ahs at pre-dawn, then pray Witr. Witr is three separate rak'ahs, then two rak'ahs before the Fajr prayer. The most beloved Salat al-Layl to them is at the end of the night.

Hadith 4504

عن زرارة قال: قلت: لأبي عبد الله (عليه السلام): ما جرت به السنة في الصلاة؟ فقال: ثمان ركعات الزوال، وركعتان بعد الظهر، وركعتان قبل العصر، وركعتان بعد المغرب، وثلاث عشرة ركعة من آخر الليل، منها الوتر، وركعتا الفجر.

From Zurarah who said: I said to Abu Abdullah (peace be upon him): What has the Sunnah established regarding prayer? He said: Eight rak'ahs at midday, two rak'ahs after Zuhr, two rak'ahs before Asr, two rak'ahs after Maghrib, thirteen rak'ahs at the end of the night, among them Witr and the two rak'ahs of Fajr.

قلت: فهذا جميع ما جرت به السنة؟ قال: نعم. فقال: أبو الخطاب: أفرأيت إن قوي فزاد؟ قال: فجلس - وكان متكئا - فقال: إن قويت فصلها كما كانت تصلى، وكما ليست في ساعة من النهار فليست في ساعة من الليل، إن الله يقول: (ومن آناء الليل فسبح).

I said: So this is all that the Sunnah has established? He said: Yes. Abu Al-Khattab said: What if one is strong and increases? He said: He sat up - and he was reclining - and said: If you are strong, pray as it used to be prayed. Just as there is no hour of the day in which there is no prayer, there is also no hour of the night. Indeed, Allah says: "And in parts of the night exalt Him".

أقول: المراد بالسنة هنا الاستحباب المؤكد لما تقدم، وتكون الزيادة السابقة مستحبة غير مؤكدة كتأكيد هذا العدد.

I (Hurr Amili) say: What is meant by Sunnah here is the emphasized recommendation based on what was previously mentioned, and the previous increase would be recommended but not emphasized like the emphasis of this number.

Hadith 4505

عن عبد الله بن سنان قال: سمعت أبا عبد الله (عليه السلام) يقول: لا تصل أقل من أربع وأربعين ركعة. قال: ورأيته يصلي بعد العتمة أربع ركعات.

From Abdullah bin Sinan who said: I heard Abu Abdullah (peace be upon him) say: Do not pray less than forty-four rak'ahs. He said: I saw him pray four rak'ahs after

Isha.

Hadith 4506

عن يحيى بن حبيب قال: سألت الرضا (عليه السلام) عن أفضل ما يتقرب به العباد إلى الله من الصلاة؟

قال: ستة وأربعون ركعة فرائضه ونوافله، قلت: هذه رواية زرارة، قال: أو ترى أحدا كان أصدع بالحق منه؟

From Yahya ibn Habib who said: I asked Al-Ridha (peace be upon him) about the best way that servants can get closer to Allah through prayer? He said: Forty-six rak'ahs including obligatory and supererogatory prayers. I said: This is the narration of Zurarah. He said: Do you see anyone who was more outspoken with the truth than him?

Hadith 4507

محمد بن علي بن الحسين قال: قال أبو جعفر (عليه السلام): كان رسول الله (صلى الله عليه وآله) لا يصلي بالنهار شيئا حتى تزول الشمس، وإذا زالت صلى ثماني ركعات وهي صلاة الأوابين. تفتح في تلك الساعة أبواب السماء ويستجاب الدعاء، وتهب الرياح، وينظر الله إلى خلقه، فإذا فاء الفئ ذراعا صلى الظهر أربعا.

Muhammad bin Ali bin Al-Husain said: Abu Ja'far (peace be upon him) said: The Messenger of Allah (peace be upon him and his family) would not pray anything during the day until the sun passed the meridian. When it passed, he would pray eight rak'ahs, which is the prayer of the penitent ones. At that hour, the gates of the sky are opened, supplications are answered, the winds blow, and Allah looks at His creation. When the shadow extended a forearm's length, he would pray Zuhr four rak'ahs.

وصلى بعد الظهر ركعتين، ثم صلى ركعتين أخراوين، ثم صلى العصر أربعا إذا فاء الفئ ذراعا، ثم لا يصلي بعد العصر شيئا حتى تئوب الشمس، فإذا آبت وهو أن تغيب صلى المغرب ثلاثا، وبعد المغرب أربعا، ثم لا يصلي شيئا حتى يسقط الشفق، فإذا سقط الشفق صلى العشاء،

After Zuhr, he would pray two rak'ahs, then pray another two rak'ahs. Then he would pray Asr four rak'ahs when the shadow extended a forearm's length. He would not pray anything after Asr until the sun set. When it set, which is when it disappears, he would pray Maghrib three rak'ahs, and after Maghrib four rak'ahs. Then he would not pray anything until the twilight disappeared. When the twilight disappeared, he would pray Isha.

ثم آوى رسول الله (صلى الله عليه وآله) إلى فراشه ولم يصل شيئا حتى يزول نصف الليل، فإذا زال نصف الليل صلى ثماني ركعات، وأوتر في الربع الأخير من الليل بثلاث ركعات، فقرأ فيهن " فاتحة الكتاب " و (قل هو الله أحد) ويفصل بين الثلاث بتسليمة، ويتكلم ويأمر بالحاجة، ولا يخرج من مصلاه حتى يصلي

الثالثة التي يوتر فيها، ويقنت فيها قبل الركوع.

Then the Messenger of Allah (peace be upon him and his family) would go to his bed and not pray anything until midnight. When midnight passed, he would pray eight rak'ahs and pray Witr in the last quarter of the night with three rak'ahs. He would recite in them Surah Al-Fatihah and "Say: He, Allah, is One". He would separate between the three with a taslim (salutation), speak and command regarding needs. He would not leave his prayer place until he prayed the third rak'ah in which he prayed Witr. He would perform qunoot in it before the ruku.

ثم يسلم ويصلي ركعتي الفجر قبل الفجر وعنده وبعيده، ثم يصلي ركعتي الصبح وهي الفجر إذا اعترض الفجر وأضاء حسنا، فهذه صلاة رسول الله (صلى الله عليه وآله) التي قبضه الله عز وجل عليها.

Then he would give salutations and pray the two rak'ahs of Fajr before dawn, near him and far from him. Then he would pray the two rak'ahs of morning which is Fajr when the dawn appeared and shone brightly. This was the prayer of the Messenger of Allah (peace be upon him and his family) upon which Allah, the Mighty and Sublime, took his soul.

Hadith 4508

عن أبي عبد الله (عليه السلام) قال - في حديث طويل -: وعليك بالصلاة الستة والأربعين، وعليك بالحج أن تهل بالافراد، وتنوي الفسخ إذا قدمت مكة، ثم قال: والذي أتاك به أبو بصير من صلاة إحدى وخمسين، والاهلال بالتمتع إلى الحج وما أمرناه به من أن يهل بالتمتع فلذلك عندنا معان وتصاريف لذلك ما يسعنا ويسعكم، ولا يخالف شئ منه الحق ولا يضاده.

From Abu Abdullah (peace be upon him) who said in a long hadith: You should perform forty-six prayers, and you should perform Hajj by declaring Ihram for Ifrad (singular Hajj), and intend to change it when you arrive in Makkah. Then he said: And what Abu Basir brought to you about fifty-one prayers, and declaring Ihram (pronouncing the Talbiyah) for Tamattu Hajj, and what we ordered him regarding declaring Ihram (pronouncing the Talbiyah) for Tamattu - for us these have meanings and interpretations that suffice us and you, and none of them contradicts or opposes the truth.

Hadith 4509

عن أبي عبد الله (عليه السلام) - في حديث - إنه دخل عليه فأوصاه بأشياء ثم قال: إذا كانت الشمس من هيهنا من العصر فصل ست ركعات.

From Abu Abdullah (peace be upon him) - in a hadith - that someone came to him seeking advice, and among the things he advised him with he said: When the sun is at this position in the afternoon, pray six rak'ahs.

أقول: ويدل على جواز النقص من النوافل ما يأتي من جواز تركها، وقد ثبت مشروعية الزيادة السابقة واستحبابها بما تقدم وغيره، على أن أحاديث النقص محتملة للتقية، ويمكن حملها عليها.

I (Hurr Amili) say: The permissibility of reducing from the supererogatory prayers is indicated by what will come regarding the permissibility of omitting them. The legitimacy of the aforementioned increase and its recommendation has been established by what has preceded and other evidence. Furthermore, the hadiths of reduction can be interpreted as taqiyyah, and it is possible to interpret them as such.

CHAPTER 15

Each Two Rak'ahs Of Supererogatory Prayers Require Tashahhud And Taslim, And The Witr Prayer Separately, Excluding The Bedouin's Prayer And Similar Cases

[Hadith 4510 to 4527]

Hadith 4510

عن أبي ولاد حفص بن سالم الحناط قال: سألت أبا عبد الله (عليه السلام) عن التسليم في ركعتي الوتر؟ فقال: نعم، وإن كانت لك حاجة فأخرج واقضها، ثم عد واركع ركعة.

From Abu Wallad Hafs bin Salim al-Hannat who said: I asked Abu Abdullah (peace be upon him) about giving taslim in the two rak'ahs of Witr? He said: Yes, and if you have a need, go out and fulfill it, then return and pray one rak'ah.

Hadith 4511

عن علي بن جعفر، عن أخيه موسى بن جعفر (عليه السلام) قال: سألته عن الرجل يصلي النافلة. أيصلح له أن يصلي أربع ركعات لا يسلم بينهن؟ قال: لا، إلا أن يسلم بين كل ركعتين.

From Ali bin Ja'far, from his brother Musa bin Ja'far (peace be upon him) who said: I asked him about a man praying supererogatory prayers, is it permissible for him to pray four rak'ahs without giving taslim between them? He said: No, except by giving taslim between every two rak'ahs.

Hadith 4512

عن أبي بصير قال: قال أبو جعفر (عليه السلام) - في حديث -: وافصل بين كل ركعتين من نوافلك بالتسليم.

From Abu Basir who said: Abu Ja'far (peace be upon him) said - in a hadith -: Separate between every two rak'ahs of your supererogatory prayers with taslim.

Hadith 4513

عن أبي ولاد حفص بن سالم الحناط أنه قال: سمعت أبا عبد الله (عليه السلام) يقول: لا بأس بأن يصلي الرجل ركعتين من الوتر ثم ينصرف فيقضي حاجته، ثم يرجع فيصلي ركعة، ولا بأس أن يصلي الرجل ركعتين من الوتر، ثم يشرب الماء، ويتكلم، وينكح، ويقضي ما شاء من حاجته، ويحدث وضوءه ثم يصلي الركعة قبل أن يصلي الغداة.

From Abu Wallad Hafs bin Salim al-Hannat who said: I heard Abu Abdullah (peace be upon him) saying: There is no problem if a man prays two rak'ahs of Witr then leaves to fulfill his need, then returns to pray one rak'ah, and there is no problem if a man prays two rak'ahs of Witr, then drinks water, speaks, has intimate relations, fulfills whatever need he has, performs wudu again then prays the remaining rak'ah before praying the dawn prayer.

Hadith 4514

عن الفضل بن شاذان، عن الرضا (عليه السلام) قال: الصلاة ركعتان ركعتان، فلذلك جعل الاذان مثنى مثنى.

From Al-Fadhl bin Shadhan, from Al-Ridha (peace be upon him) who said: Prayer is two rak'ahs by two rak'ahs, and that is why the adhan was made in pairs.

Hadith 4515

عن معاوية بن عمار قال: قلت لأبي عبد الله (عليه السلام): التسليم في ركعتي الوتر؟ فقال: توقظ الراقد وتكلم بالحاجة.

From Mu'awiyah bin Ammar who said: I said to Abu Abdullah (peace be upon him): The taslim in the two rak'ahs of Witr? He said: Wake the sleeping person and speak about needs.

Hadith 4516

عن معاوية بن عمار قال: قال لي: اقرأ في الوتر في ثلاثتهن بقل هو الله أحد، وسلم في الركعتين توقظ الراقد وتأمر بالصلاة.

From Mu'awiyah bin Ammar who said: He told me: Recite in all three rak'ahs of Witr "Say: He is Allah, One" [Quran 112:1], and give taslim in the two rak'ahs to wake the sleeping person and command prayer.

Hadith 4517

عن أبي عبد الله (عليه السلام) قال: لا بأس أن يصلي الرجل الركعتين من الوتر، ثم ينصرف فيقضي حاجته.

From Abu Abdullah (peace be upon him) who said: There is no problem if a person prays two rak'ahs of Witr, then leaves to fulfill his need.

Hadith 4518

عن سليمان بن خالد، عن أبي عبد الله (عليه السلام) قال: الوتر ثلاث ركعات تفصل بينهن، وتقرأ فيهن جميعا بقل هو الله أحد.

From Sulayman bin Khalid, from Abu Abdullah (peace be upon him) who said:

Witr is three rak'ahs separated between them, and in all of them recite Qul Huwa Allahu Ahad [Quran 112:1].

Hadith 4519

عن أبي بصير، عن أبي عبد الله (عليه السلام) قال: الوتر ثلاث ركعات، ثنتين مفصولة، وواحدة.

From Abu Basir, from Abu Abdullah (peace be upon him) who said: Witr is three rak'ahs, two separated and one.

Hadith 4520

عن أبي عبد الله (عليه السلام)، فيمن انصرف في الركعة الثانية من الوتر، هل يجوز له أن يتكلم أو يخرج من المسجد ثم يعود فيوتر؟ قال: نعم، تصنع ما تشاء وتتكلم وتحدث وضوءك، ثم تتمها قبل أن تصلي الغداة.

From Abu Abdullah (peace be upon him), regarding one who leaves after the second rak'ah of Witr, is it permissible for him to speak or exit the mosque then return to complete Witr? He said: Yes, you may do what you wish and speak and renew your wudu, then complete it before praying the dawn prayer.

Hadith 4521

عن أبي الحسن الرضا (عليه السلام)، قال: سألته عن الوتر، أفصل أم وصل؟ قال: فصل.

From Abu al-Hasan al-Ridha (peace be upon him), he said: I asked him about Witr, should it be separated or connected? He said: Separated.

Hadith 4522

عن بعض مشيخته قال: قلت لأبي عبد الله (عليه السلام): أفصل في الوتر؟ قال: نعم، قلت: فإني ربما عطشت فأشرب الماء؟ قال: نعم، وانكح.

From some of his elders who said: I said to Abu Abdullah (peace be upon him): Should I separate in Witr? He said: Yes. I said: Sometimes I get thirsty and drink water? He said: Yes, and you may even have marital relations.

Hadith 4523

عن علي بن أبي حمزة أو غيره، عمن حدثه، عن أبي عبد الله (عليه السلام)، مثله، وأسقط قوله: وانكح.

From Ali bin Abi Hamza or other than him, from whoever narrated to him, from Abu Abdullah (peace be upon him), similar to it, except omitting his saying "and you may have marital relations."

Hadith 4524

عن مولى لأبي جعفر (عليه السلام) قال: قال: ركعتا الوتر إن شاء تكلم بينهما وبين الثالثة، وإن شاء لم يفعل.

From a freed slave of Abu Ja'far (peace be upon him) who said: The two rak'ahs of Witr - if one wishes one may speak between them and the third, and if one wishes one need not do so.

———

Hadith 4525

عن يعقوب بن شعيب قال: سألت أبا عبد الله (عليه السلام) عن التسليم في ركعتي الوتر؟ فقال: إن شئت سلمت وإن شئت لم تسلم.

From Ya'qub bin Shu'ayb who said: I asked Abu Abdullah (peace be upon him) about the taslim (salutation) in the two rak'ahs of Witr prayer? He said: If you wish, give the taslim and if you wish, do not give the taslim.

———

Hadith 4526

عن معاوية بن عمار قال: قلت لأبي عبد الله (عليه السلام) (أسلم) في ركعتي الوتر، فقال: إن شئت سلمت وإن شئت لم تسلم.

From Mu'awiyah bin Ammar who said: I said to Abu Abdullah (peace be upon him) (should I give) the salam (or taslim meaning salutation) in the two rak'ahs of Witr? He said: If you wish, give the salam and if you wish, do not give the salam.

———

Hadith 4527

عن كردويه الهمداني قال: سألت العبد الصالح (عليه السلام) عن الوتر؟ فقال: صله.

From Kardawayh al-Hamdani who said: I asked the Abd al-Salih (Righteous Servant) (peace be upon him) about the Witr? He said: Pray it.

أقول: حمل الشيخ هذه الأحاديث الثلاثة على التقية، وجوز فيها أن يراد بالتسليم الصيغة المستحبة، وأن يراد به ما يستباح بالتسليم من الكلام وغيره، ويأتي ما يدل على استثناء صلاة الاعرابي وصلوات أخر في الجمعة وفي الصلوات المندوبة.

I (Hurr Amili) say: Al-Shaykh interpreted these three hadiths as taqiyyah, and it is permissible that the meaning of taslim here refers to the recommended formula, or it could mean what becomes permissible after taslim such as speaking and other things. Evidence will come later regarding the exception of the Bedouin's prayer and other prayers in Friday prayer and recommended prayers.

———

CHAPTER 16

The Permissibility Of Leaving Supererogatory Prayers
[Hadith 4528 to 4538]

Hadith 4528

عن محمد الحلبي قال: قال أبو عبد الله (عليه السلام): في الوتر: إنما كتب الله الخمس وليست الوتر مكتوبة، إن شئت صليتها، وتركها قبيح.

From Muhammad al-Halabi who said: Abu Abdullah (peace be upon him) said regarding Witr prayer: Allah only prescribed the five prayers, and Witr is not prescribed. If you wish you can pray it, though abandoning it is disliked.

Hadith 4529

عن الحسن بن موسى الحناط قال: خرجنا أنا وجميل بن دراج وعائذ الأحمسي حجاجا، فكان عائذ كثيرا ما يقول لنا في الطريق: إن لي إلى أبي عبد الله (عليه السلام) حاجة أريد أن أسأله عنها، فأقول له حتى نلقاه،

From Al-Hasan bin Musa al-Hannat who said: We went for Hajj - myself, Jameel bin Darraj and A'idh al-Ahmasi. A'idh would often tell us on the way: I have a need to ask Abu Abdullah (peace be upon him) something. I would tell him: Wait until we meet him.

فلما دخلنا عليه سلمنا وجلسنا فأقبل علينا بوجهه مبتدئا فقال: من أتى الله بما افترض عليه لم يسأله عما سوى ذلك، فغمزنا عائذ. فلما قمنا قلنا: ما كانت حاجتك؟ قال: الذي سمعتم، قلنا: كيف كانت هذه حاجتك؟ فقال: أنا رجل لا أطيق القيام بالليل فخفت أن أكون مأخوذا به فأهلك.

When we entered upon him, we greeted and sat down. He faced us and initiated by saying: Whoever fulfills what Allah has made obligatory upon him will not be questioned about anything else. A'idh gestured to us. When we got up, we asked: What was your need? He said: What you heard. We said: How was this your need? He said: I am a man who cannot manage night prayers, and I feared I would be held accountable for it and perish.

Hadith 4530

عن عبد الله بن مسكان قال: حدثني من سأل أبا عبد الله (عليه السلام) عن الرجل تجتمع عليه الصلوات؟ قال: ألقها واستأنف.

From Abdullah bin Muskan who said: Someone who asked Abu Abdullah (peace be upon him) told me about a man who has accumulated [supererogatory] prayers that he missed? He said: Drop (discard) them and start anew.

Hadith 4531

عن أبي الحسن الرضا (عليه السلام)، أن أبا الحسن (عليه السلام) كان إذا اغتم ترك الخمسين. قال الشيخ: يعني تمام الخمسين، لان الفرائض لا يجوز تركها.

From Abu al-Hasan al-Ridha (peace be upon him): When Abu al-Hasan (peace be upon him) was distressed, he would leave the fifty. The Shaykh said: This means the complete fifty, because leaving obligatory prayers is not permissible.

Hadith 4532

عن عدة من أصحابنا، أن أبا الحسن موسى (عليه السلام) كان إذا اهتم ترك النافلة.

From several of our companions: When Abu al-Hasan Musa (peace be upon him) was concerned, he would leave the supererogatory prayers.

Hadith 4533

عن عمار الساباطي قال: كنا جلوسا عند أبي عبد الله (عليه السلام) بمنى، فقال له: رجل ما تقول في النوافل؟ قال: فريضة، قال: ففزعنا وفزع الرجل. فقال أبو عبد الله (عليه السلام): إنما أعنى صلاة الليل على رسول الله (صلى الله عليه وآله)، إن الله يقول: (ومن الليل فتهجد به نافلة لك).

From Ammar al-Sabati who said: We were sitting with Abu Abdullah (peace be upon him) in Mina when a man asked him: What do you say about the supererogatory prayers? He said: Obligatory. We and the man were alarmed. Abu Abdullah (peace be upon him) then said: I only meant Salat al-Layl for the Messenger of Allah (peace be upon him and his family), as Allah says: "And during part of the night, pray Tahajjud as an additional prayer for you" [Quran 17:79].

Hadith 4534

عن عائذ الأحمسي قال: دخلت على أبي عبد الله (عليه السلام) وأنا أريد أن أسأله عن صلاة الليل - إلى أن قال - فقال من غير أن أسأله: إذا لقيت الله بالصلوات الخمس المفروضات لم يسألك عما سوى ذلك.

From A'idh al-Ahmasi who said: I entered upon Abu Abdullah (peace be upon him) wanting to ask him about Salat al-Layl - until he said - he said without me asking: If you meet Allah with the five obligatory prayers, He will not question you about anything else.

Hadith 4535

عن علي بن معبد أو غيره، عن أحدهما (عليهما السلام) قال: قال النبي (صلى الله عليه وآله): إن للقلوب إقبالا وإدبارا، فإذا أقبلت فتنفلوا، وإذا أدبرت فعليكم بالفريضة.

From Ali bin Ma'bad or others, from one of them (peace be upon them) who said: The Prophet (peace be upon him and his family) said: Indeed hearts have periods of advancement and withdrawal. When they advance, perform optional acts, and when they withdraw, stick to the obligatory acts.

Hadith 4536

عن نريح المحاربي، عن أبي عبد الله (عليه السلام) قال: (قال رجل): يا رسول الله يسأل الله عما سوى الفريضة؟ قال: لا.

From Dhuraih al-Muharibi, from Abu Abdullah (peace be upon him) who said: A man asked: O Messenger of Allah, will Allah question about anything besides the obligatory acts? He said: No.

Hadith 4537

عن عائذ الأحمسي قال: دخلت على أبي عبد الله (عليه السلام) - إلى أن قال - فقال لي: يا عائذ إذا لقيت الله عز وجل بالصلوات الخمس المفروضات لم يسألك عما سوى ذلك، قال عائذ: وكان لا يمكنني قيام الليل، وكنت خائفا أن أوخذ بذلك فأهلك، فابتدأني (عليه السلام) بجواب ما كنت أريد أن أسأله عنه.

From A'idh al-Ahmasi who said: I entered upon Abu Abdullah (peace be upon him) - until he said - he said to me: O A'idh, when you meet Allah with the five obligatory prayers, He will not question you about anything else besides that. A'idh said: I was unable to perform night prayers and was afraid I would be held accountable for that and perish, so he (peace be upon him) preemptively answered what I wanted to ask him about.

Hadith 4538

محمد بن الحسين الرضي في (نهج البلاغة) عن أمير المؤمنين (عليه السلام) أنه قال: إن للقلوب إقبالا وإدبارا. فإذا أقبلت فاحملوها على النوافل وإذا أدبرت فاقتصروا بها على الفرائض.

Muhammad bin Al-Husayn Al-Radi in (Nahj al-Balagha) from Amir al-Mu'minin (peace be upon him) that he said: Indeed hearts have periods of advancement and withdrawal. When they advance, burden them with voluntary acts, and when they withdraw, limit them to the obligatory duties.

CHAPTER 17

The Importance Of Maintaining Supererogatory Prayers And Focusing The Heart In Prayer

[Hadith 4539 to 4551]

Hadith 4539

عن الفضيل قال: سألت أبا جعفر (عليه السلام) عن قول الله عز وجل: (الذين هم على صلاتهم يحافظون)؟ قال: هي الفريضة. قلت: (الذين هم على صلاتهم دائمون) قال: هي النافلة.

From Al-Fudhayl who said: I asked Abu Ja'far (peace be upon him) about the saying of Allah, the Mighty and Majestic: "Those who carefully maintain their prayers?" [Quran, 23:9] He said: It refers to the obligatory prayers. I said: "Those who are constant in their prayers" [Quran, 70:23]. He said: It refers to the supererogatory prayers.

Hadith 4540

عن محمد بن مسلم قال: قلت لأبي عبد الله (عليه السلام): إن عمار الساباطي روى عنك رواية، قال: وما هي؟ قلت: روى أن السنة فريضة، فقال: أين يذهب، أين يذهب؟! ليس هكذا حدثته، إنما قلت له: من صلى فأقبل على صلاته لم يحدث نفسه فيها أو لم يسه فيها أقبل الله عليه ما أقبل عليها، فربما رفع نصفها أو ربعها أو ثلثها أو خمسها، وإنما أمرنا بالسنة ليكمل بها ما ذهب من المكتوبة.

From Muhammad ibn Muslim who said: I said to Abu Abdullah (peace be upon him): Ammar al-Sabati narrated a tradition from you. He asked: What is it? I said: He narrated that the Sunnah is obligatory. He said: Where is he going with this? Where is he going?! This is not how I narrated to him. What I said was: Whoever prays and focuses on his prayer without talking to himself or becoming distracted, Allah turns towards him as much as he turned towards his prayer. Sometimes half of it is raised up, or a quarter, or a third, or a fifth. We were commanded to perform supererogatory prayers to complete what was missed from the obligatory prayers.

Hadith 4541

عن أبي جعفر (عليه السلام) قال: إن العبد ليرفع له من صلاته نصفها أو ثلثها أو ربعها أو خمسها. فما يرفع له إلا ما أقبل عليه منها بقلبه، وإنما أمرنا بالنافلة ليتم لهم بها ما نقصوا من الفريضة.

From Abu Ja'far (peace be upon him) who said: Indeed half of a servant's prayer may be raised up, or a third, or a quarter, or a fifth. Only what he focused on with his heart is raised. We were commanded to perform supererogatory prayers to complete what they missed from the obligatory prayers.

Hadith 4542

عن أبي بصير، عن أبي عبد الله (عليه السلام) - في حديث - قال: يا با محمد، إن العبد يرفع له ثلث صلاته ونصفها وثلاثة أرباعها وأقل وأكثر على قدر سهوه فيها، لكنه يتم له من النوافل. قال: فقال له أبو بصير: ما أرى النوافل ينبغي أن تترك على حال، فقال أبو عبد الله (عليه السلام): أجل، لا.

From Abu Basir, from Abu Abdullah (peace be upon him) in a hadith saying: O Abu Muhammad, indeed a third of a servant's prayer is raised up, or half, or three quarters, more or less according to his level of distraction in it, but it is completed for him through supererogatory prayers. Abu Basir said to him: I don't think supererogatory prayers should ever be abandoned. Abu Abdullah (peace be upon him) said: Indeed, no.

Hadith 4543

عن أبي عبد الله (عليه السلام) قال: إن العبد يقوم فيصلي النافلة فيعجب الرب ملائكته منه، فيقول: يا ملائكتي، عبدي يقضي ما لم أفترض عليه.

From Abu Abdullah (peace be upon him) who said: When a servant stands to perform supererogatory prayer, the Lord amazes His angels with him, saying: O My angels, My servant is fulfilling what I did not make obligatory upon him.

Hadith 4544

عن أبي جعفر (عليه السلام) - في حديث - إن الله جل جلاله قال: ما يتقرب إلى عبد من عبادي بشئ أحب إلي مما افترضت عليه، وإنه ليتقرب إلي بالنافلة حتى أحبه، فإذا أحببته كنت سمعه الذي يسمع به، وبصره الذي يبصر به، ولسانه الذي ينطق به، ويده التي يبطش بها، إن دعاني أجبته، وإن سألني أعطيته.

From Abu Ja'far (peace be upon him) in a hadith: Allah, Mighty and Majestic, said: No servant draws closer to Me with anything more beloved to Me than what I made obligatory upon him. And he continues to draw closer to Me through supererogatory acts until I love him. When I love him, I become his hearing with which he hears, his sight with which he sees, his tongue with which he speaks, and his hand with which he grasps. If he calls upon Me, I answer him, and if he asks Me, I give to him.

Hadith 4545

عن زرارة عن أبي جعفر (عليه السلام)، قال: قلت له: (آناء الليل، ساجدا وقائما يحذر الآخرة ويرجو رحمة ربه) قال: يعني صلاة الليل، قال: قلت له: (وأطراف النهار لعلك ترضى)؟ قال: يعني تطوع بالنهار، قال: قلت له: (وإدبار النجوم)؟ قال: ركعتان قبل الصبح، قلت: (وأدبار السجود)؟ قال: ركعتان بعد المغرب.

From Zurarah from Abu Ja'far (peace be upon him), he said: I asked him about "Is one who is devoutly obedient during periods throughout the night, prostrating and standing, fearing the Hereafter and hoping for the mercy of his Lord" [Quran, 39:9], he said: It means Salat al-Layl. I asked him about "and at the ends of the day, perhaps you will be satisfied" [Quran, 20:130], he said: It means voluntary prayers during the day. I asked him about "and at the decline of the stars" [Quran, 52:49], he said: Two rak'ahs before dawn prayer. I asked him about "and after prostration" [Quran, 50:40], he said: Two rak'ahs after Maghrib prayer.

Hadith 4546

عن أبي بصير قال: سمعت أبا جعفر (عليه السلام) يقول: كل سهو في الصلاة يطرح منها، غير أن الله يتم بالنوافل.

From Abu Basir who said: I heard Abu Ja'far (peace be upon him) saying: Every forgetfulness in prayer is deducted from it, except that Allah completes it with supererogatory prayers.

Hadith 4547

عن أبي الحسن (عليه السلام) قال: صلاة النوافل قربان كل مؤمن.

From Abu al-Hasan (peace be upon him) who said: Supererogatory prayers are a means of nearness for every believer.

Hadith 4548

عن زرارة، عن أبي جعفر (عليه السلام) قال: إنما جعلت النافلة ليتم بها ما يفسد من الفريضة.

From Zurarah, from Abu Ja'far (peace be upon him) who said: The supererogatory prayer was only established to complete what becomes deficient in the obligatory prayer.

Hadith 4549

عن أبي بكر قال: قال لي أبو جعفر (عليه السلام): أتدري لأي شئ وضع التطوع؟ قلت ما أدري جعلت فداك؟ قال: إنه تطوع لكم، ونافلة للأنبياء، وتدري لم وضع التطوع؟ قلت: لا أدري، جعلت فداك؟ قال لأنه إن كان في الفريضة نقصان قضيت النافلة على الفريضة حتى تتم، إن الله عز وجل يقول لنبيه (صلى الله عليه وآله): (ومن الليل فتهجد به نافلة لك).

From Abu Bakr who said: Abu Ja'far (peace be upon him) said to me: Do you know why the voluntary prayer was established? I said: I do not know, may I be sacrificed for you. He said: It is voluntary for you, and obligatory for the prophets. And do you know why the voluntary prayer was established? I said: I do not know, may I be sacrificed for you. He said: Because if there is any deficiency in the obligatory prayer, the voluntary prayer makes up for the obligatory one until it is complete. Indeed Allah, the Mighty and Majestic, says to His Prophet (peace be upon him and his family): "And during part of the night, pray Tahajjud as additional worship for you" [Quran, 17:79].

Hadith 4550

عن أبي بصير قال: قال أبو عبد الله (عليه السلام): يرفع للرجل من الصلاة ربعها أو ثمنها أو نصفها أو أكثر بقدر ماسها، ولكن الله تعالى يتمم ذلك بالنوافل.

From Abu Basir who said: Abu Abdullah (peace be upon him) said: A quarter or an eighth or half or more of a person's prayer is raised according to how much they performed of it, but Allah the Exalted completes that through supererogatory prayers.

Hadith 4551

وفي (المجالس والاخبار) بإسناده عن أبي ذر، عن رسول الله (صلى الله عليه وآله) قال: يا أبا ذر ركعتان مقتصدتان في تفكر خير من قيام ليلة والقلب ساه.

And in (Al-Majalis wal-Akhbar) with its chain from Abu Dharr, from the Messenger of Allah (peace be upon him and his family) who said: O Abu Dharr, two moderate rak'ahs of prayer with contemplation are better than standing all night with a heedless heart.

CHAPTER 18

Confirmation Of The Recommendation To Make Up Missed Supererogatory Prayers, And If Unable Then Giving Charity Of One Mudd For Every Two Rak'ahs

[Hadith 4552 to 4557]

Hadith 4552

عن ابن سنان يعني عبد الله قال: سمعت أبا عبد الله (عليه السلام) يقول: إن العبد يقوم فيقضي النافلة فيعجب الرب ملائكته منه، فيقول: ملائكتي، عبدي يقضي ما لم أفترضه عليه.

From Ibn Sinan, meaning Abdullah, who said: I heard Abu Abdullah (peace be upon him) saying: When a servant makes up supererogatory prayers, the Lord shows him off to His angels saying: "My angels, My servant is making up what I did not make obligatory upon him."

Hadith 4553

عن أبي عبد الله (عليه السلام) قال: قلت له: أخبرني عن رجل عليه من صلاة النوافل مالا يدري ما هو من كثرتها، كيف يصنع؟ قال: فليصل حتى لا يدري كم صلى من كثرتها، فيكون قد قضى بقدر علمه من ذلك،

From Abu Abdullah (peace be upon him): I asked him about a man who has many missed supererogatory prayers that he cannot count, what should he do? He said: Let him pray until he loses count, so he will have made up what he knows of them.

ثم قال: قلت له: فإنه لا يقدر على القضاء، فقال إن كان شغله في طلب معيشة لابد منها، أو حاجة لأخ مؤمن فلا شئ عليه، وإن كان شغله لجمع الدنيا والتشاغل بها عن الصلاة فعليه القضاء، وإلا لقي الله وهو مستخف، متهاون، مضيع لحرمة رسول الله (صلى الله عليه وآله)،

Then I asked: What if he cannot make them up? He said: If he is occupied with necessary livelihood or helping a believing brother, then nothing is upon him. But if he is busy accumulating worldly things and being distracted from prayer, then he must make them up, otherwise he will meet Allah while being negligent and disrespecting the sanctity of the Messenger of Allah (peace be upon him and his family).

قلت: فإنه لا يقدر على القضاء فهل يجزي أن يتصدق؟ فسكت مليا ثم قال: لكم فليتصدق بصدقة. قلت: فما يتصدق؟ قال: بقدر طوله وأدنى ذلك مد لكل مسكين مكان كل صلاة، قلت: وكم الصلاة التي يجب فيها مد لكل مسكين؟ قال: لكل ركعتين من صلاة الليل مد، ولكل ركعتين من صلاة النهار مد،

I asked: If he cannot make them up, is it sufficient to give sadaqah? He was silent for a while then said: Let him give sadaqah. I asked: How much? He said: According to his ability, minimum one mudd per prayer for each poor person. I asked: For how many prayers is one mudd required? He said: One mudd for every two rak'ahs of Salat al-Layl and one mudd for every two rak'ahs of day prayer.

فقلت: لا يقدر فقال: مد إذا لكل أربع ركعات من صلاة النهار (مد لكل أربع ركعات من صلاة الليل)، قلت: لا يقدر، قال: فمد إذا لصلاة الليل ومد لصلاة النهار، والصلاة أفضل، والصلاة أفضل والصلاة أفضل.

I said: He cannot afford that. He said: Then one mudd for every four rak'ahs of day prayer and Salat al-Layl. I said: He cannot afford that. He said: Then one mudd for Salat al-Layl and one mudd for day prayer - but prayer is better, prayer is better, prayer is better.

Hadith 4554

قال الصدوق: وقال رسول الله (صلى الله عليه وآله): إن الله ليباهي ملائكته بالعبد يقضي صلاة الليل بالنهار، فيقول: يا ملائكتي، أنظروا إلى عبدي يقضي ما لم أفترضه عليه أشهدكم أني قد غفرت له.

Al-Saduq said: The Messenger of Allah (peace be upon him and his family) said: Allah boasts to His angels about the servant who makes up night prayers during the day, saying: "O My angels, look at My servant making up what I did not make obligatory upon him. I make you witness that I have forgiven him."

Hadith 4555

عن زرارة قال: دخلت على أبي جعفر (عليه السلام) وأنا شاب، فوصف لي التطوع والصوم، فرأى ثقل ذلك في وجهي، فقال لي: إن هذا ليس كالفريضة، من تركها هلك، إنما هو التطوع، إن شغلت عنه أو تركته قضيته، إنهم كانوا يكرهون أن ترفع أعمالهم يوما تاما ويوما ناقصا، إن الله عز وجل يقول: (الذين هم على صلاتهم دائمون) وكانوا يكرهون أن يصلوا شيئا حتى يزول النهار، إن أبواب السماء تفتح إذا زال النهار.

From Zurarah who said: I entered upon Abu Ja'far (peace be upon him) while I was young. He described to me supererogatory prayers and fasting. Seeing the burden on my face, he said: This is not like obligations which lead to destruction if abandoned. This is voluntary - if you are busy or leave it, make it up. They disliked their deeds being recorded complete one day and incomplete another. Allah says: "Those who are constant in their prayers" [Quran 70:23]. They disliked praying anything until the sun declined, for the gates of heaven open at that time.

Hadith 4556

عن عاصم بن حميد قال: قال أبو عبد الله (عليه السلام): إن الرب ليعجب ملائكته من العبد من عباده يراه يقضي النافلة، فيقول: أنظروا إلى عبدي يقضي ما لم أفترض عليه.

From Asim bin Humayd who said: Abu Abdullah (peace be upon him) said: The

Lord shows off to His angels the servant who makes up supererogatory prayers, saying: "Look at My servant making up what I did not make obligatory upon him."

Hadith 4557

عن علي بن جعفر، عن أخيه موسى بن جعفر (عليه السلام)، قال: سألته عن الرجل يكون في السفر فيترك النافلة وهو مجمع أن يقضي إذا أقام، هل يجزيه تأخير ذلك؟ قال: إن كان ضعيفا لا يستطيع (أن يقضي) أجزأه ذلك، وإن كان قويا فلا يؤخره.

From Ali bin Ja'far from his brother Musa bin Ja'far (peace be upon him): I asked him about a man who leaves supererogatory prayers while traveling intending to make them up when resident - is it permissible to delay them? He said: If he is weak and unable to make them up then yes, but if he is strong then he should not delay them.

CHAPTER 19

If One Does Not Know The Amount Of Missed Supererogatory Prayers, It Is Recommended To Make Them Up Until One Is Confident Or Certain Of Fulfillment

[Hadith 4558 to 4561]

Hadith 4558

عن مرازم قال: سأل إسماعيل بن جابر أبا عبد الله (عليه السلام) فقال: أصلحك الله إن علي نوافل كثيرة، فكيف أصنع؟ فقال: اقضها، فقال له: إنها أكثر من ذلك، قال: اقضها، قلت، لا أحصيها، قال: توخ.

From Marazim who said: Isma'il bin Jabir asked Abu Abdullah (peace be upon him) saying: May Allah bless you, I have many supererogatory prayers due on me, what should I do? He said: Make them up. He said: They are more than that. He said: Make them up. I said: I cannot count them. He said: Estimate them.

Hadith 4559

عن أبي عبد الله (عليه السلام) قال: سألته عن الصلاة تجتمع علي؟ قال: تحر، واقضها.

From Abu Abdullah (peace be upon him), he said: I asked him about prayers that accumulate on me? He said: Estimate and make them up.

Hadith 4560

عن علي بن جعفر، عن أخيه موسى بن جعفر (عليهما السلام) قال: سألته عن الرجل ينسى ما عليه من النافلة وهو يريد أن يقضي، (كيف يقضي)؟ قال: يقضي حتى يرى أنه قد زاد على ما عليه وأتم.

From Ali bin Ja'far, from his brother Musa bin Ja'far (peace be upon them) said: I asked him about a man who forgets how many supererogatory prayers he owes and wants to make them up, (how should he make them up)? He said: He should make them up until he sees that he has exceeded what was due on him and completed them.

Hadith 4561

وقد تقدم حديث عبد الله بن سنان قال: قلت لأبي عبد الله (عليه السلام): أخبرني عن رجل عليه من صلاة النوافل مالا يدري ما هو من كثرتها، كيف يصنع؟ قال: فليصل حتى لا يدري كم صلى من كثرتها فيكون قد قضى بقدر علمه من ذلك.

The previous hadith of Abdullah bin Sinan has already been mentioned where he said: I said to Abu Abdullah (peace be upon him): Tell me about a man who has so many supererogatory prayers due that he does not know how many they are due to their abundance, what should he do? He said: Let him pray until he does not know how many he has prayed due to their abundance, so he will have made up what he knows of that.

―――――

CHAPTER 20

Recommendation Of Making Up Supererogatory Prayers Missed Due To Illness, And That This Recommendation Is Not Strongly Emphasized

[Hadith 4562 to 4564]

Hadith 4562

عن أبي جعفر (عليه السلام) قال: قلت له: رجل مرض فترك النافلة، فقال: يا محمد، ليست بفريضة، إن قضاها فهو خير يفعله، وإن لم يفعل فلا شئ عليه.

From Abu Ja'far (peace be upon him), he said: I asked him about a man who became ill and left the supererogatory prayer. He said: O Muhammad, it is not obligatory. If he makes it up, it is good that he does so, and if he does not, there is nothing upon him.

Hadith 4563

عن مرازم بن حكيم أنه قال: مرضت أربعة أشهر لم أتنفل فيها، فقلت لأبي عبد الله (عليه السلام)، فقال: ليس عليك قضاء، إن المريض ليس كالصحيح، كل ما غلب الله عليه فالله أولى بالعذر.

From Murazim bin Hakim who said: I was ill for four months during which I did not perform supererogatory prayers, so I mentioned this to Abu Abdullah (peace be upon him). He said: You do not have to make them up. The sick person is not like the healthy one. For everything that Allah overcomes someone with, Allah is most worthy of accepting the excuse.

Hadith 4564

عن العيص بن القاسم قال: سألت أبا عبد الله (عليه السلام) عن رجل اجتمع عليه صلاة السنة من مرض؟ قال: لا يقضى.

From al-Ais bin al-Qasim who said: I asked Abu Abdullah (peace be upon him) about a man who had accumulated yearly prayers due to illness? He said: They are not to be made up.

أقول: حمله الشيخ على النوافل لما مر، ويمكن حمله على من صلى الفريضة أو النافلة في المرض جالسا أو مؤميا.

I (Hurr Amili) say: The Shaykh interpreted this as referring to supererogatory prayers, and it can also be interpreted as referring to one who prayed the obligatory or supererogatory prayers while sitting or gesturing during illness.

CHAPTER 21

Shortening Four Rak'ah Prayers To Two During Travel And Specifically Dropping Supererogatory Prayers Of Dhuhr And Asr

[Hadith 4565 to 4572]

Hadith 4565

عن محمد بن مسلم، عن أحدهما (عليهما السلام) قال: سألته عن الصلاة تطوعا في السفر؟ قال: لا تصل قبل الركعتين ولا بعدهما شيئا نهارا.

From Muhammad ibn Muslim, from one of them (peace be upon them) who said: I asked him about voluntary prayer during travel? He said: Do not pray anything before or after the two rak'ahs during daytime.

Hadith 4566

عن أبي جعفر وأبي عبد الله (عليهما السلام) أنهما قالا: الصلاة في السفر ركعتان ليس قبلهما ولا بعدهما شيئ.

From Abu Ja'far and Abu Abdullah (peace be upon them) that they both said: Prayer during travel is two rak'ahs with nothing before or after them.

Hadith 4567

عن أبي عبد الله (عليه السلام) قال: الصلاة في السفر ركعتان ليس قبلهما ولا بعدهما شيئ إلا المغرب ثلاث.

From Abu Abdullah (peace be upon him) who said: Prayer during travel is two rak'ahs with nothing before or after them except Maghrib which is three.

Hadith 4568

عن أبي يحيى الحناط قال: سألت أبا عبد الله (عليه السلام) عن صلاة النافلة بالنهار في السفر؟ فقال: يا بني ل، وصلحت النافلة في السفر تمت الفريضة.

From Abu Yahya al-Hannat who said: I asked Abu Abdullah (peace be upon him) about supererogatory prayer during daytime while traveling? He said: O my son, no. If supererogatory prayer was valid during travel, the obligatory prayer would be complete.

Hadith 4569

عن صفوان بن يحيى قال: سألت الرضا (عليه السلام) عن التطوع بالنهار وأنا في سفر؟ فقال: لا، ولكن تقضي صلاة الليل بالنهار وأنت في سفر، فقلت: جعلت فداك. صلاة النهار التي أصليها في الحضر أقضيها بالنهار في السفر؟ قال: أما أنا فلا أقضيها.

From Safwan ibn Yahya who said: I asked Al-Ridha (peace be upon him) about voluntary prayer during daytime while I am traveling? He said: No, but you can make up Salat al-Layl during day while traveling. I said: May I be sacrificed for you, can I make up the daytime prayers that I pray while resident during day while traveling? He said: As for me, I do not make them up.

Hadith 4570

عن أبي جعفر (عليه السلام) قال: لما عرج برسول الله (صلى الله عليه وآله) نزل بالصلاة عشر ركعات ركعتين ركعتين، فلما ولد الحسن والحسين زاد رسول الله (صلى الله عليه وآله) سبع ركعات شكرا لله، فأجاز الله له ذلك، وترك الفجر لم يزد فيها لضيق وقتها، لأنه يحضرها ملائكة الليل وملائكة النهار، فلما أمره الله بالتقصير في السفر وضع عن أمته ست ركعات، وترك المغرب لم ينقص منها شيئا.

From Abu Ja'far (peace be upon him) who said: When the Prophet (peace be upon him and his family) was taken on the night journey, prayer was sent down as ten rak'ahs, two by two. When Hasan and Husayn were born, the Prophet added seven rak'ahs in gratitude to Allah, and Allah permitted that for him. And Fajr was left without addition due to its tight timing, because angels of night and day attend it. When Allah commanded him to shorten prayer during travel, six rak'ahs were removed from his community, and Maghrib was left without any reduction.

Hadith 4571

عن أبي بصير، عن أبي عبد الله (عليه السلام) قال: الصلاة في السفر ركعتان ليس قبلهما ولا بعدهما شئ إلا المغرب، فإن بعدها أربع ركعات لا تدعهن في سفر ولا حضر، وليس عليك قضاء صلاة النهار، وصل صلاة الليل واقضه.

From Abu Basir, from Abu Abdullah (peace be upon him) who said: Prayer during travel is two rak'ahs with nothing before or after them except Maghrib, for after it are four rak'ahs that you should not leave whether traveling or resident. You do not have to make up daytime prayers, but pray and make up Salat al-Layl.

Hadith 4572

عن الرضا (عليه السلام)، أنه كان في السفر يصلي فرائضه ركعتين ركعتين إلا المغرب، فإنه كان يصليها ثلاثا، ولا يدع نافلتها، ولا يدع صلاة الليل، والشفع والوتر، وركعتي الفجر، في سفر ولا حضر، وكان لا يصلي من نوافل النهار في السفر شيئا.

From Al-Ridha (peace be upon him): During travel, he would pray his obligatory prayers as two rak'ahs each except Maghrib which he would pray as three rak'ahs. He would not leave its supererogatory prayers, nor would he leave Salat al-Layl, the even and odd prayers, and the two rak'ahs of Fajr - neither during travel nor at home. And he would not pray any of the daytime supererogatory prayers while traveling.

CHAPTER 22
Ruling On Making Up Supererogatory Day Prayers At Night During Travel
[Hadith 4573 to 4576]

Hadith 4573

عن معاوية بن عمار قال: قلت لأبي عبد الله (عليه السلام): أقضي صلاة النهار بالليل في السفر؟ فقال: نعم، فقال له إسماعيل بن جابر: أقضي صلاة النهار بالليل في السفر؟ فقال: لا، فقال: إنك قلت: نعم، فقال: إن ذلك يطيق وأنت لا تطيق.

From Mu'awiyah ibn Ammar, he said: I asked Abu Abdullah (peace be upon him): Should I make up the daytime prayers at night while traveling? He said: Yes. Then Ismail ibn Jabir said to him: Should I make up the daytime prayers at night while traveling? He said: No. So he said: But you said yes. He replied: That one is capable of it, and you are not capable of it.

Hadith 4574

عن عمر بن حنظلة قال: قلت لأبي عبد الله (عليه السلام): جعلت فداك، إني سألتك عن قضاء صلاة النهار بالليل في السفر؟ فقلت: لا تقضها، وسألك أصحابنا فقلت: اقضوا، فقال لي: أفأقول لهم: لا تصلوا والله ما ذاك عليهم.

From Umar ibn Hanzala, who said: I said to Abu Abdullah (peace be upon him): May I be your ransom, I asked you about making up the daytime prayers at night while traveling, and you told me: Do not make them up. But when our companions asked you, you told them: Make them up. He said to me: Should I then tell them: Do not pray? By Allah, that is not something I would impose upon them.

Hadith 4575

عن أبي عبد الله (عليه السلام)، قال: قال له بعض أصحابنا: إنا كنا نقضي صلاة النهار إذا نزلنا بين المغرب والعشاء الآخرة؟ فقال: لا، الله أعلم بعباده حين رخص لهم، إنما فرض الله على المسافر ركعتين لا قبلهما ولا بعدهما شيء إلا صلاة الليل على بعيرك حيث توجه بك.

From Abu Abdullah (peace be upon him) that one of our companions said to him: We used to make up the day prayers when we would stop between Maghrib and Isha prayers? He said: No, Allah knows best about His servants when He gave them allowance. Allah only obligated two rak'ah on the traveler with nothing before or after them except Salat al-Layl on your mount wherever it faces.

Hadith 4576

عن سدير قال: قال أبو عبد الله (عليه السلام): كان أبي يقضي في السفر نوافل النهار بالليل، ولا يتم صلاة فريضة.

From Sudayr who said: Abu Abdullah (peace be upon him) said: My father used to make up the supererogatory day prayers at night while traveling, but would not complete the obligatory prayer.

Shaykh Hurr Amili: . The Shaykh at times interprets these hadiths as permissibility as is apparent from them, and at times for the one who traveled after the entrance of the time as will come.

―――――――

CHAPTER 23

Recommendation Of Supererogatory Noon Prayers (Dhuhr And Asr) During Travel For Those Who Begin Travel After Their Time Has Begun

[Hadith 4577 to 4577]

Hadith 4577

عن عمار بن موسى، عن أبي عبد الله (عليه السلام)، قال: سئل عن الرجل إذا زالت الشمس وهو في منزله ثم يخرج في السفر؟ فقال: يبدأ بالزوال فيصليها، ثم يصلي الأولى بتقصير ركعتين، لأنه خرج من منزله قبل أن تحضر الأولى.

From Ammar ibn Musa, from Abu Abdullah (peace be upon him), he said: He was asked about a man [who is at home] when the sun passes the meridian (Zawal), then he leaves on a journey? He said: He begins with the [prayers of] Zawal and prays them, then he prays the First (Zuhr) with shortening to two rak'ahs, because he left his home before the First (Zuhr) arrived.

وسئل: فإن خرج بعدما حضرت الأولى؟ قال: يصلي الأولى أربع ركعات، ثم يصلي بعد النوافل ثمان ركعات، لأنه خرج من منزله بعدما حضرت الأولى، فإذا حضرت العصر صلى العصر بتقصير وهي ركعتان، لأنه خرج في السفر قبل أن تحضر العصر.

And he was asked: What if he leaves after the First (Zuhr) has arrived? He said: He prays the First (Zuhr) four rak'ahs, then he prays after [it] the Nawafil eight rak'ahs, because he left his home after the First (Zuhr) arrived. Then when Asr arrives, he prays Asr with shortening, and it is two rak'ahs, because he left for the journey before Asr arrived.

Translator: If a man departs after Zawal but before the obligation is established as a resident duty, he maintains the merit of the voluntary Nawafil but performs the Fard as a traveler. Conversely, if he remains until the obligation is present, he must complete the full residency requirement for that specific prayer, even if he departs immediately afterward.

———————

CHAPTER 24

Recommendation Of Maintaining The Supererogatory Prayers Of Maghrib And Not Omitting Them During Travel, The Impermissibility Of Shortening Maghrib And Fajr

[Hadith 4578 to 4587]

Hadith 4578

عن الحارث بن المغيرة قال: قال أبو عبد الله (عليه السلام): أربع ركعات بعد المغرب لا تدعهن في حضر ولا سفر.

From Al-Harith bin Al-Mughirah, he said: Abu Abdullah (peace be upon him) said: Four rak'ahs after Maghrib, do not leave them whether you are resident or traveling.

———————

Hadith 4579

عن أبي بصير، عن أبي عبد الله (عليه السلام) قال: الصلاة في السفر ركعتان ليس قبلهما ولا بعدهما شئ إلا المغرب، فإن بعدها أربع ركعات لا تدعهن في حضر ولا سفر، وليس عليك قضاء صلاة النهار، وصل صلاة الليل واقضه.

From Abu Basir, from Abu Abdullah (peace be upon him), he said: The prayer during travel is two rak'ahs, there is nothing before them or after them except Maghrib, for after it there are four rak'ahs that you should not leave whether you are resident or traveling. You are not obligated to make up for the day prayer, pray Salat al-Layl and make up for it.

———————

Hadith 4580

عن أبي الحارث قال: سألته - يعني الرضا (عليه السلام) - عن الأربع ركعات بعد المغرب في السفر يعجلني الجمال ولا يمكنني الصلاة على الأرض، هل أصليها في المحمل؟ فقال: نعم، صلها في المحمل.

From Abu Al-Harith, he said: I asked him - meaning Al-Ridha (peace be upon him) - about the four rak'ahs after Maghrib while traveling, the camel makes me hurry and I cannot pray on the ground, should I pray them in the carriage? He said: Yes, pray them in the carriage.

———————

Hadith 4581

عن سماعة قال: سألته عن الصلاة في السفر؟ فقال: ركعتان ليس قبلهما ولا بعدهما شئ، إلا أنه ينبغي للمسافر أن يصلي بعد المغرب أربع ركعات، وليتطوع بالليل ما شاء.

From Sama'ah, he said: I asked him about the prayer during travel. He said: Two rak'ahs, there is nothing before them or after them, except that it is recommended for the traveler to pray four rak'ahs after Maghrib, and to pray the voluntary night prayers as much as he wishes.

Hadith 4582

عن الفضل بن شاذان – في حديث العلل التي سمعها من الرضا (عليه السلام) –، قال: إن الصلاة إنما قصرت في السفر لان الصلاة المفروضة أولا إنما هي عشر ركعات، والسبع إنما زيدت فيها بعد،

From Al-Fadhl bin Shadhan - in a hadith of reasons that he heard from Al-Ridha (peace be upon him) -, he said: The prayer was shortened during travel because the obligatory prayers at first were only ten rak'ahs, and the seven were added to them afterwards.

فخفف الله عز وجل عن العبد تلك الزيادة لموضع سفره وتعبه ونصبه واشتغاله بأمر نفسه وطعنه وإقامته، لئلا يشتغل عما لابد له، من معيشته، رحمة من الله عز وجل، وتعطفا عليه، إلا صلاة المغرب، فإنها لم تقصر لأنها صلاة مقصرة في الأصل،

Allah, the Mighty and Sublime, lightened that addition from the servant due to his travel, fatigue, hardship, and preoccupation with his own matters, food, and residence, so that he would not be preoccupied from what is necessary for his livelihood, as a mercy from Allah, the Mighty and Sublime, and kindness towards him, except the Maghrib prayer, for it was not shortened because it is originally a short prayer.

قال: وإنما ترك تطوع النهار ولم يترك تطوع الليل، لان كل صلاة لا يقصر فيها (لا يقصر فيما بعدها من التطوع)، وذلك أن المغرب لا تقصير فيها فلا تقصير فيما بعدها من التطوع، وكذلك الغداة لا تقصير فيها فلا تقصير فيما قبلها من التطوع.

He said: The voluntary prayers of the day were left and the voluntary prayers of the night were not left, because every prayer in which there is no shortening (there is no shortening in the voluntary prayers that follow it), and that is because there is no shortening in Maghrib so there is no shortening in the voluntary prayers that follow it, and likewise there is no shortening in Fajr so there is no shortening in the voluntary prayers before it.

Hadith 4583

قال: وسئل الصادق (عليه السلام): لم صارت المغرب ثلاث ركعات وأربعا بعدها ليس فيها تقصير في حضر ولا سفر؟ فقال: إن الله تبارك وتعالى أنزل على نبيه كل صلاة ركعتين، فأضاف إليها رسول الله (صلى الله عليه وآله) لكل صلاة ركعتين في الحضر، وقصر فيها في السفر إلا المغرب والغداة.

He said: Al-Sadiq (peace be upon him) was asked: Why did Maghrib become three rak'ahs and four after it, with no shortening in it whether resident or traveling? He said: Allah, the Blessed and Exalted, revealed to His Prophet every prayer as two rak'ahs, then the Messenger of Allah (peace be upon him and his family) added to each prayer two rak'ahs while resident, and shortened them while traveling except Maghrib and Fajr.

فلما صلى المغرب بلغه مولد فاطمة (عليها سلام الله) فأضاف إليها ركعة شكرا لله عز وجل، فلما أن ولد الحسن (عليه السلام) أضاف إليها ركعتين شكرا لله، فلما أن ولد الحسين (عليه السلام) أضاف إليها ركعتين شكرا لله عز وجل، فقال: (للذكر مثل حظ الأنثيين) فتركها على حالها في الحضر والسفر.

When he prayed Maghrib, he was informed of the birth of Fatimah (peace of Allah be upon her), so he added one rak'ah to it in gratitude to Allah, the Mighty and Sublime. When Al-Hasan (peace be upon him) was born, he added two rak'ahs to it in gratitude to Allah. When Al-Husayn (peace be upon him) was born, he added two rak'ahs to it in gratitude to Allah, the Mighty and Sublime. He said: (For the male is the share of two females), so he left it as it was whether resident or traveling.

Hadith 4584

عن الحسن بن إبراهيم يرفعه إلى محمد بن مسلم قال: قلت لأبي عبد الله (عليه السلام): لأي علة تصلى المغرب في السفر ثلاث ركعات وسائر الصلوات ركعتين؟

From Al-Hasan bin Ibrahim, attributing it to Muhammad bin Muslim, he said: I said to Abu Abdullah (peace be upon him): For what reason is Maghrib prayed as three rak'ahs while traveling and the rest of the prayers as two rak'ahs?

فقال: لان رسول الله (صلى الله عليه وآله) فرض عليه الصلاة مثنى مثنى، وأضاف إليها رسول الله (صلى الله عليه وآله) ركعتين، ثم نقص من المغرب ركعة

He said: Because the Messenger of Allah (peace be upon him and his family) was obligated to pray in twos, then the Messenger of Allah (peace be upon him and his family) added two rak'ahs to them, then he subtracted one rak'ah from Maghrib.

ثم وضع رسول الله (صلى الله عليه وآله) ركعتين في السفر وترك المغرب، وقال: إني أستحيي أن أنقص منها مرتين فلتلك العلة تصلى ثلاث ركعات في السفر والحضر.

Then the Messenger of Allah (peace be upon him and his family) omitted two rak'ahs while traveling and left Maghrib, and he said: I am ashamed to subtract from it twice, so for that reason it is prayed as three rak'ahs while traveling and while resident.

Hadith 4585

عن أبي عبد الله (عليه السلام) قال: لا تدع أربع ركعات بعد المغرب في سفر ولا حضر وإن طلبتك الخيل.

From Abu Abdullah (peace be upon him), he said: Do not leave the four rak'ahs after Maghrib while traveling or while resident, even if the horses pursue you.

Hadith 4586

عن الحارث بن المغيرة قال: قال لي أبو عبد الله (عليه السلام): لا تدع أربع ركعات بعد المغرب في السفر ولا في الحضر.

From Al-Harith bin Al-Mughirah, he said: Abu Abdullah (peace be upon him) said to me: Do not leave the four rak'ahs after Maghrib while traveling or while resident.

Hadith 4587

عن علي بن مهزيار قال: قال بعض أصحابنا لأبي عبد الله (عليه السلام): ما بال صلاة المغرب لم يقصر فيها رسول الله (صلى الله عليه وآله) في السفر والحضر مع نافلتها؟

From Ali bin Mahziyar, he said: Some of our companions said to Abu Abdullah (peace be upon him): Why did the Messenger of Allah (peace be upon him and his family) not shorten the Maghrib prayer while traveling and while resident along with its supererogatory prayers?

فقال: لان الصلاة كانت ركعتين ركعتين فأضاف إليها رسول الله (صلى الله عليه وآله) إلى كل ركعتين ركعتين، ووضعهما عن المسافر، وأقر المغرب على وجهها في السفر والحضر، ولم يقصر في ركعتي الفجر أن يكون تمام الصلاة سبعة عشر ركعة في السفر والحضر.

He said: Because the prayers were two rak'ahs each, then the Messenger of Allah (peace be upon him and his family) added two rak'ahs to every two rak'ahs, and he omitted them from the traveler, and he affirmed Maghrib in its form while traveling and while resident. He did not shorten the two rak'ahs of Fajr so that the complete prayers would be seventeen rak'ahs while traveling and while resident.

CHAPTER 25

Recommendation Of Maintaining Night Prayer And Witr, And That They Are Not Waived During Travel, And Are Not Obligatory

[Hadith 4588 to 4593]

Hadith 4588

عن الحارث بن المغيرة - في حديث - قال: قال أبو عبد الله (عليه السلام): كان أبي لا يدع ثلاث عشرة ركعة بالليل في سفر ولا حضر.

From Al-Harith bin Al-Mughirah - in a hadith - he said: Abu Abdullah (peace be upon him) said: My father never left thirteen rak'ah at night whether traveling or at home.

————————

Hadith 4589

عن محمد بن مسلم قال: قال لي أبو جعفر (عليه السلام): صل صلاة الليل والوتر والركعتين في المحمل.

From Muhammad bin Muslim who said: Abu Ja'far (peace be upon him) said to me: Pray Salat al-Layl, Witr, and the two rak'ah in the riding mount.

————————

Hadith 4590

عن أبي عبد الله (عليه السلام) أنه سأل عن الوتر؟ فقال: سنة ليست بفريضة.

From Abu Abdullah (peace be upon him) that he was asked about Witr? He said: It is a sunnah, not an obligation.

————————

Hadith 4591

عن عبيد بن زرارة، عن أبيه، عن أبي جعفر (عليه السلام) قال: الوتر في كتاب علي (عليه السلام) واجب، وهو وتر الليل، والمغرب وتر النهار.

From Ubayd bin Zurarah, from his father, from Abu Ja'far (peace be upon him) who said: Witr in the book of Ali (peace be upon him) is obligatory, and it is the Witr of the night, and Maghrib is the Witr of the day.

قال الشيخ: يعني أنه سنة، لان المسنون إذا كان مؤكدا يسمى واجبا. أقول: ويمكن حمله على التقية.

The Shaykh said: He means it is sunnah, because emphasized sunnah is called obligatory. I (Hurr Amili) say: It can be interpreted as taqiyyah.

————————

Hadith 4592

عن معاوية بن عمار، عن أبي عبد الله (عليه السلام) قال: قال النبي (صلى الله عليه وآله) لعلي (عليه السلام): أوصيك في نفسك بخصال فاحفظها، ثم قال: اللهم أعنه - إلى أن قال - وعليك بصلاة الليل، (وعليك بصلاة الليل، وعليك بصلاة الليل).

From Mu'awiyah bin Ammar, from Abu Abdullah (peace be upon him) who said: The Prophet (peace be upon him and his family) said to Ali (peace be upon him): I advise you regarding yourself with qualities, so preserve them. Then he said: O Allah help him - until he said - and upon you is Salat al-Layl, (and upon you is Salat al-Layl, and upon you is the night prayer).

————————

Hadith 4593

عن زرارة، عن أبي جعفر (عليه السلام) قال: كان رسول الله (صلى الله عليه وآله) يصلي من الليل ثلاث عشرة ركعة، منها الوتر وركعتا الفجر، في السفر والحضر.

From Zurarah, from Abu Ja'far (peace be upon him) who said: The Messenger of Allah (peace be upon him and his family) used to pray thirteen rak'ah at night, including Witr and the two rak'ah of Fajr, whether traveling or at home.

————————

CHAPTER 26

Dislike Of Performing Supererogatory Prayers Before Isha
[Hadith 4594 to 4594]

Hadith 4594

عن الحلبي قال: سألت أبا عبد الله (عليه السلام): هل قبل العشاء الآخرة وبعدها شئ؟ قال: لا، غير أني أصلي بعدها ركعتين ولست أحسبهما من صلاة الليل.

From Al-Halabi who said: I asked Abu Abdullah (peace be upon him): Is there anything to pray before and after Isha prayer? He said: No, except that I pray two rak'ahs after it, and I do not count them as part of Salat al-Layl.

أقول: وتقدم ما يدل على ذلك في أحاديث كثيرة. فأما ما تضمن بعضها من استحباب ركعتين قبل العشاء فوجهه أنهما من نافلة المغرب، كما تقدم في نافلة العصر أيضا مثله، وذلك ظاهر.

I (Hurr Amili) say: What indicates that has preceded in many hadiths. As for what some of them included regarding the recommendation of two rak'ahs before Isha, the reason is that they are from the supererogatory prayers of Maghrib, as has preceded regarding the supererogatory prayers of Asr as well, and that is apparent.

CHAPTER 27

Recommendation Of Making Up Missed Night Supererogatory Prayers During Travel Even During Day

[Hadith 4595 to 4598]

Hadith 4595

عن ذريح قال: قلت لأبي عبدالله (عليه السلام): فاتتني صلاة الليل في السفر، أفأقضيها في النهار؟ فقال: نعم، إن أطقت ذلك.

From Dhuraih who said: I asked Abu Abdullah (peace be upon him): I missed Salat al-Layl while traveling, should I make it up during the day? He said: Yes, if you are able to do so.

———

Hadith 4596

عن معاوية بن عمّار، عن أبي عبدالله (عليه السلام) قال: كان علي بن الحسين (عليه السلام) يقول: أنّي لأُحبّ أن أدوم على العمل وإن قلّ، قال: قلنا: نقضي صلاة اللّيل بالنهار في السفر؟ قال: نعم.

From Mu'awiyah bin Ammar, from Abu Abdullah (peace be upon him) who said: Ali bin Al-Husayn (peace be upon him) used to say: I love to be consistent in good deeds even if they are few. He said: We asked: Should we make up Salat al-Layl during the day while traveling? He said: Yes.

———

Hadith 4597

عن صفوان الجمّال قال: كان أبو عبدالله (عليه السلام) يصلّي صلاة اللّيل بالنهار على راحلته أينها توجّهت به.

From Safwan Al-Jammal who said: Abu Abdullah (peace be upon him) used to pray Salat al-Layl during the day while on his mount wherever it was facing.

———

Hadith 4598

عن صفوان بن يحيى قال: سألت الرضا (عليه السلام) عن التطوّع بالنهار وأنا في سفر؟ فقال: لا، ولكن تقضي صلاة اللّيل بالنهار وأنت في سفر،

From Safwan ibn Yahya said: I asked Al-Ridha (peace be upon him) about performing voluntary prayers during the day while traveling. He said: No, but you may make up Salat al-Layl during the day while traveling.

فقلت: جعلت فداك، صلاة النهار التي أصلّيها في الحضر، أقضيها بالنهار في السفر؟ قال: أمّا أنا فلا أقضيها.

I said: May I be your ransom, the daytime voluntary prayers that I perform when at home, may I make them up during the day while traveling? He said: As for me, I do not make them up.

CHAPTER 28

Recommendation Of Consistently Performing The Noon Supererogatory Prayers While At Home

[Hadith 4599 to 4602]

Hadith 4599

عن معاوية بن عمار، عن أبي عبد الله (عليه السلام) - في (وصية النبي (صلى الله عليه وآله) لعلي (عليه السلام) - قال: وعليك بصلاة الزوال، وعليك بصلاة الزوال، وعليك بصلاة الزوال.

From Mu'awiyah bin Ammar, from Abu Abdullah (peace be upon him) - in the Prophet's (peace be upon him and his family) advice to Ali (peace be upon him) - he said: You must perform the midday (salat al-zawal) prayer, you must perform the midday prayer, you must perform the midday prayer.

———

Hadith 4600

عن يحيى بن أبي العلاء، عن أبي عبد الله (عليه السلام) قال: قال أمير المؤمنين (عليه السلام): صلاة الزوال صلاة الأوابين.

From Yahya bin Abi Al-Ala, from Abu Abdullah (peace be upon him) who said: Amir al-Mu'minin (peace be upon him) said: The midday prayer (salat al-zawal) is the prayer of those who frequently return to Allah.

———

Hadith 4601

عن أبي عبد الله (عليه السلام) - في وصية النبي (صلى الله عليه وآله) لعلي (عليه السلام) -: وعليك بصلاة الليل، يكررها أربعا، وعليك بصلاة الزوال.

From Abu Abdullah (peace be upon him) - in the Prophet's (peace be upon him and his family) advice to Ali (peace be upon him): You must perform Salat al-Layl - repeating it four times - and you must perform the midday prayer (salat al-zawal).

———

Hadith 4602

عن علي (عليهم السلام) أنه كان يقول: إذا زالت الشمس عن كبد السماء فمن صلى تلك الساعة أربع ركعات فقد وافق صلاة الأوابين، وذلك بعد نصف النهار.

From Ali (peace be upon them) that he used to say: When the sun declines from the middle of the sky, whoever prays four rak'ahs at that time has coincided with the prayer of those who frequently return to Allah, and that is after midday.

———

CHAPTER 29

Recommendation Of Maintaining The Night Prayer Supererogatory Prayers Sitting Or Standing, With Standing Being Better, And Not Abandoning Them During Travel

[Hadith 4603 to 4611]

Hadith 4603

عن زرارة قال: قال أبو جعفر (عليه السلام): من كان يؤمن بالله واليوم الآخر فلا يبيتن إلا بوتر.

From Zurarah who said: Abu Ja'far (peace be upon him) said: Whoever believes in Allah and the Last Day should not sleep except after performing Witr prayer.

Hadith 4604

محمد بن علي بن الحسين: قال النبي (صلى الله عليه وآله): من كان يؤمن بالله واليوم الآخر فلا يبيتن إلا بوتر.

Muhammad bin Ali bin Al-Husayn said: The Prophet (peace be upon him and his family) said: Whoever believes in Allah and the Last Day should not sleep except after performing Witr prayer.

Hadith 4605

عن الرضا (عليه السلام) - في حديث - قال: وإنما صارت العتمة مقصورة وليس تترك ركعتيها، لان الركعتين ليستا من الخمسين، وإنما هي زيادة في الخمسين تطوعا ليتم بهما بدل كل ركعة من الفريضة ركعتين من التطوع.

From Al-Ridha (peace be upon him) - in a hadith - he said: The Atmah (Isha) prayer became shortened but its two rak'ahs are not abandoned, because these two rak'ahs are not from the fifty, rather they are an addition to the fifty as voluntary prayers to complete with them two voluntary rak'ahs for each obligatory rak'ah.

Hadith 4606

عن زرارة بن أعين قال: قال أبو جعفر (عليه السلام): من كان يؤمن بالله واليوم الآخر فلا يبيتن إلا بوتر.

From Zurarah bin Ayan who said: Abu Ja'far (peace be upon him) said: Whoever believes in Allah and the Last Day should not sleep except after performing Witr prayer.

Hadith 4607

عن أبي جعفر (عليه السلام) قال: قال رسول الله (صلى الله عليه وآله): لا يبيتن الرجل وعليه وتر.

From Abu Ja'far (peace be upon him) who said: The Messenger of Allah (peace be upon him and his family) said: A man should not sleep while the Witr prayer is still due upon him.

Hadith 4608

عن أبي عبد الله القزويني قال: قلت لأبي جعفر محمد بن علي الباقر (عليهما السلام): لأي علة تصلى الركعتان بعد العشاء الآخرة من قعود؟ فقال: لان الله فرض سبع عشر ركعة فأضاف إليها رسول الله (صلى الله عليه وآله) مثليها فصارت إحدى وخمسين ركعة، فتعدان هاتان الركعتان من جلوس بركعة.

From Abu Abdullah Al-Qazwini who said: I asked Abu Ja'far Muhammad bin Ali Al-Baqir (peace be upon them both): For what reason are the two rak'ahs after the Isha prayer performed while sitting? He said: Because Allah prescribed seventeen rak'ahs, and the Messenger of Allah (peace be upon him and his family) added twice as many, so they became fifty-one rak'ahs, and these two rak'ahs performed while sitting count as one rak'ah.

Hadith 4609

عن أبي عبد الله (عليه السلام)، قال: قلت: أصلي العشاء الآخرة، فإذا صليت صليت ركعتين وأنا جالس؟ فقال أما إنها واحدة، ولو مت مت على وتر.

From Abu Abdullah (peace be upon him), he said: I asked: I pray the Isha prayer, and when I finish I pray two rak'ahs while sitting? He said: Indeed it counts as one, and if you were to die, you would die having performed Witr.

Shaykh Hurr Amili: What indicates that standing in it is preferred has preceded in the hadiths about the number of obligatory and supererogatory prayers.

Hadith 4610

عن أبي بصير، عن أبي عبد الله (عليه السلام) قال: من كان يؤمن بالله واليوم الآخر فلا يبيتن إلا بوتر، قال: قلت: تعني الركعتين بعد العشاء الآخرة؟ قال: نعم إنهما بركعة، فمن صلاهما ثم حدث به حدث مات على وتر، فإن لم يحدث به حدث الموت يصلي الوتر في آخر الليل،

From Abu Basir, from Abu Abdullah (peace be upon him) who said: Whoever believes in Allah and the Last Day should not sleep except after performing Witr prayer. I said: Do you mean the two rak'ahs after the last Isha prayer? He said: Yes, they are with one rak'ah. So whoever prays them and then something happens to him, he dies having performed Witr. And if death does not come to him, he prays

Witr at the end of the night (*).

فقلت: هل صلى رسول الله (صلى الله عليه وآله) هاتين الركعتين؟ قال: لا. قلت: ولم؟ قال: لان رسول الله (صلى الله عليه وآله) كان يأتيه الوحي، وكان يعلم أنه هل يموت في هذه الليلة أم لا، وغيره لا يعلم. فمن أجل ذلك لم يصلهما، وأمر بهما.

I asked: Did the Messenger of Allah (peace be upon him and his family) pray these two rak'ahs? He said: No. I asked: Why? He said: Because revelation would come to the Messenger of Allah (peace be upon him and his family), and he knew whether he would die that night or not, while others do not know. For this reason, he did not pray them but ordered others to do so.

أقول: وتقدم أنه (عليه السلام) كان يصليهما، ويأتي ما يدل عليه، فيظهر أنه كان يصليهما مدة ويتركهما مدة.

I (Hurr Amili) say: It was previously mentioned that he (peace be upon him) used to pray them, and evidence for this will come later, so it appears that he would pray them for a period and leave them for a period.

Translator: * A person can pray Witr at the end of the night only if he is sure that he won't die before then.

Hadith 4611

عن الرضا (عليه السلام) - في حديث - قال: إن أهل البصرة سألوني فقالوا: إن يونس يقول: من السنة أن يصلي الانسان ركعتين وهو جالس بعد العتمة؟ فقلت: صدق يونس.

From Al-Ridha (peace be upon him) - in a hadith - he said: The people of Basra asked me saying: Yunus says it is from the Sunnah for a person to pray two rak'ahs while sitting after the darkness (Isha)? I said: Yunus spoke the truth.

CHAPTER 30

Recommendation Of Praying One Thousand Rak'ahs Every Day And Night, Or Each Day And Each Night If Possible

[Hadith 4612 to 4620]

Hadith 4612

عن أبي عبد الله (عليه السلام) قال: إن استطعت أن تصلي في كل يوم ألف ركعة فصل، إن عليا (عليه السلام) كان في آخر عمره يصلي في كل يوم وليلة ألف ركعة.

From Abu Abdullah (peace be upon him) who said: If you can pray one thousand rak'ahs every day, then do so. Indeed Ali (peace be upon him) used to pray one thousand rak'ahs every day and night in his later years.

———————

Hadith 4613

عن أبي عبد الله (عليه السلام): قال: إن استطعت أن تصلي في شهر رمضان وغيره في اليوم والليلة ألف ركعة فافعل، فإن عليا (عليه السلام) كان يصلي في اليوم والليلة ألف ركعة.

From Abu Abdullah (peace be upon him) who said: If you can pray one thousand rak'ahs during the day and night in the month of Ramadan and other months, then do so, for Ali (peace be upon him) used to pray one thousand rak'ahs during the day and night.

———————

Hadith 4614

عن أبي جعفر (عليه السلام) قال: كان علي بن الحسين (عليه السلام) يصلي في اليوم والليلة ألف ركعة وكانت الريح تميله بمنزلة السنبلة.

From Abu Ja'far (peace be upon him) who said: Ali ibn Al-Husayn (peace be upon him) used to pray one thousand rak'ahs during the day and night, and the wind would sway him like an ear of wheat.

———————

Hadith 4615

عن عبد السلام بن صالح الهروي قال: جئت إلى باب الدار التي حبس فيها الرضا (عليه السلام) بسرخس وقد قيد واستأذنت عليه السجان فقال: لا سبيل لك عليه، قلت: ولم؟ قال: لأنه ربما صلى في يومه وليلته ألف ركعة.

From Abdul Salam ibn Salih Al-Harawi who said: I came to the door of the house where Al-Ridha (peace be upon him) was imprisoned in Sarakhs (*) while he was in chains. I sought permission from the jailer who said: There is no way to see him.

I asked: Why? He said: Because he sometimes prays one thousand rak'ahs in his day and night.

Translator: * A city located in the Khorasan Province of northeastern Iran, near the border with Turkmenistan.

Hadith 4616

عن عبد العزيز بن أبي حازم قال: سمعت أبا حازم يقول: ما رأيت هاشميا أفضل من علي بن الحسين (عليه السلام)، وكان يصلي في اليوم والليلة ألف ركعة حتى خرج بجبهته وآثار سجوده مثل كركرة البعير.

From Abdul Aziz ibn Abi Hazim who said: I heard Abu Hazim saying: I have not seen a Hashimite better than Ali ibn Al-Husayn (peace be upon him), and he used to pray one thousand rak'ahs during the day and night until his forehead developed marks from prostration like the knees of a camel.

Hadith 4617

عن حمزة بن حمران، عن أبيه عن أبي جعفر (عليه السلام) قال: كان علي بن الحسين (عليهما السلام) يصلي في اليوم والليلة ألف ركعة كما كان يفعل أمير المؤمنين (عليه السلام)، كانت له خمسمائة نخلة وكان يصلي عند كل نخلة ركعتين،

From Hamza ibn Hamran, from his father, from Abu Ja'far (peace be upon him) who said: Ali ibn Al-Husayn (peace be upon them both) used to pray one thousand rak'ahs during the day and night just as Amir al-Mu'minin (peace be upon him) used to do. He had five hundred palm trees and would pray two rak'ahs at each tree.

وكان إذا قام في صلاته غشى لونه لون آخر، وكان قيامه في صلاته قيام العبد الذليل بين يدي الملك الجليل، كانت أعضاؤه ترتعد من خشية الله، وكان يصلي صلاة مودع يرى أن لا يصلي بعدها أبدا،

When he would stand for prayer, his color would change to another color, and his standing in prayer was like that of a humble servant before a majestic king. His limbs would tremble from fear of Allah, and he would pray like someone bidding farewell, thinking he would never pray again.

وقال: إن العبد لا يقبل من صلاته إلا ما أقبل عليه منها بقلبه، فقال رجل: هلكنا؟ فقال: كلا، إن الله متمم ذلك بالنوافل.

He said: A servant's prayer is only accepted to the extent his heart is present in it. A man said: Then we are ruined? He replied: No, Allah completes it with supererogatory prayers.

Hadith 4618

عن الرضا (عليه السلام) - في حديث - أنه خلع على دعبل قميصا من خز وقال له: احتفظ بهذا القميص، فقد صليت فيه ألف ليلة كل ليلة ألف ركعة، وختمت فيه القرآن ألف ختمة.

From Al-Ridha (peace be upon him) - in a hadith - that he gave Di'bil a silk shirt and said to him: Keep this shirt, for I have prayed in it for a thousand nights, one thousand rak'ahs each night, and completed the Quran a thousand times in it.

Hadith 4619

عن أبي جعفر الباقر (عليه السلام) قال: والله إن كان علي (عليه السلام) ليأكل أكلة العبد، ويجلس جلسة العبد - إلى أن قال - وكان يصلي في اليوم والليلة ألف ركعة.

From Abu Ja'far Al-Baqir (peace be upon him) who said: By Allah, Ali (peace be upon him) would eat like a servant eats, and sit like a servant sits - and he said - and he would pray one thousand rak'ah during the day and night.

Hadith 4620

عن ابن عبد ربه قال: قيل لعلي بن الحسين (عليه السلام): ما أقل ولد أبيك؟! قال: العجب كيف ولدت له! كان يصلي في اليوم والليلة ألف ركعة فمتى كان يتفرغ للنساء؟!

From Ibn Abd Rabbih who said: It was said to Ali bin Al-Husayn (peace be upon him): How few are your father's children! He replied: The wonder is how he had any children at all! He used to pray one thousand rak'ah during the day and night, so when would he have time for women?!

CHAPTER 31

Undesirability And Non-Legislative Nature Of The Duha Prayer
[Hadith 4621 to 4626]

Hadith 4621

عن زرارة، عن أبي جعفر (عليه السلام) قال: ما صلى رسول الله (صلى الله عليه وآله) الضحى قط، قال: فقلت له: ألم تخبرني أنه كان يصلي في صدر النهار أربع ركعات؟ قال: بلى، إنه كان يجعلها من الثمان التي بعد الظهر. أقول: المراد بالظهر هنا الوقت أعني زوال الشمس، وهو ظاهر.

From Zurarah, from Abu Ja'far (peace be upon him) who said: The Messenger of Allah (peace be upon him and his family) never prayed the Duha (*) prayer at all. I said to him: Didn't you tell me that he used to pray four rak'ahs in the early part of the day? He said: Yes, but he would count them as part of the eight rak'ahs after noon. I (Hurr Amili) say: What is meant by noon here is the time, meaning when the sun passes its zenith, and this is apparent.

Translator: * A voluntary prayer that is typically performed in the morning after sunrise, usually when the sun has risen to about a spear's length in the sky. It's also known as the forenoon prayer.

Hadith 4622

عن بكير بن أعين، عن أبي جعفر (عليه السلام) قال: ما صلى رسول الله (صلى الله عليه وآله) الضحى قط.

From Bukayr ibn Ayan, from Abu Ja'far (peace be upon him) who said: The Messenger of Allah (peace be upon him and his family) never prayed the Duha prayer at all.

Hadith 4623

عن عبد الواحد بن المختار الأنصاري، عن أبي جعفر (عليه السلام) قال: سألته عن صلاة الضحى؟ فقال: أول من صلاها قومك، إنهم كانوا من الغافلين فيصلونها، ولم يصلها رسول الله (صلى الله عليه وآله)، وقال: إن عليا (عليه السلام) مر على رجل وهو يصليها، فقال علي (عليه السلام): ما هذه الصلاة؟ فقال: أدعها يا أمير المؤمنين؟ فقال علي (عليه السلام): أكون أنهى عبدا إذا صلى.

From Abdul Wahid ibn al-Mukhtar al-Ansari, from Abu Ja'far (peace be upon him) who said: I asked him about the Duha prayer? He said: Your people were the first to pray it. They were among the heedless ones who prayed it, while the Messenger of Allah (peace be upon him and his family) did not pray it. And he said: Ali (peace be upon him) passed by a man who was praying it, and Ali (peace be upon him) said:

What is this prayer? The man said: Should I leave it, Amir al-Mu'minin? Ali (peace be upon him) said: I would not forbid a servant when he prays.

Hadith 4624

عن الرضا (عليه السلام) - في حديث - قال: ما رأيته صلى الضحى في سفر ولا حضر.

From Al-Ridha (peace be upon him) - in a hadith - he said: I never saw him pray the Duha prayer whether traveling or at home.

Hadith 4625

عن زرارة والفضيل جميعا، عن أبي جعفر وأبي عبد الله (عليهما السلام)، أن رسول الله (صلى الله عليه وآله) قال: صلاة الضحى بدعة.

From Zurarah and Al-Fudhayl together, from Abu Ja'far and Abu Abdullah (peace be upon them), that the Messenger of Allah (peace be upon him and his family) said: The Duha prayer is an innovation.

Hadith 4626

ن سيف بن عميرة رفعه قال: مر أمير المؤمنين (عليه السلام) برجل يصلي الضحى في مسجد الكوفة، فغمز جنبه بالدرة وقال: نحرت صلاة الأوابين نحرك الله، قال: فأتركها؟ قال: فقال: أرأيت الذي ينهى عبدا إذا صلى. فقال أبو عبد الله (عليه السلام): وكفى بإنكار علي (عليه السلام) نهيا.

From Sayf ibn Umayra, raising it, said: Amir al-Mu'minin (peace be upon him) passed by a man praying the Duha prayer in the Kufa mosque, and he poked his side with a stick and said: You have slaughtered the prayer of the penitent ones, may Allah slaughter you. The man said: Should I leave it? He said: What do you think of one who forbids a servant when he prays? Abu Abdullah (peace be upon him) said: Ali's (peace be upon him) disapproval is sufficient as a prohibition.

Shaykh Hurr Amili: There will come what indicates that in the hadiths of the supererogatory prayers of the month of Ramadan, and what indicates the limitation of obligatory and supererogatory prayers has preceded.

CHAPTER 32

Recommendation Of Abundant Supererogatory Prayers
[Hadith 4627 to 4630]

Hadith 4627

عن أبي جعفر (عليه السلام) قال: أتى رسول الله (صلى الله عليه وآله) رجل فقال: أدع الله أن يدخلني الجنة. فقال أعني بكثرة السجود.

From Abu Ja'far (peace be upon him) who said: A man came to the Messenger of Allah (peace be upon him and his family) and said: Pray to Allah to make me enter Paradise. He said: Help me by performing many prostrations.

Hadith 4628

عن أبي جعفر العطار قال: سمعت الصادق جعفر بن محمد (عليهما السلام) يقول: جاء رجل إلى رسول الله (صلى الله عليه وآله) فقال: يا رسول الله كثرت ذنوبي وضعف عملي، فقال رسول الله (صلى الله عليه وآله): أكثر السجود فإنه يحط الذنوب كما تحط الريح ورق الشجر.

From Abu Ja'far al-Attar who said: I heard al-Sadiq Ja'far bin Muhammad (peace be upon them both) saying: A man came to the Messenger of Allah (peace be upon him and his family) and said: O Messenger of Allah, my sins have become many and my good deeds have become weak. The Messenger of Allah (peace be upon him and his family) said: Increase in prostration, for it removes sins just as wind removes leaves from trees.

Hadith 4629

عن سلمان الفارسي قال: كنا مع رسول الله (صلى الله عليه وآله) في ظل شجرة فأخذ غصنا منها فنفضه، فتساقط ورقه، فقال: ألا تسألوني عما صنعت؟ فقالوا: أخبرنا يا رسول الله، قال: إن العبد المسلم إذا قام إلى الصلاة تحاتت خطاياه كما تحاتت ورق هذه الشجرة.

From Salman Al-Farisi who said: We were with the Messenger of Allah (peace be upon him and his family) in the shade of a tree when he took a branch from it and shook it, causing its leaves to fall. He said: Will you not ask me about what I did? They said: Tell us, O Messenger of Allah. He said: When a Muslim servant stands for prayer, his sins fall off just as the leaves of this tree have fallen.

Hadith 4630

عن عنبسة بن بجاد العابد قال: سمعت أبا عبد الله (عليه السلام) وذكر عنده الصلاة، فقال: إن في كتاب علي الذي هو إملاء رسول الله (صلى الله عليه وآله): إن الله لا يعذب على كثرة الصلاة والصيام ولكن يزيده خيرا.

From Anbasa bin Bajjad al-Abid who said: I heard Abu Abdullah (peace be upon him), and prayer was mentioned in his presence, so he said: In the book of Ali which was dictated by the Messenger of Allah (peace be upon him and his family): Indeed Allah does not punish for abundance of prayer and fasting, but rather increases one in good.

———————

CHAPTER 33

Recommendation Of Maintaining The Two Rak'ahs Of Fajr And Not Abandoning Them During Travel

[Hadith 4631 to 4634]

Hadith 4631

عن أبي الحسن الرضا (عليه السلام) قال: صل ركعتي الفجر في المحمل.

From Abu Al-Hasan Al-Ridha (peace be upon him) who said: Pray the two rak'ahs of Fajr in the camel litter (*).

Translator: * Al-maḥmal refers to a type of litter or howdah, which is a seat or compartment mounted on a camel or other animal, used for traveling.

———

Hadith 4632

عن إسماعيل بن عبد الخالق قال: سمعت أبا عبد الله (عليه السلام) يقول: الركعتين اللتين بعد المغرب هما ادبار السجود، والركعتين اللتين بعد الفجر هما إدبار النجوم.

From Ismail ibn Abd al-Khaliq, who said: I heard Abu Abdullah (peace be upon him) say: The two rak'ahs after Maghrib are the "declining of prostrations" [Quran, 50:40], and the two rak'ahs after Fajr are the "declining of the stars" [Quran, 52:49].

———

Hadith 4633

عن الرضا (عليه السلام) قال: ادبار السجود أربع ركعات بعد المغرب، وادبار النجوم ركعتين قبل صلاة الصبح.

From al-Ridha (peace be upon him) that he said: The "adbar al-sujud" refers to four rak'ahs performed after the Maghrib prayer, and the "adbar al-nujum" refers to two rak'ahs performed before the Fajr prayer.

———

Hadith 4634

عن سعد أبي عمرو الجلاب قال: قلت لأبي عبد الله (عليه السلام): ركعتا الفجر تفوتني، أفأصليها؟ قال: نعم، قلت: لم، فريضة؟ قال: فقال رسول الله (صلى الله عليه وآله) سنها، فما سن رسول الله (صلى الله عليه وآله) فهو فرض.

From Sa'd Abu Amr Al-Jallab who said: I said to Abu Abdullah (peace be upon him): I miss the two rak'ahs of Fajr, should I pray them? He said: Yes. I said: Why, is it obligatory? He said: The Messenger of Allah (peace be upon him and his family) made it a tradition, and what the Messenger of Allah made a tradition is obligatory.

قال الشيخ: قوله: فرض، معناه مقدر، لان الفرض هو التقدير، وليس يريد أنه فرض يستحق تاركه العقاب.

أقول: ويمكن الحمل على تأكد الاستحباب، ويحتمل الحمل على الاستفهام الانكاري ويراد به إنكار الوجوب والفرض. وقد تقدم ما يدل على ذلك، ويأتي ما يدل عليه إن شاء الله تعالى.

The Shaykh said: His saying "obligatory" means "determined," because obligation means determination, and it does not mean that one who abandons it deserves punishment. I (Hurr Amili) say: It can be interpreted as emphasized recommendation, and possibly as rhetorical questioning meant to deny obligation. Evidence for this has preceded and will follow, insha'Allah.

Section 2
Al-Mawaqiyat (Timings)

CHAPTER 1

Obligation Of Maintaining Prayers In Their Times
[Hadith 4635 to 4661]

Hadith 4635

عن أبان بن تغلب قال: كنت صليت خلف أبي عبد الله (عليه السلام) بالمزدلفة، فلما انصرف التفت إلي فقال: يا أبان، الصلوات الخمس المفروضات من أقام حدودهن وحافظ على مواقيتهن لقي الله يوم القيامة وله عنده عهد يدخله به الجنة، ومن لم يقم حدودهن ولم يحافظ على مواقيتهن لقي الله ولا عهد له، إن شاء عذبه وإن شاء غفر له.

From Aban ibn Taghlib who said: I prayed behind Abu Abdullah (peace be upon him) at Muzdalifah. When he finished, he turned to me and said: O Aban, regarding the five obligatory prayers - whoever establishes their limits and maintains their appointed times will meet Allah on the Day of Resurrection having a covenant with Him by which He will admit him to Paradise. And whoever does not establish their limits and does not maintain their appointed times will meet Allah having no covenant - if He wills He will punish him and if He wills He will forgive him.

Hadith 4636

عن أبي بصير قال: سمعت أبا جعفر (عليه السلام) يقول: كل سهو في الصلاة يطرح منها، غير أن الله يتم بالنوافل، إن أول ما يحاسب به العبد الصلاة، فان قبلت قبل ما سواها، إن الصلاة إذا ارتفعت في أول وقتها رجعت إلى صاحبها وهي بيضاء مشرقة، تقول: حفظتني حفظك الله، وإذا ارتفعت في غير وقتها بغير حدودها رجعت إلى صاحبها وهي سوداء مظلمة تقول: ضيعتني ضيعك الله.

From Abu Basir, he said: I heard Abu Ja'far (peace be upon him) say: Every lapse in prayer diminishes it, except that Allah completes it through supererogatory prayers. Indeed, the first thing by which the servant will be held accountable is prayer; if it is accepted, whatever else he has done will also be accepted. When the prayer ascends at the beginning of its proper time, it returns to its owner white and radiant, saying: You preserved me, may Allah preserve you. But when it ascends outside its proper time and without its proper bounds, it returns to its owner dark and gloomy, saying: You neglected me, may Allah neglect you.

Hadith 4637

عن أبي جعفر (عليه السلام) قال: أيما مؤمن حافظ على الصلوات المفروضة فصلاها لوقتها فليس هذا من الغافلين.

From Abu Ja'far (peace be upon him) who said: Any believer who maintains the obligatory prayers and prays them at their time is not among the heedless.

Hadith 4638

عن أبي جعفر (عليه السلام) - في حديث -: إن ملك الموت قال لرسول الله (صلى الله عليه وآله): مامن أهل بيت مدر ولا شعر في بر ولا بحر إلا وأنا أتصفحهم في كل يوم خمس مرات عند مواقيت الصلاة.

From Abu Ja'far (peace be upon him) - in a hadith: The Angel of Death said to the Messenger of Allah (peace be upon him and his family): There is not a household of mud or fur (settled or nomadic) on land or sea except that I examine them five times every day at the times of prayer.

Hadith 4639

عن أبي عبد الله (عليه السلام) - في حديث -: إن ملك الموت قال: إنه ليس في شرقها ولا في غربها أهل بيت مدر ولا وبر إلا وأنا أتصفحهم في كل يوم خمس مرات. فقال رسول الله (صلى الله عليه وآله): إنما يتصفحهم في مواقيت الصلاة، فإن كان ممن يواظب عليها عند مواقيتها لقنه شهادة أن لا إله إلا الله وأن محمدا رسول الله (صلى الله عليه وآله)، ونحى عنه ملك الموت إبليس.

From Abu Abdullah (peace be upon him) - in a hadith: The Angel of Death said: There is not a household in the east or west, whether of mud or fur (settled or nomadic), except that I examine them five times every day. Then the Messenger of Allah (peace be upon him and his family) said: He examines them at the prayer times, so if someone regularly maintains their prayers at their proper times, he instructs them to testify that there is no god but Allah and that Muhammad is the Messenger of Allah (peace be upon him and his family), and the Angel of Death drives Iblis away from them.

Hadith 4640

عن أبي بصير، عن أبي عبد الله (عليه السلام) قال: من صلى في غير الوقت فلا صلاة له.

From Abu Basir, from Abu Abdullah (peace be upon him) who said: Whoever prays outside the time has no prayer.

Hadith 4641

عن أبي بصير، عن أبي عبد الله (عليه السلام) قال: مامن يوم سحاب يخفى فيه على الناس وقت الزوال إلا كان من الامام للشمس زجرة حتى تبدو فيحتج على أهل كل قرية من اهتم بصلاته ومن ضيعها.

From Abu Basir, from Abu Abdullah (peace be upon him) who said: There is no cloudy day when people are unable to determine the time of noon, except that the Imam has authority over the sun until it appears, so that it may be evidence against the people of every village - those who care about their prayer and those who neglect it.

Translator: On a cloudy day when the exact time of zawal is not apparent to the people, the Imam has the spiritual capacity to command the sun to appear, so that the time of zawal becomes clear, and distinction is established between those who are mindful of their prayers and those who neglect them.

Hadith 4642

عن زرارة قال: سألت أبا جعفر (عليه السلام) عن الفرض في الصلاة؟ فقال: الوقت والطهور والقبلة والتوجه والركوع والسجود والدعاء، قلت: ما سوى ذلك؟ فقال: سنة في فريضة.

From Zurarah who said: I asked Abu Ja'far (peace be upon him), about what is obligatory (fard) in the prayer. He said: The time, purification, the qiblah, the orientation (tawajjuh), the bowing (ruku), the prostration (sujud), and the supplication (du'a). I said: What about other than these? He said: It is a sunnah within an obligation.

Hadith 4643

محمد بن علي بن الحسين قال: قال الصادق (عليه السلام): تعلموا من الديك خمس خصال: محافظته على أوقات الصلوات، والغيرة، والسخاء، والشجاعة، وكثرة الطروقة.

Muhammad ibn Ali ibn Al-Husayn said: Al-Sadiq (peace be upon him) said: Learn five traits from the rooster: observing prayer times, ghayrah (possessive or protective jealousy), generosity, courage, and frequent mating.

Hadith 4644

قال: دخل رسول الله (صلى الله عليه وآله) المسجد وفيه ناس من أصحابه فقال: تدرون ما قال ربكم؟ قالوا: الله ورسوله أعلم، قال: إن ربكم يقول: إن هذه الصلوات الخمس المفروضات من صلاهن لوقتهن وحافظ عليهن لقيني يوم القيامة وله عندي عهد أدخله به الجنة. ومن لم يصلهن لوقتهن ولم يحافظ عليهن فذاك إلى، إن شئت عذبته، وإن شئت غفرت له.

He said: The Messenger of Allah (peace be upon him and his family) entered the mosque where some companions were and said: Do you know what your Lord says? They said: Allah and His Messenger know best. He said: Your Lord says: These five obligatory prayers - whoever prays them at their times and preserves them will meet Me on the Day of Resurrection with a covenant from Me to enter Paradise. And whoever does not pray them at their times and does not preserve them, then it is up to Me - if I wish I will punish him, and if I wish I will forgive him.

Hadith 4645

عن هشام الجواليقي عن أبي عبد الله (عليه السلام) قال: قال رسول الله (صلى الله عليه وآله): من صلى الصلاة لغير وقتها رفعت له سوداء مظلمة تقول: ضيعتني ضيعك الله كما ضيعتني، وأول ما يسأل العبد إذا وقف بين يدي الله تعالى عن الصلاة، فإن زكت صلاته زكا سائر عمله، وإن لم تزك صلاته لم يزك عمله.

From Hisham Al-Jawaliki from Abu Abdullah (peace be upon him) who said: The Messenger of Allah (peace be upon him and his family) said: Whoever prays outside its prescribed time, it will be raised as dark and black, saying: You neglected me, may Allah neglect you as you neglected me. The first thing a servant will be asked about when standing before Allah is prayer - if his prayer is pure his other deeds will be pure, and if his prayer is not pure his deeds will not be pure.

Hadith 4646

عن أبي عبد الله، عن أبيه، عن آبائه، عن أمير المؤمنين (عليهم السلام) قال: قال رسول الله (صلى الله عليه وآله): لا يزال الشيطان هائبا لابن آدم، ذعرا منه، ما صلى الصلوات الخمس لوقتهن، فإذا ضيعهن اجترأ عليه فأدخله في العظائم.

From Abu Abdullah, from his father, from his forefathers, from Amir al-Mu'minin (peace be upon them) who said: The Messenger of Allah (peace be upon him and his family) said: Satan continues to fear and be frightened of the son of Adam as long as he prays the five prayers at their times. But when he neglects them, Satan becomes bold against him and leads him into major sins.

Hadith 4647

عن أبي عبد الله الصادق عن آبائه (عليهم السلام) قال: قال رسول الله (صلى الله عليه وآله): لا ينال شفاعتي غدا من أخر الصلاة المفروضة بعد وقتها.

From Abu Abdullah Al-Sadiq from his forefathers (peace be upon them) who said: The Messenger of Allah (peace be upon him and his family) said: My intercession tomorrow will not reach one who delays the obligatory prayer beyond its time.

Hadith 4648

عن الرضا (عليه السلام)، عن آبائه (عليهم السلام) قال: قال رسول الله (صلى الله عليه وآله): لا يزال الشيطان ذعرا من المؤمن ما حافظ على مواقيت الصلوات الخمس، فإذا ضيعهن اجترأ عليه فأدخله في العظائم.

From Al-Ridha (peace be upon him), from his forefathers (peace be upon them) who said: The Messenger of Allah (peace be upon him and his family) said: Satan continues to be frightened of the believer as long as he preserves the times of the five prayers. But when he neglects them, Satan becomes bold against him and leads him into major sins.

Hadith 4649

عن أبي عبد الله (عليه السلام) قال: خصلتان من كانتا فيه وإلا فاعزب ثم أعزب، قيل: وما هما؟ قال: الصلاة في مواقيتها والمواظبة عليها، والمواساة.

From Abu Abdullah (peace be upon him) who said: Two traits - whoever has them [is good] and whoever doesn't then away with him, then away with him. It was asked: What are they? He said: Praying at their proper times with consistency, and helping others.

Hadith 4650

عن جعفر بن محمد (عليه السلام) قال: امتحنوا شيعتنا عند ثلاث: عند مواقيت الصلاة، كيف محافظتهم عليها؟ وعند أسرارهم، كيف حفظهم لها عند عدونا؟ وإلى أموالهم، كيف مواساتهم لإخوانهم فيها؟

From Ja'far bin Muhammad (peace be upon him) who said: Test our followers in three things: At prayer times - how do they preserve them? With their secrets - how do they protect them from our enemies? And with their wealth - how do they share it with their brothers?

Hadith 4651

عن ابن مسعود قال: سألت رسول الله (صلى الله عليه وآله): أي الاعمال أحب إلى الله؟ قال: الصلاة لوقتها. قلت: ثم أي شئ؟ قال: بر الوالدين، قلت ثم أي شئ؟ قال: الجهاد في سبيل الله.

From Ibn Masud who said: I asked the Messenger of Allah (peace be upon him and his family): Which deeds are most beloved to Allah? He said: Prayer at its prescribed time. I said: Then what? He said: Kindness to parents. I said: Then what? He said: Jihad in the way of Allah.

Hadith 4652

عن الرضا (عليه السلام) قال: في الديك الأبيض خمس خصال من خصال الأنبياء (عليهم السلام):
معرفته بأوقات الصلوات، والغيرة، والسخاء، والشجاعة، وكثرة الطروقة.

From Al-Ridha (peace be upon him) who said: The white rooster has five characteristics of the prophets (peace be upon them): Knowledge of prayer times, ghayrah (possessive or protective jealousy), generosity, bravery, and frequent mating.

Hadith 4653

وبإسناده عن علي (عليه السلام) - في حديث الأربعمائة - قال: ليس عمل أحب إلى الله عز وجل من
الصلاة، فلا يشغلنكم عن أوقاتها شئ من أمور الدنيا، فإن الله عز وجل ذم أقواما فقال: (الذين هم عن
صلاتهم ساهون)، يعني أنهم غافلون، استهانوا بأوقاتها، اعلموا أن صالحي عدوكم يرائي بعضهم بعضا، لكن
الله لا يوفقهم ولا يقبل إلا ما كان له خالصا.

And by his chain from Ali (peace be upon him) - in the hadith of the four hundred - he said: There is no deed more beloved to Allah, the Mighty and Majestic, than prayer, so do not let anything from worldly matters distract you from its prescribed times, for Allah, the Mighty and Majestic, condemned people saying "Those who are neglectful of their prayers [Quran, 107:5]," meaning they are heedless, taking its times lightly. Know that even the righteous among your enemies show off to one another, but Allah does not grant them success and only accepts what is purely for Him.

Hadith 4654

عن أبي جعفر (عليه السلام) قال: أيما مؤمن حافظ على صلاة الفريضة فصلاها لوقتها فليس هو من
الغافلين، فإن قرأ فيها بمائة آية فهو من الذاكرين.

From Abu Ja'far (peace be upon him) who said: Any believer who preserves the obligatory prayer and prays it at its time is not among the heedless. If he recites a hundred verses in it, he is among those who remember Allah.

Hadith 4655

وعن ابن محبوب رفعه إلى أبي عبد الله (عليه السلام) قال: قال رسول الله (صلى الله عليه وآله) في
مرضه الذي توفي فيه، وأغمي عليه ثم أفاق فقال: لا ينال شفاعتي من أخر الصلاة بعد وقتها.

From Ibn Mahbub, raising it to Abu Abdullah (peace be upon him) who said: The Messenger of Allah (peace be upon him and his family) said during his illness in which he passed away, and he fainted then regained consciousness and said: My intercession will not reach whoever delays prayer beyond its time.

Hadith 4656

عن مسعدة بن صدقة قال: قال أبو عبد الله (عليه السلام): امتحنوا شيعتنا عند مواقيت الصلاة، كيف محافظتهم عليها؟.

From Masada bin Sadaqa who said: Abu Abdullah (peace be upon him) said: Test our Shia in the timings of the prayer - how do they preserve/maintain them?

Hadith 4657

عن زرارة، عن أبي جعفر (عليه السلام) قال: هذه الفريضة من صلاها لوقتها عارفا بحقها لا يؤثر عليها غيرها كتب الله له براءة لا يعذبه، ومن صلاها لغير وقتها مؤثرا عليها غيرها فإن ذلك إليه إن شاء غفر له وإن شاء عذبه.

From Zurarah, from Abu Ja'far (peace be upon him) who said: This obligation - whoever prays it at its time knowing its right, not preferring anything else over it, Allah writes for them immunity from punishment. And whoever prays it outside its time, preferring other things over it, that matter is up to Him - if He wills He forgives them and if He wills He punishes them.

Hadith 4658

عن أبي عبد الله (عليه السلام) في قوله تعالى: (الذين هم عن صلاتهم ساهون) أهي وسوسة الشيطان؟ فقال: لا. كل أحد يصيبه هذا ولكن أن يغفلها ويدع أن يصلي في أول وقتها.

From Abu Abdullah (peace be upon him) regarding Allah's saying: "Those who are neglectful of their prayers" [Quran 107:5] - Is it from Satan's whispering? He said: No, this affects everyone, but it means being heedless of it and leaving it from its earliest time.

Hadith 4659

وعن أبي أسامة زيد الشحام قال: سألت أبا عبد الله (عليه السلام) عن قول الله عز وجل (الذين هم عن صلاتهم ساهون)، قال: هو الترك لها والتواني عنها.

From Abu Usama Zayd al-Shahham who said: I asked Abu Abdullah (peace be upon him) about Allah's saying "Those who are neglectful of their prayers" [Quran 107:5]. He said: It means abandoning it and being lazy about it.

Hadith 4660

وعن محمد بن الفضيل، عن أبي الحسن (عليه السلام) قال: هو التضييع لها.

From Muhammad ibn al-Fadhl, from Abu al-Hasan (peace be upon him) who said: It means wasting it.

Hadith 4661

عن أبي عبد الله (عليه السلام) قال: إذا صليت في السفر شيئا من الصلوات في غير وقتها فلا يضرك.

From Abu Abdullah (peace be upon him), he said: If you pray any of the prayers while traveling outside their prescribed time, it will not harm you.

أقول: حمله الشيخ على تأخيرها لعذر فتصير قضاءا، والأقرب حملها على تأخيرها عن وقت الفضيلة، والاتيان بها في وقت الاجزاء، ويحتمل الحمل على النوافل، ويأتي ما يدل على ذلك وعلى مضمون الباب.

I (Hurr Amili) say: The Shaykh interpreted it as referring to delaying it due to an excuse, so it becomes a make-up prayer (qada). The more probable interpretation is that it refers to delaying it beyond the time of merit (waqt al-fadila) and performing it during the time of sufficiency (waqt al-ijza). It is also possible to interpret it as referring to the supererogatory prayers (nawafil). What supports this interpretation, as well as the content of this chapter, will be mentioned later.

CHAPTER 2

Recommendation Of Sitting In The Mosque And Waiting For Prayer

[Hadith 4662 to 4671]

Hadith 4662

عن جعفر بن محمد، عن أبيه، عن آبائه في وصية النبي لعلي (عليهم السلام) قال: يا علي ثلاث درجات: إسباغ الوضوء على السبرات، والمشي بالليل والنهار إلى الجماعات، وانتظار الصلاة بعد الصلاة.

From Ja'far ibn Muhammad, from his father, from his forefathers, regarding the Prophet's counsel to Ali (peace be upon them all), he said: O Ali, three things are of elevated ranks: performing ablution thoroughly in the bitter cold, walking by night and day to the congregational prayers, and awaiting the next prayer after a prayer.

Hadith 4663

قال: وقال الصادق (عليه السلام) كان رسول الله (صلى الله عليه وآله) يقول: من حبس نفسه على صلاة فريضة ينتظر وقتها، فصلاها في أول وقتها، فأتم ركوعها وسجودها وخشوعها، ثم مجد الله عز وجل، وعظمه، وحمده، حتى يدخل وقت صلاة أخرى، لم يلغ بينهما، كتب الله له كأجر الحاج المعتمر، وكان من أهل عليين.

He said: And al-Sadiq (peace be upon him) said: The Messenger of Allah (peace be upon him and his family) used to say: Whoever restrains himself to perform an obligatory prayer, waiting for its time, then prays it at the beginning of its time, and completes its ruku and sujud and humility, then glorifies Allah the Mighty and Majestic, and magnifies Him, and praises Him, until the time of another prayer enters, without engaging in idle talk between the two, Allah will record for him a reward like that of the one who performs Hajj and Umrah, and he will be among the people of Illiyyun.

Hadith 4664

وفي كتاب (الاخوان) بسنده عن أبي عبد الله (عليه السلام) قال: ثلاثة نفر من خالصة الله عز وجل يوم القيامة: رجل زار أخاه في الله عز وجل فهو زور الله عز وجل وعلى الله أن يكرم زوره، ويعطيه ما سأل، ورجل دخل المسجد فصلى وعقب انتظارا للصلاة الأخرى فهو ضيف الله وحق على الله أن يكرم ضيفه، والحاج والمعتمر فهما وفد الله وحق على الله أن يكرم وفده.

In the book Al-Ikhwan, with its chain to Abu Abdullah (peace be upon him), he said: Three people will be among Allah's special ones on the Day of Judgment: A man who visits his brother for the sake of Allah, so he is Allah's visitor and it is upon Allah to honor His visitor and grant him what he asks; a man who enters the mosque, prays and stays waiting for another prayer, so he is Allah's guest and it is upon Allah to honor His guest; and the one performing Hajj and Umrah, they are Allah's delegation and it is upon Allah to honor His delegation.

Hadith 4665

عن الصادق، عن آبائه (عليهم السلام) قال: قال رسول الله (صلى الله عليه وآله): الجلوس في المسجد لانتظار الصلاة عبادة ما لم يحدث. قيل: يا رسول الله وما الحدث؟ قال: الغيبة.

From Al-Sadiq, from his forefathers (peace be upon them), he said: The Messenger of Allah (peace be upon him and his family) said: Sitting in the mosque waiting for prayer is worship as long as one does not commit hadath. It was asked: O Messenger of Allah, what is hadath? He said: Backbiting.

Hadith 4666

وفي (الخصال) بإسناده عن علي (عليه السلام) - في حديث الأربعمائة - قال: المنتظر وقت الصلاة بعد الصلاة من زوار الله عز وجل، وحق على الله أن يكرم زائره، وأن يعطيه ما سأل، والحاج والمعتمر وفد الله، وحق على الله أن يكرم وفده، ويحبوه بالمغفرة.

In Al-Khisal, with its chain to Ali (peace be upon him) - in the hadith of four hundred - he said: The one waiting for prayer time after prayer is among Allah's visitors, and it is upon Allah to honor His visitor and grant him what he asks. The one performing Hajj and Umrah is Allah's delegation, and it is upon Allah to honor His delegation and bestow forgiveness upon them.

Hadith 4667

عن عيسى بن عبد الله الهاشمي، عن علي (عليه السلام) قال: قال رسول الله (صلى الله عليه وآله): انتظار الصلاة بعد الصلاة كنز من كنوز الجنة.

From Isa bin Abdullah al-Hashimi, from Ali (peace be upon him) who said: The Messenger of Allah (peace be upon him and his family) said: Waiting for prayer after prayer is a treasure from the treasures of Paradise.

Hadith 4668

عن عثمان بن مظعون - في حديث - أنه قال: لرسول الله (صلى الله عليه وآله): إني أردت أن أترهب، قال: لا تفعل يا عثمان فإن ترهب أمتي القعود في المساجد انتظار الصلاة بعد الصلاة.

From Uthman bin Madh'un - in a hadith - that he said to the Messenger of Allah (peace be upon him and his family): I want to become a monk. He said: Do not do that, O Uthman, for the monasticism of my nation is sitting in mosques waiting for prayer after prayer.

Hadith 4669

وفي (المجالس والاخبار) بإسناده عن أبي ذر، عن النبي (صلى الله عليه وآله) في وصيته له، قال: يا أبا ذر إن الله يعطيك ما دمت جالسا في المسجد بكل نفس تتنفس فيه درجة في الجنة، وتصلي عليك الملائكة، ويكتب لك بكل نفس تنفست فيه عشر حسنات، ويمحى عنك عشر سيئات.

In (Al-Majalis wal-Akhbar) with his chain from Abu Dharr, from the Prophet (peace be upon him and his family) in his advice to him, he said: O Abu Dharr, Allah grants you, as long as you are sitting in the mosque, for every breath you take in it a rank in Paradise, and the angels send blessings upon you, and for every breath you take in it ten good deeds are written for you, and ten bad deeds are erased from you.

يا أبا ذر، أتعلم في أي شئ أنزلت هذه الآية: (اصبروا وصابروا ورابطوا واتقوا الله لعلكم تفلحون)؟ قلت: لا. قال: في انتظار الصلاة خلف الصلاة. يا أبا ذر إسباغ الوضوء على المكاره من الكفارات، وكثرة الاختلاف إلى المساجد فذلكم الرباط. يا أبا ذر كل جلوس في المسجد لغو إلا ثلاثة: قراءة مصل، أو ذاكر الله تعالى، أو مسائل عن علم.

O Abu Dharr, do you know for what this verse was revealed: "Be patient and urge one another to patience and be steadfast and fear Allah that you may prosper?" [Quran, 3:200] I said: No. He said: It is for waiting for prayer after prayer. O Abu Dharr, performing thorough wudu despite hardships is among the expiations, and frequent visits to mosques, that is steadfastness. O Abu Dharr, every sitting in the mosque is futile except for three: recitation by one who prays, one who remembers Allah the Exalted, or inquiries about knowledge.

Hadith 4670

عن أبي عبد الله (عليه السلام) قال: قال علي بن الحسين (عليهما السلام): من اهتم بمواقيت الصلاة لم يستكمل لذة الدنيا.

From Abu Abdullah (peace be upon him) who said: Ali bin Al-Husayn (peace be upon them both) said: Whoever is preoccupied with the prayer times will not experience complete worldly pleasure.

Hadith 4671

عن أبي عبد الله (عليه السلام) قال: من أقام في مسجد بعد صلاته انتظارا للصلاة فهو ضيف الله، وحق على الله أن يكرم ضيفه.

From Abu Abdullah (peace be upon him) who said: Whoever stays in the mosque after his prayer waiting for the next prayer is a guest of Allah, and it is Allah's right to honor His guest.

CHAPTER 3

Recommendation Of Praying At The Beginning Of Prayer Time
[Hadith 4672 to 4691]

Hadith 4672

عن أبي الحسن موسى (عليه السلام) قال: الصلوات المفروضات في أول وقتها إذا أقيم حدودها أطيب ريحا من قضيب الاس حين يؤخذ من شجره في طيبه وريحه وطراوته، وعليكم بالوقت الأول.

From Abu Al-Hasan Musa (peace be upon him) who said: The obligatory prayers at their beginning times, when performed within their proper bounds, are more fragrant than a myrtle branch when first picked from its tree in its freshness, fragrance, and tenderness. So adhere to the first time.

Hadith 4673

عن محمد بن مسلم قال: سمعت أبا عبد الله (عليه السلام) يقول: إذا دخل وقت صلاة فتحت أبواب السماء لصعود الاعمال، فما أحب أن يصعد عمل أول من عملي، ولا يكتب في الصحيفة أحد أول مني.

From Muhammad bin Muslim who said: I heard Abu Abdullah (peace be upon him) saying: When the prayer time enters, the gates of heaven open for the ascension of deeds. I love that my deed be the first to ascend, and that no one's deed be written in the record before mine.

Hadith 4674

وعنه، عن البرقي، عن سعد بن سعد قال: قال الرضا (عليه السلام): يا فلان إذا دخل الوقت عليك فصلها فإنك لا تدري ما يكون.

From him, from Al-Barqi, from Saad bin Saad who said: Al-Ridha (peace be upon him) said: O so-and-so, when the time enters upon you, pray, for you do not know what may happen.

Hadith 4675

عن ابن سنان - يعني عبد الله - عن أبي عبد الله (عليه السلام) - في حديث - قال: لكل صلاة وقتان، وأول الوقتين أفضلهما، ولا ينبغي تأخير ذلك عمدا، ولكنه. وقت من شغل أو نسي أو سها أو نام. وليس لاحد أن يجعل آخر الوقتين وقتا إلا من عذر أو علة.

From Ibn Sinan - meaning Abdullah - from Abu Abdullah (peace be upon him) - in a hadith - he said: For every prayer there are two times, and the first of the two times is better. It is not appropriate to deliberately delay it, but it is a time for one who is busy, forgetful, mistaken, or asleep. No one should make the latter time their regular time except with an excuse or illness.

Hadith 4676

عن زرارة قال: قال أبو جعفر (عليه السلام): أحب الوقت إلى الله عز وجل أوله، حين يدخل وقت الصلاة فصل الفريضة. فإن لم تفعل فإنك في وقت منهما حتى تغيب الشمس.

From Zurarah who said: Abu Ja'far (peace be upon him) said: The most beloved time to Allah, the Mighty and Majestic, is its beginning when the prayer time enters, so pray the obligatory prayer. If you do not do so, you are still within their time until the sun sets.

Hadith 4677

عن سعيد بن الحسن قال: قال أبو جعفر (عليه السلام): أول الوقت زوال الشمس، وهو وقت الله الأول، وهو أفضلهما.

From Sa'id bin Al-Hasan who said: Abu Ja'far (peace be upon him) said: The beginning of the time is the sun's zenith, and it is Allah's first time, and it is the better of the two.

Hadith 4678

عن أبي عبد الله (عليه السلام) قال: قال رسول الله (صلى الله عليه وآله): مامن صلاة يحضر وقتها إلا نادى ملك بين يدي الله: أيها الناس، قوموا إلى نيرانكم التي أوقدتموها على ظهوركم فأطفؤوها بصلاتكم.

From Abu Abdullah (peace be upon him) who said: The Messenger of Allah (peace be upon him and his family) said: There is no prayer whose time arrives except that an angel calls out before Allah: O people, rise to your fires which you have kindled upon your backs and extinguish them with your prayers.

Hadith 4679

عن أبي عبد الله (عليه السلام) قال: قال جبرئيل لرسول الله (صلى الله عليه وآله) - في حديث -: أفضل الوقت أوله.

From Abu Abdullah (peace be upon him) who said: Jibreel said to the Messenger of Allah (peace be upon him and his family) - in a hadith: The best time is its beginning.

Hadith 4680

عن أبي بصير، قال: ذكر أبو عبد الله (عليه السلام) أول الوقت وفضله، فقلت: كيف أصنع بالثماني ركعات؟ فقال: خفف ما استطعت.

From Abu Basir who said: Abu Abdullah (peace be upon him) mentioned the beginning of prayer time and its virtue, so I said: What should I do about the eight rak'ahs? He said: Make them as light as you can.

Hadith 4681

عن زرارة قال: قال أبو جعفر (عليه السلام): اعلم أن أول الوقت أبدا أفضل فعجل الخير ما استطعت، وأحب الاعمال إلى الله ما داوم عليه العبد وإن قل.

From Zurarah who said: Abu Ja'far (peace be upon him) said: Know that the beginning of time is always better, so hasten to do good as much as you can, and the most beloved deeds to Allah are those that the servant maintains consistently even if they are few.

Hadith 4682

عن معاوية بن عمار - أو ابن وهب - قال: قال أبو عبد الله (عليه السلام): لكل صلاة وقتان وأول الوقت أفضلهما.

From Mu'awiyah bin Ammar - or Ibn Wahb - who said: Abu Abdullah (peace be upon him) said: For every prayer there are two times, and the beginning time is better of the two.

Hadith 4683

عن زرارة قال: قلت لأبي جعفر (عليه السلام): أصلحك الله، وقت كل صلاة أول الوقت أفضل أو وسطه أو آخره؟ قال: أوله، إن رسول الله (صلى الله عليه وآله) قال: إن الله عز وجل يحب من الخير ما يعجل.

From Zurarah who said: I said to Abu Ja'far (peace be upon him): May Allah keep you well, is the time of every prayer better at its beginning, middle or end? He said: Its beginning, for the Messenger of Allah (peace be upon him and his family) said: Allah loves good deeds that are hastened.

Hadith 4684

عن أبي عبد الله (عليه السلام)، قال: سمعته يقول: لكل صلاة وقتان وأول الوقت أفضله. وليس لاحد أن يجعل آخر الوقتين وقتا إلا في عذر من غير علة.

From Abu Abdullah (peace be upon him), who said: I heard him saying: For every prayer there are two times and the beginning time is better, and no one should make the latter of the two times his regular time except with a valid excuse.

Hadith 4685

قال أبو عبد الله (عليه السلام): لفضل الوقت الأول على الأخير خير للرجل من ولده وماله.

Abu Abdullah (peace be upon him) said: The virtue of the first time over the last is better for a man than his children and wealth.

Hadith 4686

عن أبي عبد الله (عليه السلام) قال: إن فضل الوقت الأول على الاخر كفضل الآخرة على الدنيا.

From Abu Abdullah (peace be upon him) who said: The virtue of the first time over the last is like the virtue of the Hereafter over this world.

Hadith 4687

قال الصادق (عليه السلام): أوله رضوان الله، وآخره عفو الله، والعفو لا يكون إلا عن ذنب.

Al-Sadiq (peace be upon him) said: Its beginning is Allah's pleasure, and its end is Allah's forgiveness, and forgiveness only comes after a sin.

Hadith 4688

عن أبي عبد الله (عليه السلام) قال: من صلى الصلوات المفروضات في أول وقتها وأقام حدودها رفعها الملك إلى السماء بيضاء نقية وهي تهتف به، تقول: حفظك الله كما حفظتني وأستودعك الله استودعتني ملكا كريما،

From Abu Abdullah (peace be upon him) who said: Whoever prays the obligatory prayers at their beginning time and establishes their proper limits, the angel raises them to heaven white and pure, and they call out saying: May Allah protect you as you protected me, and I entrust you to Allah as you entrusted me to a noble angel.

ومن صلاها بعد وقتها من غير علة ولم يقم حدودها رفعها الملك سوداء مظلمة وهي تهتف به: ضيعتني ضيعك الله كما ضيعتني، ولا رعاك الله كما لم ترعني.

And whoever prays them after their time without a valid excuse and does not establish their proper limits, the angel raises them black and dark, and they call out saying: You neglected me, may Allah neglect you as you neglected me, and may Allah not care for you as you did not care for me.

ثم قال الصادق (عليه السلام): إن أول ما يسأل عنه العبد إذا وقف بين يدي الله عز وجل الصلوات المفروضات، وعن الزكاة المفروضة، وعن الصيام المفروض، وعن الحج المفروض، وعن ولايتنا أهل البيت.

Then Al-Sadiq (peace be upon him) said: Indeed the first things that a servant will be asked about when standing before Allah the Mighty and Majestic are the obligatory prayers, the obligatory zakat, the obligatory fasting, the obligatory Hajj, and our Wilayah (allegiance/obedience)- the Ahl al-Bayt.

Hadith 4689

وفي (عيون الأخبار) بإسناده عن الفضل بن شاذان، عن الرضا (عليه السلام) - في حديث طويل - قال: والصلاة في أول الوقت أفضل.

And in (Uyun al-Akhbar) with its chain from Al-Fadhl ibn Shadhan, from Al-Ridha (peace be upon him) - in a long hadith - he said: Prayer at the beginning of its time is best.

Hadith 4690

عن الحسن بن علي بن أبي طالب، عن أبيه (عليهما السلام)، أنه قال: أوصيك يا بني بالصلاة عند وقتها.

From Al-Hasan ibn Ali ibn Abi Talib, from his father (peace be upon them both), that he said: I advise you, O my son, to pray at its proper time.

Hadith 4691

علي بن إبراهيم في (تفسيره) عن أبي عبد الله (عليه السلام) في قول الله عز وجل: (فويل للمصلين الذين هم عن صلاتهم ساهون) قال: تأخير الصلاة عن أول وقتها لغير عذر.

Ali ibn Ibrahim in his (Tafsir) from Abu Abdullah (peace be upon him) regarding Allah's words: "So woe to those who pray, Who are heedless of their prayer" [Quran 107:4-5], he said: It means delaying prayer from its first time without an excuse.

CHAPTER 4

When The Sun Passes Its Zenith, The Time For Zuhr And Asr Prayers Begins And Extends Until Sunset, With Zuhr Specifically At Its Beginning For Its Duration, And Similarly Asr At Its End

[Hadith 4692 to 4714]

Hadith 4692

عن زرارة، عن أبي جعفر (عليه السلام) قال: إذا زالت الشمس دخل الوقتان الظهر والعصر فإذا غابت الشمس دخل الوقتان المغرب والعشاء الآخرة.

From Zurarah, from Abu Ja'far (peace be upon him) who said: When the sun passes its zenith, the times for both Zuhr and Asr begin, and when the sun sets, the times for both Maghrib and Isha begin.

————

Hadith 4693

قال: وقال أبو جعفر (عليه السلام): وقت صلاة الجمعة يوم الجمعة ساعة تزول الشمس، ووقتها في السفر والحضر واحد، وهو من المضيق، وصلاة العصر في يوم الجمعة في وقت الأولى في سائر الأيام.

He said: And Abu Ja'far (peace be upon him) said: The time for Friday prayer on Friday is when the sun passes its zenith, and its timing during travel and residence is the same, and it is among the restricted times, and Asr prayer on Friday is at the time of the First prayer (Zuhr) on other days.

————

Hadith 4694

قال: وقال الصادق (عليه السلام): لا يفوت الصلاة من أراد الصلاة، لا تفوت صلاة النهار حتى تغرب الشمس، ولا صلاة الليل حتى يطلع الفجر، وذلك للمضطر والعليل والناسي.

He said: And Al-Sadiq (peace be upon him) said: Prayer is not missed by one who intends to pray, the day prayers are not missed until sunset, and the night prayers until dawn breaks, and this applies to the distressed, the sick, and the forgetful.

أقول: المراد بصلاة الليل مجموع الفرض والنافلة، وهو مجمل يأتي تفصيله إن شاء الله.

I (Hurr Amili) say: What is meant by Salat al-Layl is the combination of obligatory and supererogatory prayers, and this is a summary that will be detailed later, insha'Allah.

————

Hadith 4695

عن زرارة قال: قلت: لأبي جعفر (عليه السلام): بين الظهر والعصر حد معروف؟ فقال: لا.

From Zurarah who said: I asked Abu Ja'far (peace be upon him): Is there a known boundary between Zuhr and Asr? He said: No.

Hadith 4696

عن عبيد بن زرارة قال: سألت أبا عبد الله (عليه السلام) عن وقت الظهر والعصر، فقال: إذا زالت الشمس دخل وقت الظهر والعصر جميعا، إلا أن هذه قبل هذه، ثم أنت في وقت منهما جميعا حتى تغيب الشمس.

From Ubayd ibn Zurarah who said: I asked Abu Abdullah (peace be upon him) about the time of Zuhr and Asr, and he said: When the sun passes its zenith, the time for both Zuhr and Asr begins, except that this comes before that, and you remain in the time for both until the sun sets.

Hadith 4697

عن زرارة، عن (أبي جعفر (عليه السلام) قال: صلى رسول الله (صلى الله عليه وآله) بالناس الظهر والعصر حين زالت الشمس في جماعة من غير علة.

From Zurarah, from Abu Ja'far (peace be upon him) who said: The Messenger of Allah (peace be upon him and his family) prayed Zuhr and Asr with the people when the sun passed its zenith in congregation without any specific reason.

Hadith 4698

عن أبي عبد الله (عليه السلام) قال: إذا زالت الشمس فقد دخل وقت الظهر حتى يمضي مقدار ما يصلي المصلي أربع ركعات، فإذا مضى ذلك فقد دخل وقت الظهر والعصر حتى يبقى من الشمس مقدار ما يصلي المصلي أربع ركعات، فإذا بقي مقدار ذلك فقد خرج وقت الظهر، وبقي وقت العصر حتى تغيب الشمس.

From Abu Abdullah (peace be upon him) who said: When the sun passes its zenith, the time for Zuhr begins until the duration it takes to pray four rak'ahs passes, and when that passes, the time for both Zuhr and Asr begins until there remains of the sun the duration it takes to pray four rak'ahs, and when that much remains, the time for Zuhr ends, and the time for Asr remains until sunset.

Hadith 4699

عن الصباح بن سيابة، عن أبي عبد الله (عليه السلام) قال: إذا زالت الشمس فقد دخل وقت الصلاتين.

From Al-Sabah bin Siyabah, from Abu Abdullah (peace be upon him) who said: When the sun passes its zenith, the time for both prayers has begun.

Hadith 4700

عن سفيان بن السمط، عن أبي عبد الله (عليه السلام) قال: إذا زالت الشمس فقد دخل وقت الصلاتين.

From Sufyan bin al-Simt, from Abu Abdullah (peace be upon him) who said: When the sun passes its zenith, the time for both prayers has begun.

Hadith 4701

عن العبد الصالح (عليه السلام) قال: سمعته يقول: إذا زالت الشمس فقد دخل وقت الصلاتين.

From Al-Abd Al-Salih (peace be upon him) who said: I heard him say: When the sun passes its zenith, the time for both prayers has begun.

Hadith 4702

عن مالك الجهني قال: سألت أبا عبد الله (عليه السلام) عن وقت الظهر؟ فقال: إذا زالت الشمس فقد دخل وقت الصلاتين.

From Malik Al-Juhani who said: I asked Abu Abdullah (peace be upon him) about the time of Zuhr prayer? He said: When the sun passes its zenith, the time for both prayers has begun.

Hadith 4703

عن معاوية بن وهب قال: سألته عن رجل صلى الظهر حين زالت الشمس قال: لا بأس به.

From Mu'awiyah bin Wahb who said: I asked him about a man who prayed Zuhr when the sun passed its zenith, he said: There is no problem with that.

Hadith 4704

عن محمد بن مسلم، عن أحدهما (عليهما السلام)، في الرجل يريد الحاجة أو النوم حين تزول الشمس فجعل يصلي الأولى حينئذ، قال: لا بأس به.

From Muhammad bin Muslim, from one of them (peace be upon them), regarding a man who wants to attend to a need or sleep when the sun passes its zenith and thus performs the first prayer then, he said: There is no problem with that.

Hadith 4705

عن أبي عبد الله (عليه السلام) قال: قلت: العصر، متى أصليها إذا كنت في غير سفر؟ قال: على قدر ثلثي قدم بعد الظهر.

From Abu Abdullah (peace be upon him), I said: Asr prayer, when should I pray it when not traveling? He said: After Zuhr by the measure of two-thirds of a qadam (* foot).

Translator: * A unit of measurement sometimes used metaphorically to indicate a brief interval.

Hadith 4706

عن معاوية بن ميسرة قال: قلت لأبي عبد الله (عليه السلام): إذا زالت الشمس في طول النهار، للرجل أن يصلي الظهر والعصر؟ قال: نعم، وما أحب أن يفعل ذلك كل يوم.

From Mu'awiyah bin Maysarah who said: I said to Abu Abdullah (peace be upon him): When the sun passes its zenith during the long day, can a man pray Zuhr and Asr? He said: Yes, but I do not like him to do that every day.

Hadith 4707

عن أبي عبد الله (عليه السلام)، قال: قلت له: إني صليت الظهر في يوم غيم فانجلت، فوجدتني صليت حين زال النهار؟ قال: فقال: لا تعد، ولا تعد.

Abu Abdullah (peace be upon him) was asked: I prayed Zuhr on a cloudy day then it cleared up, and I found I had prayed right when the sun had passed its zenith? He said: Do not repeat it, do not repeat it.

أقول: النهي عن الإعادة يدل على دخول الوقت، والنهي عن العود لكونه ترك النافلة، أو لكونه صلى مع الشك في الوقت.

I (Hurr Amili) say: The prohibition against repeating indicates the time had entered, and the prohibition against returning is either because he left the supererogatory prayer or because he prayed while doubting the time.

Hadith 4708

عن أبي الحسن (عليه السلام)، أنه قال في الرجل يؤخر الظهر حتى يدخل وقت العصر: أنه يبدأ بالعصر ثم يصلي الظهر.

From Abu Al-Hasan (peace be upon him), he said regarding a man who delays Zuhr until Asr time enters: He should start with Asr then pray Zuhr.

Shaykh Hurr Amili: The Shaykh interpreted it as the constriction of the time of Asr based on what has passed and will come.

Translator: He delays Zuhr so much that only enough time remains to pray four rak'ahs before sunset.

Hadith 4709

عن الحلبي - في حديث - قال: سألته عن رجل نسي الأولى والعصر جميعا ثم ذكر ذلك عند غروب الشمس؟ فقال: إن كان في وقت لا يخاف فوت إحداهما فليصل الظهر ثم ليصل العصر، وإن هو خاف أن تفوته فليبدأ بالعصر ولا يؤخرها فتفوته فيكون قد فاتتاه جميعا، ولكن يصلي العصر فيما قد بقي من

وقتها، ثم ليصل الأولى بعد ذلك على أثرها.

From Al-Halabi - in a hadith - he said: I asked him about a man who forgot both the First (Zuhr) and Asr prayers then remembered at sunset? He said: If there is time where he does not fear missing either of them, he should pray Zuhr then Asr. If he fears missing it, he should start with Asr and not delay it so both are missed, but pray Asr in its remaining time, then pray the first one right after it.

Hadith 4710

عن علي بن رئاب قال: سمعت عبيد بن زرارة يقول لأبي عبد الله (عليه السلام): يكون أصحابنا مجتمعين في منزل الرجل منا، فيقوم بعضنا يصلي الظهر، وبعضنا يصلي العصر، وذلك كله في وقت الظهر؟ قال: لا بأس الامر واسع بحمد الله ونعمته.

Ali ibn Ri'ab said: I heard Ubayd ibn Zurarah say to Abu Abdullah (peace be upon him): Our companions gather in one of our homes, some pray Zuhr while others pray Asr, all during Zuhr time? He said: No problem, the matter is flexible by Allah's praise and blessing.

Hadith 4711

عن إسماعيل بن مهران قال: كتبت إلى الرضا (عليه السلام): ذكر أصحابنا أنه إذا زالت الشمس فقد دخل وقت الظهر والعصر، وإذا غربت دخل وقت المغرب والعشاء الآخرة، إلا أن هذه قبل هذه في السفر والحضر، وإن وقت المغرب إلى ربع الليل. فكتب: كذلك الوقت، غير أن وقت المغرب ضيق.

Isma'il ibn Mihran said: I wrote to Al-Ridha (peace be upon him): Our companions mentioned that when the sun passes its zenith, the time for both Zuhr and Asr enters, and when it sets the time for Maghrib and Isha enters, except this comes before that whether traveling or resident, and Maghrib time is until a quarter of the night. He wrote back: The timing is like that, except Maghrib time is narrow.

Translator: The window of time for performing the Maghrib prayer is relatively short compared to the other prayers. The time for Maghrib prayer begins after the sun sets (when redness disappears from the east) and lasts until a quarter of the night, suggesting that Maghrib should be prayed early within this time frame and should not be delayed without a valid reason. This is in contrast to the times for Fajr, Dhuhr, Asr, and Isha prayers, which have more flexibility in their timings.

Hadith 4712

عن عبيد بن زرارة، عن أبي عبد الله (عليه السلام) قال: إذا زالت الشمس فقد دخل وقت الصلاتين إلا أن هذه قبل هذه.

From Ubayd ibn Zurarah, from Abu Abdullah (peace be upon him) who said:

When the sun passes its zenith, the time for both prayers enters except this comes before that.

———

Hadith 4713

عن البرقي، عن القاسم مثله، وفيه: دخل وقت الظهر والعصر جميعا، وزاد: ثم أنت في وقت منهما جميعا حتى تغيب الشمس.

From Al-Barqi, from Al-Qasim similar to it, adding: The time for both Zuhr and Asr enters together, and you remain in time for both until sunset.

———

Hadith 4714

عن عبيد بن زرارة قال: كنت أنا ونفر من أصحابنا مترافقين فيهم ميسر فيما بين مكة والمدينة، فارتحلنا ونحن نشك في الزوال، فقال: بعضنا لبعض: فامشوا بنا قليلا حتى نتيقن الزوال ثم نصلي، ففعلنا، فما مشينا إلا قليلا حتى عرض لنا قطار أبي عبد الله (عليه السلام)، فقلت: أتى القطار، فرأيت محمد بن إسماعيل، فقلت له: صليتم؟ فقال لي أمرنا جدي فصلينا الظهر والعصر جميعا ثم ارتحلنا، فذهبت إلى أصحابي فأعلمتهم ذلك.

From Ubayd ibn Zurara, who said: I and a group of our companions were traveling together, among them Maysar, between Makkah and Madinah. We set out while we were uncertain whether the sun had reached its zenith. Some of us said to the others: Let us walk a little until we are certain of the zenith, and then we will pray. So we did that, and we had walked only a short distance when the caravan of Abu Abdullah (peace be upon him) came across our path. I said: The caravan has come! I then saw Muhammad ibn Ismail, and I said to him: Have you prayed? He said to me: Our grandfather ordered us, so we prayed Zuhr and Asr together, then we set out. So I went to my companions and informed them of that.

———

CHAPTER 5

Recommendation Of Delaying Supererogatory Prayers Of Zuhr And Asr From Their First Time Until Completing Their Supererogatory Prayers

[Hadith 4715 to 4728]

Hadith 4715

عن ومنصور بن حازم قال: كنا نقيس الشمس بالمدينة بالذراع، فقال أبو عبد الله (عليه السلام): ألا أنبئكم بأبين من هذا، إذا زالت الشمس فقد دخل وقت الظهر، إلا أن بين يديها سبحة، وذلك إليك إن شئت طولت وإن شئت قصرت.

From Mansur ibn Hazim who said: We used to measure the sun in Madinah by the length of a forearm, so Abu Abdullah (peace be upon him) said: Shall I not inform you of something clearer than this? When the sun passes its zenith, the time of Zuhr has entered, except that before it there is a voluntary prayer, and that is up to you - if you wish you may lengthen it and if you wish you may shorten it.

Hadith 4716

عن ومنصور بن حازم، مثله، وفيه: إليك، فإن أنت خففت سبحتك فحين تفرغ من سبحتك، وإن طولت فحين تفرغ من سبحتك.

From Mansur bin Hazim, similar to above, adding: It's up to you - if you shorten your optional prayer then when you finish it, and if you lengthen it then when you finish it.

Hadith 4717

عن ذريح المحاربي قال: قلت لأبي عبد الله (عليه السلام): متى أصلي الظهر؟ فقال: صل الزوال ثمانية، ثم صل الظهر، ثم صل سبحتك، طالت أو قصرت، ثم صل العصر.

From Dharih Al-Muharibi who said: I asked Abu Abdullah (peace be upon him): When should I pray Zuhr? He said: Pray eight units at noon, then pray Zuhr, then pray your optional prayer - whether long or short, then pray Asr.

Hadith 4718

عن مسمع بن عبد الملك قال: إذا صليت الظهر فقد دخل وقت العصر إلا أن بين يديها سبحة، فذلك إليك إن شئت طولت وإن شئت قصرت.

From Misma' bin Abdul Malik who said: When you pray Zuhr, the time for Asr has entered except there is a optional prayer before it, and that is up to you - if you wish make it long or if you wish make it short.

Hadith 4719

عن أبي عبد الله (عليه السلام) قال: إذا زالت الشمس فقد دخل وقت الظهر إلا أن بين يديها سبحة، وذلك إليك إن شئت طولت وإن شئت قصرت.

From Abu Abdullah (peace be upon him) who said: When the sun passes its zenith, the time for the Zuhr prayer has entered, except that before it there is a voluntary prayer, and that is up to you - if you wish you may lengthen it, and if you wish you may shorten it.

Hadith 4720

عن يزيد بن خليفة قال: قلت لأبي عبد الله (عليه السلام): إن عمر بن حنظلة أتانا عنك بوقت، فقال أبو عبد الله (عليه السلام): إذا لا يكذب علينا،

From Yazid bin Khalifah who said: I said to Abu Abdullah (peace be upon him): Umar bin Handhalah came to us from you with timing. Abu Abdullah (peace be upon him) said: Then he does not lie about us.

قلت: ذكر أنك قلت: إن أول صلاة افترضها الله على نبيه الظهر. وهو قول الله عز وجل: (أقم الصلاة لدلوك الشمس) فإذا زالت الشمس لم يمنعك إلا سبحتك، ثم لا تزال في وقت إلى أن يصير الظل قامة وهو آخر الوقت، فإذا صار الظل قامة دخل وقت العصر، فلم تزل في وقت العصر حتى يصير الظل قامتين، وذلك المساء؟ فقال: صدق.

I said: It has been mentioned that you said: The first prayer that Allah made obligatory upon His Prophet was the Zuhr prayer, and it is the saying of Allah, the Mighty and Glorious: "Establish the prayer from the declining of the sun" [Quran, 17:78], so when the sun passes its zenith, nothing prevents you except your voluntary prayer, and you remain within its time until the shadow reaches one qama (a person's height), and that is the last of its time. When the shadow reaches one qama, the time of Asr enters, and you remain within the time of Asr until the shadow reaches two qamas, and that is the evening. He (the Imam) said: You have spoken the truth.

Hadith 4721

عن مالك الجهني، أنه سأل أبا عبد الله (عليه السلام) عن وقت الظهر؟ فقال: إذا زالت الشمس فقد دخل وقت الصلاتين، فإذا فرغت من سبحتك فصل الظهر متى ما بدا لك.

From Malik al-Juhani, that he asked Abu Abdullah (peace be upon him) about the time of Zuhr. He said: When the sun passes its zenith, the time for both prayers has entered. So when you finish your voluntary prayer, pray the noon prayer whenever you wish.

Hadith 4722

عن عيسى بن أبي منصور قال: قال لي أبو عبد الله (عليه السلام): إذا زالت الشمس فصليت سبحتك فقد دخل وقت الظهر.

From Isa ibn Abi Mansur, who said: Abu Abdullah (peace be upon him) said to me: When the sun passes its zenith and you have performed your voluntary prayers, the time of the Zuhr prayer has entered.

Hadith 4723

عن عمر بن حنظلة قال: كنت أقيس الشمس عند أبي عبد الله (عليه السلام) فقال: يا عمر، ألا أنبئك بأبين من هذا؟ قال: قلت: بلى جعلت فداك. قال: إذا زالت الشمس فقد وقع وقت الظهر إلا أن بين يديها سبحة. وذلك إليك، فإن أنت خففت فحين تفرغ من سبحتك، وإن طولت فحين تفرغ من سبحتك.

From Umar ibn Hanzala, who said: I was measuring the sun in the presence of Abu Abdullah (peace be upon him), and he said: O Umar, shall I not inform you of something more clear than this? He said: I replied: Indeed, may I be your ransom. He said: When the sun passes its zenith, the time of Zuhr has arrived, except that before it there is a voluntary prayer, and that is up to you. If you make it brief, then when you finish your voluntary prayer, and if you make it long, then when you finish your voluntary prayer.

Hadith 4724

عن زرارة قال: قلت لأبي عبد الله (عليه السلام): أصوم فلا أقيل حتى تزول الشمس، فإذا زالت الشمس صليت نوافلي ثم صليت الظهر، ثم صليت نوافلي، ثم صليت العصر، ثم نمت، وذلك قبل أن يصلي الناس، فقال: يا زرارة إذا زالت الشمس فقد دخل الوقت، ولكني أكره لك أن تتخذه وقتا دائما.

From Zurarah, who said: I said to Abu Abdullah (peace be upon him): I fast and do not take a midday nap until the sun passes its zenith. When the sun passes its zenith, I pray my supererogatory prayers, then I pray Zuhr, then I pray my supererogatory prayers, then I pray Asr, then I sleep, and this is before the people pray. He said: O Zurarah, when the sun passes its zenith, the time has indeed entered, but I dislike for you to make it a permanent and constant practice.

Hadith 4725

عن سماعة بن مهران قال: قال لي أبو عبد الله (عليه السلام): إذا زالت الشمس فصل ثمان ركعات، ثم صل الفريضة أربعا. فإذا فرغت من سبحتك قصرت أو طولت فصل العصر.

From Samaah ibn Mihran who said: Abu Abdullah (peace be upon him) said to me: When the sun passes its zenith, pray eight rak'ahs, then pray the obligatory four rak'ahs, and when you have finished your supererogatory prayers, whether you have shortened or lengthened them, then pray the Asr prayer.

Hadith 4726

عن أبي عبد الله (عليه السلام) قال: سأل أبا عبد الله (عليه السلام) ناس وأنا حاضر، فقال: إذا زالت الشمس فهو وقت لا يحبسك منه إلا سبحتك تطيلها أو تقصرها.

From Abu Abdullah (peace be upon him) that some people asked Abu Abdullah (peace be upon him) while I was present, and he said: When the sun passes its zenith, that is the time, and nothing should delay you from it except your optional prayers, whether you lengthen them or shorten them.

Hadith 4727

عن محمد بن أحمد بن يحيى قال: كتب بعض أصحابنا إلى أبي الحسن (عليه السلام): روي عن آبائك القدم والقدمين والأربع، والقامة والقامتين، وظل مثلك، والذراع والذراعين؟ فكتب (عليه السلام): لا القدم ولا القدمين،

From Muhammad bin Ahmad bin Yahya who said: Some of our companions wrote to Abu al-Hasan (peace be upon him): It is narrated from your forefathers about one foot, two feet, four feet, one height, two heights, shadow equal to your height, one cubit and two cubits? He wrote back: Not one foot or two feet.

إذا زالت الشمس فقد دخل وقت الصلاة وبين يديها سبحة وهي ثمان ركعات، فإن شئت طولت، وإن شئت قصرت، ثم صل الظهر، فإذا فرغت كان بين الظهر والعصر سبحة، وهي ثماني ركعات، إن شئت طولت وإن شئت قصرت، ثم صل العصر.

When the sun passes the zenith, the prayer time has begun and before it are voluntary prayers of eight rak'ahs - you can make them long or short, then pray Zuhr. When you finish there are voluntary prayers between Zuhr and Asr of eight rak'ahs - you can make them long or short, then pray Asr.

Shaykh Hurr Amili: The Shaykh said: He only negated the foot and the two feet so that it would not be thought that this is a time other than which is not permissible.

Hadith 4728

عن علي بن جعفر، عن أخيه موسى بن جعفر (عليهما السلام) قال: سألته عن وقت الظهر؟ قال: نعم، إذا زالت الشمس فقد دخل وقتها، فصل إذا شئت بعد أن تفرغ من سبحتك.

From Ali ibn Ja'far, from his brother Musa ibn Ja'far (peace be upon them both), he said: I asked him about the time of Zuhr. He said: Yes, when the sun passes its zenith, its time has entered, so pray whenever you wish after you have finished your voluntary prayers.

وسألته عن وقت العصر متى هو؟ قال: إذا زالت الشمس قدمين صليت الظهر، والسبحة بعد الظهر، فصل العصر إذا شئت.

And I asked him about the time of Asr, when is it? He said: When the sun has moved two feet past the zenith, you pray Zuhr and the supererogatory prayers after Zuhr, then pray Asr whenever you wish.

CHAPTER 6

Recommendation For Travelers To Pray Zuhr And Asr At The Beginning Of Their Time, And Permissibility Of Slightly Delaying Zuhr For Combining Prayers

[Hadith 4729 to 4730]

Hadith 4729

عن زرارة، عن أبي جعفر (عليه السلام) قال: صلاة المسافر حين تزول الشمس، لأنه ليس قبلها في السفر صلاة. وإن شاء أخرها إلى وقت الظهر في الحضر. غير أن أفضل ذلك أن يصليها في أول وقتها حين تزول.

From Zurarah, from Abu Ja'far (peace be upon him), who said: The prayer of the traveler begins when the sun passes its zenith, for there is no prayer before that time during travel. And if he wishes, he may delay it until the time of the noon prayer as observed by one in residence. However, the most virtuous of that is to perform it at the first of its time when the sun passes its zenith.

Hadith 4730

وبهذا الاسناد قال: سمعت أبا جعفر (عليه السلام) يقول: إذا كنت مسافرا لم تبال أن تؤخر الظهر حتى يدخل وقت العصر فتصلي الظهر ثم تصلي العصر، وكذلك المغرب والعشاء الآخرة، تؤخر المغرب حتى تصليها في آخر وقتها وركعتين بعدها ثم تصلي العشاء.

Through the same chain of narration, he said: I heard Abu Ja'far (peace be upon him) saying: When you are traveling, there is no harm in delaying Zuhr until the time of Asr enters, then pray Zuhr followed by Asr. The same applies to Maghrib and Isha - you may delay Maghrib until its last time, pray it with two units after it, then pray Isha.

CHAPTER 7

Permissibility Of Prayer At The Beginning, Middle, And End Of Its Time, And The Dislike Of Delaying Without Excuse

[Hadith 4731 to 4740]

Hadith 4731

عن أبي جعفر (عليه السلام) قال: إن من الأشياء أشياء موسعة وأشياء مضيقة، فالصلوات مما، وسع فيه، تقدم مرة وتؤخر أخرى، والجمعة مما ضيق فيها، فإن وقتها يوم الجمعة ساعة تزول، ووقت العصر فيها وقت الظهر في غيرها.

Abu Ja'far (peace be upon him) said: Among things there are things that have been given latitude and things that have been restricted. The prayers are among those that have been given latitude, being performed early at one time and delayed at another. The Friday prayer is among those that have been restricted, for its time is on Friday at the moment the sun passes the zenith, and the time of the Asr prayer on that day is the same as the time of the Zuhr prayer on other days.

Hadith 4732

عن زرارة قال: كنت قاعدا عند أبي عبد الله (عليه السلام) أنا وحمران بن أعين، فقال له حمران: ما تقول فيما يقوله زرارة وقد خالفته فيه؟ فقال أبو عبد الله (عليه السلام): ما هو؟ قال: يزعم أن مواقيت الصلاة كانت مفوضة إلى رسول الله (صلى الله عليه وآله) هو الذي وضعها،

From Zurarah who said: I was sitting with Abu Abdullah (peace be upon him) along with Hamran bin Ayan. Hamran said to him: What do you say about what Zurarah says, as I have disagreed with him about it? Abu Abdullah (peace be upon him) said: What is it? He said: He claims that the prayer times were delegated to the Messenger of Allah (peace be upon him and his family), and he is the one who set them.

فقال أبو عبد الله (عليه السلام): فما تقول أنت؟ قلت: إن جبرئيل أتاه في اليوم الأول بالوقت الأول، وفي اليوم الأخير بالوقت الأخير، ثم قال جبرئيل (عليه السلام): ما بينهما وقت، فقال أبو عبد الله (عليه السلام): يا حمران فإن زرارة يقول: إن جبرئيل إنما جاء مشيرا على رسول الله (صلى الله عليه وآله)، وصدق زرارة، إنما جعل الله ذلك إلى محمد (صلى الله عليه وآله) فوضعه، وأشار جبرئيل عليه به.

Abu Abdullah (peace be upon him) said: So what do you say? I said: Jibreel came to him on the first day with the first time, and on the last day with the last time, then Jibreel (peace be upon him) said: What is between them is time. Abu Abdullah (peace be upon him) said: O Hamran, Zurarah says that Jibreel only came to advise the Messenger of Allah (peace be upon him and his family), and Zurarah is truthful. Indeed Allah gave this authority to Muhammad (peace be upon him and his family) to establish, and Jibreel advised him about it.

Hadith 4733

عن أبي عبد الله (عليه السلام)، قال: سأله إنسان وأنا حاضر، فقال: ربما دخلت المسجد وبعض أصحابنا يصلون العصر وبعضهم يصلي الظهر؟ فقال: أنا أمرتهم بهذا، لو صلوا على وقت واحد عرفوا فأخذوا برقابهم.

From Abu Abdullah (peace be upon him), a person asked him while I was present, saying: Sometimes I enter the mosque and some of our companions are praying Asr while others are praying Zuhr? He said: I ordered them to do this. If they had prayed at one time, they would have been recognized and seized by their necks.

Hadith 4734

عن زرارة والفضيل قالا: قلنا لأبي جعفر (عليه السلام): أرأيت قول الله عز وجل: (إن الصلاة كانت على المؤمنين كتابا موقوتا)، قال: يعني كتابا مفروضا، وليس يعني وقت فوتها، إن جاز ذلك الوقت ثم صلاها لم تكن صلاة مؤداة، لو كان ذلك كذلك لهلك سليمان بن داود (عليه السلام) حين صلاها بغير وقتها، ولكنه متى ما ذكرها صلاها.

From Zurarah and Al-Fadeel who said: We said to Abu Ja'far (peace be upon him): What do you say about Allah's words, the Mighty and Majestic: Indeed, prayer has been decreed upon the believers a decree of specified times [Quran, 4:103]. He said: It means a prescribed decree, and it does not mean the time of missing it. If that time passes and then one prays it, it would not be a prayer performed in time. If it were like that, Sulayman bin Dawud (peace be upon him) would have been ruined when he prayed it outside its time, but rather whenever he remembered it, he prayed it.

Translator: According to tradition, there was an instance when Solomon was preoccupied with his horses and missed the prescribed time for prayer. When he realized this, he prayed the missed prayer, and it was accepted by Allah. The Imam argues that if missing the prescribed time rendered the prayer invalid, then Solomon would have been "ruined" or sinful for praying outside the specified time. However, since Solomon's prayer was accepted, it shows that the prayer can still be valid even if performed after its prescribed time, as long as there is a valid excuse, and one remembers and performs it as soon as possible.

Hadith 4735

عن زرارة، عن أبي جعفر (عليه السلام) في قول الله تعالى (إن الصلاة كانت على المؤمنين كتابا موقوتا) قال: موجبا إنما يعني بذلك وجوبها على المؤمنين، ولو كان كما يقولون لهلك سليمان بن داود حين أخر الصلاة حتى توارت بالحجاب، لأنه لو صلاها قبل أن تغيب كان وقتا، وليس صلاة أطول وقتا من العصر.

From Zurarah, from Abu Ja'far (peace be upon him) regarding the words of Allah the Exalted "Indeed, prayer has been decreed upon the believers a decree of specified times" [Quran, 4:103], he said: It means obligatory, referring to its obligation upon the believers. If it were as they say, Sulayman bin Dawud would have been doomed when he delayed the prayer until it disappeared behind the veil, because if he had prayed it before it set it would have been within time. And there is no prayer that has a longer time than Asr.

Translator: See comment on previous Hadith 4734.

Hadith 4736

عن زرارة، عن أبي عبد الله (عليه السلام) قال: صلى رسول الله (صلى الله عليه وآله) بالناس الظهر والعصر حين زالت الشمس في جماعة من غير علة، وصلى بهم المغرب والعشاء الآخرة قبل سقوط الشفق من غير علة في جماعة، وإنما فعل ذلك رسول الله (صلى الله عليه وآله) ليتسع الوقت على أمته.

From Zurarah, from Abu Abdullah: The Messenger of Allah prayed Zuhr and Asr in congregation when the sun passed the zenith without any excuse, and prayed Maghrib and Isha before the twilight disappeared without excuse in congregation. The Messenger did this to expand the time for his nation.

Hadith 4737

عن أبي عبد الله (عليه السلام) قال: إنا لنقدم ونؤخر، وليس كما يقال: من أخطأ وقت الصلاة، فقد هلك، وإنما الرخصة للناسي والمريض والمدنف والمسافر والنائم في تأخيرها.

From Abu Abdullah: We pray early and late. It's not as they say that whoever misses prayer time has perished. The allowance for delay is for the forgetful, sick, severely ill, traveler, and sleeper.

Hadith 4738

عن عبيد بن زرارة، عن أبي عبد الله (عليه السلام)، قال: قلت له: يكون أصحابنا في المكان مجتمعين فيقوم بعضهم يصلي الظهر، وبعضهم يصلي العصر، قال: (كل واسع).

From Ubayd ibn Zurarah, from Abu Abdullah (peace be upon him), who said: I said to him: Our companions gather in a place, and some of them stand to pray Zuhr while others pray Asr. He said: All of it is permissible.

Hadith 4739

عن زرارة قال: قلت لأبي عبد الله (عليه السلام): الرجلان يصليان في وقت واحد، وأحدهما يعجل العصر، والاخر يؤخر الظهر؟ قال: لا بأس.

From Zurarah who said: I said to Abu Abdullah (peace be upon him): Two men pray at one time, one of them hastens to pray Asr while the other delays Zuhr? He said: There is no problem.

Hadith 4740

عن محمد بن مسلم قال: ربما دخلت على أبي جعفر (عليه السلام) وقد صليت الظهر والعصر فيقول: صليت الظهر؟ فأقول: نعم، والعصر، فيقول: ما صليت الظهر، فيقوم مترسلا غير مستعجل فيغتسل أو يتوضأ، ثم يصلي الظهر ثم يصلي العصر، وربما دخلت عليه ولم أصل الظهر (فيقول: صليت الظهر؟ فأقول: لا) فيقول: قد صليت الظهر والعصر.

From Muhammad bin Muslim who said: Sometimes I would enter upon Abu Ja'far (peace be upon him) after I had prayed Zuhr and Asr. He would ask: Have you prayed Zuhr? I would say: Yes, and Asr. He would say: You have not prayed Zuhr (*). Then he would stand unhurriedly without haste, perform ghusl or wudu, then pray Zuhr followed by Asr. And sometimes I would enter upon him when I had not prayed Zuhr. He would ask: Have you prayed Zuhr? I would say: No. He would say: I have already prayed Zuhr and Asr.

Translator: * Demonstrates the Imam's divinely granted knowledge and his ability to know the true status of a person's prayer.

CHAPTER 8

Time Of Merit For Zuhr And Asr And Their Supererogatory Prayers

[Hadith 4741 to 4775]

Hadith 4741, 4742

عن أبي جعفر وأبي عبد الله (عليهما السلام) أنهما قالا: وقت الظهر بعد الزوال قدمان، ووقت العصر بعد ذلك قدمان.

From Abu Ja'far and Abu Abdullah (peace be upon them both) that they said: The time of Zuhr is two foot-lengths (qadamayn) after the sun's decline from its zenith, and the time of Asr is two foot-lengths after that.

———

Hadith 4743, 4744

عن زرارة، عن أبي جعفر (عليه السلام)، قال: سألته عن وقت الظهر؟ فقال: ذراع من زوال الشمس، ووقت العصر ذراعا من وقت الظهر، فذاك أربعة أقدام من زوال الشمس،

From Zurarah, from Abu Ja'far (peace be upon him), he said: I asked him about the time of Zuhr? He said: One cubit (dira) from the sun's zenith, and the time of Asr is one cubit from the time of Zuhr, so that is four foot-lengths (aqdam) from the sun's zenith.

ثم قال: إن حائط مسجد رسول الله (صلى الله عليه وآله) كان قامة، وكان إذا مضى منه ذراع صلى الظهر، وإذا مضى منه ذراعان صلى العصر،

Then he said: The wall of the Prophet's mosque (peace be upon him and his family) was the height of a man (qama). When one cubit (dira) had passed from it [its shadow], he prayed Zuhr, and when two cubits had passed from it, he prayed Asr.

ثم قال: أتدري لم جعل الذراع والذرعان؟ قلت: لم جعل ذلك؟ قال: لمكان النافلة، لك أن تتنفل من زوال الشمس إلى أن يمضي ذراع، فإذا بلغ فيؤك ذراعا بدأت بالفريضة وتركت النافلة. وإذا بلغ فيؤك ذراعين بدأت بالفريضة وتركت النافلة.

Then he said: Do you know why the one cubit and two cubits were designated? I said: Why was that designated? He said: Because of the supererogatory prayer (Nafila). You may perform supererogatory prayers from the sun's zenith until one cubit passes. So when your shadow reaches one cubit, begin the obligatory prayer and leave the voluntary. And when your shadow reaches two cubits, begin the obligatory prayer and leave the supererogatory prayer.

Qama (Stature/Height): This represents the height of an average man, traditionally estimated at approximately 170-175 cm. In legal terms, one Qama is composed of 7 Aqdam (foot-lengths) or 4 Adru (cubits).

Dira (Cubit): Forearm length - the length from the elbow to the tip of the middle finger, roughly 45-50 cm. The hadith establishes that one Dira is 1/4 of a Qama.

Aqdam (Foot-Length): These are human foot-lengths. The hadith explicitly equates two Adru (cubits) with four Aqdam (foot-lengths), confirming that 1 cubit equals 2 foot-lengths in this specific measurement system.

Hadith 4745

عن معاوية بن وهب، عن أبي عبد الله (عليه السلام) أنه قال: كان المؤذن يأتي النبي (صلى الله عليه وآله) في الحر في صلاة الظهر فيقول له رسول الله (صلى الله عليه وآله): أبرد أبرد. قال الصدوق: يعني عجل عجل، وأخذ ذلك من البريد.

From Mu'awiyah bin Wahb, from Abu Abdullah (peace be upon him) that he said: The muezzin would come to the Prophet (peace be upon him and his family) in the heat for Zuhr prayer, and the Messenger of Allah (peace be upon him and his family) would say to him: Cool down, cool down (*).

* Al-Saduq said: Meaning hurry, hurry, taking this from "al-barid" (post).

Hadith 4746

عن أبي هريرة قال: قال رسول الله (صلى الله عليه وآله): إذا اشتد الحر فأبردوا بالصلاة، فإن الحر من فيح جهنم.

From Abu Hurayrah who said: The Messenger of Allah (peace be upon him and his family) said: When the heat becomes intense, delay the prayer until it cools, for indeed the intense heat is from the exhalation of Hell.

Translator: Sheikh Saduq interpreted the previous hadith to mean hastening the prayer, while this hadith recommends delaying it in intense heat. Either Sheikh Saduq's interpretation of the term "abrid" is inaccurate or the previous hadith is referring to a different situation or level of heat.

Hadith 4747

عن أبي عبد الله (عليه السلام) - في حديث - قال: كان حائط مسجد رسول الله (صلى الله عليه وآله) قبل أن يظلل قامة، وكان إذا كان الفئ ذراعا وهو قدر مربض عنز صلى الظهر. فإذا كان ضعف ذلك صلى العصر.

From Abu Abdullah (peace be upon him) - in a hadith - he said: The wall of the Messenger of Allah's mosque (peace be upon him and his family) before it was shaded was the height of a man (qama), and when the shadow was one cubit (dira), which is about the size of a goat's resting place, he would pray Zuhr. When it was double that, he would pray Asr.

Hadith 4748

عن صفوان الجمال قال: صليت خلف أبي عبد الله (عليه السلام) عند الزوال، فقلت: بأبي وأمي، وقت العصر؟ فقال: ريثما تستقبل إبلك، فقلت: إذا كنت في غير سفر، فقال: على أقل من قدم ثلثي قدم وقت العصر.

Safwan Al-Jammal said: I prayed behind Abu Abdullah (peace be upon him) at noon time, so I said: May my father and mother be sacrificed for you, what about the time of Asr prayer? He said: As long as it takes your camels to face forward. I asked: What if I'm not traveling? He said: The time of Asr is when the shadow increases by two-thirds of a foot-length (qadam) over a foot-length.

Hadith 4749

عن أبي الحسن (عليه السلام)، قال: سألته عن وقت الظهر والعصر؟ فقال: وقت الظهر إذا زاغت الشمس إلى أن يذهب الظل قامة، ووقت العصر قامة ونصف إلى قامتين.

From Abu Al-Hasan (peace be upon him), he was asked about the time of Zuhr and Asr prayers? He said: The time of Zuhr is when the sun passes its zenith until the shadow becomes the stature of a man (qama), and the time of Asr is from one and a half statures to two statures.

Hadith 4750

عن إسماعيل الجعفي، عن أبي جعفر (عليه السلام) قال: كان رسول الله (صلى الله عليه وآله) إذا كان فئ الجدار ذراعا صلى الظهر، وإذا كان ذراعين صلى العصر. قال: قلت: إن الجدار يختلف، بعضها قصير وبعضها طويل؟ فقال: كان جدار مسجد رسول الله (صلى الله عليه وآله) يومئذ قامة.

Isma'il Al-Ju'fi narrated from Abu Ja'far (peace be upon him) who said: When the shadow of the wall was one cubit (dira), the Messenger of Allah (peace be upon him and his family) would pray Zuhr, and when it was two cubits, he would pray Asr. I said: But walls differ, some are short and some are tall? He said: The wall of the Prophet's mosque at that time was one stature (a man's height).

Hadith 4751

عن إسماعيل بن عبد الخالق قال: سألت أبا عبد الله (عليه السلام) عن وقت الظهر؟ فقال: بعد الزوال بقدم أو نحو ذلك، إلا في يوم الجمعة أو في السفر، فإن وقتها حين تزول. وعنه، عن صفوان، عن ابن مسكان، مثله، إلا أنه قال: حين تزول الشمس.

From Ismail ibn Abd al-Khaliq, who said: I asked Abu Abdullah (peace be upon him) about the time of the Zuhr prayer. He said: After the sun passes the zenith by a foot-length's measure or approximately that, except on Friday or during travel, for in those cases its time begins when the sun passes the zenith. And from him, from Safwan, from Ibn Muskan, similarly, except that he said: when the sun passes the zenith.

Hadith 4752

عن أحمد بن محمد ابن أبي نصر قال: سألته عن وقت صلاة الظهر والعصر؟ فكتب: قامة للظهر وقامة للعصر.

From Ahmad bin Muhammad Ibn Abi Nasr, who said: I asked him about the time of Zuhr and Asr prayers? He wrote: One stature (a man's height) for Zuhr and one stature for Asr.

Hadith 4753

عن زرارة قال: سألت أبا عبد الله (عليه السلام) عن وقت الصلاة الظهر في القيظ؟ فلم يجبني، فلما أن كان بعد ذلك قال لعمر بن سعيد بن هلال: إن زرارة سألني عن وقت صلاة الظهر في القيظ فلم أخبره فحرجت من ذلك فاقرأه مني السلام وقل له: إذا كان ظلك مثلك فصل الظهر. وإذا كان ظلك مثليك فصل العصر.

Zurarah said: I asked Abu Abdullah (peace be upon him) about the time of Zuhr prayer during intense heat? He did not answer me. Later, he said to Umar bin Said bin Hilal: Zurarah asked me about the time of Zuhr prayer during intense heat and I did not inform him, so I felt uncomfortable about that. Give him my greetings and tell him: When your shadow becomes equal to your height, pray Zuhr, and when your shadow becomes twice your height, pray Asr.

Hadith 4754

عن علي بن حنظلة قال: قال لي أبو عبد الله (عليه السلام): القامة والقامتان الذراع والذراعان، في كتاب علي (عليه السلام).

Ali bin Handhalah said: Abu Abdullah (peace be upon him) told me: The one stature (a man's height) and two statures are one cubit (forearm length) and two cubits, according to the book of Ali (peace be upon him).

Hadith 4755

عن علي بن أبي حمزة قال: سمعت أبا عبد الله (عليه السلام) يقول: القامة هي الذراع.

From Ali bin Abi Hamza who said: I heard Abu Abdullah (peace be upon him) saying: The qama (of the riding saddle) is the forearm.

Hadith 4756

عن أبي عبد الله (عليه السلام)، قال: قال له أبو بصير: كم القامة؟ قال: فقال: ذراع، إن قامة رحل رسول الله (صلى الله عليه وآله) كانت ذراعا.

From Abu Abdullah (peace be upon him), Abu Basir asked him: How long is the qama (shadow measurement)? He replied: One cubit, indeed the qama of the Prophet's (peace be upon him and his family) riding saddle was one cubit.

———

Hadith 4757

عن سعيد الأعرج عن أبي عبد الله (عليه السلام)، قال: سألته عن وقت الظهر أهو إذا زالت الشمس؟ فقال: بعد الزوال بقدم أو نحو ذلك، إلا في السفر أو يوم الجمعة، فإن وقتها إذا زالت.

From Sa'id Al-A'raj from Abu Abdullah (peace be upon him), he said: I asked him about the time of Zuhr prayer, is it when the sun passes the zenith? He said: After the decline by a foot-length or thereabouts, except during travel or on Friday, for then its time is when it passes the zenith.

———

Hadith 4758

عن أبي عبد الله (عليه السلام)، قال: سألته عن صلاة الظهر؟ فقال: إذا كان الفئ ذراعا، (قلت: ذراعا من أي شئ؟ قال: ذراعا من فيئك، قلت فالعصر؟ قال: الشطر من ذلك، قلت: هذا شبر؟ قال: أوليس شبر كثيرا).

From Abu Abdullah (peace be upon him), he said: I asked him about the Zuhr prayer? He said: When the shadow is one cubit. I asked: A cubit of what? He said: A cubit of your shadow. I asked: And Asr? He said: Half of that. I said: This is a span? He said: Isn't a span plenty?

———

Hadith 4759

عن زرارة، عن أبي عبد الله (عليه السلام) قال: وقت الظهر على ذراع.

From Zurarah, from Abu Abdullah (peace be upon him) he said: The time of Zuhr is at one cubit.

———

Hadith 4760

عن زرارة، عن أبي جعفر (عليه السلام) قال: أتدري لم جعل الذراع والذراعان؟ قلت: لم؟ قال: لمكان الفريضة. لك أن تتنفل من زوال الشمس إلى أن تبلغ ذراعا، فإذا بلغت ذراعا بدأت بالفريضة وتركت النافلة.

From Zurarah, from Abu Ja'far (peace be upon him) he said: Do you know why one cubit (forearm length) and two cubits were set? I said: Why? He said: For the obligatory prayer, you may perform supererogatory prayers from the sun's decline until it reaches one cubit, when it reaches one cubit you start with the obligatory prayer and leave the supererogatory prayer.

Hadith 4761

عن أبي جعفر (عليه السلام) قال: أتدري لم جعل الذراع والذراعان؟ قال: قلت: لم؟ قال: لمكان الفريضة، لئلا يؤخذ من وقت هذه ويدخل في وقت هذه.

From Abu Ja'far (peace be upon him) he said: Do you know why one cubit (forearm length) and two cubits were set? I said: Why? He said: For the obligatory prayer, so that time is not taken from this prayer and entered into the time of that prayer.

Hadith 4762

عن أبي عبد الله (عليه السلام)، قال: سأل أبا عبد الله أناس وأنا حاضر - إلى أن قال - فقال بعض القوم: إنا نصلي الأولى إذا كانت على قدمين، والعصر على أربعة أقدام؟ فقال أبو عبد الله (عليه السلام): النصف من ذلك أحب إلي.

From Abu Abdullah (peace be upon him), he said: Some people asked Abu Abdullah while I was present - until he said - some of them said: We pray the first prayer when it is at two foot-lengths, and Asr at four foot-lengths? Abu Abdullah (peace be upon him) said: Half of that is more beloved to me.

Hadith 4763

عن أبي بصير، عن أبي عبد الله (عليه السلام) قال: الصلاة في الحضر ثماني ركعات إذا زالت الشمس ما بينك وبين أن يذهب ثلثا القامة. فإذا ذهب ثلثا القامة بدأت بالفريضة.

From Abu Basir, from Abu Abdullah (peace be upon him) he said: The prayer in residence is eight rak'ahs when the sun declines between you and when two-thirds of the stature (a man's height) goes, when two-thirds of the stature goes you begin with the obligatory prayer.

Hadith 4764

عن أبي عبد الله (عليه السلام) قال: كان رسول الله (صلى الله عليه وآله) يصلي الظهر على ذراع، والعصر على نحو ذلك.

From Abu Abdullah (peace be upon him) who said: The Messenger of Allah (peace be upon him and his family) would pray Zuhr when the shadow was one cubit (forearm length), and Asr similarly.

Hadith 4765

عن عبيد بن زرارة قال: سألت أبا عبد الله (عليه السلام) عن أفضل وقت الظهر؟ قال: ذراع بعد الزوال، قال: قلت: في الشتاء والصيف سواء؟ قال: نعم.

From Ubayd ibn Zurarah who said: I asked Abu Abdullah (peace be upon him) about the best time for Zuhr prayer? He said: One cubit (forearm length) after zenith. I asked: Is it the same in winter and summer? He said: Yes.

Hadith 4766

عن علي بن حنظلة قال: قال أبو عبد الله (عليه السلام): في كتاب علي (عليه السلام) القامة ذراع، والقامتان الذراعان.

From Ali ibn Handhala who said: Abu Abdullah (peace be upon him) said: In the book of Ali (peace be upon him), one height is one forearm length, and two heights are two forearm lengths.

Hadith 4767

عن زرارة قال: سمعت أبا جعفر (عليه السلام) يقول: كان حائط مسجد رسول الله (صلى الله عليه وآله) قامة، فإذا مضى من فيئه ذراع صلى الظهر، وإذا مضى من فيئه ذراعان صلى العصر. ثم قال: أتدري لم جعل الذراع والذراعان؟ قلت: لا، قال من أجل الفريضة، إذا دخل وقت الذراع والذراعين بدأت بالفريضة وتركت النافلة.

From Zurarah who said: I heard Abu Ja'far (peace be upon him) saying: The wall of the mosque of the Messenger of Allah (peace be upon him and his family) was one stature high, so when its shadow extended one cubit (forearm length) he would pray Zuhr, and when its shadow extended two cubits he would pray Asr. Then he said: Do you know why one cubit and two cubits were set? I said: No. He said: It was for the obligatory prayer, when the time of one cubit and two cubits enters, one starts with the obligatory prayer and leaves the voluntary prayer.

Hadith 4768

عن أبي جعفر (عليه السلام) قال: كان رسول الله (صلى الله عليه وآله): إذا كان الفيء في الجدار ذراعا صلى الظهر، وإذا كان ذراعين صلى العصر، قلت: الجدران تختلف، منها قصير ومنها طويل؟ قال: إن جدار مسجد رسول الله (صلى الله عليه وآله) كان يومئذ قامة، وإنما جعل الذراع والذراعان لئلا يكون تطوع في وقت فريضة.

From Abu Ja'far (peace be upon him) who said: When the shadow on the wall was one cubit (forearm length), the Messenger of Allah (peace be upon him and his family) would pray Zuhr, and when it was two cubits he would pray Asr. I said:

Walls differ, some are short and some are tall? He said: The wall of the Prophet's mosque (peace be upon him and his family) was one height tall at that time, and the one and two cubits were established so that supererogatory prayers would not be performed during obligatory prayer times.

Hadith 4769

عن محمد بن حكيم قال: سمعت العبد الصالح (عليه السلام) وهو يقول: إن أول وقت الظهر زوال الشمس، وآخر وقتها قامة من الزوال، وأول وقت العصر قامة، وآخر وقتها قامتان، قلت: في الشتاء والصيف سواء؟ قال: نعم.

From Muhammad ibn Hakim who said: I heard the Righteous Servant (peace be upon him) saying: The beginning of Zuhr time is at the sun's zenith, and its end is one height from zenith, and the beginning of Asr time is one height, and its end is two heights. I asked: Is it the same in winter and summer? He said: Yes.

Hadith 4770

عن عبد الله بن محمد قال: كتبت إليه: جعلت فداك، روى أصحابنا، عن أبي جعفر وأبي عبد الله (عليهما السلام) أنهما قالا: إذا زالت الشمس، فقد دخل وقت الصلاتين، إلا أن بين يديها سبحة، إن شئت طولت وإن شئت قصرت.

From Abdullah ibn Muhammad who said: I wrote to him: May I be sacrificed for you, our companions have narrated from Abu Ja'far and Abu Abdullah (peace be upon them) that they said: When the sun passes its zenith, the time for both prayers enters, except there is a voluntary prayer before them - you can make it long or short as you wish.

وروى بعض مواليك عنهما أن وقت الظهر على قدمين من الزوال، ووقت العصر على أربعة أقدام من الزوال، فإن صليت قبل ذلك لم يجزك. وبعضهم يقول: يجزي، ولكن الفضل في انتظار القدمين والأربعة أقدام. وقد أحببت جعلت فداك أن أعرف موضع الفضل في الوقت؟ فكتب: القدمان والأربعة أقدام صواب جميعا.

And some of your followers narrated from them that Zuhr time is at two foot-lengths from zenith, and Asr time is at four foot-lengths from zenith, and if you pray before that it won't suffice. And some say it suffices but the virtue is in waiting for the two and four foot-lengths. I would like to know, may I be sacrificed for you, the most virtuous time? He wrote back: Both the two foot-lengths and four foot-lengths are correct.

Hadith 4771

عن محمد بن الفرج قال: كتبت أسأل عن أوقات الصلاة؟ فأجاب: إذا زالت الشمس فصل سبحتك، وأحب أن يكون فراغك من الفريضة والشمس على قدمين، ثم صل سبحتك، وأحب أن يكون فراغك من العصر والشمس على أربعة أقدام، فإن عجل بك أمر فابدأ بالفريضتين واقض بعدهما النوافل، فإذا طلع الفجر فصل الفريضة ثم اقض بعد ما شئت.

From Muhammad ibn al-Faraj who said: I wrote asking about prayer times. He replied: When the sun passes its zenith, pray your voluntary prayer, and I prefer that you finish the obligatory prayer when the sun is at two foot-lengths, then pray your voluntary prayer, and I prefer that you finish Asr when the sun is at four foot-lengths. If you are rushed, start with the obligatory prayers and make up the voluntary ones after them. When dawn breaks, pray the obligatory prayer then make up whatever you wish after it.

Hadith 4772

عن إبراهيم الكرخي قال: سألت أبا الحسن موسى (عليه السلام): متى يدخل وقت الظهر؟ قال: إذا زالت الشمس، فقلت: متى يخرج وقتها؟ فقال: من بعد ما يمضي من زوالها أربعة أقدام، إن وقت الظهر ضيق ليس كغيره،

From Ibrahim al-Karkhi, he said: I asked Abu al-Hasan Musa (peace be upon him): When does the time for Zuhr prayer begin? He said: When the sun passes its zenith. I asked: When does its time end? He said: After four foot-lengths have passed since its zenith. Indeed the time for Zuhr is narrow, unlike others.

قلت: فمتى يدخل وقت العصر؟ فقال: إن آخر وقت الظهر هو أول وقت العصر، فقلت: فمتى يخرج وقت العصر؟ فقال: وقت العصر إلى أن تغرب الشمس وذلك من علة وهو تضييع،

I asked: When does the time for Asr begin? He said: The end time of Zuhr is the beginning time of Asr. I asked: When does the time of Asr end? He said: The time of Asr is until sunset, and doing otherwise is due to excuse and is negligence.

فقلت له: لو أن رجلا صلى الظهر بعد ما يمضي من زوال الشمس أربعة أقدام، أكان عندك غير مؤد لها؟ فقال: إن كان تعمد ذلك ليخالف السنة والوقت لم تقبل منه، كما لو أن رجلا أخر العصر إلى قرب أن تغرب الشمس متعمدا من غير علة لم يقبل منه،

I asked him: If someone prays Zuhr after four foot-lengths have passed since the sun's zenith, would you consider them to have not fulfilled it? He said: If they deliberately did so to oppose the Sunnah and proper timing, it would not be accepted from them, just as if someone deliberately delays Asr until near sunset without excuse, it would not be accepted from them.

إن رسول الله (صلى الله عليه وآله) قد وقت للصلوات المفروضات أوقاتا، وحد لها حدودا في سنته للناس،
فمن رغب عن سنة من سنته الموجبات كان مثل من رغب من فرائض الله.

Indeed the Messenger of Allah (peace be upon him and his family) set specific times for the obligatory prayers and established their limits in his Sunnah for people. So whoever turns away from any of his obligatory Sunnahs is like one who turns away from Allah's obligations.

Hadith 4773

عن ابن بكير قال: دخل زرارة على أبي عبد الله (عليه السلام) فقال: إنكم قلتم لنا: في الظهر والعصر على
ذراع وذراعين، ثم قلتم: أبردوا بها في الصيف، فكيف الابراد بها؟ وفتح ألواحه ليكتب ما يقول فلم يجبه أبو
عبد الله (عليه السلام) بشئ، فأطبق ألواحه وقال: إنما علينا أن نسألكم وأنتم أعلم بما عليكم وخرج،

From Ibn Bukayr, he said: Zurarah came to Abu Abdullah (peace be upon him) and said: You told us regarding Zuhr and Asr prayers about one cubit and two cubits, then you said to pray them when it's cooler in summer, so how is cooling with them? He opened his tablets to write what he would say but Abu Abdullah (peace be upon him) did not answer him anything. So he closed his tablets and said: It is only upon us to ask you and you know better what is upon you, and he left.

ودخل أبو بصير على أبي عبد الله (عليه السلام) فقال: إن زرارة سألني عن شئ فلم أجبه وقد ضقت من
ذلك، فانهب أنت رسولي إليه فقل: صل الظهر في الصيف إذا كان ظلك مثلك، والعصر إذا كان مثليك،
وكان زرارة هكذا يصلي في الصيف، ولم أسمع أحدا من أصحابنا يفعل ذلك غيره وغير ابن بكير.

Then Abu Basir came to Abu Abdullah (peace be upon him) who said: Zurarah asked me about something but I did not answer him and I felt constrained by that, so you go as my messenger to him and tell him: Pray Zuhr in summer when your shadow is equal to your height, and Asr when it is twice your height. And Zurarah used to pray like this in summer, and I have not heard anyone from our companions doing that except him and Ibn Bukayr.

Hadith 4774

عن أبي عبد الله (عليه السلام) قال: سألته عما جاء في الحديث أن صل الظهر إذا كانت الشمس قامة
وقامتين، وذراعا وذراعين، وقدما وقدمين، من هذا ومن هذا، فمتى هذا؟ وكيف هذا؟ وقد يكون الظل في
بعض الأوقات نصف قدم؟ قال: إنما قال: ظل القامة ولم يقل: قامة الظل، وذلك أن ظل القامة يختلف، مرة
يكثر، ومرة، والقامة قامة أبدا لا تختلف.

From Abu Abdullah (peace be upon him), he said: I asked him about what came in the hadith regarding praying Zuhr when the sun's shadow was one or two statures, one or two cubits, and one or two foot-lengths - from this and that. So when is this? And how is this? While sometimes the shadow can be half a foot? He said: It refers to the shadow of stature, not the stature of shadow. This is because the shadow of stature varies - sometimes more, sometimes less - while a stature remains constant and doesn't change.

ثم قال: ذراع وذراعان، وقدم وقدمان فصار ذراع وذراعان تفسيرا للقامة والقامتين في الزمان الذي يكون فيه ظل القامة ذراعا وظل القامتين ذراعين، فيكون ظل القامة والقامتين والذراع والذراعين متفقين في كل زمان، معروفين، مفسرا أحدهما بالاخر مسددا به،

Then he said: One cubit and two cubits, one foot-length and two foot-lengths became an explanation for one stature and two statures during the time when the shadow of one stature equals one cubit and the shadow of two statures equals two cubits. So the shadow of one/two statures and one/two cubits align at any time, being known and explained by each other.

فإذا كان الزمان يكون فيه ظل القامة ذراعا كان الوقت ذراعا من ظل القامة، وكانت القامة ذراعا من الظل، وإذا كان ظل القامة أقل أو أكثر كان الوقت محصورا بالذراع والذراعين، فهذا تفسير القامة والقامتين، والذراع والذراعين.

When the time comes that the shadow of a stature equals one cubit, the time is one cubit of the stature's shadow, and the stature becomes one cubit of shadow. When the shadow of stature is less or more, the time is bounded by one and two cubits. This explains the one/two statures and one/two cubits.

Manuscript Note: It appears the questioner wants to understand the meaning of what came in the hadith about determining the beginning time of obligatory Zuhr and Asr prayers - sometimes defined by the shadow becoming one or two statures, other times by one or two cubits, and other times by one or two foot-lengths. This measurement comes in different forms, so when is this time? And why these variations and differences? Sometimes the remaining shadow at zenith is half a foot, requiring a very long time to become equal to a person's height, so how can this be the beginning time? He (peace be upon him) answered that what's meant by stature isn't the person's constant physical height, but rather the measure of its shadow remaining on the ground at zenith, called "shadow of stature," which varies by time and place. It's called "stature" when its measure equals one cubit. When the shadow increases after zenith by one cubit equaling the original shadow, that's the beginning of Zuhr's preferred time. When it increases by two cubits, that's the beginning of Asr's preferred time. When the shadow of stature is less or more, the time is determined by cubits rather than statures. The measurement by two and four foot-lengths equals that of one and two cubits, as one cubit equals two foot-lengths. The mention of one/two foot-lengths refers to shortening optional prayers, though not mentioned in this hadith, perhaps due to the questioner's focus or circumstantial irrelevance. And Allah knows best.

———————

Hadith 4775

عن زرارة عن أبي جعفر (عليه السلام) قال: إنما جعلت (القدمان والأربع) والذراع والذراعان وقتا لمكان النافلة.

From Zurarah, from Abu Ja'far (peace be upon him), who said: The time of one to two foot-lengths and one to two cubits (forearm-lengths) was established only on account of the supererogatory prayers.

أقول: وتقدم ما يدل على ذلك. ويأتي ما يدل عليه، وفي هذه الأحاديث اختلاف محمول على تفاوت الفضيلة، أو اختلاف المصلين في تطويل النافلة كما أشار إليه الشيخ وغيره.

I (Hurr Amili) say: What indicates this has preceded and what indicates it will come. And in these hadiths there are differences that are interpreted as variations in virtue, or differences between those praying in lengthening the optional prayers as the Shaykh and others have indicated.

———

CHAPTER 9

On The Emphasized Dislike Of Delaying Asr Prayer Until The Shadow Becomes Six Feet Or The Sun Turns Yellow, And That This Is Not Prohibited

[Hadith 4776 to 4789]

Hadith 4776

عن أبي بصير قال: قال أبو عبد الله (عليه السلام): إن الموتور أهله وماله من ضيع صلاة العصر، قلت: وما الموتور؟ قال: لا يكون له أهل ولامال في الجنة قلت: وما تضييعها؟ قال: يدعها حتى تصفر وتغيب.

From Abu Basir who said: Abu Abdullah (peace be upon him) said: The one who loses his family and wealth is he who neglects the Asr prayer. I said: What does "loses" mean? He said: He will have no family or wealth in Paradise. I said: What is meant by neglecting it? He said: He delays it until it becomes yellow and sets.

———————

Hadith 4777

عن سليمان بن خالد، عن أبي عبد الله (عليه السلام) قال: العصر على ذراعين، فمن تركها حتى تصير على ستة أقدام فذلك المضيع.

From Sulayman bin Khalid, from Abu Abdullah (peace be upon him) who said: The Asr prayer is at two cubits (two forearm lengths), and whoever delays it until it becomes six foot-lengths (aqdam), then he is the one who has neglected it.

———————

Hadith 4778

عن مثنى، عن منصور بن حازم، عن أبي عبد الله (عليه السلام) قال: صل العصر على أربعة أقدام.

From Muthanna, from Mansur ibn Hazim, from Abu Abdullah (peace be upon him) who said: Pray Asr at four foot-lengths (aqdam).

———————

Hadith 4779

عن مثنى قال: قال لي أبو بصير: قال لي أبو عبد الله (عليه السلام): صل العصر يوم الجمعة على ستة أقدام.

From Muthanna who said: Abu Basir told me: Abu Abdullah (peace be upon him) said to me: Pray Asr on Friday at six foot-lengths (aqdam).

———————

Hadith 4780

عن صفوان الجمال، عن أبي عبد الله (عليه السلام)، قال: قلت: العصر متى أصليها إذا كنت في غير سفر؟ قال: على قدر ثلثي قدم بعد الظهر.

From Safwan al-Jammal, from Abu Abdullah (peace be upon him), who said: I asked: When should I pray Asr when I am not traveling? He said: After a measure of two-thirds of a foot-length (qadam) after Zuhr.

Hadith 4781

عن سليمان بن جعفر قال: قال الفقيه (عليه السلام): آخر وقت العصر ستة أقدام ونصف.

From Sulayman ibn Ja'far who said: The Faqih (*) (peace be upon him) said: The latest time for Asr is six and a half foot-lengths (aqdam).

Translator: * Faqih was an epithet frequently used by the Shias to refer to their Imam (peace be upon him).

Hadith 4782

عن أبي بصير، عن أبي جعفر (عليه السلام) قال: ما خدعوك فيه من شئ فلا يخدعونك في العصر، صلها والشمس بيضاء نقية فإن رسول الله (صلى الله عليه وآله) قال: الموتور أهله وماله من ضيع صلاة العصر، قيل: وما الموتور أهله وماله؟ قال: لا يكون له أهل ولامال في الجنة. قال: وما تضييعها؟ قال: يدعها والله حتى تصفر أو تغيب الشمس.

From Abu Basir, from Abu Ja'far (peace be upon him) who said: Whatever they may deceive you about, let them not deceive you regarding Asr prayer. Pray it while the sun is white and pure, for the Messenger of Allah (peace be upon him and his family) said: One who neglects the Asr prayer is deprived of his family and wealth. It was asked: What does being deprived of family and wealth mean? He said: He will have neither family nor wealth in Paradise. It was asked: What constitutes neglecting it? He said: By Allah, he leaves (delays) it until the sun turns yellow or sets.

Hadith 4783

عن أبي سلام العبدي قال: دخلت على أبي عبد الله (عليه السلام) فقلت له: ما تقول في رجل يؤخر العصر متعمدا؟ قال: يأتي يوم القيامة موتورا أهله وماله، قال: قلت: جعلت فداك، وإن كان من أهل الجنة؟ قال: وإن كان من أهل الجنة قال: قلت: فما منزله في الجنة؟ قال: موتور أهله وماله يتضيف أهلها ليس له فيها منزل.

From Abu Salam Al-Abdi who said: I entered upon Abu Abdullah (peace be upon him) and said to him: What do you say about a man who deliberately delays the Asr prayer? He said: He will come on the Day of Resurrection having lost his family and wealth. I said: May I be sacrificed for you, even if he is from the people of Paradise? He said: Even if he is from the people of Paradise. I said: So what is his dwelling in Paradise? He said: Having lost his family and wealth, he will be a guest of its people with no dwelling of his own there.

Hadith 4784

عن محمد بن هارون قال: سمعت أبا عبد الله (عليه السلام) يقول: من ترك صلاة العصر غير ناس لها حتى تفوته وتره الله أهله وماله يوم القيامة.

From Muhammad bin Harun who said: I heard Abu Abdullah (peace be upon him) saying: Whoever abandons the Asr prayer (intentionally) without forgetting it until he misses it, Allah will deprive him of his family and wealth on the Day of Resurrection.

Hadith 4785

عن أبي عبد الله (عليه السلام) قال: إن رسول الله (صلى الله عليه وآله) قال: الموتور أهله وماله من ضيع صلاة العصر، قلت: وما الموتور أهله وماله؟ قال: لا يكون له في الجنة أهل ولامال، يضيعها فيدعها متعمدا حتى تصفر الشمس وتغيب.

From Abu Abdullah (peace be upon him) who said: Indeed the Messenger of Allah (peace be upon him and his family) said: The one deprived of his family and wealth is he who neglects Asr prayer. I asked: What does it mean to be deprived of family and wealth? He said: He will have no family or wealth in Paradise, he neglects it by deliberately leaving it until the sun turns yellow and sets.

Hadith 4786

عن علي وعمر وأبي بكر وابن عباس كلهم قالوا: صل العصر والفجاج مسفرة، فإنها كانت صلاة رسول الله (صلى الله عليه وآله).

From Ali, Umar, Abu Bakr, and Ibn Abbas, all of them said: Pray Asr while the mountain paths are still bright with daylight, for that was the prayer (time) of the Messenger of Allah (peace be upon him and his family).

Hadith 4787

عن زرارة قال: قال أبو جعفر (عليه السلام): أحب الوقت إلى الله عز وجل أوله حين يدخل وقت الصلاة، فصل الفريضة، فإن لم تفعل فإنك في وقت منهما حتى تغيب الشمس.

From Zurarah who said: Abu Ja'far (peace be upon him) said: The most beloved time to Allah Mighty and Majestic is its beginning when the prayer time enters, so pray the obligatory prayer. If you do not do so, you are still within its time until the sun sets.

Hadith 4788

عن معمر بن يحيى قال: سمعت أبا جعفر (عليه السلام) يقول: وقت العصر إلى غروب الشمس.

From Muammar bin Yahya who said: I heard Abu Ja'far (peace be upon him) saying: The time for Asr prayer extends until sunset.

Hadith 4789

عن محمد بن أبي عمر قال: دخلت على أبي عبد الله (عليه السلام) فقال: كيف تركت زرارة؟ قال: تركته لا يصلي العصر حتى تغيب الشمس، قال: فأنت رسولي إليه فقل له: فليصل في مواقيت أصحابه.

From Muhammad bin Abi Umar who said: I entered upon Abu Abdullah (peace be upon him) and he said: How did you leave Zurarah? He said: I left him not praying Asr until sunset. He said: You are my messenger to him, so tell him to pray at the times his companions pray.

CHAPTER 10

Times Of The Five Prayers And Some Of Their Rulings
[Hadith 4790 to 4802]

Hadith 4790

عن يزيد بن خليفة قال: قلت لأبي عبد الله (عليه السلام): إن عمر بن حنظلة أتانا عنك بوقت؟ فقال: إذا لا يكذب علينا: قلت: ذكر أنك قلت: إن أول صلاة افترضها الله على نبيه (صلى الله عليه وآله) الظهر، وهو قول الله عز وجل (أقم الصلاة لدلوك الشمس)

From Yazid bin Khalifa who said: I said to Abu Abdullah (peace be upon him): Umar bin Hanzala came to us from you with a timing? He said: Then he does not lie about us. I said: He mentioned that you said: The first prayer that Allah made obligatory upon His Prophet (peace be upon him and his family) was the noon prayer, and it is the saying of Allah the Mighty and Majestic: "Establish prayer at the decline of the sun [Quran, 17:78]."

فإذا زالت الشمس لم يمنعك إلا سبحتك، ثم لا تزال في وقت إلى أن يصير الظل قامة وهو آخر الوقت، فإذا صار الظل قامة دخل وقت العصر فلم تزل في وقت العصر حتى يصير الظل قامتين وذلك المساء فقال: صدق.

When the sun passes its zenith, nothing prevents you except your optional prayer, then you remain in the time until the shadow becomes one stature length which is the end of the time. When the shadow becomes one stature length, the time of Asr begins and you remain in the time of Asr until the shadow becomes two stature lengths and that is the evening. He said: He spoke the truth.

Hadith 4791

وبهذا الاسناد قال: قلت: قال: وقت المغرب إذا غاب القرص إلا أن رسول الله (صلى الله عليه وآله) كان إذا جد به السير أخر المغرب ويجمع بينها وبين العشاء، فقال: صدق، قال: وقت العشاء حين يغيب الشفق إلى ثلث الليل، ووقت الفجر حين يبدو حتى يضيئ.

With this chain, I said: He said the time for Maghrib is when the disc sets, except that when the Messenger of Allah (peace be upon him and his family) was in a hurry while traveling he would delay Maghrib and combine it with Isha. He said: He spoke truth. He said: The time of Isha is from when the twilight disappears until a third of the night, and the time of Fajr is from when it appears until it brightens.

Hadith 4792

عن زرارة قال: سمعت أبا جعفر (عليه السلام) يقول: كان رسول الله (صلى الله عليه وآله) لا يصلي من النهار شيئا حتى تزول الشمس فإذا زالت قدر نصف إصبع صلى ثماني ركعات، فإذا فاء الفئ ذراعا صلى الظهر ثم صلى بعد الظهر ركعتين، ويصلي قبل وقت العصر ركعتين، فإذا فاء الفئ ذراعين صلى العصر وصلى المغرب حتى تغيب الشمس،

From Zurarah, he said: I heard Abu Ja'far (peace be upon him) saying: The Messenger of Allah (peace be upon him and his family) would not pray anything during the day until the sun declined. When it declined the measure of half a finger he would pray eight rak'ahs. When the shadow extended one cubit he would pray Zuhr then pray two rak'ahs after Zuhr, and he would pray two rak'ahs before the time of Asr. When the shadow extended two cubits he would pray Asr and pray Maghrib until the sun sets.

فإذا غاب الشفق دخل وقت العشاء، وآخر وقت المغرب إياب الشفق، فإذا آب الشفق دخل وقت العشاء، وآخر وقت العشاء ثلث الليل، وكان لا يصلي بعد العشاء حتى ينتصف الليل، ثم يصلي ثلاث عشرة ركعة منها: الوتر ومنها ركعتا الفجر قبل الغداة، فإذا طلع الفجر وأضاء صلى الغداة.

When the twilight disappeared the time of Isha entered, and the last time for Maghrib is the disappearance of twilight. When twilight disappeared the time of Isha entered, and the last time for Isha is a third of the night. He would not pray after Isha until midnight, then he would pray thirteen rak'ahs including: the Witr and the two rak'ahs of Fajr before dawn. When Fajr appeared and brightened he would pray the dawn prayer.

––––––––––

Hadith 4793

عن عبيد بن زرارة، عن أبي عبد الله (عليه السلام) في قوله تعالى: (أقم الصلاة لدلوك الشمس إلى غسق الليل) قال: إن الله افترض أربع صلوات، أول وقتها زوال الشمس إلى انتصاف الليل. منها صلاتان أول وقتهما من عند زوال الشمس إلى غروب الشمس إلا أن هذه قبل هذه، ومنها صلاتان أول وقتهما من غروب الشمس إلى انتصاف الليل إلا أن هذه قبل هذه.

From Ubayd bin Zurarah, from Abu Abdullah (peace be upon him) regarding the words of the Almighty: "Establish prayer from the declining of the sun until the darkness of the night" [Quran, 17:78], he said: Allah has prescribed four prayers, their first time is from the sun's decline until midnight. Among them are two prayers whose first time is from the sun's decline until sunset, except that this one is before that one. And among them are two prayers whose first time is from sunset until midnight, except that this one is before that one.

Translator: This hadith describes four (out of the five) obligatory prayers.

––––––––––

Hadith 4794

عن معاوية بن وهب، عن أبي عبد الله (عليه السلام) قال: أتى جبرئيل رسول الله (صلى الله عليه وآله) بمواقيت الصلاة. فأتاه حين زالت الشمس فأمره فصلى الظهر، ثم أتاه حين زاد الظل قامة فأمره فصلى العصر، ثم أتاه حين غربت الشمس فأمره فصلى المغرب، ثم أتاه حين سقط الشفق فأمره فصلى العشاء، ثم أتاه حين طلع الفجر، فأمره فصلى الصبح،

From Mu'awiyah bin Wahb, from Abu Abdullah (peace be upon him) said: Jibreel came to the Messenger of Allah (peace be upon him and his family) with prayer times. He came to him when the sun declined and ordered him to pray Zuhr, then came when the shadow increased one stature and ordered him to pray Asr, then came when the sun set and ordered him to pray Maghrib, then came when twilight fell and ordered him to pray Isha, then came when Fajr rose and ordered him to pray morning prayer.

ثم أتاه من الغد حين زاد في الظل قامة فأمره فصلى الظهر، ثم أتاه حين زاد من الظل قامتان فأمره فصلى العصر، ثم أتاه حين غربت الشمس فأمره فصلى المغرب، ثم أتاه حين ذهب ثلث الليل فأمره فصلى العشاء، ثم أتاه حين نور الصبح فأمره فصلى الصبح، ثم قال: ما بينهما وقت.

Then he came the next day when the shadow increased one stature and ordered him to pray Zuhr, then came when the shadow increased two statures and ordered him to pray Asr, then came when the sun set and ordered him to pray Maghrib, then came when a third of the night passed and ordered him to pray Isha, then came when dawn brightened and ordered him to pray morning prayer, then said: Between these two is the time.

Hadith 4795

عن معاوية بن ميسرة، عن أبي عبد الله (عليه السلام) قال: أتى جبرئيل، وذكر مثله، إلا أنه قال بدل القامة والقامتين: ذراع وذراعين.

From Mu'awiyah bin Maysara, from Abu Abdullah (peace be upon him) said: Jibreel came, and mentioned similar to it, except he said instead of one stature and two statures: one cubit and two cubits.

Hadith 4796

عن مفضل بن عمر قال: قال أبو عبد الله (عليه السلام): نزل جبرئيل، وذكر مثله، إلا أنه ذكر بدل القامة والقامتين: قدمين وأربعة أقدام.

From Mufaddal bin Umar, he said: Abu Abdullah (peace be upon him) said: Jibreel descended, and mentioned similar to it, except he mentioned instead of one stature and two statures: two foot-lengths (aqdam) and four foot-lengths.

Hadith 4797

عن ذريح، عن أبي عبد الله (عليه السلام) قال: أتى جبرئيل رسول الله (صلى الله عليه وآله) فأعلمه مواقيت الصلاة فقال: صل الفجر حين ينشق الفجر، وصل الأولى، إذا زالت الشمس، وصل العصر بعيدها، وصل المغرب إذا سقط القرص، وصل العتمة إذا غاب الشفق،

From Dhuraih, from Abu Abdullah (peace be upon him) who said: Jibreel came to the Messenger of Allah (peace be upon him and his family) and informed him of the prayer times saying: Pray Fajr when dawn breaks, pray the first prayer when the sun declines, pray Asr after it, pray Maghrib when the disc sets, and pray Isha when the twilight disappears.

ثم أتاه من الغد فقال: أسفر بالفجر فأسفر، ثم أخر الظهر، حين كان الوقت الذي صلى فيه العصر وصلى العصر بعيدها، وصلى المغرب قبل سقوط الشفق، وصلى العتمة حين ذهب ثلث الليل، ثم قال: ما بين هذين الوقتين وقت.

Then he came to him the next day and said: Delay Fajr until it brightens, then delay Zuhr until the time he had prayed Asr previously, and pray Asr after it, and pray Maghrib before twilight disappears, and pray Isha when one-third of the night has passed, then he said: The time is between these two times.

Hadith 4798

عن عبيد بن زرارة، عن أبي عبد الله (عليه السلام) قال: لا تفوت الصلاة من أراد الصلاة، لا تفوت صلاة النهار حتى تغيب الشمس، ولا صلاة الليل حتى يطلع الفجر، ولا صلاة الفجر حتى تطلع الشمس. ورواه الصدوق مرسلا، نحوه. أقول: حمل الشيخ صلاة الليل على النوافل.

From Ubayd bin Zurarah, from Abu Abdullah (peace be upon him) who said: Prayer does not expire for one who intends to pray - the day prayers do not expire until sunset, Salat al-Layl does not expire until dawn breaks, and Fajr prayer does not expire until sunrise. I (Hurr Amili) say: The Shaykh interpreted Salat al-Layl as referring to supererogatory prayers.

Hadith 4799

عن محمد الحلبي، عن أبي عبد الله (عليه السلام) في قوله تعالى: (أقم الصلاة لدلوك الشمس إلى غسق الليل، وقرآن الفجر إن قرآن الفجر كان مشهودا) قال: دلوك الشمس زوالها، وغسق الليل انتصافه، وقرآن الفجر ركعتا الفجر.

From Muhammad al-Halabi, from Abu Abdullah (peace be upon him) regarding the verse "Establish prayer at the decline of the sun until the darkness of the night and [also] the Quran of dawn. Indeed, the Quran of dawn is witnessed." [Quran 17:78] He said: The decline of the sun is its zenith, the darkness of night is its middle, and the Quran of dawn is the two units of Fajr prayer.

Hadith 4800

عن الفضل بن شاذان، عن الرضا (عليه السلام) قال: إنما جعلت الصلاة في هذه الأوقات ولم تقدم ولم تؤخر لان الأوقات المشهورة المعلومة التي تعم أهل الأرض فيعرفها الجاهل والعالم أربعة: غروب الشمس مشهور معروف تجب عنده المغرب الشفق مشهور تجب عنده العشاء، وطلوع الفجر معلوم مشهور تجب عنده الغداة، وزوال الشمس مشهور معلوم يجب عنده الظهر. ولم يكن للعصر وقت معلوم مشهور مثل هذه الأوقات الأربعة فجعل وقتها عند الفراغ من الصلاة التي قبلها،

From Al-Fadhl bin Shadhan, from Al-Ridha (peace be upon him) who said: Prayer was established at these times, not earlier or later, because the well-known and recognized times that are common to all people on earth, known to both ignorant and knowledgeable, are four: Sunset is well-known when Maghrib becomes obligatory, twilight is well-known when Isha becomes obligatory, dawn break is well-known when morning prayer becomes obligatory, and sun's zenith is well-known when Zuhr becomes obligatory. Asr did not have a well-known time like these four times so its time was set after completing the prayer before it.

وعلة أخرى: أن الله عز وجل أحب أن يبدأ الناس في كل عمل أولا بطاعته وعبادته، فأمرهم أول النهار أن يبدؤا بعبادته، ثم ينتشروا فيما أحبوا من مرمة دنياهم فأوجب صلاة الغداة عليهم، فإذا كان نصف النهار وتركوا ما كانوا فيه من الشغل وهو وقت يضع الناس فيه ثيابهم ويستريحون ويشتغلون بطعامهم وقيلولتهم فأمرهم أن يبدؤا أولا بذكره وعبادته فأوجب عليهم الظهر. ثم يتفرغوا لما أحبوا من ذلك، فإذا قضوا ظهرهم وأرادوا الانتشار في العمل آخر النهار بدأوا بعبادته أيضا، ثم صاروا إلى ما أحبوا من ذلك فأوجب عليهم العصر، ثم ينتشرون فيما شاؤوا من مرمة دنياهم،

Another reason: Allah the Mighty and Majestic loved that people begin every action first with His obedience and worship, so He commanded them at the start of day to begin with His worship before dispersing to their worldly affairs, making Fajr (*) prayer obligatory upon them. When it is midday and they leave their work, which is when people remove their clothes and rest and are occupied with food and nap, He commanded them to begin first with His remembrance and worship by making Zuhr obligatory, then they can attend to what they wish. When they complete Zuhr and want to disperse for work in late day, they again begin with His worship, so He made Asr obligatory, then they can disperse as they wish for worldly affairs.

فإذا جاء الليل ووضعوا زينتهم وعادوا إلى أوطانهم ابتدؤا أولا بعبادة ربهم، ثم يتفرغون لما أحبوا من ذلك، فأوجب عليهم المغرب، فإذا جاء وقت النوم وفرغوا مما كانوا به مشتغلين أحب أن يبدؤا أولا بعبادته وطاعته ثم يصيرون إلى ما شاؤوا أن يصيروا إليه من ذلك فيكون قد بدأوا في كل عمل بطاعته وعبادته،

فأوجب عليهم العتمة، فإذا فعلوا ذلك لم ينسوه ولم يغفلوا عنه ولم تقس قلوبهم، ولم تقل رغبتهم،

When night comes and they put aside their adornments and return home, they begin first with worshipping their Lord before attending to what they wish, so He made Maghrib obligatory. When sleep time comes and they finish their occupations, He loved that they begin first with His worship and obedience before going to what they wish, so they begin every action with His obedience and worship, making Isha obligatory. When they do this, they will not forget Him or be heedless of Him, their hearts will not harden, and their desire will not diminish.

ولما لم يكن للعصر وقت مشهور مثل تلك الأوقات أوجبها بين الظهر والمغرب، ولم يوجبها بين العتمة وبين الغداة والظهر، لأنه ليس وقت على الناس أخف ولا أيسر ولا أحرى أن يعم فيه الضعيف والقوي بهذه الصلاة من هذا الوقت، وذلك أن الناس عامتهم يشتغلون في أول النهار بالتجارات والمعاملات والذهاب في الحوائج وإقامة الأسواق،

Since Asr did not have a well-known time like those times, He made it obligatory between Zuhr and Maghrib, and not between Isha and Fajr or between Fajr and Zuhr, because there is no time easier or more suitable for both weak and strong to perform this prayer than this time, as most people are busy in early day with trade, transactions, errands and markets.

فأراد الله أن لا يشغلهم عن طلب معاشهم ومصلحة دنياهم وليس يقدر الخلق كلهم على قيام الليل ولا يشعرون به ولا يتنبهون لوقته لو كان واجبا ولا يمكنهم ذلك، فخفف الله عنهم ولم يكلفهم ولم يجعلها في أشد الأوقات عليهم، ولكن جعلها في أخف الأوقات عليهم كما قال الله عز وجل: (يريد الله بكم اليسر ولا يريد بكم العسر).

Allah wanted not to distract them from seeking their livelihood and worldly affairs. Not all creation can stand at night, nor are they aware of its time if it were obligatory, nor is it possible for them. So Allah made it light for them and did not burden them or make it at the most difficult times, but made it at the easiest times as Allah the Mighty and Majestic said: "Allah intends for you ease and does not intend for you hardship" [Quran 2:185].

Translator: * Salat Al-Ghadah refers to the Fajr prayer. The term "Ghadah" means "morning" or "early morning."

Hadith 4801

الحسن بن محمد الطوسي في (المجالس) بإسناد تقدم في كيفية الوضوء قال: لما ولى أمير المؤمنين علي بن أبي طالب (عليه السلام) محمد بن أبي بكر مصر وأعمالها كتب له كتابا وأمره أن يقرأه على أهل مصر ويعمل بما وصاه فيه - وذكر الكتاب بطوله إلى أن قال - وانظر إلى صلاتك، كيف هي؟

Al-Hasan bin Muhammad al-Tusi narrated in Al-Majalis with a chain mentioned previously regarding wudu, saying: When Amir al-Mu'minin Ali ibn Abi Talib (peace be upon him) appointed Muhammad ibn Abi Bakr over Egypt and its territories, he wrote him a letter commanding him to read it to the people of Egypt and act upon his instructions therein - and he mentioned the letter in full until he said - Look to your prayer, how is it?

فإنك إمام لقومك، أن تتمها ولا تخففها فليس من إمام يصلي بقوم يكون في صلاتهم نقصان إلا كان عليه، لا ينقص من صلاتهم شئ، وتممها وتحفظ فيها يكن لك مثل أجورهم ولا ينقص ذلك من أجورهم شيئا، ثم ارتقب وقت الصلاة فصلها لوقتها، ولا تعجل بها قبله لفراغ، ولا تؤخرها عنه لشغل،

For you are an imam for your people, complete it and do not shorten it. No imam who leads people in prayer with any deficiency except it is upon him, nothing decreases from their prayers. Complete it and preserve it, you will have reward like theirs without decreasing anything from their rewards. Then observe prayer time and pray it at its time, do not hasten it before due to free time, nor delay it due to occupation.

فإن رجلا سأل رسول الله (صلى الله عليه وآله) عن أوقات الصلاة؟ فقال: أتاني جبرئيل (عليه السلام) فأراني وقت الصلاة حين زالت الشمس فكانت على حاجبه الأيمن، ثم أراني وقت العصر وكان ظل كل شئ مثله، ثم صلى المغرب حين غربت الشمس، ثم صلى العشاء الآخرة حين غاب الشفق، ثم صلى الصبح فأغلس بها والنجوم مشتبكة،

A man asked the Messenger of Allah (peace be upon him and his family) about prayer times? He said: Jibreel (peace be upon him) came to me and showed me prayer time when the sun declined and was at his right eyebrow, then showed me Asr time when every object's shadow was equal to it, then prayed Maghrib at sunset, then prayed later Isha when twilight disappeared, then prayed morning prayer in darkness while stars were intertwined.

فصل لهذه الأوقات، والزم السنة المعروفة والطريق الواضح، ثم أنظر ركوعك وسجودك، فإن رسول الله (صلى الله عليه وآله) كان أتم الناس صلاة، وأخفهم عملا فيها، واعلم أن كل شئ من عملك تبع لصلاتك، فمن ضيع الصلاة فإنه لغيرها أضيع.

So pray at these times, and adhere to the known Sunnah and clear path. Then look at your ruku and to your sujud, for the Messenger of Allah (peace be upon him and his family) had the most complete prayer while being lightest in its actions. Know that every action of yours follows your prayer - whoever neglects prayer will more readily neglect other things.

———

Hadith 4802

محمد بن الحسين الرضي الموسوي في (نهج البلاغة) عن أمير المؤمنين (عليه السلام)، أنه قال: في كتاب كتبه إلى أمراء البلاد: أما بعد، فصلوا بالناس الظهر حتى تفئ الشمس، مثل مربض العنز، وصلوا بهم العصر والشمس بيضاء حية في عضو من النهار حين يسار فيها فرسخان،

Muhammad bin al-Husayn al-Radi al-Musawi narrated in Nahj al-Balagha that Amir al-Mu'minin (peace be upon him) said in a letter he wrote to provincial governors: As for what follows, lead people in Zuhr prayer when the sun declines the length of a goat's pen, and lead them in Asr while the sun is still bright white in a part of the day when two parasangs can be traveled.

وصلوا بهم المغرب حين يفطر الصائم ويدفع الحاج، وصلوا بهم العشاء الآخرة حين يتوارى الشفق إلى ثلث الليل، وصلوا بهم الغداة والرجل يعرف وجه صاحبه، وصلوا بهم صلاة أضعفهم، ولا تكونوا فتانين.

Lead them in Maghrib when the fasting person breaks fast and pilgrims depart, and lead them in later Isha from when twilight disappears until one-third of night, and lead them in morning prayer when a man can recognize his companion's face. Lead them in prayer according to their weakest member, and do not be causes of tribulation.

CHAPTER 11

Determining The Sun's Zenith Through Shadow Increase After Decrease And The Sun's Inclination To The Right Eyebrow

[Hadith 4803 to 4807]

Hadith 4803

عن سماعة قال: قلت لأبي عبد الله (عليه السلام): جعلت فداك، متى وقت الصلاة؟ فأقبل يلتفت يمينا وشمالا كأنه يطلب شيئا، فلما رأيت ذلك تناولت عودا، فقلت: هذا تطلب؟ قال: نعم، فأخذ العود فنصبه بحيال الشمس، ثم قال: إن الشمس إذا طلعت كان الفئ طويلا، ثم لا يزال ينقص حتى تزول، فإذا زالت زادت، فإذا استنبت الزيادة فصل الظهر، ثم تمهل قدر ذراع وصل العصر.

From Sama'ah who said: I asked Abu Abdullah (peace be upon him): May I be sacrificed for you, when is the time for prayer? He began looking right and left as if searching for something. When I saw this, I picked up a stick and said: Is this what you're looking for? He said: Yes. He took the stick and set it up facing the sun, then said: When the sun rises, the shadow is long, then it keeps decreasing until zenith. When it reaches zenith it increases. When you notice the increase, pray Zuhr, then wait for about the length of a forearm (cubit) and pray Asr.

Hadith 4804

عن علي بن أبي حمزة قال: ذكر عند أبي عبد الله (عليه السلام) زوال الشمس، قال: فقال: أبو عبد الله (عليه السلام): تأخذون عودا طوله ثلاثة أشبار وإن زاد فهو أبين، فيقام، فما دام ترى الظل ينقص فلم تزل، فإذا زاد الظل بعد النقصان فقد زالت.

From Ali ibn Abi Hamza who said: The sun's zenith was mentioned to Abu Abdullah (peace be upon him), so Abu Abdullah (peace be upon him) said: Take a stick three spans long - and if longer it's clearer - and stand it up. As long as you see the shadow decreasing, the sun hasn't reached zenith. When the shadow increases after decreasing, it has reached zenith.

Hadith 4805

عبد الله بن سنان عن أبي عبد الله (عليه السلام) قال: تزول الشمس في النصف من حزيران على نصف قدم، وفي النصف من تموز على قدم ونصف، وفي النصف من آب على قدمين ونصف، وفي النصف من أيلول على ثلاثة أقدام ونصف، وفي النصف من تشرين الأول على خمسة أقدام ونصف، وفي النصف من تشرين الاخر على سبعة ونصف، وفي النصف من كانون الأول على تسعة ونصف، وفي النصف من كانون

الاخر على سبعة ونصف، وفي النصف من شباط على خمسة ونصف، وفي النصف من آذار على ثلاثة ونصف، وفي النصف من نيسان على قدمين ونصف، وفي النصف من أيار على قدم ونصف، وفي النصف من حزيران على نصف قدم.

Abdullah ibn Sinan reported from Abu Abdullah (peace be upon him) that he said: The sun passes its zenith in the middle of Haziran (June) when the shadow is half a foot-length; in the middle of Tammuz (July) when it is one and a half foot-length; in the middle of Ab (August) when it is two and a half foot-length; in the middle of Aylul (September) when it is three and a half foot-length; in the middle of the first Tishrin (October) when it is five and a half foot-length; in the middle of the second Tishrin (November) when it is seven and a half; in the middle of the first Kanun (December) when it is nine and a half; in the middle of the second Kanun (January) when it is seven and a half; in the middle of Shubat (February) when it is five and a half; in the middle of Adhar (March) when it is three and a half; in the middle of Nisan (April) when it is two and a half feet; in the middle of Ayyar (May) when it is one and a half foot-length; and in the middle of Haziran (June) when it is half a foot-length.

أقول: ذكر صاحب المنتقى أن النظر والاعتبار يدلان على أن هذا مخصوص بالمدينة، وكذا ذكره العلامة في التذكرة.

I (Hurr Amili) say: The author of al-Muntaqa mentioned that careful examination and consideration indicate that this is specific to Madinah, and the Allamah likewise mentioned this in al-Tadhkirah.

Translator: This tradition provides a comprehensive solar calendar for determining the "fay al-zawal" (the minimum meridian shadow) throughout the year. It is crucial to understand that these measurements do not represent the start of the prayer time itself, but rather the "base shadow" that exists at solar noon. To find the actual start of "Zuhr", one must first identify this base shadow and then add the "one cubit" (two foot-lengths) mandated in other traditions.

Hadith 4806

قال الصدوق: وقال الصادق (عليه السلام): تبيان زوال الشمس أن تأخذ عودا طوله ذراع وأربع أصابع فتجعل أربع أصابع في الأرض فإذا نقص الظل حتى يبلغ غايته ثم زاد فقد زالت الشمس، وتفتح أبواب السماء وتهب الرياح، وتقضى الحوائج العظام.

Al-Saduq said: Al-Sadiq (peace be upon him) said: To determine the sun's zenith, take a stick one forearm (dira) and four fingers long and place four fingers in the ground. When the shadow decreases until reaching its minimum then increases, the sun has reached zenith. The gates of heaven open, winds blow, and great needs are fulfilled.

Hadith 4807

وقد تقدم - في حديث - أن رسول الله (صلى الله عليه وآله) قال: أتاني جبرئيل فأراني وقت الظهر حين زالت الشمس فكانت على حاجبه الأيمن.

It was previously mentioned in a hadith that the Messenger of Allah (peace be upon him and his family) said: Jibreel came to me and showed me the time of Zuhr when the sun passed zenith and was at his right eyebrow.

Shaykh Hurr Amili: It is clear that this is specific to a place whose qiblah is the point of the south or close to it, or to one who faces the south.

CHAPTER 12

Recommendation Of Glorification, Supplication And Good Deeds At The Time Of Zenith

[Hadith 4808 to 4809]

Hadith 4808

محمد بن علي بن الحسين بإسناده عن محمد بن مسلم أنه سأل أبا جعفر (عليه السلام) عن ركود الشمس؟ فقال: يا محمد، ما أصغر جثتك وأعضل مسألتك، وإنك لأهل للجواب،

Muhammad ibn Ali ibn al-Husayn, by his chain of transmission from Muhammad ibn Muslim, that he asked Abu Ja'far (peace be upon him) about the stillness of the sun. He said: O Muhammad, how small is your frame, yet how difficult is your question, and yet you are indeed worthy of an answer.

إن الشمس إذا طلعت جذبها سبعون ألف ملك بعد أن أخذ بكل شعاع منها خمسة آلاف من الملائكة من بين جاذب ودافع، حتى إذا بلغت الجو وحاذت الكو قلبها ملك النور ظهرا لبطن، فصار ما يلي الأرض إلى السماء، وبلغ شعاعها تخوم العرش،

When the sun rises, seventy thousand angels draw it, after five thousand angels have taken hold of each of its rays, some pulling and some pushing, until when it reaches the atmosphere and comes level with the opening, the angel of light flips it face to back, so that what had faced the earth now faces the sky, and its rays reach the foundations of the Throne.

فعند ذلك نادت الملائكة سبحان الله، ولا إله إلا الله والحمد لله الذي لم يتخذ صاحبة ولا ولدا، ولم يكن له شريك في الملك ولم يكن له ولي من الذل وكبره تكبيرا، فقال له: جعلت فداك، أحافظ على هذا الكلام عند زوال الشمس؟ فقال: نعم، حافظ عليه كما تحافظ على عينك.

At that point the angels call out: Glory be to God, and there is no god but God, and praise be to God "Who has not taken a companion nor a son, and Who has no partner in dominion, and Who has no protector out of weakness" [Quran, 17:111], and they exalt Him greatly. He then said to him: May I be your ransom, should I preserve these words at the time of the sun's midday decline? He said: Yes, guard them as you guard your own eye.

Translator: * The term rukood al-shams refers to the apparent stillness or slowness of the sun's movement across the sky, especially around the time of solar noon when the sun reaches its highest point in the sky (zenith) and appears to stand still before beginning its descent.

Hadith 4809

قال: وقال رسول الله (صلى الله عليه وآله): إذا زالت الشمس فتحت أبواب السماء وأبواب الجنان واستجيب الدعاء، فطوبى لمن رفع له عند ذلك عمل صالح.

He said: And the Messenger of Allah (peace be upon him and his family) said: When the sun reaches its zenith, the gates of heaven and the gates of paradise are opened, and supplications are answered. So glad tidings to those who have raised good deeds at that time.

———

CHAPTER 13

Invalidation Of Prayer Before Certainty Of Time Entry, Even If Entry Is Assumed, And The Obligation To Repeat During Time And Make Up After Time Except What Is Exempted

[Hadith 4810 to 4820]

Hadith 4810

عن أبي عبد الله (عليه السلام) - في حديث - قال: إنه ليس لأحد أن يصلي صلاة إلا لوقتها، وكذلك الزكاة - إلى أن قال - وكل فريضة إنما تؤدى إذا حلت.

From Abu Abdullah (peace be upon him) - in a hadith - he said: No one should pray any prayer except at its time, and likewise for zakat - until he said - and every obligation is only fulfilled when it becomes due.

Hadith 4811

عن زرارة قال: قلت لأبي جعفر (عليه السلام): أيزكي الرجل ماله إذا مضى ثلث السنة؟ قال: لا، أتصلي الأولى قبل الزوال؟!

From Zurarah who said: I said to Abu Ja'far (peace be upon him): Should a man pay zakat on his wealth when one-third of the year has passed? He said: No, would you pray Zuhr before noon?!

Hadith 4812

عن زرارة عن أبي جعفر (عليه السلام) - في حديث - قال: قلت: فمن صلى لغير القبلة، أو في يوم غيم لغير الوقت؟ قال: يعيد.

From Zurarah from Abu Ja'far (peace be upon him) - in a hadith - he said: I said: What about one who prays in a direction other than qiblah, or on a cloudy day outside the proper time? He said: He must repeat it.

Hadith 4813

وعن زرارة قال: قال أبو جعفر (عليه السلام): وقت المغرب إذا غاب القرص، فإن رأيته بعد ذلك وقد صليت أعدت الصلاة.

From Zurarah who said: Abu Ja'far (peace be upon him) said: The time for Maghrib prayer is when the disk (of the sun) sets, and if you see it after that and you have already prayed, repeat the prayer.

Hadith 4814

عن زرارة، عن أبي جعفر (عليه السلام)، في رجل صلى الغداة بليل، غره من ذلك القمر، ونام حتى طلعت الشمس فأخبر أنه صلى بليل، قال: يعيد صلاته.

From Zurarah, from Abu Ja'far (peace be upon him), regarding a man who prayed Fajr during night time, being deceived by the moonlight, and slept until sunrise when he was informed that he had prayed during night, he said: He must repeat his prayer.

Hadith 4815

عن سماعة بن مهران قال: قال لي أبو عبد الله (عليه السلام): إياك أن تصلي قبل أن تزول، فإنك تصلي في وقت العصر خير لك من أن تصلي قبل أن تزول.

From Sama'ah bin Mihran who said: Abu Abdullah (peace be upon him) said to me: Beware of praying before noon, for praying during Asr time is better for you than praying before noon.

Hadith 4816

عن أبي بصير، عن أبي عبد الله (عليه السلام) قال: من صلى في غير وقت فلا صلاة له.

From Abu Basir, from Abu Abdullah (peace be upon him) who said: Whoever prays outside the proper time has not prayed at all.

Hadith 4817

عن أبيه، عن أبي عبد الله (عليه السلام) قال: لئن أصلي الظهر في وقت العصر أحب إلي من أن أصلي قبل أن تزول الشمس، فإني إذا صليت قبل أن تزول الشمس لم تحسب لي، وإذا صليت في وقت العصر حسبت لي.

From his father, from Abu Abdullah (peace be upon him) who said: For me to pray Zuhr at the time of Asr is more beloved to me than praying before the sun's zenith, because if I pray before the sun's zenith it will not be counted for me, but if I pray during Asr time it will be counted for me.

Hadith 4818

عن عبيد الله الحلبي، عن أبي عبد الله (عليه السلام) قال: إذا صليت في السفر شيئا من الصلوات في غير وقتها فلا يضرك.

From Ubaydullah al-Halabi, from Abu Abdullah (peace be upon him) who said: If you pray any of the prayers during travel outside their times, there is no harm upon you.

أقول: حمله الشيخ على خروج الوقت فتكون قضاءاً، ويحتمل الحمل على وقت الفضيلة لا الاجزاء.

I (Hurr Amili) say: The Shaykh interpreted this as referring to praying after the time has passed making it a makeup prayer, and it could also be interpreted as referring to the preferred time rather than the obligatory time.

Hadith 4819

عن أبي بصير، عن أبي عبد الله (عليه السلام) قال: من صلى في غير وقت فلا صلاة له.

From Abu Basir, from Abu Abdullah (peace be upon him) who said: Whoever prays outside the proper time, his prayer is not accepted.

Hadith 4820

محمد بن علي بن الحسين قال: قال أبو جعفر (عليه السلام): لان أصلي بعد ما مضى الوقت أحب إلي من أن أصلي وأنا في شك من الوقت، وقبل الوقت.

Muhammad bin Ali bin al-Husayn said: Abu Ja'far (peace be upon him) said: For me to pray after the time has passed is more beloved to me than praying while I am in doubt about the time, or before the time.

Shaykh Hurr Amili: What indicates this has been mentioned before, and what indicates it and the exemption of a case - which is when the time enters before finishing the prayer after having started it assuming its entrance - will be mentioned.

CHAPTER 14

Relying On Rooster's Crow To Determine Prayer Times Due To Necessity, And The Dislike Of Cursing It

[Hadith 4821 to 4825]

Hadith 4821

عن الحسين بن المختار قال: قلت للصادق (عليه السلام): إني مؤذن، فإذا كان يوم غيم لم أعرف الوقت؟

فقال: إذا صاح الديك ثلاثة أصوات ولاء فقد زالت الشمس و دخل وقت الصلاة.

From Al-Husayn bin Al-Mukhtar, he said: I said to Al-Sadiq (peace be upon him): I am a muezzin, and when it's a cloudy day I don't know the time? He said: When the rooster crows three consecutive times, the sun has passed its zenith and the prayer time has entered.

———

Hadith 4822

ورواه الشيخ بإسناده عن سهل بن زياد، عن محمد بن إبراهيم عن النوفلي، عن الحسين بن المختار، عن رجل، عن أبي عبد الله (عليه السلام).

The Shaykh narrated it through his chain from Sahl bin Ziyad, from Muhammad bin Ibrahim from Al-Nawfali, from Al-Husayn bin Al-Mukhtar, from a man, from Abu Abdullah (peace be upon him).

Translator: In the original arabic, only a chain is mentioned here, without any hadith.

———

Hadith 4823

عن الصادق جعفر بن محمد، عن آبائه (عليهم السلام) - في حديث المناهي - قال: نهى رسول الله (صلى الله عليه وآله) عن سب الديك، وقال: إنه يوقظ للصلاة.

From Al-Sadiq Ja'far bin Muhammad, from his forefathers (peace be upon them) - in the hadith of prohibitions - he said: The Messenger of Allah (peace be upon him and his family) forbade cursing the rooster, and said: Indeed it awakens for prayer.

———

Hadith 4824

قال الصدوق: وقال الصادق (عليه السلام): تعلموا من الديك خمس خصال: محافظته على أوقات الصلاة، والغيرة، والسخاء، والشجاعة، وكثرة الطروقة.

Al-Saduq said: And Al-Sadiq (peace be upon him) said: Learn from the rooster five qualities: its preservation of prayer times, ghayrah (possessive jealousy), generosity, courage, and frequent mating.

———

Hadith 4825

عن أبي عبد الله الفراء، عن أبي عبد الله (عليه السلام)، قال: قال له رجل من أصحابنا: ربما اشتبه الوقت علينا في يوم الغيم؟ فقال: تعرف هذه الطيور التي تكون عندكم بالعراق يقال لها: الديكة؟ فقلت: نعم، قال: إذا ارتفعت أصواتها وتجاوبت فقد زالت الشمس، أو قال: فصله. ورواه الصدوق بإسناده عن أبي عبد الله الفراء، إلا أنه قال: فعند ذلك فصل.

From Abu Abdullah Al-Farra, from Abu Abdullah (peace be upon him), he said: A man from our companions said to him: Sometimes the time becomes unclear to us on a cloudy day? He said: Do you know these birds that you have in Iraq called roosters? I said: Yes. He said: When their voices rise and respond to each other, the sun has passed its zenith - or he said: pray. And Al-Saduq narrated it through his chain from Abu Abdullah Al-Farra, except that he said: At that time, pray.

CHAPTER 15

Recommendation To Shorten The Supererogatory Noon Prayer When The Time Of Virtue Is Limited

[Hadith 4826 to 4826]

Hadith 4826

عن أبي بصير قال: ذكر أبو عبد الله (عليه السلام) أول الوقت وفضله، فقلت: كيف أصنع بالثماني ركعات؟ قال: خفف ما استطعت.

From Abu Basir who said: Abu Abdullah (peace be upon him) mentioned the beginning of prayer time and its virtue, so I said: What should I do about the eight rak'ahs (of supererogatory prayer)? He said: Make them as light [short] as you can.

CHAPTER 16

The Beginning Time Of Maghrib Prayer Is At Sunset, Known By The Disappearance Of Eastern Redness

[Hadith 4827 to 4856]

Hadith 4827

عن أبي جعفر (عليه السلام) قال: إذا غابت الحمرة من هذا الجانب يعني من المشرق فقد غابت الشمس من شرق الأرض وغربها.

From Abu Ja'far (peace be upon him), he said: When the redness disappears from this side, meaning from the east, then the sun has set from the east of the earth and its west.

———

Hadith 4828

عن أبي ولاد قال: قال أبو عبد الله (عليه السلام): إن الله خلق حجابا من ظلمة مما يلي المشرق، ووكل به ملكا، فإذا غابت الشمس اغترف ذلك الملك غرفة بيديه، ثم استقبل بها المغرب يتبع الشفق ويخرج من بين يديه قليلا قليلا، ويمضي فيوافي المغرب عند سقوط الشفق فيسرح الظلمة، ثم يعود إلى المشرق، فإذا طلع الفجر نشر جناحيه فاستاق الظلمة من المشرق إلى المغرب حتى يوافي بها المغرب عند طلوع الشمس.

From Abu Wallad who said: Abu Abdullah (peace be upon him) said: Allah created a veil of darkness from the direction of the east, and appointed an angel over it. When the sun sets, that angel scoops darkness with both hands, then faces the west following the twilight, releasing it gradually before him. He proceeds until reaching the west at the fall of twilight and releases the darkness, then returns to the east. When dawn breaks, he spreads his wings and drives the darkness from east to west until reaching the west at sunrise.

———

Hadith 4829

عن أبي عبد الله (عليه السلام)، قال: سمعته يقول: وقت المغرب إذا ذهبت الحمرة من المشرق، وتدري كيف ذلك؟ قلت: لا. قال: لان المشرق مطل على المغرب هكذا ورفع يمينه فوق يساره، فإذا غابت هاهنا ذهبت الحمرة من هاهنا.

From Abu Abdullah (peace be upon him) who said: I heard him say: The time of Maghrib is when the redness disappears from the east. Do you know how that is? I said: No. He said: Because the east overlooks the west like this - and he raised his right hand above his left - so when it sets here, the redness disappears from here.

———

Hadith 4830

عن أبي عبد الله (عليه السلام) قال: وقت سقوط القرص ووجوب الافطار (من الصيام) أن تقوم بحذاء القبلة وتتفقد الحمرة التي ترتفع من المشرق، فإذا جازت قمة الرأس إلى ناحية المغرب فقد وجب الافطار وسقط القرص.

From Abu Abdullah (peace be upon him) who said: The time of the setting of the disc (sun) and the obligation to break the fast (from fasting) is that you stand facing the qiblah and observe the redness that rises from the east, so when it passes over the top of the head towards the west, then breaking the fast becomes obligatory and the disc (sun) has set.

Hadith 4831

عن أبان بن تغلب قال: قلت لأبي عبد الله (عليه السلام): أي ساعة كان رسول الله (صلى الله عليه وآله) يوتر؟ فقال: على مثل مغيب الشمس إلى صلاة المغرب.

From Aban ibn Taghlib who said: I asked Abu Abdullah (peace be upon him): At what hour did the Messenger of Allah (peace be upon him and his family) pray Witr? He said: Similar to the time between sunset and Maghrib prayer.

Hadith 4832

عن أبي عبد الله (عليه السلام)، أنه سأله سائل عن وقت المغرب؟ فقال: إن الله يقول في كتابه لإبراهيم: (فلما جن عليه الليل رأى كوكبا قال هذا ربي) وهذا أول الوقت، وآخر ذلك غيبوبة الشفق، وأول وقت العشاء الآخرة ذهاب الحمرة، وآخر وقتها إلى غسق الليل يعني نصف الليل.

From Abu Abdullah (peace be upon him), that someone asked him about the time of Maghrib prayer? He said: Indeed Allah says in His Book regarding Ibrahim: When the night covered him, he saw a star and said "This is my Lord" [Quran, 6:76] and this is the beginning of the time, and its end is the disappearance of twilight, and the beginning of the time of the latter Isha is the disappearance of redness, and its end is until the darkness of night, meaning midnight.

أقول: ذكر بعض المحققين أنه موافق لما تقدم، لان ذهاب الحمرة المشرقية يستلزم رؤية كوكب غالبا، ويجوز حمله على عدم ظهور المشرق والمغرب.

I (Hurr Amili) say: Some scholars mentioned that this agrees with what preceded, because the disappearance of eastern redness usually necessitates seeing a star, and it can be interpreted as the non-appearance of both east and west.

Hadith 4833

عن بريد بن معاوية العجلي قال: سمعت أبا جعفر (عليه السلام) يقول: إذا غابت الحمرة من هذا الجانب يعني ناحية المشرق فقد غابت الشمس من شرق الأرض ومن غربها.

From Burayd ibn Mu'awiyah al-Ijli who said: I heard Abu Ja'far (peace be upon him) saying: When the redness disappears from this side, meaning the direction of the east, then the sun has set from the east and west of the earth.

Hadith 4834

عن محمد بن علي قال: صحبت الرضا (عليه السلام) في السفر فرأيته يصلي المغرب إذا أقبلت الفحمة من المشرق يعني السواد.

From Muhammad ibn Ali who said: I accompanied Al-Ridha (peace be upon him) during travel and saw him praying Maghrib when darkness came from the east, meaning the blackness.

Hadith 4835

عن شهاب بن عبد ربه قال: قال أبو عبد الله (عليه السلام): يا شهاب إني أحب إذا صليت المغرب أن أرى في السماء كوكبا.

From Shihab ibn Abd Rabbih who said: Abu Abdullah (peace be upon him) said: O Shihab, I prefer when I pray Maghrib to see a star in the sky.

Hadith 4836

عن عمار الساباطي: عن أبي عبد الله (عليه السلام) قال: إنما أمرت أبا الخطاب أن يصلي المغرب حين زالت الحمرة (من مطلع الشمس)، فجعل هو الحمرة التي من قبل المغرب، وكان يصلي حين يغيب الشفق.

From Ammar al-Sabati from Abu Abdullah (peace be upon him) who said: I only ordered Abu al-Khattab to pray Maghrib when the redness disappeared from the sun's rising place, but he considered it the redness from the west, and he would pray when the twilight disappeared.

Hadith 4837

عن أحدهما (عليه السلام) قال: إذا غابت الحمرة من المشرق فقد غابت الشمس من شرق الأرض وغربها.

From one of them (peace be upon him) who said: When the redness disappears from the east, then the sun has set from the east and west of the earth.

Hadith 4838

عن أبي عبد الله (عليه السلام)، قال: سألته عن وقت المغرب؟ فقال: إذا تغيرت الحمرة في الأفق، وذهبت الصفرة، وقبل أن تشتبك النجوم.

From Abu Abdullah (peace be upon him), he said: I asked him about the time of Maghrib? He said: When the redness changes on the horizon, and the yellowness goes away, and before the stars become intertwined.

Hadith 4839

عن أبي عبد الله (عليه السلام)، قال: قال لي: مسوا بالمغرب قليلا فإن الشمس تغيب من عندكم قبل أن تغيب من عندنا.

From Abu Abdullah (peace be upon him), he said to me: Delay Maghrib slightly because the sun sets for you before it sets for us.

Hadith 4840

عن عبد الله بن وضاح قال: كتبت إلي العبد الصالح (عليه السلام) يتوارى القرص ويقبل الليل ثم يزيد الليل ارتفاعا، وتستتر عنا الشمس، وترتفع فوق الليل حمرة، ويؤذن عندنا المؤذنون، أفأصلي حينئذ وأفطر إن كنت صائما؟ أو أنتظر حتى تذهب الحمرة التي فوق الجبل؟ فكتب إلى: أرى لك أن تنتظر حتى تذهب الحمرة، وتأخذ بالحائطة لدينك.

From Abdullah ibn Wadhah who said: I wrote to the Righteous Servant (peace be upon him): The disk disappears and night approaches, then night increases in height, and the sun is hidden from us, and redness rises above the night, and our muezzins call for prayer - should I pray then and break my fast if I am fasting? Or should I wait until the redness above the mountain disappears? He wrote back: I advise you to wait until the redness disappears, and take precaution for your religion.

Hadith 4841

عن جارود قال: قال لي أبو عبد الله (عليه السلام): يا جارود، ينصحون فلا يقبلون، وإذا سمعوا بشيئ نادوا به، أو حدثوا بشيئ أذاعوه، قلت لهم: مسوا بالمغرب قليلا فتركوها حتى اشتبكت النجوم فأنا الان أصليها إذا سقط القرص.

From Jarud who said: Abu Abdullah (peace be upon him) said to me: O Jarud, they are advised but do not accept, and when they hear something they announce it, or when they are told something they spread it. I told them: Delay Maghrib slightly, but they left it until the stars became intertwined, so now I pray it when the disk falls.

أقول: قوله: مسوا بالمغرب قليلا يدل على المقصود، وآخره يدل على عمله بالتقية بقرينة ذكر الإذاعة.

ويأتي ما يؤيد هذه الأحاديث في الصوم وغيره إن شاء الله.

I (Hurr Amili) say: His saying "delay Maghrib slightly" indicates the intended meaning, and its end indicates his practice of taqiyyah due to mentioning the spreading. Support for these hadiths will come in fasting and other topics, insha'Allah.

واعلم أنه يتعين العمل بما تقدم في هذه الأحاديث وفي العنوان: أما أولا: فلأنه أقرب إلى الاحتياط للدين في الصلاة والصوم. وأما ثانيا: فلأن فيه جمعا بين الأدلة عملا وبجميع الأحاديث من غير طرح شئ منها. وأما ثالثا: فلما فيه من حمل المجمل على المبين والمطلق على المقيد. وأما رابعا: فلاحتمال معارضه للتقية وموافقته للعامة. وأما خامسا: فلعدم احتماله للنسخ مع احتمال بعض معارضاته له. وأما سادسا: فلأنه أشهر فتوى بين الأصحاب. وأما سابعا: فلكونه أوضح دلالة من معارضه، إن لم يصرح فيه بعدم اشتراط ذهاب الحمرة، فما دل على اعتباره أوضح دلالة وأبعد من التأويل. وما تخيله بعضهم من حمله على الاستحباب يرده ما تقدم وما يأتي من عدم جواز تأخير المغرب طلبا لفضلها وغير ذلك، والله أعلم.

Know that acting upon what preceded in these hadiths and in the title is necessary: First, because it is closer to religious precaution in prayer and fasting. Second, because it combines all evidence practically and all hadiths without discarding any. Third, because it interprets the ambiguous based on the clear, and the absolute based on the restricted. Fourth, due to possibility of opposition being taqiyyah and agreement with the general public. Fifth, because it cannot be abrogated while some of its opposition may be. Sixth, because it is more famous in rulings among companions. Seventh, because it has clearer evidence than its opposition, as it does not explicitly state non-requirement of redness disappearing. What indicates its consideration has clearer evidence and is further from interpretation. What some imagined about interpreting it as recommended is rejected by what preceded and what will come about impermissibility of delaying Maghrib seeking its virtue and other matters, and Allah knows best.

Hadith 4842

عن أبي عبد الله (عليه السلام)، قال: سمعته يقول: وقت المغرب إذا غربت الشمس فغاب قرصها.

From Abu Abdullah (peace be upon him), who said: I heard him say: The time for Maghrib prayer is when the sun has set and its disk has disappeared.

Hadith 4843

عن زرارة قال: قال أبو جعفر (عليه السلام): وقت المغرب إذا غاب القرص، فإن رأيت بعد ذلك وقد صليت أعدت الصلاة. ومضى صومك وتكف عن الطعام إن كنت أصبت منه شيئا.

From Zurarah who said: Abu Ja'far (peace be upon him) said: The time for Maghrib is when the disk has disappeared. If you see it after having prayed, repeat the prayer. Your fast remains valid but refrain from food if you had consumed any.

أقول: قد عرفت أنه محمول على المغيب الذي يعلم بذهاب الحمرة المشرقية، وكذا أمثاله.

I (Hurr Amili) say: It is known that this refers to the setting that is known by the disappearance of the eastern redness, and similarly for its like cases.

Hadith 4844

محمد بن علي بن الحسين قال: قال أبو جعفر (عليه السلام): وقت المغرب إذا غاب القرص.

Muhammad bin Ali bin Al-Husayn said: Abu Ja'far (peace be upon him) said: The time for Maghrib is when the disk has disappeared.

Hadith 4845

قال: وقال الصادق (عليه السلام): إذا غابت الشمس فقد حل الافطار ووجبت الصلاة، وإذا صليت المغرب فقد دخل وقت العشاء الآخرة إلى انتصاف الليل.

He said: And Al-Sadiq (peace be upon him) said: When the sun sets, breaking the fast becomes permissible and prayer becomes obligatory, and when you pray Maghrib, the time for Isha prayer begins until midnight.

Hadith 4846

عن عمرو بن شمر، عن جابر، عن أبي جعفر (عليه السلام) قال: قال رسول الله (صلى الله عليه وآله) إذا غاب القرص أفطر الصائم ودخل وقت الصلاة.

From Amr bin Shimr, from Jabir, from Abu Ja'far (peace be upon him) who said: The Messenger of Allah (peace be upon him and his family) said: When the disk disappears, the fasting person breaks their fast and the prayer time begins.

Hadith 4847

عن داود بن أبي يزيد قال: قال الصادق جعفر بن محمد (عليه السلام): إذا غابت الشمس فقد دخل وقت المغرب.

From Dawud bin Abi Yazid who said: Al-Sadiq Ja'far bin Muhammad (peace be upon him) said: When the sun sets, the time for Maghrib has begun.

Hadith 4848

عن عبيد الله بن زرارة، عن أبي عبد الله (عليه السلام)، قال: سمعته يقول: صحبني رجل كان يمسي بالمغرب ويغلس بالفجر، وكنت أنا أصلي المغرب إذا غربت الشمس وأصلي الفجر إذا استبان لي الفجر.

From Ubaydullah bin Zurarah, from Abu Abdullah (peace be upon him), who said: I heard him say: A man accompanied me who would delay Maghrib until darkness and pray Fajr in the darkness before dawn, while I would pray Maghrib when the sun set and pray Fajr when dawn became clear to me.

فقال لي الرجل: ما يمنعك أن تصنع مثل ما أصنع؟ فإن الشمس تطلع على قوم قبلنا وتغرب عنا وهي طالعة على قوم آخرين بعد، قال: فقلت: إنما علينا أن نصلي إذا وجبت الشمس عنا، وإذا طلع الفجر عندنا، ليس علينا إلا ذلك، وعلى أولئك أن يصلوا إذا غربت عنهم.

The man said to me: What prevents you from doing as I do? For the sun rises for some people before us and sets for us while it is still rising for others afterward. He said: I replied: We are only obligated to pray when the sun sets for us and when dawn breaks for us, nothing more than that, and those others must pray when it sets for them.

أقول: لعل الرجل كان من أصحاب أبي الخطاب، وكان يصلي المغرب عند ذهاب الحمرة المغربية، وكان الصادق (عليه السلام) يصليها عند ذهاب الحمرة المشرقية، ومعلوم أن الشمس في ذلك الوقت تكون طالعة على قوم آخرين، إلا أنه لا يعتبر أكثر من ذلك القدر.

I (Hurr Amili) say: Perhaps the man was from the companions of Abu Al-Khattab, and he would pray Maghrib at the disappearance of the western redness, while Al-Sadiq (peace be upon him) would pray it at the disappearance of the eastern redness, and it is known that the sun at that time would be rising for other people, except that nothing more than that amount is considered.

Hadith 4849

عن الربيع بن سليمان، وأبان بن أرقم وغيرهم قالوا: أقبلنا من مكة حتى إذا كنا بوادي الأخضر إذا نحن برجل يصلي ونحن ننظر إلى شعاع الشمس، فوجدنا في أنفسنا، فجعل يصلي ونحن ندعو عليه (حتى صلى ركعة ونحن ندعو عليه)

From Al-Rabi' bin Sulayman, and Aban bin Arqam and others who said: We were coming from Makkah until when we were at Wadi Al-Akhdar, we saw a man praying while we could still see the sun's rays. We felt disapproval in ourselves and began invoking against him while he prayed (until he prayed one rak'ah while we were invoking against him)

ونقول: هذا من شباب أهل المدينة، فلما أتيناه إذا هو أبو عبد الله جعفر بن محمد (عليه السلام)، فنزلنا

فصلينا معه وقد فاتتنا ركعة، فلما قضينا الصلاة قمنا إليه فقلنا: جعلنا فداك هذه الساعة تصلي؟! فقال:

إذا غابت الشمس فقد دخل الوقت.

And we said: This must be from the youth of Madinah. When we approached him, it was Abu Abdullah Ja'far bin Muhammad (peace be upon him). We dismounted and prayed with him though we had missed one rak'ah. When we finished the prayer, we went to him and said: May we be sacrificed for you, you pray at this hour?! He said: When the sun sets, the time has begun.

أقول: صدر الحديث يدل على أنه كان مقررا عند الشيعة أنه لا يدخل الوقت قبل مغيب الحمرة المشرقية. ولعله (عليه السلام) صلى ذلك الوقت للتقية ويحتمل كونه صلى بعد ذهاب الحمرة بالنسبة إلى الوادي، ويكون الشعاع خلف الجبل إلى ناحية المغرب، وقد رآه الجماعة من أعلى الجبل.

I (Hurr Amili) say: The beginning of the hadith indicates that it was established among the Shia that the time does not begin before the disappearance of the eastern redness, and perhaps he (peace be upon him) prayed at that time out of taqiyyah. It's also possible that he prayed after the disappearance of the redness relative to the valley, with the rays being behind the mountain towards the west, which the group saw from the top of the mountain.

Hadith 4850

عن عبيد بن زرارة، عن أبي عبد الله (عليه السلام) قال: إذا غربت الشمس فقد دخل وقت الصلاتين إلى نصف الليل، إلا أن هذه قبل هذه، وإذا زالت الشمس فقد دخل وقت الصلاتين، إلا أن هذه قبل هذه.

From Ubayd bin Zurarah, from Abu Abdullah (peace be upon him) who said: When the sun sets, the time for both prayers enters until midnight, except that this one comes before that one. And when the sun passes its zenith, the time for both prayers enters, except that this one comes before that one.

Hadith 4851

وعنه، عن علي بن الحكم، عمن حدثه، عن أحدهما (عليهما السلام)، أنه سئل عن وقت المغرب؟ فقال: إذا غاب كرسيها، قلت: وما كرسيها؟ قال: قرصها، فقلت: متى يغيب قرصها؟ قال: إذا نظرت إليه فلم تره.

From him, from Ali bin Al-Hakam, from who narrated to him, from one of them (peace be upon them), that he was asked about the time of Maghrib prayer? He said: When its throne disappears. I asked: What is its throne? He said: Its disk. I asked: When does its disk disappear? He said: When you look for it and cannot see it.

أقول: هذه مع احتماله للتقية يحتمل أن يراد نفى رؤية القرص ورؤية أثره، وهو الشعاع والحمرة المشرقية لما تقدم.

I (Hurr Amili) say: This, while possibly being taqiyyah, could mean the inability to see both the disk and its effects, which are the rays and eastern redness as previously mentioned.

Hadith 4852

عن أبي عبد الله (عليه السلام) قال: وقت المغرب من حين تغيب الشمس إلى أن تشتبك النجوم.

From Abu Abdullah (peace be upon him) who said: The time of Maghrib is from when the sun sets until the stars become intertwined.

Hadith 4853

عن أبي عبد الله (عليه السلام) قال: كان رسول الله (صلى الله عليه وآله) يصلي المغرب حين تغيب الشمس حيث تغيب حاجبها.

From Abu Abdullah (peace be upon him) who said: The Messenger of Allah (peace be upon him and his family) would pray Maghrib when the sun set, when its disk would disappear.

أقول: هذا وبعض ما مر يحتمل النسخ، ولفظ كان يشعر بالزوال، ويحتمل الحمل على ما مر.

I (Hurr Amili) say: This and some of what passed could be abrogated, and the term "was" indicates cessation, and it could be interpreted as previously mentioned.

Hadith 4854

عن أبي بصير، عن أبي عبد الله (عليه السلام) قال: وقت المغرب حين تغيب الشمس.

From Abu Basir, from Abu Abdullah (peace be upon him) who said: The time of Maghrib is when the sun sets.

Hadith 4855

عن أبي عبد الله (عليه السلام)، قال: سألته عن وقت المغرب؟ قال: ما بين غروب الشمس إلى سقوط الشفق.

From Abu Abdullah (peace be upon him), he said: I asked him about the time of Maghrib? He said: It is between the setting of the sun until the disappearance of twilight.

Hadith 4856

عن عمرو بن أبي نصر قال: سمعت أبا عبد الله (عليه السلام) يقول: في المغرب: إذا توارى القرص كان وقت الصلاة، وأفطر.

From Amr bin Abi Nasr who said: I heard Abu Abdullah (peace be upon him) saying regarding Maghrib: When the disk disappears, it becomes time for prayer and breaking the fast.

أقول: قد عرفت وجهه، وليس في شئ من الأحاديث كما ترى تصريح بأن وقت المغرب يدخل قبل ذهاب الحمرة المشرقية، وكلها يحتمل الحمل على ذلك لما مر، فهذا ظاهر وذلك نص صريح، وهذا يحتمل التقية أيضا كما مر.

I (Hurr Amili) say: You have known its aspect, and there isn't in any of these hadiths, as you see, an explicit statement that Maghrib time enters before the eastern redness disappears, and all of them could be interpreted according to what passed, for this is apparent and that is explicitly clear, and this could also be taqiyyah as mentioned.

Translator: The narrations in this chapter establish that the legal definition of sunset (al-ghurub) involves more than the mere disappearance of the solar disk from the observer's line of sight. While several hadiths use the phrasing "when the disk disappears," the Imams clarify that the sun has not truly set - and the disk has not disappeared from both the "east and the west of the earth" - until the eastern redness (al-humrah al-mashriqiyyah) vanishes. This ruling is explained through a spatial analogy in which the east "overlooks" the west: as long as the sun's reflection remains visible in the eastern sky, the sun is still technically above the horizon in a manner that prevents the onset of Maghrib. Accordingly, in the eyes of the Law, the disk has not "disappeared" (refer to Hadith 4839) until its atmospheric effects have been fully removed - that is, until its glow has retreated entirely from the eastern horizon.

A central theme in the hadith is the distinction between the "apparent" sunset and the "true" religious sunset. Standing toward the qiblah and observing the redness rising from the east provides a definitive marker: the time for breaking the fast and praying Maghrib only arrives when that redness passes over the zenith (the top of the head) toward the west. This requirement serves as a safeguard for the believer's religion, ensuring that the prayer is not performed prematurely.

Shaykh Hurr Amili notes that hadiths which seem to permit praying immediately upon the disk's disappearance should be understood as "apparent" (zahir) meanings that are further clarified or restricted by the "explicit" (nass) requirement of the disappearance of eastern redness. He also notes that, the potential contradictions can be addressed by categorizing certain "early" prayer narrations as being influenced by taqiyyah to align with general public practice.

The Imams emphasize that the disappearance of the eastern redness typically coincides with the appearance of the first stars. However, they also warn against excessive delay, noting that the time for Maghrib is "narrow" and remains only until the "intertwining of the stars" or the fall of the western twilight (al-shafaq). Refer to Hadith 4874 in Chapter 18.

Also refer to the comments in Hadith 13014 (Vol. 10, Section 2, Chapter 52) on the timing for breaking a fast.

———————

CHAPTER 17

The Beginning Time Of Maghrib And Isha Is Sunset, And Their End Is Midnight, With Maghrib Having Priority At The Beginning And Isha At The End

[Hadith 4857 to 4870]

Hadith 4857

عن زرارة، عن أبي جعفر (عليه السلام) قال: إذا زالت الشمس دخل الوقتان الظهر والعصر، وإذا غابت الشمس دخل الوقتان المغرب والعشاء الآخرة.

From Zurarah, from Abu Ja'far (peace be upon him), who said: When the sun passes its zenith, the two times enter: Zuhr and Asr. And when the sun sets, the two times enter: Maghrib and Isha al-Akhirah.

———

Hadith 4858

قال: وقال الصادق (عليه السلام): إذا غابت الشمس فقد حل الافطار ووجبت الصلاة، وإذا صليت المغرب فقد دخل وقت العشاء الآخرة إلى انتصاف الليل.

He said: And Al-Sadiq (peace be upon him) said: When the sun sets, breaking the fast becomes permissible and prayer becomes obligatory, and when you pray Maghrib, the time for Isha al-Akhirah enters until midnight.

———

Hadith 4859

قال: وقال أبو جعفر (عليه السلام): ملك موكل يقول: من بات عن العشاء الآخرة إلى نصف الليل فلا أنام الله عينه.

He said: And Abu Ja'far (peace be upon him) said: An appointed angel says: May Allah not grant sleep to the eyes of one who delays Isha al-Akhirah until midnight.

———

Hadith 4860

عن أبي عبد الله (عليه السلام) قال: إذا غابت الشمس فقد دخل وقت المغرب حتى يمضي مقدار ما يصلي المصلي ثلاث ركعات، فإذا مضى ذلك فقد دخل وقت المغرب والعشاء الآخرة حتى يبقى من انتصاف الليل مقدار ما يصلي المصلي أربع ركعات، وإذا بقي مقدار ذلك فقد خرج وقت المغرب وبقي وقت العشاء إلى انتصاف الليل.

From Abu Abdullah (peace be upon him) who said: When the sun sets, the time for Maghrib enters until the duration it takes for one to pray three rak'ahs passes.

When that passes, the time for both Maghrib and Isha al-Akhiraj enters until there remains before midnight the duration it takes to pray four rak'ahs. When that amount remains, the time for Maghrib exits and the time for Isha remains until midnight.

Hadith 4861

عن ابن مسكان رفعه إلى أبي عبد الله (عليه السلام) قال: من نام قبل أن يصلي العتمة فلم يستيقظ حتى يمضي نصف الليل فليقض صلاته وليستغفر الله.

From Ibn Muskan, who raised it to Abu Abdullah (peace be upon him) who said: Whoever sleeps before praying Isha and does not wake up until after midnight passes should make up their prayer and seek forgiveness from Allah.

Hadith 4862

وقد تقدم، في حديث بكر بن محمد، عن أبي عبد الله (عليه السلام) قال: وأول وقت العشاء ذهاب الحمرة، وآخر وقتها إلى غسق الليل نصف الليل.

And it has preceded in the hadith of Bakr bin Muhammad, from Abu Abdullah (peace be upon him) who said: The beginning time of Isha is when the redness disappears, and its latest time is until the darkness of night, which is midnight.

Hadith 4863

عن أبي بصير، عن أبي جعفر (عليه السلام) قال: قال رسول الله (صلى الله عليه وآله): لولا أني أخاف أن أشق على أمتي لاخرت العتمة إلى ثلث الليل، وأنت في رخصة إلى نصف الليل وهو غسق الليل، فإذا مضى الغسق نادى ملكان: من رقد عن صلاة المكتوبة بعد نصف الليل فلا رقدت عيناه.

From Abu Basir, from Abu Ja'far (peace be upon him) who said: The Messenger of Allah (peace be upon him and his family) said: Were it not that I fear it would be difficult for my community, I would have delayed Isha until a third of the night, and you have a concession until midnight which is the darkness of night. When the darkness passes, two angels call out: May the eyes of whoever sleeps past the prescribed prayer after midnight never find rest.

Hadith 4864

عن أبي عبد الله (عليه السلام) قال: آخر وقت العتمة نصف الليل.

From Abu Abdullah (peace be upon him) who said: The latest time for Isha prayer is midnight.

Hadith 4865

عن أبي عبد الله (عليه السلام) قال: العتمة إلى ثلث الليل أو إلى نصف الليل، وذلك التضييع.

From Abu Abdullah (peace be upon him) who said: Isha time extends until one-third of the night or until midnight, and delaying beyond that is negligence.

Hadith 4866

عن أبي عبد الله (عليه السلام) - في حديث -: إن رسول الله (صلى الله عليه وآله) قال: لولا أني أكره أن أشق على أمتي لاخرتها، يعني العتمة إلى ثلث الليل.

From Abu Abdullah (peace be upon him) in a hadith: The Messenger of Allah (peace be upon him and his family) said: Were it not that I would make it difficult for my community, I would have delayed it - meaning Isha prayer - until one-third of the night.

Hadith 4867

عن عبيد بن زرارة، عن أبي عبد الله (عليه السلام): قال إذا غربت الشمس دخل وقت الصلاتين إلا أن هذه قبل هذه. ورواه الشيخ بإسناده عن عبيد بن زرارة، مثله، إلا أنه قال: دخل وقت الصلاتين إلى نصف الليل.

From Ubayd ibn Zurarah, from Abu Abdullah (peace be upon him), who said: When the sun sets, the time for the two prayers enters, except that this one comes before that one. The Shaykh also narrated it through his chain of transmission from Ubayd ibn Zurarah, similarly, except that he said: the time for the two prayers enters until midnight.

Hadith 4868

عن أبي بصير، عن أبي جعفر (عليه السلام) قال: قال رسول الله (صلى الله عليه وآله): لولا أن أشق على أمتي لاخرت العشاء إلى ثلث الليل.

From Abu Basir, from Abu Ja'far (peace be upon him) who said: The Messenger of Allah (peace be upon him and his family) said: Were it not that I would make it difficult for my community, I would have delayed Isha until one-third of the night.

Hadith 4869

قال الكليني: وروي أيضا إلى نصف الليل.

Al-Kulayni said: It has also been narrated until midnight.

Hadith 4870

عن إسماعيل بن مهران قال: كتبت إلى الرضا (عليه السلام): ذكر أصحابنا أنه إذا زالت الشمس فقد دخل وقت الظهر والعصر، وإذا غربت دخل وقت المغرب والعشاء الآخرة، إلا أن هذه قبل هذه في السفر والحضر، وأن وقت المغرب إلى ربع الليل. فكتب: كذلك الوقت غير أن وقت المغرب ضيق.

From Isma'il ibn Mihran who said: I wrote to Al-Ridha (peace be upon him): Our companions have mentioned that when the sun passes its zenith, the time for Zuhr and Asr prayers enters, and when it sets, the time for Maghrib and Isha prayers enters, except that this comes before that during travel and residence, and that the time for Maghrib extends until a quarter of the night. He wrote back: The timing is like that, except that the time for Maghrib is narrow.

———

CHAPTER 18

Emphasis Of Performing Maghrib Prayer At Its Earliest Time, The Dislike Of Delaying It Except With An Excuse, The Prohibition Of Delaying It Seeking Its Merit, And That The End Of Its Preferred Time Is The Disappearance Of The Western Redness

[Hadith 4871 to 4894]

Hadith 4871

عن زيد الشحام قال: سألت أبا عبد الله (عليه السلام) عن وقت المغرب؟ فقال: إن جبرئيل أتى النبي (صلى الله عليه وآله) لكل صلاة بوقتين غير صلاة المغرب فإن وقتها واحد، وإن وقتها وجوبها.

From Zayd al-Shahham, he said: I asked Abu Abdullah (peace be upon him) about the time of Maghrib prayer. He said: Indeed Jibreel came to the Prophet (peace be upon him and his family) with two times for every prayer except Maghrib prayer, for it has one time, and its time is when it becomes obligatory.

Translator: The declaration by the Imams that Maghrib possesses only "one time" refers to the fact that its period of merit (Fadilah) and its "obligatory" beginning are functionally identical. While Jibreel (peace be upon him) brought two distinct times for the other four daily prayers - essentially a preferred window and a wider secondary window of choice - he brought only one for Maghrib, which is the moment the obligation starts. This unique "one time" represents the immediate window for the healthy resident, emphasizing that the command to pray becomes "present" as soon as the eastern redness disappears. Unlike Zuhr, where a believer has a broad span to perform the act while still being within the "primary" time, the time for Maghrib is characterized as "narrow".

It is essential to distinguish this from the start of Maghrib. The traditions in Chapter 16 establish that the prayer time begins when the redness in the eastern sky vanishes. Therefore, the entire span of the Maghrib obligation is measured by the movement of these two atmospheric effects: it begins when the eastern redness disappears and ends when the western redness disappears. Therefore, although a physical duration exists between the two atmospheric events, the Hukm (ruling) treats this entire span as a single, urgent obligation for the resident rather than two distinct legal periods of choice.

Hadith 4872

عن زرارة والفضيل قالا: قال أبو جعفر (عليه السلام): إن لكل صلاة وقتين غير المغرب فإن وقتها واحد، ووقتها وجوبها، ووقت فوتها سقوط الشفق.

From Zurarah and Al-Fudhayl, they said: Abu Ja'far (peace be upon him) said: Every prayer has two times except Maghrib, for it has one time, and its time is when it becomes obligatory, and the time of missing it (expiration) is the disappearance of the twilight.

Translator: The "disappearance of twilight" ("suqut al-shafaq") refers specifically to the disappearance of the redness from the western sky. This visual marker is used to define the absolute expiration of the "Maghrib" prayer window. In practical terms, the "disappearance of twilight" occurs when the red glow on the western horizon - which remains visible for a period after the sun has set - finally fades and turns into a dull whiteness. This transition from red to white signifies the technical end of the time for "Maghrib" and the moment the prayer is considered "missed" ("fawt") for a resident in normal circumstances. It also marks the beginning of the time for the "Isha" prayer.

In a practical sense, from the start of Maghrib which is approximately fifteen minutes after the solar disk vanishes (once the eastern redness has cleared the "zenith"), a believer typically has a remaining window of thirty to seventy-five minutes before the "Hukm" of "fawt" (missing) applies. This narrow timeframe emphasizes the "Ahl al-Bayt's" insistence that "Maghrib" possesses a unique structural urgency, where its start and "obligatory" times are essentially one and the same.

Hadith 4873

قال الكليني: وروى أيضا أن لها وقتين، آخر وقتها سقوط الشفق. أقول: جمع الكليني بينهما بالحمل على تقارب ما بين الوقتين.

Al-Kulayni said: It is also narrated that it has two times, and its last time is the disappearance of twilight.

Shaykh Hurr Amili: Al-Kulayni reconciled between them by interpreting it as the closeness between the two times.

Hadith 4874

عن إسماعيل بن مهران قال: كتبت إلى الرضا (عليه السلام) - إلى أن قال - فكتب: كذلك الوقت غير أن وقت المغرب ضيق، وآخر وقتها ذهاب الحمرة، ومصيرها إلى البياض في أفق المغرب.

From Isma'il ibn Mihran, he said: I wrote to Al-Ridha (peace be upon him) - and he said - so he wrote: The time is like that except that the time for Maghrib is narrow, and the end of its time is the disappearance of redness and its turning to whiteness in the western horizon.

Translator: The "Ahl al-Bayt" describe the total window of the Maghrib prayer as "narrow". The traditions emphasize that while the disappearance of the western twilight (redness) is the final legal boundary, delaying the prayer to this point is a concession reserved only for the "traveler", the "sick", the "fearful", or those with a "pressing need". For a healthy resident, the "Maghrib" prayer should be performed much earlier, as delaying it until the "stars become intertwined" - which occurs before the western redness fully fades - is condemned as a practice of heretical groups like the "Khattabiyyah". Thus, in practical application, the "disappearance of twilight" is the point of no return where the prayer shifts from being performed on time to being an overdue obligation.

In a practical sense, from the start of Maghrib which is approximately fifteen minutes after the solar disk vanishes (once the eastern redness has cleared the "zenith"), a believer typically has a remaining window of thirty to seventy-five minutes before the "Hukm" of "fawt" (missing) applies. This narrow timeframe emphasizes the "Ahl al-Bayt's" insistence that "Maghrib" possesses a unique structural urgency, where its start and "obligatory" times are essentially one and the same.

Hadith 4875

عن أبي عبد الله (عليه السلام) أنه قال: كان رسول الله (صلى الله عليه وآله) يصلي المغرب ويصلي معه حي من الأنصار يقال لهم: بنو سلمة، منازلهم على نصف ميل، فيصلون معه، ثم ينصرفون إلى منازلهم وهم يرون مواضع سهامهم.

From Abu Abdullah (peace be upon him) that he said: The Messenger of Allah (peace be upon him and his family) would pray Maghrib and a tribe from the Ansar called Banu Salamah would pray with him, and their homes were half a mile away. They would pray with him then return to their homes while still being able to see where their arrows would land.

Hadith 4876

قال: وقال الصادق (عليه السلام): ملعون ملعون من أخر المغرب طلبا لفضلها.

He said: And Al-Sadiq (peace be upon him) said: Cursed, cursed is the one who delays Maghrib seeking its merit.

Hadith 4877

قال: وقيل له: إن أهل العراق يؤخرون المغرب حتى تشتبك النجوم؟ فقال: هذا من عمل عدو الله أبي الخطاب.

He said: And it was said to him: The people of Iraq delay Maghrib until the stars intertwine (become densely clustered)? He said: This is from the work of Allah's enemy Abu al-Khattab.

Hadith 4878

عن زيد الشحام قال سمعت أبا عبد الله (عليه السلام) يقول: من أخر المغرب حتى تشتبك النجوم من غير علة فأنا إلى الله منه بريء.

From Zayd Al-Shahham, he said: I heard Abu Abdullah (peace be upon him) saying: Whoever delays the Maghrib prayer until the stars become intertwined (densely clustered) without a valid reason, I am disassociated from him before Allah.

Hadith 4879

عن أبي عبد الله (عليه السلام) قال: كان رسول الله (صلى الله عليه وآله) لا يؤثر على صلاة المغرب شيئا إذا غربت الشمس حتى يصليها.

Abu Abdullah (peace be upon him) said: The Messenger of Allah (peace be upon him and his family) would not give preference to anything over the Maghrib prayer when the sun had set, until he had prayed it.

Hadith 4880

عن أبي عبد الله (عليه السلام) - في حديث - قال: وقت المغرب حين تجب الشمس إلى أن تشتبك النجوم.

From Abu Abdullah (peace be upon him) - in a hadith - he said: The time for Maghrib prayer is from when the sun sets until the stars become intertwined (densely clustered).

Hadith 4881

عن أديم بن الحر قال: سمعت أبا عبد الله (عليه السلام) يقول: إن جبرئيل أمر رسول الله (صلى الله عليه وآله) بالصلوات كلها فجعل لكل صلاة وقتين إلا المغرب، فإنه جعل لها وقتا واحدا.

From, Adeem ibn al-Hurr, he said: He heard Abu Abdullah (peace be upon him) say: Indeed Jibreel instructed the Messenger of Allah (peace be upon him and his family) regarding all prayers and set two times for each prayer except Maghrib, for which he set only one time.

Hadith 4882

عن ذريح قال: قلت: لأبي عبد الله (عليه السلام): إن أناسا من أصحاب أبي الخطاب يمسون بالمغرب حتى تشتبك النجوم؟ قال: أبرأ إلى الله ممن فعل ذلك متعمدا.

From Dhuraih, he said: I said to Abu Abdullah (peace be upon him): Some followers of Abu al-Khattab delay the Maghrib prayer until the stars become intertwined (densely clustered)? He said: I seek disassociation with Allah from whoever does this deliberately.

Hadith 4883

عن أبي عبد الله (عليه السلام): إن جبرئيل أتى النبي (صلى الله عليه وآله) في الوقت الثاني في المغرب قبل سقوط الشفق.

From Abu Abdullah (peace be upon him): Jibreel came to the Prophet (peace be upon him and his family) at the second time period for Maghrib before the disappearance of twilight.

Hadith 4884

عن أبي عبد الله (عليه السلام)، قال: سألته عن وقت المغرب؟ قال: ما بين غروب الشمس إلى سقوط الشفق.

Abu Abdullah (peace be upon him) was asked about the time of Maghrib prayer. He said: It is between sunset and the disappearance of twilight.

Hadith 4885

عن أبي عبد الله (عليه السلام) قال: وقت المغرب من حين تغيب الشمس إلى أن تشتبك النجوم.

From Abu Abdullah (peace be upon him) who said: The time for Maghrib prayer is from when the sun sets until the stars become intertwined (densely clustered).

Hadith 4886

عن الصباح بن سيابة وأبي أسامة قالا: سألوا الشيخ (عليه السلام) عن المغرب فقال بعضهم: جعلني الله فداك، ننتظر حتى يطلع كوكب؟ فقال: خطابية؟! إن جبرئيل نزل بها على محمد (صلى الله عليه وآله) حين سقط القرص.

From Al-Sabah bin Siyabah and Abu Usamah who said: They asked the Shaykh (peace be upon him) about Maghrib prayer, and some said: May Allah make me your ransom, should we wait until a star appears? He said: Are you Khattabites (*) ?! Indeed, Jibreel descended with it (prayer time) to Muhammad (peace be upon him and his family) when the disk (sun) had set.

أقول: معلوم أنه بعد ذهاب الحمرة المشرقية إذا اتفق عدم رؤية الكوكب لا يجب انتظاره، بل لا يجوز، وأما ما تقدم فقد عرفت وجهه، ولعل الكواكب بصيغة الجمع هي الواقعة في السؤال لما مضى ويأتي، أو لعل المراد كوكب خاص كما يأتي أيضا.

I (Hurr Amili) say: It is known that after the eastern redness disappears, if the star is not visible, waiting for it is not obligatory, rather it is not permissible. As for what preceded, you have known its aspect, and perhaps the stars in plural form occurred in the question as mentioned before and will come, or perhaps a specific star is meant as will also come.

Translator: * Followers of Abu Al-Khattab, whose full name was Muhammad ibn Abi Zaynab al-Ajda' al-Asadi, was a controversial figure during the time of Imam Jafar al-Sadiq. He was known for his extreme views and interpretations of Islamic teachings, which eventually led to his separation from mainstream Shia thought. He founded a sect called the Khattabiyya, which held beliefs that were considered heretical by both Sunni and mainstream Shia Muslims. Imam Jafar al-Sadiq eventually disavowed Abu Al-Khattab and his teachings, publicly cursing him and warning his followers against associating with the Khattabiyya.

Hadith 4887

عن أبي عبد الله (عليه السلام)، قال: ذكر أبو الخطاب، فلعنه، ثم قال: إنه لم يكن يحفظ شيئا حدثته، إن رسول الله (صلى الله عليه وآله) غابت له الشمس في مكان كذا وكذا، وصلى المغرب بالشجرة وبينهما ستة أميال، فأخبرته بذلك في السفر فوضعه في الحضر.

From Abu Abdullah (peace be upon him), he said: Abu al-Khattab was mentioned, and he cursed him, then said: He did not preserve anything I told him. Indeed, when the sun set for the Messenger of Allah (peace be upon him and his family) in such and such place, he prayed Maghrib at the tree while there were six miles between them. I informed him of this regarding travel, but he applied it to residence.

Hadith 4888

عن أبي أسامة الشحام قال: قال رجل لأبي عبد الله (عليه السلام): أؤخر المغرب حتى تستبين النجوم؟ قال: فقال خطابية؟! إن جبرئيل نزل بها على محمد (صلى الله عليه وآله) حين سقط القرص.

From Abu Usama al-Shahham, he said: A man asked Abu Abdullah (peace be upon him): "Should I delay the Maghrib prayer until the stars clearly appear?" He replied: "Are you from the Khattabiyyah?! Indeed, Jibreel descended with it (the timing) to Muhammad (peace be upon him and his family) when the disc (of the sun) sets."

Hadith 4889

عن الرضا (عليه السلام) قال: إن أبا الخطاب قد كان أفسد عامة أهل الكوفة، وكانوا لا يصلون المغرب حتى يغيب الشفق، وإنما ذلك للمسافر والخائف ولصاحب الحاجة.

From Al-Ridha (peace be upon him) who said: Indeed Abu al-Khattab had corrupted most of the people of Kufa, and they would not pray Maghrib until the twilight disappeared, while that is only for the traveler, the fearful, and one with a need.

Translator: Delaying the prayer until the western twilight vanishes is permitted only for the "traveler", the "fearful", the "sick", or those with a "pressing need". For the resident in a state of ease, the window technically expires much earlier, often associated with the moment the "stars become intertwined". In fact, the "Ahl al-Bayt" expressed total "disassociation" from those who deliberately wait for the stars to appear or for the western redness to fade without a valid excuse.

Hadith 4890

عن أبي عبد الله (عليه السلام) قال: ملعون من أخر المغرب طلب فضلها.

From Abu Abdullah (peace be upon him) who said: Cursed is the one who delays Maghrib seeking its virtue.

Hadith 4891

وقد سبق في حديث بكر بن محمد، عن أبي عبد الله (عليه السلام)، أن آخر وقت المغرب غيبوبة الشفق.

And it was previously mentioned in the hadith of Bakr bin Muhammad, from Abu Abdullah (peace be upon him), that the last time for Maghrib is the disappearance of twilight.

Hadith 4892

عن معمر بن خلاد قال: قال أبو الحسن (عليه السلام): إن أبا الخطاب أفسد أهل الكوفة فصاروا لا يصلون المغرب حتى تغيب الشفق ولم يكن ذلك، إنما ذاك للمسافر وصاحب العلة.

From Mu'ammar bin Khallad who said: Abu al-Hasan (peace be upon him) said: Indeed Abu al-Khattab corrupted the people of Kufa so they became ones who would not pray Maghrib until the twilight disappeared, while that was not the case. That is only for the traveler and the sick person.

Hadith 4893

عن زرارة، عن أبي عبد الله (عليه السلام) - في حديث - قال: أما أبو الخطاب فكذب وقال: إني أمرته أن لا يصلي هو وأصحابه المغرب حتى يروا كوكب كذا يقال له: القيداني، والله أن ذلك الكوكب ما أعرفه.

From Zurarah, from Abu Abdullah (peace be upon him) - in a hadith - he said: As for Abu al-Khattab, he lied and said that I ordered him and his companions not to pray Maghrib until they see such and such star called Al-Qaidani, and by Allah, I do not even know that star.

Hadith 4894

عن صفوان بن مهران الجمال قال: قلت لأبي عبد الله (عليه السلام): إن معي شبه الكرش المنثور، فأؤخر صلاة المغرب حتى عند غيبوبة الشفق ثم أصليهما جميعا يكون ذلك أرفق بي؟ فقال: إذا غاب القرص فصل المغرب، فإنما أنت ومالك لله.

From Safwan bin Mihran Al-Jammal, he said: I said to Abu Abdullah (peace be upon him): I have a lot of disorganized affairs and responsibilities (*), so may I delay the Maghrib prayer until the twilight disappears and then pray both of them (Maghrib and Isha) together as that would be more convenient for me? He said: When the disk (of the sun) sets, pray Maghrib, for you and your wealth belong to Allah.

Translator: * The term shibh al-kirsh al-manthur literally translates to "something like a scattered stomach" or "resembling a spread-out rumen." In this context, it's a metaphorical expression referring to scattered or disorganized affairs or responsibilities.

CHAPTER 19

Permissibility Of Delaying Maghrib Prayer Until After Twilight Disappears, And Even Later With Valid Excuse, And Its Dislike Without Excuse

[Hadith 4895 to 4910]

Hadith 4895

عن عمر بن يزيد قال: قال أبو عبد الله (عليه السلام): وقت المغرب في السفر إلى ثلث الليل.

From Umar bin Yazid who said: Abu Abdullah (peace be upon him) said: The time for Maghrib prayer during travel extends until one-third of the night.

———————

Hadith 4896

عن أبي عبد الله (عليه السلام) قال: وقت المغرب في السفر إلى ربع الليل.

From Abu Abdullah (peace be upon him) who said: The time for Maghrib prayer during travel extends until one-fourth of the night.

———————

Hadith 4897

قال الكليني: وروي أيضا إلى نصف الليل. أقول: المراد إلى أن يبقى لنصف الليل مقدار العشائين لما يأتي، وقد تقدم ما يدل على ذلك.

Al-Kulayni said: It is also narrated that it extends until half of the night. I (Hurr Amili) say: What is meant is until there remains enough time before midnight for the two evening prayers, as will be explained, and evidence for this has preceded.

———————

Hadith 4898

عن أبي عبد الله (عليه السلام) قال: لا بأس أن تؤخر المغرب في السفر حتى يغيب، الشفق.

From Abu Abdullah (peace be upon him) who said: There is no problem in delaying the Maghrib prayer during travel until the twilight disappears.

———————

Hadith 4899

عن عمر بن يزيد قال: قال أبو عبد الله (عليه السلام): وقت المغرب في السفر إلى ربع الليل.

From Umar bin Yazid who said: Abu Abdullah (peace be upon him) said: The time for Maghrib prayer during travel extends until one-fourth of the night.

———————

Hadith 4900

عن أبي بصير قال: قال أبو عبد الله (عليه السلام): أنت في وقت من المغرب في السفر إلى خمسة أميال من بعد غروب الشمس.

From Abu Basir who said: Abu Abdullah (peace be upon him) said: You are within the time for Maghrib prayer during travel up to five miles after sunset.

Hadith 4901

عن إسماعيل بن جابر قال: كنت مع أبي عبد الله (عليه السلام) حتى إذا بلغنا بين العشائين قال: يا إسماعيل، امض مع الثقل والعيال حتى ألحقك، وكان ذلك عند سقوط الشمس، فكرهت أن أنزل فأصلي وأدع العيال، وقد أمرني أن أكون معهم، فسرت ثم لحقني أبو عبد الله (عليه السلام) فقال: يا إسماعيل، هل صليت المغرب بعد؟ فقلت: لا، فنزل عن دابته وأذن وأقام وصلى المغرب وصليت معه، وكان من الموضع الذي فارقته فيه إلى الموضع الذي لحقني ستة أميال.

From Isma'il bin Jabir who said: I was with Abu Abdullah (peace be upon him) until we reached between the two evening prayers. He said: O Isma'il, go ahead with the belongings and family until I catch up with you. This was at sunset. I disliked stopping to pray while leaving the family, as he had ordered me to stay with them. So I continued traveling, then Abu Abdullah (peace be upon him) caught up with me and said: O Isma'il, have you prayed Maghrib yet? I said: No. So he dismounted his animal, gave the adhan and iqamah, and prayed Maghrib, and I prayed with him. The distance between where he left me and where he caught up with me was six miles.

Hadith 4902

عن عمر بن يزيد قال: سألت أبا عبد الله (عليه السلام) عن وقت المغرب؟ فقال: إذا كان أرفق بك، وأمكن لك في صلاتك، وكنت في حوائجك فلك أن تؤخرها إلى ربع الليل، فقال: قال لي: هذا وهو شاهد في بلده.

Umar bin Yazid said: I asked Abu Abdullah (peace be upon him) about the time of Maghrib prayer. He said: If it is more convenient for you, more suitable for your prayer, and you are busy with your needs, you may delay it until a quarter of the night. He said to me: This applies when one is present in their town.

Hadith 4903

عن أبي همام إسماعيل بن همام قال: رأيت الرضا (عليه السلام) - وكنا عنده - لم يصل المغرب حتى ظهرت النجوم، ثم قام فصلى بنا على باب دار ابن أبي محمود.

Abu Hammam Isma'il bin Hammam said: I saw Al-Ridha (peace be upon him) - while we were with him - he did not pray Maghrib until the stars appeared, then he stood and led us in prayer at the door of Ibn Abi Mahmoud's house.

Hadith 4904

عن داود الصرمي قال: كنت عند أبي الحسن الثالث (عليه السلام) يوما فجلس يحدث حتى غابت الشمس، ثم دعا بشمع وهو جالس يتحدث، فلما خرجت من البيت نظرت وقد غاب الشفق قبل أن يصلي المغرب، ثم دعا بالماء فتوضأ وصلى.

Dawud al-Sarmi said: I was with Abu al-Hasan the Third (peace be upon him) one day, and he sat talking until the sun set. Then he called for a candle while still sitting and talking. When I left the house, I noticed that the twilight had disappeared before he prayed Maghrib. Then he called for water, performed wudu and prayed.

———

Hadith 4905

عن عمر بن يزيد قال: قلت لأبي عبد الله (عليه السلام): أكون مع هؤلاء وأنصرف من عندهم عند المغرب فأمر بالمساجد فأقيمت الصلاة، فإن أنا نزلت أصلي معهم لم أستمكن من الأذان والإقامة وافتتاح الصلاة، فقال: إئت منزلك وانزع ثيابك وإن أردت أن تتوضأ فتوضأ وصل فإنك في وقت إلى ربع الليل.

Umar bin Yazid said: I said to Abu Abdullah (peace be upon him): I am with these people and leave them at Maghrib time, then I pass by mosques where prayer is being established. If I stop to pray with them, I won't be able to do the adhan, iqamah, and start the prayer properly. He said: Go to your home, take off your clothes, and if you want to perform wudu, do so and pray, for you are still within the time until a quarter of the night.

———

Hadith 4906

عن أبي عبد الله (عليه السلام) قال: سألته عن صلاة المغرب إذا حضرت، هل يجوز أن تؤخر ساعة؟ قال: لا بأس، إن كان صائما أفطر (ثم صلى)، وإن كانت له حاجة قضاها ثم صلى.

Abu Abdullah (peace be upon him) was asked about the Maghrib prayer when its time comes, is it permissible to delay it for a while? He said: There is no problem. If one is fasting, let them break their fast (then pray), and if they have a need, let them fulfill it then pray.

———

Hadith 4907

عن جميل بن دراج قال: قلت لأبي عبد الله (عليه السلام): ما تقول في الرجل يصلي المغرب بعد ما يسقط الشفق؟ فقال: لعلة، لا بأس. قلت: فالرجل يصلي العشاء الآخرة قبل أن يسقط الشفق؟ قال: لعلة، لا بأس.

Jamil bin Darraj said: I said to Abu Abdullah (peace be upon him): What do you say about a man who prays Maghrib after the twilight disappears? He said: For a valid reason, there is no problem. I asked: What about a man who prays Isha before the twilight disappears? He said: For a valid reason, there is no problem.

———

Hadith 4908

عن عمر بن يزيد قال: قلت لأبي عبد الله (عليه السلام) أكون في جانب المصر فتحضر المغرب وأنا أريد المنزل فإن أخرت الصلاة حتى أصلي في المنزل كان أمكن لي، وأدركني المساء أفأصلي في بعض المساجد؟ فقال: صل في منزلك.

Umar bin Yazid said: I said to Abu Abdullah (peace be upon him): I am at the edge of the city when Maghrib time comes, and I want to go home. If I delay the prayer until I pray at home it would be more convenient for me, but evening catches up with me - should I pray in one of the mosques? He said: Pray in your home.

Hadith 4909

عن علي بن يقطين: قال: سألته عن الرجل تدركه صلاة المغرب في الطريق، أيؤخرها إلى أن يغيب الشفق؟ قال: لا بأس بذلك في السفر، فأما في الحضر فدون ذلك شيئا.

Ali bin Yaqtin said: I asked him about a man who encounters Maghrib prayer time while on the road, can he delay it until the twilight disappears? He said: There is no problem with that while traveling, but while resident it should be somewhat before that.

Hadith 4910

عن جعفر، عن أبيه (عليهما السلام) أن النبي (صلى الله عليه وآله) كان في الليلة المطيرة يؤخر من المغرب ويعجل من العشاء فيصليهما جميعا ويقول: من لا يرحم لا يرحم.

From Ja'far from his father (peace be upon them) that the Prophet (peace be upon him and his family) used to delay the Maghrib prayer on a rainy night and hasten the Isha prayer, and he would pray them together and say: Whoever does not show mercy will not be shown mercy.

CHAPTER 20

On Not Being Required To Climb Mountains To Observe Sunset, Rather What Matters Is The Setting Of The Disk And Disappearance Of Redness

[Hadith 4911 to 4912]

Hadith 4911

عن سماعة بن مهران قال: قلت لأبي عبد الله (عليه السلام) في المغرب إنا ربما صلينا ونحن نخاف أن تكون الشمس خلف الجبل أو قد سترنا منها الجبل؟ قال: فقال: ليس عليك صعود الجبل.

From Sama'ah bin Mihran who said: I said to Abu Abdullah (peace be upon him) regarding Maghrib prayer that sometimes we pray while we fear that the sun might be behind the mountain or that the mountain has blocked our view of it? He said: You are not required to climb the mountain.

Hadith 4912

عن حريز، عن أبي أسامة أو غيره قال: صعدت مرة جبل أبي قبيس والناس يصلون المغرب، فرأيت الشمس لم تغب إنما توارت خلف الجبل عن الناس، فلقيت أبا عبد الله (عليه السلام) فأخبرته بذلك، فقال لي: ولم فعلت ذلك؟! بئس ما صنعت، إنما تصليها إذا لم ترها خلف جبل، غابت أو غارت ما لم يتجللها سحاب أو ظلمة تظلها. وإنما عليك مشرقك ومغربك، وليس على الناس أن يبحثوا.

From Hareez, from Abu Usama or other who said: Once I climbed Mount Abu Qubays while people were praying Maghrib. I saw that the sun had not set but was merely hidden behind the mountain from the people's view. Then I met Abu Abdullah (peace be upon him) and informed him of this. He said to me: Why did you do that?! What you did was wrong. You only pray it when you cannot see the sun behind a mountain, whether it has set or disappeared, as long as it is not covered by clouds or darkness that shades it. You are only responsible for your east and your west, and people are not required to investigate.

قال الشيخ: هذا لا ينافي ما اعتبرناه من غيبوبة الحمرة المشرقية لأنه لا يمتنع أن تكون قد زالت الحمرة والشمس باقية خلف الجبل، لأنها تغرب عن قوم وتطلع على آخرين، وإنما نهى عن صعود الجبل لأنه غير واجب، بل الواجب عليه مراعاة مشرقه ومغربه.

The Shaykh said: This does not contradict what we considered regarding the disappearance of eastern redness, because it's possible that the redness had disappeared while the sun remained behind the mountain, as it sets for some people while rising for others. He only prohibited climbing the mountain because it's not obligatory; rather, what's obligatory is to observe one's eastern and west horizons.

أقول: ويحتمل الحمل على التقية، على أنه قال: إنما عليك مشرقك ومغربك، فعلم أن المعتبر سقوط القرص من المغرب وذهاب الحمرة من المشرق، وإلا لم يكن لذكر المشرق هنا فائدة، واحتمال اعتباره في وقت الصبح بعيد جدا، بل لاوجه له، والله أعلم. وقد تقدم ما يدل على المقصود.

I (Hurr Amili) say: This might be interpreted as taqiyyah, as he said "You only need to concern yourself with your east and west," so it's known that what matters is the setting of the disk in the west and the disappearance of redness from the east. Otherwise, mentioning the east here would serve no purpose. The possibility of considering it for the time of dawn prayer is very unlikely, rather there is no basis for it, and Allah knows best. What was intended has been previously mentioned.

———

CHAPTER 21

Emphasis On The Recommendation Of Delaying Isha Prayer Until The Disappearance Of Evening Twilight, And That Its Preferred Time Extends Until One-Third Of The Night

[Hadith 4913 to 4919]

Hadith 4913

عن عبد الله بن سنان قال: سمعت أبا عبد الله (عليه السلام) يقول: وقت المغرب إذا غربت الشمس فغاب قرصها، قال: وسمعته يقول: أخر رسول الله (صلى الله عليه وآله) ليلة من الليالي العشاء الآخرة ما شاء الله، فجاء عمر فدق الباب، فقال: يا رسول الله نام النساء نام الصبيان، فخرج رسول الله (صلى الله عليه وآله) فقال: ليس لكم أن تؤذوني ولا تأمروني، وإنما عليكم أن تسمعوا وتطيعوا.

From Abdullah bin Sinan, he said: I heard Abu Abdullah (peace be upon him) say: The time for Maghrib prayer is when the sun sets and its disk disappears. He said: And I heard him say: One night, the Messenger of Allah (peace be upon him and his family) delayed the latter Isha prayer for as long as Allah willed. Umar came and knocked on the door saying: O Messenger of Allah, the women have slept, the children have slept. The Messenger of Allah (peace be upon him and his family) came out and said: It is not for you to harm me or command me; rather, it is upon you to listen and obey.

Hadith 4914

عن أبي بصير، عن أبي جعفر (عليه السلام) قال: قال رسول الله (صلى الله عليه وآله): لولا أني أخاف أن أشق على أمتي لاخرت العشاء إلى ثلث الليل. وأنت في رخصة إلى نصف الليل وهو غسق الليل فإذا مضى الغسق نادى ملكان من رقد عن صلاة المكتوبة بعد نصف الليل فلا رقدت عيناه.

From Abu Basir, from Abu Ja'far (peace be upon him) who said: The Messenger of Allah (peace be upon him and his family) said: If I did not fear causing hardship for my nation, I would have delayed Isha until one-third of the night. And you have leeway until midnight, which is the darkness of night. When the darkness passes, two angels call out: May the eyes of one who sleeps through the prescribed prayer after midnight never find rest.

Hadith 4915

قال الكليني: وروي إلى ربع الليل.

Al-Kulayni said: And it has been narrated until one-fourth of the night.

Hadith 4916

عن معاوية بن عمار في رواية: أن وقت العشاء الآخرة إلى ثلث الليل. قال الصدوق: وكان الثلث هو الأوسط، والنصف هو آخر الوقت.

Mu'awiyah bin Ammar narrated in a report: The time for the latter Isha prayer extends until one-third of the night. Al-Saduq said: And the third was the middle, and the half was the end of the time.

Hadith 4917

عن أبي بصير، عن أبي جعفر (عليه السلام) قال: قال رسول الله (صلى الله عليه وآله): لولا أن أشق على أمتي لاخرت العشاء إلى نصف الليل.

From Abu Basir, from Abu Ja'far (peace be upon him) who said: The Messenger of Allah (peace be upon him and his family) said: If I did not fear causing hardship for my nation, I would have delayed Isha until midnight.

Hadith 4918

عن أبي بصير، عن أبي عبد الله (عليه السلام) قال: قال رسول الله (صلى الله عليه وآله): لولا نوم الصبي وغلبة الضعيف لاخرت العتمة إلى ثلث الليل.

From Abu Basir, from Abu Abdullah (peace be upon him), who said: The Messenger of Allah (peace be upon him and his family) said: Were it not for the sleep of the young child and the overwhelming weakness of the feeble, I would have delayed the Isha prayer until one third of the night.

Hadith 4919

عن الزهري أنه طلب من العمري أن يوصله إلى صاحب الزمان (عليه السلام) فأوصله، وذكر أنه سأله فأجابه عن كل ما أراد، ثم قام ودخل الدار قال: فذهبت لأسأل فلم يستمع وما كلمني بأكثر من أن قال: ملعون ملعون من أخر العشاء إلى أن تشتبك النجوم، ملعون ملعون من أخر الغداة إلى أن تنقضي النجوم، ودخل الدار.

From Al-Zuhri, he asked Al-Amri to take him to the Master of Time (peace be upon him), so he took him. He mentioned that he asked him and he answered everything he wanted. Then he stood up and entered the house. He said: I went to ask but he did not listen and did not speak to me more than saying: Cursed, cursed is the one who delays Isha until the stars intertwine; cursed, cursed is the one who delays the morning prayer until the stars fade, and he entered the house.

أقول: لعل المراد من أخر العشائين، ويكون اللعن باعتبار تأخير المغرب لما تقدم، أو يكون مخصوصا بمن يؤخر العشاء بعد الفراغ من المغرب معتقدا وجوب التأخير لما مر، وكذا الغداة، والله أعلم. وتقدم ما يدل على المقصود في عدة أحاديث هنا، وفي أعدد الفرائض ونوافلها، ويأتي ما يدل عليه.

I (Hurr Amili) say: Perhaps what is meant is delaying the two evening prayers, and the curse is due to delaying Maghrib as previously mentioned, or it is specific to one who delays Isha after finishing Maghrib believing in the obligation of delay as mentioned before, and likewise for the morning prayer, and Allah knows best. What has been mentioned indicates the intended meaning in several hadiths here, in the numbers of obligatory prayers and their supererogatory prayers, and what will come will indicate it.

CHAPTER 22

Permissibility Of Offering Isha Prayer Before The Disappearance Of Twilight, Though Disliked Without An Excuse

[Hadith 4920 to 4927]

Hadith 4920

عن أبي عبد الله (عليه السلام) قال: لا بأس بأن تؤخر المغرب في السفر حتى يغيب الشفق، ولا بأس بأن تعجل العتمة في السفر قبل أن يغيب الشفق.

From Abu Abdullah (peace be upon him) who said: There is no harm in delaying Maghrib prayer while traveling until the twilight disappears, and there is no harm in hastening the Isha prayer while traveling before the twilight disappears.

Hadith 4921

عن زرارة، عن أبي عبد الله (عليه السلام) قال: صلى رسول الله (صلى الله عليه وآله) بالناس المغرب والعشاء الآخرة قبل الشفق من غير علة في جماعة، وإنما فعل ذلك ليتسع الوقت على أمته.

From Zurarah, from Abu Abdullah (peace be upon him) who said: The Messenger of Allah (peace be upon him and his family) led people in Maghrib and Isha prayers before twilight without any excuse in congregation, and he did this to create ease in timing for his community.

Hadith 4922

عن أبي عبيدة قال: سمعت أبا جعفر (عليه السلام) يقول: كان رسول الله (صلى الله عليه وآله) إذا كانت ليلة مظلمة وريح ومطر صلى المغرب ثم مكث قدر ما يتنفل الناس، ثم أقام مؤذنه ثم صلى العشاء الآخرة ثم انصرفوا.

From Abu Ubayda who said: I heard Abu Ja'far (peace be upon him) saying: When there was a dark night with wind and rain, the Messenger of Allah (peace be upon him and his family) would pray Maghrib, then wait for the duration people would pray supererogatory prayers, then his muezzin would make the iqamah, then he would pray Isha, then they would depart.

Hadith 4923

عن أبي عبد الله (عليه السلام) - في حديث - قال: لا بأس بأن تعجل العشاء الآخرة في السفر قبل أن يغيب الشفق.

From Abu Abdullah (peace be upon him) - in a hadith - he said: There is no harm in hastening the Isha prayer while traveling before the twilight disappears.

Hadith 4924

عن زرارة قال: سألت أبا جعفر وأبا عبد الله (عليهما السلام) عن الرجل يصلي العشاء الآخرة قبل سقوط الشفق؟ فقالا: لا بأس به.

From Zurarah who said: I asked Abu Ja'far and Abu Abdullah (peace be upon them both) about a man who prays Isha before the disappearance of twilight? They both said: There is no harm in it.

Hadith 4925

عن عبيد الله وعمران ابني علي الحلبيين قالا: كنا نختصم في الطريق في الصلاة صلاة العشاء الآخرة قبل سقوط الشفق، وكان منا من يضيق بذلك صدره، فدخلنا على أبي عبد الله فسألناه عن صلاة العشاء الآخرة قبل سقوط الشفق؟ فقال: لا بأس بذلك، قلنا: وأي شئ الشفق؟ فقال: الحمرة.

From Ubaydullah and Imran, sons of Ali al-Halabi, who said: We were disputing on the road about praying Isha before the disappearance of twilight, and some of us were troubled by this. So we went to Abu Abdullah and asked him about praying Isha before the disappearance of twilight? He said: There is no harm in that. We asked: And what is twilight? He said: The redness.

Hadith 4926

وعنه، عن إسحاق البطيخي قال: رأيت أبا عبد الله (عليه السلام) صلى العشاء الآخرة قبل سقوط الشفق ثم ارتحل.

And from him, from Ishaq al-Batikhi who said: I saw Abu Abdullah (peace be upon him) pray Isha before the disappearance of twilight then he departed.

Hadith 4927

عن إسحاق بن عمار قال: سألت أبا عبد الله (عليه السلام): تجمع بين المغرب والعشاء في الحضر قبل أن يغيب الشفق من غير علة؟ قال: لا بأس.

From Ishaq bin Ammar who said: I asked Abu Abdullah (peace be upon him): Can one combine Maghrib and Isha prayers while at home before the twilight disappears without any excuse? He said: There is no problem with that.

CHAPTER 23

Twilight Considered For The Preferred Time Of Isha Prayer Is The Western Redness Not The Whiteness That Follows It

[Hadith 4928 to 4930]

Hadith 4928

عن عمران بن علي الحلبي قال: سألت أبا عبد الله (عليه السلام) متى تجب العتمة؟ قال: إذا غاب الشفق، والشفق الحمرة، فقال عبيد الله أصلحك الله إنه يبقى بعد ذهاب الحمرة ضوء شديد معترض، فقال أبو عبد الله (عليه السلام): إن الشفق إنما هو الحمرة، وليس الضوء من الشفق.

From Imran bin Ali al-Halabi who said: I asked Abu Abdullah (peace be upon him) when does the Isha prayer become obligatory? He said: When the twilight disappears, and the twilight is the redness. Then Ubaydullah said: May Allah keep you well, after the redness disappears there remains a strong transverse light. So Abu Abdullah (peace be upon him) said: Indeed the twilight is only the redness, and the light is not part of the twilight.

Hadith 4929

عن ابن فضال قال: سأل علي بن أسباط أبا الحسن (عليه السلام) ونحن نسمع: الشفق الحمرة أو البياض؟ فقال: الحمرة، لو كان البياض كان إلى ثلث الليل.

From Ibn Faddal who said: Ali bin Asbat asked Abu al-Hasan (peace be upon him) while we were listening: Is the twilight the redness or the whiteness? He said: The redness. If it were the whiteness it would last until a third of the night.

Hadith 4930

عبد الله بن جعفر في (قرب الإسناد): عن أحمد بن إسحاق، عن بكر بن محمد، عن أبي عبد الله (عليه السلام) قال: سألته عن وقت صلاة المغرب؟ فقال: إذا غاب القرص. ثم سألته عن وقت العشاء الآخرة؟ فقال: إذا غاب الشفق، قال: وآية الشفق الحمرة، ثم قال بيده: هكذا.

Abdullah bin Ja'far in (Qurb al-Isnad): From Ahmad bin Ishaq, from Bakr bin Muhammad, from Abu Abdullah (peace be upon him) who said: I asked him about the time of Maghrib prayer? He said: When the disc sets. Then I asked him about the time of the latter Isha? He said: When the twilight disappears. He said: And the sign of twilight is the redness, then he gestured with his hand like this.

CHAPTER 24

Time Of Maghrib And Isha For One Who Cannot See The East And West

[Hadith 4931 to 4931]

Hadith 4931

عن علي بن الريان قال: كتبت إليه، الرجل يكون في الدار تمنعه حيطانها النظر إلى حمرة المغرب ومعرفة مغيب الشفق ووقت صلاة عشاء الآخرة، متى يصليها؟ وكيف يصنع؟ فوقع (عليه السلام) يصليها إذا كان على هذه الصفة عند قصرة النجوم، والمغرب عند اشتباكها وبياض مغيب الشمس.

From Ali bin Al-Rayyan who said: I wrote to him asking about a man who is in a house where its walls prevent him from seeing the redness of Maghrib and knowing when the twilight disappears and the time of Isha prayer - when should he pray them and what should he do? He (peace be upon him) wrote: When in this situation, he should pray Isha when the stars are clear, and Maghrib when they become intermingled and when the whiteness of sunset remains.

ورواه الشيخ بإسناده عن سهل بن زياد، إلا أنه قال في إحدى روايتيه: والعشاء عند اشتباكها. ورواه عبد الله بن جعفر الحميري، عن علي بن الريان، مثله، إلا أنه قال: عند اشتباك النجوم والمغرب عند قصر النجوم. قال الشيخ والكليني: معنى قصر النجوم بيانها.

The Shaykh narrated it through his chain from Sahl bin Ziyad, except that in one of his two narrations he said: And Isha at their intermingling. And Abdullah bin Ja'far Al-Himyari narrated it from Ali bin Al-Rayyan similarly, except that he said: At the intermingling of stars and Maghrib at the clarity of stars. Shaykh and Kulayni said: The meaning of clarity of stars is their appearance.

CHAPTER 25

About One Who Prays Thinking The Prayer Time Has Begun When It Had Not, Then The Time Enters While They Are Praying, It Is Sufficient

[Hadith 4932 to 4932]

Hadith 4932

عن أبي عبد الله (عليه السلام) قال: إذا صليت وأنت ترى أنك في وقت ولم يدخل الوقت فدخل الوقت وأنت في الصلاة فقد أجزأت عنك.

From Abu Abdullah (peace be upon him) who said: If you pray while believing you are in the prayer time but the time had not yet begun, then the time enters while you are in prayer, it counts as sufficient for you.

———

CHAPTER 26

The Time Of Dawn Prayer Is From Dawn Break Until Sunrise
[Hadith 4933 to 4940]

Hadith 4933

عن أبي عبد الله (عليه السلام) قال: وقت الفجر حين ينشق الفجر إلى أن يتجلل الصبح السماء ولا ينبغي تأخير ذلك عمدا ولكنه وقت لمن شغل أو نسي أو نام.

From Abu Abdullah (peace be upon him) who said: The time of dawn is from when dawn breaks until morning light spreads across the sky. One should not deliberately delay it beyond this, but this timing is for one who is busy, forgetful, or sleeping.

Translator: Refer to the comments in Hadith 4937.

Hadith 4934

عن زرارة، عن أبي جعفر (عليه السلام) - في حديث - قال: إذا طلع الفجر فقد دخل وقت الغداة.

From Zurarah, from Abu Ja'far (peace be upon him) who said in a hadith: When dawn breaks, the time for the morning prayer has begun.

Hadith 4935

عن أبي عبد الله (عليه السلام) قال: وقت الفجر حين يبدو حتى يضئ.

From Abu Abdullah (peace be upon him) who said: The time of dawn is from when it appears until it becomes bright.

Hadith 4936

عن محمد بن مسلم قال: قلت لأبي عبد الله (عليه السلام): رجل صلى الفجر حين طلع الفجر، فقال: لا بأس.

From Muhammad bin Muslim who said: I asked Abu Abdullah (peace be upon him) about a man who prayed Fajr when dawn broke, and he said: There is no problem with that.

Hadith 4937

عن أبي عبد الله (عليه السلام) قال: لكل صلاة وقتان، وأول الوقتين أفضلهما، وقت صلاة الفجر حين ينشق الفجر إلى أن يتجلل الصبح السماء، ولا ينبغي تأخير ذلك عمدا، ولكنه وقت من شغل أو نسي أو سها أو نام. ووقت المغرب حين تجب الشمس إلى أن تشتبك النجوم. وليس لأحد أن يجعل آخر الوقتين

وقتا إلا من عذر أو من علة.

From Abu Abdullah (peace be upon him) who said: Every prayer has two times, and the first of the two times is better. The time for dawn prayer is from when dawn breaks until morning light spreads across the sky. One should not deliberately delay it beyond this, but this timing is for one who is busy, forgetful, confused, or sleeping. And the time for Maghrib is from when the sun sets until the stars become intertwined, and no one should make the latter time their regular time except with an excuse or illness.

Translator: The series of traditions in this chapter defines the legislative boundaries of the morning prayer through specific celestial markers. The obligation begins at the precise "break of dawn", which is the moment the first light "splits" the darkness of the night sky. However, the Infallible Guides establish a narrow window of primary merit that concludes when the morning light "spreads across the sky" or becomes fully bright.

While the absolute expiration of the prayer time - the point at which it is officially "missed" ("fawt") - is the appearance of the solar disk at sunrise, the reports emphasize that this extension is not a general permission for everyone. Instead, the period between the spreading of light and the rising of the sun is a specific concession reserved exclusively for those who are busy, forgetful, or overcome by sleep. Deliberately delaying the "Salat" into this secondary window is explicitly discouraged, as the "Ahl-al-Bayt" categorize "Fajr" similarly to "Maghrib", requiring that the act be finalized before the atmosphere undergoes its final transition into full daylight.

By focusing on the spreading of light as the practical boundary for the observant believer, these traditions establish that the functional "sunrise" for prayer is the moment the morning light dominates the horizon, while the physical appearance of the solar disk serves only as the final technical limit for those with a valid excuse.

Hadith 4938

عن زرارة، عن أبي جعفر (عليه السلام) قال: وقت صلاة الغداة ما بين طلوع الفجر إلى طلوع الشمس.

From Zurarah, from Abu Ja'far (peace be upon him) who said: The time for morning prayer is between dawn break and sunrise.

Hadith 4939

عن أبي عبد الله (عليه السلام) في الرجل إذا غلبته عينه أو عاقه أمر أن يصلي (المكتوبة من) الفجر ما بين أن يطلع الفجر إلى أن تطلع الشمس، وذلك في المكتوبة خاصة.

From Abu Abdullah (peace be upon him) regarding a man who is overcome by sleep or prevented by some matter, he may pray the prescribed dawn prayer between dawn break and sunrise, and this applies specifically to the prescribed prayer.

Hadith 4940

وقد تقدم في حديث عبيد بن زرارة، عن أبي عبد الله (عليه السلام) قال: لا تفوت صلاة الفجر حتى تطلع الشمس.

It was previously mentioned in the hadith of Ubayd ibn Zurarah, from Abu Abdullah (peace be upon him) who said: The Fajr prayer is not missed until the sun rises.

CHAPTER 27

Beginning Time Of Fajr Is The Rising Of The Second Dawn That Appears Horizontally Across The Horizon, Not The First Vertical Dawn

[Hadith 4941 to 4946]

Hadith 4941

عن أبي بصير ليث المرادي قال: سألت أبا عبد الله (عليه السلام) فقلت: متى يحرم الطعام والشراب على الصائم وتحل الصلاة صلاة الفجر؟ فقال: إذا اعترض الفجر فكان كالقبطية البيضاء، فثم يحرم الطعام على الصائم وتحل الصلاة صلاة الفجر قلت: أفلسنا في وقت إلى أن يطلع شعاع الشمس؟ قال: هيهات أين يذهب بك، تلك صلاة الصبيان.

From Abu Basir Layth al-Muradi, he said: I asked Abu Abdullah (peace be upon him) saying: When does food and drink become forbidden for the fasting person and when does the Fajr prayer become permissible? He said: When the dawn appears horizontally like a white Egyptian (*) cloth, at that point food becomes forbidden for the fasting person and the Fajr prayer becomes permissible. I said: Are we not still within the time until the sun's rays appear? He said: Far from it! Where are you going with this? That is the prayer of children.

Translator: * A high-quality, white linen fabric that was historically produced in Egypt by Coptic weavers. The comparison of the true dawn to it is meant to convey the idea of a distinct, unmistakable white light that spreads horizontally across the horizon, in contrast to the false dawn (al-fajr al-kadhib) which is described as being vertically elongated and likened to a wolf's tail.

Hadith 4942

عن أبي عبد الله (عليه السلام) أنه قال: الصبح هو الذي إذا رأيته كان معترضا كأنه بياض نهر سوراء.

From Abu Abdullah (peace be upon him) that he said: The morning is when you see it appearing horizontally like the whiteness of the Sawra river.

Hadith 4943

قال: وروي أن وقت الغداة إذا اعترض الفجر فأضاء حسنا، وأما الفجر الذي يشبه ذنب السرحان فذاك الفجر الكاذب، والفجر الصادق هو المعترض كالقبطي.

It has been narrated that the time of morning prayer is when dawn appears horizontally and illuminates beautifully. As for the dawn that resembles a wolf's tail, that is the false dawn. The true dawn is the horizontal one like Egyptian cloths.

Translator: * See comment on Hadith 4941.

Hadith 4944

عن علي بن مهزيار قال: كتب أبو الحسن بن الحصين إلى أبي جعفر الثاني (عليه السلام) معي: جعلت فداك قد اختلف موالوك في صلاة الفجر، فمنهم من يصلي إذا طلع الفجر الأول المستطيل في السماء، ومنهم من يصلي إذا اعترض في أسفل الأفق واستبان،

From Ali ibn Mahziyar, he said: Abu al-Hasan ibn al-Husayn wrote with me to Abu Ja'far the Second (peace be upon him): May I be sacrificed for you, your followers have differed regarding the Fajr prayer. Some pray when the first vertical dawn appears in the sky, while others pray when it appears horizontally across the lower horizon and becomes clear.

ولست أعرف أفضل الوقتين فأصلي فيه، فإن رأيت أن تعلمني أفضل الوقتين وتحده لي، وكيف أصنع مع القمر والفجر لاتبيين معه، حتى يحمر ويصبح، وكيف أصنع مع الغيم وما حد ذلك في السفر والحضر؟ فعلت إن شاء الله،

I do not know which of the two times is better to pray in. If you could teach me the better of the two times and specify it for me, and how should I deal with the moon and dawn when it's not clear until it reddens and morning comes, and what should I do with clouds, and what is the limit of that during travel and residence? May Allah will it.

فكتب (عليه السلام) بخطه وقرأته: الفجر يرحمك الله هو الخيط الأبيض المعترض، وليس هو الأبيض صعدا فلا تصل في سفر ولا حضر حتى تبينه، فإن الله تبارك وتعالى لم يجعل خلقه في شبهة من هذا، فقال: (وكلوا واشربوا حتى يتبين لكم الخيط الأبيض من الخيط الأسود من الفجر)، فالخيط الأبيض هو المعترض الذي يحرم به الأكل والشرب في الصوم، وكذلك هو الذي يوجب به الصلاة.

He (peace be upon him) wrote in his handwriting which I read: The dawn, may Allah have mercy on you, is the white horizontal thread, not the white vertical one. Do not pray during travel or residence until you can clearly see it, for Allah the Blessed and Exalted has not left His creation in doubt about this, saying [Quran 2:187]. The white thread is the horizontal one which makes food and drink forbidden during fasting, and likewise it is what makes prayer obligatory.

Hadith 4945

عن زرارة، عن أبي جعفر (عليه السلام) قال: كان رسول الله (صلى الله عليه وآله) يصلي ركعتي الصبح - وهي الفجر - إذا اعترض الفجر وأضاء حسنا.

From Zurarah, from Abu Ja'far (peace be upon him) who said: The Messenger of

Allah (peace be upon him and his family) would pray the two rak'ahs of morning - which is Fajr - when dawn appeared horizontally and illuminated beautifully.

Hadith 4946

عن أبي الحسن الماضي (عليه السلام) قال: سألته عن وقت صلاة الفجر؟ فقال: حين يعترض الفجر فتراه مثل نهر سوراء.

From Abu al-Hasan al-Madhi (peace be upon him), he said: I asked him about the time of Fajr prayer? He said: When dawn appears horizontally and you see it like the Sawra river.

CHAPTER 28

Emphasis On The Recommendation Of Performing Fajr Prayer At Its Earliest Time

[Hadith 4947 to 4949]

Hadith 4947

عن إسحاق بن عمار قال: قلت لأبي عبد الله (عليه السلام): أخبرني عن أفضل المواقيت في صلاة الفجر، قال: مع طلوع الفجر إن الله تعالى يقول (إن قرآن الفجر كان مشهودا) يعني صلاة الفجر تشهده ملائكة الليل وملائكة النهار، فإذا صلى العبد صلاة الصبح مع طلوع الفجر أثبت له مرتين، تثبته ملائكة الليل وملائكة النهار.

From Ishaq ibn Ammar who said: I said to Abu Abdullah (peace be upon him): Tell me about the most virtuous time for the dawn prayer. He said: With the break of dawn, for Allah the Exalted says "Indeed, the recitation of dawn is witnessed" [Quran, 17:78], meaning the dawn prayer is witnessed by the angels of the night and the angels of the day. So when a servant prays the morning prayer at the break of dawn, it is recorded for him twice - recorded by the angels of the night and the angels of the day.

Hadith 4948

عن أبي بصير المكفوف قال: سألت أبا عبد الله (عليه السلام) عن الصائم متى يحرم عليه الطعام؟ فقال: إذا كان الفجر كالقبطية البيضاء، قلت: فمتى تحل الصلاة؟ فقال: إذا كان كذلك، فقلت: ألست في وقت من تلك الساعة إلى أن تطلع الشمس؟ فقال: لا، إنما نعدها صلاة الصبيان، ثم قال: إنه لم يكن يحمد الرجل أن يصلي في المسجد ثم يرجع فينبه أهله وصبيانه.

From Abu Basir the blind who said: I asked Abu Abdullah (peace be upon him) about when food becomes forbidden for the fasting person. He said: When the dawn appears like white Egyptian (*) cloth. I asked: When does the prayer become permissible? He said: At that time. I said: Am I not in time from that hour until sunrise? He said: No, we only consider that the prayer of children. Then he said: It was not praiseworthy for a man to pray in the mosque then return to wake up his family and children.

Translator: * See comment on Hadith 4941.

Hadith 4949

وفي (المجالس والاخبار) بإسناده الآتي عن رزيق، عن أبي عبد الله (عليه السلام) أنه كان يصلي الغداة بغلس عند طلوع الفجر الصادق أول ما يبدو قبل أن يستعرض. وكان يقول: (وقرآن الفجر إن قرآن الفجر كان مشهودا) إن ملائكة الليل تصعد وملائكة النهار تنزل عند طلوع الفجر، فأنا أحب أن تشهد ملائكة الليل وملائكة النهار صلاتي. وكان يصلي المغرب عند سقوط القرص قبل أن تظهر النجوم.

From Ruzayq, from Abu Abdullah (peace be upon him) that he would pray the dawn prayer in darkness at the time of true dawn when it first appears before it spreads, and he would say: "And the recitation of dawn. Indeed, the recitation of dawn is witnessed" [Quran, 17:78]. Indeed, the angels of night ascend and the angels of day descend at the break of dawn, so I love that both the angels of night and angels of day witness my prayer. And he would pray the Maghrib prayer at the setting of the disk (sun) before the stars appear.

———

CHAPTER 29

On The Dislike Of Sleeping Before Isha Prayer And Talking After It, And That Whoever Sleeps Through It Until Midnight Must Make It Up And Perform Expiation By Fasting That Day

[Hadith 4950 to 4958]

Hadith 4950

عن الصادق، عن آبائه (عليهم السلام) في وصية النبي (صلى الله عليه وآله) لعلي (عليه السلام) قال: وكره النوم بين العشائين لأنه يحرم الرزق.

From Al-Sadiq, from his forefathers (peace be upon them), in the Prophet's (peace be upon him and his family) counsel to Ali (peace be upon him), he said: And he disliked sleeping between the two evening prayers (Maghrib and Isha) because it prevents sustenance.

Hadith 4951

قال: وقال أبو جعفر (عليه السلام): ملك موكل يقول: من بات عن العشاء الآخرة إلى نصف الليل فلا أنام الله عينه.

Abu Ja'far (peace be upon him) said: An appointed angel says: Whoever delays the Isha prayer until midnight, may Allah not let his eyes sleep.

Hadith 4952

قال: وروي في من نام عن العشاء الآخرة إلى نصف الليل أنه يقضي ويصبح صائما عقوبة، وإنما وجب ذلك عليه لنومه عنها إلى نصف الليل.

He said: And it has been narrated regarding one who sleeps past the Isha prayer until midnight that he should make it up and begin fasting the next day as a punishment, and this was only made obligatory upon him due to his sleeping past it until midnight.

Hadith 4953

عن الصادق، عن أبيه، عن آبائه (عليهم السلام) عن رسول الله (صلى الله عليه وآله) قال: إن الله كره لكم أيتها الأمة أربعا وعشرين خصلة ونهاكم عنها - إلى أن قال - وكره النوم قبل العشاء الآخرة، وكره الحديث بعد العشاء الآخرة.

From Al-Sadiq, from his father, from his forefathers (peace be upon them), from the Messenger of Allah (peace be upon him and his family) who said: Indeed Allah has disliked twenty-four characteristics for you, O nation, and has forbidden you from them - then he said - and He disliked sleeping before the Isha prayer, and disliked conversation after the Isha prayer.

Hadith 4954

عن زرارة، عن أبي جعفر (عليه السلام) قال: ملك موكل يقول: من نام عن العشاء إلى نصف الليل فلا أنام الله عينه.

From Zurarah, from Abu Ja'far (peace be upon him) who said: An appointed angel says: For whoever sleeps through Isha until midnight, may Allah not let his eye sleep.

Hadith 4955

عن ابن مسكان رفعه إلى أبي عبد الله (عليه السلام) قال: من نام قبل أن يصلي العتمة فلم يستيقظ حتى يمضي نصف الليل فليقض صلاته وليستغفر الله.

From Ibn Muskan, raising it to Abu Abdullah (peace be upon him) who said: Whoever sleeps before praying the Isha and does not wake up until half the night has passed should make up his prayer and seek forgiveness from Allah.

Hadith 4956

عن أبي عبد الله، عن آبائه (عليهم السلام) قال: قال رسول الله (صلى الله عليه وآله): دخلت الجنة فرأيت فيها قصرا من ياقوت أحمر، فقلت: يا جبرئيل لمن هذا؟ قال: لمن أطاب الكلام، وأدام الصيام، وأطعم الطعام، وتهجد بالليل والناس نيام، ثم قال: وتدري ما التهجد بالليل والناس نيام؟ قلت: الله ورسوله أعلم، قال: لا ينام حتى يصلى العشاء الآخرة، ويريد بالناس هنا اليهود والنصارى، لأنهم ينامون بين الصلاتين.

From Abu Abdullah, from his forefathers (peace be upon them) who said: The Messenger of Allah (peace be upon him and his family) said: I entered Paradise and saw therein a palace of red ruby, so I said: O Jibreel, for whom is this? He said: For whoever speaks good words, maintains fasting, feeds food, and performs tahajjud at night while people are sleeping. Then he said: Do you know what tahajjud at night while people are sleeping means? I said: Allah and His Messenger know best. He said: One does not sleep until he prays the Isha prayer, and what is meant by people here are the Jews and Christians, because they sleep between the two prayers.

Hadith 4957

عن أبي عبد الله (عليهم السلام)، في رجل نام عن العتمة فلم يقم إلى انتصاف الليل، قال: يصليها ويصبح صائما.

From Abu Abdullah (peace be upon him), regarding a man who slept through Isha prayer and did not wake up until midnight, he said: He should pray it and begin fasting in the morning.

Hadith 4958

وقد تقدم حديث أبي بصير، عن أبي جعفر (عليه السلام) قال: إذا مضى الغسق نادى ملكان: رقد عن صلاة المكتوبة بعد نصف الليل فلا رقدت عيناه.

Abu Basir transmitted from Abu Ja'far (peace be upon him), who said: When darkness has passed, two angels call out: One who sleeps missing the prescribed prayer after midnight, may his eyes find no rest.

CHAPTER 30

Regarding One Who Prays One Rak'ah Then Time Expires Should Complete Their Prayer As Performance, And The Ruling On Menstruation Occurring At The Beginning And End Of Time

[Hadith 4959 to 4963]

Hadith 4959

عن أبي عبد الله (عليه السلام) - في حديث - قال: فإن صلى ركعة من الغداة ثم طلعت الشمس فليتم وقد جازت صلاته.

From Abu Abdullah (peace be upon him) - in a hadith - he said: If one prays one rak'ah of the morning prayer then the sun rises, they should complete it and their prayer is valid.

———

Hadith 4960

عن الأصبغ بن نباتة قال: قال أمير المؤمنين (عليه السلام): من أدرك من الغداة ركعة قبل طلوع الشمس فقد أدرك الغداة تامة.

From Al-Asbagh bin Nubatah who said: Amir al-Mu'minin (peace be upon him) said: Whoever catches one rak'ah of the morning prayer before sunrise has caught the complete morning prayer.

———

Hadith 4961

عن أبي عبد الله (عليه السلام) - في حديث - قال: فإن صلى من الغداة ركعة ثم طلعت الشمس فليتم الصلاة وقد جازت صلاته، وإن طلعت الشمس قبل أن يصلي ركعة فليقطع الصلاة ولا يصلي حتى تطلع الشمس ويذهب شعاعها.

From Abu Abdullah (peace be upon him) - in a hadith - he said: If one prays one rak'ah of the morning prayer and then the sun rises, let him complete the prayer and his prayer is valid. But if the sun rises before he prays one rak'ah, he should stop the prayer and not pray until the sun has risen and its rays have spread.

———

Hadith 4962

محمد بن مكي الشهيد في (الذكرى) قال: روي عن النبي (صلى الله عليه وآله) أنه قال: من أدرك ركعة من الصلاة فقد أدرك الصلاة.

Muhammad bin Makki Al-Shaheed said in (Al-Dhikra): It is narrated from the Prophet (peace be upon him and his family) that he said: Whoever catches one

221

rak'ah of the prayer has caught the prayer.

Hadith 4963

قال: وعنه (عليه السلام) من أدرك ركعة من العصر قبل أن يغرب الشمس فقد أدرك العصر.

From him (peace be upon him): Whoever catches one rak'ah of Asr prayer before the sun sets has caught Asr prayer.

CHAPTER 31

Permissibility Of Combining Two Prayers At One Time In Congregation Or Individually Due To An Excuse

[Hadith 4964 to 4970]

Hadith 4964

عن عبد الله بن سنان قال: شهدت صلاة المغرب ليلة مطيرة في مسجد رسول الله (صلى الله عليه وآله)، فحين كان قريبا من الشفق ثاروا وأقاموا الصلاة فصلوا المغرب، ثم أمهلوا الناس حتى صلوا ركعتين ثم قام المنادي في مكانه في المسجد فأقام الصلاة فصلوا العشاء ثم انصرف الناس إلى منازلهم، فسألت أبا عبد الله (عليه السلام) عن ذلك؟ فقال: نعم قد كان رسول الله (صلى الله عليه وآله) عمل بهذا.

From Abdullah ibn Sinan, he said: I attended the Maghrib prayer on a rainy night in the mosque of the Messenger of Allah (peace be upon him and his family). When it was close to twilight, they arose and established the prayer and prayed Maghrib. Then they gave people time until they prayed two rak'ahs. Then the caller stood in his place in the mosque and established the prayer, and they prayed Isha. Then people departed to their homes. I asked Abu Abdullah (peace be upon him) about that and he said: Yes, indeed the Messenger of Allah (peace be upon him and his family) had done this.

Hadith 4965

عن صفوان الجمال قال: صلى بنا أبو عبد الله (عليه السلام) الظهر والعصر عندما زالت الشمس بأذان وإقامتين، وقال: إني على حاجة فتنفلوا.

From Safwan al-Jammal, he said: Abu Abdullah (peace be upon him) led us in the Zuhr and Asr prayers together when the sun had passed its zenith, with one adhan and two iqamahs, and he said: I have a matter to attend to, so perform your supererogatory prayers.

Hadith 4966

عن أبي عبد الله (عليه السلام) قال: كان رسول الله (صلى الله عليه وآله) إذا كان في سفر أو عجلت به حاجة يجمع بين الظهر والعصر، وبين المغرب والعشاء الآخرة، قال: وقال أبو عبد الله (عليه السلام): لا بأس أن تعجل العشاء الآخرة في السفر قبل أن يغيب الشفق.

From Abu Abdullah (peace be upon him), he said: When the Messenger of Allah (peace be upon him and his family) was traveling or had an urgent need, he would combine Zuhr and Asr, and Maghrib and Isha prayers. He said: And Abu Abdullah (peace be upon him) said: There is no harm in hastening the Isha prayer during travel before the twilight disappears.

Hadith 4967

عن معاذ بن جبل أن رسول الله (صلى الله عليه وآله) جمع بين الظهر والعصر والمغرب والعشاء عام تبوك.

From Mu'adh ibn Jabal that the Messenger of Allah (peace be upon him and his family) combined Zuhr and Asr, and Maghrib and Isha during the year of Tabuk.

Hadith 4968

عن جعفر بن محمد، عن أبيه، (عليهما السلام) أنه كان يأمر الصبيان يجمعون بين الصلاتين: الأولى والعصر، والمغرب والعشاء، يقول: ما داموا على وضوء قبل أن يشتغلوا.

From Ja'far ibn Muhammad, from his father (peace be upon them both) that he used to instruct the children to combine the two prayers: the First (Zuhr) and Asr, and Maghrib and Isha, saying: As long as they maintain their wudu before becoming occupied.

Hadith 4969

عن علي (عليهم السلام) قال: كان رسول الله (صلى الله عليه وآله) يجمع بين المغرب والعشاء في الليلة المطيرة. فعل ذلك مرارا.

From Ali (peace be upon them), he said: The Messenger of Allah (peace be upon him and his family) would combine Maghrib and Isha on rainy nights, he did this multiple times.

Hadith 4970

عن أبي عبد الله (عليه السلام) أن رسول الله (صلى الله عليه وآله) كان في السفر يجمع بين المغرب والعشاء والظهر والعصر، إنما يفعل ذلك إذا كان مستعجلا. وقال (عليه السلام): وتفريقهما أفضل.

From Abu Abdullah (peace be upon him), that the Messenger of Allah (peace be upon him and his family) would combine Maghrib and Isha, and Zuhr and Asr while traveling, he would only do this when he was in haste. And he (peace be upon him) said: Praying them separately is better.

CHAPTER 32
Permissibility Of Combining Prayers Without An Excuse
[Hadith 4971 to 4981]

Hadith 4971

عن الصادق (عليه السلام) أن رسول الله (صلى الله عليه وآله) جمع بين الظهر والعصر بأذان وإقامتين،
وجمع بين المغرب والعشاء في الحضر من غير علة بأذان واحد وإقامتين.

From Al-Sadiq (peace be upon him): The Messenger of Allah (peace be upon him and his family) combined Zuhr and Asr prayers with one adhan and two iqamas, and combined Maghrib and Isha prayers while at home without any reason with one adhan and two iqamas.

———————

Hadith 4972

عن أبي عبد الله (عليه السلام) قال: إن رسول الله (صلى الله عليه وآله) صلى الظهر والعصر في مكان
واحد من غير علة ولا سبب، فقال له عمر - وكان أجرأ القوم عليه -: أحدث في الصلاة شئ؟ قال: لا،
ولكن أردت أن أوسع على أمتي.

From Abu Abdullah (peace be upon him) who said: Indeed the Messenger of Allah (peace be upon him and his family) prayed Zuhr and Asr in one place without any illness or reason. Then Umar - who was the most daring of the people towards him - said to him: Has something new occurred in the prayer? He said: No, but I wanted to make things easier for my nation.

———————

Hadith 4973

عن أبي عبد الله (عليه السلام) قال: قلت له: أجمع بين الصلاتين من غير علة؟ قال: قد فعل ذلك رسول
الله (صلى الله عليه وآله)، أراد التخفيف عن أمته.

From Abu Abdullah (peace be upon him), he said: I said to him: Can I combine two prayers without any reason? He said: The Messenger of Allah (peace be upon him and his family) had done that, he wanted to make it easier for his nation.

———————

Hadith 4974

عن ابن عباس قال: جمع رسول الله (صلى الله عليه وآله) بين الظهر والعصر من غير خوف ولا سفر،
فقال: أراد أن لا يحرج أحد من أمته.

From Ibn Abbas who said: The Messenger of Allah (peace be upon him and his family) combined Zuhr and Asr prayers without fear or travel. He said: He wanted that no one from his nation should be put in difficulty.

Hadith 4975

عن ابن عباس، أن رسول الله (صلى الله عليه وآله) جمع بين الظهر والعصر والمغرب والعشاء عن غير مطر ولا سفر، فقل لابن عباس: ما أراد به؟ قال: أراد التوسيع لامته.

From Ibn Abbas: The Messenger of Allah (peace be upon him and his family) combined Zuhr with Asr and Maghrib with Isha without rain or travel. It was said to Ibn Abbas: What did he intend by this? He said: He intended to make things easy for his nation.

Hadith 4976

عن ابن عباس أن رسول الله (صلى الله عليه وآله) جمع بين الظهر والعصر والمغرب والعشاء في السفر والحضر.

From Ibn Abbas: The Messenger of Allah (peace be upon him and his family) combined Zuhr and Asr, and Maghrib and Isha during travel and while at home.

Hadith 4977

عبد الله بن عمر أن النبي (صلى الله عليه وآله) صلى بالمدينة مقيما غير مسافر (جميعا وتماما جمعا).

Abdullah ibn Umar: The Prophet (peace be upon him and his family) prayed in Madinah while resident, not traveling (combined and complete prayers together).

Hadith 4978

عن زرارة، عن أبي عبد الله (عليه السلام) قال: صلى رسول الله (صلى الله عليه وآله) بالناس الظهر والعصر حين زالت الشمس في جماعة من غير علة، وصلى بهم المغرب والعشاء الآخرة قبل سقوط الشفق من غير علة في جماعة، وإنما فعل رسول الله (صلى الله عليه وآله) ليتسع الوقت على أمته.

From Zurarah, from Abu Abdullah (peace be upon him) who said: The Messenger of Allah (peace be upon him and his family) prayed Zuhr and Asr with people in congregation when the sun declined without any reason, and he prayed Maghrib and Isha before the disappearance of twilight without any reason in congregation. The Messenger of Allah (peace be upon him and his family) did this to create ease in timing for his nation.

Hadith 4979

عن عباس الناقد قال: تفرق ما كان في يدي وتفرق عني حرفائي فشكوت، ذلك إلى أبي محمد (عليه السلام) فقال لي: اجمع بين الصلاتين الظهر والعصر ترى ما تحب.

From Abbas al-Naqid who said: What was in my possession dispersed and my associates scattered away from me, so I complained about this to Abu Muhammad (peace be upon him). He said to me: Combine the two prayers of Zuhr and Asr, and you will see what you like.

Hadith 4980

عن إسحاق بن عمار قال: سألت أبا عبد الله (عليه السلام) نجمع بين المغرب والعشاء في الحضر قبل أن يغيب الشفق من غير علة؟ قال: لا بأس.

From Ishaq bin Ammar who said: I asked Abu Abdullah (peace be upon him): Can we combine Maghrib and Isha prayers while at home before the twilight disappears without any reason? He said: There is no problem with that.

Hadith 4981

عن رهط منهم الفضيل وزرارة، عن أبي جعفر (عليه السلام) أن رسول الله (صلى الله عليه وآله) جمع بين الظهر والعصر بأذان وإقامتين، وجمع بين المغرب والعشاء بأذان واحد وإقامتين.

From a group including Al-Fadhl and Zurarah, from Abu Ja'far (peace be upon him) that the Messenger of Allah (peace be upon him and his family) combined Zuhr and Asr with one adhan and two iqamas, and combined Maghrib and Isha with one adhan and two iqamas.

CHAPTER 33

Recommendation Of Delaying Supererogatory Prayers When Combining Prayers And The Permissibility Of Performing Them Between Combined Prayers

[Hadith 4982 to 4985]

Hadith 4982

عن أبان بن تغلب قال: صليت خلف أبي عبد الله (عليه السلام) المغرب بالمزدلفة. فلما انصرف أقام الصلاة فصلى العشاء الآخرة لم يركع بينهما، ثم صليت معه بعد ذلك بسنة فصلى المغرب ثم قام فتنفل بأربع ركعات، ثم أقام فصلى العشاء الآخرة.

From Aban ibn Taghlib who said: I prayed Maghrib behind Abu Abdullah (peace be upon him) at Muzdalifah. When he finished, he established the prayer and prayed Isha without praying any optional prayers between them. Then I prayed with him a year later and he prayed Maghrib, then stood and prayed four optional rak'ahs, then established and prayed Isha.

Hadith 4983

عن أبي الحسن (عليه السلام) قال: سمعته يقول: إذا جمعت بين صلاتين فلا تطوع بينهما.

From Abu al-Hasan (peace be upon him) who said: I heard him say: When you combine two prayers, do not pray optional prayers between them.

Hadith 4984

عن محمد بن حكيم قال: سمعت أبا الحسن (عليه السلام) يقول: الجمع بين الصلاتين إذا لم يكن بينهما تطوع فإذا كان بينهما تطوع فلا جمع.

From Muhammad ibn Hakim who said: I heard Abu al-Hasan (peace be upon him) say: Combining two prayers is when there are no optional prayers between them. If there are optional prayers between them, then it is not combining.

Hadith 4985

عن جعفر بن محمد (عليه السلام) قال: رأيت أبي وجدي القاسم بن محمد يجمعان مع الأئمة المغرب والعشاء في الليلة المطيرة ولا يصليان بينهما شيئا.

From Ja'far ibn Muhammad (peace be upon him) who said: I saw my father and my grandfather al-Qasim ibn Muhammad combining Maghrib and Isha prayers with the imams on a rainy night, and they would not pray anything between them.

CHAPTER 34

Recommendation Of Combining The Two Night Prayers At Muzdalifah With One Adhan And Two Iqamas

[Hadith 4986 to 4986]

Hadith 4986

عن أبي عبد الله (عليه السلام) قال: سألته عن صلاة المغرب والعشاء بجمع؟ فقال: بأذان وإقامتين، لا
تصل بينهما شيئا هكذا صلى الله رسول الله (صلى الله عليه وآله).

From Abu Abdullah (peace be upon him), he said: I asked him about praying Maghrib and Isha at Muzdalifah? He said: With one adhan and two iqamas, do not pray anything between them - this is how the Messenger of Allah (peace be upon him and his family) prayed.

————————

CHAPTER 35

Permissibility Of Supererogatory Prayers During The Time Of Obligatory Prayers

[Hadith 4987 to 4997]

Hadith 4987

عن سماعة قال: سألته عن الرجل يأتي المسجد وقد صلى أهله أيبتدي بالمكتوبة أو يتطوع؟ فقال: إن كان في وقت حسن فلا بأس بالتطوع قبل الفريضة، وإن كان خاف الفوت من أجل ما مضى من الوقت فليبدأ بالفريضة وهو حق الله ثم ليتطوع ما شاء الا.

From Sama'ah who said: I asked him about a man who comes to the mosque after its people have prayed - should he start with the obligatory prayer or pray voluntary prayers? He said: If there is ample time, there is no harm in praying voluntary prayers before the obligatory prayer. But if he fears missing the prayer due to the time that has passed, he should start with the obligatory prayer as it is the right of Allah, then pray whatever voluntary prayers he wishes.

هو موسع أن يصلي الانسان في أول دخول وقت الفريضة النوافل، إلا أن يخاف فوت الفريضة والفضل إذا صلى الانسان وحده أن يبدأ بالفريضة إذا دخل وقتها ليكون فضل أول الوقت للفريضة، وليس بمحظور عليه أن يصلي النوافل من أول الوقت إلى قريب من آخر الوقت.

It is permissible for a person to pray supererogatory prayers at the beginning of the obligatory prayer time, unless he fears missing the obligatory prayer. When praying alone, it is preferable to start with the obligatory prayer when its time begins so that the virtue of the early time goes to the obligatory prayer. However, it is not forbidden to pray supererogatory prayers from the beginning of the time until near its end.

Hadith 4988

عن إسحاق بن عمار قال: قلت: أصلي في وقت فريضة نافلة؟ قال: نعم، في أول الوقت إذا كنت مع إمام تقتدي به، فإذا كنت وحدك فابدأ بالمكتوبة.

From Ishaq bin Ammar who said: I asked: Can I pray supererogatory prayers during the time of an obligatory prayer? He said: Yes, at the beginning of the time if you are with an imam you follow. But if you are alone, start with the obligatory prayer.

Hadith 4989

عن أبي جعفر (عليه السلام) قال: قال لي رجل من أهل المدينة: يا أبا جعفر مالي لا أراك تتطوع بين الأذان والإقامة كما يصنع الناس؟ فقلت: إنا إذا أردنا أن نتطوع كان تطوعنا في غير وقت فريضة، فإذا دخلت الفريضة فلا تطوع.

From Abu Ja'far (peace be upon him) who said: A man from Madinah said to me: O Abu Ja'far, why don't I see you praying voluntary prayers between the adhan and iqamah like other people do? I said: When we want to pray voluntary prayers, we do so outside the time of obligatory prayers. When the obligatory prayer time enters, there are no voluntary prayers.

Hadith 4990

عن أبي عبد الله (عليه السلام) قال: سمعته يقول: إذا حضرت المكتوبة فابدأ بها، فلا يضرك أن تترك ما قبلها من النافلة.

From Abu Abdullah (peace be upon him) who said: I heard him say: When the obligatory prayer is due, start with it. It will not harm you to leave the supererogatory prayers that precede it.

Hadith 4991

عن نجبة قال: قلت لأبي جعفر (عليه السلام): تدركني الصلاة ويدخل وقتها فأبدأ بالنافلة؟ قال: فقال أبو جعفر (عليه السلام): لا، ولكن ابدأ بالمكتوبة واقض النافلة.

Najabah said: I asked Abu Ja'far (peace be upon him): When prayer time comes, should I start with the supererogatory prayer? Abu Ja'far (peace be upon him) replied: No, rather start with the obligatory prayer and make up the supererogatory prayer later.

Hadith 4992

عن أديم بن الحر قال: سمعت أبا عبد الله (عليه السلام) يقول: لا يتنفل الرجل إذا دخل وقت فريضة. قال: وقال: إذا دخل وقت فريضة فابدأ بها.

From Udaym bin Al-Hurr who said: I heard Abu Abdullah (peace be upon him) say: A man should not pray supererogatory prayers when the time for an obligatory prayer has entered. He also said: When the time for an obligatory prayer enters, start with it.

Hadith 4993

عن جعفر بن محمد (عليه السلام) قال: إذا دخل وقت صلاة فريضة فلا تطوع.

From Ja'far bin Muhammad (peace be upon him) who said: When the time for an obligatory prayer enters, there are no voluntary prayers.

Hadith 4994

عن زرارة، عن أبي جعفر (عليه السلام) قال: لا تصل من النافلة شيئا في وقت الفريضة، فإنه لا تقضى نافلة في وقت فريضة، فإذا دخل وقت الفريضة فابدأ بالفريضة.

From Zurarah, from Abu Ja'far (peace be upon him) who said: Do not pray any supererogatory prayers during the time of obligatory prayer, for supererogatory prayers are not made up during the time of obligatory prayer. When the time for obligatory prayer enters, begin with the obligatory prayer.

Hadith 4995

عن عمر بن يزيد أنه سأل أبا عبد الله (عليه السلام) عن الرواية التي يروون أنه (لا يتطوع في وقت فريضة) ما حد هذا الوقت؟ قال: إذا أخذ المقيم في الإقامة. فقال له: إن الناس يختلفون في الإقامة، فقال: المقيم الذي يصلي معه.

From Umar bin Yazid, that he asked Abu Abdullah (peace be upon him) about the narration they narrate that "no voluntary prayer is performed during the time of an obligatory prayer", what is the limit of this time? He said: When the one establishing prayer begins the iqamah. He said to him: People differ regarding the iqamah. He said: The one establishing prayer is the one you pray with.

Hadith 4996

وفي (الخصال) بإسناده عن علي (عليه السلام) في - حديث الأربعمائة - قال: من أتى الصلاة عارفا بحقها غفر له، لا يصلي الرجل نافلة في وقت فريضة إلا من عذر، ولكن يقضي بعد ذلك إذا أمكنه القضاء. قال الله تعالى: (الذين هم على صلاتهم دائمون) يعني الذين يقضون ما فاتهم من الليل بالنهار، وما فاتهم من النهار بالليل، لا تقضي النافلة في وقت فريضة، ابدأ بالفريضة ثم صل ما بدا لك.

In (Al-Khisal) with his chain from Ali (peace be upon him) - in the hadith of four hundred - he said: Whoever comes to prayer knowing its right will be forgiven. A man should not pray voluntary prayer during the time of obligatory prayer except with an excuse, but he should make it up afterwards when making up is possible. Allah the Exalted said: "Those who are constant in their prayer," [Quran, 70:23] meaning those who make up what they missed from night prayer during day, and what they missed from day prayer during night. Do not make up supererogatory prayer during the time of obligatory prayer. Start with the obligatory prayer then pray whatever you wish.

Hadith 4997

عن أبي جعفر (عليه السلام) قال: أتدري لم جعل الذراع والذراعان؟ قلت: لا، قال: حتى لا يكون تطوع في وقت مكتوبة.

From Abu Ja'far (peace be upon him) who said: Do you know why one and two forearm lengths (cubits) were established? I said: No. He said: So that there would not be voluntary prayer during the time of prescribed prayer.

أقول: ما تضمن المنع محمول على ضيق الوقت أو على كراهة التنفل بغير نافلة الفريضة قبلها وبها بعد خروج وقتها، فإن الأحاديث الصريحة في الجواز كثيرة، مضى بعضها في أعداد الصلوات وغيرها، ويأتي باقيها هنا وفي الاذان وغيره.

I (Hurr Amili) say: What contains the prohibition is interpreted as applying to limited time, or to the dislike of supererogatory prayer other than the supererogatory prayers associated with obligatory prayers before them and with them after their time has passed, for there are many explicit hadiths permitting it, some of which were mentioned in the numbers of prayers and others, and the rest will come here and in the chapter on adhan and elsewhere.

CHAPTER 36

That The Virtuous Time For The Supererogatory Noon Prayer Is After Zenith Until Two Feet Of Shadow, And The Time For Supererogatory Afternoon Prayer Is Until Four Feet

[Hadith 4998 to 5004]

Hadith 4998

عن زرارة قال: قال لي أتدري لم جعل الذراع والذراعان؟ قال: قلت لم؟ قال لمكان الفريضة، لك أن تتنفل من زوال الشمس إلى أن يبلغ ذراعا، فإذا بلغ ذراعا بدأت بالفريضة وتركت النافلة. ورواه الشيخ كما مر.

From Zurarah, he said: He said to me: Do you know why one and two forearms (cubits) were established? I said: Why? He said: Because of the obligatory prayer. You can pray optional prayers from the sun's zenith until the shadow reaches one forearm. When it reaches one forearm, start with the obligatory prayer and leave the optional prayer. And the Shaykh narrated it as previously mentioned.

Hadith 4999

عن محمد بن مسلم قال: قلت لأبي عبد الله (عليه السلام): إذا دخل وقت الفريضة أتنفل أو أبدأ بالفريضة؟ قال: إن الفضل أن تبدأ بالفريضة.

From Muhammad ibn Muslim, he said: I said to Abu Abdullah (peace be upon him): When the time for the obligatory prayer enters, should I pray optional prayers or start with the obligatory? He said: The virtue is in starting with the obligatory prayer.

Hadith 5000

وبهذا الاسناد، مثله وزاد: وإنما أخرت الظهر ذراعا من عند الزوال من أجل صلاة الأوابين.

With the same chain of narration, similar to it with addition: The noon prayer was delayed by one forearm (cubit) from zenith for the sake of the prayer of the oft-returning.

Hadith 5001

عن منهال قال: سألت أبا عبد الله (عليه السلام) عن الوقت الذي لا ينبغي لي إذا جاء الزوال؟ قال: الذراع إلى مثله.

From Minhal, he said: I asked Abu Abdullah (peace be upon him) about the time that is not appropriate for me when zenith comes? He said: From one forearm length (cubit) to its like.

Hadith 5002

عن عدة أنهم سمعوا أبا جعفر (عليه السلام) يقول: كان أمير المؤمنين (عليه السلام) لا يصلي من النهار حتى تزول الشمس ولامن الليل بعد ما يصلي العشاء الآخرة حتى ينتصف الليل.

From several narrators who heard Abu Ja'far (peace be upon him) saying: Amir al-Mu'minin (peace be upon him) would not pray during the day until the sun passed zenith, and would not pray at night after praying the last evening prayer until midnight.

Hadith 5003

عن زرارة، عن أبي جعفر (عليه السلام) قال: كان علي (عليه السلام) لا يصلي من الليل شيئا إذا صلى العتمة حتى ينتصف الليل، ولا يصلي من النهار شيئا حتى تزول الشمس.

From Zurarah, from Abu Ja'far (peace be upon him) saying: Ali (peace be upon him) would not pray anything at night after praying the evening prayer until midnight, and would not pray anything during the day until the sun passed zenith.

Hadith 5004

عن زرارة قال: سمعت أبا جعفر (عليه السلام) يقول: كان رسول الله (صلى الله عليه وآله) لا يصلي من النهار شيئا حتى تزول الشمس فإذا زال النهار قدر نصف إصبع صلى ثماني ركعات.

From Zurarah, he said: I heard Abu Ja'far (peace be upon him) saying: The Messenger of Allah (peace be upon him and his family) would not pray anything during the day until the sun passed zenith. When the day passed zenith by half a finger's length, he would pray eight units.

CHAPTER 37

Permissibility Of Performing Supererogatory Prayers Of Noon And Others Before Their Times For Those Who Fear Being Unable To Perform Them, And Delaying Them

[Hadith 5005 to 5015]

Hadith 5005

عن محمد بن مسلم قال: سألت أبا جعفر (عليه السلام) عن الرجل يشتغل عن الزوال أيعجل من أول النهار؟ قال: نعم، إذا علم أنه يشتغل فيعجلها في صدر النهار كلها.

From Muhammad ibn Muslim, he said: I asked Abu Ja'far (peace be upon him) about a man who becomes busy at noon time, can he hasten to pray [the prescribed supererogatory prayers] early in the day? He said: Yes, if he knows he will be busy, he can hasten to pray all of them early in the day.

Hadith 5006

عن معاوية بن وهب قال: لما كان يوم فتح مكة ضربت على رسول الله (صلى الله عليه وآله) خيمة سوداء من شعر بالأبطح، ثم أفاض عليه الماء من جفنة يرى فيها أثر العجين، ثم تحرى القبلة ضحى، فركع ثماني ركعات لم يركعها رسول الله (صلى الله عليه وآله) قبل ذلك ولابعد.

From Mu'awiyah ibn Wahb, he said: On the day of the conquest of Makkah, a black tent made of hair was set up for the Messenger of Allah (peace be upon him and his family) in Al-Abtah. Then water was poured over him from a bowl in which traces of dough could be seen. Then he faced the qiblah in the morning and prayed eight rak'ahs which the Messenger of Allah (peace be upon him and his family) had never prayed before or after that.

Hadith 5007

عن أبي عبد الله (عليه السلام) قال: إعلم أن النافلة بمنزلة الهدية متى ما أتي بها قبلت.

From Abu Abdullah (peace be upon him), he said: Know that the supererogatory prayer is like a gift - whenever it is offered, it is accepted.

Hadith 5008

عن إسماعيل بن جابر قال: قلت لأبي عبد الله (عليه السلام): إني أشتغل، قال فاصنع كما نصنع، صل ست ركعات إذا كانت الشمس في مثل موضعها من صلاة العصر يعني ارتفاع الضحى الأكبر، واعتد بها من الزوال.

From Isma'il ibn Jabir, he said: I said to Abu Abdullah (peace be upon him): I become busy. He said: Then do as we do, pray six rak'ahs when the sun is in a position like its position at the time of the Asr prayer, meaning the higher forenoon, and count them from noon.

From Isma'il ibn Jabir, he said: I said to Abu Abdullah (peace be upon him): I become busy. He said: Do as we do - pray six rak'ahs when the sun is in a position similar to its position at Asr prayer, meaning at the greater morning elevation, and count it as the noon prayer.

Hadith 5009

عن أبي عبد الله (عليه السلام) قال: قلت له: جعلت فداك صلاة النهار صلاة النوافل في كم هي؟ قال: ست عشرة ركعة في أي ساعات النهار شئت أن تصليها صليتها، إلا أنك إذا صليتها في مواقيتها أفضل.

Abu Abdullah (peace be upon him) was asked: May I be sacrificed for you, how many rak'ahs are the optional day prayers? He said: Sixteen rak'ahs which you can pray at any hour of the day you wish, though praying them at their prescribed times is better.

Hadith 5010

عن أبي عبد الله (عليه السلام) قال: قال لي: صلاة النهار ست عشرة ركعة أي النهار شئت، إن شئت في أوله، وإن شئت في وسطه، وإن شئت في آخره.

From Abu Abdullah (peace be upon him), he said to me: The day prayer is sixteen rak'ahs at any time of day you wish - if you wish at its beginning, if you wish in its middle, and if you wish at its end.

Hadith 5011

عن عبد الأعلى قال: سألت أبا عبد الله (عليه السلام) عن نافلة النهار؟ قال: ست عشرة ركعة متى ما نشطت، إن علي بن الحسين (عليه السلام) كانت له ساعات من النهار يصلي فيها، فإذا شغله ضيعة أو سلطان قضاها إنما النافلة مثل الهدية متى ما أتي بها قبلت.

From Abdul A'la, he said: I asked Abu Abdullah (peace be upon him) about the supererogatory day prayer? He said: Sixteen rak'ahs whenever you are energetic. Ali ibn Al-Husayn (peace be upon him) used to have specific hours of the day when he would pray them, but if he was occupied by property matters or authority, he would make them up. Indeed, the supererogatory prayer is like a gift - whenever it is offered, it is accepted.

Hadith 5012

عن محمد بن عذافر قال: قال أبو عبد الله (عليه السلام): صلاة التطوع بمنزلة الهدية متى ما أتي بها قبلت، فقدم منها ما شئت، وأخر منها ما شئت.

From Muhammad ibn Athafir who said: Abu Abdullah (peace be upon him) said: Voluntary prayer is like a gift - whenever it is offered it is accepted. So perform what you wish of it earlier and delay what you wish of it.

Hadith 5013

عن علي بن جعفر، عن أخيه موسى بن جعفر (عليهم السلام) قال: نوافلكم صدقاتكم فقدموها أنى شئتم.

From Ali ibn Ja'far, from his brother Musa ibn Ja'far (peace be upon them) who said: Your supererogatory prayers are your charitable deeds, so perform them whenever you wish.

Hadith 5014

عن زرارة، عن أبي جعفر (عليه السلام) أنه قال: ما صلى رسول الله (صلى الله عليه وآله) الضحى قط، قال: فقلت له: ألم تخبرني أنه كان يصلي في صدر النهار أربع ركعات، قال: بلى إنه كان يجعلها من الثمان التي بعد الظهر.

From Zurarah, from Abu Ja'far (peace be upon him) that he said: The Messenger of Allah (peace be upon him and his family) never prayed Duha prayer at all. He said: So I said to him: Did you not tell me that he used to pray four rak'ahs in the early part of the day? He said: Yes, but he would consider it part of the eight rak'ahs after Zuhr.

أقول: المراد هنا بالظهر الزوال وهو ظاهر.

I (Hurr Amili) say: What is meant here by Zuhr is the zenith (zawal) and this is apparent.

Hadith 5015

عن أبي البختري، عن الصادق، عن أبيه - في حديث - أن أمير المؤمنين (عليه السلام) في صفين نزل فصلى أربع ركعات قبل الزوال.

From Abu al-Bakhtari, from al-Sadiq, from his father - in a hadith - that Amir al-Mu'minin (peace be upon him) during Siffin descended and prayed four rak'ahs before zawal.

CHAPTER 38

Starting Supererogatory Prayers At Sunrise, Sunset, Zenith, After Fajr, And After Asr - Is It Disliked Or Not?

[Hadith 5016 to 5029]

Hadith 5016

عن أبي عبد الله (عليه السلام) قال: لا صلاة بعد الفجر حتى تطلع الشمس، فإن رسول الله (صلى الله عليه وآله) قال: إن الشمس تطلع بين قرني الشيطان، وتغرب بين قرني الشيطان، وقال: لا صلاة بعد العصر حتى تصلى المغرب.

From Abu Abdullah (peace be upon him) who said: There is no prayer after Fajr until sunrise, for the Messenger of Allah (peace be upon him and his family) said: The sun rises between the two horns of Satan and sets between the two horns of Satan. And he said: There is no prayer after Asr until you pray Maghrib.

———

Hadith 5017

عن أبي عبد الله (عليه السلام) قال: لا صلاة بعد العصر حتى تصلى المغرب، ولا صلاة بعد الفجر حتى تطلع الشمس.

From Abu Abdullah (peace be upon him) who said: There is no prayer after Asr until you pray Maghrib, and no prayer after Fajr until sunrise.

———

Hadith 5018

عن علي بن بلال قال: كتبت إليه في قضاء النافلة من طلوع الفجر إلى طلوع الشمس، ومن بعد العصر إلى أن تغيب الشمس، فكتب لا يجوز ذلك إلا للمقتضي، فأما لغيره فلا.

From Ali ibn Bilal who said: I wrote to him asking about making up supererogatory prayers from Fajr until sunrise, and after Asr until sunset. He wrote back: That is not permissible except for making up missed (obligatory) prayers, but for others it is not allowed.

———

Hadith 5019

عن علي بن محمد، عن أبيه، رفعه قال: قال رجل لأبي عبد الله (عليه السلام): إن الشمس تطلع بين قرني الشيطان، قال: نعم إن إبليس اتخذ عرشا بين السماء والأرض، فإذا طلعت الشمس وسجد في ذلك الوقت الناس قال: إبليس لشياطينه: إن بني آدم يصلون لي.

From Ali ibn Muhammad, from his father, who raised it saying: A man said to Abu

Abdullah (peace be upon him): The sun rises between the two horns of Satan? He said: Yes, Iblis has taken a throne between the heaven and earth, so when the sun rises and people prostrate at that time, Iblis says to his devils: The children of Adam are praying to me.

Hadith 5020

عن محمد بن فرج قال: كتبت إلى العبد الصالح (عليه السلام) أسأله عن مسائل، فكتب إلى: وصل بعد العصر من النوافل ما شئت، وصل بعد الغداة من النوافل ما شئت.

From Muhammad ibn Farj who said: I wrote to the Righteous Servant (peace be upon him) asking him about some matters, and he wrote back to me: Pray whatever supererogatory prayers you wish after Asr, and pray whatever supererogatory prayers you wish after morning prayer.

Hadith 5021

عن جعفر بن محمد، عن آبائه (عليهم السلام) - في حديث المناهي - قال: ونهى رسول الله (صلى الله عليه وآله) عن الصلاة عند طلوع الشمس وعند غروبها وعند استوائها.

From Ja'far ibn Muhammad, from his forefathers (peace be upon them) - in the hadith of prohibitions - he said: The Messenger of Allah (peace be upon him and his family) prohibited prayer at sunrise, at sunset, and at the sun's zenith.

Hadith 5022

قال: وقد روي ونهي عن الصلاة عند طلوع الشمس وعند غروبها لان الشمس تطلع بين قرني شيطان، وتغرب بين قرني شيطان.

It has been narrated that prayer was prohibited at sunrise and sunset because the sun rises between the two horns of Satan and sets between the two horns of Satan.

Hadith 5023

عن أبي الحسين محمد بن جعفر الأسدي أنه ورد عليه فيما ورد من جواب مسائله عن محمد بن عثمان العمري (قدس الله روحه) وأما ما سألت عن الصلاة عند طلوع الشمس وعند غروبها فلان كان كما يقول الناس إن الشمس تطلع بين قرني شيطان، وتغرب بين قرني شيطان، فما أرغم أنف الشيطان بشئ أفضل من الصلاة فصلها، وأرغم أنف الشيطان.

From Abu Al-Husayn Muhammad bin Ja'far Al-Asadi that he received among the answers to his questions from Muhammad bin Uthman Al-Amri (may Allah sanctify his soul): As for what you asked about prayer at sunrise and sunset, if it is as people say that the sun rises between the two horns of Satan and sets between the two horns of Satan, then nothing humiliates Satan's nose better than prayer, so pray and humiliate Satan's nose.

———

Hadith 5024

عن سليمان بن جعفر الجعفري قال: سمعت الرضا (عليه السلام) يقول: لا ينبغي لاحد أن يصلي إذا طلعت الشمس، لأنها تطلع بقرني شيطان، فإذا ارتفعت وضفت فارقها، فتستحب الصلاة ذلك الوقت والقضاء وغير ذلك، فإذا انتصفت النهار قارنها، فلا ينبغي لاحد أن يصلي في ذلك الوقت، لان أبواب السماء قد غلقت فإذا زالت الشمس وهبت الريح فارقها.

From Sulayman bin Ja'far Al-Ja'fari who said: I heard Al-Ridha (peace be upon him) saying: No one should pray when the sun rises because it rises with the horns of Satan. When it rises higher and becomes bright, Satan leaves it, so prayer is recommended at that time including making up missed prayers and other prayers. When it reaches midday Satan accompanies it again, so no one should pray at that time because the gates of heaven are closed. When the sun passes its zenith and the wind blows, Satan leaves it.

———

Hadith 5025

عن عائشة قالت: صلاتان لم يتركهما رسول الله (صلى الله عليه وآله) سرا وعلانية: ركعتين بعد العصر، وركعتين قبل الفجر.

From Aisha who said: Two prayers that the Messenger of Allah (peace be upon him and his family) never left, secretly or openly: two rak'ahs after Asr prayer and two rak'ahs before Fajr prayer.

———

Hadith 5026

عن عايشة أنه دخل عليها يسألها عن الركعتين بعد العصر، قالت: والذي ذهب بنفسه يعني رسول الله (صلى الله عليه وآله) ما تركهما حتى لقي الله عز وجل، وحتى ثقل عن الصلاة وكان يصلي كثيرا من صلاته وهو قاعد. فقلت: إنه لما ولي عمر نهي عنهما، قالت: صدقت، ولكن رسول الله (صلى الله عليه وآله) كان لا يصليهما في المسجد مخافة أن يثقل على أمته، وكان يحب ما خف عليهم.

From Aisha that he came to ask her about the two rak'ahs after Asr. She said: By the One who took his soul - meaning the Messenger of Allah (peace be upon him and his family) - he never left them until he met Allah Almighty, even when prayer became difficult for him and he would pray much of his prayer while sitting. I said: When Umar took charge he forbade them. She said: You speak the truth, but the Messenger of Allah (peace be upon him and his family) would not pray them in the mosque fearing it would be burdensome for his nation, and he loved what was easy for them.

———

Hadith 5027

عن عائشة أنها قالت: كان رسول الله عندي يصلي بعد العصر ركعتين.

From Aisha who said: The Messenger of Allah would pray two rak'ahs after Asr while with me.

Hadith 5028

عن أبي بكر بن عبد الله بن قيس، عن أبيه قال: قال رسول الله (صلى الله عليه وآله): من صلى البردين دخل الجنة يعني بعد الغداة وبعد العصر.

From Abu Bakr bin Abdullah bin Qays, from his father who said: The Messenger of Allah (peace be upon him and his family) said: Whoever prays the two cool prayers will enter Paradise - meaning after morning and after Asr.

قال الصدوق: مرادي بايراد هذه الأخبار الرد على المخالفين لأنهم لا يرون بعد الغداة وبعد العصر صلاة فأحببت أن أبين أنهم قد خالفوا رسول الله (صلى الله عليه وآله) في قوله وفعله.

Al-Saduq said: My intention in presenting these reports is to refute the opponents because they do not consider prayer valid after morning and after Asr, so I wanted to show that they have contradicted the Messenger of Allah (peace be upon him and his family) in his words and actions.

Hadith 5029

عن أبي الحسن (عليه السلام) - في حديث - أنه صلى المغرب ليلة فوق سطح من السطوح. فقيل له: إن فلانا كان يفتي عن آبائك (عليهم السلام) أنه لا بأس بالصلاة بعد طلوع الفجر إلى طلوع الشمس وبعد العصر إلى أن تغيب الشمس، فقال: كذب - لعنه الله - على أبي، أو قال: على آبائي.

From Abu Al-Hasan (peace be upon him) - in a hadith - that he prayed Maghrib one night on a rooftop. It was said to him: So-and-so used to give fatwas citing your forefathers (peace be upon them) that there is no problem praying after Fajr until sunrise and after Asr until sunset. He said: He lied - may Allah curse him - about my father, or he said: about my forefathers.

أقول: حمل الشيخ النهي في هذه الأحاديث على الكراهة لما مر من أحاديث الجواز، وجوز حملها على التقية لما مر من حديث العمرى وهو الأقرب.

I (Hurr Amili) say: The Shaykh interpreted the prohibition in these hadiths as disliked based on the previous hadiths allowing it, and allowed interpreting them as taqiyyah based on the previous hadith of Al-Amri which is closer to correct.

CHAPTER 39

Permissibility Of Making Up Prayers At Any Time, Including Tawaf Prayer, Eclipse Prayer, Ihram Prayer, And Funeral Prayer

[Hadith 5030 to 5048]

Hadith 5030

عن زرارة، عن أبي جعفر (عليه السلام) أنه قال: أربع صلوات يصليها الرجل في كل ساعة: صلاة فاتتك فمتى ما ذكرتها أديتها، وصلاة ركعتي طواف الفريضة، وصلاة الكسوف، والصلاة على الميت، هذه يصليهن الرجل في الساعات كلها.

From Zurarah, from Abu Ja'far (peace be upon him) who said: There are four prayers that a person can pray at any hour: a prayer that you missed, which you should perform whenever you remember it; the two rak'ah prayer of obligatory tawaf; the eclipse prayer; and the funeral prayer. These can be prayed by a person at all hours.

———

Hadith 5031

عن حماد بن عثمان أنه سأل أبا عبد الله (عليه السلام) عن رجل فاته شئ من الصلوات فذكر عند طلوع الشمس أو عند غروبها؟ قال: فليصل حين يذكر.

From Hammad bin Uthman that he asked Abu Abdullah (peace be upon him) about a man who missed some prayers and remembered them at sunrise or sunset. He said: Let him pray when he remembers.

———

Hadith 5032

عن حبيب قال: كتبت إلى أبي الحسن الرضا (عليه السلام): تكون علي الصلاة، النافلة، متى أقضيها؟ فكتب (عليه السلام): أي ساعة شئت من ليل أو نهار.

From Habib who said: I wrote to Abu al-Hasan al-Ridha (peace be upon him): When should I make up supererogatory prayers that I owe? He wrote back (peace be upon him): At any hour you wish, during night or day.

Shaykh Hurr Amili: What indicates that has already been mentioned and what indicates it will come. What apparently prohibits making up after Asr can be interpreted as dissimulation (taqiyyah).

———

Hadith 5033

عن معاوية بن عمار قال: سمعت أبا عبد الله (عليه السلام) يقول: خمس صلاة لا تترك على حال: إذا طفت بالبيت، وإذا أردت أن تحرم، وصلاة الكسوف، وإذا نسيت فصل إذا ذكرت، وصلاة الجنازة.

From Mu'awiyah bin Ammar who said: I heard Abu Abdullah (peace be upon him) saying: Five prayers that should not be abandoned in any situation: when you perform tawaf around the House (Ka'bah), when you intend to enter ihram, the eclipse prayer, when you forget a prayer then pray it when you remember it, and the funeral prayer.

Hadith 5034

عن أبي بصير، عن أبي عبد الله (عليه السلام) قال: خمس صلوات تصليهن في كل وقت: صلاة الكسوف، والصلاة على الميت، وصلاة الاحرام، والصلاة التي تفوت، وصلاة الطواف من الفجر إلى طلوع الشمس وبعد العصر إلى الليل.

From Abu Basir, from Abu Abdullah (peace be upon him) who said: Five prayers that you can pray at any time: the eclipse prayer, the funeral prayer, the ihram prayer, a missed prayer, and the tawaf prayer from dawn until sunrise and after Asr until night.

Hadith 5035

عن محمد بن مسلم قال: سألته عن الرجل تفوته صلاة النهار؟ قال: يصليها إن شاء بعد المغرب وإن شاء بعد العشاء.

From Muhammad bin Muslim who said: I asked him about a man who misses the day prayers? He said: He can pray them after Maghrib if he wishes or after Isha if he wishes.

Hadith 5036

عن الحلبي قال: سئل أبو عبد الله (عليه السلام) عن رجل فاتته صلاة النهار متى يقضيها؟ قال: متى شاء، إن شاء بعد المغرب وإن شاء بعد العشاء.

From al-Halabi who said: Abu Abdullah (peace be upon him) was asked about a man who missed the day prayers, when should he make them up? He said: Whenever he wishes, either after Maghrib or after Isha.

Hadith 5037

عن الحسين بن مسلم قال: قلت لأبي الحسن الثاني: أكون في السوق فأعرف الوقت ويضيق علي أن أدخل فأصلي قال: إن الشيطان يقارن الشمس في ثلاثة أحوال: إذا نحرت وإذا كبدت وإذا غربت، فصل بعد الزوال، فإن الشيطان يريد أن يوقفك على حد يقطع بك دونه.

Al-Husayn bin Muslim said: I said to Abu Al-Hasan the Second: I am in the market and know the prayer time but find it difficult to enter and pray. He said: Satan accompanies the sun in three conditions: when it rises, when it is at its zenith, and when it sets, so pray after zenith, for Satan wants to stop you at a limit that cuts you off before it.

Hadith 5038

عن حسان بن مهران قال: سألت أبا عبد الله (عليه السلام) عن قضاء النوافل؟ قال: ما بين طلوع الشمس إلى غروبها.

Hasan bin Mihran said: I asked Abu Abdullah (peace be upon him) about making up supererogatory prayers? He said: Between sunrise and sunset.

Hadith 5039

عن عبد الله بن أبي يعفور، عن أبي عبد الله (عليه السلام) في قضاء صلاة الليل والوتر تفوت الرجل، أيقضيها بعد صلاة الفجر وبعد العصر؟ فقال: لا بأس بذلك.

From Abdullah bin Abi Yafur, from Abu Abdullah (peace be upon him) regarding making up Salat al-Layl and Witr that a man misses, can he make them up after Fajr prayer and after Asr? He said: There is no problem with that.

Hadith 5040

عن سليمان بن هارون قال: سألت أبا الحسن (عليه السلام) عن قضاء الصلاة بعد العصر؟ قال: إنما هي النوافل فاقضها متى ما شئت.

Sulayman bin Haroun said: I asked Abu Al-Hasan (peace be upon him) about making up prayers after Asr? He said: These are only supererogatory prayers, so make them up whenever you wish.

Hadith 5041

عن ابن أبي يعفور قال: سمعت أبا عبد الله (عليه السلام) يقول: صلاة النهار يجوز قضاؤها أي ساعة شئت من ليل أو نهار.

Ibn Abi Yafur said: I heard Abu Abdullah (peace be upon him) saying: Daytime prayers can be made up at any hour you wish, during night or day.

Hadith 5042

عن الحسين بن أبي العلاء، عن أبي عبد الله (عليه السلام) قال: اقض صلاة النهار أي ساعة شئت من ليل أو نهار كل ذلك سواء.

From Al-Husayn bin Abi Al-Ala, from Abu Abdullah (peace be upon him) who said: Make up daytime prayers at any hour you wish of night or day, all of that is the same.

Hadith 5043

عن جميل بن دراج قال: سألت أبا الحسن الأول (عليه السلام) عن قضاء صلاة الليل بعد الفجر إلى طلوع الشمس؟ قال: نعم، وبعد العصر إلى الليل فهو من سر آل محمد المخزون.

Jamil bin Darraj said: I asked Abu Al-Hasan the First (peace be upon him) about making up Salat al-Layl after Fajr until sunrise? He said: Yes, and after Asr until night - this is from the stored secrets of the family of Muhammad.

Hadith 5044

عن مفضل بن عمر قال: قلت لأبي عبد الله (عليه السلام): جعلت فداك تفوتني صلاة الليل فأصلي الفجر، فلي أن أصلي بعد صلاة الفجر ما فاتني من صلاة الليل وأنا في مصلاي قبل طلوع الشمس؟ فقال: نعم، ولكن لاتعلم به أهلك فيتخذونه سنة.

Mufaddal bin Umar said: I said to Abu Abdullah (peace be upon him): May I be sacrificed for you, I miss Salat al-Layl and pray Fajr, can I pray after Fajr prayer what I missed from Salat al-Layl while I am in my prayer place before sunrise? He said: Yes, but do not let your family know about it lest they take it as a regular practice.

Hadith 5045

عن نعمان الرازي قال: سألت أبا عبد الله (عليه السلام) عن رجل فاته شئ من الصلوات فذكر عند طلوع الشمس وعند غروبها؟ قال فليصل حين ذكره.

Nu'man al-Razi said: I asked Abu Abdullah (peace be upon him) about a man who missed some prayers and remembered them at sunrise and sunset? He said: Let him pray when he remembers them.

Hadith 5046

عن أحمد بن النضر قال: سئل أبو عبد الله (عليه السلام) عن القضاء قبل طلوع الشمس وبعد العصر؟ فقال: نعم فاقضه فإنه من سر آل محمد.

Ahmad ibn al-Nadr said: Abu Abdullah (peace be upon him) was asked about making up prayers before sunrise and after Asr? He said: Yes, make them up for it is from the secrets of the family of Muhammad.

Hadith 5047

عن أبيه إسماعيل بن عيسى قال: سألت الرضا (عليه السلام) عن الرجل يصلي الأولى ثم يتنفل فيدركه وقت العصر من قبل أن يفرغ من نافلته فيبطئ (بعد نافلته، أو يصليها بعد العصر)، أو يؤخرها حتى يصليها في وقت آخر؟ قال: يصلي العصر ويقضي نافلته في يوم آخر.

From his father Isma'il ibn Isa who said: I asked Al-Ridha (peace be upon him) about a man who prays the first prayer then starts supererogatory prayers, and the time for Asr prayer comes before he finishes his supererogatory prayers, should he delay (after his supererogatory prayers, or pray them after Asr), or postpone them to pray at another time? He said: He should pray Asr and make up the supererogatory prayers on another day.

Hadith 5048

وقد تقدم في حديث محمد بن الفرج قال: فإذا طلع الفجر فصل الفريضة ثم اقض بعدها ما شئت.

And it was previously mentioned in the hadith of Muhammad ibn al-Faraj who said: When dawn breaks, pray the obligatory prayer then make up whatever you wish after it.

Shaykh Hurr Amili: What indicates this has preceded, and what indicates it will come, and what appears to be a prohibition against praying Qadha after Asr prayer can potentially be interpreted as taqiyyah.

CHAPTER 40

If One Starts Praying A Supererogatory (Nafl) Prayer Of Zuhr Or Asr, Even If It Is Just One Rak'ah, And Then The Time For That Prayer Ends, One Should Complete The Supererogatory Prayer Before Praying The Obligatory (Fard) Prayer

[Hadith 5049 to 5049]

Hadith 5049

عن أبي عبد الله (عليه السلام) - في حديث - قال: وقت صلاة الجمعة إذا زالت الشمس شراك أو نصف،

وقال: للرجل أن يصلي الزوال ما بين زوال الشمس إلى أن يمضي قدمان،

From Abu Abdullah (peace be upon him) in a hadith, he said: The time for Friday prayer is when the sun passes the meridian (highest point) by the length of the strap of a sandal (*) or half of it. And he said: A man can pray the zawal (midday) prayer from when the sun passes the meridian until two feet (of shadow) have passed.

وإن كان قد بقي من الزوال ركعة واحدة أو قبل أن يمضي قدمان أتم الصلاة حتى يصلي تمام الركعات، فإن مضى قدمان قبل أن يصلي ركعة بدأ بالأولى ولم يصل الزوال إلا بعد ذلك،

If one rak'ah remains from the zawal prayer, or before two feet have passed, one should complete the prayer until finishing the rak'ahs. If two feet pass before praying one rak'ah, one should begin with the first (obligatory prayer) and not pray the zawal prayer until after that.

وللرجل أن يصلي من نوافل الأولى ما بين الأولى إلى أن تمضي أربعة أقدام، فإن مضت الأربعة أقدام ولم يصل من النوافل شيئا فلا يصلي النوافل، وإن كان قد صلى ركعة فليتم النوافل حتى يفرغ منها، ثم يصلي العصر.

A man can pray the supererogatory prayers of Zuhr between Zuhr until four feet (of shadow) have passed. If four feet pass and one has not prayed any of the supererogatory prayers, then one should not pray the supererogatory prayers. If one has prayed one rak'ah, then one should complete the supererogatory prayers until finishing them, then pray Asr.

وقال: للرجل أن يصلي إن بقي عليه شئ من صلاة الزوال إلى أن يمضي بعد حضور الأولى نصف قدم، وللرجل إذا كان قد صلى من نوافل الأولى شيئا قبل أن تحضر العصر فله أن يتم نوافل الأولى إلى أن يمضي بعد حضور العصر قدم، وقال: القدم بعد حضور العصر مثل نصف قدم بعد حضور الأولى في الوقت سواء.

He said: A man can pray if something remains for him from the zawal prayer until half a foot passes after the arrival of Zuhr. If a man has prayed something from the supererogatory prayers of Zuhr before Asr arrives, then he can complete the supererogatory prayers of Zuhr until one foot passes after the arrival of Asr. He said: One foot after the arrival of Asr is equivalent to half a foot after the arrival of Zuhr in terms of time.

Translator: * In the context of the hadith "shirak" refers to a shoelace or strap of a sandal. It is being used as a unit of measurement to describe a short period of time.

CHAPTER 41

Recommendation Of Being Mindful Of Times And Frequently Observing Times Of Virtue

[Hadith 5050 to 5051]

Hadith 5050

عن أبي بصير، عن أبي عبد الله (عليه السلام) قال: مامن يوم سحاب يخفى فيه على الناس وقت الزوال إلا كان من الامام للشمس زجرة حتى تبدو فيحتج على (أهل) كل قرية من اهتم بصلاته ومن ضيعها.

From Abu Basir, from Abu Abdullah (peace be upon him) who said: There is no cloudy day when the time of zawal (when the sun passes the zenith) is hidden from people except that the Imam has authority over the sun until it appears, so that it may be used as evidence against the people of every town - those who cared about their prayer and those who neglected it.

Hadith 5051

الحسن بن محمد الديلمي في (الارشاد) قال: كان علي (عليه السلام) يوما في حرب صفين مشتغلا بالحرب والقتال وهو مع ذلك بين الصفين يراقب الشمس، فقال له ابن عباس: يا أمير المؤمنين، ما هذا الفعل؟ قال: أنظر إلى الزوال حتى نصلي

Al-Hasan bin Muhammad Al-Dailami in (Al-Irshad) said: One day Ali (peace be upon him) was engaged in battle and fighting during the Battle of Siffin, and despite that, he was between the battle lines watching the sun. Ibn Abbas asked him: O Amir al-Mu'minin, what are you doing? He said: I am watching for the sun's zenith so we can pray.

فقال له ابن عباس: وهل هذا وقت الصلاة؟ إن عندنا لشغلا بالقتال عن الصلاة، فقال (عليه السلام): على ما نقاتلهم؟ إنما نقاتلهم على الصلاة، قال: ولم يترك صلاة الليل قط حتى ليلة الهرير.

Ibn Abbas said to him: Is this the time for prayer? We are too busy fighting to pray. He (peace be upon him) said: What are we fighting them for? We are fighting them for prayer. He said: And he never abandoned Salat al-Layl except on the Night of Harir (a night of intense fighting in Siffin).

CHAPTER 42

Emphasis Of Performing Zuhr Prayer At Its Earliest Time
[Hadith 5052 to 5053]

Hadith 5052

عن أبي عبد الله (عليه السلام) أنه قال: كان المؤذن يأتي النبي (صلى الله عليه وآله) في الحر في صلاة الظهر فيقول له رسول الله (صلى الله عليه وآله): أبرد أبرد. قال الصدوق: يعني عجل عجل، وأخذ ذلك من البريد.

From Abu Abdullah (peace be upon him) who said: The muezzin would come to the Prophet (peace be upon him and his family) in the heat during the noon prayer, and the Messenger of Allah (peace be upon him and his family) would say to him: Cool down, cool down. Al-Saduq said: This means hurry, hurry, derived from al-barid (postal system).

Hadith 5053

عن إبراهيم الكرخي قال: سألت أبا الحسن موسى (عليه السلام) متى يدخل وقت الظهر؟ قال: إذا زالت الشمس، فقلت: متى يخرج وقتها؟ فقال: من بعد ما يمضي من زوالها أربعة أقدام، إن وقت الظهر ضيق ليس كغيره.

From Ibrahim al-Karkhi who said: I asked Abu al-Hasan Musa (peace be upon him) when does the time of Zuhr prayer begin? He said: When the sun passes its zenith. I asked: When does its time end? He said: After four feet pass from its zenith, for the time of Zuhr is narrow unlike other prayers.

CHAPTER 43

Time For Salat Al-Layl (Night Prayer) Is After Half Of The Night Has Passed

[Hadith 5054 to 5058]

Hadith 5054

عن عبد الله بن زرارة، عن أبي عبد الله (عليه السلام) أنه قال: كان رسول الله (صلى الله عليه وآله) إذا صلى العشاء آوى إلى فراشه ولم يصل شيئا حتى ينتصف الليل.

From Abdullah bin Zurarah, from Abu Abdullah (peace be upon him) that he said: When the Messenger of Allah (peace be upon him and his family) would pray Isha, he would retire to his bed and would not pray anything until half of the night passed.

Hadith 5055

قال: وقال أبو جعفر (عليه السلام): وقت صلاة الليل ما بين نصف الليل إلى آخره.

He said: And Abu Ja'far (peace be upon him) said: The time for Salat al-Layl is between half of the night until its end.

Hadith 5056

عن فضيل، عن أحدهما أن رسول الله (صلى الله عليه وآله) كان يصلي بعد ما ينتصف الليل ثلاث عشرة ركعة.

From Fudhayl, from one of them that the Messenger of Allah (peace be upon him and his family) would pray thirteen rak'ahs after half of the night had passed.

Hadith 5057

عن أبي عبد الله (عليه السلام) قال: سمعته يقول: كان رسول الله (صلى الله عليه وآله) إذا صلى العشاء الآخرة آوى إلى فراشه فلا يصلي شيئا إلا بعد انتصاف الليل، لا في شهر رمضان ولا في غيره.

From Abu Abdullah (peace be upon him), he said: I heard him saying: When the Messenger of Allah (peace be upon him and his family) would pray the last Isha, he would retire to his bed and would not pray anything except after the middle of the night, neither in the month of Ramadan nor in other months.

Hadith 5058

عن الرجل العسكري (عليه السلام) قال: إذا انتصف الليل ظهر بياض في وسط السماء شبه عمود من حديد تضئ له الدنيا فيكون ساعة ويذهب ثم يظلم، فإذا بقي الثلث الليل الأخير ظهر بياض من قبل المشرق فأضاءت له الدنيا فيكون ساعة ثم يذهب وهو وقت صلاة الليل، ثم تظلم قبل الفجر ثم يطلع الفجر الصادق من قبل المشرق، وقال: من أراد أن يصلي في نصف الليل فيطول فذلك له.

From the man Al-Askari (peace be upon him) he said: When it becomes middle of the night, a whiteness appears in the middle of the sky like an iron pillar illuminating the world, it remains for an hour then disappears and becomes dark. When the last third of the night remains, a whiteness appears from the east illuminating the world, it remains for an hour then disappears - and this is the time for Salat al-Layl. Then it becomes dark before dawn, then the true dawn appears from the east. And he said: Whoever wants to pray at midnight and lengthen their prayer, that is for them.

CHAPTER 44

Permissibility Of Performing Salat Al-Layl And Witr Before Midnight After Isha Prayer Due To Valid Excuses Such As Travel, Youth With Heavy Sleep, Fear Of Ritual Impurity, Cold Weather, Sleep, Illness, Or Similar Reasons

[Hadith 5059 to 5077]

Hadith 5059

عن ليث المرادي قال: سألت أبا عبد الله (عليه السلام) عن الصلاة في الصيف في الليالي القصار صلاة الليل في أول الليل؟ فقال: نعم. نعم ما رأيت، ونعم ما صنعت، يعني في السفر. قال: وسألته عن الرجل يخاف الجنابة في السفر أو في البرد فيعجل صلاة الليل والوتر في أول الليل؟ فقال: نعم.

From Layth Al-Muradi, he said: I asked Abu Abdullah (peace be upon him) about praying Salat al-Layl in early night during short summer nights? He said: Yes, yes what you saw, and yes what you did, meaning during travel. I asked him about a man who fears becoming junub (in a state of major ritual impurity) during travel or in cold weather, so he hastens to pray Salat al-Layl and Witr in early night? He said: Yes.

––––––––––

Hadith 5060

عن الحلبي، عن أبي عبد الله (عليه السلام) قال: إن خشيت أن لا تقوم في آخر الليل أو كانت بك علة أو أصابك برد فصل وأوتر في الليل في السفر.

From Al-Halabi, from Abu Abdullah (peace be upon him) who said: If you fear that you won't wake up in the late night, or you have an illness, or you are affected by cold, then pray and perform Witr during the night while traveling.

––––––––––

Hadith 5061

عن الرضا (عليه السلام) - في حديث - قال: إنما جاز للمسافر والمريض أن يصليا صلاة الليل في أول الليل لاشتغاله وضعفه وليحرز صلاته فيستريح المريض في وقت راحته، وليشتغل المسافر باشتغاله وارتحاله وسفره.

From Al-Ridha (peace be upon him) in a hadith, he said: It is permitted for the traveler and the sick person to pray Salat al-Layl in early night due to their preoccupation and weakness, and to secure their prayer so that the sick person may rest during his time of rest, and the traveler may attend to his affairs, departure and journey.

––––––––––

Hadith 5062

عن علي بن سعيد أنه سأل أبا عبد الله (عليه السلام) عن صلاة الليل والوتر في السفر من أول الليل قال: نعم.

From Ali bin Sa'eed that he asked Abu Abdullah (peace be upon him) about Salat al-Layl and Witr during travel in early night, he said: Yes.

Hadith 5063

عن سماعة بن مهران أنه سأل أبا الحسن الأول (عليه السلام) عن وقت صلاة الليل في السفر؟ فقال: من حين تصلي العتمة إلى أن ينفجر الصبح.

From Sama'ah bin Mihran that he asked Abu Al-Hasan the First (peace be upon him) about the time of Salat al-Layl during travel? He said: From when you pray Isha until dawn breaks.

Hadith 5064

عن أبي جرير بن إدريس، عن أبي الحسن موسى بن جعفر (عليه السلام) قال: قال: صل صلاة الليل في السفر من أول الليل في المحمل والوتر وركعتي الفجر.

From Abu Jareer bin Idrees, from Abu Al-Hasan Musa bin Ja'far (peace be upon him) who said: Pray Salat al-Layl during travel from early night in the carriage, and the Witr and the two units of Fajr prayer.

Hadith 5065

عن عبد الرحمن بن أبي نجران - في حديث - قال: سألت أبا الحسن (عليه السلام) عن الصلاة بالليل في السفر في أول الليل؟ فقال: إذا خفت الفوت في آخره.

From Abd al-Rahman bin Abi Najran in a hadith, he said: I asked Abu Al-Hasan (peace be upon him) about Salat al-Layl during travel in early night? He said: If you fear missing it at its end.

Hadith 5066

عن الحلبي قال: سألت أبا عبد الله (عليه السلام) عن صلاة الليل والوتر في أول الليل في السفر إذا تخوفت البرد، وكانت علة؟ فقال: لا بأس، أنا أفعل (إذا تخوفت).

From Al-Halabi, he asked Abu Abdullah (peace be upon him) about Salat al-Layl and Witr at the beginning of the night while traveling if one fears cold weather or has an illness? He said: There is no problem, I do that (when I fear).

Hadith 5067

عن أبي عبد الله (عليه السلام) قال: لا بأس بصلاة الليل فيما بين أوله إلى آخره إلا أن أفضل ذلك بعد انتصاف الليل.

From Abu Abdullah (peace be upon him) who said: There is no problem with praying Salat al-Layl anytime from its beginning to its end, though the best time is after midnight.

Hadith 5068

عن أبي عبد الله (عليه السلام) قال: سألته عن الرجل يخاف الجنابة في السفر أو البرد، أيعجل صلاة الليل والوتر في أول الليل؟ قال: نعم.

Abu Abdullah (peace be upon him) was asked about a man who fears becoming junub (one in a state of major ritual impurity) while traveling or fears cold weather, can he hasten Salat al-Layl and Witr at the beginning of the night? He said: Yes.

Hadith 5069

عن أبي عبد الله (عليه السلام) قال: سألته عن صلاة الليل أصليها أول الليل؟ قال: نعم إني لافعل ذلك، فإذا أعجلني الجمال صليتها في المحمل.

Abu Abdullah (peace be upon him) was asked: Can I pray Salat al-Layl at the beginning of the night? He said: Yes, I do that, and when the camel drivers hurry me I pray it in the camel litter.

Hadith 5070

عن أبي بصير، عن أبي عبد الله (عليه السلام) قال: إذا خشيت أن لا تقوم آخر الليل أو كانت بك علة أو أصابك برد فصل صلاتك، وأوتر من أول الليل.

From Abu Basir, from Abu Abdullah (peace be upon him) who said: If you fear that you won't wake up at the end of the night, or you have an illness, or you're affected by cold weather, then pray your prayer and perform Witr at the beginning of the night.

Hadith 5071

عن الحسين بن علي بن بلال قال: كتبت إليه في وقت صلاة الليل، فكتب: عند زوال الليل وهو نصفه أفضل، فإن فات فأوله وآخره جائز.

From Al-Husain ibn Ali ibn Bilal who said: I wrote to him asking about the time of Salat al-Layl. He wrote back: At the decline of night which is its middle is best, but if that's missed then its beginning or end is permissible.

Hadith 5072

عن محمد بن عيسى قال: كتبت إليه أسأله يا سيدي روي عن جدك أنه قال: لا بأس بأن يصلي الرجل صلاة الليل في أول الليل؟ فكتب: في أي وقت صلى فهو جائز، إن شاء الله.

From Muhammad ibn Isa, he said: I wrote to him asking: O my master, it is narrated from your grandfather that he said there is no problem with a man praying Salat al-Layl at the beginning of the night? He wrote back: It is permissible to pray at any time, insha'Allah.

———

Hadith 5073

عن أبي عبد الله (عليه السلام) قال: كان أبو عبد الله (عليه السلام) يصلي ركعتين بعد العشاء يقرأ فيهما بمئة آية ولا يحتسبهما وركعتين وهو جالس يقرأ فيهما بقل هو الله أحد وقل يا أيها الكافرون، فان استيقظ من الليل صلى صلاة الليل وأوتر، وإن لم يستيقظ حتى يطلع الفجر صلى ركعة، فصارت شفعا، واحتسب بالركعتين اللتين صلاهما بعد العشاء وترا.

Abu Abdullah (peace be upon him) said: Abu Abdullah used to pray two units after Isha prayer reciting one hundred verses in them without counting them as part of Salat al-Layl, and two units while sitting reciting Surah Al-Ikhlas [Quran 112] and Surah Al-Kafirun [Quran 109]. If he woke up during the night he would pray Salat al-Layl and Witr, and if he didn't wake up until dawn he would pray one unit, making it even, and count the two units he prayed after Isha as Witr.

———

Hadith 5074

عن ليث قال: سألت أبا عبد الله (عليه السلام) عن الصلاة في الصيف في الليالي القصار، (صلاة الليل) في أول الليل؟ فقال: نعم، (نعم ما رأيت، ونعم ما صنعت).

From Layth who said: I asked Abu Abdullah (peace be upon him) about Salat al-Layl in summer during short nights, at the beginning of the night? He said: Yes, excellent is what you saw and excellent is what you did.

———

Hadith 5075

عن يعقوب الأحمر قال: سألته عن صلاة الليل (في الصيف في الليالي القصار) في أول الليل، قال: نعم نعم ما رأيت، ونعم ما صنعت ثم قال إن الشاب يكثر النوم فأنا آمرك به.

From Ya'qub al-Ahmar, he said: I asked him about Salat al-Layl in summer during short nights at the beginning of the night. He said: Yes, excellent is what you saw and excellent is what you did. Then he said: Indeed the youth sleeps a lot, so I command you to do it.

———

Hadith 5076

عن أبان بن تغلب قال: خرجت مع أبي عبد الله (عليه السلام) فيما بين مكة والمدينة فكان يقول: أما أنتم فشباب تؤخرون، وأما أنا فشيخ اعجل. فكان يصلي صلاة الليل أول الليل.

From Aban bin Taghlib, he said: I went out with Abu Abdullah (peace be upon him) between Makkah and Madinah. He used to say: As for you young people, you delay it, but as for me, I am old and hasten to do it. He would pray Salat al-Layl at the beginning of the night.

Hadith 5077

عن إبراهيم بن سيابة قال: كتب بعض أهل بيتي إلى أبي محمد (عليه السلام) في صلاة المسافر أول الليل صلاة الليل، فكتب: فضل صلاة المسافر من أول الليل كفضل صلاة المقيم في الحضر من آخر الليل.

From Ibrahim bin Siyabah, he said: Some of my family members wrote to Abu Muhammad (peace be upon him) about the traveler's Salat al-Layl at the beginning of the night. He wrote back: The virtue of the traveler's prayer at the beginning of the night is like the virtue of the resident's prayer at the end of the night when at home.

CHAPTER 45

Preference For Making Up Salat Al-Layl After Fajr Rather Than Performing It Before Midnight, And Preference For Delaying It Until The Last Third Of Night

[Hadith 5078 to 5085]

Hadith 5078

عن أبي عبد الله (عليه السلام) أنه قال: قلت له: إن رجلا من مواليك من صلحائهم شكا إلي ما يلقى من النوم، وقال: إني أريد القيام بالليل فيغلبني النوم حتى أصبح فربما قضيت صلاتي الشهر المتتابع والشهرين أصبر على ثقله، فقال: قرة عين والله، قرة عين والله، ولم يرخص في النوافل أول الليل، وقال: القضاء بالنهار أفضل.

From Abu Abdullah (peace be upon him), he said: I told him: A righteous man among your followers complained to me about what he experiences with sleep, saying: I want to perform Salat al-Layl but sleep overwhelms me until morning, so I make up my prayers for a consecutive month or two months, enduring its difficulty. He said: By Allah, it brings joy to the eyes! By Allah, it brings joy to the eyes! And he did not permit supererogatory prayers in the early night, and said: Making them up during the day is better.

Hadith 5079

ورواه الشيخ بإسناده عن حماد بن عيسى، مثله، وزادا: قلت فإن من نسائنا أبكارا الجارية تحب الخير وأهله وتحرص على الصلاة فيغلبها النوم حتى ربما قضت وربما ضعفت عن قضائه وهي تقوى عليه أول الليل فرخص لهن في الصلاة أول الليل إذا ضعفن وضيعن القضاء.

The Shaykh narrated it through his chain from Hammad bin Isa, similarly, with this addition: I said: Among our women are virgins who love goodness and its people and are eager for prayer, but sleep overwhelms them until sometimes they make it up and sometimes they are too weak to make it up, though they have strength for it in early night. So he permitted them to pray in early night if they are weak and unable to make it up.

Hadith 5080

عن عمر بن حنظلة أنه قال لأبي عبد الله (عليه السلام): إني مكثت ثمانية عشر ليلة أنوي القيام فلا أقوم أفأصلي أول الليل؟ قال: لا، اقض بالنهار فإني أكره أن تتخذ ذلك خلقا.

From Umar bin Hanzala that he said to Abu Abdullah (peace be upon him): I remained for eighteen nights intending to perform Salat al-Layl but could not get up - should I pray in early night? He said: No, make it up during the day for I dislike that you make this a habit.

Hadith 5081

قال: وقال الصادق (عليه السلام): قضاء صلاة الليل بعد الغداة وبعد العصر من سر آل محمد (صلى الله عليه وآله) المخزون.

He said: Al-Sadiq (peace be upon him) said: Making up Salat al-Layl after morning prayer and after Asr prayer is among the hidden secrets of the family of Muhammad (peace be upon him and his family).

Hadith 5082

عن أحدهما قال: قلت: الرجل من أمره القيام بالليل تمضي عليه الليلة والليلتان والثلاث لا يقوم فيقضي أحب إليك أم يعجل الوتر أول الليل؟ قال: لا، بل يقضي وإن كان ثلاثين ليلة.

From one of them, he said: I asked: For a man whose practice is Salat al-Layl but one night, two nights or three nights pass without him performing it - is making it up more beloved to you or hastening to pray Witr in early night? He said: No, rather he should make it up even if it was thirty nights.

Hadith 5083

عن أبي عبد الله (عليه السلام) قال: قلت له: متى أصلي صلاة الليل؟ فقال: صلها آخر الليل، قال: فقلت: فاني لا أستنبه، فقال تستنبه مرة فتصليها وتنام فتقضيها، فإذا اهتممت بقضائها بالنهار استنبهت.

From Abu Abdullah (peace be upon him), he said: I asked him: When should I pray Salat al-Layl? He said: Pray it in late night. I said: But I don't wake up. He said: You wake up once and pray it, then sleep and make it up, and when you are concerned about making it up during the day, you will wake up.

Hadith 5084

عن محمد بن مسلم قال: سألته عن الرجل لا يستيقظ من آخر الليل حتى يمضي لذلك العشر والخمس عشرة فيصلي أول الليل أحب إليك أم يقضي؟ قال: لا، بل يقضي أحب إلي إني أكرهه أن يتخذ ذلك خلقا. وكان زرارة يقول: كيف تقضى صلاة لم يدخل وقتها؟ إنما وقتها بعد نصف الليل.

From Muhammad bin Muslim who said: I asked him about a man who does not wake up in late night, and this continues for ten or fifteen days - is praying in early night more beloved to you or making it up? He said: No, rather making it up is more beloved to me as I dislike that this becomes a habit. And Zurarah used to say: How can a prayer be made up before its time comes? Its time is only after midnight.

Hadith 5085

عن أخيه موسى بن جعفر (عليه السلام) قال: سألته عن الرجل يتخوف أن لا يقوم من الليل، أيصلي صلاة الليل إذا انصرف من العشاء الآخرة؟ وهل يجزيه ذلك أم عليه قضاء؟ قال: لا صلاة حتى يذهب الثلث الأول من الليل والقضاء بالنهار أفضل من تلك الساعة.

From his brother Musa bin Ja'far (peace be upon him) who said: I asked him about a man who fears he will not wake up during the night, can he pray Salat al-Layl after finishing the last Isha prayer? And would that suffice or does he need to make it up? He said: No prayer until the first third of the night has passed, and making it up during the day is better than praying at that hour.

أقول: المراد أنه يستحب تأخير التقديم إلى ثلث الليل لا أنه وقتها بدليل تفصيل القضاء عليه، وتقدم ما يدل على ذلك.

I (Hurr Amili) say: What is meant is that it is recommended to delay the advance prayer until a third of the night, not that this is its designated time, as evidenced by the details about making it up, and what was previously mentioned indicates this.

CHAPTER 46

The Last Time For Salat Al-Layl Is Dawn, And The Recommendation To Shorten It When Time Is Limited And To Delay It After Witr When Fearing Missing It

[Hadith 5086 to 5096]

Hadith 5086

عن عبد الله بن سنان قال: قلت لأبي عبد الله (عليه السلام): إني أقوم آخر الليل وأخاف الصبح، قال: اقرأ الحمد واعجل واعجل.

From Abd Allah ibn Sinan, who said: I said to Abu Abdullah (peace be upon him): I rise in the last part of the night and I fear the dawn will come. He said: Recite al-Hamd and hasten, hasten.

Hadith 5087

عن أبي جعفر (عليه السلام) قال: سألته عن الرجل يقوم من آخر الليل وهو يخشى أن يفجأه الصبح، أيبدأ بالوتر أو يصلي الصلاة على وجهها حتى يكون الوتر آخر ذلك؟! قال بل يبدأ بالوتر، وقال: أنا كنت فاعلا ذلك.

From Abu Ja'far (peace be upon him): I asked him about a man who stands in the last part of the night and fears that dawn might surprise him, should he start with Witr or pray the prayer in its proper sequence until Witr is the last of it? He said: Rather, he should start with Witr, and he said: I used to do that.

Hadith 5088

عن معاوية بن وهب قال: سمعت أبا عبد الله (عليه السلام) يقول: أما يرضى أحدكم أن يقوم قبل الصبح ويوتر ويصلي ركعتي الفجر ويكتب له بصلاة الليل.

From Mu'awiyah ibn Wahb, he said: I heard Abu Abdullah (peace be upon him) saying: Would not one of you be pleased to stand before dawn, perform Witr, pray the two rak'ahs of Fajr, and have Salat al-Layl recorded for him?

Hadith 5089

عن أبي عبد الله (عليه السلام) قال: إذا قام الرجل من الليل فظن أن الصبح قد ضاء فأوتر ثم نظر فرأى أن عليه ليلا، قال: يضيف إلى الوتر ركعة، ثم يستقبل صلاة الليل ثم يوتر بعده.

From Abu Abdullah (peace be upon him): If a man stands at night thinking dawn has broken and performs Witr, then looks and sees that it is still night, he should add one rak'ah to the Witr, then resume Salat al-Layl and perform Witr after it.

Hadith 5090

عن الرضا (عليه السلام) قال: قال الرضا (عليه السلام): إذا كنت في صلاة الفجر فخرجت ورأيت الصبح فزد ركعة إلى الركعتين اللتين صليتهما قبل واجعله وترا.

From Al-Ridha (peace be upon him): Al-Ridha said: If you are in Fajr prayer and you go out and see the dawn, add one rak'ah to the two rak'ahs you prayed before and make it Witr.

Hadith 5091

عن إسماعيل بن جابر قال: قلت لأبي عبد الله (عليه السلام): أوتر بعدما يطلع الفجر؟ قال: لا.

From Isma'il ibn Jabir, he said: I said to Abu Abdullah (peace be upon him): Should I perform Witr after dawn breaks? He said: No.

Hadith 5092

عن أبي الحسن الرضا (عليه السلام) قال: سألته عن الرجل يكون في بيته وهو يصلي وهو يرى أن عليه ليلا ثم يدخل عليه الاخر من الباب، فقال: قد أصبحت، هل يصلي الوتر أم لا، أو يعيد شيئا من صلاته؟ قال: يعيد إن صلاها مصبحا.

From Abu Al-Hasan Al-Ridha (peace be upon him): I asked him about a man who is in his house praying, thinking it is still night, then another person enters through the door saying: Dawn has broken, should he pray Witr or not, or should he repeat any of his prayer? He said: He should repeat it if he prayed it after dawn.

Hadith 5093

عن علي بن عبد العزيز قال: قلت لأبي عبد الله (عليه السلام): أقوم وأنا أتخوف الفجر، قال: فأوتر، قلت: فأنظر وإذا علي ليل، قال: فصل صلاة الليل.

From Ali bin Abdul Aziz who said: I said to Abu Abdullah (peace be upon him): I get up while fearing dawn, he said: Then pray Witr, I said: But I look and there is still night, he said: Then pray Salat al-Layl.

Hadith 5094

وعنه، عن الحسن بن علي بن بنت إلياس، عن عبد الله بن سنان قال: سمعت أبا عبد الله (عليه السلام) يقول: إذا قمت وقد طلع الفجر فابدأ بالوتر، ثم صل الركعتين، ثم صل الركعات إذا أصبحت.

From him, from Al-Hasan bin Ali bin Bint Ilyas, from Abdullah bin Sinan who said: I heard Abu Abdullah (peace be upon him) saying: If you rise and dawn has broken, then start with Witr, then pray the two rak'ahs, then pray the remaining rak'ahs when morning comes.

Hadith 5095

محمد بن علي بن الحسين قال: قال أبو جعفر (عليه السلام): وقت صلاة الليل ما بين نصف الليل إلى آخره.

Muhammad bin Ali bin Al-Husayn said: Abu Ja'far (peace be upon him) said: The time for Salat al-Layl is between middle of the night until its end.

Hadith 5096

عن ابن عمر، عن رسول الله (صلى الله عليه وآله) قال: صلاة الليل مثنى مثنى، فإذا خفت الصبح فأوتر بواحدة، إن الله عز وجل يحب الوتر لأنه واحد.

From Ibn Umar, from the Messenger of Allah (peace be upon him and his family) who said: The Salat al-Layl is two by two, and when you fear morning then pray one rak'ah of Witr, for Allah the Mighty and Majestic loves Witr because He is One.

CHAPTER 47

Recommendation To Complete Four Units Of Salat Al-Layl In A Shortened Form Before The Obligatory Prayer If Dawn Breaks

[Hadith 5097 to 5098]

Hadith 5097

عن أبي جعفر الأحول محمد بن النعمان قال: قال أبو عبد الله (عليه السلام): إذا كنت أنت صليت أربع ركعات من صلاة الليل قبل طلوع الفجر فأتم الصلاة طلع أم لم يطلع.

From Abu Ja'far al-Ahwal Muhammad bin al-Numan who narrated that Abu Abdullah (peace be upon him) said: If you have prayed four units of Salat al-Layl before dawn breaks, complete the prayer whether dawn has broken or not.

———————

Hadith 5098

عن ابن مسكان، عن يعقوب البزاز قال: قلت له: أقوم قبل طلوع الفجر بقليل فاصلي أربع ركعات، ثم أتخوف أن ينفجر الفجر: أبدأ بالوتر أو أتم الركعات؟ فقال: لا بل أوتر وأخر الركعات حتى تقضيها في صدر النهار.

From Ibn Muskan, from Ya'qub al-Bazzaz who said: I said to him: I wake up shortly before dawn and pray four units, then I fear dawn will break - should I start with the Witr prayer or complete the units? He said: No, rather pray Witr and delay the units until you can make them up in the early part of the day.

أقول: هذا محمول على الفضيلة، والأول على الجواز قاله الشيخ، ويمكن الجمع بخوف الفوت وعدمه لما مضى ويأتي.

I (Hurr Amili) say: This ruling is based on preference, while the first one indicates permissibility as stated by the Shaykh. These can be reconciled based on whether one fears missing the prayer or not, as explained previously and will be explained later.

———————

CHAPTER 48

Recommendation Of Salat Al-Layl And Brief Witr Before Morning Prayer For One Who Wakes After Dawn As Long As Time Is Not Constrained, And The Dislike Of Making It A Habit

[Hadith 5099 to 5105]

Hadith 5099

عن أبي عبد الله (عليه السلام) قال: سألته عن صلاة الليل والوتر بعد طلوع الفجر؟ فقال: صلها بعد الفجر حتى يكون في وقت تصلي الغداة في آخر وقتها، ولا تعمد ذلك في كل ليلة. وقال: أوتر أيضا بعد فراغك منها.

From Abu Abdullah (peace be upon him), he said: I asked him about Salat al-Layl and Witr after the rise of dawn? He said: Pray them after dawn until it becomes time to pray the morning prayer in its latest time, but do not make this intentional every night. And he said: Also perform Witr after finishing it.

Hadith 5100

عن إسماعيل بن سعد الأشعري - في حديث - قال: سألت أبا الحسن الرضا (عليه السلام) عن الوتر بعد الصبح؟ قال: نعم قد كان أبي ربما أوتر بعد ما انفجر لصبح.

From Isma'il bin Sa'd al-Ash'ari - in a hadith - he said: I asked Abu al-Hasan al-Ridha (peace be upon him) about Witr after dawn? He said: Yes, my father would sometimes pray Witr after dawn had broken.

Hadith 5101

عن سليمان بن خالد، قال: قال لي أبو عبد الله (عليه السلام): ربما قمت وقد طلع الفجر فأصلي صلاة الليل والوتر والركعتين قبل الفجر ثم أصلي الفجر قال: قلت: أفعل أنا ذا؟ قال: نعم، ولا يكون منك عادة.

From Sulayman bin Khalid, he said: Abu Abdullah (peace be upon him) said to me: Sometimes I wake up after dawn has risen and I pray Salat al-Layl, Witr, and the two units before dawn, then I pray the dawn prayer. I said: Should I do this? He said: Yes, but do not make it a habit.

Hadith 5102

عن المفضل بن عمر قال: قلت لأبي عبد الله (عليه السلام): أقوم وأنا أشك في الفجر. فقال: صل على شكك، فإذا طلع الفجر فأوتر وصل الركعتين وإذا أنت قمت وقد طلع الفجر فابدأ بالفريضة، ولا تصل غيرها، فإذا فرغت فاقض ما فاتك، ولا يكون هذا عادة، وإياك أن تطلع على هذا أهلك فيصلون على ذلك ولا يصلون

بالليل.

From al-Mufaddal bin Umar who said: I said to Abu Abdullah (peace be upon him): I wake up and I am unsure about dawn. He said: Pray in your state of doubt. When dawn rises, pray Witr and pray the two units. When you wake up and dawn has already risen, start with the obligatory prayer and do not pray anything else. When you finish, make up what you missed, but do not make this a habit. And beware of letting your family know about this lest they pray like this and abandon Salat al-Layl.

Hadith 5103

عن عمر بن يزيد قال: قلت لأبي عبد الله (عليه السلام): أقوم وقد طلع الفجر، فإن أنا بدأت بالفجر صليتها في أول وقتها، وإن بدأت بصلاة الليل والوتر صليت الفجر في وقت هؤلاء، فقال: ابدأ بصلاة الليل والوتر ولا تجعل ذلك عادة.

From Umar bin Yazid who said: I said to Abu Abdullah (peace be upon him): I wake up after dawn has risen. If I start with dawn prayer I pray it at its earliest time, and if I start with Salat al-Layl and Witr I pray dawn prayer at their time. He said: Start with Salat al-Layl and Witr but do not make it a habit.

Hadith 5104

عن إسحاق بن عمار قال: قلت لأبي عبد الله (عليه السلام): أقوم وقد طلع الفجر ولم أصل صلاة الليل، فقال: صل صلاة الليل وأوتر وصل ركعتي الفجر.

From Ishaq bin Ammar who said: I said to Abu Abdullah (peace be upon him): I wake up after dawn has risen and have not prayed Salat al-Layl. He said: Pray Salat al-Layl, Witr, and pray the two rak'ahs of dawn.

Hadith 5105

محمد بن علي بن الحسين قال: وقد رويت رخصة في أن يصلي الرجل صلاة الليل بعد طلوع الفجر المرة بعد المرة ولا يتخذ ذلك عادة.

Muhammad bin Ali bin al-Husayn said: There is a concession allowing a man to pray Salat al-Layl after dawn rises occasionally but not make it a habit.

أقول: وتقدم ما يدل على جواز تقديم النوافل وتأخيرها، وعلى جواز التنفل أداء وقضاء في وقت الفريضة ما لم يتضيق، وما تضمن النهي قد عرفت وجهه.

I (Hurr Amili) say: What was previously mentioned indicates the permissibility of advancing or delaying supererogatory prayers, and the permissibility of supererogatory prayers - both on time and makeup - during obligatory prayer time as long as time is not constrained, and you have learned the reason for what included prohibition.

———————

CHAPTER 49

Recommendation Of Delaying The Making Up Of Salat Al-Layl After The Midday Supererogatory Prayers And After Zuhr Prayer When Remembered After Noon

[Hadith 5106 to 5106]

Hadith 5106

عبد الله بن جعفر في (قرب الإسناد): عن عبد الله بن الحسن، عن جده علي بن جعفر، عن أخيه موسى بن جعفر (عليه السلام) قال: سألته عن رجل نسي صلاة الليل والوتر فيذكر إذا قام في صلاة الزوال، فقال: يبدأ بالنوافل فإذا صلى الظهر صلى صلاة الليل، وأوتر ما بينه وبين العصر، أو متى أحب.

Abdullah ibn Ja'far in (Qurb al-Isnad): From Abdullah ibn al-Hasan, from his grandfather Ali ibn Ja'far, from his brother Musa ibn Ja'far (peace be upon him) said: I asked him about a man who forgot Salat al-Layl and Witr prayer, then remembers when he stands for the midday optional prayer. He said: He should begin with the supererogatory prayers, then after he prays Zuhr he should pray Salat al-Layl, and pray Witr anytime between then and Asr prayer, or whenever he wishes.

CHAPTER 50

Recommendation Of Performing The Two Rak'ahs Of Fajr Before Dawn After Salat Al-Layl Or Generally

[Hadith 5107 to 5114]

Hadith 5107

عن أحمد بن محمد بن أبي نصر قال: سألت الرضا (عليه السلام) عن ركعتي الفجر؟ فقال: احشوا بهما صلاة الليل.

From Ahmad ibn Muhammad ibn Abi Nasr, he said: I asked Al-Ridha (peace be upon him) about the two rak'ahs of Fajr? He said: Include them with Salat al-Layl.

Hadith 5108

عن أبي بصير قال: قلت لأبي عبد الله (عليه السلام): متى أصلي ركعتي الفجر؟ قال: فقال لي: بعد طلوع الفجر قلت له. إن أبا جعفر (عليه السلام) أمرني أن أصليهما قبل طلوع الفجر، فقال: يا أبا محمد، إن الشيعة أتوا أبي مسترشدين فأفتاهم بمر الحق، وأتوني شكاكا فأفتيتهم بالتقية. أقول: يعني أن عدم جواز تقديم ركعتي الفجر إنما حكموا به للتقية لا جواز التأخير لما مضى ويأتي.

From Abu Basir, he said: I said to Abu Abdullah (peace be upon him): When should I pray the two rak'ahs of Fajr? He said: After the break of dawn. I said to him: Abu Ja'far (peace be upon him) ordered me to pray them before the break of dawn. He said: O Abu Muhammad, the Shia came to my father seeking guidance, so he gave them the pure truth, and they came to me with doubts, so I gave them a precautionary answer. Comment: This means that the ruling against performing the two rak'ahs of Fajr early was given out of precaution, not that delaying them is permissible, as explained before and will be explained later.

Hadith 5109

عن زرارة، عن أبي جعفر (عليه السلام) قال: سألته عن ركعتي الفجر قبل الفجر أو بعد الفجر؟ فقال: قبل الفجر إنهما من صلاة الليل ثلاث عشرة ركعة صلاة الليل، أتريد أن تقايس؟ لو كان عليك من شهر رمضان، أكنت تطوع إذا دخل عليك وقت الفريضة، فابدأ بالفريضة.

From Zurarah, from Abu Ja'far (peace be upon him): I asked him about the two rak'ahs of Fajr - before dawn or after dawn? He said: Before dawn, they are part of Salat al-Layl of thirteen rak'ahs. Do you want to make analogies? If you had to make up fasts from Ramadan, would you perform voluntary prayers when the time for obligatory prayer has entered? So begin with the obligatory prayer.

Hadith 5110

عن أبي بصير، عن أبي عبد الله (عليه السلام) قال: قلت ركعتا الفجر من صلاة الليل هي؟ قال: نعم.

From Abu Basir who narrated from Abu Abdullah (peace be upon him): I said: Are the two rak'ahs of Fajr part of Salat al-Layl? He said: Yes.

Hadith 5111

عن محمد بن مسلم قال: سألت أبا جعفر (عليه السلام) عن أول وقت ركعتي الفجر؟ فقال: سدس الليل الباقي.

From Muhammad ibn Muslim, he said: I asked Abu Ja'far (peace be upon him) about the earliest time for the two rak'ahs of Fajr? He said: The last sixth of the night.

Hadith 5112

عن أحمد بن محمد بن أبي نصر قال: قلت لأبي الحسن (عليه السلام): وركعتي الفجر أصليهما قبل الفجر أو بعد الفجر؟ فقال: قال أبو جعفر (عليه السلام): احش بهما صلاة الليل، وصلهما قبل الفجر.

From Ahmad ibn Muhammad ibn Abi Nasr, he said: I said to Abu al-Hasan (peace be upon him): Should I pray the two rak'ahs of Fajr before dawn or after dawn? He said: Abu Ja'far (peace be upon him) said: Include them with Salat al-Layl and pray them before dawn.

Hadith 5113

عن زرارة قال: قلت لأبي جعفر (عليه السلام): الركعتان اللتان قبل الغداة أين موضعهما؟ فقال: قبل طلوع الفجر، فإذا طلع الفجر فقد دخل وقت الغداة.

From Zurarah, he said: I said to Abu Ja'far (peace be upon him): The two rak'ahs before the morning prayer, where is their proper place? He said: Before the break of dawn, for when dawn breaks, the time for the morning prayer has entered.

Hadith 5114

عن علي بن مهزيار قال: قرأت في كتاب رجل إلى أبي جعفر (عليه السلام) (الركعتان اللتان) قبل صلاة الفجر من صلاة الليل هي أم من صلاة النهار؟ وفي أي وقت أصليهما؟ فكتب (عليه السلام) بخطه: احشهما في صلاة الليل حشوا.

From Ali bin Mahziyar, he said: I read in a man's letter to Abu Ja'far (peace be upon him): Are the two rak'ahs before Fajr prayer part of Salat al-Layl or the day prayer? And at what time should I pray them? So he (peace be upon him) wrote in his own handwriting: Insert them as part of Salat al-Layl.

CHAPTER 51

Extension Of The Time For The Two Rak'ahs Of Fajr After Dawn Until the Eastern Redness Appears, And The Recommendation To Repeat Them After Dawn For Those Who Prayed Them Before Dawn And Then Slept

[Hadith 5115 to 5124]

Hadith 5115

عن علي بن يقطين قال: سألت أبا الحسن (عليه السلام) عن الرجل لا يصلي الغداة حتى يسفر وتظهر الحمرة ولم يركع ركعتي الفجر أيركعهما أو يؤخرهما؟ قال: يؤخرهما.

From Ali ibn Yaqtin, he said: I asked Abu al-Hasan (peace be upon him) about a man who does not pray the morning prayer until it becomes bright and the redness appears, and he has not prayed the two rak'ahs of Fajr - should he pray them or delay them? He said: He should delay them.

———

Hadith 5116

عن سليمان بن خالد قال: سألت أبا عبد الله (عليه السلام) عن الركعتين قبل الفجر؟ قال: تركعهما حين تترك الغداة. إنهما قبل الغداة.

From Sulayman ibn Khalid, he said: I asked Abu Abdullah (peace be upon him) about the two rak'ahs before Fajr? He said: Pray them when you leave the morning prayer, for they are before the morning prayer.

———

Hadith 5117

وفي رواية أخرى: حين تنور الغداة.

In another narration: When the dawn becomes bright.

———

Hadith 5118

الحسين بن أبي العلاء، قال: قلت لأبي عبد الله (عليه السلام): الرجل يقوم وقد نور بالغداة، قال: فليصل السجدتين اللتين قبل الغداة ثم ليصل الغداة.

Al-Husayn ibn Abi al-'Ala narrated: I said to Abu Abdullah (peace be upon him): A man wakes up when dawn has already brightened. He said: He should pray the two prostrations that come before the morning prayer, then pray the morning prayer.

———

Hadith 5119

عن عبد الرحمان بن الحجاج قال: قال أبو عبد الله (عليه السلام): صلهما بعد ما يطلع الفجر.

From Abd al-Rahman ibn al-Hajjaj, he said: Abu Abdullah (peace be upon him) said: Pray them after the dawn breaks.

Hadith 5120

قال أبو عبد الله (عليه السلام): صلهما بعد الفجر، واقرأ فيهما في الأولى قل يا أيها الكافرون، وفي الثانية قل هو الله أحد.

Abu Abdullah (peace be upon him) said: Pray them after Fajr, and recite in them in the first rak'ah [Quran 109:1-6] and in the second rak'ah [Quran 112:1-4].

Hadith 5121

عن إسحاق بن عمار، عمن أخبره عنه (عليه السلام) قال: صل الركعتين ما بينك وبين أن يكون الضوء حذاء رأسك، فإن كان بعد ذلك فابدأ بالفجر.

Ishaq ibn Ammar narrated from someone who informed him from him (peace be upon him) who said: Pray the two rak'ahs any time before the light becomes directly overhead, but if it becomes after that, then start with the Fajr prayer.

Hadith 5122

عن حماد بن عثمان قال: قال لي أبو عبد الله (عليه السلام): ربما صليتهما وعلي ليل، فإن قمت ولم يطلع الفجر أعدتهما.

From Hammad ibn Uthman, he said that Abu Abdullah (peace be upon him) said to me: Sometimes I pray them while it is still night, so if I wake up and dawn has not yet broken, I repeat them.

Hadith 5123

عن زرارة قال: سمعت أبا جعفر (عليه السلام) يقول: إني لأصلي صلاة الليل وأفرغ من صلاتي وأصلي الركعتين فأنام ما شاء الله قبل أن يطلع الفجر، فإن استيقظت عند الفجر أعدتهما.

From Zurarah, he said: I heard Abu Ja'far (peace be upon him) saying: I pray Salat al-Layl and finish my prayer and pray the two rak'ahs, then I sleep as long as Allah wills before dawn breaks. If I wake up at dawn, I repeat them.

Hadith 5124

عن أبي بكر الحضرمي قال: سألت أبا عبد الله (عليه السلام) فقلت: متى أصلي ركعتي الفجر؟ فقال: حين يعترض الفجر وهو الذي تسميه العرب: الصديع.

From Abu Bakr al-Hadrami, he said: I asked Abu Abdullah (peace be upon him), saying: When should I pray the two rak'ahs of dawn? He said: When dawn spreads horizontally, which the Arabs call: Al-Sadee' (the split).

CHAPTER 52

Permissibility Of Praying The Two Rak'ahs Of Fajr Before, During, And After Dawn

[Hadith 5125 to 5130]

Hadith 5125

عن محمد بن مسلم قال: سمعت أبا جعفر (عليه السلام) يقول: صل ركعتي الفجر قبل الفجر وبعده وعنده.

From Muhammad ibn Muslim, he said: I heard Abu Ja'far (peace be upon him) saying: Pray the two rak'ahs of Fajr before dawn, during it, and after it.

Hadith 5126

عن ابن أبي يعفور قال: سألت أبا عبد الله (عليه السلام) عن ركعتي الفجر، متى أصليهما؟ فقال: قبل الفجر ومعه وبعده.

From Ibn Abi Ya'fur, he said: I asked Abu Abdullah (peace be upon him) about the two rak'ahs of Fajr, when should I pray them? He said: Before dawn, with it, and after it (*).

Translator: * Just before the start of Fajr, exactly at the start of Fajr, or after the start of Fajr.

Hadith 5127

عن محمد بن مسلم قال: سألت أبا عبد الله (عليه السلام) عن ركعتي الفجر؟ قال: صلهما قبل الفجر ومع الفجر وبعد الفجر.

From Muhammad ibn Muslim, he said: I asked Abu Abdullah (peace be upon him) about the two rak'ahs of Fajr? He said: Pray them before dawn, with dawn, and after dawn.

Hadith 5128

عن أبي جعفر (عليه السلام) قال: صلهما مع الفجر وقبله وبعده.

From Abu Ja'far (peace be upon him) who said: Pray them with dawn, before it, and after it.

Hadith 5129

عن إسحاق بن عمار قال: سألت أبا عبد الله (عليه السلام) عن الركعتين اللتين قبيل الفجر؟ قال: قبل الفجر ومعه وبعده. قلت فمتى أدعها حتى أقضيها؟ قال: قال إذا قال المؤذن، قد قامت الصلاة.

From Ishaq ibn Ammar, he said: I asked Abu Abdullah (peace be upon him) about the two rak'ahs before dawn? He said: Before dawn, with it, and after it. I asked: When should I leave them until I make them up? He said: When the muezzin says, "Prayer has been established."

Hadith 5130

محمد بن علي بن الحسين قال: قال الصادق (عليه السلام): صل ركعتي الفجر قبل الفجر وعنده وبعده وتقرأ في الأولى (الحمد) و (قل يا أيها الكافرون) وفي الثانية: (الحمد) و (قل هو الله أحد).

From Muhammad ibn Ali ibn Al-Husayn, he said: Al-Sadiq (peace be upon him) said: Pray the two rak'ahs of Fajr before dawn, during it, and after it, and recite in the first rak'ah Surah Al-Fatihah and Surah Al-Kafirun [Quran 109], and in the second rak'ah Surah Al-Fatihah and Surah Al-Ikhlas [Quran 112].

CHAPTER 53

Recommendation Of Dividing Salat Al-Layl After Its Midpoint Into Four, Four And Three Rak'ahs Like Zuhr And Maghrib

[Hadith 5131 to 5135]

Hadith 5131

عن معاوية بن وهب قال: سمعت أبا عبد الله (عليه السلام) يقول: - وذكر صلاة النبي (صلى الله عليه وآله) قال -: كان يؤتى بطهور فيخمر عند رأسه ويوضع سواكه تحت فراشه ثم ينام ما شاء الله، فإذا استيقظ جلس، ثم قلب بصره في السماء، ثم تلا الآيات من (آل عمران): (إن في خلق السماوات والأرض) الآيات،

From Mu'awiyah ibn Wahb who said: I heard Abu Abdullah (peace be upon him) saying - mentioning the prayer of the Prophet (peace be upon him and his family) he said: Pure water would be brought to him and placed covered near his head, and his siwak would be placed under his bed, then he would sleep as long as Allah willed. When he would wake up, he would sit, then turn his gaze toward the sky, then recite the verses from (Al-Imran): Indeed in the creation of the heavens and the earth [Quran 3:190] to the end of the verses.

ثم يستن ويتطهر، ثم يقوم إلى المسجد فيركع أربع ركعات على قدر قراءة ركوعه وسجوده على قدر ركوعه، يركع حتى يقال: متى يرفع رأسه؟! ويسجد حتى يقال: متى يرفع رأسه؟! ثم يعود إلى فراشه فينام ما شاء الله، ثم يستيقظ فيجلس فيتلو الآيات من (آل عمران) ويقلب بصره في السماء ثم يستن ويتطهر ويقوم إلى المسجد ويصلي الأربع ركعات كما ركع قبل ذلك،

Then he would brush his teeth and purify himself, then stand to pray in the mosque performing four units of prayer, with his recitation, ruku and sujud being equal in length - he would bow so long that it would be said "When will he raise his head?" and prostrate so long that it would be said "When will he raise his head?" Then he would return to his bed and sleep as long as Allah willed. Then he would wake up, sit and recite the verses from Al-Imran and turn his gaze to the sky, then brush his teeth and purify himself and stand to pray in the mosque performing four units as he had prayed before.

ثم يعود إلى فراشه فينام ما شاء الله ثم يستيقظ ويجلس ويتلو الآيات من (آل عمران) ويقلب بصره في السماء، ثم يستن ويتطهر، ويقوم إلى المسجد فيوتر ويصلي الركعتين، ثم يخرج إلى الصلاة.

Then he would return to his bed and sleep as long as Allah willed. Then he would wake up, sit and recite the verses from Al-Imran and turn his gaze to the sky, then brush his teeth and purify himself, and stand to pray in the mosque performing the Witr prayer and two units, then leave for prayer.

Hadith 5132

عن أبي عبد الله (عليه السلام) قال: إن رسول الله (صلى الله عليه وآله) كان إذا صلى العشاء الآخرة أمر بوضوئه وسواكه فوضع عند رأسه مخمرا فيرقد ما شاء الله، ثم يرقد،

From Abu Abdullah (peace be upon him) who said: When the Messenger of Allah (peace be upon him and his family) would pray the Isha prayer, he would ask for his wudu water and toothstick to be placed covered near his head, then he would sleep as long as Allah willed.

ثم يقوم فيستاك ويتوضأ ويصلي أربع ركعات، ثم يرقد حتى إذا كان في وجه الصبح قام فأوتر ثم صلى الركعتين، ثم قال: لقد كان لكم في رسول الله (صلى الله عليه وآله) أسوة حسنة. قلت: متى كان يقوم؟ قال: بعد ثلث الليل.

Then he would get up, brush his teeth, perform wudu and pray four units, then sleep until dawn approached when he would get up and pray the Witr followed by two units. Then he said: "Indeed in the Messenger of Allah you have an excellent example." I asked: "When would he get up?" He replied: "After a third of the night."

Hadith 5133

قال الكليني: وقال في حديث آخر: بعد نصف الليل.

Al-Kulayni said: And in another hadith it states: After half the night.

Hadith 5134

قال: وفي رواية أخرى: يكون قيامه وركوعه وسجوده سواء، ويستاك في كل مرة قام من نومه ويقرأ الآيات من (آل عمران) (إن في خلق السماوات والأرض - إلى قوله - إنك لا تخلف الميعاد).

He said: And in another narration: His standing (qiyam), ruku, and sujud would be equal in length, and he would brush his teeth (with siwak) every time he got up from sleep and recite the verses from Al-Imran "Indeed in the creation of the heavens and earth..." until "...You do not fail in Your promise" [Quran 3:190-194].

Hadith 5135

عن ابن بكير قال: قال أبو عبد الله (عليه السلام): ما كان يحمد الرجل أن يقوم من آخر الليل فيصلي صلاته ضربة واحدة ثم ينام ويذهب.

From Ibn Bukayr, who said: Abu Abdullah (peace be upon him) said: It was not praiseworthy for a man to rise at the end of the night, pray his prayer all at once, and then sleep and be done with it.

CHAPTER 54

Recommendation Of Delaying Salat Al-Layl To Its End, And Making Witr Prayer Between The Two Dawns

[Hadith 5136 to 5140]

Hadith 5136

عن معاوية بن وهب قال: سألت أبا عبد الله (عليه السلام) عن أفضل ساعات الوتر؟ فقال: الفجر أول ذلك.

From Mu'awiyah ibn Wahb who said: I asked Abu Abdullah (peace be upon him) about the best times for Witr prayer? He said: The dawn is the beginning of that.

Hadith 5137

عن أبان بن تغلب قال: قلت لأبي عبد الله (عليه السلام): أي ساعة كان رسول الله (صلى الله عليه وآله) يوتر؟ فقال: على مثل مغيب الشمس إلى صلاة المغرب.

From Aban ibn Taghlib who said: I said to Abu Abdullah (peace be upon him): At what hour did the Messenger of Allah (peace be upon him and his family) pray Witr? He said: At a time similar to the setting of the sun in relation to Maghrib prayer (*).

Translator: * In a short time window between the true and the false dawn (refer to hadith 4943) similar to the window of time between sunset and the Maghrib prayer.

Hadith 5138

عن أبي عبد الله (عليه السلام)، قال: قلت له: متى أصلي صلاة الليل؟ قال: صلها في آخر الليل.

From Abu Abdullah (peace be upon him), he said: I said to him: When should I pray Salat al-Layl? He said: Pray it at the end of the night.

Hadith 5139

عن إسماعيل بن سعد الأشعري قال: سألت أبا الحسن الرضا (عليه السلام) عن ساعات الوتر، قال: أحبها إلى الفجر الأول، وسألته عن أفضل ساعات الليل؟ قال: الثلث الباقي.

From Isma'il ibn Sa'd al-Ash'ari who said: I asked Abu al-Hasan al-Ridha (peace be upon him) about the times of Witr, he said: The most beloved of them is at the first dawn, and I asked him about the best hours of the night? He said: The last third.

Hadith 5140

عن زرارة، أن رجلا سأل أمير المؤمنين (عليه السلام) عن الوتر أول الليل؟ فلم يجبه، فلما كان بين الصبحين خرج أمير المؤمنين (عليه السلام) إلى المسجد، فنادى: أين السائل عن الوتر ثلاث مرات نعم ساعات الوتر هذه، ثم قام فأوتر.

From Zurarah, that a man asked Amir al-Mu'minin (peace be upon him) about Witr at the beginning of the night? He did not answer him, but when it was between the two dawns, Amir al-Mu'minin (peace be upon him) went out to the mosque and called out: Where is the one who asked about Witr three times? Yes, these are the hours of Witr, then he stood and prayed Witr.

CHAPTER 55

How To Know The Middle Of The Night
[Hadith 5141 to 5142]

Hadith 5141

عن عمر حنظلة، أنه سأل أبا عبد الله (عليه السلام) فقال له: زوال الشمس نعرفه بالنهار، فكيف لنا بالليل؟ فقال: لليل زوال كزوال الشمس، قال: فبأي شئ نعرفه؟ قال: بالنجوم إذا انحدرت.

From Umar Handhala, that he asked Abu Abdullah (peace be upon him): We know the sun's zenith during the day, but how can we know it during the night? He said: The night has a zenith like the zenith of the sun. He asked: How can we know it? He said: By the stars when they descend.

أقول: المراد بالنجوم التي طلعت أول الليل وتغيب في آخره.

I (Hurr Amili) say: What is meant by the stars are those that rise at the beginning of the night and set at its end.

Hadith 5142

عن أبي بصير، عن أبي جعفر (عليه السلام) قال: دلوك الشمس زوالها، وغسق الليل بمنزلة الزوال من النهار.

From Abu Basir, from Abu Ja'far (peace be upon him) who said: The declining of the sun (duluk al-shams) is its passing the zenith/meridian, and the darkness of night (ghasaq al-layl) is equivalent to the zenith/meridian of the day.

CHAPTER 56

Recommendation Of Making Up Salat Al-Layl After Morning Prayer Or After Afternoon Prayer

[Hadith 5143 to 5145]

Hadith 5143

عن جميل بن دراج قال: سألت أبا الحسن الأول (عليه السلام) عن قضاء صلاة الليل بعد الفجر إلى طلوع الشمس؟ فقال: نعم، وبعد العصر إلى الليل، فهو من سر آل محمد المخزون.

From Jamil bin Darraj who said: I asked Abu al-Hasan the First (peace be upon him) about making up Salat al-Layl between dawn and sunrise? He said: Yes, and after Asr until nightfall, and this is from the hidden secrets of the family of Muhammad.

Hadith 5144

عن مفضل بن عمر قال: قلت لأبي عبد الله (عليه السلام) جعلت فداك: تفوتني صلاة الليل فأصلي الفجر، فلي أن أصلي بعد صلاة الفجر ما فاتني من صلاة الليل وأنا في مصلاي قبل طلوع الشمس؟ قال: نعم، ولكن لاتعلم به أهلك فيتخذونه سنة.

From Mufaddal bin Umar who said: I said to Abu Abdullah (peace be upon him): May I be sacrificed for you, I miss Salat al-Layl and I pray Fajr, am I allowed to pray after Fajr prayer what I missed from Salat al-Layl while I am in my prayer place before sunrise? He said: Yes, but do not let your family know about it lest they take it as a regular practice.

أقول: الظاهر أن المراد مرجوحية الترك اكتفاء بالقضاء.

I (Hurr Amili) say: It appears that the meaning is the undesirability of abandoning (the night prayer) relying on making it up later.

Hadith 5145

محمد بن علي بن الحسين قال: قال الصادق (عليه السلام): قضاء صلاة الليل بعد الغداة وبعد العصر من سر آل محمد المخزون. أقول: وتقدم ما يدل على استحباب القضاء وعلى جوازه في كل وقت.

Muhammad ibn Ali ibn Al-Husain said: Al-Sadiq (peace be upon him) said: Making up Salat al-Layl after morning and after afternoon prayer is from the hidden secrets of the family of Muhammad. I (Hurr Amili) say: And there has preceded what indicates the recommendation of making it up and its permissibility at any time.

CHAPTER 57

Recommendation Of Hastening To Make Up Missed Prayers Of Day Even At Night, And Vice Versa, And The Permissibility Of Matching Make-up Time With Performance Time

[Hadith 5146 to 5161]

Hadith 5146

عن زرارة، عن أبي جعفر (عليه السلام) أنه سئل عن رجل صلى بغير طهور، أو نسي صلوات لم يصلها، أو نام عنها؟ فقال: يقضيها إذا ذكرها في أي ساعة ذكرها من ليل أو نهار.

From Zurarah, from Abu Ja'far (peace be upon him) that he was asked about a man who prayed without purification, or forgot prayers and did not pray them, or slept through them? He said: He should make them up whenever he remembers them, at any hour he remembers them, whether night or day.

Hadith 5147

عن عنبسة العابد قال: سألت أبا عبد الله (عليه السلام) عن قول الله عز وجل: (وهو الذي جعل الليل النهار خلفة لمن أراد أن يذكر أو أراد شكورا)؟ قال: قضاء صلاة الليل بالنهار وصلاة النهار بالليل.

From Anbasa Al-Abid who said: I asked Abu Abdullah (peace be upon him) about the saying of Allah the Mighty and Majestic: "And it is He who made the night and day in succession for whoever desires to remember or desires gratitude" [Quran, 25:62]? He said: Making up Salat al-Layl during the day and day prayer during the night.

Hadith 5148

عن أبي جعفر (عليه السلام) أنه قال: أفضل قضاء صلاة الليل في الساعة التي فاتتك آخر الليل، وليس بأس أن تقضيها بالنهار وقبل أن تزول الشمس.

From Abu Ja'far (peace be upon him) that he said: The best time to make up night prayers is in the hour you missed them at the end of night, and there is no problem making them up during the day before the sun passes its zenith.

أقول: هذا محمول على من ذكر آخر الليل أو على التقية.

I (Hurr Amili) say: This is interpreted as applying to one who remembered at the end of night or as precautionary dissimulation.

Hadith 5149

قال: وقال الصادق (عليه السلام): كل ما فاتك من صلاة الليل فاقضه بالنهار، قال الله تبارك وتعالى (وهو الذي جعل الليل والنهار خلفة لمن أراد أن يذكر أو أراد شكورا) يعني أن يقضي الرجل ما فاته بالليل بالنهار، وما فاته بالنهار بالليل، واقض ما فاتك من صلاة الليل أي وقت شئت من ليل أو نهار ما لم يكن وقت فريضة.

Al-Sadiq (peace be upon him) said: Whatever you miss from Salat al-Layl, make it up during the day. Allah, the Blessed and Exalted, said "And it is He who has made the night and the day in succession for whoever desires to remember or desires gratitude" [Quran, 25:62], meaning that a man should make up what he missed during the night in the day, and what he missed during the day in the night. And make up what you missed from Salat al-Layl at any time you wish of night or day as long as it is not the time of an obligatory prayer.

Hadith 5150

قال: وقال رسول الله (صلى الله عليه وآله): إن الله ليباهي ملائكته بالعبد يقضي صلاة الليل بالنهار فيقول: يا ملائكتي انظروا إلى عبدي يقضي ما لم أفترضه عليه، أشهدكم أني قد غفرت له.

The Messenger of Allah (peace be upon him and his family) said: Indeed Allah boasts to His angels about the servant who makes up night prayers during the day, saying: O My angels, look at My servant making up what I did not make obligatory upon him. I make you witness that I have forgiven him.

Hadith 5151

عن معاوية بن عمار قال: قال أبو عبد الله (عليه السلام): اقض ما فاتك من صلاة النهار بالنهار، وما فاتك من صلاة الليل بالليل، قلت: أقضي وترين في ليلة؟ قال: نعم، اقض وترا أبدا.

From Mu'awiyah ibn Ammar who said: Abu Abdullah (peace be upon him) said: Make up what you missed from day prayers during the day, and what you missed from night prayers during the night. I said: Should I make up two Witr prayers in one night? He said: Yes, always make up the Witr prayer.

Hadith 5152

قال أبو جعفر (عليه السلام): أفضل قضاء النوافل قضاء صلاة الليل بالليل وصلاة النهار بالنهار، قلت: ويكون وتران في ليلة؟ قال: لا، قلت: ولم تأمرني أن أوتر وترين في ليلة؟ فقال: (عليه السلام): أحدهما قضاء.

Abu Ja'far (peace be upon him) said: The best way to make up supererogatory prayers is to make up night prayers during the night and day prayers during the day. I asked: Can there be two Witr prayers in one night? He said: No. I said: Then why did you order me to pray two Witr prayers in one night? He (peace be upon him) said: Because one of them is a make-up prayer.

Hadith 5153

عن أبي عبد الله (عليه السلام) قال: إن علي بن الحسين (عليه السلام) كان إذا فاته شئ من صلاة الليل قضاه بالنهار وإن فاته شئ من اليوم قضاه من الغد، أو في الجمعة، أو في الشهر. وكان إذا اجتمعت عليه الأشياء قضاها في شعبان حتى يكمل له عمل السنة كلها كاملة.

From Abu Abdullah (peace be upon him) who said: When Ali bin Al-Husayn (peace be upon him) missed something from Salat al-Layl, he would make it up during the day, and if he missed something from the day prayer, he would make it up the next day, or during the week, or during the month. When things accumulated, he would make them up during Shaban until he completed the entire year's worship completely.

Hadith 5154

عن أبي بصير قال: قال أبو عبد الله (عليه السلام): إن قويت فاقض صلاة النهار بالليل.

Abu Basir reported that Abu Abdullah (peace be upon him) said: If you are able, make up the day prayer during the night.

Hadith 5155

وبالاسناد قال: قال أبو عبد الله (عليه السلام): إن فاتك شئ من تطوع الليل والنهار فاقضه عند زوال الشمس، وبعد الظهر عند العصر، وبعد المغرب، وبعد العتمة ومن آخر السحر.

Through the same chain, Abu Abdullah (peace be upon him) said: If you miss any voluntary prayers of the night or day, make them up at noon, after Zuhr at Asr time, after Maghrib, after Isha, and in the last part of pre-dawn.

Hadith 5156

عن زرارة قال: سألت أبا جعفر (عليه السلام) عن قضاء صلاة الليل؟ قال: اقضها في وقتها التي صليت فيه، فقال: قلت: يكون وتران في ليلة؟ قال: ليس هو وتران في ليلة، أحدهما لما فاتك.

Zurarah said: I asked Abu Ja'far (peace be upon him) about making up Salat al-Layl? He said: Make it up at its time that you usually pray it. I asked: Would there be two Witr prayers in one night? He said: It's not two Witr prayers in one night, one of them is for what you missed.

Hadith 5157

عن أبي عبد الله (عليه السلام) قال: اقض صلاة النهار أي ساعة شئت من ليل أو نهار، كل ذلك سواء.

Abu Abdullah (peace be upon him) said: Make up the day prayer at any hour you wish of night or day, it's all the same.

Hadith 5158

عن ذريح قال: قلت لأبي عبد الله (عليه السلام): فاتتني صلاة الليل في السفر، أفأقضيها بالنهار فقال: نعم إن أطقت ذلك.

Dhuraih said: I said to Abu Abdullah (peace be upon him): I missed Salat al-Layl while traveling, should I make it up during the day? He said: Yes, if you are able to do so.

Hadith 5159

عن أبي عبد الله (عليه السلام) قال: سألته عن الرجل ينام عن الفجر حتى تطلع الشمس وهو في سفر، كيف يصنع؟ أيجوز له أن يقضي بالنهار؟ قال: لا يقضي صلاة نافلة ولا فريضة بالنهار، ولا يجوز له ولا يثبت له، ولكن يؤخرها فيقضيها بالليل.

Abu Abdullah (peace be upon him) was asked about a traveling man who sleeps through Fajr until sunrise, what should he do? Is it permissible for him to make it up during the day? He said: He should not make up supererogatory or obligatory prayers during the day, it's not permissible or established for him, but he should delay it and make it up at night.

قال الشيخ: هذا خبر شاذ لا تعارض به الاخبار المطابقة لظاهر القرآن. أقول: هذا مخصوص بالسفر، فيمكن حمله على مرجوحية القضاء نهارا، لكثرة الشواغل للبال وقلة التوجه والاقبال، أو على الصلاة على الراحلة.

Shaykh said: This is an irregular report that doesn't contradict other reports that match the apparent meaning of the Quran. I (Hurr Amili) say: This is specific to travel, and can be interpreted as the undesirability of making up prayers during the day due to many distractions and less focus, or it refers to prayer while riding.

Hadith 5160

عن إسحاق بن عمار قال: لقيت أبا عبد الله (عليه السلام) بالقادسية عند قدومه على أبي العباس، فأقبل حتى انتهينا إلى طراناباد فإنا نحن برجل على ساقية يصلي، وذلك ارتفاع النهار، فوقف عليه أبو عبد الله (عليه السلام) وقال: يا عبد الله، أي شئ تصلي؟ فقال: صلاة الليل فاتتني أقضيها بالنهار.

Ishaq bin Ammar said: I met Abu Abdullah (peace be upon him) in Qadisiyyah when he was arriving to meet Abu Al-Abbas. We proceeded until we reached

Taranabad where we found a man praying by a water channel in the late morning. Abu Abdullah (peace be upon him) stopped by him and said: O servant of Allah, what prayer are you performing? He said: The Salat al-Layl that I missed, I'm making it up during the day.

فقال: يا معتب، حط رحلك حتى نتغدى مع الذي يقضي صلاة الليل، فقلت: جعلت فداك، تروي فيه شيئًا؟ فقال: حدثني أبي عن آبائه قال: قال رسول الله (صلى الله عليه وآله): إن الله يباهي بالعبد يقضي صلاة الليل بالنهار، يقول: يا ملائكتي، انظروا إلى عبدي كيف يقضي ما لم أفترضه عليه!؟ أشهدكم أني قد غفرت له.

He said: O Mu'attib, put down our loads so we can have lunch with the one who makes up Salat al-Layl. I said: May I be sacrificed for you, do you narrate anything about this? He said: My father narrated to me from his forefathers that the Messenger of Allah (peace be upon him and his family) said: Allah boasts to the angels about the servant who makes up Salat al-Layl during the day, saying: O My angels, look at My servant making up what I did not make obligatory upon him! I make you witness that I have forgiven him.

Hadith 5161

عن أبي عبد الله (عليه السلام)، قال: قال له رجل: ربما فاتتني صلاة الليل الشهر والشهرين والثلاثة فأقضيها بالنهار، أيجوز ذلك؟ قال: قرة عين لك والله - ثلاثا - إن الله يقول: (وهو الذي جعل الليل والنهار خلفة) الآية، فهو قضاء صلاة النهار بالليل، وقضاء صلاة الليل بالنهار، وهو من سر آل محمد المكنون.

From Abu Abdullah (peace be upon him), who said: A man said to him: Sometimes I miss Salat al-Layl for a month, two months, or three months, so I make it up during the day. Is this permissible? He said: By Allah, it is a comfort for your eyes - three times. Indeed Allah says "And it is He who made the night and day in succession" [Quran, 25:62]. So it is making up the day prayer at night, and making up Salat al-Layl during the day, and it is from the hidden secrets of the family of Muhammad.

CHAPTER 58

Obligation Of Knowing The Entry Of Prayer Times
[Hadith 5162 to 5165]

Hadith 5162

عن عبد الله بن عجلان قال: قال أبو جعفر (عليه السلام): إذا كنت شاكا في الزوال فصل ركعتين، فإذا استيقنت أنها قد زالت بدأت بالفريضة.

From Abdullah bin Ajlan who said: Abu Ja'far (peace be upon him) said: If you are in doubt about the sun's zenith, pray two rak'ahs. When you become certain that it has passed the zenith, begin with the obligatory prayer.

Hadith 5163

عن الصادق، عن آبائه، عن أمير المؤمنين (عليهم السلام) - في حديث طويل - إن الله تعالى إذا حجب عن عباده عين الشمس التي جعلها دليلا على أوقات الصلاة فموسع عليهم تأخير الصلوات، ليتبين لهم الوقت بظهورها، ويستيقنوا أنها قد زالت.

From Al-Sadiq, from his forefathers, from Amir al-Mu'minin (peace be upon them) - in a long hadith - Indeed when Allah the Exalted conceals from His servants the sun's eye which He made as an indicator for prayer times, He gives them flexibility to delay the prayers until they can clearly determine the time through its appearance and become certain that it has passed its zenith.

Hadith 5164

عن أبي جعفر (عليه السلام) قال: الفجر هو الخيط الأبيض المعترض، فلا تصل في سفر ولا حضر حتى تتبينه فإن الله سبحانه لم يجعل خلقه في شبهة من هذا، فقال: (وكلوا واشربوا حتى يتبين لكم الخيط الأبيض من الخيط الأسود من الفجر).

From Abu Ja'far (peace be upon him) who said: The dawn is the horizontal white thread, so do not pray in travel or residence until you clearly see it, for Allah the Glorified has not placed His creation in doubt regarding this, for He said: "and eat and drink until the white thread becomes distinct to you from the black thread of dawn" [Quran, 2:187].

Hadith 5165

محمد بن مكي الشهيد في (الذكرى) عن ابن أبي قرة بإسناده عن علي بن جعفر: عن أخيه موسى (عليه السلام)، في الرجل يسمع الاذان فيصلي الفجر ولا يدري أطلع أم لا، غير أنه يظن لمكان الاذان أنه طلع، قال: لا يجزيه حتى يعلم أنه قد طلع.

Muhammad ibn Makki al-Shahid reported in Al-Dhikra from Ibn Abi Qurrah with his chain to Ali ibn Ja'far: From his brother Musa (peace be upon him), regarding a man who hears the adhan and prays Fajr without knowing if dawn has broken or not, except that he assumes due to the adhan that it has broken, he said: It is not sufficient until he knows for certain that dawn has broken.

أقول: هذا لا ينافي ما يأتي من جواز الاعتماد على الاذان، لأنه محمول على عدم عدالة المؤذن أو مخصوص بالصبح لشرعية الاذان قبل الفجر، والله أعلم.

I (Hurr Amili) say: This does not contradict what will come regarding the permissibility of relying on the adhan, because this is interpreted as applying when the muezzin is not trustworthy, or specifically for dawn prayer since it is prescribed to give adhan before dawn, and Allah knows best.

CHAPTER 59

Permissibility Of Relying On The Time Based On Information From A Trustworthy Person Or Their Adhan

[Hadith 5166 to 5167]

Hadith 5166

عن زرارة، عن أبي جعفر (عليه السلام)، في رجل صلى الغداة بليل غره من ذلك القمر ونام حتى طلعت الشمس فأخبر أنه صلى بليل، قال: يعيد صلاته.

From Zurarah, from Abu Ja'far (peace be upon him), regarding a man who prayed the morning prayer at night being deceived by the moon, and then slept until sunrise, and was informed that he had prayed during the night, he said: He should repeat his prayer.

Hadith 5167

عن (أحمد بن عبد الله القزويني)، عن أبيه قال: دخلت على الفضل بن الربيع وهو جالس على سطح فقال لي: ادن مني، فدنوت منه حتى حاذيته، ثم قال لي: أشرف إلى البيت في الدار، فأشرفت، فقال لي: ما ترى في البيت؟ قلت: ثوبا مطروحا، فقال: أنظر حسنا، فتأملته ونظرت فتيقنت فقلت: رجل ساجد - إلى أن قال -

From Ahmad ibn Abdullah al-Qazwini, from his father who said: I entered upon Al-Fadhl ibn Al-Rabi' while he was sitting on a roof. He said to me: Come closer to me. So I approached until I was next to him. Then he said: Look down at the house in the courtyard. I looked and he asked: What do you see in the house? I said: A cloth spread out. He said: Look carefully. So I examined and looked carefully until I was certain and said: A man in prostration.

فقال: هذا أبو الحسن موسى بن جعفر (عليه السلام)، إني أتفقده الليل والنهار فلم أجده في وقت من الأوقات إلا على الحالة التي أخبرك بها، إنه يصلي الفجر فيعقب ساعة في دبر صلاته إلى أن تطلع الشمس، ثم يسجد سجدة فلا يزال ساجدا حتى تزول الشمس، وقد وكل من يترصد له الزوال، فلست أدري متى يقول الغلام: قد زالت الشمس إذ وثب فيبتدي الصلاة من غير أن يحدث وضوءا، فأعلم أنه لم ينم في سجوده، ولا أغفى ولا يزال إلى أن يفرغ من صلاة العصر،

He said: This is Abu Al-Hasan Musa ibn Ja'far (peace be upon him). I observe him day and night and I never find him at any time except in the state I am telling you about. He prays Fajr and remains engaged in post-prayer devotions until sunrise. Then he prostrates and remains in prostration until the sun passes its zenith. He has assigned someone to watch for noon time. I don't know when exactly the servant announces the sun has passed its zenith, but he immediately rises and begins prayer without renewing his wudu, so I know he neither slept nor dozed in his prostration. He remains like this until he completes the Asr prayer.

فإذا صلى العصر سجد سجدة فلا يزال ساجدا إلى أن تغيب الشمس، فإذا غابت الشمس وثب من سجدته فصلى المغرب من غير أن يحدث حدثنا، ولا يزال في صلاته وتعقيبه إلى أن يصلي العتمة. فإذا صلى العتمة أفطر على شواء يؤتى به، ثم يجدد الوضوء، ثم يسجد ثم يرفع رأسه فينام نومة خفيفة، ثم يقوم فيجدد الوضوء، ثم يقوم فلا يزال يصلي في جوف الليل حتى يطلع الفجر، فلست أدري متى يقول الغلام: إن الفجر قد طلع، إن وثب هو لصلاة الفجر فهذا دأبه منذ حول إلي.

After Asr prayer, he prostrates again and remains in prostration until sunset. When the sun sets, he rises from his prostration and prays Maghrib without performing new ablutions. He remains in his prayer and post-prayer devotions until he prays Isha. After Isha prayer, he breaks his fast with roasted meat that is brought to him. Then he renews his wudu, prostrates, raises his head, takes a light nap, then gets up and renews his wudu. He then stands and continues praying through the night until Fajr. I don't know exactly when the servant announces that Fajr has begun, but he immediately rises for the Fajr prayer. This has been his routine since he was transferred to my custody.

أقول: ويأتي ما يدل على جواز الاعتماد على أذان الثقة. وتقدم ما ظاهره المنافاة وبينا وجهه.

I (Hurr Amili) say: Evidence will come regarding the permissibility of relying on the adhan of a trustworthy person, and what has preceded that apparently contradicts this has been explained.

———————

CHAPTER 60

On Doubting Whether One Prayed Or Not Before And After The Prayer Time

[Hadith 5168 to 5169]

Hadith 5168

عن زرارة والفضيل، عن أبي جعفر (عليه السلام) - في حديث - قال: متى استيقنت أو شككت في وقت فريضة أنك لم تصلها، أو في وقت فوتها أنك لم تصلها، صليتها، وإن شككت بعد ما خرج وقت الفوت وقد دخل حائل فلا إعادة عليك من شك حتى تستيقن، فإن استيقنت فعليك أن تصليها في أي حالة كنت.

From Zurarah and Al-Fadil, from Abu Ja'far (peace be upon him) - in a hadith - he said: Whenever you become certain or doubt during the time of an obligatory prayer that you have not performed it, or during the time of its lapse that you have not performed it, you should pray it. And if you doubt after the time of lapse has passed and an intervening event (*) has occurred, then there is no obligation to repeat upon one who doubts until they become certain. If you become certain, then you must pray it in whatever state you are in.

Translator: * Such as the expiration of the prayer time or performance of the next prayer. It acts as a barrier between the time when the prayer was due and the time after it and serves as a marker to determine whether a person should act upon their doubt or not when it comes to making up missed prayers.

Hadith 5169

عن زرارة، عن أبي جعفر (عليه السلام) قال: إذا جاء يقين بعد حائل قضاه ومضى على اليقين ويقضي الحائل والشك جميعا، فإن شك في الظهر فيما بينه وبين أن يصلي العصر قضاها، وإن دخله الشك بعد أن يصلي العصر فقد مضت، إلا أن يستيقن، لان العصر حائل فيما بينه وبين الظهر، فلا يدع الحائل لما كان من الشك إلا بيقين.

From Zurarah, from Abu Ja'far (peace be upon him) who said: When certainty comes after an intervening event, one should make up for it and proceed with certainty, and make up for both the intervening event and the doubt. So if one doubts about the noon prayer before performing the afternoon prayer, they should make it up. But if doubt enters after performing the afternoon prayer, then it has passed, unless there is certainty, because the afternoon prayer is an intervening event between oneself and the noon prayer, and one should not abandon the intervening event due to doubt except with certainty.

CHAPTER 61

Permissibility Of Performing Supererogatory Prayers While Having Obligatory Prayers To Make Up, And The Recommendation To Start With The Obligatory Prayer

[Hadith 5170 to 5178]

Hadith 5170

عن أبي عبد الله (عليه السلام)، قال: سمعته يقول: إن رسول الله (صلى الله عليه وآله) رقد فغلبته عيناه فلم يستيقظ حتى آذاه حر الشمس، ثم استيقظ فعاد ناديه ساعة وركع ركعتين ثم صلى الصبح وقال: يا بلال، مالك؟ فقال بلال: أرقدني الذي أرقدك يا رسول الله، قال: وكره المقام وقال: نمتم بوادي الشيطان.

From Abu Abdullah (peace be upon him) who said: I heard him say: The Messenger of Allah (peace be upon him and his family) fell asleep and his eyes overtook him until the heat of the sun bothered him. Then he woke up and returned to his gathering for a while and prayed two units, then prayed the morning prayer and said: O Bilal, what happened to you? Bilal said: What made you sleep made me sleep O Messenger of Allah. He disliked staying there and said: You slept in the valley of Satan.

Hadith 5171

عن أبي بصير، عن أبي عبد الله (عليه السلام)، قال: سألته عن رجل نام عن الغداة حتى طلعت الشمس؟ فقال: يصلي ركعتين، ثم يصلي الغداة.

From Abu Basir, from Abu Abdullah (peace be upon him), who said: I asked him about a man who slept through the morning prayer until sunrise? He said: He should pray two units, then pray the morning prayer.

Hadith 5172

عن زرارة، عن أبي جعفر (عليه السلام)، أنه سئل عن رجل صلى بغير طهور أو نسي صلوات لم يصلها أو نام عنها؟ قال: يقضيها إذا ذكرها في أي ساعة ذكرها - إلى أن قال - ولا يتطوع بركعة حتى يقضي الفريضة.

From Zurarah, from Abu Ja'far (peace be upon him), that he was asked about a man who prayed without purification or forgot prayers he had not prayed or slept through them? He said: He should make them up when he remembers them at whatever hour he remembers - until he said - and he should not perform voluntary prayers until he makes up the obligatory prayer.

Hadith 5173

عن أبي عبد الله (عليه السلام)، قال: سألته عن الرجل ينام عن الغداة حتى تبزغ الشمس، أيصلي حين يستيقظ، أو ينتظر حتى تنبسط الشمس؟ فقال: يصلي حين يستيقظ. قلت: يوتر أو يصلي الركعتين؟ قال: بل يبدأ بالفريضة.

From Abu Abdullah (peace be upon him), who said: I asked him about a man who sleeps through the morning prayer until sunrise, should he pray when he wakes up or wait until the sun has risen high? He said: He should pray when he wakes up. I said: Should he pray the Witr or the two units? He said: Rather he should start with the obligatory prayer.

Hadith 5174

عن أبي عبد الله (عليه السلام) قال: لكل صلاة مكتوبة لها نافلة ركعتين إلا العصر فإنه يقدم نافلتها فيصيران قبلها، وهي الركعتان اللتان تمت بهما الثماني بعد الظهر، فإذا أردت أن تقضي شيئا من الصلاة مكتوبة أو غيرها فلا تصل شيئا حتى تبدأ فتصلي قبل الفريضة التي حضرت ركعتين نافلة لها، ثم اقض ما شئت.

From Abu Abdullah (peace be upon him) who said: For every prescribed prayer there is a supererogatory prayer of two rak'ahs except for Asr, for its supererogatory prayer is moved forward and performed before it, and these are the two rak'ahs that complete the eight after Zuhr. If you want to make up any missed prayer, whether prescribed or otherwise, do not pray anything until you begin by praying two supererogatory rak'ahs for the prescribed prayer whose time has come, then make up whatever you wish.

يحتمل أن يكون المراد أنك إذا أردت قضاء فريضة في وقت حاضرة صليت قبل الحاضرة نافلة ركعتين ثم صليت الفريضة، ويكفيك هاتان الركعتان لنافلة القضاء أيضا، فاقض بعد الفريضة ما شئت. أو المراد أنك إذا أردت القضاء في وقت الفريضة فقدم ركعتين من القضاء لنافلة، وأخر عنها سائرها، ويحتمل أن يكون المراد بالفريضة التي حضرت صلاة القضاء بأن يكون المراد أنه يستحب لكل قضاء نافلة، ويحتمل أن يكون القضاء بمعنى الفعل ويحتمل أن يكون المراد أن لكل صلاة نافلة يختص بها إلا العصر فإنه اكتفى فيها ركعتين من نافلة الظهر لقربهما منها وهذا بناء على أن الثمان ركعات قبل الظهر ليست بنافلة الظهر ولكنها بهذا توقتت والثمان التي بعدها نافلة للظهر إما جميعها أو بعضها كما يحتمل أن يكون المراد أن كل صلاة بعدها نافلة وان لمم يكن متصلا بها إلا العصر فإنها قبلها وليس بعدها إلى المغرب نافلة. أو المراد أن كل فريضة لها نافلة متصلة بها سواء كان قبلها أو بعدها إلا العصر فإنه يجوز الفصل بينها وبين الركعتين لاختلاف وقتيهما. (هامش المخطوط م - ق - ر) وخط الهامش لا يشبه خط المصنف. ٦ - الذكرى: ٤٣١.

Footnote in manuscript: It's possible that this means when you want to make up a missed prayer during the time of a present prayer, you should pray two rak'ahs of nafilah before the present prayer, then pray the obligatory prayer, and these two rak'ahs would suffice for the nafilah of the makeup prayer as well, then make up whatever you wish after the obligatory prayer. Or it means that when you want to make up prayers during the time of an obligatory prayer, perform two rak'ahs of the makeup prayer as nafilah first, and delay the rest. It could also mean that the "present obligatory prayer" refers to the makeup prayer itself, suggesting that every makeup prayer should have a nafilah. The term "making up" could also mean simply performing the prayer. It could also mean that every prayer has its specific nafilah except Asr, which suffices with two rak'ahs from Zuhr's nafilah due to their proximity, based on the understanding that the eight rak'ahs before Zuhr are not Zuhr's nafilah but are timed as such, and the eight after it are Zuhr's nafilah, either all or some of them. It could also mean that every prayer has a nafilah after it, even if not immediately connected, except Asr which has it before and has no nafilah until Maghrib. Or it means that every obligatory prayer has a connected nafilah, whether before or after, except Asr where separation between it and the two rakahs is permitted due to their different timings. (Manuscript margin m - q - r) The marginal writing does not match the author's handwriting. 6 - Al-Dhikra: 134.

Hadith 5175

عن زرارة، عن أبي جعفر (عليه السلام) قال: قال رسول الله (صلى الله عليه وآله): إذا دخل وقت صلاة مكتوبة فلا صلاة نافلة حتى يبدأ بالمكتوبة، قال: فقدمت الكوفة، فأخبرت الحكم بن عتيبة وأصحابه فقبلوا ذلك مني.

From Zurarah, from Abu Ja'far (peace be upon him) who said: The Messenger of Allah (peace be upon him and his family) said: When the time for an obligatory prayer enters, there is no supererogatory prayer until one begins with the obligatory prayer. He said: So I went to Kufa and informed Al-Hakam bin Utayba and his companions and they accepted that from me.

فلما كان في القابل لقيت أبا جعفر (عليه السلام) فحدثني أن رسول الله (صلى الله عليه وآله) عرس في بعض أسفاره وقال: من يكلؤنا؟ فقال بلال: أنا، فنام بلال وناموا حتى طلعت الشمس، فقال: يا بلال ما أرقدك؟ فقال: يا رسول الله أخذ بنفسي الذي أخذ بأنفاسكم.

When the following year came, I met Abu Ja'far (peace be upon him) and he told me that the Messenger of Allah (peace be upon him and his family) camped during one of his journeys and said: Who will watch over us? Bilal said: I will. Then Bilal slept and they slept until the sun rose. He said: O Bilal what made you sleep? He said: O Messenger of Allah, what overtook your breaths overtook mine.

فقال رسول الله (صلى الله عليه وآله): قوموا فتحولوا عن مكانكم الذي أصابكم فيه الغفلة، وقال: يا بلال

أذن، فأذن، فصلى رسول الله (صلى الله عليه وآله) ركعتي الفجر، وأمر أصحابه فصلوا ركعتي الفجر، ثم قام فصلى بهم الصبح.

The Messenger of Allah (peace be upon him and his family) said: Get up and move from your place where heedlessness overtook you, and said: O Bilal, make the call to prayer. So he made the call, and the Messenger of Allah (peace be upon him and his family) prayed the two rak'ahs of Fajr, and ordered his companions to pray the two rak'ahs of Fajr, then he stood and led them in the morning prayer.

وقال: من نسي شيئا من الصلاة فليصليها إذا ذكرها، فإن الله عز وجل يقول: (وأقم الصلاة لذكري)، قال زرارة: فحملت الحديث إلى الحكم وأصحابه فقالوا: نقضت حديثك الأول، فقدمت على أبي جعفر (عليه السلام) فأخبرته بما قال القوم، فقال: يا زرارة، ألا أخبرتهم أنه قد فات الوقتان جميعا، وأن ذلك كان قضاء من رسول الله (صلى الله عليه وآله).

And he said: Whoever forgets any prayer should pray it when he remembers it, for Allah the Mighty and Majestic says: [Quran 20:14]. Zurarah said: I took the hadith to Al-Hakam and his companions and they said: You have contradicted your first hadith. So I went to Abu Ja'far (peace be upon him) and informed him of what the people said. He said: O Zurarah, why didn't you tell them that both times had passed, and that was a make-up prayer from the Messenger of Allah (peace be upon him and his family).

Hadith 5176

محمد بن الحسين الرضي في (نهج البلاغة) عن أمير المؤمنين (عليه السلام)، أنه قال: لا قربة بالنوافل إذا أضرت بالفرائض.

Muhammad bin Al-Husayn Al-Radhi in (Nahj al-Balagha) from Amir al-Mu'minin (peace be upon him), that he said: There is no nearness through supererogatory prayers when they harm the obligatory prayers.

Hadith 5177

قال: وقال (عليه السلام): إذا أضرت النوافل بالفرائض فارفضوها.

He said: He (peace be upon him) said: When supererogatory acts interfere with obligatory duties, abandon them.

Hadith 5178

عن زرارة، عن أبي جعفر (عليه السلام)، قال: قلت له: رجل عليه دين من صلاة قام يقضيه فخاف أن يدركه الصبح ولم يصل صلاة ليلته تلك؟ قال: يؤخر القضاء ويصلي صلاة ليلته تلك.

From Zurarah, from Abu Ja'far (peace be upon him), he said: I asked him about a man who has to make up missed prayers and starts making them up, but fears dawn will arrive before he can perform that night's prayer? He said: He should delay making up the missed prayers and perform that night's prayer.

CHAPTER 62

Permissibility Of Making Up Obligatory Prayers During The Time Of A Present Obligatory Prayer As Long As Time Is Not Constrained

[Hadith 5179 to 5186]

Hadith 5179

عن زرارة، عن أبي جعفر - في حديث - قال: إذا دخل وقت صلاة ولم يتم ما قد فاته فليقض ما لم يتخوف أن يذهب وقت هذه الصلاة التي قد حضرت، وهذه أحق بوقتها فليصلها، فإذا قضاها فليصل ما فاته مما قد مضى.

From Zurarah, from Abu Ja'far who said in a hadith: When the time for prayer enters while one has not completed making up missed prayers, they should make them up as long as they do not fear losing the time of the present prayer. The present prayer has more right to its time, so pray it, then after completing it, make up what was missed from the past.

Hadith 5180

عن أبي جعفر (عليه السلام) قال: إذا فاتتك صلاة فذكرتها في وقت أخرى، فإن كنت تعلم أنك إذا صليت التي فاتتك كنت من الأخرى في وقت، فابدأ بالتي فاتتك، فإن الله عز وجل يقول: (أقم الصلاة لذكري) وإن كنت تعلم أنك إذا صليت التي فاتتك فاتتك التي بعدها فابدأ بالتي أنت في وقتها واقض الأخرى.

From Abu Ja'far (peace be upon him) who said: If you miss a prayer and remember it during the time of another prayer, then if you know that when you pray the one you missed you will still have time for the current one, start with the one you missed, for Allah the Mighty and Majestic says "Establish prayer for My remembrance" [Quran, 20:14]. But if you know that if you pray the one you missed you will miss the current one, then start with the one whose time is current and make up the other one later.

Hadith 5181

عن أبي بصير، عن أبي عبد الله (عليه السلام) قال: إن نام رجل ولم يصل صلاة المغرب والعشاء أو نسي، فإن استيقظ قبل الفجر قدر ما يصليهما كلتيهما فليصلهما، وإن خشي أن تفوته إحداهما فليبدأ بالعشاء الآخرة. وإن استيقظ بعد الفجر فليبدأ فليصل الفجر ثم المغرب ثم العشاء الآخرة قبل طلوع الشمس. فإن خاف أن تطلع الشمس فتفوته إحدى الصلاتين فليصل المغرب ويدع العشاء الآخرة حتى تطلع الشمس ويذهب شعاعها، ثم ليصلها.

From Abu Basir, from Abu Abdullah (peace be upon him) who said: If a man sleeps and does not pray Maghrib and Isha or forgets them, then if he wakes up before Fajr with enough time to pray both of them, he should pray them both. If he fears missing one of them, he should start with Isha. If he wakes up after Fajr, he should start by praying Fajr, then Maghrib, then Isha before sunrise. If he fears the sun will rise causing him to miss one of the two prayers, he should pray Maghrib and leave Isha until after the sun rises and its rays disperse, then pray it.

Hadith 5182

عن أبي عبد الله (عليه السلام) قال: إن نام رجل أو نسي أن يصلي المغرب والعشاء الآخرة، فإن استيقظ قبل الفجر قدر ما يصليهما كلتيهما فليصلهما، وإن خاف أن تفوته إحداهما فليبدأ بالعشاء الآخرة، وإن استيقظ بعد الفجر فليصل الصبح، ثم المغرب، ثم العشاء الآخرة قبل طلوع الشمس.

From Abu Abdullah (peace be upon him) who said: If a man sleeps or forgets to pray Maghrib and Isha, then if he wakes up before Fajr with enough time to pray both of them, he should pray them both. If he fears missing one of them, he should start with Isha. If he wakes up after Fajr, he should pray Fajr, then Maghrib, then Isha before sunrise.

أقول: حمل الشيخ ما تضمنه الخبران من تأخير القضاء إلى بعد طلوع الشمس على التقية لما تقدم من جواز القضاء في كل وقت، وما تضمنه ظاهرهما من امتداد وقت العشائين إلى طلوع الفجر محمول على التقية أيضا لموافقته للعامة، مع كونه غير صريح في الأداء.

I (Hurr Amili) say: The Shaykh interpreted the postponement of makeup prayers until after sunrise mentioned in these two reports as being due to taqiyyah, based on the previous ruling that makeup prayers are permitted at any time. The apparent meaning that the time for the two night prayers extends until Fajr is also interpreted as taqiyyah since it agrees with the general Muslim view, while not being explicit about being on time.

Hadith 5183

عن أبي عبد الله (عليه السلام)، قال: سألته عن الرجل تفوته المغرب حتى تحضر العتمة؟ فقال: إن حضرت العتمة وذكر أن عليه صلاة المغرب، فإن أحب أن يبدأ بالمغرب بدأ، وإن أحب بدأ بالعتمة ثم صلى المغرب بعد.

From Abu Abdullah (peace be upon him): I asked him about a man who misses Maghrib until Isha time enters. He said: If Isha time enters and he remembers he hasn't prayed Maghrib, he can start with whichever he prefers - either Maghrib first or Isha first and then Maghrib after.

قال الشيخ: هذا خبر شاذ، والعمل على ما قدمناه من أنه إذا كان الوقت واسعا ينبغي أن يبدأ بالفائتة وإن

كان الوقت مضيقا بدء بالحاضرة، وليس هنا وقت يكون الانسان فيه مخيرا. قال: ويمكن حمل الخبر على الجواز، والاخبار الأولى على الفضل والاستحباب. أقول: ويحتمل الحمل على التقية.

I (Hurr Amili) say: The Shaykh said: This is an irregular report, and practice should follow what we presented earlier - that with ample time one should start with the missed prayer, and with constrained time start with the present prayer. There is no time where one has a choice. He said it's possible to interpret this report as permissibility while the earlier reports indicate preference and recommendation. I say it may be interpreted as taqiyyah.

Hadith 5184

عن أبي عبد الله (عليه السلام)، قال: قلت: تفوت الرجل الأولى والعصر والمغرب ويذكر بعد العشاء؟ قال: يبدأ بصلاة الوقت الذي هو فيه، فإنه لا يأمن الموت فيكون قد ترك الفريضة في وقت قد دخل، ثم يقضي ما فاته الأول فالأول. أقول: وتقدم الوجه في مثله.

From Abu Abdullah (peace be upon him): I said: A man misses Zuhr, Asr and Maghrib and remembers after Isha? He said: He should start with the prayer of the current time, for he is not safe from death and would have left an obligatory prayer in its time, then make up what he missed in order. Commentary: The reasoning for this was explained earlier.

Hadith 5185

عن أبي الحسن (عليه السلام)، قال: سألته عن رجل نسي الظهر حتى غربت الشمس، وقد كان صلى العصر؟ فقال: كان أبو جعفر (عليه السلام) أو كان أبي يقول: إن أمكنه أن يصليها قبل أن تفوته المغرب بدأ بها، وإلا صلى المغرب، ثم صلاها.

From Abu al-Hasan (peace be upon him): I asked him about a man who forgot Zuhr until sunset, though he had prayed Asr? He said: Abu Ja'far or my father used to say: If he can pray it before missing Maghrib he should start with it, otherwise he should pray Maghrib then make it up.

Hadith 5186

عن أبي بصير قال: سألته عن رجل نسي الظهر حتى دخل وقت العصر، قال: يبدأ بالظهر وكذلك الصلوات تبدأ بالتي نسيت إلا أن تخاف أن يخرج وقت الصلاة فتبدأ بالتي أنت في وقتها ثم تقضي التي نسيت.

From Abu Basir who said: I asked him about a man who forgot the Zuhr prayer until the time of Asr entered'. He said: He should start with Zuhr, and likewise for all prayers one should start with the forgotten prayer, except if you fear that the current prayer time will expire, then start with the prayer whose time you are in, then make up the forgotten prayer.

CHAPTER 63

Obligation Of Maintaining Order Between Obligatory Prayers In Performance And Making Up, And The Obligation Of Changing Intention To The Previous Prayer If Remembered During Prayer, Whether Performing Or Making Up, In Congregation Or Individually

[Hadith 5187 to 5192]

Hadith 5187

عن زرارة، عن أبي جعفر (عليه السلام) قال: إذا نسيت صلاة أو صليتها بغير وضوء وكان عليك قضاء صلوات فابدأ بأولهن فأذن لها وأقم ثم صلها، ثم صل ما بعدها بإقامة إقامة لكل صلاة، وقال: قال أبو جعفر (عليه السلام): وإن كنت قد صليت الظهر وقد فاتتك الغداة فذكرتها فصل الغداة أي ساعة ذكرتها ولو بعد العصر ومتى ما ذكرت صلاة فاتتك صليتها.

From Zurarah, from Abu Ja'far (peace be upon him) who said: If you forget a prayer or pray without wudu and you have prayers to make up, start with the first one by giving adhan and iqamah for it then pray it, then pray what comes after it with an iqamah for each prayer. Abu Ja'far (peace be upon him) said: If you have prayed Zuhr and missed Fajr then remembered it, pray Fajr at whatever hour you remember it even after Asr, and whenever you remember a missed prayer, pray it.

وقال: إذا نسيت الظهر حتى صليت العصر فذكرتها وأنت في الصلاة أو بعد فراغك فانوها الأولى ثم صل العصر، فإنما هي أربع مكان أربع وإن ذكرت أنك لم تصل الأولى وأنت في صلاة العصر وقد صليت منها ركعتين (فانوها الأولى) ثم صل الركعتين الباقيتين وقم فصل العصر،

He said: If you forget Zuhr until you pray Asr then remember it while you are in prayer or after finishing, intend it as the first one then pray Asr, for it is four rak'ahs in place of four. If you remember that you did not pray the first one while you are in Asr prayer and have prayed two rak'ahs of it, intend it as the first one then complete the remaining two rak'ahs and stand to pray Asr.

وإن كنت قد ذكرت أنك لم تصل العصر حتى دخل وقت المغرب ولم تخف فوتها فصل العصر ثم صل المغرب، فإن كنت قد صليت المغرب فقم فصل العصر وإن كنت قد صليت من المغرب ركعتين ثم ذكرت العصر فانوها العصر (ثم قم فأتمها ركعتين) ثم تسلم ثم تصلي المغرب.

If you remember that you did not pray Asr until Maghrib time entered and you do not fear missing it, pray Asr then pray Maghrib. If you have prayed Maghrib, stand and pray Asr, and if you have prayed two rak'ahs of Maghrib then remembered Asr, intend it as Asr then stand and complete it as two rak'ahs then say the salam then pray Maghrib.

فإن كنت قد صليت العشاء الآخرة ونسيت المغرب فقم فصل المغرب، وإن كنت ذكرتها وقد صليت من العشاء الآخرة ركعتين أو قمت في الثالثة فانوها المغرب ثم سلم ثم قم فصل العشاء الآخرة، فإن كنت قد نسيت العشاء الآخرة حتى صليت الفجر فصل العشاء الآخرة، وإن كنت ذكرتها وأنت في الركعة الأولى أو في الثانية من الغداة فانوها العشاء ثم قم فصل الغداة وأذن وأقم،

If you have prayed Isha and forgot Maghrib, stand and pray Maghrib, and if you remembered it after praying two rak'ahs of Isha or stood up for the third, intend it as Maghrib then say salam then stand and pray Isha. If you forgot Isha until you prayed Fajr, pray Isha, and if you remembered it while in the first or second rak'ah of Fajr, intend it as Isha then stand and pray Fajr with adhan and iqamah.

وإن كانت المغرب والعشاء قد فاتتاك جميعا فابدأ بهما قبل أن تصلي الغداة، ابدأ بالمغرب ثم العشاء فان خشيت أن تفوتك الغداة إن بدأت بهما فابدأ بالمغرب ثم صل الغداة ثم صل العشاء، وإن خشيت أن تفوتك الغداة إن بدأت بالمغرب فصل الغداة ثم صل المغرب والعشاء، ابدأ بأولهما، لأنهما جميعا قضاء أيهما ذكرت فلا تصلهما إلا بعد شعاع الشمس. قال: قلت: ولم ذاك؟ قال: لأنك لست تخاف فوتها.

If both Maghrib and Isha were missed, start with them before praying Fajr - begin with Maghrib then Isha. If you fear missing Fajr by starting with them, begin with Maghrib then pray Fajr then pray Isha. If you fear missing Fajr by starting with Maghrib, pray Fajr then pray Maghrib and Isha, starting with the first of them, because they are both make-up prayers. Whichever you remember, do not pray them except after sunrise. I asked: And why is that? He said: Because you do not fear missing them.

Hadith 5188

عن عبد الرحمن بن أبي عبد الله قال: سألت أبا عبد الله (عليه السلام) عن رجل نسي صلاة حتى دخل وقت صلاة أخرى؟ فقال: إذا نسي الصلاة أو نام عنها صلى حين يذكرها، فإذا ذكرها وهو في صلاة بدأ بالتي نسي،

From Abd al-Rahman bin Abu Abdullah who said: I asked Abu Abdullah (peace be upon him) about a man who forgot a prayer until the time of another prayer entered? He said: If he forgets the prayer or sleeps through it, he should pray when he remembers it. If he remembers it while he is in another prayer, he should start with the forgotten one.

وإن ذكرها مع إمام في صلاة المغرب أتمها بركعة ثم صلى المغرب ثم صلى العتمة بعدها، وإن كان صلى العتمة وحده فصلى منها ركعتين ثم ذكر أنه نسي المغرب أتمها بركعة فتكون صلاته للمغرب ثلاث ركعات ثم يصلي العتمة بعد ذلك.

And if he remembers it while praying with an imam in Maghrib prayer, he should complete it with one rak'ah then pray Maghrib then pray Isha after it. And if he had prayed Isha alone and prayed two rak'ahs of it, then remembered that he forgot Maghrib, he should complete it with one rak'ah so his prayer for Maghrib becomes three rak'ahs, then he should pray Isha after that.

Hadith 5189

عن الحلبي قال: سألت أبا عبد الله (عليه السلام) عن رجل أم قوما في العصر فذكر وهو يصلي بهم أنه لم يكن صلى الأولى؟ قال: فليجعلها الأولى التي فاتته ويستأنف العصر وقد قضى القوم صلاتهم.

From Al-Halabi, he said: I asked Abu Abdullah (peace be upon him) about a man who led people in Asr prayer then remembered while leading them that he had not prayed the first prayer (Zuhr)? He said: He should make it the first prayer he missed and restart Asr, while the people have completed their prayer.

Hadith 5190

عن الحلبي قال: سألته عن رجل نسي أن يصلي الأولى حتى صلى العصر، قال: فليجعل صلاته التي صلى الأولى ثم ليستأنف العصر.

From Al-Halabi, he said: I asked him about a man who forgot to pray the first prayer (Zuhr) until he prayed Asr. He said: He should consider the prayer he prayed as the first one then restart Asr.

Hadith 5191

عن الحسن بن زياد الصيقل قال: سألت أبا عبد الله (عليه السلام) عن رجل نسي الأولى حتى صلى ركعتين من العصر، قال: فليجعلها الأولى وليستأنف العصر، قلت: فإنه نسي المغرب حتى صلى ركعتين من العشاء ثم ذكر قال: فليتم صلاته ثم ليقض بعد المغرب.

From Al-Hasan ibn Ziyad al-Sayqal, he said: I asked Abu Abdullah (peace be upon him) about a man who forgot the first prayer until he prayed two units of Asr. He said: He should make it the first one and restart Asr. I asked: What if he forgot Maghrib until he prayed two units of Isha then remembered? He said: He should complete his prayer then make up Maghrib afterwards.

قلت له: جعلت فداك، قلت – حين نسي الظهر ثم ذكر وهو في العصر –: يجعلها الأولى ثم يستأنف، وقلت لهذا: يتم صلاته ثم ليقض بعد المغرب؟! فقال: ليس هذا مثل هذا، إن العصر ليس بعدها صلاة، والعشاء بعدها صلاة.

I said: May I be sacrificed for you, you said when he forgot Zuhr and remembered during Asr to make it the first one and restart, but for this one you said complete the prayer and make up Maghrib afterwards? He said: This is not like that, there is no prayer after Asr, but there is a prayer after Isha.

أقول: هذا محمول على تضييق وقت العشاء دون العصر، لما تقدم، لان ذلك أوضح دلالة وأوثق وأكثر وهو الموافق لعمل الأصحاب

I (Hurr Amili) say: This is interpreted as applying when the time for Isha is tight unlike Asr, based on what preceded, because that is clearer in evidence, more reliable, more prevalent and agrees with the practice of the companions.

Hadith 5192

عن زرارة، عن أبي جعفر (عليه السلام) في رجل دخل مع قوم ولم يكن صلى هو الظهر والقوم يصلون العصر يصلي معهم، قال: يجعل صلاته التي صلى معهم الظهر، ويصلي هو بعد العصر.

From Zurarah, from Abu Ja'far (peace be upon him) regarding a man who joined people while he had not prayed Zuhr and the people were praying Asr with them. He said: He should make the prayer he prayed with them Zuhr, and he should pray Asr afterwards.

Section 3
Al-Qiblah

CHAPTER 1
Obligation Of Facing The Qiblah In Prayer
[Hadith 5193 to 5198]

Hadith 5193

عن زرارة قال: سألت أبا جعفر (عليه السلام) عن الفرض في الصلاة؟ فقال: الوقت، والطهور، والقبلة، والتوجه، والركوع، والسجود، والدعاء. قلت: ما سوى ذلك؟ فقال: سنة في فريضة.

From Zurarah who said: I asked Abu Ja'far (peace be upon him), about what is obligatory (fard) in the prayer. He said: The time, purification, the qiblah, the orientation (tawajjuh), the bowing (ruku), the prostration (sujud), and the supplication (du'a). I said: What about other than these? He said: They are sunnah within an obligation (faridhah).

————

Hadith 5194

عن أبي بصير يعني المرادي، عن أبي عبد الله (عليه السلام) قال: سألته عن قول الله عز وجل: (فأقم وجهك للدين حنيفا)؟ قال: أمره أن يقيم وجهه للقبلة ليس فيه شئ من عبادة الأوثان خالصا مخلصا.

From Abu Basir Al-Muradi, from Abu Abdullah (peace be upon him) who said: I asked him about Allah's saying [Quran 10:105]: "So direct your face toward the religion as a hanif." He said: He commanded him to direct his face toward the qiblah, with nothing in it from idol worship, purely and sincerely.

————

Hadith 5195

عن أبي بصير، عن أبي عبد الله (عليه السلام) قال: سألته عن قول الله عز وجل: (وأقيموا وجوهكم عند كل مسجد)؟ قال: هذه القبلة أيضا.

From Abu Basir, from Abu Abdullah (peace be upon him) who said: I asked him about the words of Allah the Mighty and Majestic: [Quran 7:29] "And direct your faces at every mosque," he said: This also refers to the qiblah.

————

Hadith 5196

عن أبي بصير، عن أبي عبد الله (عليه السلام) قال: سألته عن قول الله عز وجل: (وما جعلنا القبلة التي كنت عليها إلا لنعلم من يتبع الرسول ممن ينقلب على عقبيه) أمره به؟ قال: نعم، إن رسول الله (صلى الله عليه وآله) كان يقلب وجهه في السماء فعلم الله عز وجل ما في نفسه، فقال: (قد نرى تقلب وجهك في السماء فلنولينك قبلة ترضيها).

From Abu Basir, from Abu Abdullah (peace be upon him) who said: I asked him about the words of Allah the Mighty and Majestic: [Quran 2:143] "And We did not make the qiblah which you used to face except that We might make evident who would follow the Messenger from who would turn back on his heels" - did He command him with it? He said: Yes, indeed the Messenger of Allah (peace be upon him and his family) used to turn his face toward the sky, so Allah the Mighty and Majestic knew what was in his heart, and said: [Quran 2:144] "We have certainly seen the turning of your face toward the heaven, and We will surely turn you to a qiblah with which you will be pleased."

Hadith 5197

عن أبي عبد الله (عليه السلام) في قوله تعالى: (أقيموا وجوهكم عند كل مسجد) قال: مساجد محدثة، فأمروا أن يقيموا وجوههم شطر المسجد الحرام.

From Abu Abdullah (peace be upon him) regarding the words of the Almighty: "Direct your faces at every mosque" [Quran 7:29], he said: These are newly established mosques, so they were commanded to direct their faces toward the Sacred Mosque.

Hadith 5198

عن أبي عبد الله (عليه السلام) في قول الله عز وجل: (فأقم وجهك للدين حنيفا) قال: تقيم في الصلاة ولا تلتفت يمينا وشمالا.

From Abu Abdullah (peace be upon him) regarding the words of Allah the Mighty and Majestic: "So direct your face toward the religion inclining to truth" [Quran 10:105], he said: Stand straight in prayer and do not turn right or left.

CHAPTER 2

The Qiblah Is The Ka'bah When Near, And Its Direction When Far

[Hadith 5199 to 5215]

Hadith 5199

عن أبي عبد الله (عليه السلام) قال: قلت له: متى صرف رسول الله (صلى الله عليه وآله) إلى الكعبة؟

قال: بعد رجوعه من بدر.

From Abu Abdullah (peace be upon him) who said: I said to him: When did the Messenger of Allah (peace be upon him and his family) change direction to the Ka'bah? He said: After his return from Badr.

Hadith 5200

عن أبي بصير، عن أحدهما (عليه السلام) - في حديث - قال: قلت له: إن الله أمره أن يصلي إلى بيت المقدس؟ قال: نعم، ألا ترى أن الله يقول: (وما جعلنا القبلة التي كنت عليها إلا لنعلم من يتبع الرسول) الآية!؟

From Abu Basir, from one of them (peace be upon him) - in a hadith - he said: I said to him: Did Allah command him to pray towards Bayt al-Maqdis? He said: Yes, do you not see that Allah says "And We did not make the qiblah which you used to face except that We might know who would follow the Messenger" [Quran, 2:143]?

ثم قال: إن بني عبد الأشهل أتوهم وهم في الصلاة قد صلوا ركعتين إلى بيت المقدس، فقيل لهم: إن نبيكم صرف إلى الكعبة فتحول النساء مكان الرجال، والرجال مكان النساء، وجعلوا الركعتين الباقيتين إلى الكعبة فصلوا صلاة واحدة إلى قبلتين، فلذلك سمي مسجدهم مسجد القبلتين.

Then he said: The Banu Abd al-Ashhal came while they were in prayer having prayed two rak'ahs towards Bayt al-Maqdis, and they were told: Your Prophet has been directed towards the Ka'bah, so the women switched places with the men, and the men switched places with the women, and they performed the remaining two rak'ahs towards the Ka'bah, thus they prayed one prayer towards two qiblas, and for this reason their mosque was named the Mosque of the Two Qiblas.

Hadith 5201

وعن معاوية بن عمار قال: قلت لأبي عبد الله (عليه السلام): متى صرف رسول الله (صلى الله عليه وآله) إلى الكعبة؟ قال: بعد رجوعه من بدر، وكان يصلي في المدينة إلى بيت المقدس سبعة عشر شهرا ثم أعيد إلى الكعبة.

From Mu'awiyah bin Ammar who said: I asked Abu Abdullah (peace be upon him): When did the Messenger of Allah (peace be upon him and his family) turn towards the Ka'bah? He said: After his return from Badr, and he had prayed in Madinah towards Bayt al-Maqdis for seventeen months, then it was changed to the Ka'bah.

Hadith 5202

عن أبي عبد الله (عليه السلام) قال: سألته هل كان رسول الله (صلى الله عليه وآله) يصلي إلى بيت المقدس؟ قال: نعم، فقلت: أكان يجعل الكعبة خلف ظهره؟ فقال: أما إذا كان بمكة فلا، وأما إذا هاجر إلى المدينة فنعم حتى حول إلى الكعبة.

From Abu Abdullah (peace be upon him) who said: I asked him whether the Messenger of Allah (peace be upon him and his family) used to pray towards Bayt al-Maqdis? He said: Yes. So I asked: Would he put the Ka'bah behind his back? He said: When he was in Makkah, no, but when he migrated to Madinah, yes, until he was directed towards the Ka'bah.

Hadith 5203

عن أبي عبد الله (عليه السلام) قال: - وقد أنكر عليه الطواف بالكعبة -: وهذا بيت استعبد الله به خلقه ليختبر طاعتهم في إتيانه فحثهم على تعظيمه وزيارته وجعله محل أنبيائه وقبلة للمصلين إليه.

From Abu Abdullah (peace be upon him) who said, when the tawaf of the Ka'bah was denied: This is a house through which Allah made His creation worship Him to test their obedience in coming to it, and He urged them to venerate it and visit it, and made it the place of His prophets and the qiblah for those who pray towards it.

Hadith 5204

عن أبي عبد الله (عليه السلام) - في حديث - إن الله بعث جبرئيل إلى آدم فانطلق به إلى مكان البيت، وأنزل عليه غمامة فأظلت مكان البيت، فقال: يا آدم، خط برجلك حيث أظلت هذه الغمامة فإنه سيخرج لك بيت من مهاة يكون قبلتك وقبلة عقبك من بعدك.

From Abu Abdullah (peace be upon him) - in a hadith - Allah sent Jibreel to Adam and took him to the location of the House (Ka'bah), and sent down a cloud which shaded the location of the House. Then he said: O Adam, mark with your foot where this cloud has cast its shadow, for a house of pearl will emerge for you which will be your qiblah and the qiblah of your descendants after you.

Hadith 5205

عن أبي عبد الله (عليه السلام) - في حديث - إن الله بعث جبرئيل إلى آدم فنزل غمام من السماء فأظل
مكان البيت، فقال جبرئيل: يا آدم، خط برجلك حيث أظل الغمام فإنه قبلة لك ولآخر عقبك من ولدك.

From Abu Abdullah (peace be upon him) - in a hadith - Allah sent Jibreel to Adam, and a cloud descended from the sky and shaded the location of the House (Ka'bah). Jibreel said: O Adam, mark with your foot where the cloud has shaded, for it is the qiblah for you and for the last of your descendants from your children.

Hadith 5206

محمد بن علي بن الحسين قال: قال النبي (صلى الله عليه وآله): لن يعمل ابن آدم عملا أعظم عند الله عز
وجل من رجل قتل نبيا، أو هدم الكعبة التي جعلها الله عز وجل قبلة لعباده، أو أفرغ ماءه في امرأة حراما.

Muhammad bin Ali bin Al-Husain said: The Prophet (peace be upon him and his family) said: The son of Adam will not commit any deed more grievous in the sight of Allah, the Mighty and Majestic, than a man who kills a prophet, or demolishes the Ka'bah which Allah, the Mighty and Majestic, has made as a qiblah (direction of prayer) for His servants, or discharges his semen into a woman unlawfully.

Hadith 5207

عن زرارة، عن أبي جعفر (عليه السلام) أنه قال: لا صلاة إلا إلى القبلة. قال: قلت: وأين حد القبلة؟ قال: ما
بين المشرق والمغرب قبلة كله.

From Zurarah, from Abu Ja'far (peace be upon him) that he said: There is no prayer except towards the qiblah. He said: I asked: And what are the bounds of the qiblah? He said: Everything between the east and the west is all qiblah.

قال الشهيد في (الذكرى): هذا نص في الجهة. أقول: وقد تقدم حديث بمضمونه في الصلاة على جنازة
المصلوب.

Al-Shaheed said in (Al-Dhikra): This text is regarding the direction. I (Hurr Amili) say: A hadith with similar content has preceded regarding prayer over a crucified person.

Hadith 5208

عن الصادق (عليه السلام) أنه قال: إن الله عز وجل حرمات ثلاثا ليس مثلهن شئ كتابه وهو حكمة ونور،
وبيته الذي جعله قبلة للناس لا يقبل من أحد توجها إلى غيره، وعترة نبيكم (صلى الله عليه وآله).

From Al-Sadiq (peace be upon him) who said: Allah has made three sacred things unlike anything else - His Book which is wisdom and light, His House which He made as qiblah for people and He does not accept anyone turning to other than it, and the family of your Prophet (peace be upon him and his family).

Hadith 5209

علي بن الحسين المرتضى علم الهدى في (رسالة المحكم والمتشابه) بإسناده الآتي عن أمير المؤمنين (عليه السلام) أن رسول الله (صلى الله عليه وآله) كان في أول مبعثه يصلي، إلى بيت المقدس جميع أيام مقامه بمكة وبعد هجرته إلى المدينة بأشهر.

Ali bin Al-Husayn Al-Murtadha Alam Al-Huda in his treatise Al-Muhkam wa Al-Mutashabih through his chain from Amir Al-Mu'mineen (peace be upon him) that the Messenger of Allah (peace be upon him and his family) used to pray towards Bayt Al-Maqdis during his early mission throughout his stay in Makkah and for months after his migration to Madinah.

فعيرته اليهود وقالوا: إنك تابع لقبلتنا فأحزنه ذلك فأنزل الله عز وجل - وهو يقلب وجهه في السماء وينتظر الامر -: (قد نرى تقلب وجهك في السماء فلنولينك قبلة ترضيها فول وجهك شطر المسجد الحرام وحيث ما كنتم فولوا وجوهكم شطره).

The Jews taunted him saying: You follow our qiblah. This saddened him, so Allah revealed - while he was turning his face towards the sky awaiting the command: "We have certainly seen the turning of your face toward the heaven, and We will surely turn you to a qiblah with which you will be pleased. So turn your face toward al-Masjid al-Haram. And wherever you are, turn your faces toward it" [Quran 2:144].

Hadith 5210

محمد بن علي بن الحسين قال: صلى رسول الله (صلى الله عليه وآله) إلى بيت المقدس بعد النبوة ثلاثة عشر سنة بمكة، وتسعة عشر شهرا بالمدينة، ثم عيرته اليهود فقالوا له: إنك تابع لقبلتنا فاغتم لذلك غما شديدا،

Muhammad bin Ali bin Al-Husayn said: After prophethood, the Messenger of Allah (peace be upon him and his family) prayed towards Bayt Al-Maqdis for thirteen years in Makkah and nineteen months in Madinah. Then the Jews taunted him saying: You follow our qiblah. This deeply saddened him.

فلما كان في بعض الليل خرج (عليه السلام) يقلب وجهه في آفاق السماء فلما أصبح صلى الغداة، فلما صلى من الظهر ركعتين جاء جبرئيل (عليه السلام) فقال له: (قد نرى تقلب وجهك في السماء فلنولينك قبلة ترضيها فول وجهك شطر المسجد الحرام) الآية. ثم أخذ بيد النبي (صلى الله عليه وآله) فحول وجهه إلى الكعبة وحول من خلفه وجوههم حتى قام الرجال مقام النساء، والنساء مقام الرجال.

One night he went out turning his face towards the horizons of the sky. When morning came he prayed the dawn prayer. When he prayed two rak'ahs of the noon prayer, Jibreel (peace be upon him) came and said: "We have certainly seen the turning of your face toward the heaven..." [Quran 2:144]. Then he took the Prophet's hand and turned his face towards the Ka'bah, and those behind him turned their faces until the men stood in the women's place and the women in the men's place.

فكان أول صلاته إلى بيت المقدس وآخرها إلى الكعبة وبلغ الخبر مسجدا بالمدينة. وقد صلى أهله من العصر ركعتين، فحولوا نحو القبلة وكان أول صلاتهم إلى بيت المقدس وآخرها إلى الكعبة، فسمي ذلك المسجد مسجد القبلتين.

The first part of his prayer was towards Bayt Al-Maqdis and its end towards the Ka'bah. The news reached a mosque in Madinah while its people had prayed two rak'ahs of Asr prayer, so they turned towards the qiblah - the first part of their prayer was towards Bayt Al-Maqdis and its end towards the Ka'bah. That mosque was named the Mosque of Two Qiblas.

Hadith 5211

عن أبي عبد الله بن علي، عن جده عبد الله، علي بن موسى، عن أبيه، عن آبائه، عن علي (عليه السلام) قال: لما صرفت القبلة أتى رجل قوما في الصلاة فقال: إن القبلة قد صرفت وتحولوا وهم ركوع.

From Abu Abdullah bin Ali, from his grandfather Abdullah, Ali bin Musa, from his father, from his forefathers, from Ali (peace be upon him) who said: When the qiblah was changed, a man came to some people while they were in prayer and said: The qiblah has been changed, so they turned while in ruku (bowing).

Hadith 5212

أحمد بن علي بن أبي طالب الطبرسي في (الاحتجاج) بإسناده عن العسكري في احتجاج النبي (صلى الله عليه وآله) على المشركين قال: إنا عباد الله مخلوقون مربوبون نأتمر له فيما أمرنا وننزجر له عما زجرنا - إلى أن قال - فلما أمرنا أن نعبده بالتوجه إلى الكعبة أطعنا، ثم أمرنا بعبادته بالتوجه نحوها في سائر البلدان التي تكون بها فأطعناه، فلم نخرج في شئ من ذلك من اتباع أمره.

Ahmad bin Ali bin Abi Talib Al-Tabarsi in Al-Ihtijaj through his chain from Al-Askari regarding the Prophet's (peace be upon him and his family) argument against the polytheists said: We are Allah's servants, created and nurtured. We follow His commands and abstain from what He forbids. When He commanded us to worship Him by facing the Ka'bah we obeyed, then He commanded us to worship Him by facing it from all lands we may be in, so we obeyed Him. We did not deviate in any of this from following His command.

Hadith 5213

عن أبي الحسن موسى، عن أبيه أن رسول الله (صلى الله عليه وآله) قال لعلي (عليه السلام): إنما مثلك في الأمة مثل الكعبة التي نصبها الله علما، وإنما تؤتى من كل فج عميق ونأي سحيق، ولا تأتي.

From Abi Al-Hasan Musa, from his father that the Messenger of Allah (peace be upon him and his family) said to Ali (peace be upon him): Your example in the nation is like that of the Ka'bah which Allah has established as a landmark; it is approached from every deep mountain path and distant place [Quran, 22:27], but it does not approach.

Hadith 5214

محمد بن محمد بن النعمان المفيد في (مسار الشيعة) قال: في النصف من من رجب سنة اثنتين من الهجرة حولت القبلة من البيت المقدس إلى الكعبة، وكان الناس في صلاة العصر فتحولوا فيها إلى البيت الحرام.

Muhammad bin Muhammad bin Al-Nu'man Al-Mufid reported in (Masar Al-Shi'a) saying: In the middle of Rajab in the second year after Hijra, the qiblah was changed from Bayt Al-Maqdis (Jerusalem) to the Ka'bah, while people were in the Asr prayer and they turned towards Bayt al-Haram (The Sacred House) during it.

Hadith 5215

عن أبي البختري، عن جعفر بن محمد، عن أبيه أن رسول الله (صلى الله عليه وآله) استقبل بيت المقدس تسعة عشر شهرا ثم صرف إلى الكعبة وهو في العصر.

Abu Al-Bakhtari narrated from Ja'far bin Muhammad, from his father that the Messenger of Allah (peace be upon him and his family) faced Bayt Al-Maqdis for nineteen months then was directed to the Ka'bah while he was in Asr prayer.

أقول: هذا محمول على ما بعد الهجرة لما مر، وقد تقدم ما يدل على ذلك، ويأتي ما يدل عليه، ويأتي ما ظاهره المنافاة ونبين وجهه.

I (Hurr Amili) say: This is interpreted as referring to the period after Hijra based on what has passed, and evidence for this has preceded and will follow, and what appears to contradict this will come and we will explain its aspect.

CHAPTER 3

The Ka'bah Is The Qiblah For Those In The Mosque, The Mosque Is The Qiblah For Those In The Haram, And The Haram Is The Qiblah For The World, And The Extent Of The Ka'bah's Alignment Direction

[Hadith 5216 to 5219]

Hadith 5216

عن أبي عبد الله (عليه السلام) إن الله تعالى جعل الكعبة قبلة لأهل المسجد، وجعل المسجد قبلة لأهل الحرم، وجعل الحرم قبلة لأهل الدنيا.

From Abu Abdullah (peace be upon him): Indeed Allah the Exalted made the Ka'bah the qiblah for the people of the mosque, and made the mosque the qiblah for the people of the Haram (Sacred Sanctuary), and made the Haram the qiblah for the people of the world.

———

Hadith 5217

عن جعفر بن محمد (عليه السلام) قال: سمعته يقول: البيت قبلة لأهل المسجد، والمسجد قبلة لأهل الحرم، والحرم قبلة للناس جميعا.

From Ja'far bin Muhammad (peace be upon him), he said: I heard him saying: The House (Ka'bah) is the qiblah for the people of the Mosque, and the Mosque is the qiblah for the people of the Haram (Sacred Sanctuary), and the Haram is the qiblah for all people.

———

Hadith 5218

محمد بن علي بن الحسين قال: قال الصادق (عليه السلام) إن الله تبارك وتعالى جعل الكعبة قبلة لأهل المسجد، وجعل المسجد قبلة لأهل الحرم، وجعل الحرم قبلة لأهل الدنيا.

Muhammad bin Ali bin Al-Husayn said: Al-Sadiq (peace be upon him) said: Indeed Allah, the Blessed and Exalted, made the Ka'bah the qiblah for the people of the Mosque, and made the Mosque the qiblah for the people of the Haram (Sacred Sanctuary), and made the Haram the qiblah for the people of the world.

———

Hadith 5219

عن أبي غرة قال: قال لي أبو عبد الله (عليه السلام): البيت قبلة المسجد، والمسجد قبلة مكة، ومكة قبلة الحرم، والحرم قبلة الدنيا.

From Abu Ghurrah who said: Abu Abdullah (peace be upon him) said to me: The House (Ka'bah) is the qiblah of the mosque, and the mosque is the qiblah of Makkah, and Makkah is the qiblah of the Haram (Sacred Sanctuary), and the Haram is the qiblah of the world.

أقول: ويأتي ما يدل على التياسر، وهو يؤيد ذلك، لأنه مبني على التوجه إلى الحرم كما يأتي، وقد ذكر بعض المحققين أنه لا نزاع هنا ولا اختلاف بين أحاديث هذا الباب، والذي قبله، لان جهة المحاذاة مع البعد متسعة، وهذه الأحاديث وما دل على أن ما بين المشرق والمغرب قبلة وما دل على استقبال المسجد الحرام من الآية والرواية وغير ذلك كله إشارة إلى اتساع جهة المحاذاة وتسهيل الامر ودفع الوسواس ويؤيده الاكتفاء شرعا لأهل إقليم عظيم بعلامة واحدة كما يأتي، والله أعلم.

I (Hurr Amili) say: There will come evidence about turning slightly left, which supports this, because it is based on facing the Haram (Sacred Sanctuary) as will come. Some scholars have mentioned that there is no dispute or difference between the hadiths of this chapter and the previous one, because the direction of alignment becomes wider with distance. These hadiths, along with what indicates that what is between east and west is qiblah, and what indicates facing the Sacred Mosque from the verse and narration and other things, all point to the breadth of the alignment direction, making the matter easier and removing doubts. This is supported by the legal sufficiency of one sign for the people of a great region as will come, and Allah knows best.

———————

CHAPTER 4

Recommendation Of Slight Left Inclination For The People Of Iraq And Those Allied With Them

[Hadith 5220 to 5222]

Hadith 5220

عن علي بن محمد قال: قيل لأبي عبد الله (عليه السلام): لم صار الرجل ينحرف في الصلاة إلى اليسار؟ فقال: لان للكعبة ستة حدود، أربعة منها على يسارك، واثنان منها على يمينك، فمن أجل ذلك وقع التحريف على اليسار.

From Ali ibn Muhammad, he said: It was asked to Abu Abdullah (peace be upon him): Why does a person incline to the left in prayer [from Iraq]? He said: Because the Ka'bah has six boundaries, four of them are on your left and two of them are on your right, and for this reason the inclination occurs to the left.

Hadith 5221

عن المفضل بن عمر أنه سأل أبا عبد الله (عليه السلام) عن التحريف لأصحابنا ذات اليسار عن القبلة وعن السبب فيه؟ فقال: إن الحجر الأسود لما أنزل من الجنة ووضع في موضعه جعل أنصاب الحرم من حيث يلحقه النور نور الحجر.

Al-Mufaddal ibn Umar asked Abu Abdullah (peace be upon him) about the inclination of our companions [in Iraq] to the left from the qiblah and its reason? He said: When the Black Stone was sent down from Paradise and placed in its position, the boundaries of the Haram (Sacred Sanctuary) were set from where its light - the light of the Stone - reached.

فهي عن يمين الكعبة أربعة أميال، وعن يسارها ثمانية أميال، كله اثنى عشر ميلا، فإذا انحرف الانسان ذات اليمين خرج عن حد القبلة لقلة انصاب الحرم، وإذا انحرف الانسان ذات اليسار لم يكن خارجا من حد القبلة.

So it is four miles on the right of the Ka'bah and eight miles on its left, twelve miles in total. Thus when a person inclines to the right they exit the boundary of the qiblah due to the few markers of the Haram, but when they incline to the left they do not exit the boundary of the qiblah.

Translator: This hadith is discussing the deviation from the qibla direction, and the context suggests this is from the perspective of someone in Iraq where Imam Ja'far al-Sadiq had many followers, including Al-Mufaddal ibn Umar who is narrating this hadith. For the people in Iraq, a slight deviation to the left (west) would still keep one within the acceptable range of the qibla, while a deviation to the right (east) would take one outside the acceptable range more quickly. It is worthwhile to note that the hadith does not indicate the range of the qibla in the north-south direction.

Hadith 5222

محمد بن الحسن في (النهاية) قال: من توجه إلى القبلة من أهل العراق والمشرق قاطبة فعليه أن يتياسر قليلا ليكون متوجها إلى الحرم، بذلك جاء الأثر عنهم (عليهم السلام).

Muhammad ibn al-Hasan said in (al-Nihaya): Whoever faces the qiblah from the people of Iraq and the East in general should incline slightly to the left to be facing the Haram, as has been reported in traditions from them (peace be upon them).

CHAPTER 5
Obligation Of Using Polaris In Determining The Qiblah
[Hadith 5223 to 5226]

Hadith 5223

عن محمد بن مسلم، عن أحدهما (عليهما السلام) قال: سألته عن القبلة؟ فقال: ضع الجدي في قفاك وصل.

From Muhammad ibn Muslim, from one of them (peace be upon them) who said: I asked him about the qiblah? He said: Put Polaris behind your back and pray.

Hadith 5224

محمد بن علي بن الحسين قال: قال رجل للصادق (عليه السلام): إني أكون في السفر ولا أهتدي إلى القبلة بالليل، فقال: أتعرف الكوكب الذي يقال له الجدي؟ قلت: نعم، قال: اجعله علي يمينك، وإذا كنت في طريق الحج فاجعله بين كتفيك.

Muhammad ibn Ali ibn Al-Husayn said: A man said to Al-Sadiq (peace be upon him): I am on a journey and cannot find the qiblah at night. He said: Do you know the star called Polaris? I said: Yes. He said: Place it on your right, and when you are on the Hajj route, place it between your shoulders.

قال صاحب المدارك: الأولى العلامة الأولى والثالثة على أطراف العراق الغربية كسنجار وما والاها، وحمل الثانية على أوساط العراق كالكوفة وبغداد، وأما أطرافه الشرقية كالبصرة وما ساواها فيحتاج فيها إلى زيادة انحراف نحو المغرب وكذا القول في بلاد خراسان.

The author of Al-Madarik said: The first and third signs are for the western edges of Iraq like Sinjar and its surroundings, and the second is for central Iraq like Kufa and Baghdad. As for its eastern edges like Basra and its equivalents, they require additional westward adjustment, and the same applies to the lands of Khorasan.

Hadith 5225

عن جعفر بن محمد، عن آبائه (عليهم السلام) قال: قال رسول الله (صلى الله عليه وآله): (وبالنجم هم يهتدون) قال: هو الجدي لأنه نجم لا يزول، وعليه بناء القبلة، وبه يهتدي أهل البر والبحر.

From Ja'far ibn Muhammad, from his forefathers (peace be upon them) who said: The Messenger of Allah (peace be upon him and his family) said regarding "And by the stars they are guided" [Quran 16:16], he said: It is Polaris because it is a star that does not move, and upon it the qiblah is built, and by it the people of land and sea are guided.

Hadith 5226

وعنه، عن أبي عبد الله (عليه السلام) في قوله: (وعلامات وبالنجم هم يهتدون) قال: ظاهر وباطن، الجدي عليه تبني القبلة وبه يهتدي أهل البر والبحر لأنه نجم لا يزول.

From him, from Abu Abdullah (peace be upon him) regarding His saying: "And landmarks and by the stars they are guided" [Quran 16:16], he said: Apparent and hidden, Polaris is what the qiblah is built upon, and by it the people of land and sea are guided because it is a star that does not move.

CHAPTER 6

Obligation Of Striving To Determine The Qiblah When Uncertain, Following The Prayer Niche Of The Infallible And Similar Guides, And Acting Upon Best Judgment

[Hadith 5227 to 5231]

Hadith 5227

عن زرارة قال: قال أبو جعفر (عليه السلام): يجزئ التحري أبدا إذا لم يعلم أين وجه القبلة.

From Zurarah who said: Abu Ja'far (peace be upon him) said: Making an effort to determine the direction is always sufficient when one does not know the direction of the qiblah.

Hadith 5228

عن سماعة قال: سألته عن الصلاة بالليل والنهار إذا لم ير الشمس ولا القمر ولا النجوم؟ قال: اجتهد رأيك وتعمد القبلة جهدك.

From Sama'ah who said: I asked him about prayer during night and day when one cannot see the sun, moon, or stars? He said: Exercise your judgment and strive your utmost to face the qiblah.

Hadith 5229

عن سماعة بن مهران أنه سأله عن الصلاة بالليل والنهار إذا لم تر الشمس والقمر ولا النجوم؟ فقال: تجهد رأيك وتعتمد القبلة بجهدك.

From Sama'ah bin Mihran that he asked him about prayer during the night and day when you cannot see the sun, moon, or stars? He said: Exert your judgment and determine the direction of qiblah to the best of your ability.

Hadith 5230

عن الصادق عن آبائه (عليهم السلام) في قوله تعالى: (فول وجهك شطر المسجد الحرام)، قال: معنى شطره نحوه إن كان مرئيا، وبالدلائل والاعلام إن كان محجوبا، فلو علمت القبلة لوجب استقبالها والتولي والتوجه إليها ولو لم يكن الدليل عليها موجودا حتى تستوي الجهات كلها فله حينئذ أن يصلي باجتهاده حيث أحب واختار حتى يكون على يقين من الدلالات المنصوبة والعلامات المبثوثة.

From al-Sadiq from his forefathers (peace be upon them) regarding His saying: "Direct your face toward Masjid al-Haram (The Sacred Mosque)" [Quran, 2:144], he said: The meaning of "toward it" is in its direction if it is visible, and by signs and markers if it is hidden. If you know the qiblah, it is obligatory to face it and turn towards it. If there is no evidence for its direction such that all directions appear equal, then at that time one may pray according to their best judgment in whichever direction they prefer and choose until they become certain through erected indicators and dispersed signs.

فإن مال عن هذا التوجه مع ما ذكرناه حتى يجعل الشرق غربا والغرب شرقا زال معنى اجتهاده وفسد حال اعتقاده، قال: وقد جاء عن النبي (صلى الله عليه وآله) خبر منصوص مجمع عليه أن الأدلة المنصوبة إلى بيت الله الحرام لا تذهب بكليتها حادثة من الحوادث، منا من الله تعالى على عباده في إقامة ما افترض عليهم.

If one deviates from this direction along with what we mentioned, to the extent of making the east west and the west east, the meaning of his ijtihad becomes void and his belief becomes corrupt. He said: There is an explicitly reported and unanimously agreed upon narration from the Prophet (peace be upon him and his family) that the signs established towards the Sacred House of Allah (Baitullah al-Haram) cannot be completely eliminated by any event, as a blessing from Allah the Exalted upon His servants in establishing what He has made obligatory upon them.

Hadith 5231

أبو الفضل شاذان بن جبرئيل القمي في (رسالة القبلة) قال: قد تعلم القبلة بالمشاهدة، أو يخبر عن مشاهدة توجب العلم (بأن ينصب النبي (صلى الله عليه وآله) مسجدا) كقبلة المدينة وقبا، وفي بعض أسفاره وغزواته.

Abu Al-Fadhl Shadhan bin Jibreel Al-Qummi said in (Risalat Al-qiblah): The qiblah can be known through direct observation, or through information from an observation that necessitates knowledge (such as when the Prophet (peace be upon him and his family), established a mosque), like the qiblah of Madinah and Quba, and in some of his journeys and military expeditions.

وهي مساجد معروفة إلى الان مثل مسجد الفضيخ ومسجد الأعمى، ومسجد الإجابة، ومسجد البغلة، ومسجد الفتح وسلع وغيرها من المواضع التي صلى فيها النبي (صلى الله عليه وآله)، وكالقبور المرفوعة بحضوره مثل قبر إبراهيم ابن رسول الله (صلى الله عليه وآله) وفاطمة بنت أسد، وقبر حمزة سيد الشهداء بأحد وغيره أو نصبها أحد من الأئمة (عليهم السلام) مثل الكوفة، والبصرة أو غيرهما، أو يحكم بأنهم صلوا إليها (صلى الله عليهم)، فإنه بجميع ذلك تعلم القبلة.

These are well-known mosques that exist until now such as Masjid Al-Fadikh, Masjid Al-A'ma, Masjid Al-Ijaba, Masjid Al-Baghla, Masjid Al-Fath and Sal' and other places where the Prophet (peace be upon him and his family) prayed, and like the raised graves in his presence such as the grave of Ibrahim son of the Messenger of Allah (peace be upon him and his family) and Fatimah bint Asad, and the grave of Hamza master of martyrs at Uhud and others, or those established by one of the Imams (peace be upon them) such as in Kufa, Basra or elsewhere, or those judged that they (peace be upon them) prayed towards them, for through all of these the qiblah can be known.

––––––––––

CHAPTER 7

Obligation Of The Blind Person To Follow The Direction Of One Who Knows The Qiblah

[Hadith 5232 to 5234]

Hadith 5232

عن أبي عبد الله (عليه السلام) قال: لا بأس بأن يصلي الأعمى بالقوم وإن كانوا هم الذين يوجهونه.

From Abu Abdullah (peace be upon him) who said: There is no problem with a blind person leading people in prayer even if they are the ones guiding him to the direction.

Hadith 5233

عن زرارة، عن أبي جعفر (عليه السلام) - في حديث - قال: قلت: أصلي خلف الأعمى؟ قال: نعم إذا كان له من يسدده وكان أفضلهم.

From Zurarah, from Abu Ja'far (peace be upon him) - in a hadith - he said: I asked: Can I pray behind a blind person? He replied: Yes, if he has someone to guide him and if he is the most virtuous among them.

Hadith 5234

عن أبي عبد الله (عليه السلام) قال: قال أمير المؤمنين (عليه السلام) - في حديث -: لا يؤم الأعمى في الصحراء إلا أن يوجه إلى القبلة.

From Abu Abdullah (peace be upon him) who said: Amir al-Mu'minin (peace be upon him) said - in a hadith: A blind person should not lead prayer in an open space unless he is directed towards the qiblah.

CHAPTER 8

Obligation Of Praying Towards Four Directions When Uncertain And Unable To Determine Direction, And That One Direction Suffices When Time Is Limited

[Hadith 5235 to 5240]

Hadith 5235

محمد بن علي بن الحسين قال: روي فيمن لا يهتدي إلى القبلة في مفازة أنه يصلي إلى أربعة جوانب.

Muhammad bin Ali bin Al-Husayn said: It has been narrated regarding one who cannot determine the direction of qiblah in an open area that they should pray towards four directions.

Hadith 5236

عن أبي جعفر (عليه السلام) أنه قال: يجزي المتحير أبدا أينما توجه إذا لم يعلم أين وجه القبلة.

From Abu Ja'far (peace be upon him) who said: It suffices for the confused person to pray in whichever direction they face when they do not know the direction of qiblah.

أقول: حمله بعض الأصحاب على عدم التمكن من الصلاة إلى أربع جهات لما مضى ويأتي.

I (Hurr Amili) say: Some companions interpreted this as applying to situations where praying in four directions is not possible, based on previous and upcoming evidence.

Hadith 5237

عن زرارة قال: سألت أبا جعفر (عليه السلام) عن قبلة المتحير، فقال: يصلي حيث يشاء.

From Zurarah who said: I asked Abu Ja'far (peace be upon him) about the qiblah for the confused person, and he said: They may pray in whichever direction they wish.

Hadith 5238

قال: وروي أيضا أنه يصلي إلى أربع جوانب.

He said: It has also been narrated that one should pray towards four directions.

Hadith 5239

عن أبي عبد الله (عليه السلام) قال: قلت: جعلت فداك إن هؤلاء المخالفين علينا يقولون: إذا أطبقت علينا أو أظلمت فلم نعرف السماء كنا وأنتم سواء في الاجتهاد، فقال: ليس كما يقولون، إذا كان ذلك فليصل لأربع وجوه.

From Abu Abdullah (peace be upon him) who said: I said: May I be sacrificed for you, these opponents of ours say that if the sky is overcast or darkened and we cannot recognize it, then we and you are equal in making ijtihad (effort) to determine direction. He said: It is not as they say. When that happens, one should pray in four directions.

أقول: هذا محمول إما على تساوي الجهات وعدم الترجيح، وإما على كون التحير في الحكم الشرعي لا في جهة القبلة فقط، كما إذا لم يعلم أنه يجوز له العمل في هذه الحالة بالظن أم لا فيتعين عليه الصلاة إلى أربع جهات لليقين بشغل الذمة فلابد من الخروج من العهدة.

I (Hurr Amili) say: This is interpreted either as applying when all directions are equal with no preferable direction, or when the uncertainty is about the religious ruling rather than just the qiblah direction, such as when one doesn't know if relying on speculation is permissible in this situation, so praying in four directions becomes necessary to ensure fulfillment of obligation with certainty.

Hadith 5240

وقد تقدم في حديث زرارة عن أبي جعفر (عليه السلام) قال: ولا تنقض اليقين أبدا بالشك، وإنما تنقضه بيقين آخر.

And it was previously mentioned in Zurarah's hadith from Abu Ja'far (peace be upon him) who said: Never invalidate certainty with doubt, rather invalidate it only with another certainty.

CHAPTER 9

Invalidation Of Prayer When Deliberately Praying In A Direction Other Than The Qiblah And The Obligation To Repeat It

[Hadith 5241 to 5245]

Hadith 5241

عن زرارة قال: قال أبو جعفر (عليه السلام): لا تعاد الصلاة إلا من خمسة: الطهور، والوقت، والقبلة، والركوع، والسجود.

From Zurarah, who said: Abu Jafar (peace be upon him) said: The prayer is not to be repeated except on account of five things: purification, time, qiblah, ruku, and sujud.

Hadith 5242

عن أبي جعفر (عليه السلام) أنه قال: لا صلاة إلا إلى القبلة قال: قلت أين حد القبلة؟ قال: ما بين المشرق والمغرب قبلة كله، قال: قلت: فمن صلى لغير القبلة أو في يوم غيم في غير الوقت؟ قال: يعيد.

From Abu Ja'far (peace be upon him) that he said: There is no prayer except facing the qiblah. I asked: What are the boundaries of the qiblah? He said: Everything between east and west is qiblah. I asked: What about someone who prays in a direction other than the qiblah or on a cloudy day outside the prayer time? He said: They must repeat it.

Hadith 5243

وعنه، عن أبي جعفر (عليه السلام) أنه قال له: استقبل القبلة بوجهك، ولا تقلب بوجهك عن القبلة فتفسد صلاتك، فإن الله عز وجل يقول لنبيه في الفريضة: (فول وجهك شطر المسجد الحرام وحيث ما كنتم فولوا وجوهكم شطره) وقم منتصبا فإن رسول الله (صلى الله عليه وآله) قال: من لم يقم صلبه في صلاته فلا صلاة له، واخشع ببصرك لله عز وجل، ولا ترفعه إلى السماء، وليكن حذاء وجهك في موضع سجودك.

From him, from Abu Ja'far (peace be upon him) that he said to him: Face the qiblah with your face, and do not turn your face away from the qiblah as it invalidates your prayer, for Allah the Mighty and Majestic says to His Prophet regarding the obligatory prayer: "Turn your face toward the Masjid al-Haram (Sacred Mosque), and wherever you are, turn your faces toward it" [Quran 2:144]. Stand upright, for the Messenger of Allah (peace be upon him and his family) said: Whoever does not straighten their spine in prayer has no prayer. Lower your gaze in humility to Allah the Mighty and Majestic, and do not raise it to the sky, and let your gaze be directed at your place of prostration.

Hadith 5244

عن أبي بصير، عن أبي عبد الله (عليه السلام) قال: إن تكلمت أو صرفت وجهك عن القبلة فأعد الصلاة.

From Abu Basir, from Abu Abdullah (peace be upon him) who said: If you speak or turn your face away from the qiblah, then repeat the prayer.

Hadith 5245

عن عمر بن يحيى قال: سألت أبا عبد الله (عليه السلام) عن رجل صلى على غير القبلة، ثم تبينت القبلة وقد دخل وقت صلاة أخرى؟ قال: يعيدها قبل أن يصلي هذه التي قد دخل وقتها.

From Umar ibn Yahya who said: I asked Abu Abdullah (peace be upon him) about a man who prayed in a direction other than the qiblah, then the correct qiblah became clear after the time for another prayer had begun? He said: He should repeat it before praying the prayer whose time has begun.

أقول: هذا محمول إما على العمد، أو على ترك الاجتهاد، أو على الاستحباب، لما يأتي.

I (Hurr Amili) say: This applies either to intentional cases, or to cases where one did not make an effort to determine the direction, or it is recommended, as will be explained later.

CHAPTER 10

One Who Made An Effort To Find The Qiblah And Prayed Based On Assumption, Then Learned He Had Deviated From It Within The Range Between East And West - His Prayer Is Valid And Need Not Be Repeated

[Hadith 5246 to 5250]

Hadith 5246

عن معاوية بن عمار أنه سأل الصادق (عليه السلام) عن الرجل يقوم في الصلاة ثم ينظر بعدما فرغ، فيرى أنه قد انحرف عن القبلة يمينا أو شمالا؟ فقال له: قد مضت صلاته، وما بين المشرق والمغرب قبلة.

From Mu'awiyah bin Ammar who asked Al-Sadiq (peace be upon him) about a man who stands in prayer then looks after finishing and sees that he had deviated from the qiblah to the right or left? He said to him: His prayer is complete, and what lies between the east and west is qiblah.

Hadith 5247

عن زرارة، عن أبي جعفر (عليه السلام) قال: لا صلاة إلا إلى القبلة، قال: قلت: أين حد القبلة؟ قال: ما بين المشرق والمغرب قبلة كله.

From Zurarah, from Abu Ja'far (peace be upon him) who said: There is no prayer except facing the qiblah. I said: What are the bounds of the qiblah? He said: All that lies between the east and west is qiblah.

Hadith 5248

عن القاسم بن الوليد قال: سألته عن رجل تبين له وهو في الصلاة أنه على غير القبلة؟ قال: يستقبلها إذا أثبت ذلك، وإن كان فرغ منها فلا يعيدها.

From Al-Qasim bin Al-Walid who said: I asked him about a man who realizes during prayer that he is not facing the qiblah? He said: He should face it when he confirms that, and if he had finished the prayer he need not repeat it.

Hadith 5249

عن أبي عبد الله (عليه السلام) قال: في رجل صلى على غير القبلة فيعلم وهو في الصلاة قبل أن يفرغ من صلاته، قال: إن كان متوجها فيما بين المشرق والمغرب فليحول وجهه إلى القبلة ساعة يعلم، وإن كان متوجها إلى دبر القبلة فليقطع الصلاة ثم يحول وجهه إلى القبلة ثم يفتتح الصلاة.

From Abu Abdullah (peace be upon him) regarding a man who prayed not facing the qiblah and realizes while still in prayer before finishing: He said: If he was facing within the range between east and west, he should turn his face toward the qiblah as soon as he realizes, but if he was facing opposite to the qiblah he should stop the prayer then turn his face to the qiblah and start the prayer anew.

Hadith 5250

عن علي (عليهم السلام)، أنه كان يقول: من صلى على غير القبلة وهو يرى أنه على القبلة ثم عرف بعد ذلك فلا إعادة عليه إذا كان فيما بين المشرق والمغرب.

From Ali (peace be upon him), that he used to say: Whoever prayed not facing the qiblah while thinking he was facing it, then realized afterwards - he need not repeat if he was within the range between east and west.

CHAPTER 11

Obligation To Repeat Prayer Within Its Time, Not After, If One Discovers They Prayed In A Direction Other Than The Qiblah While Thinking It Was Correct

[Hadith 5251 to 5260]

Hadith 5251

عن أبي عبد الله (عليه السلام) قال: إذا صليت وأنت على غير القبلة واستبان لك أنك صليت وأنت على غير القبلة وأنت في وقت فأعد، وإن فاتك الوقت فلا تعد.

From Abu Abdullah (peace be upon him) who said: If you pray in a direction other than the qiblah and it becomes clear to you that you prayed in the wrong direction while still within the prayer time, then repeat it. If the time has passed, do not repeat it.

———————

Hadith 5252

عن يعقوب بن يقطين قال: سألت عبدا صالحا عن رجل صلى في يوم سحاب على غير القبلة ثم طلعت الشمس وهو في وقت، أيعيد الصلاة إذا كان قد صلى على غير القبلة؟ وإن كان قد تحرى القبلة بجهده، أتجزيه صلاته؟ فقال: يعيد ما كان في وقت، فإذا ذهب الوقت فلا إعادة عليه.

From Ya'qub ibn Yaqtin who said: I asked a righteous servant about a man who prayed on a cloudy day in a direction other than the qiblah, then the sun came out while still within the prayer time - should he repeat the prayer if he had prayed in the wrong direction? And if he had tried his best to determine the qiblah, would his prayer suffice? He said: He should repeat it if still within the time, but if the time has passed, he does not need to repeat it.

———————

Hadith 5253

عن زرارة، عن أبي جعفر (عليه السلام) قال: إذا صليت على غير القبلة فاستبان لك قبل أن تصبح أنك صليت على غير القبلة فأعد صلاتك.

From Zurarah, from Abu Ja'far (peace be upon him) who said: If you pray in a direction other than the qiblah and it becomes clear to you before morning that you prayed in the wrong direction, then repeat your prayer.

———————

Hadith 5254

عن محمد بن الحصين قال: كتبت إلى عبد صالح: الرجل يصلي في يوم غيم في فلاة من الأرض ولا يعرف القبلة، فيصلي حتى إذا فرغ من صلاته بدت له الشمس، فإذا هو قد صلى لغير القبلة، أيعتد بصلاته أم يعيدها؟ فكتب: يعيدها ما لم يفته الوقت، أو لم يعلم أن الله يقول وقوله الحق: (فأينما تولوا فثم وجه الله)!؟

From Muhammad ibn Al-Husayn who said: I wrote to a righteous servant: About a man who prays on a cloudy day in an open land and doesn't know the qiblah, so he prays, and when he finishes his prayer the sun appears and he realizes he had prayed in the wrong direction - should his prayer count or should he repeat it? He wrote back: He should repeat it if the time hasn't passed. Or hasn't he known that Allah says, and His word is truth: "Wherever you turn, there is the Face of Allah" [Quran 2:115]?!

Hadith 5255

عن أبي عبد الله (عليه السلام) قال: إذا صليت وأنت على غير القبلة واستبان لك أنك على غير القبلة وأنت في وقت فأعد، وإن فاتك فلا تعد.

From Abu Abdullah (peace be upon him) who said: If you pray in a direction other than the qiblah and it becomes clear to you that you're facing the wrong direction while still within the time, then repeat it. If the time has passed, do not repeat it.

Hadith 5256

عن سليمان بن خالد قال: قلت لأبي عبد الله (عليه السلام): الرجل يكون في قفر من الأرض في يوم غيم فيصلي لغير القبلة، ثم تصحى فيعلم أنه صلى لغير القبلة، كيف يصنع؟ قال: إن كان في وقت فليعد صلاته، وإن كان مضى الوقت فحسبه اجتهاده.

From Sulayman ibn Khalid who said: I asked Abu Abdullah (peace be upon him): What about a man who is in a desolate land on a cloudy day and prays in the wrong direction, then it clears up and he realizes he prayed in the wrong direction - what should he do? He said: If it's still within the time, he should repeat his prayer, and if the time has passed, his effort is sufficient.

Hadith 5257

عن أبي عبد الله (عليه السلام)، في الأعمى يؤم القوم وهو على غير القبلة، قال: يعيد ولا يعيدون فإنهم قد تحروا.

From Abu Abdullah (peace be upon him), regarding a blind man leading people in prayer while facing the wrong direction, he said: He should repeat but they should not repeat, for they made their best effort to determine the direction.

Hadith 5258

عن عبد الرحمن بن أبي عبد الله، أنه سئل الصادق (عليه السلام) عن رجل أعمى صلى على غير القبلة؟

فقال: إن كان في وقت فليعد، وإن كان قد مضى الوقت فلا يعد. قال: وسألته عن رجل صلى وهي مغيمة

ثم تجلت فعلم أنه صلى على غير القبلة؟ فقال: إن كان في وقت فليعد، وإن كان الوقت قد مضى فلا

يعيد.

From Abd al-Rahman bin Abu Abdullah, who asked Al-Sadiq (peace be upon him) about a blind man who prayed in a direction other than the qiblah? He said: If it is still within the prayer time, he should repeat it, and if the time has passed, he should not repeat it. He said: And I asked him about a man who prayed when it was cloudy, then it cleared and he realized he had prayed in a direction other than the qiblah? He said: If it is still within the prayer time, he should repeat it, and if the time has passed, he should not repeat it.

Hadith 5259

عن أبي بصير، عن أبي عبد الله (عليه السلام) قال: الأعمى إذا صلى لغير القبلة فإن كان في وقت فليعد،

وإن كان قد مضى الوقت فلا يعيد.

From Abu Basir, from Abu Abdullah (peace be upon him) who said: When a blind person prays in a direction other than the qiblah, if it is still within the prayer time, he should repeat it, and if the time has passed, he should not repeat it.

Hadith 5260

محمد بن الحسن في (النهاية) قال: قد رويت رواية، أنه إذا كان صلى إلى استدبار القبلة ثم علم بعد

خروج الوقت وجب عليه إعادة الصلاة، وهذا هو الأحوط وعليه العمل.

Muhammad bin Al-Hasan in (Al-Nihayah) said: A narration has been reported that if one prays facing away from the qiblah and then learns of this after the prayer time has passed, it is obligatory upon him to repeat the prayer, and this is the more precautionary approach and this is what should be practiced.

CHAPTER 12

Dislike Of Spitting And Expectorating Towards The Qiblah, Facing A Wall Seeping From A Drain During Prayer, The Obligation Of Facing The Qiblah When Slaughtering When Possible, The Prohibition Of Facing Or Turning One's Back To It When Relieving Oneself, And The Dislike Of Both During Intimacy

[Hadith 5261 to 5266]

Hadith 5261

عن أبي الحسن الأول (عليه السلام) أنه قال: إذا ظهر النز من خلف الكنيف وهو في القبلة يستره بشيء.

From Abu Al-Hasan Al-Awwal (peace be upon him) who said: If moisture (seepage) appears from behind the toilet and it is in the direction of the qiblah, cover it with something.

———

Hadith 5262

قال: ونهى رسول الله (صلى الله عليه وآله) عن البزاق في القبلة.

He said: The Messenger of Allah (peace be upon him and his family) forbade spitting towards the qiblah.

———

Hadith 5263

قال: ونهى عن الجماع مستقبل القبلة ومستدبرها.

He said: And he forbade having intimate relations while facing or turning one's back to the qiblah.

———

Hadith 5264

قال: ونهى عن استقبال القبلة ببول أو غائط.

He said: And he forbade facing the qiblah while urinating or defecating.

———

Hadith 5265

قال: وقال أبو جعفر (عليه السلام): لا يبزقن أحدكم في الصلاة قبل وجهه، ولاعن يمينه، وليبزق عن يساره وتحت قدمه اليسرى.

He said: And Abu Ja'far (peace be upon him) said: None of you should spit during prayer in front of him or to his right, but should spit to his left and under his left foot.

Hadith 5266

قال: وقال الصادق (عليه السلام): من حبس ريقه إجلالا لله تعالى في صلاته أورثه الله تعالى صحة حتى الممات.

He said: And Al-Sadiq (peace be upon him) said: Whoever holds back their saliva out of reverence for Allah the Exalted during their prayer, Allah the Exalted will grant them health until death.

CHAPTER 13

Permissibility Of Prayer On A Ship, In Congregation Or Individually, Even If Not Facing The Qiblah Out Of Necessity

[Hadith 5267 to 5283]

Hadith 5267

عن عبيد الله بن علي الحلبي، أنه سأل أبا عبد الله (عليه السلام) عن الصلاة في السفينة؟ فقال: يستقبل القبلة، ويصف رجليه، فإذا دارت واستطاع أن يتوجه إلى القبلة وإلا فليصل حيث توجهت به، وإن أمكنه القيام فليصل قائما، وإلا فليقعد ثم يصلي.

From Ubaydullah ibn Ali al-Halabi, he asked Abu Abdullah (peace be upon him) about prayer in a ship. He replied: Face the qiblah and keep your feet in line. If the ship turns and you can face the qiblah then do so, otherwise pray in whatever direction the ship faces. If you can stand then pray standing, otherwise sit and pray.

Hadith 5268

عن زرارة، أنه سأل أبا جعفر (عليه السلام) في الرجل يصلي النوافل في السفينة؟ قال: يصلي نحو رأسها.

From Zurarah, who asked Abu Ja'far (peace be upon him) about praying supererogatory prayers in a ship. He said: Pray towards its bow.

Hadith 5269

عن جميل بن دراج، أنه قال لأبي عبد الله (عليه السلام): تكون السفينة قريبة من الجد فأخرج وأصلي؟ فقال: صل فيها، أما ترضى بصلاة نوح (عليه السلام).

From Jamil ibn Darraj, who said to Abu Abdullah (peace be upon him): If the ship is close to land, should I disembark and pray? He replied: Pray in it - are you not satisfied with the prayer of Noah (peace be upon him)?

Hadith 5270

عن إبراهيم بن ميمون، أنه قال لأبي عبد الله (عليه السلام): نخرج إلى الأهواز في السفن، فنجمع فيها الصلاة؟ قال: نعم. ليس به بأس فقال له: فأسجد على ما فيها وعلى القير؟ فقال: لا بأس به.

From Ibrahim ibn Maymun, who said to Abu Abdullah (peace be upon him): We travel to Ahwaz in ships, can we pray congregational prayers in them? He said: Yes, there is no problem with that. He asked: Can I prostrate on what is in it and on the tar? He replied: There is no problem with that.

Hadith 5271

عن يونس بن يعقوب، أنه سأل أبا عبد الله (عليه السلام) عن الصلاة في الفرات، وما هو أصغر منه من الأنهار، في السفينة؟ فقال: إن صليت فحسن، وإن خرجت فحسن.

From Yunus ibn Ya'qub, who asked Abu Abdullah (peace be upon him) about praying in the Euphrates and smaller rivers while in ships. He replied: If you pray in it that is good, and if you disembark that is also good.

Hadith 5272

قال: وسأله عن الصلاة المكتوبة في السفينة وهي تأخذ شرقا وغربا؟ فقال: استقبل القبلة، ثم كبر، ثم در مع السفينة حيث دارت بك.

He asked him about the obligatory prayer in a ship while it is turning east and west. He replied: Face the qiblah, then say the opening takbir, then turn with the ship wherever it turns with you.

Hadith 5273

قال: وروي أنه إذا عصفت الريح بمن في السفينة ولم يقدر على أن يدور إلى القبلة صلى إلى صدر السفينة.

It is narrated that if strong winds affect those in the ship and they cannot turn towards the qiblah, they should pray towards the bow of the ship.

Hadith 5274

عن علي بن إبراهيم قال: سألته عن الصلاة في السفينة؟ قال: يصلي وهو جالس إذا لم يمكنه القيام في السفينة، ولا يصلي في السفينة وهو يقدر على الشط، وقال: يصلي في السفينة، يحول وجهه إلى القبلة ثم يصلي كيف ما دارت.

From Ali ibn Ibrahim who said: I asked him about prayer in the ship? He said: One should pray while sitting if standing is not possible in the ship, and one should not pray in the ship if they can reach the shore. And he said: Pray in the ship by turning towards the qiblah then pray however it turns.

Hadith 5275

عن أبي عبد الله (عليه السلام) قال: لا بأس بالصلاة في جماعة في السفينة.

From Abu Abdullah (peace be upon him) who said: There is no problem with praying in congregation on the ship.

Hadith 5276

عن صالح بن الحكم قال: سألت أبا عبد الله (عليه السلام) عن الصلاة في السفينة؟ فقال: إن رجلا سأل أبي عن الصلاة في السفينة؟ فقال له: أترغب عن صلاة نوح (عليه السلام)؟! فقلت له: آخذ معي مدرة أسجد عليها؟ فقال: نعم.

From Salih ibn al-Hakam who said: I asked Abu Abdullah (peace be upon him) about prayer on the ship? He said: A man asked my father about prayer on the ship? He replied: Do you dislike the prayer of Noah (peace be upon him)?! So I said: Should I take with me some clay to prostrate on? He said: Yes.

Hadith 5277

عن المفضل بن صالح قال: سألت أبا عبد الله (عليه السلام) عن الصلاة في الفرات، وما هو أضعف منه من الأنهار، في السفينة؟ فقال: إن صليت فحسن، وإن خرجت فحسن.

From Al-Mufaddal ibn Salih who said: I asked Abu Abdullah (peace be upon him) about prayer in the Euphrates and weaker rivers than it, in ships? He said: If you pray in it that is good, and if you leave it that is good.

Hadith 5278

عن إبراهيم بن ميمون أنه سأل أبا عبد الله (عليه السلام) عن الصلاة في جماعة في السفينة؟ فقال: لا بأس.

From Ibrahim ibn Maymun that he asked Abu Abdullah (peace be upon him) about praying in congregation on the ship? He said: There is no problem.

Hadith 5279

عن أبي عبد الله (عليه السلام)، أنه سئل عن الصلاة في السفينة؟ فقال: يستقبل القبلة، فإذا دارت فاستطاع أن يتوجه إلى القبلة فليفعل، وإلا فليصل حيث توجهت به. قال: فإن أمكنه القيام فليصل قائما، وإلا فليقعد ثم ليصل.

From Abu Abdullah (peace be upon him), that he was asked about prayer on the ship? He said: Face the qiblah, and if it turns and you can face the qiblah then do so, otherwise pray in whatever direction it faces. He said: If standing is possible then pray standing, otherwise sit and pray.

Hadith 5280

وعنه، عن أبيه، عن حماد بن عيسى قال: سمعت أبا عبد الله (عليه السلام) يسأل عن الصلاة في السفينة؟ فيقول: إن استطعتم أن تخرجوا إلى الجدد فأخرجوا، فإن لم تقدروا فصلوا قياما، فإن لم تستطيعوا فصلوا قعودا وتحروا القبلة.

From him, from his father, from Hammad ibn Isa who said: I heard Abu Abdullah (peace be upon him) being asked about prayer on the ship? He said: If you can disembark to firm ground then do so, if you cannot then pray standing, if you cannot then pray sitting and try to face the qiblah.

Hadith 5281

عن أبي عبد الله (عليه السلام)، في الرجل يكون في السفينة فلا يدري أين القبلة؟ قال: يتحرى، فإن لم يدر صلى نحو رأسها.

From Abu Abdullah (peace be upon him), regarding a man on a ship who does not know where the qiblah is? He said: He should try his best, if he still does not know then pray towards its front.

Hadith 5282

علي بن جعفر في كتابه عن أخيه موسى (عليه السلام)، قال: سألته عن قوم في سفينة لا يقدرون أن يخرجوا إلا لطين وماء، هل يصلح لهم أن يصلوا الفريضة في السفينة؟ قال: نعم.

Ali ibn Ja'far in his book from his brother Musa (peace be upon him) said: I asked him about people on a ship who cannot disembark except into mud and water - is it permissible for them to pray the obligatory prayer on the ship? He said: Yes.

Hadith 5283

عن زرارة قال: قلت لأبي عبد الله (عليه السلام): الصلاة في السفر في السفينة والمحمل سواء؟ قال: النافلة كلها سواء، تومئ إيماء أينما توجهت دابتك وسفينتك، والفريضة تنزل لها عن المحمل إلى الأرض إلا من خوف، فإن خفت أومأت، وأما السفينة فصل فيها قائما وتوخ القبلة بجهدك، فإن نوحا (عليه السلام) قد صلى الفريضة فيها قائما متوجها إلى القبلة وهي مطبقة عليهم،

From Zurarah who said: I asked Abu Abdullah (peace be upon him): Is prayer during travel the same in a ship and in a howdah? He said: All supererogatory prayers are the same - you gesture wherever your mount or ship faces. For obligatory prayer, you must descend from the howdah to the ground except out of fear. If you are afraid, then gesture. As for the ship, pray standing in it and strive towards the qiblah to your best ability, for indeed Noah (peace be upon him) prayed the obligatory prayer standing in it facing the qiblah while it covered them.

قلت: وما كان علمه بالقبلة فيتوجهها وهي مطبقة عليهم؟ قال: كان جبرئيل (عليه السلام) يقومه نحوها، قال: قلت: فأتوجه نحوها في كل تكبيرة؟ قال: أما في النافلة فلا، إنما تكبر على غير القبلة (الله أكبر)، ثم قال: كل ذلك قبلة للمتنفل (أينما تولوا فثم وجه الله).

I asked: How did he know the qiblah direction to face it while it covered them? He said: Jibreel (peace be upon him) would position him towards it. I asked: Should I face it for every takbir? He said: Not in supererogatory prayer. You say takbir (Allahu Akbar) not facing qiblah. Then he said: All directions are qiblah for supererogatory prayer [Wherever you turn, there is the Face of Allah] [Quran 2:115].

أقول: ويأتي ما يدل على ذلك في أحاديث القيام وغير ذلك، وعلى صلاة الخوف وحكمها في محله، إن شاء الله تعالى.

I (Hurr Amili) say: And there will come what indicates this in the hadiths about standing and other matters, and about the prayer of fear and its rulings in its place, insha'Allah.

CHAPTER 14

Impermissibility Of Performing Obligatory And Vowed Prayers On A Mount Or In A Litter By Choice, Its Permissibility In Necessity, And The Obligation To Face The Qiblah When Possible

[Hadith 5284 to 5294]

Hadith 5284

عن أبي عبد الله (عليه السلام) قال: لا يصلي على الدابة الفريضة إلا مريض يستقبل به القبلة، ويجزيه فاتحة الكتاب، ويضع بوجهه في الفريضة على ما أمكنه من شئ، ويومئ في النافلة ايماء.

From Abu Abdullah (peace be upon him) who said: One should not pray obligatory prayers on a mount except if sick, in which case one should face the qiblah. Reciting the Opening of the Book suffices, and one should place their face on whatever is possible for obligatory prayer, while making gestures for supererogatory prayers.

Hadith 5285

عن محمد بن عذافر - في حديث - قال: قلت لأبي عبد الله (عليه السلام): رجل يكون في وقت الفريضة لا تمكنه الأرض من القيام عليها ولا السجود عليها من كثرة الثلج والماء والمطر والوحل، أيجوز له أن يصلي الفريضة في المحمل؟ قال: نعم، هو بمنزلة السفينة، إن أمكنه قائما وإلا قاعدا، وكل ما كان من ذلك فالله أولى بالعذر، يقول الله عز وجل (بل الانسان على نفسه بصيرة).

From Muhammad ibn Adhafir in a hadith saying: I asked Abu Abdullah (peace be upon him): If a man is in the time of obligatory prayer and cannot stand or prostrate on the ground due to excessive snow, water, rain and mud, is it permissible for him to pray the obligatory prayer in the litter? He said: Yes, it is like being on a ship - standing if possible, otherwise sitting. In all such cases, Allah is most worthy of accepting the excuse. Allah the Mighty and Majestic says "Rather, man is clear evidence against himself" [Quran 75:14].

Hadith 5286

عن أحدهما (عليهما السلام) قال: سألته عن المرأة تزامل الرجل في المحمل، يصليان جميعا؟ فقال: لا، ولكن يصلي الرجل فإذا فرغ صلت المرأة.

From one of them (peace be upon them) saying: I asked him about a woman sharing a litter with a man, can they both pray together? He said: No, but the man should pray first and when he finishes the woman can pray.

Hadith 5287

عن عبد الله بن سنان قال: قلت لأبي عبد الله (عليه السلام): أيصلي الرجل شيئا من المفروض راكبا؟

فقال: لا، إلا من ضرورة.

From Abdullah ibn Sinan who said: I asked Abu Abdullah (peace be upon him): Can a man pray any obligatory prayers while riding? He said: No, except out of necessity.

Hadith 5288

عن الحميري يعني عبد الله بن جعفر قال: كتبت إلى أبي الحسن (عليه السلام): روى، جعلني الله فداك، مواليك عن آبائك أن رسول الله (صلى الله عليه وآله) صلى الفريضة على راحلة في يوم مطير، ويصيبنا المطر ونحن في محاملنا والأرض مبتلة والمطر يؤذي، فهل يجوز لنا يا سيدي أن نصلي في هذه الحال في محاملنا أو على دوابنا الفريضة. إن شاء الله؟ فوقع (عليه السلام): يجوز ذلك مع الضرورة الشديدة.

From al-Himyari, meaning Abdullah ibn Ja'far, who said: I wrote to Abu al-Hasan (peace be upon him): Your followers have narrated from your forefathers that the Messenger of Allah (peace be upon him and his family) prayed obligatory prayer on his mount on a rainy day. When rain affects us while we are in our litters and the ground is wet and the rain is harmful, is it permissible for us, O my master, to pray obligatory prayers in this condition in our litters or on our mounts, if Allah wills? He wrote back: That is permissible in cases of severe necessity.

Hadith 5289

عن علي بن جعفر، عن أخيه موسى (عليه السلام)، قال: سألته عن رجل جعل لله عليه أن يصلي كذا وكذا، هل يجزيه أن يصلي ذلك على دابته وهو مسافر؟ قال: نعم.

From Ali ibn Ja'far, from his brother Musa (peace be upon him), who said: I asked him about a man who made a vow to Allah to pray such and such prayers, would it suffice for him to pray these while on his mount while traveling? He said: Yes.

Hadith 5290

عن أبي عبد الله (عليه السلام) قال: لا تصل شيئا من المفروض راكبا. قال النضر في حديثه: إلا أن يكون مريضا.

From Abu Abdullah (peace be upon him) who said: Do not pray any obligatory prayers while riding. Al-Nadr added in his narration: Unless one is sick.

Hadith 5291

عن مندل بن علي قال: سمعت أبا عبد الله (عليه السلام) يقول: صلى رسول الله (صلى الله عليه وآله) على راحلته الفريضة في يوم مطير.

Mandal ibn Ali said: I heard Abu Abdullah (peace be upon him) say: The Messenger of Allah (peace be upon him and his family) prayed the obligatory prayer on his mount on a rainy day.

Hadith 5292

عن جميل بن دراج قال: سمعت أبا عبد الله (عليه السلام) يقول: صلى رسول الله (صلى الله عليه وآله) الفريضة في المحمل في يوم وحل ومطر.

Jamil ibn Darraj said: I heard Abu Abdullah (peace be upon him) say: The Messenger of Allah (peace be upon him and his family) prayed the obligatory prayer in the carriage on a muddy and rainy day.

Hadith 5293

عن منصور بن حازم قال: سأله أحمد بن النعمان فقال: أصلي في محملي وأنا مريض؟ قال: فقال: أما النافلة فنعم، وأما الفريضة فلا. قال: وذكر أحمد شدة وجعه، فقال: أنا كنت مريضا شديد المرض فكنت آمرهم إذا حضرت الصلاة ينيخوني فاحتمل بفراشي فأوضع وأصلي، ثم احتمل بفراشي فأوضع في محملي.

Mansur ibn Hazim said: Ahmad ibn al-Nu'man asked him saying: Can I pray in my carriage while I am sick? He replied: As for supererogatory prayers, yes, but as for obligatory prayers, no. Ahmad mentioned the severity of his pain, so he said: I was severely ill and when prayer time came, I would order them to make my camel kneel down, then I would be carried with my bedding to be placed down to pray, then I would be carried with my bedding to be placed back in my carriage.

Shaykh Hurr Amili: Al-Shaykh said: This is interpreted as being recommended.

Hadith 5294

أحمد بن علي بن أبي طالب الطبرسي في (الاحتجاج): عن محمد بن عبد الله بن جعفر الحميري، عن صاحب الزمان (عليه السلام)، أنه كتب إليه يسأله عن رجل يكون في محمله والثلج كثير بقامة رجل فيتخوف إن نزل الغوص فيه، وربما يسقط الثلج وهو على تلك الحال، ولا يستوي له أن يلبد شيئا منه لكثرته وتهافته، هل يجوز أن يصلي في المحمل الفريضة؟ فقد فعلنا ذلك أياما. فهل علينا فيه إعادة أم لا؟ فأجاب: لا بأس به عند الضرورة والشدة.

Ahmad ibn Ali ibn Abi Talib al-Tabarsi reported in (al-Ihtijaj): From Muhammad ibn Abdullah ibn Ja'far al-Himyari, from the Master of Time (peace be upon him), that he wrote to him asking about a man who is in his carriage while there is heavy snow reaching a man's height, and he fears sinking if he descends, and sometimes snow falls while he is in that state, and he cannot compact any of it due to its abundance and continuous falling - is it permissible for him to pray the obligatory prayer in the carriage? We have done this for days, so do we need to repeat the prayers or not? He answered: There is no problem with it in cases of necessity and hardship.

———

CHAPTER 15

Permissibility Of Offering Supererogatory Prayers While Riding A Mount Or In A Carriage By Gesturing, Whether With Or Without Excuse, Even If Not Facing The Qiblah, During Travel Or At Home

[Hadith 5295 to 5318]

Hadith 5295

عن عبد الرحمن بن الحجاج، أنه سأل أبا عبد الله (عليه السلام) عن الرجل يصلي النوافل في الأمصار وهو على دابته حيث ما توجهت به؟ قال: لا بأس.

From Abd al-Rahman ibn al-Hajjaj, he asked Abu Abdullah (peace be upon him) about a man who prays supererogatory prayers in cities while on his mount wherever it faces. He replied: There is no problem with that.

Hadith 5296

عن أبي عبد الله (عليه السلام) أنه قال له: إني أقدر أن أتوجه نحو القبلة في المحمل، فقال: هذا الضيق، أما لكم في رسول الله (صلى الله عليه وآله) أسوة؟!

He said to Abu Abdullah (peace be upon him): I am able to face the qiblah in the carriage. He replied: This is constraint. Do you not have an example in the Messenger of Allah (peace be upon him and his family)!?

Hadith 5297

عن سعد بن سعد، أنه سأل أبا الحسن الرضا (عليه السلام) عن الرجل تكون معه المرأة الحائض في المحمل، أيصلي وهي معه؟ قال: نعم.

From Saad ibn Saad, he asked Abu al-Hasan al-Ridha (peace be upon him) about a man who has a menstruating woman with him in the carriage, can he pray while she is with him? He replied: Yes.

Hadith 5298

عن سعيد بن يسار، أنه سأل أبا عبد الله (عليه السلام) عن الرجل يصلي صلاة الليل وهو على دابته، وله أن يغطي وجهه وهو يصلي؟ فقال: أما إذا قرأ فنعم، وأما إذا أومأ بوجهه للسجود فليكشفه حيث أومت به الدابة.

From Said ibn Yasar, he asked Abu Abdullah (peace be upon him) about a man who prays Salat al-Layl while on his mount, is it permissible for him to cover his face while praying? He replied: When reciting yes, but when gesturing prostration with his face, he should uncover it wherever the mount turns.

Hadith 5299

عن محمد بن مسلم قال: قال لي أبو جعفر (عليه السلام): صل صلاة الليل والوتر والركعتين في المحمل.

From Muhammad ibn Muslim, he said: Abu Ja'far (peace be upon him) said to me: Pray Salat al-Layl, Witr, and the two units in the carriage.

Hadith 5300

عن الحلبي أنه سأل أبا عبد الله (عليه السلام) عن صلاة النافلة على البعير والدابة؟ فقال: نعم، حيث كان متوجها، وكذلك فعل رسول الله (صلى الله عليه وآله).

From Al-Halabi, he asked Abu Abdullah (peace be upon him) about supererogatory prayers on a camel or mount? He replied: Yes, wherever it faces, and this is what the Messenger of Allah (peace be upon him and his family) did.

Hadith 5301

عن محمد بن سنان، مثله، وزاد: قلت على البعير والدابة؟ قال: نعم، حيث ما كنت متوجها. قلت: أستقبل القبلة إذا أردت التكبير؟ قال: لا، ولكن تكبر حيثما كنت متوجها، وكذلك فعل رسول الله (صلى الله عليه وآله).

From Muhammad ibn Sinan similarly, and added: I asked: On a camel and mount? He said: Yes, wherever you are facing. I asked: Should I face the qiblah when wanting to say the opening takbir? He said: No, but say takbir wherever you are facing, and this is what the Messenger of Allah (peace be upon him and his family) did.

Translator: In the Arabic edition, Hadith 5300 and 5301 are recorded together as a single hadith.

Hadith 5302

عن علي بن مهزيار قال: قرأت في كتاب لعبد الله بن محمد إلى أبي الحسن (عليه السلام): اختلف أصحابنا في رواياتهم عن أبي عبد الله (عليه السلام) في ركعتي الفجر في السفر، فروى بعضهم أن صلهما في المحمل. وروى بعضهم لا تصلهما إلا على الأرض، فأعلمني، كيف نصنع أنت لأقتدي بك في ذلك؟ فوقع (عليه السلام): موسع عليك بأية عملت.

From Ali ibn Mahziyar, he said: I read in a letter from Abdullah ibn Muhammad to Abu Al-Hasan (peace be upon him): Our companions differed in their narrations from Abu Abdullah (peace be upon him) regarding the two rak'ahs of Fajr during travel - some narrated to pray them in the carriage, and others narrated not to pray them except on the ground, so inform me what you do so I may follow your example in this? He (peace be upon him) wrote back: You have flexibility to act upon either way.

Hadith 5303

عن أبي عبد الله (عليه السلام)، في الصلاة في المحمل، فقال: صل متربعا، وممدود الرجلين، وكيف أمكنك.

From Abu Abdullah (peace be upon him), regarding prayer in the carriage, he said: Pray while sitting cross-legged, with legs extended, or however you are able.

Hadith 5304

عن أبي الحسن الأول (عليه السلام)، في الرجل يصلي النافلة وهو على دابته في الأمصار، قال: لا بأس.

From Abu Al-Hasan the First (peace be upon him), regarding a man praying supererogatory prayers while on his mount in cities, he said: There is no problem with it.

Hadith 5305

عن معاوية بن وهب قال: سمعت أبا عبد الله (عليه السلام) يقول: كان أبي يدعو بالطهور في السفر وهو في محمله، فيؤتى بالتور فيه الماء، فيتوضأ ثم يصلي الثماني والوتر في محمله، فإذا نزل صلى الركعتين والصبح.

From Mu'awiyah ibn Wahb, he said: I heard Abu Abdullah (peace be upon him) saying: My father would ask for water for purification during travel while in his carriage. A vessel with water would be brought to him, he would perform wudu then pray the eight (rak'ahs) and Witr in his carriage. When he would dismount he would pray the two rak'ahs and Fajr prayer.

Hadith 5306

عن أبي الحسن (عليه السلام) قال: سألته عن صلاة النافلة في الحضر على ظهر الدابة إذا خرجت قريبا من أبيات الكوفة، أو كنت مستعجلا بالكوفة؟ فقال: إن كنت مستعجلا لا تقدر على النزول وتخوفت فوت ذلك إن تركته وأنت راكب، فنعم، وإلا فإن صلاتك على الأرض أحب إلى.

From Abu Al-Hasan (peace be upon him): I asked him about voluntary prayers while in town on the back of a mount when going near the houses of Kufa, or when in a hurry in Kufa? He said: If you are in a hurry and unable to dismount and fear missing it if you leave it while riding, then yes. Otherwise, your prayer on the ground is more beloved to me.

Hadith 5307

عن عبد الرحمن بن أبي نجران قال: سألت أبا الحسن (عليه السلام) عن الصلاة بالليل في السفر في المحمل، قال: إذا كنت على غير القبلة فاستقبل القبلة ثم كبر وصل حيث ذهب بك بعيرك. قلت: جعلت فداك في أول الليل؟ فقال: إذا خفت الفوت في آخره.

From Abd al-Rahman ibn Abi Najran, he said: I asked Abu Al-Hasan (peace be upon him) about Salat al-Layl during travel in the carriage. He said: If you are not facing the qiblah, then face the qiblah, say takbir, then pray wherever your camel takes you. I said: May I be sacrificed for you, in the early night? He said: If you fear missing it in its latter part.

Hadith 5308

عن سماعة قال: سألته عن الصلاة في السفر - إلى أن قال - وليتطوع بالليل ما شاء إن كان نازلا، وإن كان راكبا فليصل على دابته وهو راكب، ولتكن صلاته ايماء، وليكن رأسه حيث يريد السجود أخفض من ركوعه.

From Sama'ah, he said: I asked him about prayer during travel - until he said - and one may pray voluntary prayers at night as much as he wishes if stationary, and if riding then pray on his mount while riding, and let his prayer be by gesturing, and let his head when intending sujud be lower than his ruku.

Hadith 5309

عن يعقوب بن شعيب قال: سألت أبا عبد الله (عليه السلام) عن الرجل يصلي على راحلته، قال: يومئ ايماء، يجعل السجود أخفض من الركوع.

From Ya'qub ibn Shu'ayb, he said: I asked Abu Abdullah (peace be upon him) about a man praying on his mount. He said: He gestures, making the sujud lower than the ruku.

Hadith 5310

عن علي بن النعمان، عمن ذكره، عن أبي عبد الله (عليه السلام) في الرجل يصلي وهو على دابته متلثما يومئ قال: يكشف موضع السجود.

From Ali bin al-Nu'man, from someone he mentioned, from Abu Abdullah (peace be upon him) regarding a man who prays while on his mount with his face covered, making gestures, he said: He should uncover the place of prostration.

Hadith 5311

وعن علي بن الحكم عمن ذكره قال: رأيت أبا عبد الله (عليه السلام) في المحمل يسجد على القرطاس وأكثر ذلك يومئ ايماء.

And from Ali bin al-Hakam from someone he mentioned who said: I saw Abu Abdullah (peace be upon him) in the carriage prostrating on paper, and most often he would gesture with motions.

Hadith 5312

الفضل بن الحسن الطبرسي في (مجمع البيان) عن أبي جعفر وأبي عبد الله (عليهما السلام) في قوله تعالى: (فأينما تولوا فثم وجه الله) إنها ليست بمنسوخة، وأنها مخصوصة بالنوافل في حال السفر.

Al-Fadhl bin al-Hasan al-Tabarsi in Majma' al-Bayan from Abu Ja'far and Abu Abdullah (peace be upon them) regarding the words of the Almighty: "So wherever you turn, there is the Face of Allah" [Quran 2:115], they said it is not abrogated, and it is specific to supererogatory prayers during travel.

Hadith 5313

محمد بن الحسن في (النهاية) عن الصادق (عليه السلام) في قوله تعالى: (فأينما تولوا فثم وجه الله) قال: هذا في النوافل خاصة في حال السفر، فأما الفرائض فلابد فيها من استقبال القبلة.

Muhammad bin al-Hasan in Al-Nihaya from Al-Sadiq (peace be upon him) regarding the words of the Almighty: "So wherever you turn, there is the Face of Allah" [Quran 2:115], he said: This is specifically for supererogatory prayers during travel, as for obligatory prayers, facing the qiblah is necessary.

Hadith 5314

عن حماد بن عيسى قال: سمعت أبا عبد الله (عليه السلام) يقول: خرج رسول الله (صلى الله عليه وآله) إلي تبوك فكان يصلي على راحلته صلاة الليل حيث توجهت به ويومئ ايماء.

From Hammad bin Isa who said: I heard Abu Abdullah (peace be upon him) say: The Messenger of Allah (peace be upon him and his family) went out to Tabuk and would pray Salat al-Layl on his mount wherever it faced, making gestures.

Hadith 5315

عن جعفر بن محمد، عن أبيه عن علي (عليهم السلام) أن رسول الله (صلى الله عليه وآله) أوتر على راحلته في غزاة تبوك. قال: وكان علي (عليه السلام) يوتر على راحلته إذا جد به السير.

From Ja'far bin Muhammad, from his father, from Ali (peace be upon them) that the Messenger of Allah (peace be upon him and his family) performed Witr prayer on his mount during the Tabuk expedition. He said: And Ali (peace be upon him) would perform Witr on his mount when traveling quickly.

Hadith 5316

عن فيض بن مطر قال: دخلت على أبي جعفر (عليه السلام) وأنا أريد أن أسأله عن صلاة الليل في المحمل، قال: فابتدأني فقال: كان رسول الله (صلى الله عليه وآله) يصلي على راحلته حيث توجهت به.

From Fayd bin Matar who said: I entered upon Abu Ja'far (peace be upon him) wanting to ask him about Salat al-Layl in the carriage. He said: He initiated the conversation saying: The Messenger of Allah (peace be upon him and his family) would pray on his mount wherever it faced.

Hadith 5317

محمد بن مسعود العياشي في تفسيره عن حريز قال: قال أبو جعفر (عليه السلام): أنزل الله هذه الآية في التطوع خاصة: (فأينما تولوا فثم وجه الله إن الله واسع عليم) وصلى رسول (صلى الله عليه وآله) إيماء على راحلته أينما توجهت به حيث خرج إلى خيبر، وحين رجع من مكة، وجعل الكعبة خلف ظهره.

Muhammad bin Mas'ud al-Ayyashi in his Tafsir from Hareez who said: Abu Ja'far (peace be upon him) said: Allah revealed this verse specifically about voluntary prayers: "So wherever you turn, there is the Face of Allah. Indeed, Allah is all-Encompassing and Knowing" [Quran 2:115], and the Messenger (peace be upon him and his family) prayed with gestures on his mount wherever it faced when he went to Khaybar, and when he returned from Makkah, with the Ka'bah behind his back.

Hadith 5318

عن ابن عمر قال: كان رسول الله (صلى الله عليه وآله) يصلي على راحلته حيث توجهت به.

From Ibn Umar, he said: The Messenger of Allah (peace be upon him and his family) would pray on his mount wherever it faced.

CHAPTER 16

Permissibility Of Performing Obligatory Prayers While Walking When Necessary, And Supererogatory Prayers Unconditionally, And The Obligation To Face The Qiblah As Much As Possible Even If Only For The Opening Takbir

[Hadith 5319 to 5325]

Hadith 5319

عن أبي عبد الله (عليه السلام) قال: لا بأس بأن يصلي الرجل صلاة الليل في السفر وهو يمشي، ولا بأس إن فاتته صلاة الليل أن يقضيها بالنهار وهو يمشي يتوجه إلى القبلة ثم يمشي ويقرأ. فإذا أراد أن يركع حول وجهه إلى القبلة وركع وسجد ثم مشى.

From Abu Abdullah (peace be upon him) who said: There is no problem if a man performs Salat al-Layl while walking during travel, and there is no problem if he misses Salat al-Layl to make it up during the day while walking. He should face the qiblah then walk and recite, and when he wants to perform ruku, he should turn his face to the qiblah, bow and prostrate, then continue walking.

Hadith 5320

عن أبي عبد الله (عليه السلام) قال: إن صليت وأنت تمشي كبرت ثم مشيت فقرأت، فإذا أردت أن تركع أومأت، ثم أومأت بالسجود فليس في السفر تطوع.

From Abu Abdullah (peace be upon him) who said: If you pray while walking, say the takbir then walk and recite, and when you want to bow, gesture for it, then gesture for prostration, for there is no voluntary prayer during travel.

Hadith 5321

عن يعقوب بن شعيب قال: سألت أبا عبد الله (عليه السلام) عن الصلاة في السفر وأنا أمشي؟ قال: أوم إيماء واجعل السجود أخفض من الركوع.

From Ya'qub bin Shu'ayb who said: I asked Abu Abdullah (peace be upon him) about praying while walking during travel? He said: Make gestures and make the sujud lower than the ruku.

Hadith 5322

عن يعقوب بن شعيب قال: سألت أبا عبد الله (عليه السلام) - إلى أن قال - قلت: يصلي وهو يمشي؟
قال: نعم، يومئ إيماء وليجعل السجود أخفض من الركوع.

From Ya'qub bin Shu'ayb who said: I asked Abu Abdullah (peace be upon him) - until he said - I asked: Can one pray while walking? He said: Yes, making gestures and making the sujud lower than the ruku.

Hadith 5323

عن أبي جعفر (عليه السلام) أنه كان لا يرى بأسا بأن يصلي الماشي وهو يمشي ولكن لا يسوق الإبل.

From Abu Ja'far (peace be upon him) that he saw no problem with a walking person praying while walking but should not be driving camels.

Hadith 5324

عن أبي عبد الله (عليه السلام) قال: سألته عن الرجل يصلي وهو يمشي تطوعا؟ قال: نعم.

From Abu Abdullah (peace be upon him) who said: I asked him about a man praying voluntarily while walking? He said: Yes.

Hadith 5325

محمد بن محمد المفيد في (المقنعة) قال: سئل عن الرجل يجد به السير أيصلي على راحلته؟ قال: لا بأس بذلك ويومئ ايماء، وكذلك الماشي إذا اضطر إلى الصلاة.

Muhammad bin Muhammad al-Mufid in (al-Muqni'ah) said: He was asked about a man who needs to travel, can he pray on his mount? He said: There is no problem with that and he should make gestures, and likewise for the walker when compelled to pray.

Shaykh Hurr Amili: Evidence for that will come in the prayer of fear.

CHAPTER 17

Dislike Of Performing Obligatory Prayer In The Ka'bah, The Recommendation Of Supererogatory Prayer In It, And Facing All Its Walls

[Hadith 5326 to 5334]

Hadith 5326

عن محمد بن مسلم، عن أحدهما (عليهما السلام) قال: لا تصل المكتوبة في الكعبة.

From Muhammad ibn Muslim, from one of them (peace be upon them) said: Do not perform the prescribed prayer in the Ka'bah.

Hadith 5327

قال الكليني: وروي في حديث آخر يصلي في أربع جوانبها إذا اضطر إلى ذلك. قال الشهيد في الذكرى: هذا إشارة إلى أن القبلة إنما هي جميع الكعبة فإذا صلى في الأربع عند الضرورة فكأنه استقبل جميع الكعبة.

Al-Kulayni said: It is reported in another hadith that one may pray in its four corners when compelled to do so. Al-Shahid said in Al-Dhikra: This indicates that the qiblah is the entire Ka'bah, so when one prays in the four corners out of necessity, it is as if he faced the entire Ka'bah.

Hadith 5328

عن أبي عبد الله (عليه السلام) قال: لا تصل المكتوبة في جوف الكعبة فإن النبي (صلى الله عليه وآله) لم يدخل الكعبة في حج ولا عمرة ولكنه دخلها في الفتح فتح مكة، وصلى ركعتين بين العمودين ومعه أسامة بن زيد.

From Abu Abdullah (peace be upon him) said: Do not perform the prescribed prayer inside the Ka'bah, for the Prophet (peace be upon him and his family) did not enter the Ka'bah during Hajj or Umrah, but he entered it during the Conquest of Makkah, and prayed two rak'ahs between the two pillars with Usama ibn Zayd.

Hadith 5329

عن العلاء، عن محمد، عن أحدهما (عليهما السلام) قال: لا تصلح صلاة المكتوبة في جوف الكعبة.

From Al-Ala, from Muhammad, from one of them (peace be upon them) said: The prescribed prayer is not proper inside the Ka'bah.

Hadith 5330

عن محمد بن مسلم، عن أحدهما (عليهما السلام) قال: تصلح الصلاة المكتوبة في جوف الكعبة.

From Muhammad ibn Muslim, from one of them (peace be upon them) said: The prescribed prayer is proper inside the Ka'bah.

أقول: لفظة (لا) هنا غير موجودة في النسخة التي قوبلت بخط الشيخ، وهي موجودة في بعض النسخ وعلى تقدير عدم وجودها فهو محمول على الجواز، وما تقدم على الكراهة.

I (Hurr Amili) say: The word "not" is not present in the copy compared with Shaykh's handwriting, though it exists in some copies. Assuming its absence, it indicates permissibility, while what preceded indicates dislike.

Hadith 5331

عن يونس بن يعقوب قال: قلت: لأبي عبد الله (عليه السلام): حضرت الصلاة المكتوبة وأنا في الكعبة، أفأصلي فيها؟ قال: صل.

From Yunus ibn Ya'qub who said: I said to Abu Abdullah (peace be upon him): The time for prescribed prayer has come while I am in the Ka'bah, should I pray in it? He said: Pray.

قال الشيخ: هذا محمول على الضرورة على أن ذلك مكروه غير محظور لما مر.

Note: The Shaykh said: This applies to necessity, though it is disliked but not forbidden, as previously mentioned.

Hadith 5332

عن محمد بن عبد الله بن مروان قال: رأيت يونس بمنى يسأل أبا الحسن (عليه السلام) عن الرجل إذا حضرته صلاة قلت: الفريضة وهو في الكعبة فلم يمكنه الخروج من الكعبة استلقى على قفاه وصلى ايماء، وذكر قول الله عز وجل: (فأينما تولوا فثم وجه الله).

From Muhammad ibn Abdullah ibn Marwan who said: I saw Yunus at Mina asking Abu Al-Hasan (peace be upon him) about a man when the time for obligatory prayer comes while he is in the Ka'bah and cannot exit, he should lie on his back and pray with gestures, and he mentioned Allah's saying "Wherever you turn, there is the Face of Allah" [Quran 2:115].

أقول: حمله بعض أصحابنا على الضرورة والعجز عن القيام.

I (Hurr Amili) say: Some of our companions interpreted this as applying to necessity and inability to stand.

Hadith 5333

عن جعفر بن محمد، عن أبيه (عليهما السلام) أنه رأى علي بن الحسين (عليه السلام) يصلي في الكعبة ركعتين.

Ja'far bin Muhammad narrated from his father (peace be upon them) that he saw Ali bin Al-Husayn (peace be upon him) praying two rak'ahs in the Ka'bah.

Hadith 5334

محمد بن محمد المفيد في (المقنعة) قال: قال (عليه السلام): لا تصل المكتوبة في جوف الكعبة، ولا بأس أن تصلي فيها النافلة.

Muhammad bin Muhammad Al-Mufid said in (Al-Muqni'ah): He (peace be upon him) said: Do not pray the obligatory prayers inside the Ka'bah, but there is no problem with praying supererogatory prayers in it.

CHAPTER 18

Permissibility Of Praying On Abu Qubays Mountain And Similar Places Higher Or Lower Than The Ka'bah While Facing Its Direction

[Hadith 5335 to 5337]

Hadith 5335

عن أبي عبد الله (عليه السلام) قال: سأله رجل قال: صليت فوق أبي قبيس العصر فهل يجزي ذلك والكعبة تحتي؟ قال: نعم إنها قبلة من موضعها إلى السماء.

From Abu Abdullah (peace be upon him): A man asked him saying: I prayed Asr prayer on top of Abu Qubays (*) while the Ka'bah was below me, is that sufficient? He replied: Yes, it is a qiblah from its position up to the sky.

Translator: * A famous mountain (about 1,320 feet tall) near the eastern side of the Masjid al-Haram.

Hadith 5336

عن خالد بن أبي إسماعيل قال: قلت لأبي عبد الله (عليه السلام): الرجل يصلي على أبي قبيس مستقبل القبلة، فقال: لا بأس.

From Khalid bin Abi Isma'il who said: I asked Abu Abdullah (peace be upon him) about a man who prays on Abu Qubays mountain while facing the qiblah. He said: There is no problem with that.

Hadith 5337

محمد بن علي بن الحسين قال: قال الصادق (عليه السلام): أساس البيت من الأرض السابعة السفلى إلى الأرض السابعة العليا.

Muhammad bin Ali bin Al-Husayn said: Al-Sadiq (peace be upon him) said: The foundation of the House (Ka'bah) extends from the lowest seventh earth to the highest seventh earth.

Shaykh Hurr Amili: Evidence has preceded for that in general and absolute terms, and evidence for it will come.

CHAPTER 19
Ruling On Praying On The Roof Of The Ka'bah
[Hadith 5338 to 5339]

Hadith 5338

عن الصادق، عن آبائه (عليهم السلام) - في حديث المناهي - قال: نهى رسول الله (صلى الله عليه وآله) عن الصلاة على ظهر الكعبة.

From Al-Sadiq, from his forefathers (peace be upon them) - in the hadith of prohibitions - he said: The Messenger of Allah (peace be upon him and his family) forbade praying on top of the Ka'bah.

Hadith 5339

عن الرضا (عليه السلام) في الذي تدركه الصلاة وهو فوق الكعبة قال: إن قام لم يكن له قبلة، ولكن يستلقي على قفاه ويفتح عينيه إلى السماء ويعقد بقلبه القبلة التي في السماء البيت المعمور، ويقرأ فإذا أراد أن يركع غمض عينيه، وإذا أراد أن يرفع رأسه من الركوع فتح عينيه، والسجود على نحو ذلك.

From Al-Ridha (peace be upon him) regarding one who encounters prayer time while being on top of the Ka'bah, he said: If he stands, he will have no qiblah, but he should lie on his back and open his eyes toward the sky and establish in his heart the qiblah that is in the sky - the Bayt Al-Ma'mur - and recite. When he wants to perform ruku, he closes his eyes, and when he wants to raise his head from ruku, he opens his eyes, and sujud is done similarly.

أقول: ادعى الشيخ الاجماع على مضمونه، وقد توقف فيه جماعة من المتأخرين، لأنه ينافي وجوب القيام والركوع والسجود واستقبال الكعبة فحكموا أن من صلى على ظهر الكعبة أبرز بين يديه منها شيئا، ولا يخفى أنه لا تصريح فيه بالفريضة فيمكن حمله على النافلة أو على العجز عن القيام، أو على الضرورة مع عدم إمكان إبراز شئ بين يديه لما مر إلا أن تأويله موقوف على وجود المعارض الخاص ولو وجد لأمكن حمله على التقية، وحديث عبد السلام غير موافق للتقية، والله أعلم.

I (Hurr Amili) say: The Shaykh claimed consensus on its content, though a group of later scholars hesitated about it, because it contradicts the obligation of standing (qiyam), ruku, sujud, and facing the Ka'bah. So they ruled that whoever prays on top of the Ka'bah should place something from it in front of him. It is not hidden that there is no explicit mention of it being an obligatory prayer, so it can be interpreted as applying to supererogatory prayer, or to inability to stand, or to necessity when unable to place anything in front, except that its interpretation depends on finding specific contradicting evidence.

Section 4
Libas Al-Musalli (Clothing of the Praying Person)

CHAPTER 1

Prohibition Of Prayer In Dead Animal Hide Even If Tanned

[Hadith 5340 to 5343]

Hadith 5340

عن محمد بن مسلم قال: سألته عن الجلد الميت أيلبس في الصلاة إذا دبغ؟ قال: لا، ولو دبغ سبعين مرة.

From Muhammad bin Muslim who said: I asked him about praying while wearing tanned dead animal hide. He said: No, even if it was tanned seventy times.

Hadith 5341

عن أبي عبد الله (عليه السلام) في الميتة قال: لا تصل في شئ منه ولا شسع.

From Abu Abdullah (peace be upon him) regarding dead animals, he said: Do not pray in anything from it, not even a sandal strap (or shoelace).

Hadith 5342

محمد بن علي بن الحسين قال: سئل الصادق (عليه السلام) عن قول الله عز وجل لموسى: (فاخلع نعليك إنك بالواد المقدس طوى) قال: كانتا من جلد حمار ميت.

Muhammad bin Ali bin Al-Husayn said: Al-Sadiq (peace be upon him) was asked about Allah's words to Moses: "Take off your sandals, for you are in the sacred valley of Tuwa" [Quran 20:12]. He said: They were made from dead donkey hide.

Hadith 5343

عن أبي عبد الله (عليه السلام) قال: قال الله عز وجل لموسى (فاخلع نعليك) لأنها كانت من جلد حمار ميت.

From Abu Abdullah (peace be upon him) who said: Allah told Moses "Take off your sandals" [Quran 20:12] because they were made from dead donkey hide.

أقول: هذا وإن أشعر بلبس جلد الميتة في غير الصلاة يحتمل الحمل على التقية في الرواية، وله نظائر. فقد روى الصدوق في كتاب (إكمال الدين) حديثا طويلا عن صاحب الزمان (عليه السلام) في إنكار هذه الرواية ونسبتها إلى العامة. ويمكن الحمل على كونه منسوخا فإن تلك الشريعة ليست بحجة علينا، على

أنه ليس فيه دلالة على أنه كان يلبس نعليه في الصلاة، ولا فيه إشعار بأنه كان عالما بكونهما ميتة، بل هو دال على مضمون الباب للامر بالخلع. وتقدم ما يدل على ذلك، ويأتي ما يدل عليه في أحاديث من يستحل الميتة بالدباغ، وفي أحاديث جلود السباع وغير ذلك، إن شاء الله.

I (Hurr Amili) say: Although this suggests wearing dead animal hide outside of prayer, the narration can be interpreted as taqiyyah, and it has similar examples. Al-Saduq has narrated in Ikmal Al-Din a long hadith from the Master of Time (peace be upon him) rejecting this narration and attributing it to the Aammah (general non-Shia muslims). It can also be interpreted as being abrogated since that legislation is not binding upon us. Moreover, there is no indication that he wore his sandals during prayer, nor any suggestion that he knew they were from dead animals. Rather, it demonstrates the chapter's message through the command to remove them. What was previously mentioned indicates this, and what will come later will further support it in hadiths about those who consider tanned dead animals permissible, and in hadiths about predator hides and others, insha'Allah.

CHAPTER 2

Permissibility Of Prayer In Fur, Leather, Wool, Hair, Animal Hair And Similar Materials If From Edible Animals With The Condition Of Proper Slaughter For Leather

[Hadith 5344 to 5351]

Hadith 5344

عن ابن بكير قال: سأل زرارة أبا عبد الله (عليه السلام) عن الصلاة في الثعالب والفنك، والسنجاب وغيره من الوبر؟ فأخرج كتابا زعم أنه إملاء رسول الله (صلى الله عليه وآله): أن الصلاة في وبر كل شئ حرام أكله فالصلاة في وبره وشعره وجلده وبوله وروثه وكل شئ منه فاسد، لاتقبل تلك الصلاة حتى يصلي في غيره مما أحل الله أكله،

From Ibn Bukayr who said: Zurarah asked Abu Abdullah (peace be upon him) about praying in fox fur, fennec fox fur, squirrel fur and other animal hair. He brought out a book which he claimed was dictated by the Messenger of Allah (peace be upon him and his family): Prayer in the hair of any animal forbidden to eat - its hair, fur, skin, urine, dung and everything from it is invalid. Such prayer is not accepted until one prays in something Allah has made permissible to eat.

ثم قال: يا زرارة، هذا عن رسول الله (صلى الله عليه وآله) فاحفظ ذلك يا زرارة، فإن كان مما يؤكل لحمه فالصلاة في وبره وبوله وشعره وروثه وألبانه وكل شئ منه ذكي جائز إذا علمت أنه ذكي قد ذكاه الذبح. وإن كان غير ذلك مما قد نهيت عن أكله وحرم عليك أكله فالصلاة في كل شئ منه فاسد، ذكاه الذبح أو لم يذكه.

Then he said: O Zurarah, this is from the Messenger of Allah (peace be upon him and his family), so remember this O Zurarah. If it is from what is permissible to eat, then prayer in its hair, urine, fur, dung, milk and everything from it is permissible when you know it was properly slaughtered. If it is from what you are forbidden to eat, then prayer in anything from it is invalid, whether slaughtered properly or not.

Hadith 5345

عن علي بن أبي حمزة قال: سألت أبا عبد الله (عليه السلام) أو أبا الحسن (عليه السلام) عن لباس الفراء والصلاة فيها؟ فقال: لا تصل فيها إلا ما كان منه ذكيا. قال: قلت: أوليس الذكي مما ذكي بالحديد؟ قال: بلى إذا كان مما يؤكل لحمه.

From Ali ibn Abi Hamza, he said: I asked Abu Abdullah or Abu al-Hasan (peace be upon them) about wearing fur and praying in it. He said: Do not pray in it except what was properly slaughtered. I asked: Isn't proper slaughter what is slaughtered with iron? He said: Yes, when it is from what is permissible to eat.

Hadith 5346

عن أبي تمامة قال: قلت لأبي جعفر الثاني (عليه السلام): إن بلادنا بلاد باردة فما تقول في لبس هذا الوبر؟ فقال: إلبس منها ما أكل وضمن.

From Abu Tamama, he said: I said to Abu Ja'far the Second (peace be upon him): Our land is cold, so what do you say about wearing this animal hair? He said: Wear from it what is eaten and guaranteed.

Hadith 5347

عن إبراهيم بن محمد الهمداني قال: كتبت إليه: يسقط على ثوبي الوبر والشعر مما لا يؤكل لحمه من غير تقية ولا ضرورة، فكتب: لا تجوز الصلاة فيه.

From Ibrahim ibn Muhammad al-Hamdani, I wrote to him (the Imam): Animal hair and fur from inedible animals falls on my clothes without taqiyyah or necessity. He wrote back: Prayer in it is not permissible.

Hadith 5348

عن الحسن بن علي الوشاء قال: كان أبو عبد الله (عليه السلام) يكره الصلاة في وبر كل شئ لا يؤكل لحمه.

From Al-Hasan ibn Ali al-Washa, he said: Abu Abdullah (peace be upon him) disliked prayer in the hair of anything whose meat is not eaten.

Hadith 5349

عن جعفر بن محمد، عن آبائه، (عليهم السلام) في وصية النبي (صلى الله عليه وآله) لعلي (عليه السلام) قال: يا علي، لا تصل في جلد مالا يشرب لبنه ولا يؤكل لحمه.

From Ja'far ibn Muhammad, from his forefathers (peace be upon them), in the Prophet's (peace be upon him and his family) advice to Ali (peace be upon him) said: O Ali, do not pray in the skin of what its milk is not drunk and its meat is not eaten.

Hadith 5350

عن محمد بن إسماعيل بإسناده يرفعه إلى أبي عبد الله (عليه السلام) قال: لا تجوز الصلاة في شعر ووبر ما لا يؤكل لحمه لان أكثرها مسوخ.

From Muhammad ibn Isma'il, with his chain reaching to Abu Abdullah (peace be upon him) said: Prayer is not permissible in the hair and fur of what is not permissible to eat because most of them are transformed beings.

Hadith 5351

الحسن بن علي بن شعبة في (تحف العقول) عن الصادق (عليه السلام) - في حديث - قال: وكل ما أنبتت الأرض فلا بأس بلبسه والصلاة فيه. وكل شئ يحل لحمه فلا بأس بلبس جلده الذكي منه وصوفه وشعره ووبره، وإن كان الصوف والشعر والريش والوبر من الميتة وغير الميتة ذكيا فلا بأس بلبس ذلك والصلاة فيه.

From Al-Hasan bin Ali bin Shu'bah in (Tuhaf al-Uqul), from Al-Sadiq (peace be upon him) who said in a hadith: Everything that grows from the earth is permissible to wear and pray in, and everything whose meat is permissible to eat, it is also permissible to wear its tanned hide, wool, hair and fur. If the wool, hair, feathers and fur are from a dead animal or from a non-slaughtered animal but have been tanned, then it is permissible to wear them and pray in them.

CHAPTER 3

Permissibility Of Prayer In Squirrel Fur, Fur Garments, And Crop Pelts

[Hadith 5352 to 5358]

Hadith 5352

عن الحلبي عن أبي عبد الله (عليه السلام) أنه سأل عن أشياء منها الفرا والسنجاب؟ فقال: لا بأس بالصلاة فيه.

From Al-Halabi, from Abu Abdullah (peace be upon him) that he asked about various things including fur and squirrel fur. He replied: There is no problem praying in it.

———

Hadith 5353

عن مقاتل بن مقاتل قال: سألت أبا الحسن (عليه السلام) عن الصلاة في السمور والسنجاب والثعلب؟ فقال: لا خير في ذا كله ما خلا السنجاب فإنه دابة لا تأكل اللحم.

From Muqatil bin Muqatil, he said: I asked Abu Al-Hasan (peace be upon him) about praying in sable, squirrel, and fox fur. He said: There is no good in any of these except squirrel fur, for it is a creature that does not eat meat.

———

Hadith 5354

عن علي بن أبي حمزة قال: سألت أبا عبد الله وأبا الحسن (عليهما السلام) عن لباس الفراء والصلاة فيها؟ فقال: لا تصل فيها إلا ما كان منه ذكيا، قال: قلت: أوليس الذكي مما ذكي بالحديد؟ قال: بلى، إذا كان مما يؤكل لحمه، قلت: وما لا يؤكل لحمه من غير الغنم؟ قال: لا بأس بالسنجاب فإنه دابة لا تأكل اللحم، وليس هو مما نهى عنه رسول الله (صلى الله عليه وآله)، إن نهى عن كل ذي ناب ومخلب.

From Ali bin Abi Hamza he said: I asked Abu Abdullah and Abu Al-Hasan (peace be upon them) about wearing fur garments and praying in them. He said: Do not pray in them except what was properly slaughtered. I asked: Isn't proper slaughter what is slaughtered with iron? He said: Yes, if it is from what its meat can be eaten. I asked: What about those whose meat is not eaten other than sheep? He said: There is no problem with squirrel fur for it is a creature that does not eat meat, and it is not from what the Messenger of Allah (peace be upon him and his family) prohibited when he prohibited every beast with fangs and claws.

———

Hadith 5355

عن بشير بن بشار قال: سألته عن الصلاة في الفنك والفرا والسنجاب والسمور والحواصل التي تصاد ببلاد الشرك أو بلاد الاسلام (أن أصلي) فيه لغير تقية؟ قال: فقال: صل في السنجاب والحواصل الخوارزمية، ولا تصل في الثعالب ولا السمور.

From Bashir bin Bashar, he said: I asked him about praying in fennec fox fur, fur garments, squirrel fur, sable, and crop pelts that are hunted in polytheist lands or Muslim lands (to pray) in them without taqiyyah? He said: Pray in squirrel fur and Khwarazmian crop pelts, but do not pray in fox or sable fur.

Hadith 5356

عن أبي علي ابن راشد قال: قلت لأبي جعفر (عليه السلام): ما تقول في الفراء أي شئ يصلي فيه؟ قال: أي الفراء؟ قلت: الفنك والسنجاب والسمور، قال: فصل في الفنك والسنجاب، فأما السمور فلا تصل فيه.

From Abu Ali ibn Rashid he said: I said to Abu Ja'far (peace be upon him): What do you say about fur garments, which ones can one pray in? He said: Which furs? I said: Fennec fox, squirrel, and sable. He said: Pray in fennec fox and squirrel fur, but as for sable, do not pray in it.

Hadith 5357

عن يحيى بن أبي عمران أنه قال: كتبت إلى أبي جعفر الثاني (عليه السلام) في السنجاب والفنك والخز، وقلت: جعلت فداك أحب أن لا تجيبني بالتقية في ذلك، فكتب بخطه إلي: صل فيها.

From Yahya bin Abi Imran, he said: I wrote to Abu Ja'far the Second (peace be upon him) about squirrel fur, fennec fox fur, and silk blend, saying: May I be sacrificed for you, I would like you not to answer me with taqiyyah in this matter. He wrote back in his handwriting: Pray in them.

Hadith 5358

عن الوليد بن أبان قال: قلت للرضا (عليه السلام): أصلي في الفنك والسنجاب؟ قال: نعم.

From Al-Walid bin Aban, he said: I said to Al-Ridha (peace be upon him): Should I pray in fennec fox and squirrel fur? He said: Yes.

CHAPTER 4

Prohibition Of Prayer While Wearing Sable And Fennec Fox Fur Except In Taqiyya And Necessity

[Hadith 5359 to 5364]

Hadith 5359

عن الرضا (عليه السلام) قال: سألته عن جلود السمور؟ فقال: أي شئ هو ذاك الادبس؟ فقلت: هو الأسود، فقال: يصيد؟ قلت: نعم، يأخذ الدجاج والحمام، فقال: لا.

From Al-Ridha (peace be upon him): I asked him about sable furs? He said: What is that dark thing? I said: It is black. He asked: Does it hunt? I said: Yes, it catches chickens and pigeons. He said: No.

Hadith 5360

عن أبي عبد الله (عليه السلام) قال: سألته عن الفرا والسمور والسنجاب والثعالب وأشباهه؟ قال: لا بأس بالصلاة فيه. أقول: حكم ما عدا السنجاب والفرا هنا محمول على التقية لما مضى ويأتي، ذكره الشيخ وغيره.

From Abu Abdullah (peace be upon him): I asked him about fox fur, sable, squirrel, and similar furs? He said: There is no problem praying in them. I (Hurr Amili) say: The ruling for all except squirrel and fox fur here is interpreted as taqiyyah based on previous and upcoming evidence, as mentioned by Shaykh and others.

Hadith 5361

عن محمد بن علي بن عيسى، قال: كتبت إلى الشيخ يعني الهادي (عليه السلام) أسأله عن الصلاة في الوبر أي أصنافه أصلح؟ فأجاب: لا أحب الصلاة في شئ منه، قال: فرددت الجواب إنا مع قوم في تقية وبلادنا بلاد لا يمكن أحدا أن يسافر فيها بلا وبر ولا يأمن على نفسه إن هو نزع وبره، وليس يمكن للناس ما يمكن للأئمة فما الذي ترى أن نعمل به في هذا الباب؟ قال فرجع الجواب إلي: تلبس الفنك والسمور.

From Muhammad bin Ali bin Isa: I wrote to the Shaykh meaning Al-Hadi (peace be upon him) asking about prayer in fur - which types are most appropriate? He responded: I do not like prayer in any of them. I replied explaining we are among people requiring taqiyyah and our lands are such that none can travel without fur nor feel safe if they remove their fur, and people cannot do what the Imams can do, so what do you advise us to do in this matter? His response came back: Wear fennec and sable.

Hadith 5362

عن سفيان بن السمط - في حديث - قال: وقرأت في كتاب محمد بن إبراهيم إلى أبي الحسن (عليه السلام) يسأله عن الفنك يصلي فيه؟ فكتب: لا بأس به. وكتب يسأله عن جلود الأرانب، فكتب: مكروهة.

From Sufyan bin al-Samt in a hadith: I read in Muhammad bin Ibrahim's letter to Abu al-Hasan (peace be upon him) asking about praying in fennec fur? He wrote back: There is no problem with it. And he wrote asking about rabbit skins, he wrote back: It is disliked.

Hadith 5363

الحسن بن الفضل الطبرسي في (مكارم الأخلاق) قال: وسئل الرضا (عليه السلام) عن جلود الثعالب والسنجاب والسمور؟ فقال: قد رأيت السنجاب على أبي، ونهاني عن الثعالب والسمور.

Al-Hasan bin al-Fadhl al-Tabarsi reported in Makarim al-Akhlaq: Al-Ridha (peace be upon him) was asked about fox, squirrel and sable furs? He said: I saw squirrel fur on my father, and he forbade me from fox and sable.

Hadith 5364

عن أخيه موسى بن جعفر (عليهم السلام) قال: سألته عن لبس السمور والسنجاب والفنك؟ فقال: لا يلبس ولا يصلى فيه إلا أن يكون ذكيا.

From his brother Musa bin Ja'far (peace be upon them): I asked him about wearing sable, squirrel and fennec? He said: It should not be worn nor prayed in unless it is properly slaughtered.

أقول: هذا مخصوص بالسنجاب لما مر، وحكم غيره محمول إما على التقية، أو الضرورة لما تقدم.

I (Hurr Amili) say: This applies specifically to squirrel based on what preceded, and the ruling for others is interpreted either as taqiyyah or necessity based on what was presented earlier.

CHAPTER 5

Permissibility Of Wearing Skins Of Animals Whose Meat Is Not Eaten If Properly Slaughtered, And Their Hair, Fur And Wool

[Hadith 5365 to 5370]

Hadith 5365

عن علي بن يقطين قال: سألت أبا الحسن (عليه السلام) عن لباس الفراء والسمور والفنك والثعالب وجميع الجلود؟ قال: لا بأس بذلك.

From Ali ibn Yaqtin, he said: I asked Abu al-Hasan (peace be upon him) about wearing fur of sable, ermine, fennec fox, foxes and all types of skins? He said: There is no problem with that.

Hadith 5366

عن الريان بن الصلت قال: سألت أبا الحسن الرضا (عليه السلام) عن لبس فراء السمور والسنجاب والحواصل وما أشبهها، والمناطق والكيمخت والمحشو بالقز والخفاف من أصناف الجلود؟ فقال: لا بأس بهذا كله إلا بالثعالب.

From Al-Rayyan ibn al-Salt who said: I asked Abu al-Hasan al-Ridha (peace be upon him) about wearing fur of sable, squirrel, pouches and similar items, and belts, treated leather, silk-filled items and shoes made from various types of leather? He said: There is no problem with any of these except foxes.

Hadith 5367

عن سماعة قال: سألته عن لحوم السباع وجلودها؟ فقال: أما لحوم السباع فمن الطير والدواب فإنا نكرهه، وأما الجلود فاركبوا عليها ولا تلبسوا منها شيئا تصلون فيه.

From Sama'ah who said: I asked him about the meat of predatory animals and their skins? He said: As for the meat of predatory animals, whether birds or beasts, we dislike it, and as for the skins, you may ride upon them but do not wear anything from them in which you pray.

Hadith 5368

عن سماعة قال: سئل أبو عبد الله (عليه السلام) عن جلود السباع؟ فقال: اركبوها ولا تلبسوا منها شيئا تصلون فيه.

From Sama'ah who said: Abu Abdullah (peace be upon him) was asked about the skins of predatory animals? He said: Ride upon them but do not wear anything from them while you pray.

Translator: In the arabic edition, Hadith 5367 and 5368 are combined into a single hadith.

Hadith 5369

عن علي بن جعفر، عن أخيه قال: سألته عن ركوب جلود السباع؟ فقال: لا بأس ما لم يسجد عليها.

From Ali ibn Ja'far, from his brother who said: I asked him about riding on predator skins? He said: There is no problem as long as one does not prostrate on them.

Hadith 5370

عن سماعة قال: سئل أبو عبد الله (عليه السلام) عن جلود السباع؟ فقال: اركبوها ولا تلبسوا شيئا منها تصلون فيه.

From Sama'ah who said: Abu Abdullah (peace be upon him) was asked about the skins of predatory animals? He said: Ride on them but do not wear anything from them while praying.

أقول: هذا مخصوص بوقت الصلاة كما مر في هذه الرواية بعينها، ويحتمل الحمل على عدم الذكاة، وعلى الكراهة لما مر، ويأتي ما يدل على ذلك، وتقدم ما يدل على نجاسة الكلب والخنزير والميتة.

I (Hurr Amili) say: This is specific to prayer time as mentioned in this very narration, and it could mean when not properly slaughtered, or indicate dislike as mentioned before, and evidence for this will come later, and previous narrations indicated the impurity of dogs, pigs and carrion.

CHAPTER 6

Prohibition Of Prayer In Predatory Animal Skins, Their Hair, Fur, And Wool

[Hadith 5371 to 5374]

Hadith 5371

عن إسماعيل بن سعد بن الأحوص قال: سألت أبا الحسن الرضا (عليه السلام) عن الصلاة في جلود السباع؟ فقال: لا تصل فيها.

From Isma'il bin Sa'd bin Al-Ahwas who said: I asked Abu Al-Hasan Al-Ridha (peace be upon him) about praying in predatory animal skins? He said: Do not pray in them.

Hadith 5372

عن قاسم الخياط أنه قال: سمعت موسى بن جعفر (عليه السلام) يقول: ما أكل الورق والشجر فلا بأس بأن يصلي فيه، وما أكل الميتة فلا تصل فيه.

From Qasim Al-Khayyat who said: I heard Musa bin Ja'far (peace be upon him) saying: Whatever eats leaves and trees, there is no problem praying in it, and whatever eats carrion, do not pray in it.

Hadith 5373

عن الفضل بن شاذان، عن الرضا (عليه السلام) في كتابه إلى المأمون قال: ولا يصلى في جلود السباع.

From Al-Fadhl bin Shadhan, from Al-Ridha (peace be upon him) in his letter to Al-Ma'mun said: And one should not pray in predatory animal skins.

Hadith 5374

عن جعفر بن محمد (عليه السلام) - في حديث شرائع الدين - قال: ولا يصلى في جلود الميتة وإن دبغت سبعين مرة ولا في جلود السباع.

From Ja'far bin Muhammad (peace be upon him) - in a hadith about religious laws - he said: One should not pray in dead animal skins even if tanned seventy times, nor in predatory animal skins.

CHAPTER 7

Prohibition Of Prayer In Fox And Rabbit Skins And Their Fur Even If Slaughtered Properly, The Dislike Of Praying In Clothes That Touch Them, And The Permissibility Of Wearing Them Outside Prayer When Properly Slaughtered

[Hadith 5375 to 5386]

Hadith 5375

عن محمد بن مسلم قال: سألت أبا عبد الله (عليه السلام) عن جلود الثعالب أيصلي فيها؟ فقال: ما أحب أن أصلي فيها.

From Muhammad bin Muslim, he said: I asked Abu Abdullah (peace be upon him) about fox skins, can one pray in them? He said: I do not like to pray in them.

Hadith 5376

وعنه، عن محمد بن إبراهيم قال: كتبت إليه أسأله عن الصلاة في جلود الأرانب؟ فكتب: مكروه. أقول: الكراهة محمولة على التحريم، أو على الضرورة، أو التقية: لما مضى ويأتي.

From him, from Muhammad bin Ibrahim who said: I wrote to him asking about praying in rabbit skins? He wrote back: It is disapproved. I (Hurr Amili) say: The disapproval here implies prohibition, or applies to cases of necessity or taqiyyah, based on what has preceded and what will follow.

Hadith 5377

عن علي بن مهزيار قال: كتب إليه إبراهيم بن عقبة: عندنا جوارب وتكك تعمل من وبر الأرانب، فهل تجوز الصلاة في وبر الأرانب، من غير ضرورة ولا تقية؟ فكتب (عليه السلام): لا تجوز الصلاة فيها.

From Ali bin Mahziyar who said: Ibrahim bin Uqbah wrote to him: We have socks and waistbands made from rabbit fur, is prayer permitted in rabbit fur without necessity or taqiyyah? He (peace be upon him) wrote back: Prayer is not permitted in them.

Hadith 5378

عن أبي علي بن راشد - في حديث - قال: قلت لأبي جعفر (عليه السلام): الثعالب يصلى فيها؟ قال: لا ولكن تلبس بعد الصلاة، قلت أصلي في الثوب الذي يليه؟ قال: لا.

From Abu Ali bin Rashid - in a hadith - who said: I asked Abu Ja'far (peace be upon him): Can one pray in fox skins? He said: No, but they can be worn after prayer. I asked: Can I pray in clothes that touch it? He said: No.

Hadith 5379

عن أحمد بن إسحاق الأبهري قال: كتبت إليه: جعلت فداك عندنا جوارب وتكك تعمل من وبر الأرانب، فهل تجوز الصلاة في وبر الأرانب من غير ضرورة ولا تقية؟ فكتب: لا تجوز الصلاة فيها.

From Ahmad bin Ishaq al-Abhari, he said: I wrote to him: May I be your ransom, we have socks and waistbands made from rabbit fur, is prayer permitted in rabbit fur without necessity or taqiyyah? He wrote: Prayer is not permitted in them.

Hadith 5380

عن جعفر بن محمد بن أبي زيد قال: سأل الرضا (عليه السلام) عن جلود الثعالب الذكية؟ قال: لا تصل فيها.

From Ja'far bin Muhammad bin Abi Zayd who said: Al-Ridha (peace be upon him) was asked about properly slaughtered fox skins? He said: Do not pray in them.

Hadith 5381

عن الوليد بن أبان - في حديث - قال: قلت للرضا (عليه السلام): يصلي في الثعالب إذا كانت ذكية؟ قال: لا تصل فيها.

From Al-Walid bin Aban - in a hadith - who said: I said to Al-Ridha (peace be upon him): Can one pray in fox skins if they are properly slaughtered? He said: Do not pray in them.

Hadith 5382

عن علي بن مهزيار، عن رجل سأل الماضي (عليه السلام) عن الصلاة في جلود الثعالب؟ فنهي عن الصلاة فيها وفي الثوب الذي يليه، فلم أدر أي الثوبين الذي يلصق بالوبر أو الذي يلصق بالجلد؟ فوقع بخطه: الثوب الذي يلصق بالجلد. قال: وذكر أبو الحسن يعني علي بن مهزيار أنه سأله عن هذه المسألة، فقال: لا تصل في الذي فوقه ولا في الذي تحته.

From Ali ibn Mahziyar, from a man who asked Al-Madhi (peace be upon him) about praying in fox skins? He prohibited praying in them and in the garment next to it. I did not know which of the two garments - the one touching the fur or the one touching the skin? He wrote in his handwriting: The garment that touches the skin. Ali ibn Mahziyar, meaning Abu Al-Hasan, mentioned that he asked him about this matter, and he said: Do not pray in what is above it nor in what is below it.

Hadith 5383

عن أبي عبد الله (عليه السلام) قال: سألته عن الصلاة في جلود الثعالب؟ فقال، إذا كانت ذكية فلا بأس.

قال الشيخ: يجوز أن يكون ورد لضرب من التقية لأنه موافق لمذهب جميع العامة.

From Abu Abdullah (peace be upon him), he said: I asked him about praying in fox skins? He said: If they are properly slaughtered, there is no problem. The Shaykh said: This may have been said as a form of taqiyyah because it agrees with the doctrine of all the Aammah (general sunni public).

Hadith 5384

عن أبي عبد الله (عليه السلام) قال: سألته عن جلود الثعالب إذا كانت ذكية أيصلي فيها؟ قال: نعم.

From Abu Abdullah (peace be upon him), he said: I asked him about fox skins if they are properly slaughtered, can one pray in them? He said: Yes.

Hadith 5385

عن عبد الرحمن بن الحجاج قال: سألته عن اللحاف من الثعالب أو الجرز منه أيصلي فيها أم لا؟ قال: إن كان ذكيا فلا بأس به.

From Abd al-Rahman ibn Al-Hajjaj, he said: I asked him about blankets made of fox fur or pieces of it, can one pray in them or not? He said: If it is properly slaughtered, there is no problem with it.

Hadith 5386

أحمد بن علي بن أبي طالب الطبرسي في (الاحتجاج): عن محمد بن عبد الله بن جعفر الحميري، عن صاحب الزمان (عليه السلام) أنه كتب إليه: قد سأل بعض العلماء عن معنى قول الصادق (عليه السلام): لا تصل في الثعلب ولا في الأرنب ولا في الثوب الذي يليه؟ فقال (عليه السلام): إنما عنى الجلود دون غيرها.

Ahmad ibn Ali ibn Abi Talib Al-Tabarsi in (Al-Ihtijaj): From Muhammad ibn Abdullah ibn Ja'far Al-Himyari, from the Master of the Time (peace be upon him) that it was written to him: Some scholars asked about the meaning of Al-Sadiq's (peace be upon him) statement: "Do not pray in fox skin, nor in rabbit skin, nor in the garment next to it?" He (peace be upon him) said: He only meant the skins, not anything else.

CHAPTER 8

Permissibility Of Praying In Pure Khazz Fur And Its Pure Fleece
[Hadith 5387 to 5392]

Hadith 5387

عن سليمان بن جعفر الجعفري أنه قال رأيت الرضا (عليه السلام) يصلي في جبة خز.

From Sulayman bin Ja'far al-Ja'fari, he said: I saw Al-Ridha (peace be upon him) praying while wearing a khazz cloak.

Hadith 5388

عن علي بن مهزيار قال: رأيت أبا جعفر الثاني (عليه السلام) يصلي الفريضة وغيرها في جبة خز طاروي، وكساني جبة خز وذكر أنه لبسها على بدنه وصلى فيها وأمرني بالصلاة فيها.

From Ali bin Mahziyar who said: I saw Abu Ja'far the Second (peace be upon him) performing obligatory and other prayers while wearing a Tarawi khazz cloak. He gave me a khazz cloak and mentioned that he wore it on his body and prayed in it, and he ordered me to pray in it.

Hadith 5389

عن زرارة قال: خرج أبو جعفر (عليه السلام) يصلي على بعض أطفالهم وعليه جبة خز صفراء ومطرف خز أصفر.

From Zurarah who said: Abu Ja'far (peace be upon him) went out to pray for one of their children while wearing a yellow khazz cloak and a yellow khazz shawl.

Hadith 5390

عن ابن أبي يعفور قال: كنت عند أبي عبد الله (عليه السلام) إذ دخل عليه رجل من الخزازين فقال له: جعلت فداك ما تقول في الصلاة في الخز؟ فقال: لا بأس بالصلاة فيه،

From Ibn Abi Yafur who said: I was with Abu Abdullah (peace be upon him) when a khazz merchant entered and said to him: May I be sacrificed for you, what do you say about praying in khazz? He replied: There is no problem praying in it.

فقال له الرجل: جعلت فداك إنه ميت وهو علاجي وأنا أعرفه، فقال له أبو عبد الله (عليه السلام): أنا أعرف به منك، فقال له الرجل: إنه علاجي وليس أحد أعرف به مني فتبسم أبو عبد الله (عليه السلام) ثم قال له: أتقول: إنه دابة تخرج من الماء أو تصاد من الماء فتخرج فإذا فقد الماء مات؟ فقال الرجل: صدقت جعلت فداك هكذا هو،

The man said: May I be sacrificed for you, it is dead and it is my trade and I know about it. Abu Abdullah (peace be upon him) said: I know more about it than you. The man said: It is my trade and no one knows more about it than me. Abu Abdullah (peace be upon him) smiled and said to him: Are you saying it is a creature that comes out of water or is hunted from water, and when it loses water it dies? The man said: You speak the truth, may I be sacrificed for you, that is how it is.

فقال له أبو عبد الله (عليه السلام): فإنك تقول: إنه دابة تمشي على أربع وليس هو في حد الحيتان فتكون ذكاته خروجه من الماء، فقال الرجل: أي والله هكذا أقول، فقال له أبو عبد الله (عليه السلام): فإن الله تعالى أحله وجعل ذكاته موته كما أحل الحيتان وجعل ذكاتها موتها.

Abu Abdullah (peace be upon him) said to him: You are saying it is a creature that walks on four legs and is not in the category of fish so its slaughter would be its exit from water? The man said: Yes, by Allah, that is what I say. Abu Abdullah (peace be upon him) said: Indeed Allah the Exalted has made it permissible and made its death its slaughter just as He made fish permissible and made their death their slaughter.

أقول: ذكر جماعة من علمائنا أنه ليس المراد هنا حل لحمه، لما يأتي، بل حل استعمال جلده ووبره والصلاة فيهما.

I (Hurr Amili) say: A group of our scholars mentioned that what is meant here is not the permissibility of its meat, as will be discussed later, but rather the permissibility of using its skin and fur and praying in them.

Hadith 5391

عن معمر بن خلاد قال: سألت أبا الحسن الرضا (عليه السلام) عن الصلاة في الخز؟ فقال: صل فيه.

From Muammar bin Khallad who said: I asked Abu al-Hasan al-Ridha (peace be upon him) about praying in khazz? He said: Pray in it.

Hadith 5392

وقد تقدم حديث دعبل أن الرضا (عليه السلام) خلع عليه قميصا من خز وقال له: احتفظ بهذا القميص فقد صليت فيه ألف ليلة كل ليلة ألف ركعة.

The previous hadith of Di'bil has been mentioned that Al-Ridha (peace be upon him) gave him a khazz shirt and said to him: Keep this shirt for I have prayed in it for a thousand nights, a thousand rak'ahs each night.

CHAPTER 9

Impermissibility Of Praying In Adulterated Khazz With The Fleece Of Rabbits, Foxes, And Similar Animals

[Hadith 5393 to 5394]

Hadith 5393

عن أيوب بن نوح رفعه قال: قال أبو عبد الله (عليه السلام): الصلاة في الخز الخالص لا بأس به، فأما الذي يخلط فيه وبر الأرانب أو غير ذلك مما يشبه هذا فلا تصل فيه.

From Ayyub bin Nuh, raising it, he said: Abu Abdullah (peace be upon him) said: Praying in pure khazz (*), there is no problem with it. As for that in which rabbit fleece or other than that which resembles this is mixed, do not pray in it.

Translator: * See Hadith 5390 for a description of khazz.

Hadith 5394

عن بشر بن بشار قال: سألته عن الصلاة في الخز يغش بوبر الأرانب؟ فكتب: يجوز ذلك.

From Bishr bin Bashar who said: I asked him about praying in khazz adulterated with rabbit fleece? He wrote: That is permissible.

أقول: حمله الشيخ على التقية لما مر، ويمكن الحمل على الضرورة، وعلى الانكار، ويأتي ما يدل على المقصود.

I (Hurr Amili) say: The Shaykh interpreted it as taqiyyah due to what has passed, and it is possible to interpret it as necessity, and as denial, and there will come what indicates the intended meaning.

CHAPTER 10

Permissibility Of Wearing The Skin Of Khazz And Its Fleece Even If It Is Adulterated With Silk

[Hadith 5395 to 5410]

Hadith 5395

عن عبد الرحمان بن الحجاج قال: سأل أبا عبد الله (عليه السلام) رجل وأنا عنده عن جلود الخز؟ فقال: ليس بها بأس، فقال الرجل: جعلت فداك إنها علاجي وإنما هي كلاب تخرج من الماء، فقال أبو عبد الله (عليه السلام): إذا خرجت من الماء تعيش خارجة من الماء؟ فقال الرجل: لا، قال: (ليس به بأس).

From Abdur Rahman bin al-Hajjaj who said: A man asked Abu Abdullah (peace be upon him) while I was with him about the skins of khazz (*)? He said: There is no problem with them. The man said: May I be your ransom, it is my profession and they are just dogs that come out of the water. Abu Abdullah (peace be upon him) said: When they come out of the water, do they live outside of the water? The man said: No. He said: (There is no problem with it).

Translator: * See Hadith 5390 for a description of khazz.

Hadith 5396

عن أبي داود ابن يوسف بن إبراهيم قال: دخلت على أبي عبد الله (عليه السلام) وعلي قباء خز وبطانته خز وطيلسان خز مرتفع، فقلت: إن علي ثوبا أكره لبسه، فقال: وما هو؟ قلت طيلساني هذا، قال: وما بال الطيلسان؟ قلت: هو خز، قال: وما بال الخز؟ قلت: سداه إبريسم: قال: وما بال الإبريسم؟ قال: لا تكره أن يكون سدا الثوب إبريسم.

From Abu Dawud Ibn Yusuf bin Ibrahim who said: I entered upon Abu Abdullah (peace be upon him) while wearing a khazz robe with a khazz lining and a high khazz cloak. I said: I am wearing a garment I dislike wearing. He said: And what is it? I said: This cloak of mine. He said: And what's wrong with the cloak? I said: It is khazz. He said: And what's wrong with khazz? I said: Its warp is silk. He said: And what's wrong with silk? He said: Do not dislike that the warp of the garment is silk.

Hadith 5397

عن أبي جعفر (عليه السلام) قال: إنا معاشر آل محمد نلبس الخز واليمنة.

From Abu Ja'far (peace be upon him) who said: We, the family of Muhammad, wear khazz and Yemeni garments.

Hadith 5398

عن جعفر بن عيسى قال: كتبت إلى أبي الحسن الرضا (عليه السلام) أسأله عن الدواب التي يعمل الخز من وبرها، أسباع هي؟ فكتب: لبس الخز الحسين بن علي ومن بعده جدي (صلوات الله عليهم).

From Ja'far bin Isa who said: I wrote to Abu al-Hasan al-Ridha (peace be upon him) asking him about the animals from whose fleece khazz is made, are they predators? He wrote: Al-Husayn bin Ali and my grandfather after him wore khazz (peace be upon them).

Hadith 5399

عن أبي الحسن الرضا (عليه السلام) قال: كان علي بن الحسين (عليه السلام) يلبس الجبة الخز بخمسين دينارا والمطرف الخز بخمسين دينارا.

From Abu al-Hasan al-Ridha (peace be upon him) who said: Ali bin al-Husayn (peace be upon him) used to wear a khazz cloak for fifty dinars and a khazz shawl for fifty dinars.

Hadith 5400

عن أبي الحسن الرضا (عليه السلام) قال: سمعته يقول: كان علي بن الحسين (عليه السلام) يلبس في الشتاء الجبة الخز والمطرف الخز والقلنسوة الخز فيشتو فيه ويبيع المطرف في الصيف ويتصدق بثمنه ثم يقول: (حرم زينة الله التي أخرج لعباده والطيبات من الرزق).

From Abu al-Hasan al-Ridha (peace be upon him) who said: I heard him say: Ali bin al-Husayn (peace be upon him) used to wear in winter a khazz cloak, a khazz shawl, and a khazz cap. He would spend winter in it and sell the shawl in summer and give its price in sadaqah. Then he would say: (Who has forbidden the adornment of Allah which He has brought forth for His servants, and the good things of His provision).

Hadith 5401

عن يوسف بن إبراهيم قال: دخلت على أبي عبد الله (عليه السلام) وعلي جبة خز وطيلسان خز فنظر إلي فقلت: جعلت فداك علي جبة خز وطيلساني هذا خز، فما تقول فيه؟ فقال: وما بأس بالخز، فقلت: وسداه إبريسم، قال: وما بأس بالإبريسم، قد أصيب الحسين (عليه السلام) وعليه جبة خز.

From Yusuf bin Ibrahim who said: I entered upon Abu Abdullah (peace be upon him) while wearing a khazz cloak and a khazz shawl. He looked at me and I said: May I be your ransom, I am wearing a khazz cloak and this shawl of mine is khazz, so what do you say about it? He said: And what's wrong with khazz? I said: And its warp is silk. He said: And what's wrong with silk? Al-Husayn (peace be upon him) was martyred while wearing a khazz cloak.

Hadith 5402

عن أبي جعفر (عليه السلام) قال: قتل الحسين بن علي (عليه السلام) وعليه جبة خز دكناء فوجدوا فيها ثلاثة وستين من بين ضربة بسيف أو طعنة برمح أو رمية بسهم.

From Abu Ja'far (peace be upon him) who said: Al-Husayn bin Ali (peace be upon him) was killed while wearing a dark khazz cloak, and they found in it sixty-three wounds between sword strikes, spear thrusts, and arrow shots.

Hadith 5403

عن يعقوب بن جعفر أنه كان عند أبي إبراهيم فاحتج على راهب بكلام طويل حتى أسلم فدعى أبو إبراهيم (عليه السلام) بجبة خز وقميص قوهي وطيلسان وخف وقلنسوة فأعطاه إياه.

From Ya'qub bin Ja'far that he was with Abu Ibrahim who argued with a monk in a long discourse until he converted to Islam. Then Abu Ibrahim (peace be upon him) called for a khazz cloak, a Quhi shirt, a shawl, shoes, and a cap, and gave them to him.

Hadith 5404

عن الرضا (عليه السلام) في حديث أن علي بن الحسين (عليه السلام) كان يلبس الجبة الخز بخمسمائة درهم والمطرف الخز بخمسين دينارا فيشتو فيه فإذا خرج الشتاء باعه وتصدق بثمنه.

From al-Ridha (peace be upon him) in a hadith that Ali bin al-Husayn (peace be upon him) used to wear a khazz cloak for five hundred dirhams and a khazz shawl for fifty dinars. He would spend winter in it, and when winter ended, he would sell it and give its price in sadaqah.

Hadith 5405

عن حفص بن محمد مؤذن علي بن يقطين قال: رأيت أبا عبد الله (عليه السلام) في الروضة وعليه جبة خز سفر جلية. ورواه الكليني عن عدة من أصحابنا، عن سهل بن زياد، عن محمد بن عيسى، عن حفص بن عمر أبي محمد، مثله، إلا أنه قال: وهو يصلي في الروضة.

From Hafs bin Muhammad, the muezzin of Ali bin Yaqtin, who said: I saw Abu Abdullah (peace be upon him) in the Rawdah wearing a light-colored travel khazz cloak. Al-Kulayni narrated it from a number of our companions, from Sahl bin Ziyad, from Muhammad bin Isa, from Hafs bin Umar Abu Muhammad, similar to it, except that he said: And he was praying in the Rawdah.

Hadith 5406

عن جعفر بن محمد، عن أبيه قال: كسا علي (عليه السلام) الناس بالكوفة فكان في الكسوة برنس خز، فسأله إياه الحسن فأبي أن يعطيه إياه وأسهم عليه بين المسلمين فصار لفتى من همدان فانقلب به الهمداني، فقيل له: إن حسنا كان سأله أباه فمنعه إياه، فأرسل به الهمداني إلى الحسن فقبله.

From Ja'far bin Muhammad, from his father who said: Ali (peace be upon him) clothed the people in Kufa, and among the clothing was a khazz hood. Al-Hasan asked him for it, but he refused to give it to him and distributed it by lots among the Muslims. It went to a young man from Hamdan who left with it. It was said to him: Al-Hasan had asked his father for it, but he refused him. So the Hamdani sent it to Al-Hasan, who accepted it.

Hadith 5407

عن الحلبي قال: سألته عن لبس الخز فقال: لا بأس به، إن علي بن الحسين (عليه السلام) كان يلبس الكساء الخز في الشتاء فإذا جاء الصيف باعه وتصدق بثمنه، وكان يقول: إني لأستحيي من ربي أن آكل ثمن ثوب قد عبدت الله فيه.

From al-Halabi who said: I asked him about wearing khazz and he said: There is no problem with it. Ali bin al-Husayn (peace be upon him) used to wear a khazz cloak in winter, and when summer came, he would sell it and give its price in sadaqah. He used to say: I am ashamed before my Lord to eat the price of a garment in which I have worshipped Allah.

Hadith 5408

عن الرضا (عليه السلام) قال: سألته عن جلود الخز؟ فقال: هو ذا نحن نلبس، فقلت: ذاك الوبر جعلت فداك قال: إن حل وبره حل جلده.

From al-Ridha (peace be upon him) who said: I asked him about the skins of khazz? He said: Here we are wearing it. I said: That is the fleece, may I be your ransom. He said: When its fleece is permissible, its skin is permissible.

Hadith 5409

أحمد بن علي بن أبي طالب الطبرسي في (الاحتجاج): عن محمد بن عبد الله الحميري، عن صاحب الزمان (عليه السلام) أنه كتب إليه: روي لنا عن صاحب العسكر (عليه السلام) أنه سئل عن الصلاة في الخز الذي يغش بوبر الأرانب؟

Ahmad bin Ali bin Abi Talib al-Tabarsi in (al-Ihtijaj): From Muhammad bin Abdullah al-Himyari, from the Master of the Time (peace be upon him) that he wrote to him: It has been narrated to us from the Master of al-Askar (peace be upon him) that he was asked about praying in khazz that is adulterated with rabbit fleece?

فوقع: يجوز. وروي عنه أيضا أنه لا يجوز، فبأي الخبرين نعمل؟ فأجاب (عليه السلام): إنما حرم في هذه الأوبار والجلود، فأما الأوبار وحدها فكل حلال.

He wrote: It is permissible. And it has also been narrated from him that it is not permissible. So which of the two reports should we act upon? He (peace be upon him) answered: The prohibition is only in these fleeces and skins, but as for the fleeces alone, all is permissible.

أقول: لعل التحريم في الجلود مخصوص بالأرانب، والرخصة في وبرها محمولة على التقية.

I (Hurr Amili) say: Perhaps the prohibition in skins is specific to rabbits, and the permission in their fleece is based on dissimulation.

Hadith 5410

عن عمر بن علي، عن أبيه زين العابدين علي بن الحسين (عليهما السلام) أنه كان يشتري كساء الخز بخمسين دينارا فإذا صاف تصدق به ولا يرى بذلك بأسا. ويقول: (قل من حرم زينة الله) الآية.

From Umar bin Ali, from his father Zayn al-Abidin Ali bin al-Husayn (peace be upon them both): He would buy a khazz cloak for fifty dinars, and when summer came he would give it in sadaqah, and he saw no problem with that, and he would recite: "Say, who has forbidden the adornment of Allah [Quran, 7:32]."

CHAPTER 11

Prohibition Of Men Praying In Pure Silk, Permissibility Of Selling It, And Prohibition Of Wearing It And Similarly Raw Silk

[Hadith 5411 to 5422]

Hadith 5411

عن إسماعيل بن سعد الأحوص - في حديث - قال: سألت أبا الحسن الرضا (عليه السلام) هل يصلي الرجل في ثوب إبريسم؟ فقال: لا.

From Isma'il bin Saad Al-Ahwas - in a hadith: I asked Abu Al-Hasan Al-Ridha (peace be upon him) whether a man can pray in a silk garment? He said: No.

Hadith 5412

عن محمد بن عبد الجبار قال: كتبت إلى أبي محمد (عليه السلام) أسأله هل يصلى في قلنسوة حرير محض أو قلنسوة ديباج؟ فكتب (عليه السلام): لا تحل الصلاة في حرير محض.

From Muhammad ibn Abdul-Jabbar who said: I wrote to Abu Muhammad (peace be upon him) asking him if one can pray while wearing a pure silk cap or a brocade cap? So he wrote (peace be upon him): Prayer is not permissible in pure silk.

Hadith 5413

عن أبي جعفر (عليه السلام) قال: لا يصلح لباس الحرير والديباج، فأما بيعهما فلا بأس.

Abu Ja'far (peace be upon him) said: Wearing silk and brocade is not proper, but there is no problem in selling them.

Hadith 5414

عن العباس بن موسى، عن أبيه (عليه السلام) قال: سألته عن الإبريسم والقز؟ قال: هما سواء.

From Al-Abbas bin Musa, from his father (peace be upon him) who said: I asked him about silk and raw silk? He said: They are the same.

Hadith 5415

عن أبي جعفر (عليه السلام) أن رسول الله (صلى الله عليه وآله) قال لعلي (عليه السلام): إني أحب لك ما أحب لنفسي، وأكره لك ما أكره لنفسي فلا تختم بخاتم ذهب - إلى أن قال - ولا تلبس الحرير فيحرق الله جلدك يوم تلقاه.

From Abu Ja'far (peace be upon him) that the Messenger of Allah (peace be upon him and his family) said to Ali (peace be upon him): I love for you what I love for myself, and I dislike for you what I dislike for myself, so do not wear a gold ring - and he continued - and do not wear silk for Allah will burn your skin on the day you meet Him.

Hadith 5416

قال: وقد وردت الاخبار بالنهي عن لبس الديباج والحرير والإبريسم المحض والصلاة فيه للرجال.

He said: Reports have been narrated prohibiting men from wearing brocade, silk, and pure silk, and from praying while wearing them.

Hadith 5417

عن أبي الحارث قال: سألت الرضا (عليه السلام) هل يصلي الرجل في ثوب إبريسم؟ قال: لا.

From Abu Al-Harith who said: I asked Al-Ridha (peace be upon him) whether a man can pray in a silk garment? He said: No.

Hadith 5418

عن أبي عبد الله (عليه السلام) - في حديث - قال: وعن الثوب يكون علمه ديباجا؟ قال: لا يصلي فيه.

From Abu Abdullah (peace be upon him) - in a hadith - he was asked about a garment that has silk brocade as its marking? He said: One should not pray in it.

أقول: هذا محمول على ما يكون باقيه حريرا أو قزا أو على الكراهة، لما مضى ويأتي.

I (Hurr Amili) say: This is interpreted as applying to when the rest of it is silk or raw silk, or it indicates disapproval, based on what has preceded and what will follow.

Hadith 5419

عن أبي عبد الله (عليه السلام) أنه كان يكره أن يلبس القميص المكفوف بالديباج، ويكره لباس الحرير ولباس الوشي ويكره الميثرة الحمراء فإنه ميثرة إبليس.

From Abu Abdullah (peace be upon him) that he disliked wearing a shirt trimmed with silk brocade, and he disliked wearing silk and embroidered clothing, and he disliked the red saddle cushion for it is the cushion of Iblis.

أقول: الكراهة محمولة على التحريم في الحرير خاصة لما مضى ويأتي، إن شاء الله.

I (Hurr Amili) say: The dislike here is interpreted as prohibition specifically regarding silk based on what has preceded and what will follow, insha'Allah.

Hadith 5420

عن محمد بن إسماعيل بن بزيع، قال: سألت أبا الحسن (عليه السلام) عن الصلاة في ثوب ديباج؟ فقال: ما لم يكن فيه التماثيل فلا بأس.

From Muhammad bin Isma'il bin Bazi, he said: I asked Abu Al-Hasan (peace be upon him) about prayer in a silk brocade garment? He said: As long as there are no images in it, there is no problem.

قال الشيخ: هذا مخصوص بحال الحرب دون حال الاختيار، قال: ويجوز أن يكون إذا كان الديباج سداه قطنا أو كتانا. أقول: ويحتمل الحمل على التقية.

The Shaykh said: This is specific to the state of war, not the state of choice, he said: And it is permissible if the silk brocade's warp is cotton or linen. I (Hurr Amili) say: It can be interpreted as taqiyyah.

Hadith 5421

عن جعفر بن محمد، عن أبيه أن رسول الله (صلى الله عليه وآله) نهاهم عن سبع: منها لباس الإستبرق والحرير والقز والأرجوان.

From Ja'far bin Muhammad, from his father that the Messenger of Allah (peace be upon him and his family) forbade them from seven things: among them wearing brocade, silk, raw silk, and purple silk.

Hadith 5422

عن علي بن جعفر، عن أخيه موسى بن جعفر (عليهم السلام) قال: سألته عن الرجل هل يصلح له لبس الطيلسان فيه الديباج، والبركان عليه حرير؟ قال: لا.

From Ali bin Ja'far, from his brother Musa bin Ja'far (peace be upon them) who said: I asked him about whether it is permissible for a man to wear a tailasan (cloak) containing silk brocade, and a burkan (garment) with silk on it? He said: No.

أقول: (هذا محمول على كونه حريرا محضا أو على الكراهة). ويأتي ما يدل على ذلك.

I (Hurr Amili) say: This applies to cases where it is pure silk or indicates disapproval. Evidence for this will follow.

CHAPTER 12

Permissibility Of Men Wearing Silk In War And Necessity Specifically

[Hadith 5423 to 5428]

Hadith 5423

عن أبي عبد الله (عليه السلام) قال: لا يصلح للرجل أن يلبس الحرير إلا في الحرب.

From Abu Abdullah (peace be upon him) who said: It is not proper for a man to wear silk except in war.

Hadith 5424

عن أبي عبد الله (عليه السلام) قال: لا يلبس الرجل الحرير والديباج إلا في الحرب.

From Abu Abdullah (peace be upon him) who said: A man should not wear silk and brocade except in war.

Hadith 5425

عن سماعة بن مهران قال: سألت أبا عبد الله (عليه السلام) عن لباس الحرير والديباج، فقال: أما في الحرب فلا بأس به، وإن كان فيه تماثيل.

From Sama'ah bin Mihran who said: I asked Abu Abdullah (peace be upon him) about wearing silk and brocade. He said: As for during war, there is no problem with it, even if it has images on it.

Hadith 5426

محمد بن علي بن الحسين قال: لم يطلق النبي (صلى الله عليه وآله) لبس الحرير لاحد من الرجال إلا لعبد الرحمن بن عوف وذلك إنه كان رجلا قملا.

Muhammad bin Ali bin Al-Husain said: The Prophet (peace be upon him and his family) did not permit wearing silk for any man except for Abdur-Rahman bin Awf, and that was because he had lice.

Hadith 5427

عن جعفر، عن أبيه (عليهما السلام) أن عليا كان لا يرى بلباس الحرير والديباج في الحرب إذا لم يكن فيه التماثيل بأسا.

From Ja'far, from his father (peace be upon them) that Ali did not see any problem with wearing silk and brocade in war if it did not have images on it.

أقول: هذا محمول على نفي التحريم والكراهة، وحديث سماعة محمول على نفي التحريم وإن بقيت الكراهة بالتمثيل، أو ذاك محمول على عدم الصلاة في الثوب.

I (Hurr Amili) say: This is interpreted as negating prohibition and dislike, and the hadith of Sama'ah is interpreted as negating prohibition even if dislike remains due to the images, or that is interpreted as not praying in the garment.

Hadith 5428, 5429, 5430

ويدل على جواز لبس الحرير في الضرورة أحاديث أخر عامة تأتي في القيام وفي قضاء المغمى عليه وفي كتاب الأطعمة وغيره مثل قولهم (عليهم السلام): ليس شئ مما حرم الله إلا وقد أحله لمن اضطر إليه، وقولهم (عليهم السلام): كلما غلب الله عليه فالله أولى بالعذر، وقوله (عليه السلام): رفع عن أمتي الخطأ والنسيان وما أكرهوا عليه، ومالا يطيقون وغير ذلك.

The permissibility of wearing silk in necessity is indicated by other general hadiths that will come in the chapters on standing, making up prayers for one who fainted, in the book of foods, and others, such as their saying (peace be upon them): There is nothing that Allah has forbidden except that He has permitted it for one who is compelled to it, and their saying (peace be upon them): Whatever Allah has overpowered, Allah is more worthy of excuse, and his saying (peace be upon him): My nation has been pardoned for mistakes, forgetfulness, and what they are compelled to do, and what they cannot bear, and other than that.

Translator: In the Arabic edition, this hadith is combined under the numbers 5428, 5429, and 5430.

CHAPTER 13

Permissibility Of Wearing Non-Pure Silk When Mixed With Materials Valid For Prayer, Even If Silk Is More Than Half

[Hadith 5431 to 5438]

Hadith 5431

سأل الحسين بن قياما أبا الحسن (عليه السلام) عن الثوب الملحم بالقز والقطن والقز أكثر من النصف، أيصلي فيه؟ قال: لا بأس، قد كان لأبي الحسن (عليه السلام) منه جبات.

Al-Husayn bin Qiyama asked Abu Al-Hasan (peace be upon him) about cloth woven with silk and cotton where silk is more than half, can one pray in it? He said: There is no problem. Abu Al-Hasan (peace be upon him) had robes made of it.

———

Hadith 5432

عن عبيد بن زرارة، عن أبي عبد الله (عليه السلام) قال: لا بأس بلباس القز، إذا كان سداه أو لحمته من قطن أو كتان.

From Ubayd bin Zurarah, from Abu Abdullah (peace be upon him) who said: There is no problem wearing silk if its warp or weft is made of cotton or linen.

———

Hadith 5433

عن أبي عبد الله (عليه السلام) قال: سأله أبو سعيد عن الخميصة وأنا عنده سداها إبريسم، أيلبسها؟ وكان وجد البرد؟ فأمره أن يلبسها.

From Abu Abdullah (peace be upon him): Abu Sa'id asked him while I was present about a decorated garment with silk warp, can he wear it? And he was feeling cold? So he ordered him to wear it.

———

Hadith 5434

عن أبي عبد الله (عليه السلام) في الثوب يكون فيه الحرير، فقال: إن كان فيه خلط فلا بأس.

From Abu Abdullah (peace be upon him) regarding cloth containing silk, he said: If it is mixed with something else, there is no problem.

———

Hadith 5435

عن زرارة قال: سمعت أبا جعفر (عليه السلام) ينهى عن لباس الحرير للرجال والنساء إلا ما كان من حرير مخلوط بخز لحمته أو سداه خز أو كتان أو قطن، وإنما يكره الحرير المحض للرجال والنساء.

From Zurarah, he said: I heard Abu Ja'far (peace be upon him) prohibiting silk clothing for men and women except silk mixed with fur where its weft or warp is fur, linen, or cotton. Pure silk is disliked for both men and women.

أقول: ذكر بعض الأصحاب أن المراد بالكراهة هنا المرجوحية وأنها بمعنى التحريم في حق الرجال دون النساء، جمعا بين الأحاديث كما مضى ويأتي.

I (Hurr Amili) say: Some companions mentioned that dislike here means less preferred and it means prohibition for men but not women, reconciling between hadiths as mentioned before and will come later.

Hadith 5436

عن أبي عبد الله (عليه السلام) قال: لا بأس بالثوب أن يكون سداه وزره وعلمه حريرا، وإنما كره الحرير المبهم للرجال.

From Abu Abdullah (peace be upon him) who said: There is no problem with cloth having silk in its warp, buttons and marks. Pure silk is what is disliked for men.

Hadith 5437

عن علي بن مهزيار أنه كتب إلى أبي محمد الحسن (عليه السلام) يسأله عن الصلاة في القرمز وأن أصحابنا يتوقفون عن الصلاة فيه؟ فكتب: لا بأس مطلق والحمد لله. قال الصدوق: وذلك إذا لم يكن القرمز من إبريسم محض، والذي نهى عنه هو ما كان من إبريسم محض.

From Ali bin Mahziyar who wrote to Abu Muhammad Al-Hasan (peace be upon him) asking about prayer in crimson cloth and that our companions hesitate to pray in it? He wrote back: It is absolutely permitted, praise be to Allah. Al-Saduq said: This applies when the crimson is not pure silk, and what is prohibited is what is made of pure silk.

Hadith 5438

أحمد بن علي بن أبي طالب الطبرسي في (الاحتجاج): عن محمد بن عبد الله بن جعفر الحميري، عن صاحب الزمان (عليه السلام) أنه كتب إليه: يتخذ بإصفهان ثياب فيها عتابية على عمل الوشى من قز وإبريسم، هل تجوز الصلاة فيها أم لا؟ فأجاب (عليه السلام) لا تجوز الصلاة إلا في ثوب سداه أو لحمته قطن أو كتان.

From Ahmad bin Ali bin Abi Talib al-Tabarsi in (al-Ihtijaj): From Muhammad bin Abdullah bin Ja'far al-Himyari, from the Master of the Time (peace be upon him) that he wrote to him: In Isfahan, there are clothes made with striped patterns woven from silk and pure silk. Is prayer permissible in them or not? He (peace be upon him) answered: Prayer is not permissible except in garments whose warp or weft is cotton or linen.

أقول: وتقدم في أحاديث الخز ما يدل على جواز لبس الحرير الممزوج به، وتقدم أيضا ما يدل على المقصود، ويأتي ما يدل عليه.

I (Hurr Amili) say: And it has been mentioned previously in the hadiths about al-khazz (silk blend) what indicates the permissibility of wearing silk mixed with it, and what indicates the intended meaning has also preceded, and what indicates it will come.

———

CHAPTER 14

Ruling On What Is Insufficient For Prayer When Alone If It Is Silk, Impure, Dead Animal, Or From What Is Not Eaten

[Hadith 5439 to 5444]

Hadith 5439

عن محمد بن عبد الجبار قال: كتبت إلى أبي محمد (عليه السلام) أسأله هل يصلي في قلنسوة حرير محض أو قلنسوة ديباج؟ فكتب (عليه السلام): لا تحل الصلاة في حرير محض.

From Muhammad ibn Abdul-Jabbar who said: I wrote to Abu Muhammad (peace be upon him) asking him if one can pray wearing a pure silk cap or a brocade cap? He wrote back (peace be upon him): Prayer is not permissible in pure silk.

Hadith 5440

عن أبي عبد الله (عليه السلام) قال: كل مالا تجوز الصلاة فيه وحده فلا بأس بالصلاة فيه، مثل التكة الإبريسم والقلنسوة والخف والزنار يكون في السراويل ويصلي فيه.

From Abu Abdullah (peace be upon him) who said: Everything in which prayer alone is not permissible, there is no harm in praying while wearing it, such as a silk waistband, cap, leather socks, and a belt that is in the trousers and praying in it.

Hadith 5441

عن علي بن مهزيار قال: كتب إليه إبراهيم بن عقبة: عندنا جوارب وتكك تعمل من وبر الأرانب فهل تجوز الصلاة في وبر الأرانب من غير ضرورة ولا تقية؟ فكتب لا تجوز الصلاة فيها.

From Ali ibn Mahziyar who said: Ibrahim ibn Uqbah wrote to him: We have socks and waistbands made from rabbit fur - is prayer permitted in rabbit fur without necessity or taqiyyah? He wrote back: Prayer in them is not permitted.

Hadith 5442

عن محمد بن عبد الجبار قال: كتبت إلى أبي محمد (عليه السلام) أسأله هل يصلي في قلنسوة عليها وبر ما لا يؤكل لحمه أو تكة حرير محض أو تكة من وبر الأرانب؟ فكتب: لا تحل الصلاة في الحرير المحض وإن كان الوبر ذكيا حلت الصلاة فيه، إن شاء الله.

From Muhammad ibn Abdul-Jabbar who said: I wrote to Abu Muhammad (peace be upon him) asking if one can pray in a cap that has fur from an animal whose meat is not eaten, or a pure silk waistband, or a waistband made of rabbit fur? He wrote: Prayer is not permissible in pure silk, and if the fur is from a properly slaughtered animal then prayer in it is permissible, insha'Allah.

Hadith 5443

عن الريان بن الصلت أنه سأل الرضا (عليه السلام) عن أشياء منها الخفاف من أصناف الجلود، فقال: لا بأس بهذا كله إلا الثعالب.

From Al-Rayyan ibn Al-Salt that he asked Al-Ridha (peace be upon him) about various things including leather socks made from different types of leather, and he said: There is no problem with all of these except fox leather.

Hadith 5444

عن غير واحد، عن أبي عبد الله (عليه السلام) في الميتة قال: لا تصل في شئ منه ولاشسع.

From multiple narrators, from Abu Abdullah (peace be upon him) regarding dead animals, he said: Do not pray in anything from it, not even sandal straps.

أقول: قد فهم بعض الأصحاب من هذه الأحاديث كراهة مالا تتم الصلاة فيه من الحرير وغير مأكول اللحم وحملوها على ذلك جمعا، وذهب جماعة إلى المنع وحملوا الجواز على التقية وهو الأحوط. وقد تقدم ما يدل على حكم نجاسة هذه الأشياء وجواز الصلاة فيها في النجاسات.

I (Hurr Amili) say: Some companions understood from these hadiths that what is insufficient for prayer alone like silk and meat of animals not eaten is disliked and they interpreted them as such to reconcile the narrations, while a group went towards prohibition and interpreted the permission as taqiyyah which is more precautionary. What indicates the ruling on the impurity of these things and permissibility of prayer in them has preceded in the chapter on impurities.

CHAPTER 15

Permissibility Of Using Silk As Bedding, Praying On It, Using It As Quran Cover, And Ruling On Garments Bordered With Silk, And The Ka'bah's Brocade

[Hadith 5445 to 5447]

Hadith 5445

عن علي بن جعفر قال: سألت أبا الحسن (عليه السلام) عن الفراش الحرير ومثله من الديباج والمصلى الحرير، هل يصلح للرجل النوم عليه والتكأة والصلاة؟ قال: يفترشه ويقوم عليه ولا يسجد عليه .

From Ali bin Ja'far who said: I asked Abu al-Hasan (peace be upon him) about silk bedding and similar items made of brocade and silk prayer mats - is it permissible for a man to sleep on it, recline on it, and pray on it? He said: He may lie on it (use it as bedding) and stand on it but should not prostrate on it.

Hadith 5446

عن أبي عبد الله (عليه السلام) أنه قال: لا بأس أن يأخذ من ديباج الكعبة فيجعله غلاف مصحف، أو يجعله مصلى يصلي عليه .

From Abu Abdullah (peace be upon him) that he said: There is no harm in taking from the Ka'bah's brocade to use as a Quran cover or as a prayer mat to pray on.

Hadith 5447

وقد تقدم حديث جراح المدائني، عن أبي عبد الله (عليه السلام) أنه كان يكره أن يلبس القميص المكفوف بالديباج .

And previously mentioned in the hadith of Jarrah Al-Madaini, from Abu Abdullah (peace be upon him) that he disliked wearing shirts bordered with brocade.

CHAPTER 16

Permissibility Of Women Wearing Pure Silk And Others, And The Ruling On Their Prayer While Wearing It

[Hadith 5448 to 5456]

Hadith 5448

عن أبي عبد الله (عليه السلام) - في حديث - قال: قلت له: طيلساني هذا خز، قال: وما بال الخز؟ قلت: وسداه إبريسم، قال: وما بال الإبريسم؟ قال لا تكره أن يكون سدى الثوب إبريسم ولازره ولاعلمه إنما يكره المصمت من الإبريسم للرجال ولا يكره للنساء.

From Abu Abdullah (peace be upon him) - in a hadith - he said: I said to him: This is my silk cloak. He said: What about silk? I said: Its warp is silk. He said: What about silk? He said: There is no dislike in having silk as the warp of the garment, nor its buttons, nor its marks. What is disliked is solid silk for men, but it is not disliked for women.

Hadith 5449

عن ليث المرادي قال: قال أبو عبد الله (عليه السلام): إن رسول الله (صلى الله عليه وآله) كسا أسامة بن زيد حلة حرير فخرج فيها فقال: مهلا يا أسامة، إنما يلبسها من لأخلاق له فاقسمها بين نساءك.

From Layth al-Muradi who said: Abu Abdullah (peace be upon him) said: The Messenger of Allah (peace be upon him and his family) gave Usama bin Zayd a silk garment, and he went out wearing it. The Prophet said: Take it easy, O Usama, this is only worn by those who have no morals, so distribute it among your women.

Hadith 5450

عن أبي عبد الله (عليه السلام) قال: النساء يلبسن الحرير والديباج إلا في الاحرام.

From Abu Abdullah (peace be upon him) who said: Women can wear silk and brocade except during ihram.

Hadith 5451

عن أبي عبد الله (عليه السلام) قال: لا ينبغي للمرأة أن تلبس الحرير المحض وهي محرمة، فأما في الحر والبرد فلا بأس.

From Abu Abdullah (peace be upon him) who said: It is not appropriate for a woman to wear pure silk while she is in the state of ihram, but in heat and cold there is no problem.

Hadith 5452

عن آبائه (عليهم السلام) - في حديث المناهي - قال: نهى رسول الله (صلى الله عليه وآله) عن لبس الحرير والديباج والقز للرجال، فأما النساء فلا بأس.

From his forefathers (peace be upon them) - in the hadith of prohibitions - he said: The Messenger of Allah (peace be upon him and his family) prohibited men from wearing silk, brocade, and raw silk, but for women there is no problem.

Hadith 5453

عن جابر الجعفي قال: سمعت أبا جعفر (عليه السلام) يقول: ليس على النساء أذان - إلى أن قال - ويجوز للمرأة لبس الديباج والحرير في غير صلاة وإحرام، وحرم ذلك على الرجال إلا في الجهاد، ويجوز أن تتختم بالذهب وتصلي فيه، وحرم ذلك على الرجال إلا في الجهاد.

From Jabir al-Jufi who said: I heard Abu Ja'far (peace be upon him) saying: There is no adhan for women - until he said - and it is permissible for women to wear brocade and silk except during prayer and ihram, while it is forbidden for men except during jihad, and it is permissible for her to wear gold rings and pray while wearing them, while it is forbidden for men except during jihad.

Hadith 5454

قال الصدوق: قد وردت الاخبار بجواز لبس النساء الحرير ولم ترد بجواز صلاتهن فيه، انتهى.

Al-Saduq said: Reports have come regarding the permissibility of women wearing silk, but none have come regarding the permissibility of their praying in it, end quote.

Hadith 5455

وقد تقدم في حديث زرارة، عن أبي جعفر (عليه السلام) قال: وإنما يكره الحرير المبهم للرجال والنساء.

It has been previously mentioned in the hadith of Zurarah, from Abu Ja'far (peace be upon him) who said: Pure silk is disliked for both men and women.

Hadith 5456

عن علي بن جعفر، عن أخيه موسى بن جعفر (عليه السلام) قال: سألته عن الديباج هل يصلح لبسه للنساء؟ قال: لا بأس.

From Ali bin Ja'far, from his brother Musa bin Ja'far (peace be upon him) who said: I asked him about brocade, is it permissible for women to wear it? He said: There is no problem with it.

CHAPTER 17

Ruling On Prayer In Clothing That Has Hair From Animals Whose Meat Is Not Permissible To Eat

[Hadith 5457 to 5458]

Hadith 5457

عن إبراهيم بن محمد الهمداني قال: كتبت إليه: يسقط على ثوبي الوبر والشعر مما لا يؤكل لحمه من غير تقية ولا ضرورة، فكتب: لا تجوز الصلاة فيه.

From Ibrahim bin Muhammad Al-Hamdani who said: I wrote to him asking: Hair and fur from animals whose meat is not permissible falls on my clothes without taqiyyah or necessity. He wrote back: Prayer is not permissible in it.

Hadith 5458

عن الحسن بن علي الوشاء قال: كان أبو عبد الله (عليه السلام) يكره الصلاة في وبر كل شئ لا يؤكل لحمه.

From Al-Hasan bin Ali Al-Washaa who said: Abu Abdullah (peace be upon him) disliked praying in clothing that had hair from any animal whose meat is not permissible to eat.

أقول: وتقدم ما يدل على الجواز فيما لا تتم الصلاة فيه، وهو لا ينافي الكراهة لكن يحتمل التقية.

I (Hurr Amili) say: What was mentioned earlier indicates permissibility for what is not required for prayer, and while this does not negate the dislike, it may be a case of taqiyyah.

CHAPTER 18

Permissibility Of Praying In A Garment That Has Human Hair And Nails On It

[Hadith 5459 to 5460]

Hadith 5459

عن علي بن الريان بن الصلت أنه سأل أبا الحسن الثالث (عليه السلام) عن الرجل يأخذ من شعره وأظفاره، ثم يقوم إلى الصلاة من غير أن ينفضه من ثوبه ؟ فقال: لا بأس.

From Ali ibn Al-Rayyan ibn Al-Salt, that he asked Abu Al-Hasan the Third (peace be upon him) about a man who cuts his hair and nails, then stands for prayer without shaking them off his garment? He said: There is no problem with that.

———

Hadith 5460

عن علي بن الريان قال: كتبت إلى أبي الحسن (عليه السلام): هل تجوز الصلاة في ثوب يكون فيه شعر من شعر الانسان وأظفاره من قبل أن ينفضه ويلقيه عنه ؟ فوقع يجوز.

From Ali ibn Al-Rayyan who said: I wrote to Abu Al-Hasan (peace be upon him): Is prayer permissible in a garment that has human hair and nails on it before shaking them off and removing them? He wrote back: It is permissible.

———

CHAPTER 19

Dislike Of Wearing Black Except In Socks, Turban And Cloak, Removal Of Dislike Due To Dissimulation, And Impermissibility Of Imitating Enemies In Dress And Other Matters

[Hadith 5461 to 5470]

Hadith 5461

عن أبي عبد الله (عليه السلام) قال: يكره السواد إلا في ثلاثة: الخف، والعمامة، والكساء.

From Abu Abdullah (peace be upon him) who said: Black is disliked except in three things: khuff (leather socks), turban (amaamah), and cloak (kisa').

Translator: The narrations compiled in this chapter present a remarkably severe and unified stance against the wearing of black clothing. The language utilized by the Imams is not merely one of mild aesthetic discouragement; rather, it attaches heavy theological and historical stigma to the color, explicitly labeling it the "dress of Pharaoh" (Hadith 5465), the "clothing of the people of hellfire" (Hadith 5467), and the attire of the enemies of the Ahl al-Bayt (Hadith 5468). For a reader reflecting on these primary texts, the sheer weight of these descriptions establishes a clear, blanket order: black is fundamentally discouraged as a standard color for the garments of a believer - regardless of the intention or occasion.

The structural consistency of the exceptions highlights the strictness of this rule. Multiple narrations independently restrict the permissibility of black to exactly three functional items: the turban, the cloak, and the socks. A comprehensive review of the canonical hadith collections reveals that there are absolutely no narrations that permit or encourage wearing black for any other reason. The texts presented here do not offer open-ended allowances or situational caveats.

In later eras, scholars operating within the Rationalist jurisprudence have attempted to formulate exceptions to this universal rule. Some Rationalist jurists have argued that if a believer's "niyyah" (intention) is specifically to mourn the Imams, the prohibition is lifted. Others have argued that the hadiths were merely forbidding the adoption of black as a regular, daily uniform - as was the oppressive custom of the Abbasid dynasty - meaning it remains permissible to wear occasionally, especially during periods of mourning.

However, an objective reading of the primary texts does not support these claims. We find no hadith in the Shia corpus that conditions the prohibition of black clothing on the wearer's intention, nor do we find any narration that creates a specific carve-out permitting black attire during days of mourning. Crucially, we also find no hadith where the Imams explicitly recommended wearing black during periods of mourning, nor did they ever mention any extra reward for adorning black when mourning the Imams. Furthermore, the texts do not distinguish between everyday wear and occasional wear.

When the Imams themselves wore full black - as seen in the narrations of Hudhaifa bin Mansur (Hadith 5467) and Dawud Al-Raqqi (Hadith 5469) - it was explicitly framed as an extreme act of "taqiyyah" (dissimulation). The Imams were forced to navigate the intense political pressure of the Abbasid caliphate. The fact that an Imam felt compelled to secretly dye the inner cotton of his garments black just to prove his compliance to a hostile, spying regime underscores a critical reality: wearing full black was an oppressive political imposition that they endured for survival, not a permissible occasional practice or an internal religious ideal that they willingly embraced.

This intense climate of taqiyyah extended directly to how the community was instructed to conduct itself. The Imams would never recommend any public practice or expressions (of protest) that would irk the tyrant rulers and jeopardize their followers. Because of this, they actively directed the community to keep mourning as a profoundly private, inward expression. In fact, on the most tragic day of Ashura itself, the Imams explicitly recommended believers to mourn in the complete seclusion of their homes, away from the public eye (Hadith 10156 in Vol. 8).

In conclusion, when we synthesize the strict, general commands prohibiting black attire with the complete absence of any instructions or promised rewards for wearing it during mourning, the reality becomes remarkably clear. The idea of adopting a distinct, public uniform for grief entirely contradicts the protective methodology of the Ahl al-Bayt. Given all of this, relying strictly on the preserved texts, we find no scriptural or historical grounds for the modern cultural practice of wearing black.

Hadith 5462

عن بعض أصحابه رفعه قال: كان رسول الله (صلى الله عليه وآله) يكره السواد إلا في ثلاث: الخف، والعمامة، والكساء.

From some of his companions who raised it to say: The Messenger of Allah (peace be upon him and his family) disliked black except in three things: khuff, turban (amaamah), and cloak (kisa).

Hadith 5463

عن أبي جعفر (عليه السلام) قال: قتل الحسين بن علي (عليه السلام) وعليه جبة خز دكناء. أقول، هذا محمول على الجواز ونفي التحريم.

From Abu Ja'far (peace be upon him) who said: Husayn bin Ali (peace be upon him) was killed while wearing a dark silk jubbah (*). I (Hurr Amili) say: This indicates permissibility and negates prohibition.

Translator: * A jubbah is a traditional outer garment that has been worn throughout

Islamic history. It is typically a long, loose-fitting robe, open in the front with wide sleeves and worn over other clothing as an outer layer.

Hadith 5464

قال: الكليني: وروي لا تصل في ثوب أسود فأما الخف أو الكساء أو العمامة فلا بأس.

Al-Kulayni said: It is narrated: Do not pray in black clothing, but there is no problem with black socks, cloak, or turban.

Hadith 5465

محمد بن علي بن الحسين قال: قال أمير المؤمنين (عليه السلام) فيما علم أصحابه: لا تلبس السواد فإنه لباس فرعون.

Muhammad bin Ali bin Al-Husayn said: Amir al-Mu'minin (peace be upon him) said while teaching his companions: Do not wear black for it is the dress of Pharaoh.

Translator: Refer to comments in Hadith 5461.

Hadith 5466

قال: وروي: أن جبرئيل (عليه السلام) هبط على رسول الله (صلى الله عليه وآله) في قباء أسود ومنطقة فيها خنجر، فقال: يا جبرئيل ما هذا؟ فقال: زي ولد عمك العباس يا محمد، ويل لولدك من ولد عمك العباس.

It is narrated: Jibreel (peace be upon him) descended upon the Messenger of Allah (peace be upon him and his family) wearing a black cloak and a belt containing a dagger. He asked: O Jibreel, what is this? He replied: This is the attire of your cousin Al-Abbas's children, O Muhammad. Woe to your children from your cousin Al-Abbas's children.

Hadith 5467

عن حذيفة بن منصور أنه قال: كنت عند أبي عبد الله (عليه السلام) بالحيرة فأتاه رسول أبي العباس الخليفة يدعوه فدعا بممطر أحد وجهيه أسود والآخر أبيض فلبسه، ثم قال (عليه السلام): أما أني ألبسه وأنا أعلم أنه لباس أهل النار.

From Hudhayfa bin Mansur who said: I was with Abu Abdullah (peace be upon him) in Al-Hira when a messenger from Abu Al-Abbas the Caliph came calling for him. He asked for a coat that was black on one side and white on the other and wore it, then said (peace be upon him): I wear this while knowing it is the clothing of the people of hellfire.

أقول: ذكر الصدوق أنه (عليه السلام) لبس السواد للتقية.

I (Hurr Amili) say: Al-Saduq mentioned that he (peace be upon him) wore black for taqiyyah.

Translator: Refer to comments in Hadith 5461.

Hadith 5468

عن إسماعيل بن مسلم، عن الصادق (عليه السلام) قال: إنه أوحى الله إلى نبي من أنبيائه قل للمؤمنين: لا تلبسوا لباس أعدائي، ولا تطعموا مطاعم أعدائي، ولا تسلكوا مسالك أعدائي فتكونوا أعدائي كما هم أعدائي.

From Isma'il bin Muslim, from Al-Sadiq (peace be upon him) who said: Allah revealed to one of His prophets: Tell the believers: Do not wear the clothes of My enemies, do not eat the food of My enemies, and do not follow the ways of My enemies, lest you become My enemies just as they are My enemies.

Hadith 5469

عن داود الرقي قال: كانت الشيعة تسأل أبا عبد الله (عليه السلام) عن لبس السواد؟ قال: فوجدناه قاعدا عليه جبة سوداء وقلنسوة سوداء، وخف أسود مبطن بسواد، ثم فتق ناحية منه وقال: أما أن قطنه أسود وأخرج منه قطنا أسود، ثم قال: بيض قلبك والبس ما شئت.

From Dawud Al-Raqqi who said: The Shia used to ask Abu Abdullah (peace be upon him) about wearing black? He said: We found him sitting wearing a black robe, a black cap, and black leather socks lined with black. Then he tore a part of it and said: Indeed its cotton is black, and he pulled out black cotton, then said: Purify your heart and wear whatever you wish.

قال الصدوق: فعل ذلك كله تقية لأنه كان متهما عند الأعداء بأنه لا يرى لبس السواد فأحب أن يتقي بأجهد ما يمكنه، فصبغ القطن بالسواد. أقول: ويمكن حمله على إرادة الجواز ونفي التحريم بقرينة آخره.

Al-Saduq said: He did all of that out of taqiyyah because he was accused by enemies that he did not approve wearing black, so he wanted to practice taqiyyah to the maximum extent possible, so he dyed the cotton black. I (Hurr Amili) say: It can be interpreted as permissibility and negation of prohibition based on the context of its ending.

Translator: Refer to comments in Hadith 5461.

Hadith 5470

عن أبي جعفر (عليه السلام) قال: كأني بعبد الله بن شريك العامري عليه عمامة سوداء ذؤابتاها بين كتفيه مصعدا في لحف الجبل بين يدي قائمنا أهل البيت في أربعة آلاف يكبرون ويكررون.

From Abu Ja'far (peace be upon him) who said: It is as if I can see Abdullah bin Sharik Al-Amiri wearing a black turban with its two ends between his shoulders, ascending the mountain slope in front of our Ahl al-Bayt's Qaim (rising one) among four thousand people who are saying takbir and repeating it.

أقول: ويأتي ما يدل على ذلك، وعلى عدم كراهة الخف الأسود.

I (Hurr Amili) say: Evidence for this will come later, and for the non-disliked status of black leather socks.

———

CHAPTER 20

Dislike Of Praying While Wearing A Black Cap And Other Black Clothes Except What Has Been Exempted

[Hadith 5471 to 5473]

Hadith 5471

عن أبي عبد الله (عليه السلام) قال: قلت له: أصلي في القلنسوة السوداء؟ فقال: لا تصل فيها فإنها لباس أهل النار.

From Abu Abdullah (peace be upon him) who said: I said to him: Should I pray in a black cap? He said: Do not pray in it for it is the clothing of the people of the Fire.

———————

Hadith 5472

قال الكليني: وروي لا تصل في ثوب أسود، فأما الخف أو الكساء أو العمامة فلا بأس.

Al-Kulayni said: It has been narrated: Do not pray in black clothes, but there is no problem with black khuff (leather socks), cloak (kisa'), or turban (amaamah).

———————

Hadith 5473

عن أبي عبد الله (عليه السلام) قال: قلت له: أصلي في القلنسوة السوداء؟ قال: لا تصل فيها فإنها لباس أهل النار.

From Abu Abdullah (peace be upon him) who said: I said to him: Can I pray wearing a black cap? He said: Do not pray in it for it is the clothing of the people of the Fire.

———————

CHAPTER 21
Prohibition Of Prayer In Thin Clothing That Does Not Cover The Awrah And Women Wearing Transparent Clothing

[Hadith 5474 to 5478]

Hadith 5474

عن محمد بن مسلم قال: قلت لأبي جعفر (عليه السلام): الرجل يصلي في قميص واحد؟ فقال: إذا كان كثيفا فلا بأس به، والمرأة تصلي في الدرع والمقنعة إذا كان الدرع كثيفا، يعني إذا كان ستيرا.

From Muhammad bin Muslim, he said: I asked Abu Ja'far (peace be upon him) about a man praying in a single shirt? He replied: If it is thick, there is no problem with it. And a woman prays in a long dress and head covering if the dress is thick, meaning if it provides proper concealment (coverage).

Hadith 5475

عن أبي عبد الله (عليه السلام) قال: لا يصلح للمرأة المسلمة أن تلبس من الخمر والدروع ما لا يواري شيئا. أقول: وتقدم في آداب الحمام أحاديث كثيرة تتضمن النهي عن لبس المرأة الثياب الرقاق، ونهى الرجل عن الاذن لها في ذلك.

From Abu Abdullah (peace be upon him) who said: It is not appropriate for a Muslim woman to wear veils and dresses that do not conceal anything. I (Hurr Amili) say: Many hadith have preceded in the etiquette of bathing that include prohibition of women wearing thin clothes and prohibiting men from allowing them to do so.

Hadith 5476

وعن محمد بن يحيى قال: قال أبو عبد الله (عليه السلام): لا تصل فيما شف أوسف يعني الثوب الصقيل.

From Muhammad bin Yahya who said: Abu Abdullah (peace be upon him) said: Do not pray in what is transparent or thin (revealing), meaning polished cloth.

Hadith 5477

عن أحمد بن حماد، عبد الله (عليه السلام) قال: لا تصل فيما شف أو صف، يعني الثوب المصقل. وذكره الشهيد في (الذكرى)، ثم قال: أو وصف بواوين أي حكى الحجم. وفي خط الشيخ أو صف بواو واحد.

From Ahmad bin Hammad, from Abdullah (peace be upon him) who said: Do not pray in what is transparent or thin (revealing), meaning polished cloth. And it was mentioned by Al-Shaheed in (Al-Dhikra), then he said: "wasafa" with two waws means it shows the size, and in the Shaykh's writing it is "safa" with one waw.

Hadith 5478

محمد بن علي بن الحسين في (الخصال) بإسناده الآتي عن علي (عليه السلام) - في حديث الأربعمائة - قال: عليكم بالصفيق من الثياب فإن من رق ثوبه رق دينه، لا يقومن أحدكم بين يدي الرب جل جلاله وعليه ثوب يشف، تجزئ الصلاة للرجل في ثوب واحد يعقد طرفيه على عنقه، وفي القميص الصفيق يزره عليه.

Muhammad bin Ali bin Al-Husayn in Al-Khisal with his chain from Ali (peace be upon him) - in the hadith of the four hundred - said: You must wear thick clothing, for whoever has thin clothing has thin religion. None of you should stand before the Lord, Majestic is His Glory, wearing transparent clothing. Prayer is sufficient for a man in a single garment tied at both ends around his neck, and in a thick buttoned shirt.

أقول: ويدل على ذلك جميع ما دل على وجوب ستر العورة، وقد سبق في آداب الحمام، ويأتي ما يدل عليه، إن شاء الله.

I (Hurr Amili) say: This is supported by all evidence indicating the obligation of covering the awrah, as mentioned previously in bathing etiquette, and more evidence will come, insha'Allah.

CHAPTER 22

Permissibility Of Praying In A Single Garment If It Covers What Must Be Covered, Whether As Imam Or Follower

[Hadith 5479 to 5494]

Hadith 5479

عن محمد بن مسلم قال: رأيت أبا جعفر (عليه السلام) صلى في إزار واحد ليس بواسع قد عقده على عنقه. فقلت له: ما ترى للرجل يصلي في قميص واحد؟ فقال: إذا كان كثيفا فلا بأس به.

From Muhammad bin Muslim who said: I saw Abu Ja'far (peace be upon him) pray in a single wrap that wasn't wide, which he had tied around his neck. I asked him: What do you think about a man praying in a single shirt? He replied: If it is thick, then there is no problem with it.

———

Hadith 5480

عن أبي عبد الله (عليه السلام) قال: سألته عن الرجل يصلي في قميص واحد أو قباء طاق، أو في قباء محشو وليس عليه أزرار؟ فقال: إذا كان عليه قميص صفيق أو قباء ليس بطويل الفرج فلا بأس، والثوب الواحد يتوشح به، والسراويل كل ذلك لا بأس به، وقال: إذا لبس السراويل فليجعل على عاتقه شيئا ولو حبلا.

From Abu Abdullah (peace be upon him) who said: I asked him about a man who prays in a single shirt, or an unlined (single-layered) cloak, or in a padded cloak without buttons? He said: If he is wearing a thick shirt or a cloak that does not have long slits then there is no problem, and a single garment that he wraps around himself, and trousers - all of these are permissible. And he said: If he wears trousers, he should place something on his shoulder even if it is a rope.

———

Hadith 5481

عن رفاعة قال: حدثني من سمع أبا عبد الله (عليه السلام) عن الرجل يصلي في ثوب واحد متزرا به، قال: لا بأس به إذا رفعه إلى الثندوتين.

From Rifa'a who said: Someone who heard Abu Abdullah (peace be upon him) told me about a man who prays in a single garment using it as a waist wrap. He said: There is no problem with it if he raises it up to the chest.

———

Hadith 5482

عن جميل قال: سأل مرازم أبا عبد الله (عليه السلام) وأنا معه حاضر عن الرجل الحاضر يصلي في إزار مؤتزرا به؟ قال: يجعل على رقبته منديلا أو عمامة يتردى به.

Jameel said: Murazim asked Abu Abdullah (peace be upon him) while I was present with him about a settled person praying while wearing only a waist wrap? He said: He should put a cloth or turban around his neck to cover himself with.

Hadith 5483

عن أبي عبد الله (عليه السلام) قال: الرجل إذا اتزر بثوب واحد إلى ثندوته صلى فيه.

From Abu Abdullah (peace be upon him) who said: When a man wraps a single garment up to his chest, he may pray in it.

Hadith 5484

عن عبيد بن زرارة، عن أبيه قال: صلى بنا أبو جعفر (عليه السلام) في ثوب واحد.

From Ubayd bin Zurarah, from his father who said: Abu Ja'far (peace be upon him) led us in prayer wearing a single garment.

Hadith 5485

عن أبي مريم الأنصاري - في حديث - قال: صلى بنا أبو جعفر (عليه السلام) في قميص بلا إزار ولا رداء، فقال: إن قميصي كثيف فهو يجزئ أن لا يكون على إزار ولا رداء.

From Abu Maryam al-Ansari - in a hadith - who said: Abu Ja'far (peace be upon him) led us in prayer wearing only a shirt without a wrap or upper garment. He said: My shirt is thick, so it is sufficient without having to wear a wrap or upper garment.

Hadith 5486

عن علي بن جعفر أنه سأل أخاه موسى بن جعفر (عليهما السلام) عن الرجل، هل يصلي بالقوم وعليه سراويل ورداء؟ قال: لا بأس به.

From Ali bin Ja'far, he asked his brother Musa bin Ja'far (peace be upon them both) about a man leading people in prayer while wearing trousers and a robe? He said: There is no problem with it.

Hadith 5487

عن زرارة، عن أبي جعفر (عليه السلام) أنه قال: إن آخر صلاة صلاها رسول الله (صلى الله عليه وآله) بالناس في ثوب واحد قد خالف بين طرفيه، ألا أريك الثوب؟ قلت: بلى، قال: فأخرج ملحفة فذرعتها وكانت سبعة أذرع في ثمانية أشبار.

From Zurarah, from Abu Ja'far (peace be upon him) who said: The last prayer that the Messenger of Allah (peace be upon him and his family) led with people was in a single garment which he wrapped around himself. Should I show you the garment? I said: Yes. He brought out a sheet and I measured it - it was seven cubits (forearm lengths) by eight spans.

Hadith 5488

عن أبي بصير أنه قال لأبي عبد الله (عليه السلام): ما يجزي الرجل من الثياب أن يصلي فيه؟ فقال: صلى الحسين بن علي (عليه السلام) في ثوب قد قلص عن نصف ساقه، وقارب ركبتيه، ليس على منكبه منه إلا قدر جناحي الخطاف وكان إذا ركع سقط عن منكبيه، وكلما سجد يناله عنقه فرده على منكبيه بيده، فلم يزل ذلك دأبه ودأبه مشتغلا به حتى انصرف.

From Abu Basir that he said to Abu Abdullah (peace be upon him): What is sufficient clothing for a man to pray in? He said: Husayn bin Ali (peace be upon him) prayed in a garment that reached halfway down his shin and near his knees, with only the size of swallow wings covering his shoulders. When he bowed, it would fall from his shoulders, and whenever he prostrated it would reach his neck, so he would return it to his shoulders with his hand. This remained his manner throughout until he finished.

Hadith 5489

علي بن جعفر في كتابه عن أخيه موسى بن جعفر (عليه السلام) قال: سألته عن الرجل هل يصلح له أن يصلي في قميص واحد أو قباء وحده؟ قال: ليطرح على ظهره شيئا.

Ali bin Ja'far in his book from his brother Musa bin Ja'far (peace be upon him) said: I asked him if it is permissible for a man to pray in a single shirt or in a cloak alone? He said: He should put something on his back.

Hadith 5490

قال: وسألته عن الرجل هل يصلح له أن يؤم في ممطر وحده أو جبة وحدها؟ قال: إذا كان تحتها قميص فلا بأس.

He said: And I asked him if it is permissible for a man to lead prayer in just a raincoat or just a jubba? He said: If there is a shirt underneath then it is fine.

Hadith 5491

قال: وسألته عن الرجل يؤم في قباء وقميص؟ قال: إذا كانا ثوبين فلا بأس.

He said: And I asked him about a man leading prayer in a cloak and shirt? He said: If they are two garments then it is fine.

Hadith 5492

قال: وسألته عن السراويل هل تجزي مكان الإزار؟ قال: نعم.

He said: And I asked him if trousers can substitute for a waist wrap? He said: Yes.

Hadith 5493

قال: وسألته عن الرجل هل يصلح له أن يؤم في سراويل وقلنسوة؟ قال: لا يصلح.

He said: And I asked him if it is permissible for a man to lead prayer in trousers and a cap? He said: It is not permissible.

Hadith 5494

قال: وسألته عن الرجل، هل يصلح له أن يؤم في سراويل ورداء؟ قال: لا بأس به.

He said: And I asked him about a man, is it permissible for him to lead prayer wearing trousers and an upper garment? He said: There is no problem with it.

CHAPTER 23

Permissibility Of Men Praying With Unfastened Buttons And Loose Garment While Covering The Awrah, Though Disliked

[Hadith 5495 to 5503]

Hadith 5495

عن أبي جعفر (عليه السلام) قال: لا بأس أن يصلي أحدكم في الثوب الواحد وأزراره محللة إن دين محمد حنيف.

From Abu Ja'far (peace be upon him) who said: There is no harm if one of you prays in a single garment with unfastened buttons, indeed the religion of Muhammad is naturally inclined to ease.

———

Hadith 5496

عن أبي عبد الله (عليه السلام) قال: لا بأس أن يصلي الرجل وثوبه على ظهره ومنكبيه فيسبله إلى الأرض، ولا يلتحف به، وأخبرني من رآه يفعل ذلك.

From Abu Abdullah (peace be upon him) who said: There is no harm if a man prays with his garment on his back and shoulders letting it fall to the ground without wrapping it around himself, and someone informed me that they saw him doing this.

———

Hadith 5497

عن جعفر، عن أبيه (عليه السلام) قال: لا يصلي الرجل محلول الازرار إذا لم يكن عليه إزار.

From Ja'far, from his father (peace be upon him) who said: A man should not pray with unfastened buttons if he is not wearing a waist wrap.

أقول: حمله الشيخ على الاستحباب، ويمكن حمله على التقية، وعلى عدم ستر العورة في بعض الحالات.

I (Hurr Amili) say: The Shaykh interpreted this as recommended, and it can be interpreted as taqiyyah, and as not covering the awrah in some cases.

———

Hadith 5498

عن رجل قال: قلت لأبي عبد الله (عليه السلام): إن الناس يقولون: إن الرجل إذا صلى وأزراره محلولة ويداه داخلة في القميص إنما يصلي عريانا، قال: لا بأس.

From a man who said: I said to Abu Abdullah (peace be upon him): People say that when a man prays with his buttons unfastened and his hands inside his shirt, he is praying as if naked. He said: There is no harm in it.

———

Hadith 5499

عن إبراهيم الأحمري قال: سألت أبا عبد الله (عليه السلام) عن رجل يصلي وأزراره محللة، قال: لا ينبغي ذلك.

From Ibrahim Al-Ahmari who said: I asked Abu Abdullah (peace be upon him) about a man who prays with unfastened buttons. He said: That is not appropriate.

Hadith 5500

عن أبي جعفر (عليه السلام) - حديث - إن حل الازرار في الصلاة من عمل قوم لوط.

From Abu Ja'far (peace be upon him) - a hadith - that unfastening buttons during prayer is from the practices of the people of Lut.

Hadith 5501

عن عبد الله بن بكير أنه سأل أبا عبد الله (عليه السلام) عن الرجل يصلي ويرسل جانبي ثوبه؟ قال: لا بأس.

From Abdullah bin Bukayr that he asked Abu Abdullah (peace be upon him) about a man who prays while letting the sides of his garment loose? He said: There is no harm in it.

Hadith 5502

عن موسى بن جعفر (عليه السلام) قال: سألته عن الرجل يقوم في الصلاة فيطرح على ظهره ثوبا يقع طرفه خلفه وأمامه الأرض لا يضمنه عليه، أيجزيه ذلك؟ قال: نعم.

From Musa bin Ja'far (peace be upon him), he said: I asked him about a man who stands in prayer and puts a garment on his back with its ends falling behind him and in front of him on the ground without securing it on himself, is this sufficient for him? He said: Yes.

Hadith 5503

وبالاسناد قال: وسألته عن الرجل يتوشح بالثوب في الصلاة يقع على الأرض أو يجاوز عاتقه، أيصلح ذلك؟ قال: لا بأس.

And with the same chain of transmission, he said: And I asked him about a man who wraps himself with a garment in prayer that falls on the ground or extends beyond his shoulder, is this permissible? He said: There is no problem with it.

CHAPTER 24

Dislike Of Wearing A Wrap Over The Shirt And Wearing A Waist-Wrap Over It Especially For The Prayer Leader, And That It Is Not Prohibited

[Hadith 5504 to 5515]

Hadith 5504

عن أبي بصير، عن أبي عبد الله (عليه السلام) قال: لا ينبغي أن تتوشح بإزار فوق القميص (وأنت تصلي، ولا تتزر بإزار فوق القميص) إذا أنت صليت فإنه من زي الجاهلية.

From Abu Basir, from Abu Abdullah (peace be upon him) who said: One should not wear a wrap over the shirt while praying, nor wear a waist-wrap over the shirt when praying, for this was a practice of pre-Islamic times.

———

Hadith 5505

عن أبي عبد الله (عليه السلام) قال: سئل عن الرجل يؤم بقوم يجوز له أن يتوشح؟ قال: لا يصلي الرجل بقوم وهو متوشح فوق ثيابه، وإن كانت عليه ثياب كثيرة، لأن الامام لا تجوز له الصلاة وهو متوشح.

From Abu Abdullah (peace be upon him) who said: He was asked about whether it is permissible for a man leading people in prayer to wear a wrap? He said: A man should not lead people in prayer while wearing a wrap over his clothes, even if he is wearing many clothes, because it is not permissible for the imam to pray while wearing a wrap.

———

Hadith 5506

عن محمد بن إسماعيل، عن بعض أصحابنا، عن أحدهما (عليهما السلام) قال: قال: الارتداء فوق التوشح في الصلاة مكروه، والتوشح فوق القميص مكروه.

From Muhammad bin Isma'il, from some of our companions, from one of them (peace be upon them) who said: Wearing a robe over a wrap in prayer is disliked, and wearing a wrap over the shirt is disliked.

———

Hadith 5507

عن أبي جعفر (عليه السلام) قال: سأله رجل وأنا حاضر عن الرجل يخرج من الحمام أو يغتسل فيتوشح ويلبس قميصه فوق الإزار فيصلي وهو كذلك؟ قال: هذا عمل قوم لوط، قلت: قال: فإنه يتوشح فوق القميص؟ قال: هذا من التجبر، قال: قلت: إن القميص رقيق يلتحف به؟ قال: نعم، ثم قال: إن حل الازرار في الصلاة، والخذف بالحصى، ومضغ الكندر في المجالس وعلى ظهر الطريق من عمل قوم لوط.

From Abu Ja'far (peace be upon him): A man asked him while I was present about a man who leaves the bathhouse or performs ghusl, then wears a wrap and puts his shirt over the waist-wrap and prays in this state? He said: This is the practice of the people of Lut. I asked: What if he wears the wrap over the shirt? He said: This is from arrogance. I said: What if the shirt is thin and he wraps himself with it? He said: Yes. Then he said: Undoing buttons during prayer, throwing pebbles, and chewing gum in gatherings and on the road are from the practices of the people of Lut.

Hadith 5508

عن موسى بن عمر بن بزيع قال: قلت للرضا (عليه السلام) أشد الازرار والمنديل فوق قميصي في الصلاة؟ فقال: لا بأس به.

From Musa bin Umar bin Buzay, he said: I asked Al-Ridha (peace be upon him): Can I fasten buttons and wear a scarf over my shirt in prayer? He said: There is no problem with it.

Hadith 5509

عن موسى بن القاسم قال: رأيت أبا جعفر الثاني (عليه السلام) يصلي في قميص قد اتزر فوقه بمنديل وهو يصلي.

From Musa bin Al-Qasim, he said: I saw Abu Ja'far the Second (peace be upon him) praying in a shirt with a scarf wrapped over it while he was praying.

Hadith 5510

عن حماد بن عيسى قال: كتب الحسن بن علي بن يقطين إلى العبد الصالح: هل يصلي الرجل الصلاة وعليه إزار متوشح به فوق القميص؟ فكتب: نعم.

From Hammad bin Isa, he said: Al-Hasan bin Ali bin Yaqtin wrote to the Righteous Servant asking: Can a man pray while wearing a wrap over his shirt? He wrote back: Yes.

قال الشيخ: المراد بهذه الأحاديث أن يتوشح بالإزار ليغطي ما قد كشف منه ويستر ما تعرى من بدنه. أقول: الأقرب الحمل على نفى التحريم، وحمل ما تقدم على الكراهة.

The Shaykh said: The meaning of these hadiths is that one wraps with a cover to conceal what has been exposed and cover the bare parts of his body. I (Hurr Amili) say: The closest interpretation is that it negates prohibition, and what preceded indicates dislike.

Hadith 5511

محمد بن علي بن الحسين قال: قد رويت رخصة في التوشح بالإزار فوق القميص عن العبد الصالح، وعن أبي الحسن الثالث، وعن أبي جعفر الثاني (عليهم السلام).

Muhammad bin Ali bin Al-Husayn said: A concession has been narrated regarding wrapping the waist wrap over the shirt from Al-Abd Al-Salih, and from Abu Al-Hasan the Third, and from Abu Ja'far the Second (peace be upon them).

Hadith 5512

وفي (الخصال) بإسناده عن علي (عليه السلام) - في حديث الأربعمائة - قال: لا يصلي الرجل في قميص متوشحا به فإنه من أفعال قوم لوط.

In (Al-Khisal), with its chain of narration from Ali (peace be upon him) - in the hadith of the four hundred - he said: A man should not pray in a shirt while wrapping it around himself, for it is from the actions of the people of Lut.

Hadith 5513

عن أبي عبد الله (عليه السلام): قال: إنما كره التوشح فوق القميص لأنه من فعل الجبابرة.

From Abu Abdullah (peace be upon him), he said: Wrapping over the shirt was disliked because it is from the actions of tyrants.

Hadith 5514

عن أبي جعفر وأبي عبد الله (عليهما السلام) أنه سئل ما العلة التي من أجلها لا يصلي الرجل وهو متوشح فوق القميص؟ فقال: لعلة الكبر في موضع الاستكانة والذل.

From Abu Ja'far and Abu Abdullah (peace be upon them), they were asked: What is the reason for which a man should not pray while wrapping over his shirt? They said: Because of arrogance in a place meant for humility and submission.

Hadith 5515

علي بن جعفر في كتابه عن أخيه قال: سألته عن الرجل يتوشح بالثوب فيقع على الأرض أو يجاوز عاتقه أيصلح ذلك؟ قال: لا بأس به.

Ali bin Ja'far in his book from his brother said: I asked him about a man who wraps himself with a cloth that falls to the ground or extends past his shoulders, is this permissible? He said: There is no problem with it.

CHAPTER 25

Dislike Of Letting The Robe Hang Down, Wearing It Without An Opening, Gathering Its Ends On The Left Side, And The Recommendation Of Gathering Them On The Right Side Or Leaving Them

[Hadith 5516 to 5523]

Hadith 5516

عن زرارة، عن أبي جعفر (عليه السلام) أنه قال: إياك والتحاف الصماء، قلت: وما التحاف الصماء؟ قال: أن تدخل الثوب من تحت جناحك فتجعله على منكب واحد.

From Zurarah, from Abu Ja'far (peace be upon him) who said: Beware of wearing the samma. I asked: What is wearing the samma? He said: It is when you insert the garment from under your arm and place it on one shoulder.

Hadith 5517

عن سماعة قال: سألته عن الرجل يشتمل في صلاته بثوب واحد؟ قال: لا يشتمل بثوب واحد، فأما أن يتوشح فيغطي منكبيه فلا بأس.

From Sama'ah who said: I asked him about a man who wraps himself in one garment during prayer. He replied: One should not wrap in a single garment, but if he covers his shoulders with it there is no problem.

Hadith 5518

عن زرارة قال: قال أبو جعفر (عليه السلام) خرج أمير المؤمنين (عليه السلام) على قوم فرآهم يصلون في المسجد قد سدلوا أرديتهم، فقال لهم: مالكم قد سدلتم ثيابكم كأنكم يهود قد خرجوا من فهرهم؟! يعني بيعتهم إياكم وسدل ثيابكم.

From Zurarah who said: Abu Ja'far (peace be upon him) said: Amir al-Mu'minin (peace be upon him) came upon a group of people and saw them praying in the mosque with their robes hanging down. He said to them: What is wrong with you that you let your clothes hang down as if you were Jews coming out of their fahr (meaning their synagogue)? Beware of letting your clothes hang down.

Hadith 5519

عن عبد الله بن بكير أنه سأل أبا عبد الله (عليه السلام) عن الرجل يصلي ويرسل جانبي ثوبه؟ قال: لا بأس.

From Abdullah bin Bukayr that he asked Abu Abdullah (peace be upon him) about a man who prays while letting the sides of his garment hang down. He said: There is no problem with that.

Hadith 5520

وفي (معاني الأخبار): عن القاسم بن سلام رفعه عن النبي (صلى الله عليه وآله) أنه نهى عن لبستين: اشتمال الصماء، وأن يحتبي الرجل بثوب ليس بين فرجه وبين السماء شئ.

In Ma'ani al-Akhbar: From Al-Qasim bin Sallam, raising it to the Prophet (peace be upon him and his family) that he prohibited two types of dress: wearing the samma, and for a man to sit with his knees drawn up wrapped in a single garment with nothing between his farj (genitals) and the sky.

Hadith 5521

قال: وقال الصادق (عليه السلام): التحاف الصماء هو أن يدخل الرجل رداءه تحت إبطه ثم يجعل طرفيه على منكب واحد.

He said: And Al-Sadiq (peace be upon him) said: Wearing the samma is when a man puts his robe under his armpit then places its ends on one shoulder.

Hadith 5522

عن موسى بن جعفر (عليهما السلام)، قال: سألته عن الرجل، هل يصلح له أن يجمع طرفي ردائه على يساره؟ قال: لا يصلح جمعهما على اليسار، ولكن اجمعهما على يمينك، أودعهما.

From Musa bin Ja'far (peace be upon them both), he said: I asked him about a man, is it proper for him to gather the ends of his robe on his left side? He said: It is not proper to gather them on the left, rather gather them on your right or leave them.

Hadith 5523

عن جعفر بن محمد، عن أبيه (عليهما السلام) قال: إنما كره السدل على الازر بغير قميص، فأما على القمص والجباب فلا بأس.

From Ja'far bin Muhammad, from his father (peace be upon them both) who said: What is disliked is to drape garments over the waist wrap without wearing a shirt, but if worn over shirts and robes then there is no problem with it.

CHAPTER 26

Dislike Of Neglecting To Wrap The Turban Under The Chin When Wearing It, When Pursuing A Need, And When Traveling

[Hadith 5524 to 5535]

Hadith 5524

عن أبي عبد الله (عليه السلام) قال: من تعمم ولم يحنك فأصابه داء لا دواء له فلا يلومن إلا نفسه.

From Abu Abdullah (peace be upon him) who said: Whoever wears a turban without wrapping it under his chin (tahannuk) and is afflicted with an illness that has no cure, he should blame none but himself.

Hadith 5525

عن أبي عبد الله (عليه السلام) قال: من اعتم فلم يدر العمامة تحت حنكه فأصابه ألم لا دواء له فلا يلومن إلا نفسه.

From Abu Abdullah (peace be upon him) who said: Whoever wears a turban without wrapping it under his chin (hanak) and is afflicted with a pain that has no cure, he should blame none but himself.

Hadith 5526

عن علي بن الحكم رفعه إلى أبي عبد الله (عليه السلام) قال: من خرج من منزله معتما تحت حنكه يريد سفرا لم يصبه في سفره سرق ولا حرق ولا مكروه.

From Ali ibn al-Hakam, raising it to Abu Abdullah (peace be upon him) who said: Whoever leaves his house wearing a turban wrapped under his chin (hanak) intending to travel will not be afflicted during his journey by theft, fire, or any harm.

Hadith 5527

قال الكليني: وروي: أن الطابقية عمة إبليس.

Al-Kulayni said: It is narrated that the Tabiqiyyah (*) is the turban of Iblis.

Translator: * The tabiqiyyah is when the turban is simply wrapped around the head without the traditional hanging part (loose flowing end) for chin wrapping. It likely falls in the category of the "iqti'at" style mentioned in Hadith 5532. The term itself comes from the root "ta-ba-qa" (relating to layers or covering) referring to how this style simply covers the head in layers without the proper Islamic method of letting the ends flow freely for wrapping them under the chin.

Hadith 5528

عن أبي عبد الله (عليه السلام)، أنه قال: من خرج في سفر فلم يدر حنكه تحت العمامة فأصابه ألم لا دواء له فلا يلومن إلا نفسه.

From Abu Abdullah (peace be upon him), who said: Whoever sets out on a journey without wrapping the turban under his chin (hanak) and is afflicted with a pain that has no cure, he should blame none but himself.

Hadith 5529

قال: وقال الصادق (عليه السلام): ضمنت لمن خرج من بيته معتما أن يرجع إليهم سالما.

He said: And Al-Sadiq (peace be upon him) said: I guarantee that whoever leaves his house wearing a turban will return to them safely.

Hadith 5530

قال: وقال الصادق (عليه السلام): إني لأعجب ممن يأخذ في حاجة وهو معتم تحت حنكه، كيف لا تقضى حاجته؟!

He said: And Al-Sadiq (peace be upon him) said: I am amazed at one who pursues a need while wearing a turban under his chin (hanak), how could his need not be fulfilled?!

Hadith 5531

قال: وقال النبي (صلى الله عليه وآله): الفرق بين المسلمين والمشركين التلحي بالعمائم. قال الصدوق: وذلك في أول الاسلام وابتدائه.

And the Prophet (peace be upon him and his family) said: The distinction between Muslims and polytheists is wearing turbans wrapped around the chin (*). Al-Saduq said: And this was during the beginning and early days of Islam.

Translator: * This refers to the Al-talahhi style of wrapping a turban in which a part of the turban under the chin, where the loose end is brought around and under the chin. See Hadith 5532 for the other style which is prohibited.

Hadith 5532

قال: وقد نقل عنه (صلى الله عليه وآله) أهل الخلاف أيضا أنه أمر بالتلحي ونهى عن الاقتعاط.

And it was also narrated by those who differ from us that he (peace be upon him and his family) ordered wearing turbans under the chin (talahhi) and prohibited wearing them without doing so (iqti'at).

Translator: This hadith discusses two styles of wearing turbans. 1. Al-talahhi - wrapping part of the turban under the chin, where the loose end is brought around and under the chin. 2. Al-iqti'at - wrapping the turban around the head without bringing any part under the chin, also referred to as "tabiqiyyah" in Hadith 5527.

Hadith 5533

عن جعفر بن محمد، عن أبيه (عليهما السلام) أن رسول الله (صلى الله عليه وآله) قال: الفرق بيننا وبين المشركين في العمائم الالتحاء بالعمائم.

From Ja'far bin Muhammad, from his father (peace be upon them both) that the Messenger of Allah (peace be upon him and his family) said: The distinction between us and the polytheists regarding turbans is wrapping them under the chin.

Hadith 5534

أحمد بن أبي عبد الله البرقي في (المحاسن) قال: وروى: أن المسومين المعتمين.

Ahmad bin Abu Abdullah al-Barqi reported in (Al-Mahasin): It was narrated that the "musawwamim" (marked ones) are those wearing turbans.

Hadith 5535

قال: وروى: الطابقية عمة إبليس.

And it was narrated: The Tabiqiyyah is the turban of Iblis.

أقول: ويأتي ما يدل على كيفية تعمم النبي (صلى الله عليه وآله) والأئمة (عليهم السلام)، إن شاء الله تعالى، وذلك ينافي هذه الأحاديث ظاهرا، ويندفع بأن هذه الأحاديث لا تدل على حكم غير وقت التعمم والخروج إلى السفر والحاجة، وقد ذكر جملة من علمائنا، منهم الشيخ بهاء الدين، أنهم لم يجدوا نصا على استحباب التحنك في حال الصلاة، والله أعلم.

I (Hurr Amili) say: And there will come what indicates the manner of wearing the turban of the Prophet (peace be upon him and his family) and the Imams (peace be upon them), insha'Allah, and this apparently contradicts these hadiths. This contradiction is resolved by noting that these hadiths do not indicate a ruling outside the time of wearing the turban and going out for travel and need. A group of our scholars, including Shaykh Baha al-Din, have mentioned that they did not find any explicit text regarding the recommendation of wearing the turban under the chin during prayer. And Allah knows best.

Translator: The traditions compiled in this chapter establish a definitive legislative emphasis on the "tahannuk" or "hanak", which is the practice of wrapping a portion of the turban cloth under the chin. This specific method, often referred to in the texts as "al-talahhi", is characterized by taking the loose end of the turban and securing it beneath the jaw. According to the "Infallible" Guides, this structural "Adab" serves as a primary "distinction" between the believers and the polytheists. Beyond its symbolic value, the "Ahl al-Bayt" describe the "tahannuk" as a functional safeguard that protects the wearer from incurable illnesses, ensures safety from theft and fire during travel, and facilitates the fulfillment of one's needs when pursued in this manner.

In direct opposition to the recommended "Sunnah" is the "iqti'at" or "tabiqiyyah" style, which involves wrapping the cloth solely around the head in layers without any part passing under the chin. These reports categorize the "tabiqiyyah" as the "turban of Iblis", and the Imams issue severe warnings that any individual who adopts this style and is subsequently afflicted with a chronic ailment should "blame none but himself". The technical definition of "tabiqiyyah" provided in the lexicons of these traditions refers to a method of simply layering the cloth atop the head while neglecting the flowing end required for the chin-wrap. This creates a sharp "ontological" boundary between the headgear of the "Mu'min" and the styles attributed to the enemies of Allah.

While some scholars have historically analyzed these reports through various lenses, the primary texts remain focused on the physical manner of the wrap and the resulting spiritual or physical consequences. For instance, Al-Saduq noted that the distinction regarding the polytheists was particularly emphasized in the early days of Islam, while Shaykh Hurr al-Amili points out that some jurists, such as those from the Rationalist school, have debated whether the recommendation for "tahannuk" applies specifically during the state of "Salat" or if it is restricted to travel and general daily needs. However, the literal reports in this chapter link the "tahannuk" to the very act of leaving one's house or setting out on a journey. It is left to the discerning reader to audit the styles of headgear of the modern scholars, against these specific textual markers, and determine whether the contemporary practices align with the mandated "Sunnah" or if they inadvertently mirror the layered "tabiqiyyah" method condemned by the "Ahl al-Bayt".

CHAPTER 27

Obligation Of Covering The Awrah During Prayer And Otherwise, And The Prayer Not Being Invalid If Left Uncovered Unknowingly, And The Extent Of The Awrah

[Hadith 5536 to 5536]

Hadith 5536

عن علي بن جعفر، عن أخيه قال: سألته عن الرجل صلى وفرجه خارج لا يعلم به، هل عليه إعادة أو ما حاله؟ قال: لا إعادة عليه، وقد تمت صلاته.

From Ali bin Ja'far, from his brother, he said: I asked him about a man who prayed while his private part was exposed without him knowing it, does he have to repeat the prayer or what is his situation? He said: He does not have to repeat it, and his prayer is complete.

———

CHAPTER 28

Impermissibility Of Prayer For A Mature Free Woman Without A Dir'a (Robe/Gown) And Head Cover Or Single Garment That Covers Her Entire Body Except Face, Hands And Feet, And Likewise For A Partially Freed Slave Woman

[Hadith 5537 to 5553]

Hadith 5537

عن أبي جعفر (عليه السلام) قال: صلت فاطمة (عليها السلام) في درع وخمارها على رأسها، ليس عليها أكثر مما وارت به شعرها وأذنيها.

From Abu Ja'far (peace be upon him), he said: Fatimah (peace be upon her) prayed wearing a dir'a (*) and her headcover on her head, with nothing more upon her than what concealed her hair and ears.

Translator: * The dir'a refers to a woman's long dress or garment that covers the body from the shoulders down. It's essentially a full-length garment similar to what we might call a gown or robe today.

Hadith 5538

عن علي بن جعفر، أنه سأل أخاه موسى بن جعفر (عليه السلام) عن المرأة ليس لها إلا ملحفة واحدة، كيف تصلي؟ قال: تلتف فيها وتغطي رأسها وتصلي، فإن خرجت رجلها وليس تقدر على غير ذلك فلا بأس.

From Ali ibn Ja'far, that he asked his brother Musa ibn Ja'far (peace be upon him) about a woman who has only one sheet, how should she pray? He said: She should wrap herself in it and cover her head and pray. If her leg becomes exposed and she cannot do better than that, then there is no problem.

Hadith 5539

عن أبي جعفر (عليه السلام) قال: المرأة تصلي في الدرع والمقنعة إذا كان كثيفا، يعني ستيرا.

From Abu Ja'far (peace be upon him), he said: A woman can pray wearing a dir'a (full-length garment/gown) and head covering when they are thick, meaning concealing.

Hadith 5540

وبإسناده عن يونس بن يعقوب، أنه سأل أبا عبد الله (عليه السلام) عن الرجل يصلي في ثوب واحد؟ قال:
نعم. قال: قلت: فالمرأة؟ قال: لا، ولا يصلح للحرة إذا حاضت إلا الخمار، إلا أن لا تجده.

And by his chain from Yunus ibn Ya'qub, that he asked Abu Abdullah (peace be upon him) about a man praying in one garment? He said: Yes. He said: I asked: What about a woman? He said: No, and it is not proper for a free woman when she menstruates except with a head cover, unless she cannot find one.

Hadith 5541

عن أبي عبد الله (عليه السلام) قال: سألته عن المرأة تصلي في درع وملحفة ليس عليها إزار ولا مقنعة؟
قال: لا بأس إذا التفت بها، وإن لم تكن تكفيها عرضا جعلتها طولا.

From Abu Abdullah (peace be upon him) who said: I asked him about a woman praying in a dir'a (full-length garment/gown) and sheet without wearing a waist-wrap or head covering? He said: There is no problem if she wraps herself with it, and if its width is not sufficient she can use it lengthwise.

Hadith 5542

قال: وقال النبي (صلى الله عليه وآله): ثمانية لا يقبل الله لهم صلاة، منهم المرأة المدركة تصلي بغير خمار.

He said: And the Prophet (peace be upon him and his family) said: There are eight whose prayers Allah does not accept, among them is the mature woman who prays without a head cover.

Hadith 5543

عن محمد بن مسلم - في حديث - قال: قلت لأبي جعفر (عليه السلام): ما ترى للرجل يصلي في قميص
واحد؟ فقال: إذا كان كثيفا فلا بأس به، والمرأة تصلي في الدرع والمقنعة إذا كان الدرع كثيفا، يعني إذا كان ستيرا.

From Muhammad bin Muslim - in a hadith - he said: I asked Abu Ja'far (peace be upon him): What do you say about a man praying in a single shirt? He said: If it is thick then there is no problem with it, and a woman prays in a dir'a (full-length garment/gown) and head covering if the dir'a is thick, meaning if it is concealing.

Hadith 5544

عن ابن أبي يعفور قال: قال أبو عبد الله (عليه السلام): تصلي المرأة في ثلاثة أثواب: إزار، ودرع، وخمار، ولا يضرها بأن تقنع بالخمار، فإن لم تجد فثوبين تتزر بأحدهما وتقنع بالآخر، قلت: فإن كان درع وملحفة، ليس عليها مقنعة؟ فقال: لا بأس إذا تقنعت بملحفة، فإن لم تكفها فتلبسها طولا.

From Ibn Abi Ya'fur who said: Abu Abdullah (peace be upon him) said: A woman prays in three garments: a waist wrap, a dir'a (full-length garment/gown), and a head cover. It does not harm her to cover with the head cover. If she cannot find three then two garments - she wraps one and covers with the other. I asked: What if she has a dress and a sheet but no head cover? He said: No problem if she covers with the sheet, and if it's not enough she can wear it lengthwise.

Hadith 5545

عن زرارة قال: سألت أبا جعفر (عليه السلام) عن أدنى ما تصلي فيه المرأة؟ قال: درع وملحفة فتنشرها على رأسها، وتجلل بها.

From Zurarah who said: I asked Abu Ja'far (peace be upon him) about the minimum clothing in which a woman can pray? He said: A dir'a (full-length garment/gown) and a sheet which she spreads over her head and wraps around herself.

Hadith 5546

عن أبي الحسن (عليه السلام) قال: ليس على الإماء أن يتقنعن في الصلاة، ولا ينبغي للمرأة أن تصلي إلا في ثوبين.

From Abu al-Hasan (peace be upon him) who said: Female slaves are not required to cover their heads in prayer, but a woman should not pray except in two garments.

Hadith 5547

عن جميل بن دراج قال: سألت أبا عبد الله (عليه السلام) عن المرأة تصلي في درع وخمار؟ فقال: يكون عليها ملحفة تضمها عليها.

From Jamil bin Darraj who said: I asked Abu Abdullah (peace be upon him) about a woman praying in a dir'a (full-length garment/gown) and head cover? He said: She should have a wrap that she draws around herself.

قال الشيخ: هذا محمول على زيادة الفضل والثواب، أو على كون الدرع والخمار لا يواريان شيئا لما تقدم.

The Shaykh said: This is interpreted as being for additional virtue and reward, or for when the dir'a and head cover do not conceal properly based on what was previously mentioned.

Hadith 5548

عن هشام بن سالم، عن حمزة بن حمران، عن أحدهما (عليهما السلام)، قال: سألته عن الرجل أعتق نصف جاريته - إلى أن قال - قلت: فتغطي رأسها منه حين أعتق نصفها؟ قال: نعم، وتصلي، هي مخمرة الرأس.

From Hisham bin Salem, from Hamza bin Hamran, from one of them (peace be upon them), who said: I asked him about a man who freed half (*) of his slave girl - until he said - I asked: Should she cover her head from him when half of her is freed? He said: Yes, and she prays with her head covered.

Translator: * The owner relinquishes half of their ownership rights over the slave. The slave might work for the owner for half the time and be free the other half.

Hadith 5549

عن جعفر بن محمد، عن أبيه، عن علي (عليهم السلام) قال: إذا حاضت الجارية فلا تصلي إلا بخمار.

From Ja'far bin Muhammad, from his father, from Ali (peace be upon them) who said: When a girl experiences menstruation, she should not pray except with a head cover.

أقول: المراد بالجارية الصبية الحرة، والحيض المراد به البلوغ، وأنها تصلي بعد انقطاعه إن بلغت به وذلك كله ظاهر.

I (Hurr Amili) say: The girl refers to a free young woman, and menstruation refers to puberty, meaning she prays after it stops if she reached puberty through it, and all this is apparent.

Hadith 5550

وعن عبد الله بن الحسن، عن جده علي بن جعفر، عن أخيه موسى بن جعفر (عليهم السلام)، قال: سألته عن المرأة الحرة، هل يصلح لها أن تصلي في درع ومقنعة؟ قال: لا يصلح لها إلا في ملحفة إلا أن لا تجد بدا.

From Abdullah bin Al-Hasan, from his grandfather Ali bin Ja'far, from his brother Musa bin Ja'far (peace be upon them), he said: I asked him about the free woman, is it permissible for her to pray in a dir'a (full-length garment/gown) and head covering? He said: It is not permissible for her except in a full covering wrap unless she has no alternative.

Hadith 5551

علي بن جعفر في كتابه، عن أخيه موسى بن جعفر (عليه السلام)، قال: سألته عن المرأة، هل يصلح لها أن تصلي في ملحفة ومقنعة ولها درع؟ قال: لا يصلح لها إلا أن تلبس درعها.

Ali bin Ja'far in his book, from his brother Musa bin Ja'far (peace be upon him), who said: I asked him about a woman, is it proper for her to pray in a sheet and head cover when she has a dir'a (full-length garment/gown)? He said: It is not proper unless she wears her dir'a.

Hadith 5552

قال: وسألته عن المرأة، هل يصلح لها أن تصلي في إزار وملحفة ومقنعة ولها درع؟ قال: إذا وجدت فلا يصلح لها الصلاة إلا وعليها درع.

He said: And I asked him about a woman, is it permissible for her to pray wearing a waist wrap, sheet, and head cover while she has a dir'a (full-length garment/gown) available? He said: If she has one available, it is not permissible for her to pray except while wearing a dir'a.

Hadith 5553

قال: وسألته عن المرأة، هل يصلح لها أن تصلي في إزار وملحفة تقنع بها ولها درع؟ قال: (لا يصلح) أن تصلي حتى تلبس درعها.

He said: And I asked him about a woman, is it permissible for her to pray wearing a waist wrap and sheet which she uses as head covering while she has a dir'a (full-length garment/gown) available? He said: It is not permissible for her to pray until she wears her dir'a.

CHAPTER 29

Non-Requirement Of Female Slaves To Cover Their Heads In Prayer, And Likewise Free Pre-Pubescent Girls, Umm Al-Walad, Mudabbarah, And Conditional Mukatibah

[Hadith 5554 to 5564]

Hadith 5554

عن أبي جعفر (عليه السلام) - في حديث -، قال: قلت: الأمة تغطي رأسها إذا صلت؟ فقال: ليس على الأمة قناع.

From Abu Ja'far (peace be upon him) in a hadith, I asked: Should a female slave cover her head when she prays? He said: A female slave is not required to wear head covering.

———

Hadith 5555

عن أبي الحسن (عليه السلام) - في حديث - قال: ليس على الإماء أن يتقنعن في الصلاة.

From Abu Al-Hasan (peace be upon him) in a hadith, he said: Female slaves are not required to cover their heads in prayer.

Hadith 5556

عن أبي بصير، عن أبي عبد الله (عليه السلام)، أنه قال: على الصبي إذا احتلم الصيام، وعلى الجارية إذا حاضت الصيام والخمار، إلا أن تكون مملوكة فإنه ليس عليها خمار إلا أن تحب أن تختمر، وعليها الصيام.

From Abu Basir, from Abu Abdullah (peace be upon him), he said: A boy must fast when he reaches puberty, and a girl must fast and wear head covering when she menstruates, unless she is enslaved in which case she is not required to wear head covering except if she wishes to cover herself, but she must fast.

———

Hadith 5557

عن أبي عبد الله (عليه السلام) قال: قلت له: الأمة تغطي رأسها؟ فقال: لا، ولا على أم الولد أن تغطي رأسها إذا لم يكن لها ولد.

From Abu Abdullah (peace be upon him), I said to him: Should a female slave cover her head? He said: No, and neither should Umm Al-Walad (*) cover her head if she does not have a child.

Translator: * Literally "mother of the child", referring to a female slave who has borne a child to her master. According to this hadith she does not need to cover her head if she doesn't have a child (presumably, if the child has passed away or if she hasn't given birth yet).

Hadith 5558

عن أبي عبد الله (عليه السلام) قال: لا بأس بالمرأة المسلمة الحرة أن تصلي وهي مكشوفة الرأس.

From Abu Abdullah (peace be upon him), he said: There is no harm if a free Muslim woman prays with her head uncovered.

Hadith 5559

عن أبي عبد الله (عليه السلام) قال: لا بأس أن تصلي المرأة المسلمة و ليس على رأسها قناع.

From Abu Abdullah (peace be upon him), he said: There is no harm if a Muslim woman prays without head covering.

قال الشيخ: يحتمل أن يكون المراد بهذين الخبرين الصغيرة من النساء دون البالغات، ويمكن أن يكون إنما سوغ لهن هذا في حال لا يقدرن على القناع، ويحتمل أن يكون المراد تصلي بغير قناع إذا كان عليها ثوب يسترها من رأسها إلى قدميها. قال: والخبر الثاني ليس فيه ذكر الحرة فيحمل على الأمة.

The Shaykh said: These two reports possibly refer to young pre-pubescent girls rather than adult women, or it could mean this is allowed when they cannot find head covering, or it could mean praying without specific head covering when wearing a garment that covers from head to feet. He said: The second report does not mention "free woman" so it applies to female slaves.

Hadith 5560

عن أبي جعفر (عليه السلام) قال: ليس على الأمة قناع في الصلاة، ولا على المدبرة قناع في الصلاة، ولا على المكاتبة، إذا اشترط عليها مولاها، قناع في الصلاة. وهي مملوكة حتى تؤدي جميع مكاتبتها، ويجري عليها ما يجري على المملوك في الحدود كلها. قال: وسألته عن الأمة إذا ولدت، عليها الخمار؟ قال: لو كان عليها لكان عليها إذا هي حاضت، وليس عليها التقنع في الصلاة.

From Abu Ja'far (peace be upon him), he said: A female slave does not need head covering in prayer, nor does a Mudabbarah (*) need head covering in prayer, nor does a Mukatibah (**) need head covering in prayer if her master made it a condition, and she remains a slave until she completes all her Mukatibah payments, and prescribed punishments apply to her as they do to slaves in all cases. I asked him about a female slave who gives birth, does she need head covering? He said: If it was required of her, it would have been required when she menstruated, but she does not need to cover her head in prayer.

Translator: * Mudabbarah refers to a female slave whose master has promised to free her upon his death. ** Mukatibah refers to a female slave who has entered into a contract of manumission with her master. In this agreement, the slave pays a certain amount of money or performs specific tasks over a period of time to earn her freedom.

Hadith 5561

عن أبي عبد الله (عليه السلام)، قال: سألته عن الخادم تقنع رأسها في الصلاة؟ قال: اضربوها، حتى تعرف الحرة من المملوكة.

From Abu Abdullah (peace be upon him), he said: I asked him about a female servant covering her head in prayer? He said: Strike her, until the free woman is distinguished from the slave woman.

Hadith 5562

عن حماد اللحام قال: سألت أبا عبد الله (عليه السلام) عن المملوكة تقنع رأسها في الصلاة؟ قال: لا، قد كان أبي إذا رأى الخادم تصلي وهي مقنعة ضربها، لتعرف الحرة من المملوكة.

From Hammad al-Lahham who said: I asked Abu Abdullah (peace be upon him) about a female slave covering her head in prayer? He said: No, my father used to strike the servant when he saw her praying with her head covered, to distinguish the free woman from the slave woman.

Hadith 5563

عن موسى بن جعفر (عليه السلام)، قال: سألته عن الأمة، هل يصلح لها أن تصلي في قميص واحد؟ قال: لا بأس.

From Musa bin Ja'far (peace be upon him), he said: I asked him about a female slave, is it permissible for her to pray in one garment? He said: There is no problem.

Hadith 5564

عن أبي خالد القماط قال: سألت أبا عبد الله (عليه السلام) عن الأمة، أتقنع رأسها؟ قال: إن شاءت فعلت، وإن شاءت لم تفعل، سمعت أبي يقول: كن يضرب بن فيقال لهن: لا تشبهن بالحرائر.

From Abu Khalid al-Qammat who said: I asked Abu Abdullah (peace be upon him) about a female slave, should she cover her head? He said: If she wishes she may do so, and if she wishes she may not do so. I heard my father saying: They used to be struck and told: Do not imitate the free women.

CHAPTER 30

Prohibition Of Men Wearing Gold Including Rings, Praying While Wearing It, Its Permissibility For Women And Children, And Related Prohibitions

[Hadith 5565 to 5575]

Hadith 5565

عن أبي عبد الله (عليه السلام) قال: قال رسول الله (صلى الله عليه وآله) لأمير المؤمنين (عليه السلام):
لا تختم بالذهب فإنه زينتك في الآخرة.

From Abu Abdullah (peace be upon him) who said: The Messenger of Allah (peace be upon him and his family) said to Amir al-Mu'minin (peace be upon him): Do not wear a gold ring for it will be your adornment in the hereafter.

Hadith 5566

عن أبي عبد الله (عليه السلام) قال: لا تجعل في يدك خاتما من ذهب.

From Abu Abdullah (peace be upon him) who said: Do not put a gold ring on your hand.

Hadith 5567

عن أبي عبد الله (عليه السلام)، أن النبي (صلى الله عليه وآله) تختم في يساره بخاتم من ذهب، ثم خرج على الناس، فطفق الناس ينظرون إليه، فوضع يده اليمنى على خنصره اليسرى حتى رجع إلى البيت فرمى به فما لبسه.

From Abu Abdullah (peace be upon him): The Prophet (peace be upon him and his family) wore a gold ring on his left hand, then went out to the people. The people began looking at it, so he placed his right hand over his left pinky until he returned home and threw it away, never wearing it again.

أقول: هذا محمول إما على النسخ لما في آخره، أو على كونه مختصا به، ولذلك كتمه لئلا يقتدى به.

I (Hurr Amili) say: This is interpreted either as being abrogated as indicated by its ending, or as being specific to him, hence he concealed it so others would not follow his example.

Hadith 5568

عن أبي عبد الله (عليه السلام) - في حديث - قال: لا يلبس الرجل الذهب، ولا يصلي فيه، لأنه من لباس أهل الجنة.

From Abu Abdullah (peace be upon him) in a hadith saying: A man should not wear gold nor pray while wearing it, because it is from the clothing of the people of Paradise.

Hadith 5569

عن أبي عبد الله (عليه السلام)، في الحديد: إنه حلية أهل النار، والذهب إنه حلية أهل الجنة، وجعل الله الذهب في الدنيا زينة النساء فحرم على الرجال لبسه والصلاة فيه.

From Abu Abdullah (peace be upon him) regarding iron: It is the ornament of the people of Hell, and gold is the ornament of the people of Paradise, and Allah made gold in this world as an adornment for women and prohibited men from wearing it and praying in it.

Hadith 5570

عن أبي جعفر (عليه السلام)، أن النبي (صلى الله عليه وآله) قال لعلي (عليه السلام): إني أحب لك ما أحب لنفسي، وأكره لك ما أكره لنفسي، لا تتختم بخاتم ذهب، فإنه زينتك في الآخرة.

From Abu Ja'far (peace be upon him): The Prophet (peace be upon him and his family) said to Ali (peace be upon him): I love for you what I love for myself, and I dislike for you what I dislike for myself. Do not wear a gold ring, for it will be your adornment in the hereafter.

Hadith 5571

عن أبي عبد الله (عليه السلام) قال: قال علي (عليه السلام): نهاني رسول الله (صلى الله عليه وآله)، ولا أقول نهاكم، عن التختم بالذهب، وعن ثياب القسي، وعن ميائر الأرجوان، وعن الملاحف المفدمة، وعن القراءة وأنا راكع. قال حمزة بن محمد: القسي: ثياب يؤتى بها من مصر فيها حرير.

From Abu Abdullah (peace be upon him), who said: Ali (peace be upon him) said: The Messenger of Allah (peace be upon him and his family) forbade me - and I do not say he forbade you all - from wearing rings of gold, from al-Qassi garments, from al-mayathir al-arjuwan (purple saddle cloths), from al-malahif al-mufaddama (red-dyed garments), and from reciting Quran while I am in the bowing position (ruku). Hamza ibn Muhammad said: al-Qassi refers to garments brought from Egypt that contain silk.

Hadith 5572

عن البراء بن عازب قال: نهى رسول الله (صلى الله عليه وآله) عن سبع، وأمر بسبع. نهانا أن نتختم بالذهب، وعن الشرب في آنية الذهب والفضة. وقال: من شرب فيها في الدنيا لم يشرب فيها في الآخرة، وعن ركوب المياثر، وعن لبس القسي، وعن لبس الحرير والديباج والإستبرق، وأمرنا باتباع الجنائز، وعيادة المريض، وتسميت العاطس، ونصرة المظلوم، وإفشاء السلام، وإجابة الداعي، وإبرار القسم.

From Al-Bara' bin 'Azib said: The Messenger of Allah (peace be upon him and his family) prohibited seven things and commanded seven things: He prohibited us from wearing gold rings, from drinking from gold and silver vessels, and said: whoever drinks from them in this world will not drink from them in the hereafter, from riding on silk saddle cloths, from wearing silk garments called Qassi, from wearing silk, brocade and thick silk, and he commanded us to follow funeral processions, visit the sick, respond to one who sneezes, help the oppressed, spread greetings of peace, accept invitations, and fulfill oaths.

Hadith 5573

عن جعفر بن محمد، عن أبيه (عليهما السلام) أن رسول الله (صلى الله عليه وآله) نهاهم عن سبع. منها التختم بالذهب.

From Ja'far bin Muhammad, from his father (peace be upon them both): The Messenger of Allah (peace be upon him and his family) prohibited them from seven things, among them wearing gold rings.

Hadith 5574

عن أخيه موسى بن جعفر (عليهما السلام)، قال: سألته عن الرجل هل يصلح له الخاتم الذهب؟ قال: لا. ورواه علي بن جعفر في كتابه، إلا أنه قال: هل يصلح له أن يتختم بالذهب؟ قال: لا.

From his brother Musa bin Ja'far (peace be upon them both), he said: I asked him whether it is permissible for a man to wear a gold ring? He said: No. And Ali bin Ja'far reported it in his book, except he said: Is it permissible for him to wear a gold ring? He said: No.

Hadith 5575

عن أبي عبد الله (عليه السلام) قال: سمعته يقول: قال النبي (صلى الله عليه وآله) لعلي (عليه السلام): إياك أن تتختم بالذهب، فإنه حليتك في الجنة، وإياك أن تلبس القسي.

From Abu Abdullah (peace be upon him) said: I heard him say: The Prophet (peace be upon him and his family) said to Ali (peace be upon him): Beware of wearing gold rings, for it will be your ornament in Paradise, and beware of wearing Qassi garments.

CHAPTER 31

Permissibility Of Fastening Teeth With Gold When Necessary, Binding Them With It, And Replacing A Tooth With One From A Ritually Slaughtered Or Dead Person

[Hadith 5576 to 5580]

Hadith 5576

عن أبي جعفر (عليه السلام) - في حديث - أن أسنانه استرخت فشدها بالذهب.

From Abu Ja'far (peace be upon him) - in a hadith - that his teeth became loose so he fastened them with gold.

Hadith 5577

عن الحلبي، عن أبي عبد الله (عليه السلام)، قال: سألته عن الثنية تنفصم، أيصلح أن تشبك بالذهب؟ وإن سقطت يجعل مكانها ثنية شاة؟ قال: نعم إن شاء فليضع مكانها ثنية شاة، بعد أن تكون ذكية.

From Al-Halabi, from Abu Abdullah (peace be upon him), he said: I asked him about a front tooth that breaks, is it permissible to bind it with gold? And if it falls out, can it be replaced with a sheep's tooth? He said: Yes, if he wishes he may put a sheep's tooth in its place, provided it is from a ritually slaughtered animal.

Hadith 5578

عن أبي عبد الله (عليه السلام) قال: سألته عن الرجل ينفصم سنه، أيصلح له أن يشدها بالذهب؟ وإن سقطت، أيصلح أن يجعل مكانها سن شاة؟ قال: نعم إن شاء ليشدها بعد أن تكون ذكية.

From Abu Abdullah (peace be upon him), he said: I asked him about a man whose tooth breaks, is it permissible for him to fasten it with gold? And if it falls out, is it permissible to replace it with a sheep's tooth? He said: Yes, if he wishes let him fasten it, provided it is from a ritually slaughtered animal.

Hadith 5579

وعن زرارة، عن أبي عبد الله (عليه السلام)، قال: سأله أبي وأنا حاضر عن الرجل يسقط سنه، فأخذ سن إنسان ميت فيجعله مكانه؟ قال: لا بأس.

From Zurarah, from Abu Abdullah (peace be upon him), he said: My father asked him while I was present about a man whose tooth falls out, and he takes a tooth from a dead person to put in its place? He said: There is no problem with that.

Hadith 5580

عن الحلبي قال: سألته عن الثنية تنفصم وتسقط، أيصلح أن يجعل مكانها سن شاة؟ فقال: إن شاء فليضع مكانها سنا بعد أن تكون ذكية.

From Al-Halabi who said: I asked him about a front tooth that breaks and falls out, is it permissible to put a sheep's tooth in its place? He said: If he wishes he may put a tooth in its place provided it is from a ritually slaughtered animal.

CHAPTER 32

Dislike Of Praying In Exposed Iron Without Necessity, And In A Copper Or Iron Ring Other Than Chinese Iron, And In A Khomahan Stone

[Hadith 5581 to 5591]

Hadith 5581

عن السكوني عن أبي عبد الله (عليه السلام) قال: قال رسول الله (صلى الله عليه وآله) لا يصلي الرجل وفي يده خاتم حديد.

From Al-Sakuni from Abu Abdullah (peace be upon him), he said: The Messenger of Allah (peace be upon him and his family) said: A man should not pray while wearing an iron ring on his hand.

Hadith 5582

عن أبي عبد الله (عليه السلام) قال: لا يصلي الرجل وفي تكته مفتاح حديد.

From Abu Abdullah (peace be upon him), he said: A man should not pray while having an iron key in his waistband.

Hadith 5583

قال الكليني: وروي: إذا كان المفتاح في غلاف فلا بأس.

Al-Kulayni said: And it is narrated: If the key is in a case, then no problem.

Shaykh Hurr Amili: And what indicates that will come in the hadiths about praying with a sword.

Hadith 5584

عن أبي عبد الله (عليه السلام) قال: قال أمير المؤمنين (عليه السلام): لا تختموا بغير الفضة، فإن رسول الله (صلى الله عليه وآله) قال: ما طهرت كف فيها خاتم من حديد.

From Abu Abdullah (peace be upon him) who said: Amir al-Mu'minin (peace be upon him) said: Do not wear rings made of anything other than silver, for the Messenger of Allah (peace be upon him and his family) said: A hand is not pure if it has an iron ring on it.

Hadith 5585

عن أبي عبد الله (عليه السلام)، في الرجل يصلي وعليه خاتم حديد، قال: لا، ولا يتختم به الرجل، فإنه من لباس أهل النار.

From Abu Abdullah (peace be upon him), regarding a man who prays while wearing an iron ring, he said: No, and a man should not wear it as a ring, for it is from the attire of the people of the Fire.

Hadith 5586

عن أبي عبد الله (عليه السلام) في الحديد إنه حلية أهل النار – إلى أن قال – وجعل الله الحديد في الدنيا زينة الجن والشياطين، فحرم على الرجل المسلم أن يلبسه في الصلاة، إلا أن يكون قبال عدو فلا بأس به،

From Abu Abdullah (peace be upon him) regarding iron, that it is the ornament of the people of Hell - until he said - and Allah made iron in this world an adornment for the jinn and devils, so He prohibited the Muslim man from wearing it during prayer, except if he is facing an enemy then there is no harm in it.

قلت: فالرجل يكون في السفر معه السكين في خفه، لا يستغني عنها، أو في سراويله مشدودا، والمفتاح يخشي إن وضعه ضاع، أو يكون في وسطه المنطقة من حديد؟ قال: لا بأس بالسكين والمنطقة للمسافر في وقت ضرورة، وكذلك المفتاح إذا خاف الضيعة والنسيان، ولا بأس بالسيف وكل آلة السلاح في الحرب، وفي غير ذلك لا تجوز الصلاة في شئ من الحديد، فإنه نجس ممسوخ.

I said: What about a man who is traveling and has a knife in his shoe that he cannot do without, or tied to his trousers, and a key that he fears would be lost if he puts it down, or has an iron belt around his waist? He said: There is no harm in having the knife and belt for the traveler in times of necessity, and likewise the key if he fears loss and forgetfulness. There is no harm in carrying a sword and all weapons during war. Other than these circumstances, prayer is not permissible while wearing anything made of iron, for it is impure and transformed.

أقول: تقدم في النجاسات حكم الحديد وطهارته، وأن النجاسة هنا محمولة على الكراهة، أو المعنى اللغوي، أعني عدم النظافة والنزاهة.

I (Hurr Amili) say: The ruling on iron and its purity has preceded in the chapter on impurities, and that the impurity here is interpreted as dislike, or the linguistic meaning, I mean lack of cleanliness and purity.

Hadith 5587

عن جعفر بن محمد، عن آبائه (عليهم السلام) – في حديث المناهي – قال: نهى رسول الله (صلى الله عليه وآله) عن التختم بخاتم صفر أو حديد.

From Ja'far ibn Muhammad, from his forefathers (peace be upon them) - in the hadith of prohibitions - he said: The Messenger of Allah (peace be upon him and his family) forbade wearing rings of brass or iron.

Hadith 5588

وعن رسول الله (صلى الله عليه وآله) قال: لا يصلي الرجل وفي يده خاتم حديد.

And from the Messenger of Allah (peace be upon him and his family), he said: A man should not pray while wearing an iron ring on his hand.

Hadith 5589

قال: وقال (عليه السلام): ما طهر الله يدا فيها خاتم حديد.

He said: And he (peace be upon him) said: Allah does not purify a hand with an iron ring on it.

Hadith 5590

عن عبد خير قال: كان لعلي بن أبي طالب (عليه السلام) أربعة خواتيم يتختم بها: ياقوت لنبله، وفيروزج لنصرته، والحديد الصيني لقوته، وعقيق لحرزه.

From Abd Khayr, he said: Ali ibn Abi Talib (peace be upon him) had four rings he used to wear: ruby for his nobility, turquoise for his victory, Chinese iron for his strength, and agate (aqeeq) for his protection.

أقول: هذا محمول على بيان الجواز ونفي التحريم، أو على اللبس في غير الصلاة، أو مخصوص بالحديد الصيني لما مر.

I (Hurr Amili) say: This is interpreted as showing permissibility and negating prohibition, or wearing outside of prayer, or specific to Chinese iron as mentioned before.

Hadith 5591

أحمد بن علي بن أبي طالب الطبرسي في (الاحتجاج) عن محمد بن عبد الله بن جعفر الحميري أنه كتب إلى صاحب الزمان (عليه السلام) يسأله عن الفص الخماهن، هل تجوز فيه الصلاة فيه إذا كان في إصبعه؟ فكتب الجواب: فيه كراهية أن تصلي فيه، وفيه أيضا إطلاق، والعمل على الكراهية. وسأله عن الرجل يصلي وفي كمه أو سراويله سكين أو مفتاح حديد، هل يجوز ذلك؟ فكتب في الجواب: جائز. وفي نسخة: عن الفص الجوهر بدل الخماهن.

Ahmad bin Ali bin Abi Talib al-Tabarsi in (al-Ihtijaj) from Muhammad bin Abdullah bin Ja'far al-Himyari that he wrote to the Master of Time (peace be upon him) asking him about the khamahan (*) stone ring, is prayer permissible while wearing it on one's finger? He wrote in response: There is dislike in praying while wearing it, and there is also permissibility regarding it, but acting upon the dislike is preferred. And he asked him about a man who prays while having a knife or an iron key in his sleeve or trousers, is that permissible? He wrote in response: It is permissible. And in another version: about the jewel stone ring instead of khamahan.

Translator: * A blue-green colored onyx or agate gemstone and sometimes described as a stone that changes color or has multiple colors.

CHAPTER 33

Non-obligation Of Women Covering Their Faces During Prayer, Rather It Is Recommended For Them To Uncover It

[Hadith 5592 to 5592]

Hadith 5592

عن سماعة قال: سألته عن المرأة تصلي متنقبة؟ قال: إذا كشفت عن موضع السجود فلا بأس به، وإن أسفرت فهو أفضل.

From Sama'ah, who said: I asked him about a woman praying while wearing a face veil. He said: If she uncovers the place of prostration, there is no objection to it, and if she unveils her face, that is preferable.

———

CHAPTER 34

Ruling Of Uncovering The Place Of Prostration During Gesturing And Other Situations

[Hadith 5593 to 5594]

Hadith 5593

عن أبي عبد الله (عليه السلام)، في الرجل يصلي وهو يومئ على دابته، قال: يكشف موضع السجود.

From Abu Abdullah (peace be upon him), regarding a man praying while gesturing on his mount, he said: He should uncover the place of prostration.

ورواه الشيخ بإسناده عن محمد بن يعقوب، مثله، إلا أنه قال: على دابته متعمما.

And Al-Shaykh narrated it with his chain from Muhammad ibn Ya'qub, similar to it, except that he said: on his mount while wearing a turban.

———————

Hadith 5594

محمد بن علي بن الحسين بإسناده عن سعيد بن يسار، أنه سأل أبا عبد الله (عليه السلام) عن الرجل يصلي صلاة الليل وهو على دابته، أله أن يغطي وجهه وهو يصلي؟ قال: أما إذا قرأ فنعم، وأما إذا أومأ بوجهه للسجود فليكشفه حيث أومأت به الدابة.

Muhammad ibn Ali ibn Al-Husayn with his chain from Sa'id ibn Yasar, that he asked Abu Abdullah (peace be upon him) about a man praying Salat al-Layl while on his mount, is it permissible for him to cover his face while praying? He said: As for when he is reciting, yes, but when he gestures with his face for prostration, he should uncover it where the mount directs him.

———————

CHAPTER 35

Dislike Of Covering The Mouth For Men If It Does Not Prevent Recitation, Otherwise It Is Forbidden In Prayer, And The Permissibility Of Face Veil For Women In Prayer Despite Being Disliked

[Hadith 5595 to 5600]

Hadith 5595

عن أبي جعفر (عليه السلام) قال: قلت له: أيصلي الرجل وهو متلثم؟ فقال: أما على الأرض فلا، وأما على الدابة فلا بأس.

From Abu Ja'far (peace be upon him), he said: I asked him: Can a man pray while covering his mouth? He said: Not while on the ground, but there is no problem while on a mount.

Hadith 5596

عن عبد الله بن سنان، أنه سأل أبا عبد الله (عليه السلام): هل يقرأ الرجل في صلاته وثوبه على في فيه؟ فقال: لا بأس بذلك.

From Abdullah bin Sinan, that he asked Abu Abdullah (peace be upon him): Can a man recite in his prayer while his garment is over his mouth? He said: There is no problem with that.

Hadith 5597

عن الحلبي قال: سألت أبا عبد الله (عليه السلام): هل يقرأ الرجل في صلاته وثوبه على فيه؟ فقال: لا بأس بذلك إذا سمع الهمهمة.

From Al-Halabi who said: I asked Abu Abdullah (peace be upon him): Can a man recite in his prayer while his garment is over his mouth? He said: There is no problem with that if the mumbling can be heard.

Hadith 5598

عن الحسن بن علي، عن أحدهما (عليهما السلام)، أنه قال. لا بأس بأن يقرأ الرجل في الصلاة وثوبه على فيه.

From Al-Hasan bin Ali, from one of them (peace be upon them both), that he said: There is no problem with a man reciting in prayer while his garment is over his mouth.

Hadith 5599

عن سماعة قال: سألت أبا عبد الله (عليه السلام) عن الرجل يصلي ويقرأ القرآن وهو متلثم؟ فقال: لا بأس.

From Sama'ah who said: I asked Abu Abdullah (peace be upon him) about a man praying and reciting the Quran while covering his mouth? He said: There is no problem.

Hadith 5600

عن سماعة، قال: سألته عن الرجل يصلي فيتلوا القرآن وهو متلثم؟ فقال: لا بأس به، وإن كشف عن فيه فهو أفضل. قال: وسألته عن المرأة تصلي متنقبة؟ قال: إن كشفت عن موضع السجود فلا بأس به، وإن وإن أسفرت فهو أفضل.

From Sama'ah who said: I asked him about a man praying and reciting the Quran while covering his mouth? He said: There is no problem with it, though uncovering his mouth is better. He said: And I asked him about a woman praying while wearing a face veil? He said: If she uncovers the place of prostration there is no problem with it, though showing her face is better.

CHAPTER 36

Prohibition Of A Man Praying With Tied Hair And The Obligation To Repeat The Prayer

[Hadith 5601 to 5601]

Hadith 5601

عن أبي عبد الله (عليه السلام)، في الرجل صلى صلاة فريضة وهو معقص الشعر، قال: يعيد صلاته.

From Abu Abdullah (peace be upon him), regarding a man who prayed an obligatory prayer while his hair was tied in a knot, he said: He should repeat his prayer.

ورواه الشيخ بإسناده عن محمد بن يعقوب. أقول: نقل عن الشيخ في (الخلاف) أنه حكى انعقاد الاجماع على التحريم هنا.

The Shaykh narrated this with his chain of transmission from Muhammad bin Ya'qub. I (Hurr Amili) say: It was reported from the Shaykh in (Al-Khilaf) that he related there was consensus on the prohibition in this matter.

———

CHAPTER 37

Recommendation Of Praying In Clean And Pure Sandals
[Hadith 5602 to 5610]

Hadith 5602

عن أبي عبد الله (عليه السلام)، أنه قال: إذا صليت فصل في نعليك إذا كانت طاهرة، فإن ذلك من السنة.

From Abu Abdullah (peace be upon him), he said: When you pray, pray in your sandals if they are clean, for that is from the sunnah.

———————

Hadith 5603

عن الحسن بن علي بن فضال قال: رأيت أبا الحسن (عليه السلام) عند رأس النبي (صلى الله عليه وآله) صلى ست ركعات أو ثمان ركعات في نعليه.

From Al-Hasan bin Ali bin Fadhal, he said: I saw Abu Al-Hasan (peace be upon him) at the head of the Prophet (peace be upon him and his family) pray six or eight rak'ahs in his sandals.

———————

Hadith 5604

عن محمد بن إسماعيل قال: رأيته يصلي في نعليه لم يخلعهما، وأحسبه قال: ركعتي الطواف.

From Muhammad bin Isma'il, he said: I saw him praying in his sandals without taking them off, and I think he said: the two rak'ahs of tawaf.

———————

Hadith 5605

عن معاوية بن عمار قال: رأيت أبا عبد الله (عليه السلام) يصلي في نعليه غير مرة ولم أره ينزعهما قط.

From Mu'awiyah bin Ammar, he said: I saw Abu Abdullah (peace be upon him) praying in his sandals multiple times and I never saw him remove them.

———————

Hadith 5606

عن أبي عبد الله (عليه السلام) قال: إذا صليت فصل في نعليك إذا كانت طاهرة، فإنه يقال: ذلك من السنة.

From Abu Abdullah (peace be upon him), he said: When you pray, pray in your sandals if they are clean, for it is said: that is from the sunnah.

———————

Hadith 5607

عن علي بن مهزيار قال: رأيت أبا جعفر (عليه السلام) صلى حين زالت الشمس يوم التروية ست ركعات خلف المقام، وعليه نعلاه لم ينزعهما.

From Ali bin Mahziyar, he said: I saw Abu Ja'far (peace be upon him) pray six rak'ahs behind Maqam when the sun declined on the day of Tarwiyah, wearing his sandals without removing them.

Hadith 5608

عن عبد الله بن المغيرة قال: قال: إذا صليت فصل في نعليك إذا كانت طاهرة، فإن ذلك من السنة.

From Abdullah bin Al-Mughirah who said: When you pray, pray in your sandals if they are clean, for that is from the sunnah.

Hadith 5609

عن شيخ من أصحابنا يقال له: عبد الله بن رزين - في حديث - أنه رأى أبا جعفر الثاني (عليه السلام) يصلي في مسجد رسول الله (صلى الله عليه وآله) عند بيت فاطمة (عليها السلام)، يخلع نعليه ويصلي، وأنه رآه في ذلك الموضع الذي كان يصلي فيه يصلي في نعليه ولم يخلعهما حتى فعل ذلك أياما.

From one of our companions called Abdullah bin Razin - in a hadith - that he saw Abu Ja'far the Second (peace be upon him) praying in the mosque of the Messenger of Allah (peace be upon him and his family) near the house of Fatimah (peace be upon her), removing his sandals to pray, and he saw him in that same place praying in his sandals without removing them, and he continued doing this for days.

Hadith 5610

عن بعض الطالبيين يلقب برأس المذري قال: سمعت الرضا (عليه السلام) يقول: أفضل موضع القدمين للصلاة النعلان.

From one of the Talibites known as Ra's al-Madhri who said: I heard Al-Ridha (peace be upon him) say: The best position for the feet during prayer is in sandals.

Shaykh Hurr Amili: And what indicates that will come in the hadiths about wearing many clothes in prayer, and what indicates the condition of ritual slaughter has preceded.

CHAPTER 38

Permissibility Of Prayer In Leather Socks, Boots And Similar Footwear With Uppers, Ruling On Footwear Without Uppers, And What Is Bought From The Market Or Found Discarded

[Hadith 5611 to 5617]

Hadith 5611

عن إبراهيم بن مهزيار قال: سألته عن الصلاة في جرموق؟ وأتيته بجرموق بعثت به إليه، قال: يصلى فيه.

From Ibrahim bin Mahziyar who said: I asked him about praying in boots? And I brought him boots that were sent to him. He said: One may pray in them.

Hadith 5612

عن الحلبي قال: سألت أبا عبد الله (عليه السلام) عن الخفاف التي تباع في السوق؟ فقال: اشتر وصل فيها. حتى تعلم أنه ميت بعينه.

From Al-Halabi who said: I asked Abu Abdullah (peace be upon him) about leather socks sold in the market? He said: Buy and pray in them, until you know for certain it is from a dead animal.

Hadith 5613

عن إسماعيل بن الفضل قال: سألت أبا عبد الله (عليه السلام) عن لباس الجلود، والخفاف، والنعال، والصلاة فيها، إذا لم تكن من أرض المصلين؟ فقال: أما النعال والخفاف فلا بأس بهما.

From Isma'il bin Al-Fadhl who said: I asked Abu Abdullah (peace be upon him) about wearing leather garments, leather socks, sandals and praying in them when they are not from the land of those who pray? He said: As for sandals and leather socks, there is no problem with them.

Hadith 5614

أحمد بن علي بن أبي طالب الطبرسي في (الاحتجاج) عن محمد بن عبد الله بن جعفر الحميري، أنه كتب إلى صاحب الزمان (عليه السلام) يسأله: هل يجوز للرجل أن يصلي وفي رجليه بطيط لا يغطي الكعبين، أم لا يجوز؟ فكتب في الجواب: جائز. وسأله عن لبس النعل المعطون، فإن بعض أصحابنا يذكر أن لبسه كريه، فكتب في الجواب: جائز، لا بأس به.

Ahmad bin Ali bin Abi Talib Al-Tabarsi reported in Al-Ihtijaj from Muhammad bin Abdullah bin Ja'far Al-Himyari that he wrote to the Master of Time (peace be upon him) asking: Is it permissible for a man to pray while wearing short boots that do not cover the ankles, or is it not permissible? He wrote in response: It is permissible. And he asked about wearing tanned sandals, as some of our companions mention wearing them is disliked. He wrote in response: It is permissible, there is no problem with it.

Hadith 5615

عن عبد الله بن سنان قال: سمعت أبا عبد الله (عليه السلام) يقول: أهديت لأبي جبة فرومن العراق، وكان إذا أراد أن يصلي نزعها فطرحها.

From Abdullah bin Sinan who said: I heard Abu Abdullah (peace be upon him) say: A fur cloak was gifted to my father from Iraq, and when he wanted to pray he would remove it and set it aside.

Hadith 5616

وعن عبد الله بن سنان، عن أبي عبد الله (عليه السلام) قال: ما جاءك من دباغ اليمن فصل فيه ولا تسأل عنه.

From Abdullah bin Sinan, from Abu Abdullah (peace be upon him) who said: Whatever comes to you from the tanneries of Yemen, pray in it and do not ask about it.

أقول: وتقدمت أحاديث كثيرة تدل على ذلك في النجاسات، ونقل العلامة في (المختلف) وغيره عن ابن حمزة أنه عد النعل السندي والشمشك فيما تكره الصلاة فيه.

I (Hurr Amili) say: Many hadiths preceding this indicate this regarding impurities, and the Scholar reported in Al-Mukhtalif and elsewhere from Ibn Hamza that he counted Sindhi sandals and Shamshak among things in which prayer is disliked.

Hadith 5617

قال: وروي أن الصلاة محظورة في نعل السندي والشمشك، واختار الشيخ وجماعة كراهة ذلك.

He said: It is narrated that prayer is prohibited in Sindhi and Shamshak sandals, though the Shaykh and a group chose to consider it merely disliked.

Translator: Na'l as-Sindhi likely refers to a type of sandal or shoe that originates from Sindh, a region in present-day Pakistan. Ash-Shamshak is another type of footwear, though its exact nature is less clear. It might be a regional or cultural variant of shoe or sandal.

CHAPTER 39

Permissibility Of Prayer For One Who Has Applied Dye Whether Male Or Female When Able To Prostrate And Recite, Even With Dye Wrapping, Though Disliked When Removal Is Possible

[Hadith 5618 to 5626]

Hadith 5618

عن أخيه موسى بن جعفر (عليه السلام)، قال: سألته عن الرجل والمرأة يختضبان، أيصليان وهما بالحناء والوسمة؟ فقال: إذا أبرز الفم والمنخر فلا بأس.

From his brother Musa bin Ja'far (peace be upon him), he said: I asked him about a man and woman who apply dye, can they pray while having henna and wasma? He said: If the mouth and nostrils are exposed then there is no problem.

Hadith 5619

عن رفاعة قال: سألت أبا الحسن (عليه السلام) عن المختضب إذا تمكن من السجود والقراءة أيضا أيصلي في حنائه؟ قال: نعم، إذا كانت خرقته طاهرة وكان متوضئا.

From Rifaa who said: I asked Abu Al-Hasan (peace be upon him) about one who has applied dye, if they can prostrate and recite, can they pray with their henna? He said: Yes, if their wrapping is pure and they have performed wudu.

Hadith 5620

عن أبيه عن أبي الحسن (عليه السلام) قال: سألته: أيصلي الرجل في خضابه إذا كان على طهر؟ فقال: نعم.

From his father from Abu Al-Hasan (peace be upon him) who said: I asked him: Can a man pray while having dye if he has ritual purity? He said: Yes.

Hadith 5621

عن عمار الساباطي قال: سألت أبا عبد الله (عليه السلام) عن المرأة تصلي ويداها مربوطتان بالحناء؟ فقال: إن كانت توضأت للصلاة قبل ذلك فلا بأس بالصلاة وهي مختضبة ويداها مربوطتان.

From Ammar Al-Sabati who said: I asked Abu Abdullah (peace be upon him) about a woman praying while her hands are wrapped with henna? He said: If she performed wudu for prayer before that, then there is no problem praying while dyed and with hands wrapped.

Hadith 5622

عن أبي بكر الحضرمي قال: سألت أبا عبد الله (عليه السلام) عن الرجل يصلي وعليه خضابه؟ قال: لا يصلي وهو عليه، ولكن ينزعه إذا أراد أن يصلي. قلت: إن حناءه وخرقته نظيفة، فقال: لا يصلي وهو عليه، والمرأة أيضا لا تصلي وعليها خضابها.

From Abu Bakr Al-Hadhrami who said: I asked Abu Abdullah (peace be upon him) about a man praying while having dye on? He said: He should not pray while it is on him, but should remove it when he wants to pray. I said: What if his henna and wrapping are clean? He said: He should not pray while it is on him, and likewise a woman should not pray while having dye on.

Hadith 5623

عن الصادق (عليه السلام) قال: لا بأس أن تصلي المرأة وهي مختضبة ويداها مربوطتان.

From Al-Sadiq (peace be upon him) who said: There is no problem for a woman to pray while dyed and her hands wrapped.

Hadith 5624

عن مسمع بن عبد الملك قال: سمعت أبا عبد الله (عليه السلام) يقول: لا يصلي المختضب، قلت: جعلت فداك ولم؟ قال: لأنه محتضر.

From Masma bin Abdul Malik who said: I heard Abu Abdullah (peace be upon him) saying: One who has applied dye should not pray. I said: May I be sacrificed for you, why? He said: Because he is restricted.

Hadith 5625

عن مسمع بن عبد الملك قال: سمعت أبا عبد الله (عليه السلام) يقول: لا يختضب الجنب ولا يجامع المختضب ولا يصلي المختضب، قلت جعلت فداك لم لا يجامع المختضب ولا يصلي؟ قال: لأنه محتضر.

From Misma' bin Abdul Malik who said: I heard Abu Abdullah (peace be upon him) saying: The person in state of janabah (major ritual impurity) should not apply henna dye, and one who has applied henna dye should not have intimate relations, and one who has applied henna dye should not pray. I said: May I be sacrificed for you, why should one who has applied henna not have relations or pray? He said: Because he is restricted.

أقول: هذا محمول على عدم التمكن من بعض الواجبات، لما يأتي، أو على الكراهة.

I (Hurr Amili) say: This is interpreted as being due to inability to perform some obligations, as will be explained later, or as being disliked.

Hadith 5626

عن جماعة من أصحابنا قال: سئل أبو عبد الله (عليه السلام) ما العلة التي من أجلها لا يحل للرجل أن يصلي وعلى شاربه الحناء؟ قال: لأنه لا يتمكن من القراءة والدعاء.

From a group of our companions who said: Abu Abdullah (peace be upon him) was asked what is the reason that it is not permissible for a man to pray while there is henna on his mustache? He said: Because he cannot properly recite and make supplications.

CHAPTER 40

Permissibility Of Keeping Hands Under Clothes During Prostration And Other Prayer Positions

[Hadith 5627 to 5630]

Hadith 5627

عن أبي جعفر (عليه السلام) قال: سألته عن الرجل يصلي ولا يخرج يديه من ثوبه؟ قال: إن أخرج يديه فحسن، وإن لم يخرج فلا بأس.

From Abu Ja'far (peace be upon him), he said: I asked him about a man who prays without taking his hands out of his garment? He said: If he takes out his hands it is good, and if he does not take them out there is no problem.

———

Hadith 5628

عن الحسن بن علي بن فضال، عن رجل قال: قلت لأبي عبد الله (عليه السلام): إن الناس يقولون: إن الرجل إذا صلى وأزراره محلولة ويداه داخلة في القميص إنما يصلي عريانا، قال: لا بأس.

From Al-Hasan bin Ali bin Fadhal, from a man who said: I said to Abu Abdullah (peace be upon him): People say that when a man prays with his buttons unfastened and his hands inside his shirt, it is as if he is praying naked. He said: There is no problem.

———

Hadith 5629

وعنه، عن ابن أبي عمير، عن عبد الرحمان بن الحجاج قال: رأيت أبا عبد الملك القمي يسأل أبا عبد الله (عليه السلام) عن إدخال يده في الثوب في الصلاة في السجود؟ فقال: إن شئت، ثم قال: إني والله ليس من هذا وشبهه أخاف عليكم.

From him, from Ibn Abi Umayr, from Abd al-Rahman bin Al-Hajjaj who said: I saw Abu Abdul Malik Al-Qummi asking Abu Abdullah (peace be upon him) about putting hands inside the garment during prayer in prostration? He said: If you wish, then he said: By Allah, I do not fear for you regarding this and similar matters.

———

Hadith 5630

عن أبي عبد الله (عليه السلام) قال: سألته عن الرجل يصلي فيدخل (يده في ثوبه)؟ قال: إن كان عليه ثوب آخر إزار أو سراويل فلا بأس وإن لم يكن فلا يجوز له ذلك، وإن أدخل يدا واحدة ولم يدخل الأخرى فلا بأس.

From Abu Abdullah (peace be upon him), he said: I asked him about a man who prays and puts (his hand inside his garment)? He said: If he has another garment, a lower-garment or trousers, there is no problem, and if he does not it is not permissible for him, and if he puts in one hand and not the other there is no problem.

From Abu Abdullah (peace be upon him), he said: I asked him about a man who prays and puts his hand in his garment? He said: If he is wearing another garment like a waist wrap or trousers then there is no problem, and if he is not then it is not permissible for him, and if he puts in one hand and not the other then there is no problem.

أقول حمله الشيخ على الاستحباب، ويمكن حمله على التقية، وعلى عدم حصول ستر العورة في بعض الحالات.

I (Hurr Amili) say: The Shaykh interpreted this as recommended, and it can be interpreted as taqiyyah, and as not achieving covering of the awrah (private parts) in some cases.

CHAPTER 41

Permissibility Of Praying While Having Musk Pods
[Hadith 5631 to 5632]

Hadith 5631

عن أخيه موسى (عليه السلام) قال: سألته عن فارة المسك تكون مع من يصلي وهي في جيبه أو ثيابه ؟
فقال: لا بأس بذلك .

From his brother Musa (peace be upon him) who said: I asked him about having musk pods with someone who prays while it is in their pocket or clothes? He said: There is no problem with that.

Hadith 5632

عن عبد الله بن جعفر قال: كتبت إليه يعني أبا محمد (عليه السلام): يجوز للرجل أن يصلي ومعه فارة المسك ؟ فكتب: لا بأس به إذا كان ذكيا.

From Abdullah bin Ja'far who said: I wrote to him, meaning Abu Muhammad (peace be upon him): Is it permissible for a man to pray while having musk pods with him? He wrote back: There is no problem with it if it is pure.

CHAPTER 42

Disliking Wearing The Bartala And Permissibility Of Praying In It

[Hadith 5633 to 5634]

Hadith 5633

عن أبي عبد الله (عليه السلام) أنه كره لباس البرطلة.

From Abu Abdullah (peace be upon him) that he disliked wearing the bartala (*).

Translator: * A type of headgear or head covering. Some scholars describe it as a kind of cap or small turban. It's believed to have been a non-Arab style of headwear, possibly of Persian or Byzantine origin.

Hadith 5634

عن يونس بن يعقوب قال: سألت أبا عبد الله (عليه السلام) عن الرجل يصلي وعليه البرطلة؟ فقال: لا يضره.

From Yunus bin Ya'qub who said: I asked Abu Abdullah (peace be upon him) about a man praying while wearing the bartala? He said: It does not harm him.

CHAPTER 43

Recommendation Of Using Musk And Other Perfumes For Prayer
[Hadith 5635 to 5639]

Hadith 5635

عن أبي عبد الله (عليه السلام) قال: كانت لرسول الله (صلى الله عليه وآله) ممسكة إذا هو توضأ أخذها بيده وهي رطبة، فكان إذا خرج عرفوا أنه رسول الله (صلى الله عليه وآله) برائحته.

From Abu Abdullah (peace be upon him) who said: The Messenger of Allah (peace be upon him and his family) had a musk container that he would take in his hand while it was moist after performing wudu. When he would go out, people would recognize him as the Messenger of Allah (peace be upon him and his family) by his fragrance.

Hadith 5636

وعن علي بن إبراهيم رفعه عن أبي عبد الله (عليه السلام) - في حديث - قال: صلاة متطيب أفضل من سبعين صلاة بغير طيب.

From Ali ibn Ibrahim, who raised it to Abu Abdullah (peace be upon him) - in a hadith - who said: A prayer performed while wearing perfume is better than seventy prayers without perfume.

Hadith 5637

عن أبي الحسن (عليه السلام) قال: كان يعرف موضع سجود أبي عبد الله (عليه السلام) بطيب ريحه.

From Abu al-Hasan (peace be upon him) who said: The place of prostration of Abu Abdullah (peace be upon him) was known by its pleasant fragrance.

Hadith 5638

عن عبد الله بن الحارث قال: كانت لعلي بن الحسين (عليه السلام) قارورة مسك في مسجده فإذا دخل إلى الصلاة أخذ منه فتمسح به.

From Abdullah ibn al-Harith who said: Ali ibn al-Husayn (peace be upon him) had a bottle of musk in his mosque, and when he would enter for prayer, he would take from it and apply it on himself.

Hadith 5639

عن المفضل بن عمر، عن الصادق (عليه السلام) قال: ركعتان يصليهما متعطرا أفضل من سبعين ركعة يصليها غير متعطر.

From al-Mufaddal ibn Umar, from al-Sadiq (peace be upon him) who said: Two rak'ahs prayed while wearing perfume are better than seventy rak'ahs prayed without perfume.

———

CHAPTER 44

Permissibility Of Prayer In Crimson Clothing If Not Pure Silk, Otherwise Not Permitted

[Hadith 5640 to 5641]

Hadith 5640

عن علي بن مهزيار قال: كتبت إلى أبي محمد (عليه السلام) أسأله عن الصلاة في القرمز وأن أصحابنا يتوقفون عن الصلاة فيه، فكتب: لا بأس به، مطلق والحمد لله.

From Ali ibn Mahziyar, who said: I wrote to Abu Muhammad (peace be upon him) asking him about praying in crimson-dyed garments, and that our companions were hesitant to pray in them. He wrote back: There is no objection to it, it is permitted, and praise be to God.

قال الصدوق: وذلك إذا لم يكن القرمز من إبريسم محض، والذي نهي عنه ما كان من إبريسم محض.

Al-Saduq said: This is when the crimson is not made of pure silk, and what is forbidden is what is made of pure silk.

Hadith 5641

عن أبي الجارود، عن أبي جعفر (عليه السلام) أن رسول الله (صلى الله عليه وآله) قال لعلي (عليه السلام) - في حديث -: لا تلبس القرمز فإنه من أردية إبليس.

From Abu al-Jaroud, from Abu Ja'far (peace be upon him), that the Messenger of Allah (peace be upon him and his family) said to Ali (peace be upon him) - in a hadith - : Do not wear crimson garments, for they are among the robes of Iblis.

CHAPTER 45

Dislike Of Praying With Statues And Images, Whether On Clothing Or Carrying Them Or Facing Them, Unless They Are Changed, Covered, Under Foot, Or One Is Compelled

[Hadith 5642 to 5665]

Hadith 5642

عن محمد بن مسلم قال: سألت أحدهما (عليهما السلام) عن التماثيل في البيت؟ فقال: لا بأس إذا كانت عن يمينك وعن شمالك وعن خلفك أو تحت رجليك، وإن كانت في القبلة فألق عليها ثوبا.

From Muhammad bin Muslim who said: I asked one of them (peace be upon them) about statues in the house? He said: There is no problem if they are on your right, your left, behind you, or under your feet. If they are in the direction of qiblah, throw a cloth over them.

Translator: In classical Arabic, the terms "Tamatheel" (the plural of "Timthal") and "Surah" are closely related but possess slight linguistic distinctions. Generally, a "Timthal" implies a physical, embodied figure or statue, whereas a "Surah" is a broader term encompassing any form, picture, or image. However, as demonstrated by the hadith in this chapter, the Imams and the classical narrators use these two terms interchangeably when discussing the jurisprudence of representation. For the English reader, it is vital to understand that within this textual context, both terms serve as an umbrella category specifically for the artificial representation of animate, living beings. This is evidenced by the narrations explicitly mentioning predatory animals, birds, and fish, as well as defining a problematic image as one that possesses "two eyes".

The texts also clearly establish that the scope of these terms is not restricted by artistic medium or dimensionality. The concepts of "Tamatheel" and "Surah" apply equally to three-dimensional objects and two-dimensional artwork. On one hand, the narrations address physical statues, explicitly instructing believers to "break" or "cut off the heads" of the figures if they have no choice but to pray while facing them, which denotes a tangible, three-dimensional object. On the other hand, the exact same terminology is applied to flat, two-dimensional designs. The Imams use these words to describe representations that are embroidered into the fabric of clothing, woven into the patterns of carpets and pillows, engraved onto the metal surfaces of silver and black dirhams, or painted on household curtains.

Ultimately, the language used in these narrations focuses on the existence of the animate form itself rather than the material it is crafted from. By understanding that "Tamatheel" and "Surah" encompass this entire spectrum - from a carved statue to a woven bird on a rug - the reader can better grasp the structural consistency of the legal questions being asked by the early companions. The fundamental focus of the texts in this chapter is not to pass a singular judgment on art, but rather to establish the etiquette of the prayer space. The narrations manage how the presence of these animate forms interacts with the worshipper's environment, specifically addressing their position relative to the direction of prayer (the qiblah), whether they are covered or altered, and whether they are placed in a position of subordination, such as beneath the feet.

Hadith 5643

عن أبي عبد الله (عليه السلام) أنه كره أن يصلي وعليه ثوب فيه تماثيل.

From Abu Abdullah (peace be upon him) that he disliked praying while wearing clothes containing images.

Hadith 5644

عن أبي عبد الله (عليه السلام) أنه سئل عن الدراهم السود تكون مع الرجل وهو يصلي مربوطة أو غير مربوطة؟ فقال: ما أشتهي أن يصلي ومعه هذه الدراهم التي فيها التماثيل، ثم قال (عليه السلام): ما للناس بد من حفظ بضائعهم، فإن صلى وهي معه فلتكن من خلفه ولا يجعل شيئا منها بينه وبين القبلة.

From Abu Abdullah (peace be upon him) that he was asked about black dirhams that a person has while praying, whether tied or untied? He said: I do not like that one prays while having these dirhams that contain images. Then he said: People have no choice but to protect their goods. If one prays with them, they should be behind him and nothing of them should be between him and the qiblah.

Hadith 5645

عن أبي الحسن الرضا (عليه السلام) أنه سأله عن الصلاة في الثوب المعلم؟ فكره ما فيه من التماثيل.

From Abu Al-Hasan Al-Ridha (peace be upon him) that he was asked about praying in marked clothes? He disliked what contained images in them.

Hadith 5646

وفي (الخصال) بإسناده الآتي عن علي (عليه السلام) - في حديث الأربعمائة - قال: لا يسجد الرجل على صورة ولا على بساط فيه صورة، ويجوز أن تكون الصورة تحت قدميه، أو يطرح عليها ما يواريها، (و) لا يعقد الرجل الدارهم التي فيها صورة في ثوبه وهو يصلي، ويجوز أن تكون الدراهم في هميان أو في ثوب إذا خاف ويجعلها في ظهره.

In Al-Khisal with his coming chain from Ali (peace be upon him) - in the hadith of the four hundred - he said: A man should not prostrate on an image or on a carpet containing an image, but it is permissible for the image to be under his feet, or to throw something over it to cover it, and a man should not tie dirhams containing images in his clothes while praying, but it is permissible to have the dirhams in a purse or in clothes if he is afraid and puts them behind his back.

Hadith 5647

عن محمد بن مسلم قال: قلت لأبي جعفر (عليه السلام): أصلي والتماثيل قدامي وأنا أنظر إليها؟ قال: لا، اطرح عليها ثوبا. ولا بأس بها إذا كانت عن يمينك أو شمالك أو خلفك أو تحت رجلك أو فوق رأسك، وإن كانت في القبلة فألق عليها ثوبا وصل.

From Muhammad bin Muslim who said: I said to Abu Ja'far (peace be upon him): Should I pray while images are in front of me and I am looking at them? He said: No, throw a cloth over them. There is no problem if they are on your right or left or behind you or under your foot or above your head. If they are in the direction of qiblah, throw a cloth over them and pray.

Hadith 5648

عن أبي عبد الله (عليه السلام) قال: سألته عن التماثيل تكون في البساط لها عينان وأنت تصلي؟ فقال: إن كان لها عين واحدة فلا بأس، وإن كان لها عينان فلا. ورواه الكليني، عن ابن أبي عمير، مثله، إلا أنه قال: تقع عينك عليه وأنت تصلي.

From Abu Abdullah (peace be upon him), he said: I asked him about images on a carpet that have two eyes while you are praying? He said: If it has one eye there is no problem, but if it has two eyes then no. Al-Kulayni narrated it from Ibn Abi Umayr, similar to it, except he said: your eye falls on it while you are praying.

Hadith 5649

عن حماد بن عثمان قال: سألت عبد الله (عليه السلام) عن الدراهم السود فيها التماثيل، أيصلي الرجل وهي معه؟ فقال: لا بأس بذلك إذا كانت مواراة.

From Hammad bin Uthman who said: I asked Abdullah (peace be upon him) about black dirhams that have images on them, can a man pray while having them? He said: There is no problem with that if they are covered.

Hadith 5650

عن محمد بن مسلم قال: سألت أبا جعفر (عليه السلام) عن الرجل يصلي وفي ثوبه دراهم فيها تماثيل؟ فقال: لا بأس بذلك.

From Muhammad bin Muslim who said: I asked Abu Ja'far (peace be upon him) about a man who prays while having dirhams with images on them in his clothes? He said: There is no problem with that.

Hadith 5651

عن محمد بن مسلم، عن أبي جعفر (عليه السلام) قال: لا بأس أن تصلي على كل التماثيل إذا جعلتها تحتك.

From Muhammad bin Muslim, from Abu Ja'far (peace be upon him) who said: There is no problem praying on any images if you place them beneath you.

Hadith 5652

عن ليث المرادي قال: قلت لأبي عبد الله (عليه السلام) الوسائد تكون في البيت فيها التماثيل عن يمين أو شمال، فقال: لا بأس ما لم تكن تجاه القبلة فإن كان شئ منها مما بين يديك مما يلي القبلة فغطه وصل، وإذا كانت معك دراهم سود فيها تماثيل فلا تجعلها من بين يديك واجعلها من خلفك.

From Layth Al-Muradi who said: I said to Abu Abdullah (peace be upon him) about pillows in the house that have images on them to the right or left, so he said: There is no problem as long as they are not facing the qiblah, but if there is something with images in front of you towards the qiblah then cover it and pray, and if you have black dirhams with images on them, do not place them in front of you but place them behind you.

Hadith 5653

عن أبي جعفر (عليه السلام) قال: لا بأس بأن تصلي على المثال إذا جعلته تحتك.

From Abu Ja'far (peace be upon him) who said: There is no problem praying on an image if you place it beneath you.

Hadith 5654

عن أبي جعفر (عليه السلام) قال: لا بأس أن تكون التماثيل في الثوب إذا غيرت الصورة منه.

From Abu Ja'far (peace be upon him) who said: There is no problem having images on clothes if the image form is altered.

Hadith 5655

عن سعد بن إسماعيل، عن أبيه قال: سألت أبا الحسن الرضا (عليه السلام) عن المصلى والبساط يكون عليه تماثيل، أيقوم عليه فيصلي أم لا؟ فقال: والله إني لأكره. وعن رجل دخل على رجل عنده بساط عليه تمثال؟ فقال: (أتجد هاهنا مثالا)، فقال: لا تجلس عليه ولا تصل عليه.

From Saad bin Isma'il, from his father who said: I asked Abu Al-Hasan Al-Ridha (peace be upon him) about prayer rugs and carpets that have images on them, should one stand on them to pray or not? He said: By Allah, I dislike it. And about a man who entered upon another man who had a carpet with an image? He said: Do you find an image here? Then he said: Do not sit on it and do not pray on it.

Shaykh Hurr Amili: The Sheikh said this is interpreted as dislike based on what we have presented.

Hadith 5656

عن أبي عبد الله (عليه السلام) - في حديث - عن الثوب يكون في علمه مثال طير أو غير ذلك، أيصلي فيه؟ قال: لا، وعن الرجل يلبس الخاتم فيه نقش مثال الطير أو غير ذلك، قال: لا تجوز الصلاة فيه.

From Abu Abdullah (peace be upon him) - in a hadith - about clothes that have images of birds or other things embroidered on them, can one pray in them? He said: No. And about a man wearing a ring that has an engraving of a bird or other things, he said: Prayer is not permitted while wearing it.

Hadith 5657

عن علي بن جعفر، عن أبيه قال: سألته عن الرجل يصلح أن يصلي في بيت على بابه ستر خارج فيه تماثيل ودونه مما يلي البيت ستر آخر ليس فيه تماثيل، هل يصلح أن يؤخر الستر الذي ليس فيه تماثيل حتى يحول بينه وبين الستر الذي فيه التماثيل أو يجيف الباب دونه ويصلي فيه؟ قال: لا بأس.

From Ali bin Ja'far, from his father who said: I asked him about a man praying in a house that has a curtain outside its door containing images, and behind it facing the house is another curtain without images - is it permissible to pull back the curtain without images to create a barrier between him and the curtain with images, or to close the door and pray there? He said: There is no problem.

قال: وسألته عن الثوب يكون فيه التماثيل أو في علمه، أيصلى فيه؟ قال: لا يصلى فيه.

He said: I asked him about clothing that has images on it or as part of its design, can one pray in it? He said: One should not pray in it.

Hadith 5658

عن موسى بن جعفر (عليهما السلام)، وذكر مثله وزاد: قال: وسألته عن الرجل، هل يصلح أن يصلي في بيت فيه أنماط فيها تماثيل قد غطاها؟ قال: لا بأس.

From Musa bin Ja'far (peace be upon them both), who mentioned similar and added: He said: I asked him about a man - is it permissible to pray in a house containing carpets with covered images? He said: There is no problem.

Hadith 5659

وبالاسناد قال: وسألته عن البيت قد صور فيه طير أو سمكة أو شبهه يلعب به أهل البيت، هل تصلح الصلاة فيه؟ قال: لا حتى يقطع رأسه أو يفسده، وإن كان قد صلى فليس عليه إعادة.

With the same chain he said: I asked him about a house with pictures of birds or fish or similar things that the household plays with, is prayer valid in it? He said:

Not until its head is cut off or it is damaged, but if one has already prayed there is no need to repeat the prayer.

Hadith 5660

وبالاسناد قال: وسألته عن البيت فيه الدراهم السود في كيس أو تحت فراش أو موضوعة في جانب البيت فيه التماثيل. هل تصلح الصلاة فيه؟ قال: لا بأس.

With the same chain he said: I asked him about a house containing black dirhams in a pouch or under bedding or placed in a corner of the house that has images, is prayer valid in it? He said: There is no problem.

Hadith 5661

وبالاسناد قال: وسألته عن رجل كان في بيته تماثيل أو في ستر ولم يعلم بها وهو يصلي في ذلك البيت ثم علم، ما عليه؟ قال: ليس عليه فيما لا يعلم شئ، فإذا علم فلينزع الستر وليكسر رؤوس التماثيل.

And by the same chain of transmission he said: I asked him about a man who had images or figures in his house, or on a curtain, and he was unaware of them while praying in that house, and then he came to know of them. What is required of him? He said: There is nothing upon him for what he did not know. But when he comes to know, let him remove the curtain and let him break the heads of the figures.

Hadith 5662

وبالاسناد قال: وسألته عن الدار والحجرة فيها التماثيل، أيصلي فيها؟ قال: لا تصلي فيها وشئ منها مستقبلك إلا أن لا تجد بدا فتقطع رؤوسها وإلا فلا تصلى.

With the same chain he said: I asked him about a house and room containing images, can one pray in them? He said: Do not pray in them while facing any of the images unless you have no choice, then cut off their heads, otherwise do not pray.

Hadith 5663

وبالاسناد قال: وسألته عن المسجد يكون فيه المصلى تحته الفلوس والدراهم البيض أو السود، هل يصلح القيام عليها وهو في الصلاة؟ قال: لا بأس.

With the same chain he said: I asked him about a mosque where the prayer area has copper coins and white or black dirhams beneath it, is it permissible to stand on them during prayer? He said: There is no problem.

Hadith 5664

وبالاسناد قال: وسألته عن الخاتم يكون فيه نقش تماثيل سبع أو طير أيصلى فيه؟ قال: لا بأس.

With the same chain he said: I asked him about a ring that has engravings of predatory animals or birds, can one pray while wearing it? He said: There is no problem.

Hadith 5665

وقد تقدم حديث سماعة، عن أبي عبد الله (عليه السلام) في لباس الحرير والديباج فقال: أما في الحرب فلا بأس وإن كان فيه التماثيل.

From Sama'ah, from Abu Abdullah (peace be upon him) regarding wearing silk and brocade, he said: As for during war, there is no harm in it even if it contains images.

CHAPTER 46

Permissibility Of Wearing A Ring That Contains An Image Or Figure Of A Rose, Crescent, Animal, Or Bird, And Praying While Wearing It Despite It Being Disliked

[Hadith 5666 to 5668]

Hadith 5666

عن أبي الحسن الرضا (عليه السلام) - في حديث - أنه أراه خاتم أبي الحسن (عليه السلام) وفيه وردة وهلال في أعلاه.

From Abu Al-Hasan Al-Ridha (peace be upon him) - in a hadith - that he showed him the ring of Abu Al-Hasan (peace be upon him) and it had a rose and a crescent at its top.

Hadith 5667

عن جعفر بن محمد، عن أبيه (عليهما السلام) - في حديث المناهي - قال: نهى رسول الله (صلى الله عليه وآله) أن ينقش شئ من الحيوان على الخاتم.

From Ja'far ibn Muhammad, from his father (peace be upon them both) - in the hadith of prohibitions - he said: The Messenger of Allah (peace be upon him and his family) forbade engraving any animal on a ring.

Hadith 5668

وقد تقدم في حديث عمار عن أبي عبد الله (عليه السلام) أنه سأله عن الرجل يلبس الخاتم فيه نقش مثال الطير أو غير ذلك؟ قال: لا تجوز الصلاة فيه.

And it was previously mentioned in the hadith of Ammar from Abu Abdullah (peace be upon him) that he asked him about a man wearing a ring with an engraving of a bird or something else? He said: Prayer is not permissible while wearing it.

CHAPTER 47

Permissibility Of Praying In A Garment Padded With Raw Silk
[Hadith 5669 to 5672]

Hadith 5669

عن الحسين بن سعيد قال: قرأت (في) كتاب محمد بن إبراهيم إلى الرضا (عليه السلام) يسأله عن الصلاة في ثوب حشوه قز؟ فكتب إليه قرأته: لا بأس بالصلاة فيه.

From al-Husayn ibn Sa'id who said: I read in the letter of Muhammad ibn Ibrahim to al-Ridha (peace be upon him) asking him about praying in a garment padded with raw silk. He wrote back, as I read it: There is no problem in praying in it.

Hadith 5670

عن الريان بن الصلت أنه سأل الرضا (عليه السلام) عن أشياء منها المحشو بالقز؟ فقال: لا بأس بهذا كله.

From al-Rayyan ibn al-Salt that he asked al-Ridha (peace be upon him) about various things including that which is padded with raw silk. He said: There is no problem with all of this.

Hadith 5671

عن سفيان بن السمط - في حديث - قال: قرأت في كتاب محمد بن إبراهيم إلى أبي الحسن (عليه السلام) يسأله عن ثوب حشوة قز يصلي فيه؟ فكتب: لا بأس به.

From Sufyan ibn al-Simt - in a hadith - who said: I read in the letter of Muhammad ibn Ibrahim to Abu al-Hasan (peace be upon him) asking him about a garment padded with raw silk, can one pray in it? He wrote: There is no problem with it.

Hadith 5672

عن إبراهيم بن مهزيار أنه كتب إلى أبي محمد (عليه السلام): الرجل يجعل في جبته بدل القطن قزا، هل يصلي فيه؟ فكتب: نعم لا بأس به.

From Ibrahim ibn Mahziyar that he wrote to Abu Muhammad (peace be upon him): A man puts raw silk in his cloak instead of cotton, can he pray in it? He wrote: Yes, there is no problem with it.

CHAPTER 48

Dislike Of Riding On Red Cushions And Its Non-Prohibition

[Hadith 5673 to 5678]

Hadith 5673

عن أبي عبد الله (عليه السلام) ويكره أن يلبس القميص المكفوف بالديباج، ويكره لباس الحرير، ولباس الوشي، ويكره الميثرة الحمراء فإنها ميثرة إبليس.

From Abu Abdullah (peace be upon him): It is disliked to wear a shirt trimmed with silk brocade, and silk clothing is disliked, and embroidered clothing is disliked, and the red cushion is disliked for it is the cushion of Iblis.

عن النضر بن سويد، مثله، إلا أنه قال: ولباس القسي.

From Al-Nadr bin Suwayd, similar to the above, except he said: and Qassi clothing.

Hadith 5674

عن أبي عبد الله (عليه السلام) أن علي بن الحسين (عليهما السلام) كان يركب على قطيفة حمراء.

From Abu Abdullah (peace be upon him): Ali bin Al-Husayn (peace be upon them both) used to ride on a red velvet.

Hadith 5675

عن أبيه، عن حنان قال: سمعت أبا عبد الله (عليه السلام) يقول: قال النبي (صلى الله عليه وآله) لعلي: (عليه السلام): إياك أن تركب ميثرة حمراء فإنها ميثرة إبليس.

From his father, from Hanan who said: I heard Abu Abdullah (peace be upon him) saying: The Prophet (peace be upon him and his family) said to Ali (peace be upon him): Beware of riding on a red cushion for it is the cushion of Iblis.

Hadith 5676

عن أبي جعفر (عليه السلام) أن رسول الله (صلى الله عليه وآله) قال لعلي (عليه السلام) - في حديث - لا تركب بميثرة حمراء فإنها من مراكب إبليس. ورواه في (العلل) كما تقدم في أحاديث الحرير.

From Abu Ja'far (peace be upon him): The Messenger of Allah (peace be upon him and his family) said to Ali (peace be upon him) - in a hadith - do not ride with a red cushion for it is among the mounts of Iblis. And it was narrated in (Al-Ilal) as previously mentioned in the hadiths about silk.

Hadith 5677

عن جعفر بن محمد، عن أبيه أن رسول الله (صلى الله عليه وآله) نهاهم عن سبع، منها: المآثر الحمر.

From Ja'far bin Muhammad, from his father: The Messenger of Allah (peace be upon him and his family) forbade them from seven things, among them were the red cushions.

Hadith 5678

عن أبي عبد الله (عليه السلام) قال: قال النبي (صلى الله عليه وآله) لعلي (عليه السلام) في حديث إياك أن تركب ميثرة حمراء فإنها من مآثر إبليس.

From Abu Abdullah (peace be upon him) who said: The Prophet (peace be upon him and his family) said to Ali (peace be upon him) in a hadith: Beware of riding on a red cushion for it is among the cushions of Iblis.

CHAPTER 49

Permissibility Of Praying In Women's Clothes And Its Dislike When She Is Suspect, And Likewise For Men, And The Ruling On Praying In Others' Clothes With And Without Permission

[Hadith 5679 to 5681]

Hadith 5679

عن أبي عبد الله (عليه السلام) في الرجل يصلي في إزار المرأة وفي ثوبها وبعتم بخمارها، قال: إذا كانت مأمونة.

From Abu Abdullah (peace be upon him) regarding a man praying in a woman's wrap and in her garment and wearing her head covering as a turban, he said: If she is trustworthy.

———

Hadith 5680

عن محمد بن يحيى رفعه عن أبي عبد الله (عليه السلام) قال: صل في منديلك الذي تتمندل به، ولا تصل في منديل يتمندل به غيرك.

From Muhammad bin Yahya, raising it to Abu Abdullah (peace be upon him) who said: Pray in your own towel that you use, and do not pray in a towel that others use.

أقول: هذا محمول على كون الغير متهما بالنجاسة، فيستحب اجتناب منديله، أو على الكراهة، لما مضى ويأتي.

I (Hurr Amili): This is interpreted to mean when the other person is suspected of impurity, so it is recommended to avoid their towel, or it indicates dislike, based on what has passed and what will come.

———

Hadith 5681

عن أبي عبد الله (عليه السلام) قال: قلت له: منديل يتمندل به، أيجوز أن يضعه الرجل على منكبيه أو يتزر به ويصلي؟ قال: لا بأس.

From Abu Abdullah (peace be upon him), I said to him: A towel that is used for drying, is it permissible for a man to place it on his shoulders or wrap it around himself and pray? He said: There is no problem.

———

CHAPTER 50

Obligation Of Covering The Awrah In Prayer Even If With Grass Or The Like, And If One Cannot Find A Cover, They Should Pray Naked, Gesturing While Standing If No One Is Watching, And Sitting If Someone Is, Placing Their Hand Over Their Awrah

[Hadith 5682 to 5688]

Hadith 5682

عن أخيه موسى (عليهم السلام)، قال: سألته عن الرجل قطع عليه أو غرق متاعه فبقي عريانا وحضرت الصلاة، كيف يصلي؟ قال: إن أصاب حشيشا يستر به عورته أتم صلاته بالركوع والسجود، وإن لم يصب شيئا يستر به عورته أومأ وهو قائم.

From his brother Musa (peace be upon them), he said: I asked him about a man whose belongings were cut off or drowned, so he remained naked and the prayer time came, how should he pray? He said: If he can find grass to cover his awrah (private parts), he should complete his prayer with ruku and sujud, and if he cannot find anything to cover his awrah, he should gesture while standing.

———————

Hadith 5683

عن أبي عبد الله (عليه السلام) قال: العاري الذي ليس له ثوب إذا وجد حفيرة دخلها (ويسجد فيها ويركع).

From Abu Abdullah (peace be upon him), he said: The naked person who has no garment, if he finds a hole, he should enter it (and prostrate and bow in it).

———————

Hadith 5684

عن أبي عبد الله (عليه السلام) في الرجل يخرج عريانا فتدركه الصلاة، قال: يصلي عريانا قائما إن لم يره أحد، فإن رآه أحد صلى جالسا.

From Abu Abdullah (peace be upon him) regarding a man who goes out naked and the prayer time comes upon him, he said: He should pray naked while standing if no one sees him, and if someone sees him, he should pray sitting.

———————

Hadith 5685

عن أبي عبد الله (عليه السلام) أنه قال - في حديث - وإن كان معه سيف وليس معه ثوب فليتقلد السيف ويصلي قائما.

From Abu Abdullah (peace be upon him) that he said - in a hadith - and if he has a sword with him and no garment, he should wear the sword and pray standing.

Hadith 5686

قال: وروي في الرجل يخرج عريانا فتدركه الصلاة أنه يصلي عريانا قائما إن لم يره أحد، فإن رآه أحد صلى جالسا.

He said: And it is narrated regarding a man who goes out naked and the prayer time comes upon him that he should pray naked while standing if no one sees him, and if someone sees him, he should pray sitting.

Hadith 5687

عن زرارة قال: قلت لأبي جعفر (عليه السلام): رجل خرج من سفينة عريانا أو سلب ثيابه ولم يجد شيئا يصلي فيه، فقال: يصلي ايماء، وكانت امرأة جعلت يدها على فرجها، وإن كان رجلا وضع يده على سوأته ثم يجلسان فيؤميان ايماء ولا يسجدان ولا يركعان فيبدو ما خلفهما، تكون صلاتهما ايماء برؤوسهما.

From Zurara who said: I said to Abu Ja'far (peace be upon him): A man who came out of a ship naked, or whose clothes were taken from him, and he finds nothing to pray in. He said: He should pray by gesturing, and if it was a woman, she should place her hand on her farj (genitals), and if it was a man, he should place his hand on his private area. Then they should sit and gesture by gesturing, and they should not prostrate nor bow lest what is behind them be exposed. Their prayer should be by gesturing with their heads.

قال: وإن كانا في ماء أو بحر لجي لم يسجدا عليه، وموضوع عنهما التوجه فيه يؤميان في ذلك ايماء، رفعهما توجه ووضعهما.

He said: And if they were in water or a deep sea, they should not prostrate on it, and they are exempted from facing the qiblah in it. They should gesture in that, raising their heads is facing [the qibla] and lowering them [is prostration].

Hadith 5688

عن أبي جعفر (عليه السلام) في رجل عريان ليس معه ثوب، قال: إذا كان حيث لا يراه أحد فليصل قائما.

From Abu Ja'far (peace be upon him) regarding a naked man who has no garment with him, he said: If he is where no one can see him, he should pray standing.

CHAPTER 51

Recommendation Of Congregational Prayer For The Naked And Its Method

[Hadith 5689 to 5690]

Hadith 5689

عن أبي عبد الله (عليه السلام) قال: سألته عن قوم صلوا جماعة وهم عراة ؟ قال: يتقدمهم الامام بركبتيه ويصلي بهم جلوسا وهو جالس.

From Abu Abdullah (peace be upon him), he said: I asked him about people who prayed in congregation while they were naked? He said: The imam leads them on his knees and prays with them while sitting, and he is seated.

Hadith 5690

عن إسحاق بن عمار قال: قلت لأبي عبد الله (عليه السلام): قوم قطع عليهم الطريق وأخذت ثيابهم فبقوا عراتا وحضرت الصلاة، كيف يصنعون ؟ فقال: يتقدمهم إمامهم فيجلس ويجلسون خلفه فيومئ إيماء بالركوع والسجود، وهم يركعون ويسجدون خلفه على وجوههم.

From Ishaq bin Ammar, he said: I said to Abu Abdullah (peace be upon him): A group of people were ambushed on the road and their clothes were taken, so they remained naked and the prayer time came, what should they do? He said: Their imam leads them by sitting and they sit behind him. He gestures for the ruku and sujud, while they perform ruku and sujud behind him on their faces.

CHAPTER 52

Recommendation For The Naked Person To Delay Prayer Until The End Of Time While Hoping To Find Clothing

[Hadith 5691 to 5691]

Hadith 5691

عن جعفر بن محمد، عن أبيه (عليهما السلام) أنه قال: من غرقت ثيابه فلا ينبغي له أن يصلي حتى يخاف ذهاب الوقت يبتغي ثيابا. فإن لم يجد صلى عريانا جالسا يومئ ايماء يجعل سجوده أخفض من ركوعه، فان كانوا جماعة تباعدوا في المجالس، ثم صلوا كذلك فرادى.

From Ja'far bin Muhammad, from his father (peace be upon them both) who said: Whoever has their clothes soaked should not pray until they fear the time will expire while seeking clothes. If they cannot find any, they should pray naked while sitting, gesturing with gestures, making their sujud lower than their ruku. If they are a group, they should distance themselves in their sitting places, then pray like this individually.

Shaykh Hurr Amili: And what indicates the recommendation of congregation here has preceded, and this is interpreted as permissible with the first being preferable, or as taqiyya (precautionary dissimulation).

CHAPTER 53

Dislike Of Leading Prayer Without A Cloak, Its Recommendation For The Imam And For One Who Prays In A Single Garment, And The Minimum Being A Waistband Or Sword, And That It Is Not Obligatory

[Hadith 5692 to 5698]

Hadith 5692

عن سليمان بن خالد قال: سألت أبا عبد الله (عليه السلام) عن رجل أم قوما في قميص ليس عليه رداء؟ فقال: لا ينبغي إلا أن يكون عليه رداء أو عمامة يرتدي بها.

From Sulayman bin Khalid who said: I asked Abu Abdullah (peace be upon him) about a man who leads people in prayer wearing a shirt without a cloak? He said: It is not appropriate unless he has a cloak or a turban to wrap with.

Hadith 5693

عن أخيه موسى بن جعفر (عليهما السلام) قال: سألته عن الرجل، هل يصلح له أن يؤم في سراويل وقلنسوة؟ قال: لا يصلح. وسألته عن السراويل، هل يجوز مكان الإزار؟ قال: نعم.

From his brother Musa bin Ja'far (peace be upon them both) who said: I asked him about a man, is it proper for him to lead prayer in trousers and a cap? He said: It is not proper. And I asked him about trousers, can they take the place of a waist-wrap? He said: Yes.

Hadith 5694

عن عبد الله بن سنان قال: سئل أبو عبد الله (عليه السلام) عن رجل ليس معه إلا سراويل؟ قال يحل التكة منه فيطرحها على عاتقه ويصلي، قال: وإن كان معه سيف وليس معه ثوب فليتقلد السيف ويصلي قائما.

From Abdullah bin Sinan who said: Abu Abdullah (peace be upon him) was asked about a man who has nothing but trousers? He said: He should untie the waistband and put it on his shoulder and pray. He said: And if he has a sword but no garment, he should wear the sword and pray standing.

Hadith 5695

عن جميل قال: سأل مرازم أبا عبد الله (عليه السلام) وأنا معه حاضر عن الرجل الحاضر يصلي في إزار مؤتزرا به؟ قال: يجعل على رقبته منديلا أو عمامة يرتدي به.

From Jamil who said: Murazim asked Abu Abdullah (peace be upon him) while I was present with him about a man who prays in a waist-wrap wearing it? He said: He should put a handkerchief or turban on his neck to wrap with.

Hadith 5696

وعن علي بن محمد رفعه عن أبي عبد الله (عليه السلام) في رجل يصلي في سراويل ليس معه غيره، قال: يجعل التكة على عاتقه.

From Ali bin Muhammad raising it to Abu Abdullah (peace be upon him) regarding a man who prays in trousers having nothing else, he said: He should put the waistband on his shoulder.

Hadith 5697

عن زرارة، عن أبي جعفر (عليه السلام) قال: أدنى ما يجزيك أن تصلي فيه بقدر ما يكون على منكبيك مثل جناحي الخطاف.

From Zurarah, from Abu Ja'far (peace be upon him) who said: The minimum that suffices you to pray in is what covers your shoulders like the wings of a swallow.

Hadith 5698

عن موسى بن جعفر (عليهما السلام) قال: سألته عن الرجل يؤم بغير رداء؟ فقال: قد أم رسول الله (صلى الله عليه وآله) في ثوب واحد متوشح به. قال: وسألته عن الرجل، هل يصلح له أن يصلي في سراويل واحد وهو يصيب ثوبا؟ قال: لا يصلح.

From Ali bin Ja'far, from his brother Musa bin Ja'far (peace be upon them both) who said: I asked him about a man leading prayer without a cloak? He said: The Messenger of Allah (peace be upon him and his family) led prayer in a single garment wrapped around him. He said: And I asked him about a man, is it proper for him to pray in just trousers while he can find a garment? He said: It is not proper.

Shaykh Hurr Amili: And what indicates that has preceded in the hadiths about praying in a single garment.

CHAPTER 54

Recommendation Of Wearing The Coarsest And Thickest Clothes In Prayer When Alone, And The Finest And Most Beautiful Among People, And The Disapproval Of Protecting One's Clothes During Prayer

[Hadith 5699 to 5705]

Hadith 5699

عن محمد بن الحسين، عن أبيه قال: رأيت أبا عبد الله (عليه السلام) وعليه قميص غليظ خشن تحت ثيابه وفوقه جبة صوف وفوقها قميص غليظ فمسستها فقلت: جعلت فداك إن الناس يكرهون لباس الصوف، فقال: كلا كان أبي محمد بن علي (عليهما السلام) يلبسها، وكان علي بن الحسين (عليهما السلام) يلبسها وكانوا (عليهم السلام) يلبسون أغلظ ثيابهم إذا قاموا إلى الصلاة، ونحن نفعل ذلك.

From Muhammad ibn al-Husayn, from his father who said: I saw Abu Abdullah (peace be upon him) wearing a thick coarse shirt under his clothes and over it a woolen cloak and over that a thick shirt. I touched it and said: May I be sacrificed for you, people dislike wearing wool. He said: Not at all, my father Muhammad ibn Ali (peace be upon them) used to wear it, and Ali ibn al-Husayn (peace be upon them) used to wear it, and they (peace be upon them) would wear their thickest clothes when they stood for prayer, and we do the same.

Hadith 5700

عن حريز عن أبي عبد الله (عليه السلام) قال: اتخذ مسجدا في بيتك فإذا خفت شيئا فالبس ثوبين غليظين من أغلظ ثيابك فصل فيهما.

From Hareez from Abu Abdullah (peace be upon him) who said: Take a prayer place in your house, and when you fear something, wear two thick garments from your thickest clothes and pray in them.

Hadith 5701

عن محمد بن حسين بن كثير، عن أبيه قال: رأيت على أبي عبد الله (عليه السلام) جبة صوف بين ثوبين غليظين، فقلت له في ذلك، فقال: رأيت أبي يلبسها، إنا إذا أردنا أن نصلي لبسنا أخشن ثيابنا.

From Muhammad ibn Husayn ibn Kathir, from his father who said: I saw Abu Abdullah (peace be upon him) wearing a woolen cloak between two thick garments, so I asked him about that. He said: I saw my father wearing it. When we want to pray, we wear our coarsest clothes.

Hadith 5702

محمد بن علي بن الحسين قال: قال رسول الله (صلى الله عليه وآله): من اتقى على ثوبه في صلاته فليس لله اكتسى.

Muhammad ibn Ali ibn al-Husayn said: The Messenger of Allah (peace be upon him and his family) said: Whoever protects his clothes during his prayer has not dressed for Allah.

Hadith 5703

الفضل بن الحسن الطبرسي في (مجمع البيان) عن أبي جعفر (عليه السلام) في قوله تعالى: (خذوا زينتكم عند كل مسجد) قال: أي خذوا ثيابكم التي تتزينون بها للصلاة في الجمعات والأعياد.

Al-Fadhl ibn al-Hasan al-Tabarsi in Majma' al-Bayan from Abu Ja'far (peace be upon him) regarding the words of the Almighty: "Take your adornment at every place of prayer" [Quran 7:31] he said: That is, take your clothes that you adorn yourself with for prayer in Friday prayers and festivals.

Hadith 5704

قال: وروى العياشي باسناده عن الحسن بن علي (عليه السلام) أنه كان إذا قام إلى الصلاة لبس أجود ثيابه، فقيل له: يا بن رسول الله، لم تلبس أجود ثيابك؟ فقال: إن الله جميل يحب الجمال، فأتجمل لربي، وهو يقول: (خذوا زينتكم عند كل مسجد) فأحب أن ألبس أجمل ثيابي.

He said: And al-Ayyashi narrated with his chain from al-Hasan ibn Ali (peace be upon him) that when he would stand for prayer, he would wear his finest clothes. He was asked: O son of the Messenger of Allah, why do you wear your finest clothes? He said: Indeed Allah is beautiful and loves beauty, so I beautify myself for my Lord, and He says: "Take your adornment at every place of prayer" [Quran 7:31], so I love to wear my most beautiful clothes.

Hadith 5705

عن أبي عبد الله (عليه السلام) قال: كان لأبي ثوبان خشنان يصلي فيهما صلاته، وإذا أراد أن يسأل الحاجة لبسهما وسأل الله حاجته.

From Abu Abdullah (peace be upon him) who said: My father had two coarse garments in which he would pray his prayers, and when he wanted to ask for something, he would wear them and ask Allah for his need.

CHAPTER 55

Permissibility Of Praying In Clothes Purchased From Muslim Markets

[Hadith 5706 to 5709]

Hadith 5706

عن أحمد بن محمد قال: سألته عن الرجل يأتي السوق فيشتري جبة فراء لا يدري أذكية هي أم غير ذكية، أيصلي فيها؟ فقال: نعم، ليس عليكم المسألة، إن أبا جعفر (عليه السلام) كان يقول: إن الخوارج ضيقوا على أنفسهم بجهالتهم، إن الدين أوسع من ذلك.

From Ahmad bin Muhammad who said: I asked him about a man who goes to the market and buys a fur coat, not knowing whether it is from a properly slaughtered animal or not - can he pray in it? He said: Yes, you don't need to question it. Abu Ja'far (peace be upon him) used to say: The Khawarij restricted themselves due to their ignorance, but religion is broader than that.

Hadith 5707

عن علي بن أبي حمزة أن رجلا سأل أبا عبد الله (عليه ال لام) وأنا عنده عن الرجل يتقلد السيف ويصلي فيه؟ قال: نعم، فقال الرجل: إن فيه الكيمخت، قال: ما الكيمخت؟ فقال: جلود دواب منه ما يكون ذكيا ومنه ما يكون ميتة، فقال: ما علمت أنه ميتة فلا تصل فيه.

From Ali bin Abi Hamza that a man asked Abu Abdullah (peace be upon him) while I was with him about a man wearing a sword and praying with it? He said: Yes. The man said: But it has kimakht in it. He asked: What is kimakht? The man said: Animal skins, some from properly slaughtered animals and some from dead ones. He said: What you know is from dead animals, don't pray in it.

Hadith 5708

عن إسحاق بن عمار، عن العبد الصالح (عليه السلام) أنه قال: لا بأس بالصلاة في الفرا اليماني وفيما صنع في أرض الاسلام، قلت: فإن كان فيها غير أهل الاسلام؟ قال: إذا كان الغالب عليها المسلمين فلا بأس.

From Ishaq bin Ammar, from Al-Abd Al-Salih (peace be upon him) that he said: There is no problem praying in Yemeni fur and what is made in Islamic lands. I asked: What if there are non-Muslims there? He said: If Muslims are the majority there, then there is no problem.

Hadith 5709

عن جعفر بن محمد بن يونس أن أباه كتب إلى أبي الحسن (عليه السلام) يسأله عن الفرو والخف، ألبسه وأصلي فيه ولا أعلم أنه ذكي؟ فكتب: لا بأس به.

From Ja'far bin Muhammad bin Yunus that his father wrote to Abu Al-Hasan (peace be upon him) asking about fur and leather socks - can I wear them and pray in them when I don't know if they are from properly slaughtered animals? He wrote back: There is no problem with it.

———

CHAPTER 56

Permissibility Of Prayer In What Does Not Contain Life From Edible Dead Animals Such As Wool, Hair, And Fur When Cut

[Hadith 5710 to 5714]

Hadith 5710

عن أبي عبد الله (عليه السلام) قال: لا بأس بالصلاة فيما كان من صوف الميتة، إن الصوف ليس فيه روح.

From Abu Abdullah (peace be upon him), he said: There is no problem praying in what is from the wool of dead animals, as wool does not contain a soul.

Hadith 5711

عن أبي جرير القمي قال: سألت الرضا (عليه السلام) عن الريش، أذكي هو؟ فقال: كان أبي يتوسد الريش.

From Abu Jarir Al-Qummi, he said: I asked Al-Ridha (peace be upon him) about feathers, whether they need to be purified? He said: My father used to use feathers as a pillow.

Hadith 5712

وقد تقدم حديث زرارة عن أبي عبد الله (عليه السلام) قال: الشعر والصوف والريش وكل نابت لا يكون ميتا.

The previous hadith of Zurarah from Abu Abdullah (peace be upon him) has already been mentioned where he said: Hair, wool, feathers, and everything that grows does not become dead.

Hadith 5713

عن أبيه (عليهما السلام) قال: قال جابر بن عبد الله الأنصاري: إن دباغة الصوف والشعر غسله بالماء، وأي شئ يكون أطهر من الماء.

From his father (peace be upon them both), he said: Jabir ibn Abdullah Al-Ansari said: The tanning of wool and hair is washing them with water, and what could be more purifying than water.

Hadith 5714

عن أبي البختري، عن جعفر، عن أبيه (عليهما السلام) أن عليا (عليه السلام) قال: غسل الصوف الميت ذكاته. أقول: هذا مخصوص بغير الجز وقد تقدم ما يدل عل ذلك، ويأتي ما يدل على هذا المعنى.

From Abu Al-Bakhtari, from Ja'far, from his father (peace be upon them both) that Ali (peace be upon him) said: Washing dead wool is its purification.

CHAPTER 57

Permissibility Of Prayer While Wearing A Sword, Bow, And Kimkht, And The Dislike Of Sword For The Imam Except Out Of Necessity, And Facing It During Prayer

[Hadith 5715 to 5719]

Hadith 5715

عن موسى (عليه السلام) - في حديث - قال: سألته عن السيف، هل يجري مجرى الرداء يؤم القوم في السيف؟ قال: لا يصلح أن يؤم في السيف إلا في الحرب.

From Musa (peace be upon him) - in a hadith - he said: I asked him about the sword, does it serve like a cloak when leading people in prayer with the sword? He said: It is not proper to lead prayer with a sword except in war.

Hadith 5716

عن جعفر، عن أبيه (عليهما السلام) أن عليا (عليه السلام) قال: السيف بمنزلة الرداء تصلي فيه ما لم تر فيه دما، والقوس بمنزلة الرداء

From Ja'far, from his father (peace be upon them) that Ali (peace be upon him) said: The sword is like a cloak, you can pray in it as long as you don't see blood on it, and the bow is like a cloak.

Hadith 5717

ورواه الصدوق مرسلا عن أمير المؤمنين (عليه السلام) وزاد: إلا أنه لا يجوز للرجل أن يصلي وبين يديه سيف، لان القبلة أمن. قال: وروي ذلك عن أمير المؤمنين (عليه السلام).

Al-Saduq narrated it as mursal from Amir al-Mu'minin (peace be upon him) and added: However, it is not permissible for a man to pray while having a sword in front of him, because the qiblah is security. He said: And this has been narrated from Amir al-Mu'minin (peace be upon him).

Hadith 5718

وقد سبق حديث عبد الله بن سنان، عن أبي عبد الله (عليه السلام) قال: إن كان معه سيف وليس معه ثوب فليتقلد السيف ويصلي قائما.

The previous hadith of Abdullah ibn Sinan, from Abu Abdullah (peace be upon him) said: If he has a sword with him and has no garment, he should wear the sword and pray standing.

Hadith 5719

وحديث الريان بن الصلت أنه سئل الرضا (عليه السلام) عن أشياء منها الكيمخت؟ فقال: لا بأس بهذا كله .

From Al-Rayyan ibn Al-Salt that he asked Al-Ridha (peace be upon him) about several things including kimkht (processed leather)? He said: There is no harm in all of this.

CHAPTER 58

Dislike Of Woman Praying Without Ornaments
[Hadith 5720 to 5721]

Hadith 5720

عن غياث بن إبراهيم، عن جعفر، عن أبيه، عن علي (عليه السلام) قال: لا تصلي المرأة عطلا.

From Ghiyath bin Ibrahim, from Ja'far, from his father, from Ali (peace be upon him) who said: A woman should not pray unadorned.

Hadith 5721

محمد بن علي بن الحسين قال: قال الصادق (عليه السلام): لا ينبغي للمرأة أن تعطل نفسها ولو أن تعلق في عنقها قلادة، ولا ينبغي لها أن تدع يدها من الخضاب ولو أن تمسحها بالحناء مسحا وإن كانت مسنة.

Muhammad bin Ali bin Al-Husayn said that Al-Sadiq (peace be upon him) said: It is not appropriate for a woman to leave herself unadorned, even if it is just wearing a necklace around her neck. And she should not leave her hands without dye, even if she just wipes them lightly with henna, even if she is elderly.

CHAPTER 59

Dislike Of Praying In Red, Saffron-dyed, Safflower-dyed, And Deeply Saturated Garments

[Hadith 5722 to 5724]

Hadith 5722

عن مالك بن أعين قال: دخلت على أبي جعفر (عليه السلام) وعليه ملحفة حمراء شديدة الحمرة فتبسمت حين دخلت، فقال: كأني أعلم لم ضحكت؟ ضحكت من هذا الثوب الذي هو علي إن الثقفية أكرهتني عليه وأنا أحبها فأكرهتني على لبسها، ثم قال: إنا لا نصلي في هذا ولا تصلوا في المشبع المضرج.

From Malik bin Ayan who said: I entered upon Abu Ja'far (peace be upon him) while he was wearing a bright red wrap. I smiled when I entered, so he said: I think I know why you laughed? You laughed at this garment I am wearing. The Thaqafiyyah woman (his wife) compelled me to wear it, and I love her so she made me wear it. Then he said: We do not pray in this, and do not pray in deeply saturated red garments.

قال: ثم دخلت عليه وقد طلقها فقال. سمعتها تبرأ من علي (عليه السلام) فلم يسعني أن أمسكها وهي تبرأ منه.

He said: Then I entered upon him after he had divorced her (the Thaqafiyyah woman), and he said: I heard her doing tabarra'a (disavowing) Ali (peace be upon him), so I could not keep her while she did tabarra'a (disavowed) on him.

Hadith 5723

عن أبي عبد الله (عليه السلام) قال: تكره الصلاة في الثوب المصبوغ المشبع المقدم.

From Abu Abdullah (peace be upon him) who said: It is disliked to pray in dyed garments that are deeply saturated.

Hadith 5724

عن أبي عبد الله (عليه السلام) أنه كره الصلاة في المشبع بالعصفر والمضرج بالزعفران.

From Abu Abdullah (peace be upon him) that he disliked praying in garments deeply dyed with safflower or saturated with saffron.

CHAPTER 60

Dislike Of Having Animal Hide Containers Or Footwear Made From Donkey Or Mule Leather During Prayer Without Necessity, And Similarly Having A Bird In One's Sleeve

[Hadith 5725 to 5728]

Hadith 5725

عن أبي الحسن (عليه السلام) قال: سألته عن رجل صلى وفي كمه طير؟ قال: إن خاف الذهاب عليه فلا بأس.

From Abu Al-Hasan (peace be upon him): I asked him about a man who prays with a bird in his sleeve? He said: If he fears it will escape, then there is no problem.

Hadith 5726, 5727

عن موسى بن جعفر (عليه السلام)، مثله وزاد: قال: وسألته عن الرجل يصلي ومعه دبة من جلد الحمار أو بغل؟ قال: لا يصلح أن يصلي وهي معه، إلا أن يتخوف عليها ذهابها، فلا بأس أن يصلي وهي معه. قال: وسألته عن الرجل هل يصلح أن يصلي وفي فيه الخرز واللؤلؤ؟ قال: إن كان يمنعه من قراءته فلا، وإن كان لا يمنعه فلا بأس.

From Musa bin Ja'far (peace be upon him), similar to above and he added: I asked him about a man who prays while having a container made of donkey or mule leather? He said: It is not proper to pray while having it, unless he fears it will be lost, then there is no problem praying with it. I asked him about a man - is it proper for him to pray while having beads and pearls in his mouth? He said: If it prevents him from his recitation then no, but if it doesn't prevent him then there is no problem.

Hadith 5728

عن موسى (عليه السلام) - في حديث - قال: وسألته عن الرجل صلى ومعه دبة من جلد حمار، وعليه نعل من جلد حمار، هل تجزيه صلاته، أو عليه إعادة؟ قال: لا يصلح له أن يصلي وهي معه، إلا أن يتخوف عليها ذهابا، فلا بأس أن يصلي وهي معه.

From Musa (peace be upon him) - in a hadith - he said: I asked him about a man who prayed while having a container made of donkey leather, and wearing shoes made of donkey leather - is his prayer sufficient or must he repeat it? He said: It is not proper for him to pray while having it, unless he fears it will be lost, then there is no problem praying with it.

CHAPTER 61

Dislike Of Praying In Leather Purchased From A Muslim Who Considers Dead Animal Skins Lawful After Tanning

[Hadith 5729 to 5731]

Hadith 5729

عن أبي عبد الله (عليه السلام) قال: تكره الصلاة في الفراء إلا ما صنع في أرض الحجاز، أو ما علمت منه ذكاة.

From Abu Abdullah (peace be upon him), he said: Prayer is disliked in furs except what is made in the land of Hijaz, or what you know has been properly slaughtered.

Hadith 5730

عن محمد بن الحسين الأشعري قال: كتب بعض أصحابنا إلى أبي جعفر الثاني (عليه السلام): ما تقول في الفرو يشترى من السوق؟ فقال: إذا كان مضمونا فلا بأس.

From Muhammad bin Al-Husayn Al-Ash'ari, he said: Some of our companions wrote to Abu Ja'far the Second (peace be upon him): What do you say about fur purchased from the market? He said: If it is guaranteed, then there is no problem.

Hadith 5731

عن أبي بصير قال: سألت أبا عبد الله (عليه السلام) عن الصلاة في الفراء؟ فقال: كان علي بن الحسين (عليه السلام) رجلا صردا، لا يدفئه فراء الحجاز، لان دباغها بالقرظ، فكان يبعث إلى العراق فيؤتى مما قبلكم بالفرو، فيلبسه، فإذا حضرت الصلاة ألقاه وألقى القميص الذي يليه، فكان يسأل عن ذلك؟ فقال: إن أهل العراق يستحلون لباس الجلود الميتة، ويزعمون أن دباغه ذكاته.

From Abu Basir, he said: I asked Abu Abdullah (peace be upon him) about praying in furs? He said: Ali bin Al-Husayn (peace be upon him) was a person sensitive to cold, the furs of Hijaz would not keep him warm because they were tanned with qaraz. He would send to Iraq and would be brought furs from your region, and he would wear it. When prayer time came, he would remove it and remove the shirt underneath it. When he was asked about this, he said: The people of Iraq consider wearing dead animal skins lawful, and they claim that tanning it makes it pure.

CHAPTER 62

Dislike Of Anklets That Make Sound For Women And Children, And The Permissibility Of Wearing Those That Do Not Make Sound

[Hadith 5732 to 5732]

Hadith 5732

عن أخيه أبي الحسن (عليه السلام) - في حديث -، قال: سألته عن الخلاخل، هل يصلح للنساء والصبيان لبسها؟ فقال: إذا كانت صماء فلا بأس، وإن كان لها صوت فلا.

From his brother Abu Al-Hasan (peace be upon him) - in a hadith - he said: I asked him about anklets, is it permissible for women and children to wear them? He said: If they are solid (without sound) then there is no problem, but if they make sound then no.

ورواه الصدوق بإسناده عن علي بن جعفر، مثله، إلا أنه قال: فلا يصلح.

And Al-Saduq narrated it through his chain from Ali bin Ja'far, similar to it, except that he said: then it is not permissible.

CHAPTER 63

Recommendation Of Wearing Many Clothes During Prayer
[Hadith 5733 to 5734]

Hadith 5733

عن علي (عليهم السلام) قال: إن الانسان إذا كان في الصلاة فإن جسده وثيابه وكل شئ حوله يسبح.

From Ali (peace be upon him), he said: When a person is in prayer, his body, clothes, and everything around him glorifies Allah.

———————

Hadith 5734

عن جعفر بن محمد، عن أبيه (عليهما السلام) قال: إن لكل شئ عليك، تصلي فيه، يسبح معك، قال: وكان رسول الله (صلى الله عليه وآله) إذا أقيمت الصلاة لبس نعليه وصلى فيهما.

From Ja'far bin Muhammad, from his father (peace be upon them both), he said: Everything you wear while praying glorifies with you. He said: When prayer was established, the Messenger of Allah (peace be upon him and his family) would put on his sandals and pray in them.

———————

CHAPTER 64

Recommendation Of Wearing A Turban And Trousers During Prayer

[Hadith 5735 to 5737]

Hadith 5735

الحسن بن الفضل الطبرسي في (مكارم الأخلاق) عن النبي (صلى الله عليه وآله) قال: ركعتان مع العمامة خير من أربع ركعات بغير عمامة.

Al-Hasan bin Al-Fadhl Al-Tabarsi reported in (Makarim Al-Akhlaq) from the Prophet (peace be upon him and his family) who said: Two rak'ah wearing a turban are better than four rak'ah without a turban.

Refer to Hadith 5535 in Chapter 26 on the manner of wrapping the turban.

Hadith 5736

محمد بن مكي الشهيد في (الذكرى) قال: روي ركعة بسراويل تعدل أربعا بغيره.

Muhammad bin Makki Al-Shahid reported in (Al-Dhikra) saying: It is narrated that one rak'ah wearing trousers equals four without them.

Hadith 5737

قال: وكذا روي في العمامة.

He said: And similarly it was narrated regarding the turban.

END OF VOLUME 4

A Note To Our Readers

As we conclude the English translation of "Wasa'il al-Shia, Volume 4", we praise Allah (swt) for granting us the success (tawfiq) to facilitate your engagement with the explicit words of the Ahl al-Bayt (a.s.).

We have undertaken this translation project with the utmost diligence and strict fidelity to the original Arabic text. Our team has worked tirelessly to ensure that the profound nuances of the Imams' guidance are preserved, permanently removing linguistic barriers so you may connect directly with their pure teachings.

While the words of the Infallibles are perfect and absolutely free from error, the act of translation is inherently a human endeavor. Should you find any shortcomings, typographical errors, or areas for refinement in the English text, we humbly request your corrections. Your sincere feedback is a vital contribution to the ongoing perfection of this monumental project.

For those seeking to conduct deeper research, verify the original Arabic manuscripts, or review the complete transmission chains (isnad) that were excluded from this print edition, we invite you to visit our companion website at https://wasail-al-shia.net.

We pray that the traditions contained within this volume have fortified your faith and illuminated your path. May Allah (swt) accept this humble service, and may He hasten the reappearance of our Master, the Twelfth Imam, so that the earth may be filled with divine justice.

With sincere prayers,

Shia Heritage Foundation